GOLF CLUB REPAIR IN PICTURES

By
RALPH MALTBY
With Mark Wilson

Photography by Randall D. Williams

First Edition - *108 pages*
January, 1978
Revised Edition - *150 pages*
January, 1980
Third edition - *185 pages*
August, 1982
Fourth edition - *365 pages*
May, 1988

ISBN 0-9606792-8-6

*Published by
Ralph Maltby Enterprises, Inc.
Book Manufactured in the
United States of America*

Book Trade Distribution By:

Ralph Maltby Enterprises, Inc.
P.O. Box 3008
4820 Jacksontown Road
Newark, Ohio 43055-7199

**Other books published by and
available from The GolfWorks®:**

Golf Club Design, Fitting, Alteration and Repair
(Revised Second Ed.) 720 Pages, Hardcover

Golf Club Assembly Manual
40 Pages, Hardcover

The Golf Club Identification Guide
520 Pages, Softcover

The Complete Golf Club Fitting Plan,
The Eleven Important Fitting Variables and Your Swing
14 booklets in Notebook and includes Fitting Forms

INTRODUCTION

Golf Club Repair in Pictures - **Fourth Edition**
The first edition of *Golf Club Repair in Pictures*, published in January, 1978, was an immediate best seller and has continued to be so with its unending international customer demand. It has helped thousands of people to learn and perform virtually any repair on golf clubs. Revised editions in 1980 and 1982 expanded the book to 182 pages and more than 725 photographs. Now, totally rewritten, this new fourth edition has been updated and expanded to over 350 pages and contains over 1,600 photographs, charts and tables.

Golf Club Repair in Pictures is the best place to start for the handyman thinking about golf club repair either as a hobby or business, as well as the experienced repairman wanting to expand his skills and knowledge. Fully equipped shops, or those with only the basic necessities, will benefit by its information. Included among the many expanded subjects is how to use the back of heel to first step dimension charts, a refinishing section that has grown from 80 to over 300 carefully selected step-by-step photographs, face insert installations, the most up-to-date techniques utilizing the best new tools and more.

From the novice to the expert, this expanded 1988 edition will provide valuable procedures, charts, tables, technical information and methods for everyone interested in golf club repair.

If *Golf Club Repair in Pictures* creates even more interest to understand virtually every aspect of golf clubs, then I recommend that the reader obtain a copy of *Golf Club Design, Fitting, Alteration and Repair*. This hardbound book has over 720 pages and 1,500 illustrations and photographs.

Ralph Maltby

Ralph Maltby
May, 1988

TABLE OF CONTENTS

GOLF CLUB REPAIR IN PICTURES

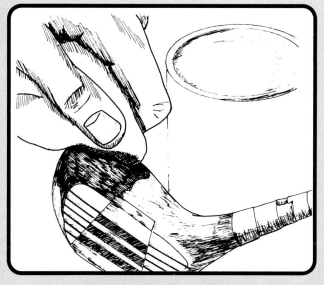

SECTION 1

GOLF WOOD CLUB REPAIRS AND ALTERATIONS

1

REFINISHING WOODS

The application of a clear polyurethane coating to a properly prepared clubhead will enhance the beauty of the wood stain and also provide a durable covering for the head. The steps involved in achieving a beautiful finish require practice; but once a sound technique has been developed, the results can be outstanding. Refinishing can be performed using many different methods . . . for example, the methods for sanding a clubhead range from time-consuming hand sanding to the use of motorized machinery for maximum speed. Regardless of the method, if done correctly, the end result can be the same. The methods shown in the ensuing pages are taught in The GolfWorks® Repair Schools and have proven to be very successful.

Refinishing "woods" has become a bit more complex with the introduction of inorganic materials (stainless steel, aluminum, byzanium alloy, graphite and plastic) into the traditional persimmon and laminated maple club lines. Fortunately, in most cases, the refinishing steps are similar. The steps required for refinishing materials other than wood are covered in the latter part of this chapter.

Almost all finishes consist of a water- or alcohol-based dye stain, a wood filler (which is either oil, water, or a urethane base) applied over or under the stain, a color cote (usually only with black finishes), and three to five coats of a clear polyurethane applied by either dipping or spraying.

A word about polyurethane coatings. There are two basic types of polyurethane available — moisture cure and oil modified. However, there are many variations of these two types commercially available through hardware and department stores. Unless the polyurethane has been developed expressly for golf club heads, you would be wise to avoid the store-bought types. This type of polyurethane may look good for a short while, but may soon crack, chip or peel upon impact with a topped ball or "fat" shot. If you are pioneering a new brand, test it thoroughly; otherwise, stick with a reputable maker or supplier of specially formulated polyurethanes for golf woods.

IMPORTANT NOTE: Product compatability is always a question. Use the table at the end of this chapter if you use either The GolfWorks® products or Mira products. Also, different products require different drying times. Again, the table at the end of this chapter should be used as a guide in determining correct drying times for both room temperature and force dry conditions.

Many times a club is received with simple instructions for a straight refinish. Never assume the club requires a simple refinish! You should thoroughly inspect the club to determine if it requires other head repairs. Failure to perform this clubhead inspection may lead to future problems with the customer. For instance, if a new finish is applied to a clubhead with a loose insert or soleplate, the finish will eventually peel or chip around these components. The customer will not understand this, though, and he will come back to you demanding an explanation. Your reputation will be hurt simply because you neglected to inspect the clubhead before refinishing and inform the customer of the possible consequences should he not agree to the additional necessary repairs. Decisions such as these should always be made by the customer so there are no hidden costs or surprises when he picks the club up.

In addition to the head inspection, there are other features on a club that should be noted prior to a refinish. These features, plus the general head inspection, are covered extensively in this chapter. Remember this: Your goal as a refinisher is to apply a finish to the clubhead that is as good, if not better, than the original factory finish.

1-1 First, check and record swingweight. Refinishing will reduce swingweight 1-2 points. This loss of weight must be compensated by perferably adding additional weight under the soleplate or as a last resort down the shaft. See Chapter 13 for weighting procedures.

1-2 Carefully cut through whipping and remove. Do not make deep cuts into the hosel. If club has a plastic whipping cover, do not remove it unless you desire to convert to whipping. Photos 2-35 thru 2-47 in Chapter 2 show how to do this.

1-3 Inspect the head to see if it is loose on the shaft. Grasp the head in one hand and the grip in the other, then twist in opposite directions. Sometimes you may only hear a squeak, which indicates the head is loose. See Chapter 8 for repairing a loose wood head.

1-4 Inspect the hosel for cracks. Minor hairline cracks are OK as long as the shaft is bonded securely to the head. Major cracks will require removal and reinstallation of the shaft to properly repair the crack. Refer to Chapter 9 for repairing cracks in necks.

1-5 Examine the head for any cracks or breaks. The head shown above will eventually break into two pieces. See Chapter 9 for the procedure on repairing cracked or broken heads.

1-6 Look carefully at this photo. This condition is known as **"dry rot"** or **"weathering."** Chapter 5 will show you how to repair this rotted area.

1-7 If the club has a brass or lead backweight, check to make sure it is set properly. A loose brass weight will need to be reset, while the lead weight will most likely need to be replaced. Chapter 14 outlines both repair procedures.

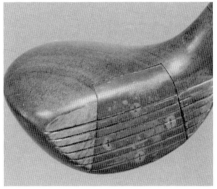

1-8 Inspect for a loose insert and reset if necessary. Follow the instructions shown in Chapter 4.

1-9 Inspect for a loose or open soleplate. If necessary, reset as outlined in Chapter 3. **Note: A very loose soleplate or insert can be an indication that a crack in the head is beginning to form.**

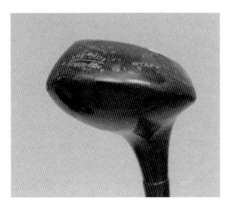

1-10 Before the finish is removed, the **color should be recorded** (if the head is to be refinished in the same color). **Make note of the decal(s) and decal position.** Recording this information will make it much easier to remember it at a later stage.

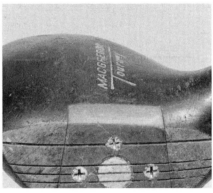

1-11 If the clubhead has a stamping in the crown or wood area of the sole, make a note of the paint color used to fill the stamping.

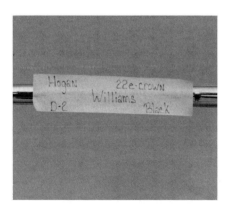

1-12 On a piece of tape (masking tape works well) attached to the shaft, record the club's swingweight, color, decal, type, decal color (if applicable), decal placement and the customer's name. This is an efficient practice regardless of the size of your shop.

1-13 Old polyurethane, varnish, shellac or lacquer finish is best removed by brushing a paste stripper onto the head.

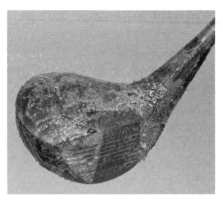

1-14 Be careful to keep the stripper off plastic inserts, whipping covers, and ferrules. Brief contact is OK, but prolonged contact will allow the stripping agent to ruin the plastic parts. Stripper has no effect on inserts such as fiber, melamine, gamma-fire, phenolic, etc. Until you can identify these different types, keep stripper off the insert.

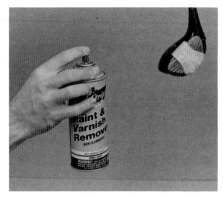

1-15 Stripper is now available in an aerosol can. The same precautions must still be taken concerning plastic components. Because you are unable to control the application as easily as with a brush, be sure to cover the insert and plastic whipping cover. Ferrules should also be covered. Masking tape works well for this.

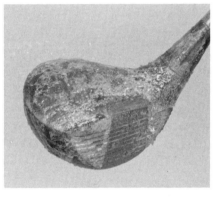

1-16 After the stripper has been on the finish for a few minutes, minor surface rippling to major bubbling will occur. Stripper and loosened finish should then be removed with . . .

1-17 . . . a stiff bristle Stripping Brush or . . .

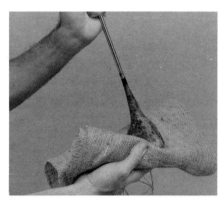

1-18 . . . vigorous wiping with burlap or . . .

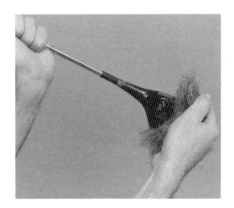

1-19 . . . coarse steel wool. **Note: The stripper can cause skin irritation. Immediately wash off any stripper from hands, arms, etc. Disposable plastic gloves work very well for stripping operations.**

1-20 Another method which is very quick is to remove the finish with **Scotchbrite**™ **Wheels.** These wheels will remove the finish without removing the wood. They are most effective when used in conjunction with the paste stripper. Instructions for use are found at the end of this chapter.

1-21 Observe properly stripped clubheads. Small patches of finish left on the head are acceptable, as our goal here is to remove the majority of the finish. Sandpaper usage will be lessened as a result of removing most of the finish with a stripper.

1-22 To check and record the horizontal face bulge, place a Face Radius Gauge horizontally across the bottom of the face and slide the gauge upwards towards the top of the face.

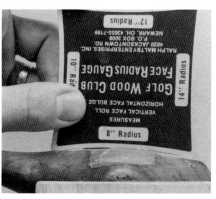

1-23 In this photo, the face does not adequately conform to the 8″ radius side; therefore, the face is flatter or has less radius than 8″.

1-24 Shown here, the face has more curvature or radius than the 14″ side. Somewhere in between these two readings is the measurement that will allow the clubface to properly match up to one side of the gauge.

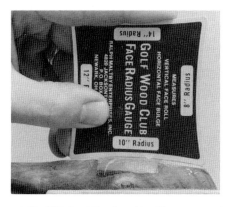

1-25 With the 10″ radius side of the gauge resting on the face, the two radius match. This is referred to as a 10″ radius horizontal face bulge or 10″ bulge.

1-26 Most manufacturers intentionally leave the top, heel portion of the face, higher or flatter in radius. This is done for cosmetic purposes and the bulge reading should not be taken along the top line of the face. Also, do not file this slightly higher area more than is necessary. This area affects the look of the face in the playing position.

1-27 Another reading to take is the vertical face roll. Again we look for that side of the gauge that allows the face to fit flush against the gauge. In this case, the 12″ radius side properly does so. Table 10-2 in Chapter 10 gives standard bulge and roll readings.

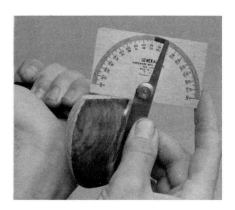

1-28 Loft should also be checked. Loft is always specified in degrees. Hold arm of protractor tight against soleplate and adjust protractor head so that it touches the face at ½ its vertical height. Photo shows protractor head resting below the halfway point so the loft reading would be less or stronger than it really is.

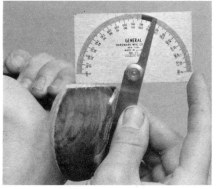

1-29 This photo shows the protractor head resting above the halfway point so the loft reading is greater or weaker than it really is.

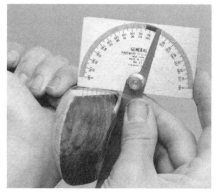

1-30 The correct positioning of the protractor head is shown here. The degree of loft is read directly off the gauge. **Note: The gauge arm is flat on the sole and the gauge head is touching the clubface at ½ its vertical height.**

1-31 Once the bulge, roll and loft angle have been determined, your goal will be to remove the finish without changing these readings, unless desired. Select a medium or fine cut file and file across the face from the heel . . .

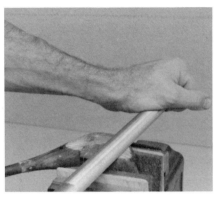

1-32 . . . towards the toe. It is best to move the file away from the hosel to prevent accidental marring of the hosel. Work the file in a radiusing motion for best results.

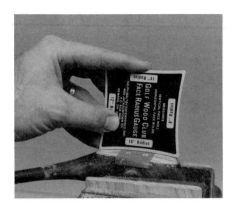

1-33 As you file, periodically check the face bulge and roll to make sure these specifications are as desired.

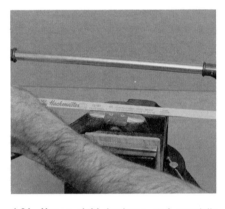

1-34 Use a rigid hacksaw and specially made, narrow width blade to clean out or slightly deepen existing face lines. The best approach is to begin in a heel side scoring line and use short cutting strokes as the blade is drawn through the line. **KEEP THE HACKSAW BLADE INSIDE THE LINES.**

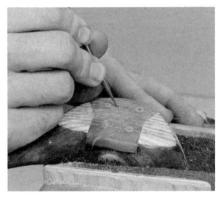

1-35 A **scriber** works well for cleaning the scoring lines in between and around the insert screws; however, it should not be used to deepen lines.

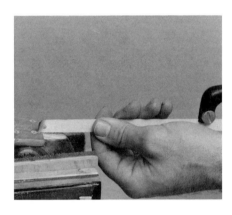

1-36 A **Mini Hacksaw** is available that will hold a blade that has been ground to a point. This enables you to deepen scoring lines around the screws.

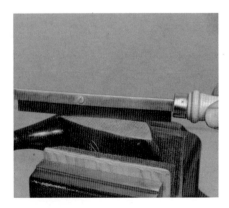

1-37 Cutting special narrow face lines on a number of older (1920's, 30's, and some 1940's) woods. The face scoring is very narrow and requires the use of a **Razor Saw** to cut them to a proper, original width.

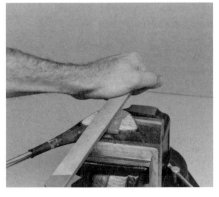

1-38 Next, lightly file the face with a flat mill or fine cut file. This will remove deeper marks left from use of the coarse cut file. No further smoothing of the face is necessary at this time.

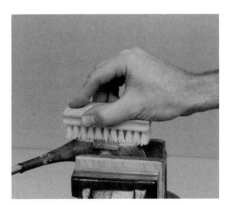

1-39 Brush the face to remove debris from the face lines and screw head recesses.

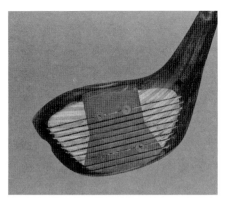

1-40 A properly prepared face will look like this. Note the clean, well defined scoring lines.

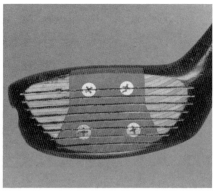

1-41 A sure sign of a novice at work. Cutting face lines through the insert screws is an **unacceptable practice.**

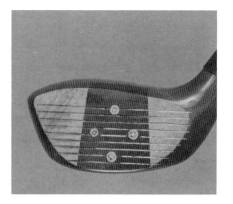

1-42 Sometimes original insert screws are damaged or the heads have become too small as a result of excessive filing. Most screws are easily turned out using a small **Reed and Prince screwdriver.** If difficulties are encountered, refer to Chapter 4, for further instructions on removing face screws.

1-43 Once the screws are removed, the face is filed as previously shown.

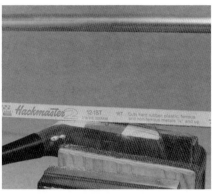

1-44 Also, cut in scoring lines as shown in photo 1-34.

1-45 Next, insert a countersink into the screw hole. Hold the shank in your fingers as shown, and twirl the countersink quickly. This is all that is necessary to enlarge the holes to accept the small face screw heads. **BE CAREFUL NOT TO MAKE HOLES WIDER THAN SCREW HEADS.** The countersink may be held in a drill chuck for faster work.

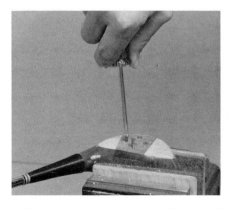

1-46 Install new insert screws. A very small dab of epoxy on the screw tip will permanently lock it in place, if desired. See Table 4-1 in Chapter 4 for recommended screw size. If insert screw pilot hole is too shallow, use a ³⁄₃₂″ drill bit to deepen it.

1-47 File the screw heads flush with the face. A properly countersunk hole will allow the head of the screw to be seated slightly above the face. This will give a professional look once the heads are filed down flush with the face.

1-48 The face is shown here with new insert screws. The additional effort required to replace the screws was well worth it. Note the screw slots have been positioned parallel and perpendicular to the scoring lines. This is a nice, professional touch.

1-49 Next, the soleplate needs to be resurfaced. First, the soleplate stampings should be cleaned. Remove dirt, paint, and old finish from the stamping using a scriber or sharpened awl. **Keep the tool inside the stamping.**

1-50 Position the clubhead in a vise as shown. Draw a fine cut file across the soleplate from the heel towards the toe. Remove as many scratches, dings and dents as possible without removing stampings. Usually, all but the very deepest dings can be removed.

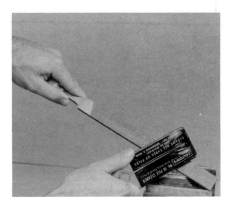

1-51 Lengthy filing will cause "loading." This occurs when metal collects between the teeth of the file. Failure to remove these metal clots will result in deep gouges inflicted on the soleplate as the file is drawn across the plate. **A good file cleaner should be kept close by and used frequently.**

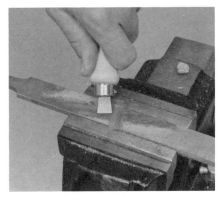

1-52 Stubborn metal or old epoxy can be removed using a piece of soft brass. Tighten the file in the vise and push the brass across the file face. This will push the residue from the file. A piece from an old brass soleplate works well for this.

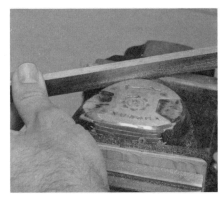

1-53 Not only must the bottom of the soleplate be refurbished, but the sides of the soleplate as well. This photo shows the trailing edge and . . .

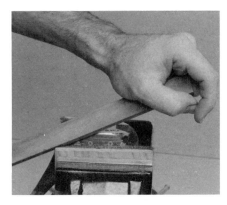

1-54 . . . the leading edge being filed. Use a radiusing motion with the file for best results. Maintain a defined edge around the soleplate.

1-55 A properly resurfaced soleplate will look like this. Note the file marks are running in the same direction on the bottom of the plate (toe to heel).

1-56 An alternative to filing is to use a belt sander. Using this machine will substantially speed up this step. For safest and fastest results, hold the club as shown. **Always wear eye protection when working around motorized machinery.**

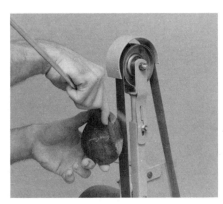

1-57 As before, lightly sand the leading edge . . .

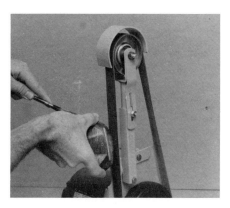

1-58 . . . and the trailing edge. **As with any motorized operation, a little practice first on junk golf clubs is highly recommended.**

1-59 This is a good example of how the bottom and edges of a soleplate should look after grinding. A smooth and uniform filing or grinding will save excess sanding and sandpaper wear later on.

1-60 Here is the typical valuable classic club. Most of these soleplate dings can be removed. The deep ding by the number stamp should not be removed as most of the number would be removed in the process. The value of the club would then drop.

1-61 **To preserve a wood stamping,** apply paste stripper once again to the stamping after the finish is removed. Refinishing a classic club is an acceptable practice as long as proper care is taken to preserve the head stampings and maintain originality.

1-62 Wait five minutes then wipe the stripper from the head. Be careful to keep the stripper off plastic inserts.

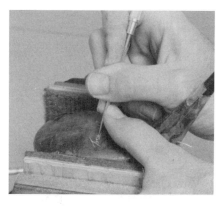

1-63 Re-etching the stamping involves a two-step process. First, simply etch the old paint from the stamp. The second step requires the stamp to be deepened. Carefully push the scriber through the stamp. **DO NOT ALLOW THE SCRIBER TO SLIDE OUT OF THE STAMP WHILE ETCHING.**

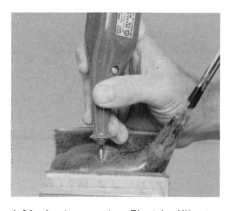

1-64 An inexpensive **Electric Vibrator Engraver** will also work, as long as the engraver has a fine point. Some engravers have a point that is too blunt and serious damage will result to the stamping. With the proper point, set engraver knob on "FINE" setting and proceed slowly and carefully.

1-65 **A properly etched stamping will look like this.** The paint has been removed and the stamping deepened. It is necessary to deepen the stamping as some depth will be lost through the sanding step. The discoloration around the stamp is normal and will sand out. The clubhead is now ready for sanding.

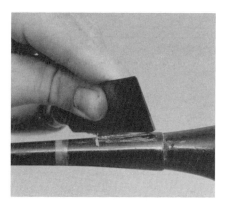

1-66 **A club with a plastic whipping cover requires additional steps before sanding.** Most covers have several coats of polyurethane. Scrape the cover lightly with a knife. If the scrapings are black, there is no polyurethane coverage. If the scrapings are clear or yellow, there is a polyurethane coating.

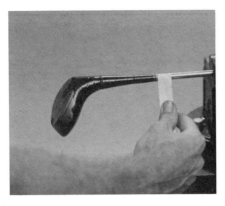

1-67 If there is no polyurethane coating, proceed to photo 1-73. If your cover has a coating, it must be removed before the clubhead is sanded. First, wrap a layer of masking tape around the shaft above the plastic ferrule.

1-68 Brush on a light coat of stripper. Cover both the ferrule and whipping cover.

1-69 Leave the stripper on the cover and ferrule until minor surface rippling is noticed. This will usually occur within the first 25 seconds after application. The purpose of the stripper is to soften the polyurethane without damaging the plastic.

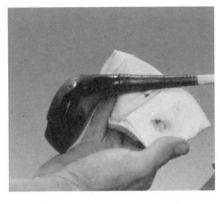

1-70 Once you notice the minor rippling, wipe the stripper off the plastic cover and ferrule. If you wait too long, the stripper will eat into the plastic. Never leave the stripper on the cover longer than 40 seconds.

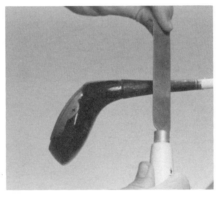

1-71 The softened polyurethane may now be removed through filing or light scraping with a **Detail Knife.** Be careful not to dig into the plastic.

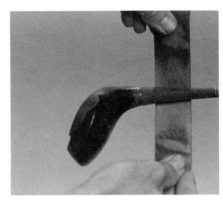

1-72 Lightly sand the cover with 150 grit sandpaper. Sanding will remove the scratches and flat spots left from filing or scraping.

1-73 Rub the cover and ferrule with fine 000 steel wool. Steel wool will eliminate the scratches left from use of the sandpaper. The ferrule should be very smooth but somewhat dull in appearance after this step.

1-74 Dampen a paper towel with acetone and quickly wipe the cover and ferrule. This will bring out the attractive deep plastic gloss.

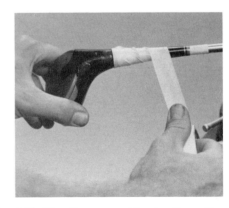

1-75 Wrap the cover and ferrule with masking tape. During the ensuing sanding steps, take great care to avoid the cover. Later, after sanding, refer to photos 1-104 and 1-105 which show how to finish the area where the wood head and plastic hosel cover meet.

1-76 The Golf Club Refinishing Machine utilizes double sponge-backed sanding drums. These sanding procedures apply to all sanding sleeve type sanders, both sponge rubber and pneumatic. It also applies to sanding cones and sanding belts as shown in photos 1-101 and 1-102.

1-77 The goal here is to preserve the original shape of the clubhead. 80 to 100 grit sandpaper is used for rough sanding. 120 or 150 paper is used for fine sanding and 180 or 220 for very fine sanding.

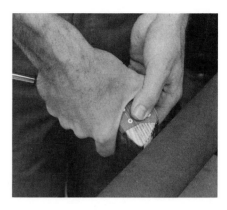

1-78 Grasp the clubhead as shown. Rotate the toe into the sanding sleeve from the edge of the face . . .

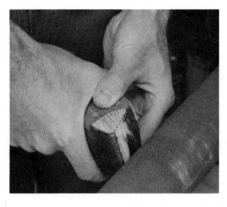

1-79 . . . outward to the middle of the toe. Sand from the top line around the toe down to the bottom line around the sole. **DO NOT SAND ON THE FACE.**

1-80 Position the club as shown. Sand from the middle of the toe to the back side of the club and . . .

1-81 . . . around to the back of the hosel. Now sand up to the heel side of the face.

1-82 The side portion of the club should look like this. It is not necessary to remove all of the color at this point. Simply remove the majority of the leftover finish and most of the color while preserving the shape of the clubhead.

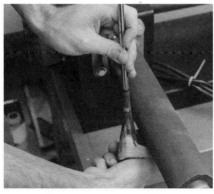

1-83 Hold the clubhead as shown. Place the back top portion of the clubhead against the sanding sleeve and . . .

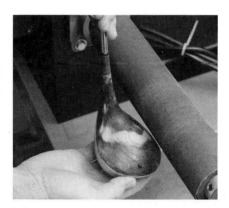

1-84 . . . rotate the clubhead away from the sleeve. This will create a sanded area from the back of the club to the front. Sanding from back to front will ensure that the sanding marks are running parallel with the grain on persimmon heads.

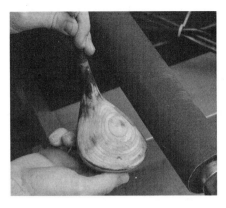

1-85 Repeat the back to front movement across the top of the clubhead until the entire top is sanded.

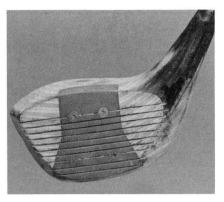

1-86 When sanding the top of the clubhead, great care must be taken along the line separating the face from the top of the clubhead.

1-87 This line should not be straight or concave as shown here. Rather, the line should have a smooth symmetrical look as shown in the previous photo. Every effort should be made to avoid pulling this top line down. **The rule of thumb for sanding is again applied: preserve the original clubhead shape.**

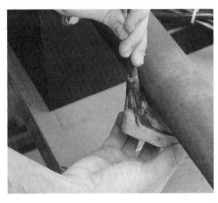

1-88 The hosel should now be sanded (except clubs with whipping covers). Place the hosel lightly against the sanding sleeve, supporting the head with one hand while holding the shaft with the other hand.

1-89 Smoothly rotate the hosel while light to medium pressure is maintained against the sleeve.

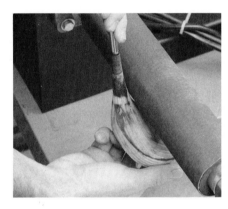

1-90 Continue to rotate the head while sanding the hosel. Keep the club constantly turning to eliminate the chance of flat spots in the hosel. The entire hosel, from the top down to the hosel/head radius is sanded.

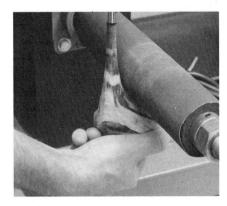

1-91 When sanding the base of the hosel (hosel radius), move the sleeve over the top of the head to ensure a smooth transition from the hosel into the head area. This eliminates ridges.

1-92 The sanded hosel should look like this. Note the presence of a stained area in the hosel. This indicates that the outside curvature of the sanding sleeve did not fit perfectly into the hosel radius. Never force the sleeve into the hosel radius. Light hand sanding will remove this excess finish.

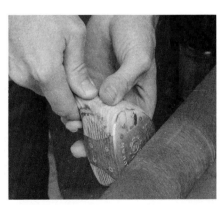

1-93 Even though the sole has been filed, we must still machine sand the sole to make sure the sanding and filing marks are running in one direction — from heel to toe. Sanding will also blend in the filing marks.

1-94 The leading edge and trailing edge are also lightly sanded. This again will blend in the filing marks.

1-95 The rough-sanded club should look like this. Notice there is finish around the edges of the clubhead. This is acceptable at this stage, as this indicates the shape has not been altered. The previous sanding steps would now be repeated using the medium 120 or 150 grit paper, followed by 180 or 220 paper.

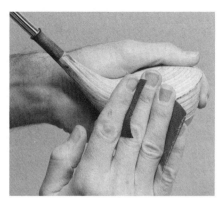

1-96 After final sanding, the edges will be sharp. Lightly radius the edges with a strip of 180 or 220 grit paper as shown. Radiusing the edges is often referred to as "blocking."

1-97 Some refinishers prefer to use a **Sand-O-Flex** for the blocking step. The sharp edge is turned into the rotating "loose" sandpaper, thus removing the sharp edge. Be sure to use a very fine grit loading.

1-98 Machine sanding the hosel will sometimes create ridges in the hosel. These are easily removed by holding the clubhead as shown. Rotate the club while sanding the hosel up and down. **"Blocking" the edges and this step are final sanding detailing steps which assure that everything is completely blended together.**

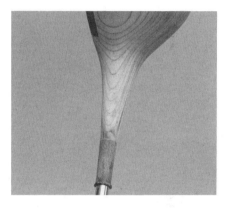

1-99 A properly sanded hosel will be smooth and possess a nice even taper from top to bottom. There should be no bulges or irregularities. This club is now ready for face masking as detailed in photos 1-115 thru 1-123.

1-100 An alternative to the Golf Club Refinishing Machine is the **Economy Sanding Machine.** This unit is ideal for shops with limited space. It can easily be mounted to a sturdy bench and is then ready for use.

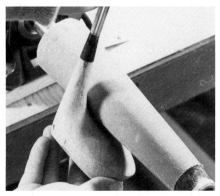

1-101 The old finish can also be removed on a sanding cone using 80 or 100 grit paper. Use 120 or 150 grit for medium sanding and 180 or 220 for final sanding. Although excellent results can be obtained with a cone, it has two drawbacks. First, the replacement sanding sleeves are expensive and second, the felt backing does not conform to the head shape as easily as the sponge rubber type backing.

1-102 A 3″ wide by 132″ long sanding belt is used to remove old finish. The same grits are used as in previous sanding steps. A belt idler unit is located on the floor. Sander is powered by a ⅓ H.P. motor. Belts are commercially available.

1-103 Sand-O-Flex wheel can also be used to strip off old finish and final sand head. For best results, use model 550A Sand-O-Flex powered by a ½ H.P. motor at 1725 RPM. Model 350 Sand-O-Flex can be used with a ⅓ H.P. motor, but is slower in removing the finish than the 550A model.

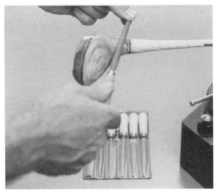

1-104 After sanding a club with a plastic whipping cover, there will be some finish around the base of the cover. This cannot be removed on a sanding machine. Place the club in a vise as shown and lightly file the excess finish from the hosel. A small flat file works best.

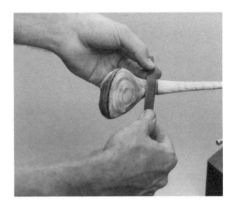

1-105 After finish is removed, lightly sand the hosel with 180 grit or finer paper. This will blend in any file marks and/or flat spots.

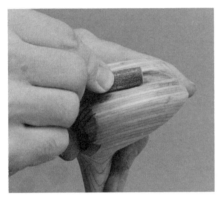

1-106 Occasionally, you will find a slot running through the toe or back portion of a club. A slot is best cleaned by first running a ½" or smaller round file through the slot. Then, lightly sand the slot with fine sandpaper wrapped around the file.

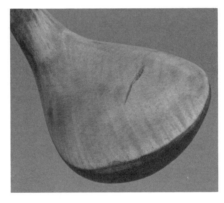

1-107 You may not be able to sand out some deep indentations in the wood head. The dent can sometimes be repaired by using the following technique, which works best on persimmon heads.

1-108 Lay a wet cloth over the damaged area. Iron the cloth directly over the dent. The dent will be infused with moisture and the steam created will raise the wood grain. This step is best performed after the rough sanding step. Once the wood grain has raised, proceed to the next sanding step.

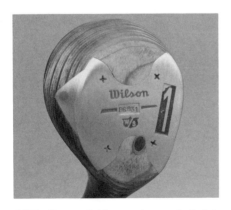

1-109 Some refinishers prefer a satin look to the soleplate. This is best accomplished by . . .

1-110 . . . lightly pressing the soleplate against the face of a **Scotchbrite Wheel.** This step is performed just prior to stain application.

1-111 In rare cases, a customer may wish to have the soleplate polished. Proceed as follows to buff soleplate: apply compound to **Stitched Buffing Wheel.** (See Table 1-2 at the end of this chapter for selection of proper buffing compound.)

1-112 Buff soleplate to desired lustre. After polishing, remove buffing compound from sole-plate by wiping with alcohol. Be careful not to get compound on wood portion of sole unless the wood will be covered with an opaque paint. If compound residue remains on the wood, wipe the wood with alcohol or acetone.

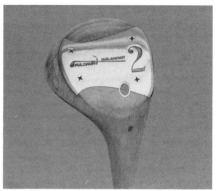

1-113 The results of a polished soleplate can be outstanding; however, the ensuing coats of finish adhere best to a somewhat rougher sur-face. Adhesion problems may occur as a result of polishing the metal.

1-114 This is a professionally sanded club-head. Note some of the original stain is still pres-ent in the wood. There are three possible reasons for this. . . .

1. The refinisher will stain the club using an identical color. Therefore, it is not necessary to remove all of the original stain.
2. A color-cote will be applied to the head. This means a coating of opaque paint will cover the old stain.
3. The original factory staining did not evenly penetrate the wood. This can be caused by imperfect sanding, wood imperfection or various absorption differences in the grain hardness, or inconsistency in the stain itself.

Many beginning refinishers will look at the club pictured in photo 1-114 and immediately assume more sanding is necessary. This is not the case. Further sanding will only reduce the size of the clubhead and, in the end, some of the stain would probably still be present.

Pursuing this course could also ruin the club, as some refinishers have been known to press the stained area against the face of a sander until the area is clean. This creates a clean head but the clubhead shape is less than desirable.

Be reasonable in your expectations of what will and won't sand out. Also, adopt a policy of advising your customer of the possible consequences should he decide to change the color of his club from a dark stain to a lighter stain.

Some commercial bleaching agents can help remove excess stain. Experiment carefully with a bleach before attempting to use it on a customer's club.

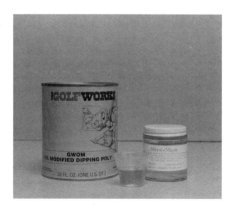

1-115 Before the clubhead can be stained, a protective coating must be applied to the face and insert. The material used for coating can be polyurethane, primer sealer or Mira-Mask, a product made expressly for this. Old, thickened polyurethane works best. The poly seeps into the wood pores and prevents stain penetration into the face.

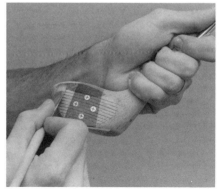

1-116 The material is spread onto the face us-ing either a stiff bristled artist's brush or your finger. Here we are using the brush. Apply a small portion of the masking material to the up-per portion of the face. Spread this evenly along the top of the face out to the toe. Keep the mask-ing material in the face outline only.

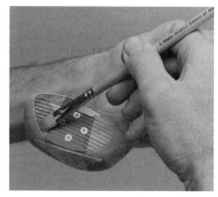

1-117 Brush the mask from the top of the toe to the bottom of the face. This is the easiest portion of the face to mask, as there should be a well-defined line between the face and toe por-tion of the clubhead. Note the brush is always inside the face. This helps prevent accidental spreading outside the face.

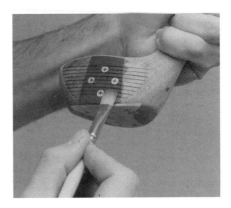

1-118 We're halfway finished. Notice the insert is also covered. Stain can penetrate deeply into fibrous type inserts. It will not penetrate into plastic, aluminum, or epoxy inserts. Until you are able to identify the different insert types, all inserts should be masked.

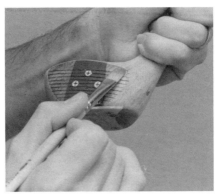

1-119 Brush the mask from the insert toward the heel. This area is more difficult to mask, as the line between the face and hosel area is not always defined. Some refinishers choose to pencil in the shape of the face prior to masking.

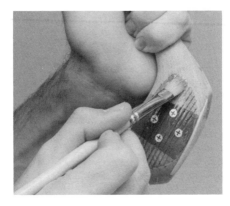

1-120 Spread the mask from the bottom of the face to the top of the face, working the mask slowly back into the heel area until the desired shape is achieved. Practice will help develop an "eye" for a properly shaped face.

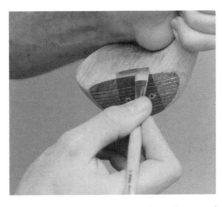

1-121 Carefully apply the mask to the top of the insert. Remember, any area coming in contact with the mask will not take stain. Keep the mask on the insert.

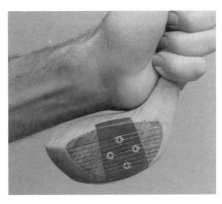

1-122 This is a properly masked face. The toe and heel of the face are well defined, with good shape.

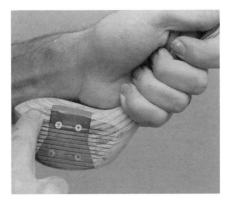

1-123 Some refinishers prefer to apply the mask with a finger. Although somewhat messier, they feel more in control using a finger instead of a brush. Experiment and see which method you like best. Results can be comparable. **Now the clubhead is ready for staining.**

1-124 Water or alcohol base stains work best. Table 1-4 at the end of this chapter offers complete information on various refinishing products regarding compatibility, application type and average drying times.

At The GolfWorks®, we feel it is easier to work with water base stains.

1-125 **For even stain coverage, completely submerge the clubhead into a container of stain for five seconds.** Repeated dippings will produce a darker color. For best results, though, wait a few minutes between coats. The plastic container shown is most convenient for holding stains and fillers for both storage and dipping.

1-126 Remove clubhead from stain and allow excess stain to drip back into can. Note the stain does not penetrate into the masked face.

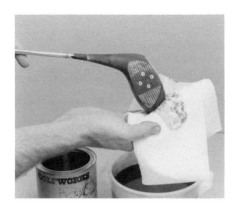

1-127 Wait 30 seconds then use a paper towel to blot excess stain from head. **DO NOT WIPE THE STAIN, BLOT IT.** Excess stain will also collect in scoring lines. Place the paper towel at the end of the face and force the collected stain onto the towel by blowing along the scoring lines.

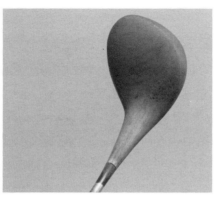

1-128 Stain dries quickly. Immediately after the clubhead is removed from the stain, it has a bright shine. As the stain dries, the clubhead will take on a duller, drier look as shown. This is to be expected. The clubhead may be advanced to the next step after drying. Drying times will vary from 4 to 12 hours depending on stain type and drying temperature. See table 1-4.

1-129 Stain may also be applied by brushing. It is difficult to achieve a uniform even color through brushing. Brushing stain is best if you wish to highlight or gradually tone an area with concentrated stain.

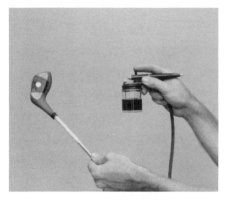

1-130 Stain can be applied by spraying, using an airbrush and small compressor. The disposable spraying unit with screw-on jars also works quite well and will spray up to 16 ounces of stain in one aerosol pack.

1-131 Stain can be applied by blotting or wiping. Cotton cloth or cheesecloth works well.

1-132 Filling the clubhead is the next finishing step. Fillers are available in an oil, polyurethane, or water base. See table 1-4. Oil base fillers are the most common and easiest to work with.

1-133 The filler serves to fill in the open pores in the wood head and provides a relatively smooth surface for the upcoming finish coats. Natural and less intense black filler are used the most. Natural retains the existing stain color while less intense black darkens the existing stain color by a few shades.

1-134 Dip the toe of the clubhead into the filler. It is not necessary to submerge the entire clubhead. Note the use of plastic gloves. Using these gloves will prevent the filler from coming in contact with your hands. Filler can stain skin and clothes, not to mention the mess under one's fingernails.

1-135 Remove toe of clubhead from the container. Wipe the filler over the entire head. Be sure to cover all wood areas with the filler.

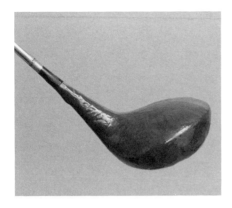

1-136 The covered clubhead will look like this. Do not remove the excess filler until the filler has "flashed off" for at least 10 minutes but not longer than 15 minutes. Flash off refers to the solvent evaporation the filler undergoes when exposed to the air. As solvents evaporate, the filler becomes a more solid coating.

1-137 If Mira-Filler is used, which is a polyurethane base filler, it may be first tinted with Mira-Stain. Note a portion of the filler has been removed from the can prior to changing the color. You won't want to color the entire can.

1-138 After the 10 minute flash off period, the filler will look quite different. It will have a dull cast to it.

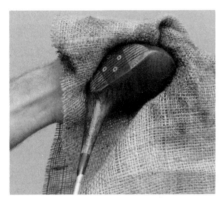

1-139 The excess filler is now wiped from the head with burlap, cheesecloth, or other coarse cloth. Rub the head briskly; failure to remove excess filler is the number one cause of finish adhesion problems.

1-140 Wipe only with clean burlap. The clubhead surface should feel smooth and polished after wiping.

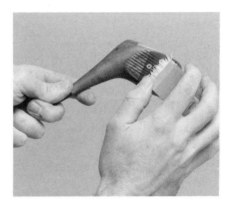

1-141 Filler will collect in scoring lines. Brush scoring lines briskly with a **stiff bristled brush** to remove excess. The clubhead is advanced to the next step after drying. Oil type fillers require 6-12 hours and polyurethane fillers require 2-5 hours. See table 1-4.

1-142 The clubhead will look dull at this stage. Every step hereafter will improve the cosmetics dramatically.

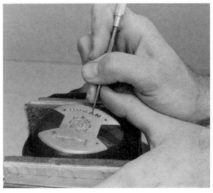

1-143 The filling step has resulted in the wood and metal stampings being filled also. **Carefully pick the excess filler from the soleplate stampings using a scriber or sharpened awl.** Keep the instrument inside the stamping. Sometimes, brisk brushing with a stiff fingernail brush will remove all filler from the soleplate engravings.

1-144 Wood stampings must also be cleaned. Use the same procedure as shown in photos 1-63 thru 1-65. Again, take great care with this step. Do not wait longer than 4 hours before cleaning stampings, as the filler will become hard and more difficult to work with.

1-145 After the filler has dried, the residue left on the soleplate (and backweight) must be removed. This residue can be removed by rubbing with fine 000 steel wool. When steel wooling the soleplate, rub from heel to toe and back again. Never from side to side.

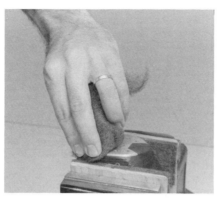

1-146 **The leading edge and trailing edge of the soleplate must also be cleaned.** Keep the steel wool on the metal surface — rubbing the wood portion of the club may remove some of the color.

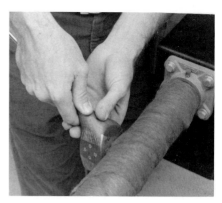

1-147 **The Golf Club Refinishing Machine is easily converted for steel wooling.** Slide the steel wool sleeve on and tighten the nut. Press the soleplate and backweight lightly against the turning steel wool. Filler residue is quickly removed.

1-148 The soleplate and backweight will now look much better. There is a small amount of oil packed into the steel wool which prevents the steel wool from oxidizing. Traces of this oil have now been thinly deposited over the soleplate and backweight or anywhere the steel wool has touched the head.

1-149 To remove the oily residue, dampen a paper towel with acetone. Wipe the towel over the soleplate and backweight only. Also, using some naphtha, lightly wipe the wood surrounding the soleplate and backweight. Do not use acetone for this.

The refinishing steps discussed thus far are identical for clubs of all colors. At this point, however, the refinishing steps will vary depending upon whether or not the club is to receive a color-cote. The purpose of a color-cote is to cover or hide the wood grain, or any surface imperfections, with an opaque coating. Black or blue finished clubs normally receive this paint color coating, while clubs of other colors usually do not.

If the club will be color-coated, continue on to step 1-150.

If the club will not be color-coated, continue on to step 1-196.

1-150 **On a color-coated club, the soleplate, backweight, and top of the insert must be covered prior to paint application.** Either a clear cellophane tape or masking tape can be used. **Cellophane tape** is preferred because it is easier to see through, but will sometimes leave a sticky residue on metal. Masking tape will not leave a residue, but is more difficult to see through and consequently to work with.

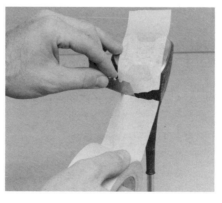

1-151 Lay a piece of tape across the soleplate. The tape should be at least 2″ wide and extend over the heel and toe portion of the sole.

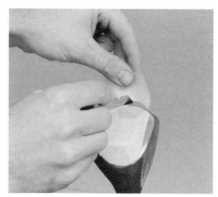

1-152 With a razor blade, carefully cut around the edge of the sole through the tape.

1-153 The bottom of the club should look like this. Two-inch wide masking tape is being used here.

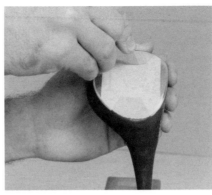

1-154 Now, carefully trace around the edge of the toe portion of the soleplate and . . .

1-155 . . . around the heel portion of the soleplate. Do not allow the razor blade to slip onto the metal, as a permanent scratch will result. **Note: Best results are obtained by using a very sharp blade.**

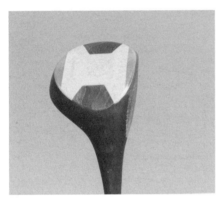

1-156 A properly outlined soleplate will look like this. Note the precise cuts that have been made around the heel and toe. A jagged edge will give an unprofessional appearance.

1-157 The trailing and leading edges must also be covered. Tear off a 5″ piece of ½″ or ¾″ masking tape.

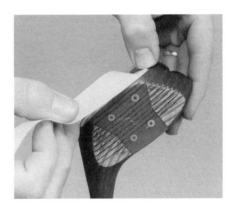

1-158 Place one end of the tape against a soleplate corner. Lay the edge of the tape against the edge of the soleplate. Wrap the tape around the leading edge, keeping the tape edge butted against the soleplate edge.

1-159 Once tape has been positioned around the front edge, place your thumbnail against the tape, inside the soleplate corner, and . . .

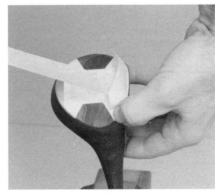

1-160 . . . quickly tear the excess tape. A razor blade also works well for this.

1-161 Fold the remaining portion of tape onto the soleplate. This will cover any exposed area of the soleplate on this side. Repeat steps shown in photo 1-157 thru 1-161 for the trailing edge.

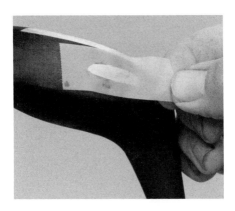

1-162 Any backweights must also be covered. Again, clear cellophane or masking tape will work. Shown here is cellophane tape.

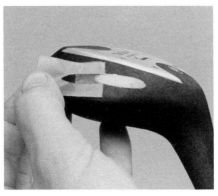

1-163 Tear off a strip of tape that will completely cover the weight. Carefully trace around the edge of the weight and remove the excess tape.

1-164 Scrape the top of the insert lightly with a **Detail Knife** to remove the polyurethane mask.

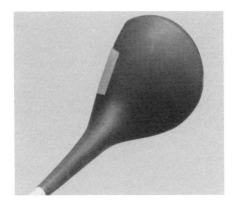

1-165 If the insert you are working with is made of ABS plastic, do the following. After scraping the top of the insert . . .

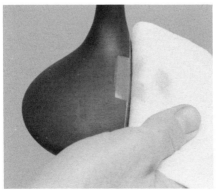

1-166 . . . dampen a paper towel or cloth with acetone and wipe the top of the insert. This will substantially brighten the plastic.

1-167 Next, lay a strip of tape across the top of the insert. One edge of the tape should butt up to the back edge of the insert. Cellophane tape should be used for this.

1-168 With a razor blade, cut and remove the excess tape around the sides of the insert. The extra tape overhanging the face may be folded down onto the face.

1-169 The club is now ready to be color-coated. The face does not need a tape masking because a polyurethane coating is already masking it.

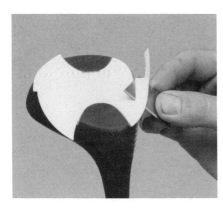

1-170 Some wood head manufacturers sell die-cut soleplate masks to fit their own brands. This is the easiest way to mask a soleplate. Once the mask is applied to the soleplate, the edges must still be masked as already shown, using ½" or ¾" masking tape or cellophane tape.

1-171 Color-cote may be applied by brushing, dipping, or spraying. There are different types of color-cotes available. Check Table 1-4 at the end of this chapter for product compatibility.

1-172 A few refinishers choose to brush the color-cote onto the head. It is difficult to achieve an even coat without streaks using this method. It works, but it is not recommended.

1-173 Spraying the color-cote allows the refinisher to control the depth of the coat and achieve an even coat. When spraying the color-cote from an aerosol can, keep the can approximately 15″ from the clubhead surface.

1-174 For best results, adopt a spraying technique that utilizes broad sweeping motions with the can. Turn the clubhead to expose unsprayed areas of the head.

1-175 The main concern is to avoid a heavy build-up. A properly sprayed surface will not have a glossy look. Instead, the sprayed surface will have a rough, dull appearance. This is normal and no steps should be taken to smooth it out.

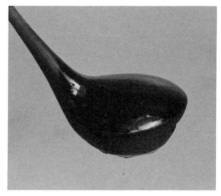

1-176 This is an example of a clubhead that has received a coating that is too heavy. If left as is, problems will develop once the next finish coat is applied. The entire head should be wiped with an acetone dampened towel to remove all the color-cote, and then reapply.

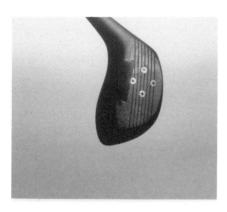

1-177 There is a fine line between too light and just right. Generally, if you are still able to see through to the face, the coating is too light. Although the above club has a coat that is too light, this can be remedied by spraying an additional light coat. Several light coats are far better than one heavy coat.

1-178 Do not be fooled if you can see the laminations on laminated maple heads. Applying more coats is a common mistake. These rings will disappear as the polyurethane coats are applied later. What happens here is that the lamination glue lines and the wood itself are not the same roughness; hence the color-cote looks smoother on each glue line vertically enhancing the lamination layers.

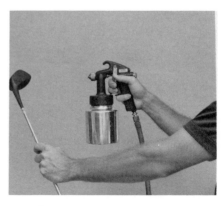

1-179 Color-cote may also be applied with an airbrush or commercial spray gun. The aerosol can method is more economical and the results are basically the same. See Table 1-4 at the end of this chapter for drying times.

1-180 After the color-cote has dried, remove the tape that covers the top of the insert. There should now be a sharp, well defined line between the insert and the color-coted wood.

1-181 Fasten the shaft, or the head, securely in a vise. Select a fine cut file. Note the use of clean felt vise pads to protect the finish. The purpose of this step is to create a reasonably clean face by removing the color-cote, if used, and the polyurethane face mask.

1-182 File carefully toward the toe. Gentle strokes are sufficient to clean the face. Remember, you are only cleaning off the face with the file and removing very little material from the face itself.

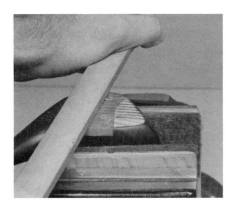

1-183 File back in the direction of the heel until the insert is clean.

1-184 Carefully work the file into the heel area. Cleaning the heel side of the face is far more difficult than the toe side. If you file into the hosel, you will have to touch-up the affected area with stain and/or colorcoat.

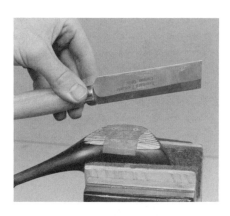

1-185 The tool shown here is called a **Detail Knife**. The Detail Knife is used to create a sharp, well-defined face.

1-186 The club may be fastened in a vise, or held as shown. Scrape with the back side of the blade, not the cutting edge. Begin at the bottom of the heel side of the face and work . . .

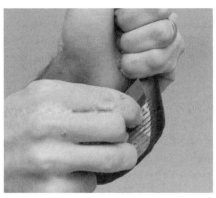

1-187 . . . up toward the top of the face. Short scraping strokes work best.

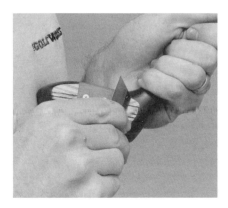

1-188 Turn the corner at the top of the face and . . .

1-189 . . . continue across the top of the face toward the toe.

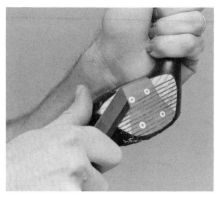

1-190 After reaching the toe, place the blade at the bottom of the face and scrape toward the top.

1-191 **This is how a properly detailed face, which was color-coted, should look.** Note the symmetrical look of the face. Drawing the knife repeatedly across the face will remove all of the file marks and create a smooth face. No face sanding will be necessary.

1-192 The sharp edge of the Detail Knife may be used for removing build-up in the scoring lines. **The Detail Knife is one of the refinisher's best friends and is one of the secrets to professional refinishes.**

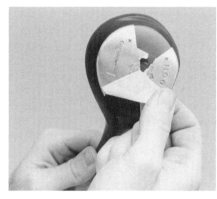

1-193 Now that the face is detailed, remove the tape from the soleplate and backweight.

1-194 Occasionally, the color-cote will bleed onto the soleplate. This is easily removed with a piece of cheese cloth and acetone. Wrap the cloth tightly around your index finger, dampen with acetone, and wipe off the excess. Keep the dampened cloth on the soleplate only. If it comes in contact with the wood, the color-cote, if any, will be removed.

1-195 As with the face, our goal is to have a well-defined outline between the color-coted wood and the soleplate. Avoid a fuzzy definition. This club is now ready for the next finishing step. Proceed to photo 1-201.

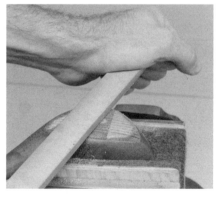

1-196 **A club that was not color-coted must also have the face cleaned.** This is easier to do than with color-coted clubs because the outline of the face is clearly seen.

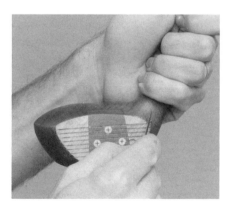

1-197 Proceed detailing the face in basically the same manner as for color-coted clubs. **Review photos 1-185 thru 1-191 for use of the Detail Knife which works best for outlining faces professionally.**

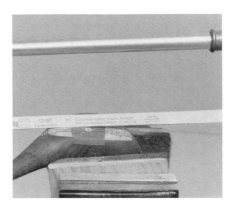

1-198 Scoring lines can be cleaned with a hacksaw blade. Keep blade in scoring lines. Note: An old broken piece of a scoring line blade held in the fingers works well for this also.

1-199 This is what a properly detailed face looks like on a non color-coted club.

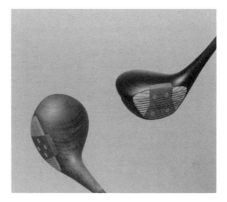

1-200 Color-coted clubs and non color-coted clubs follow identical steps from this point forward.

1-201 The two most widely used types of polyurethanes are Moisture Cure (MC) and Oil Modified (OM). The OM poly will be used here because it best serves the average refinisher and is easier to work with when learning refinishing techniques. Read "Additional Information" at the end of this chapter for descriptions of the various polyurethane types.

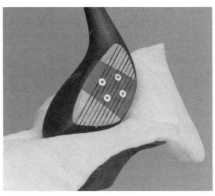

1-202 First, lightly wipe the head with a tack rag to remove any dust particles, lint, etc. An alternative to the tack rag is use of Naphtha. Wipe the head lightly with a towel dampened with this solvent. This will remove a wide range of contaminants.

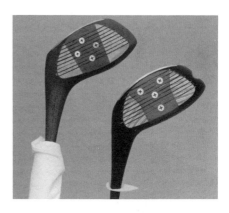

1-203 Fold a paper towel and attach it to the shaft with tape, positioning it at the top of the hosel. This towel will collect the poly runoff. Another method used to catch the polyurethane as it runs off the head is to use small rubber "dippers" available from club repair suppliers. They stretch over the grip and are slid down the shaft into position.

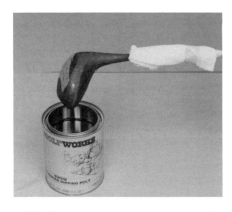

1-204 The clubhead is now ready for the 1st dipping. Note the level of the poly in the can is approximately 1½" below the rim. This will allow the clubhead to fully submerge without poly overflow. The can will arrive full. Pour enough out to reach the level shown. Excess poly can be used for masking faces.

1-205 Submerge the entire clubhead into the can and then . . .

1-206 . . . remove the club as **quickly** as possible. Speed in dipping is essential. Allow excess poly to run off the head and back into the can until the poly stops running and begins to drip. Immediately after the poly begins to drip . . .

1-207 . . . turn the head up with the face cocked slightly open. This will facilitate proper poly runoff and flow from the head. It is important that the 1st poly coat be as thin as possible. After the toe has been turned up . . .

1-208 . . . using your finger, wipe poly down uncovered hosel and blow briskly across the clubhead surface toward the hosel. This will decrease the thickness of the poly coating. A poly coat that is too thick will invite solvent entrapment problems which are explained in detail at the end of this chapter in the "Additional Information For Refinishing Woods" section.

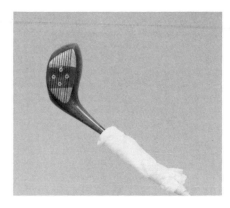

1-209 Hold the clubhead in this position until the runoff stops (usually 60 to 90 seconds). It is important to hold the clubhead as shown in this photo.

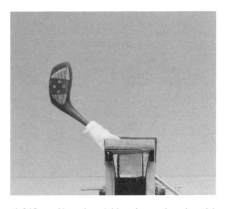

1-210 Now the clubhead may be placed in a drying rack or held in a vise for 30 minutes. Most of the solvents in the poly will evaporate during this drying period.

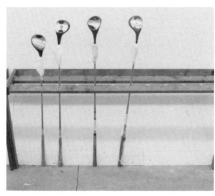

1-211 The club may then be placed under force dry conditions to accelerate the curing process or left at room temperature to dry. Table 1-4 at the end of this chapter provides average drying time information.

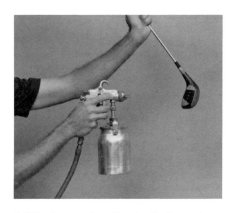

1-212 As an alternative to dipping, polyurethane is often applied by using adequate spray equipment consisting of a compressor, spray gun and spray booth.

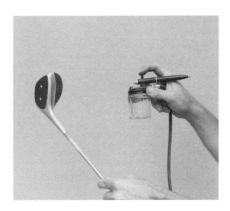

1-213 An inexpensive **Airbrush** can also be used effectively. A fine nozzle works best for proper spray dispersion.

1-214 Polyurethane is also available in an aerosol can. Serious refinishers doing any sort of volume work should avoid this as an alternative to dipping. The aerosol poly can, however, be used effectively for touch-up purposes and should be kept on hand even in larger shops.

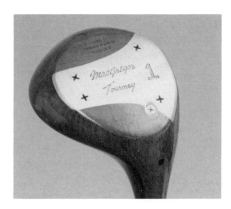

1-215 After the 1st poly coat has dried, wood and metal stampings should be paintfilled. Additional coats of poly will fill in the stamping and make paintfilling later on impossible.

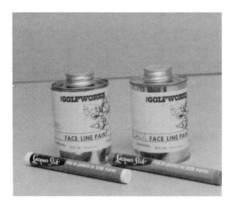

1-216 Scoring line paint and lacquer sticks are commonly used for filling stampings. Lacquer sticks are preferred because they are easier to work with and are not as messy as paint. Also, lacquer sticks dry quickly.

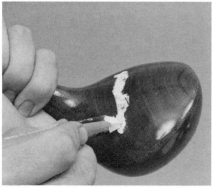

1-217 Lightly rub the **lacquer stick** into the stampings until the stamping is completely filled.

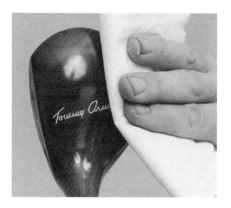

1-218 Immediately after filling the stamping, wipe the excess from the head with a paper towel. Do not smear the paint all over the head.

1-219 Any residue left around the stamping is easily removed by . . .

1-220 . . . rubbing lightly with 000 steel wool.

1-221 This is a sample of a properly filled wood stamping. **Allow the lacquer stick to dry a minimum of two hours before applying the 2nd coat of poly.** There are solvents that must evaporate before the next poly coat is applied.

1-222 The soleplate stampings are also filled in the same manner. Scoring line paint and a brush are used to fill the stampings this time. Simply fill the stampings and wipe away the excess with a paper towel.

1-223 Photo shows properly paintfilled soleplate stampings. When paintfilling stampings, try to use original colors.

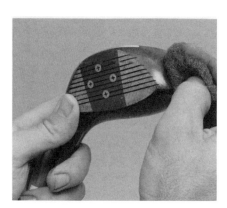

1-224 **After the polyurethane coating has dried and after any stampings are paintfilled, lightly steel wool the surface with 000 steel wool.** Abrading the surface allows the next poly coat a better "hold." This light abrading will turn the high gloss finish to a dull satin look. Do not steel wool the clubhead edges to prevent going through this 1st thin coat of poly.

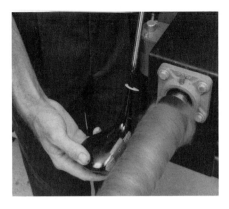

1-225 Machine steel wooling with 000 steel wool is faster. A light touch is required when working with a machine. Take the same care with the clubhead edges.

1-226 If a decal(s) is needed, proceed as follows: Fold a paper towel in half and place on a flat surface. Saturate the paper towel with water, but do not allow the water to puddle.

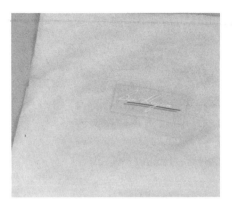

1-227 Place the decal with the image up and the back of the decal in complete contact with the wet towel. Allow the decal to absorb moisture and soften for a minute or two. When the decal slides freely on the paper backing, it may then be applied to the head. Dampen the area of the head where the decal will be applied.

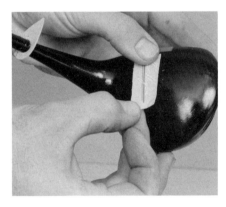

1-228 Slide the decal off the backing and onto the desired location. See "Additional Information" at the end of this chapter for more information on positioning decals. Note the positioning of the hands. A thumb is placed on one end of the decal while . . .

1-229 . . . the backing is pulled out from underneath the decal. If the decal is a reverse image type, substitute decal solvent for water. It is not possible to slide reverse image decals in place. Reverse image decals are placed in their exact position and the backing paper is lifted off the decal.

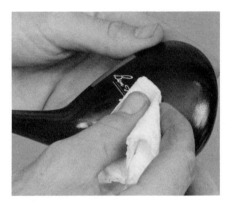

1-230 Water slide-off type decals may be moved around on the clubhead surface up to 45 seconds before permanently setting. Once the decal is set, pat the decal firmly with a damp paper towel or cloth. This will force out any air bubbles from beneath the decal.

1-231 The clubhead is **tack ragged** or wiped with **Naphtha** once again before the 2nd poly coating.

1-232 Dip the 2nd coat of polyurethane. Turn the club up once the poly runoff begins to drip. It is not necessary to blow on the finish after the 1st poly coat.

1-233 Allow the club to dry in this position at room temperature for one hour. A **Golf Club Drying Rack** as shown works best.

1-234 **After the one-hour drying period, dip the 3rd coat of polyurethane.** Do not abrade the surface before dipping this coat. The 2nd coat is tacky enough to give the 3rd coat a good bonding surface.

1-235 After the initial 30 minute flash-off period, again place the club under room temperature dry or force dry conditions.

1-236 After the 3rd coat is completely dry, the poly will have a sufficient build-up to allow some leveling of the surface. **A 400 grit silicone-backed wet or dry paper works best.** Cut strips of sandpaper approximately 1½" wide and wrap around the two middle fingers as shown.

1-237 Use a circular sanding motion for best results. Sand the entire clubhead until the finish begins to look like dust or chalk. If the finish "balls," this is an indication that the poly has not dried long enough. Hand sanding between coats is the secret to a super smooth finish and the deepest gloss.

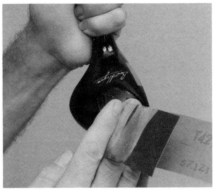

1-238 If you find a run or sag on the surface, concentrate sanding directly on top of this polyurethane build-up. Be careful not to sand the surrounding area, as the finish is much thinner there.

1-239 **Sand lightly over decals and do not sand the clubhead edges.**

1-240 This is an example of a properly sanded head. The small high gloss areas must be left as is. These spots indicate low points in the finish. If these small areas are sanded at this stage, you will sand through the poly into the wood.

1-241 Next, either hand or machine steel wool the entire head with fine 000 grade to smooth out the hand-sanding marks. Note that steel wooling does not take the place of hand sanding. Both are necessary for an excellent finish.

1-242 The same head after steel wooling. Note the even, dull appearance.

1-243 Tack rag the head or wipe with Naphtha.

1-244 Dip the 4th polyurethane coat using the same techniques as used for the previous coats. After the 30 minute flash-off period, allow the club to thoroughly dry under room temperature or force dry conditions as before.

1-245 After the poly has dried, hand sand clubhead with 400 or 600 grit sandpaper.

1-246 This is a properly sanded club. Note the even, gray appearance. This indicates there are no low spots and the polyurethane coatings have been leveled properly. Steel wool the clubhead and then lightly wipe the head with the tack rag or Naphtha.

1-247 Dip the 5th and final coat. After the 30 minute flash-off priod, allow the club to dry overnight under room or force dry conditions.

1-248 If there is a small run or surface imperfection on the final poly coat, it is not necessary to sand, steel wool and apply another coat. To rid the surface of this problem, wait three days for the poly to fully cure and then . . .

1-249 . . . put two or three **unstitched buffing wheels** together and attach them to a motor shaft and an arbor. The buffing wheel should spin no faster than 1725 R.P.M. A slower speed, between 600-900 R.P.M., is preferred. Friction created when operating at higher speeds increases the likelihood of buffing through the finish.

1-250 First, remove the run or imperfection from the surface through controlled sanding. Note the 400 or 600 grit sandpaper is wrapped around one finger instead of two.

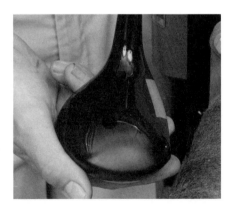

1-251 Lightly steel wool this area to blend in the sanding marks.

1-252 Apply **Glanz Wach** to the **unstitched buffing wheels** as they are turning. Apply just enough Glanz Wach to coat the wheels.

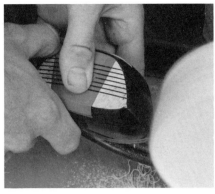

2-253 Lightly press the flawed area of the clubhead against the buffing wheel. Keep the clubhead moving at all times. After buffing the area in one direction . . .

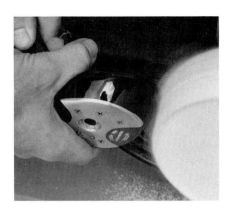

1-254 . . . lightly buff in the other direction. Repeat this until the scratches from the sandpaper and steel wool are completely gone and the repaired area has a high gloss.

1-255 The repaired area will look as if another coating of polyurethane was applied. This procedure works because enough surface friction (heat) is created to rearrange the surface molecules and polish to a bright gloss. Because so much heat is generated, the clubhead must be constantly moving to avoid burning through the finish.

1-256 Face lines are paintfilled by wiping or brushing quick drying enamel into the grooves. Scoring line paint is available from golf component suppliers.

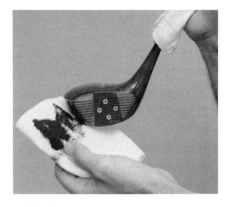

1-257 Wipe off excess paint with a paper towel which is alternately folded back and forth to expose a clean surface. Allow face paint to dry 12 hours. If all the paint is not removed, wipe again with a paper towel lightly dampened with Naphtha.

1-258 This is the finished product. With practice you can achieve a finished clubhead that is far better than most factory finishes. The club is now ready to be whipped. See Chapter 2 for correct whipping procedure.

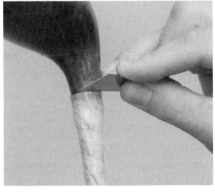

1-259 If the club has a plastic whipping cover, first cut through the polyurethane underneath the cover.

1-260 Next, unwind the masking tape covering that was wrapped prior to sanding the head.

1-261 This is the best a refinisher can expect from a club with a plastic whipping cover. Removing tape prior to dipping the poly would result in heavy runs on the cover. If the plastic needs to be touched up with acetone, do not allow it to come in contact with the polyurethane.

1-262 Refinishing Graphite Heads. In recent years, woods have been manufactured from materials other than the traditional persimmon or laminated maple. One of these new materials is graphite. Do not be intimidated by a graphite head, as most of the steps for refinishing it are identical to those for conventional woods.

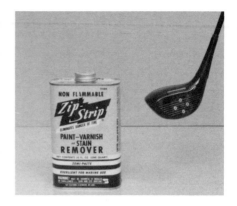

1-263 Never apply a stripping agent to a graphite head. Many graphite heads have a plastic content. The stripper will attack the plastic and permanently damage the head. Therefore, sand the old finish off the head. These steps also apply to plastic molded heads.

1-264 Remove whipping, file the face (see photos 1-22 thru 1-33), recut scoring lines (photo 1-34) and file the soleplate (photos 1-50 thru 1-59) to remove nicks.

1-265 The procedure for sanding a graphite head is identical to those steps shown in photos 1-78 thru 1-99. The key in sanding graphite is to keep the sandpaper sharp. Use 100, 150 and 220 grit sandpaper.

1-266 If the clubhead is sanded with dull, worn paper, a sag in the graphite may result. To remove this sag, sand the area with sharp paper until the sag disappears.

1-267 This is a properly sanded head. Even though we have used very fine sandpaper during the last sanding step, there are still scratches that need to be removed.

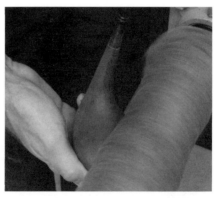

1-268 Vigorously steel wool the entire head to reduce the scratches left from sanding. Keep the steel wool moving over the head to avoid sags created by too much heat. 000 grade steel wool works best here.

1-269 The graphite head should look like this after steel wooling. Graphite heads are not stained or filled. If the clubhead had a colorcote . . .

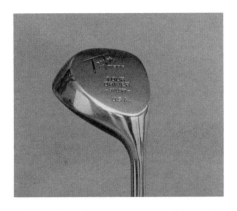

1-306 Photo shows a properly polished clubhead. All scratches have been removed to provide a mirror-like, factory new appearance.

1-307 Carefully apply tape over the polished areas. Use ⅛″ masking tape to accurately outline these areas.

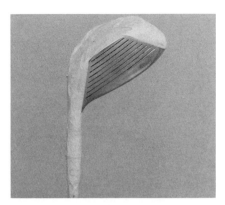

1-308 Apply ¾″ masking tape to fill in the remaining exposed polished metal surface. Make sure the tape is tight. Club is now ready for sandblasting.

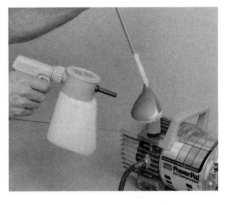

1-309 Sandblast the exposed surface by using 150 grade aluminum oxide sand at 40 to 60 P.S.I. A sandblast cabinet is best suited for this procedure, but a sandblast gun with tank-type compressor or the pictured **Power Pal compressor and accessory sandblast gun** will do the job.

1-310 Photo shows the sandblasted head. Note the even appearance of the surface. Try not to touch the head at this point.

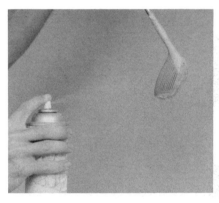

1-311 Without removing the tape, apply 2 or 3 light coats of **Primer Sealer**. Allow 30 minutes' drying time at room temperature between coats or bake the finish at 300 degrees. Baking will improve adhesion between finish and metal. The Primer Sealer is not applied to any polished metal surfaces as it will quickly wear off.

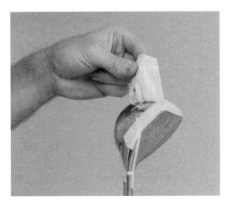

1-312 Carefully pull tape from head. There should be a defined line between the polished and sandblasted areas.

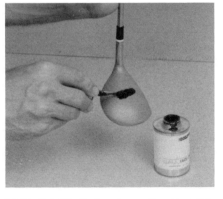

1-313 Paintfill all stampings with appropriate color paint. The coatings of Primer Sealer prevent the paint from accumulating on the head itself. After applying, quickly wipe excess paint from the head. A paper towel dampened with Grip Solvent or Naphtha will remove stubborn, dried paint.

1-314 Photo shows the finished clubhead. A professional job can be expected.

1-315 Refinishing Painted Metalwoods. Without removing the paint finish, carefully sand the entire head with a fine, 240 abrasive load in the Sand-O-Flex. Sand just enough to abrade the surface, but do not sand through it. Remember, this method makes use of the existing special primer coating.

1-316 Photo shows the properly sanded head. This step could also be performed by hand sanding with 400 wet or dry paper.

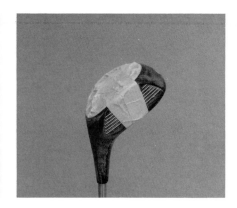

1-317 Apply tape to the clear areas on the head using ⅛″ and ¾″ masking tape. See photos 1-307 and 1-308.

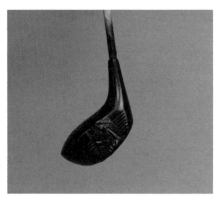

1-318 Apply several light coats of color-cote. Allow 30 minutes' drying time at room temperature between each coat. After the coats are applied, the surface will still appear rough. This is normal. Surface roughness will disappear as the consecutive poly coats are applied. Remove the masking tape from the head after drying.

1-319 After wiping the head lightly with a tack rag, dip or spray a coat of Moisture Cure Polyurethane (MC) or Oil Modified Polyurethane (OM). Allow the club to thoroughly dry.

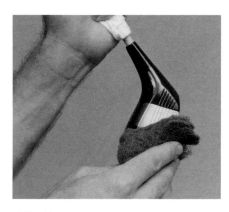

1-320 After the polyurethane coat is dry, steel wool the surface using 000 grade. Lightly wipe the head with a tack rag and apply a 2nd coat of poly. Each succeeding step is identical to those starting at photo 1-233.

1-321 The finished clubhead should look like this.

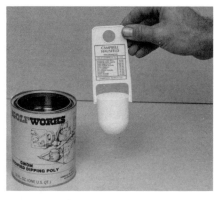

1-322 How to use a Viscosimeter. The viscosimeter will enable the refinisher to determine when the viscosity of his polyurethane is too thick for use as a clubhead coating.

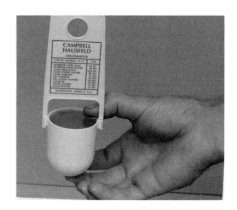

1-323 Cover the opening in the bottom of the cup with your finger or a piece of tape. Pour finish material into the cup until level with the rim.

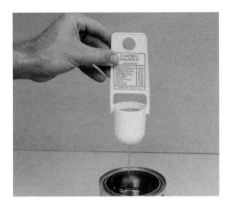 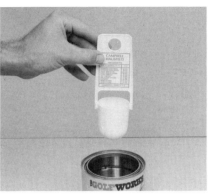

1-324 With an eye on the clock or a watch, remove your finger or tape from the opening.

1-325 Count how many seconds it takes for the contents to empty from the cup. When polyurethane registers in the low 30 second range, the refinisher should open a new can and use this old thickened poly for masking faces. **A good rule of thumb to use is: anything from 16-29 seconds is usable.**

NOTES

_____
_____
_____
_____
_____
_____
_____
_____

ADDITIONAL INFORMATION FOR REFINISHING WOODS

TABLE 1-1
Selecting The Proper Steel Wool Grade

Grade	Texture	Usage
0000	Superfine	This grade is used for most all steel wooling operations
000	Extra Fine	◄ such as leveling between coats, cleaning soleplates,
00	Very Fine	etc. Ribbon is the most common type used.
0	Fine	
1	Medium	
2	Medium Coarse	Used for removing old, softened finish after stripper has
3	Coarse	◄ been brushed on head. Pads are most commonly used.

TABLE 1-2
Selecting The Proper Buffing Compound

Grit	Compound	When to Use
Coarse	Black Emery Cake	If an extra heavy cutting action is necessary, such as removing rust, heavy nicks, deep scratches.
Medium	Tripoli Brown	For buffing items of aluminum, pewter, brass, copper, wood, bone, plastic and painted surfaces. Medium cutting action.
Fine	White Rouge	For buffing stainless steel, cast brass, aluminum, chromium, nickel and all steel articles to a bright luster. Fine cutting action.
Very Fine	Red Rouge	For buffing silverplate, gold, sterling silver and all sorts of precious metals to a bright luster. Works well on dull chrome golf shafts.

TABLE 1-3
Selecting The Proper Sandpaper Grit

Grit	Texture	Usage
40 50	Coarse	Sandpaper in this category is too abrasive for wood head refinishing. Coarse sandpaper is used to grind raw forgings or castings to weight by manufacturers.
60	Medium	
80* 100†	Medium	*Represents one possible sanding system. Would be useful for those repairmen who do not use a stripping agent to remove the finish from the clubhead prior to sanding.
120* 150† 180*	Fine	†Represents another sanding system. This system would be ideal for the repairman who does use a stripping agent and does not need the coarser 80 grit paper for finish removal.
220†	Very Fine	
240 280	Very Fine	Is generally too fine for head sanding prior to stain application. This grade of paper tends to close wood pores if dull and prevent stain absorption.
400	Extra Fine	Used between coats of polyurethane for leveling.
500 600	Extra Fine	Sometimes used prior to the final polyurethane coat or when sanding runs or sags before steel wooling and buffing.

Procedure for Installing Sandpaper, Steel Wool and Scotchbrite Wheels on Sanding Machines, Sanding Arbors and Steel Wool Arbors

This procedure has been added to eliminate much of the confusion and frustration in properly installing sanding cloth, steel wool and scotchbrite wheels on refinishing and conditioning machines. The procedure is fast and really quite simple; however, like many things, it is best to actually see how it is done to avoid all the trial and error in learning.

The world of sandpaper and sanding cloth types, grits and sizes can also be confusing. For sanding wood, either cloth-backed garnet or aluminum oxide cloth works best. Paper-backed sandpaper will not work satisfactorily; you must use a cloth backing. The grits that are most common in golf club refinishing are 80, 100, 120, 150 and 180 (see Table 1-3).

The best all around steel wool for golf clubs is 000 grade, which is quite fine. It is best obtained in spools or packages of "ribbon" and not in "pads."

Scotchbrite wheels, or discs, of a medium grade are ideally suited for the removal of finish from a golf club head. The advantage of a scotchbrite wheel, or disc, is they remove the majority of the finish without damaging any identifying stampings. Also, when used in conjunction with a paste stripper, the life of the wheel, or disc, is greatly expanded.

Remember, always wear eye protection when working around any abrasive materials.

1-326 Installing Sanding Cloth. First, wrap a strip of 2″ wide double-coated tape around sponge rubber drum.

1-327 2″ strip of tape is approximately 7″ long and should be overlapped as shown.

1-328 Place another strip of 2″ double-coated tape on opposite end.

1-329 Use a ruler to measure width of strip to be torn off. Measurement may be a little different on each make of sander.

1-330 You can first determine how much should be cut off by wrapping sanding cloth around sanding drum. It should overlap approximately ¾" to 1". Save the strips you tear off for general bench work.

1-331 Using a good quality "contact" cement, brush back side of sanding cloth with a liberal amount. **Be sure to brush cement up to the edge of the sanding cloth.**

1-332 Turn the sanding cloth over and coat the sanding surface with a liberal amount of cement. **Be sure to brush cement up to the edge of the sanding cloth. Allow contact cement to dry.**

1-333 Place the sanding cloth in position.

1-334 Work sanding cloth around sanding drum, keeping it tight against drum.

1-335 Squeeze in on sanding drum and pull sanding cloth up and over itself in the center only and press in place.

1-336 Repeat instructions in 1-335 on right side of cloth.

1-337 Repeat squeezing on left side of cloth. Note: Squeezing down on the sponge rubber drum as the sanding cloth is pressed into place helps to make it install tighter.

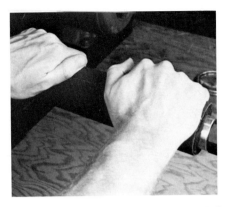

1-338 Squeeze down tightly on cemented seam to obtain a good bond.

1-339 Assembled sanding cloth should look like this. Notice how cloth overlaps which is proper because sanding drum rotates downward in front and up in the back. (counterclockwise when facing nut)

1-340 Installing Steel Wool. Wrap steel wool around drum.

1-341 As the steel wool overlaps itself, be sure it is tight.

1-342 Rotate the drum by hand and "wind on" the remaining portion of steel wool ribbon, keeping as tight as possible.

1-343 Spread apart the end of the steel wool using your fingers.

1-344 Press the spread apart ends down, as well as you can.

1-345 Place either one or two hands around steel wool and turn motor on. Your hand will shape the steel wool and lock it in place so it will not spin off. Note: If you do not want to use your hands, a rounded dowel will also work.

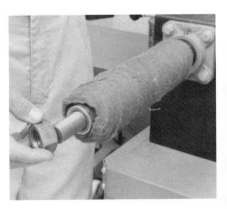

1-346 Installing Scotchbright Wheels. Remove end nut from motor shaft or arbor. The GolfWorks® Sanding Machine has a 1" diameter shaft.

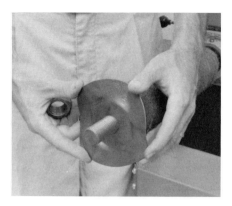

1-347 Slide 1 wavy washer over shaft. Note: Special adaptors are available so washers and wheels will also fit a ⅝" or ½" motor shaft.

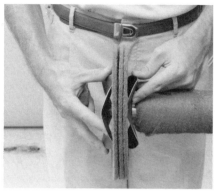

1-348 Slide 2 or 3 scotchbrite wheels over shaft. Then, slide 2nd wavy washer over shaft. Note the positioning of the 2nd washer in relation to the first.

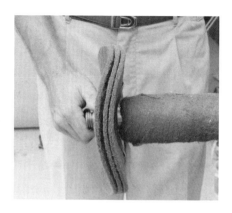

1-349 Reinstall the end nut and tighten. If wavy washers have been positioned properly, effective working area on wheels has been greatly expanded when motor is switched on. Wheels are ready for use.

Preserving Wood Head Stampings

It is important to understand how wood head stampings were put in originally at the factory and the best way of preserving them.

From time to time, confusion exists regarding the stamping in both the crown and the sole of wood heads such as, "Tommy Armour, oil hardened, 693T," etc. The value of these clubs largely depends on the readability and recognizability of the stamps in today's classic club market. (See photo 1-350.)

First of all, when the stamps were put in at the factory, they were stamped after the first and sometimes 2nd clear coat of varnish (often lacquer). Remember that the club had already been stained, filled and color-coted if the finish was to be black. When the old finish is removed during refinishing, a portion of the original stamp is removed with it because the stamp is partially in the finish as well as in the wood. Next, when the club is sanded to remove scratches and nicks, a little more of the stamp is removed. If a club has been previously refinished and is now going to be refinished again, still more of the stamp will be removed. Because of this, the stamping must be deepened before the sanding step as shown in photos 1-61 thru 1-65.

1-350

The person at the factory who originally stamped the clubs would sometimes stamp them very deep and other times quite shallow. This would depend on two factors: first, how hard he hit the stamp and second, how hard the persimmon in that particular head was. Also, a number of times human error would enter in and he would cock the stamp slightly to one side or the other thus resulting in a deep stamp on one side and shallow on the other.

Your intention should be to restore these stampings the best you can during refinishing. Obviously, you cannot restore these stamps to factory newness unless you had all the hundreds of stamps used in the past (for instance, there were 8 different Tommy Armour stamps used for stamping the MacGregor heads). However, if you become proficient with a scriber or electric engraver, you can closely match the quality of a newly stamped head.

It is very difficult if not impossible to professionally restore a hosel stamping. (See photo 1-351.) Hosel stampings are usually very shallow because the operator at the factory did not dare exert much force when stamping this relatively fragile area. Often times the stamping will disappear completely once the finish is removed because the stamp was only as deep as the finish itself. Classic club collectors generally agree, if the condition of the finish warrants a refinish, the value of the club will not drop simply because the hosel stamping is lost. It is an accepted fact that the depth of the hosel stamping does not allow it to be saved.

When a club that has wood head stampings comes in for refinishing, be sure to look it over closely to evaluate the condition of the stampings so that if necessary, you can immediately bring them to the customer's attention. Many people feel that these stampings are restamped during refinishing. Personnel in The GolfWorks® repair department use this policy: If you can see it, we can save it. With practice, you should adopt this policy also.

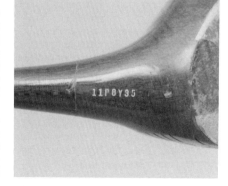

1-351

Oil Hardening

Oil hardening is a name given to a process whose sole purpose is to seal the pores of a persimmon or laminated wood turning, and help prevent the shrinking or swelling of that head due to moisture absorption or loss. The material used for this process can be boiled linseed oil, Nelsonite, resin or slight variations of these 3 materials. These materials are applied to a head by immersion or impregnation using both vacuum and pressure.

Virtually every head you encounter has been "oil hardened" and there is not a need for the head to again undergo this process. Some repairmen mistakenly believe dipping the sanded head in oil or Nelsonite will magically "harden" the wood, but this is just not so. Remember, the oil hardening process seals the wood from moisture loss or absorption but does nothing to actually harden the wood. Attempts to re-oil harden will result in a clubhead surface that a finish will have difficulty adhering to.

Moisture Cure Polyurethane vs. Oil Modified Polyurethane

Moisture cure and oil modified polyurethane represent the two most common types of poly used on golf clubs today. Each offers an excellent coating system, yet each is different in shelf life, color, odor, and curing time.

Moisture cure poly is used by approximately 95% of all golf club manufacturers and about 70% of golf club refinishers. What makes moisture cure poly very attractive is that the color is water clear. What makes moisture cure poly less attractive to some users is the tight environmental control that must be maintained during its use to ensure the product will work properly. As evidenced by the name, moisture cure poly requires the presence of moisture in the air to aid in the curing of the poly.

The moisture acts as a drying mechanism as the poly resin pulls the moisture molecules from the air and these molecules in fact become part of the poly coating. The tendency of the moisture cure poly coating is to dry from the top to the bottom, and herein lies the problem. If the top of the poly coat dries too quickly or if too heavy a coating has been applied, then as many as eight different solvents can be trapped underneath this dried film of poly. The purpose of these solvents is to aid in the blending, curing, adhesion and drying of the poly. However, the refinisher doesn't realize there are any trapped solvents until the second coat of poly is applied on top of the first coat. If the solvents in the first coat have not evaporated, the solvents in the second coat will eat through the top layer of the first coat causing a reaction between the solvents that manifests itself in the form of common wrinkling of the poly coat.

The drying characteristics of the oil modified poly are different from the moisture cure poly. Oil modified poly is made by inter-reacting the poly with a vegetable oil. The type of vegetable oil used determines the color, clarity and the flexibility of the finish. However, the addition of oil leads to a very slight amber color that is most noticeable on aluminum soleplates. This is the only drawback to oil modified poly. The drying characteristics of oil modified poly is from the bottom of the coat to the top. Primarily for this reason, you should not experience the trapped solvent problem with the oil modified poly. The other factor for this is that the poly resins are grabbing oxygen molecules from the air to aid in the curing of the poly. Oxygen will allow the solvents to evaporate much more freely than moisture will.

Which Polyurethane to Choose

The decision you make as to which type of polyurethane to choose should be based upon three points:
1. Color — Moisture cure poly is water clear while oil modified poly has a very slight amber color usually only slightly noticeable on aluminum soleplates and white inserts.
2. Working Difficulty — Oil modified poly is the easiest to work with because of the nature of the curing process. Unless the proper drying conditions are created in the use of the moisture cure poly, the refinisher may experience problems.
3. Shelf Life — After the can is first opened, oil modified poly has at least a four to six month shelf life with reasonable care and proper storage. Moisture cure poly, with the use of a preservative, should last four to eight weeks.

For the shop that works with a small number of clubs or for the part-time refinisher, the oil modified poly would suit their needs better than the moisture cure poly. For a full-time shop that has a large volume of work, the moisture cure poly would be the correct choice as the large volume shop will be refinishing enough clubs that he would run out of the moisture cure poly before it cures to a level that makes it too thick for use. Whichever poly you choose, both will give the refinisher an excellent finishing system with professional results.

How to Obtain Shelf Life

One problem which re-occurs concerns short shelf life of polyurethanes. This is especially true if the person dips because he is constantly removing and reinstalling the lid. Also, a number of smaller users may not use the polyurethane soon enough before it sets up. It should be noted that we have not found golf club polyurethanes to be defective other than accidental dirt contamination during the can filling operation. It has usually been mishandling on the user's part which allows for rapid thickening. There are a number of things you can do.
1. Always store polyurethanes in a cool location and never near direct sunlight. If material will not be used sooner than a week or two, put it in the refrigerator. This will greatly retard thickening. Remember that you must allow the material sufficient time to normalize at room temperature before using it (usually 12 hours minimum). Never use polyurethane below 65° F. An aquarium thermometer or darkroom thermometer is handy for checking it prior to use.
2. Only keep the lid off the can for the absolute minimum time. Air is the number one enemy of polyurethane and wet, humid air is even worse if you are using a moisture cure polyurethane.
3. When you receive a new can of polyurethane, pour enough in a small container so that the level in the quart can is approximately 1″ below the top. This will keep the polyurethane from running over the top. As you use it, pour the remainder back into the can to maintain this 1″ level. As the level goes below 1″, drop marbles into the can to maintain the 1″ level. This will always assure you of the minimum amount of air space in the can. *Never transfer polyurethane into glass jars or plastic containers* because glass lets in light which affects uncured polyurethane, and plastic containers let in air which promotes thickening.

   Also, once you have used a little over ½ or up to ⅔ of a can and you do not have sufficient material to dip a head in, throw the remainder out or use it for masking faces. *Never add new material to old material.* The old material will accelerate thickening and also after so many dippings it becomes contaminated. You should be able to dip 20-50 clubs 3-4 coats with one quart of polyurethane.
4. If you use spraying polyurethane or spray/dipping polyurethane, it is best to squeeze and deform the can (with the cap or lid off) as you use it up to maintain its level right up to the top. This will eliminate all air from the can which is best.

Compatibility of Various Finishing Products & Drying Times

		Drying Times		
Product	Application	Room Temp.	Force Dry*	Compatability Comments and General Notes
TABLE 1-4 Compatibility of Various Finishing Products & Drying Times				
GOLFWORKS® SYSTEMS				
GolfWorks® Water Base Stains	dip, brush, wipe or spray	4-6 hrs.	1 hr.	Can be used with anything. Dipping provides uniform coating.
GolfWorks® Oil Base Fillers	dip or brush & rub	12 hrs.	6 hrs.	Can be used with any polyurethane. Burnish well with burlap or coarse cloth when wiping. Do not steel wool.
GolfWorks® Rapid Dry Aerosol Colorcotes	aerosol	4-6 hrs.	2 hrs.	Must be used only with GolfWorks® Oil Modified or Moisture Cure Polyurethane. Do not apply heavy coat. Several light coats superior to one heavy coat. Do not sand or steel wool.
GolfWorks® Opaque Colorcotes	spray or brush	24 hrs.	12 hrs.	Must be used only with GolfWorks® Oil Modified or Moisture Cure Polyurethane. Do not apply heavy coat. If brushing, apply quickly to avoid streaks.
GolfWorks® Primer Sealer, Aerosol	aerosol	4 hrs.	1 hr.	Can be used with any polyurethane but specially formulated for Moisture Cure type polyurethane. Do not sand or steel wool.
GolfWorks® Primer Sealer, Spraying	spray	4 hrs.	1 hr.	Can be used with any polyurethane but specially formulated for Moisture Cure type polyurethane. Do not sand or steel wool.
GolfWorks® Oil Modified Dipping Polyurethane	dip or spray	8 hrs.	4 hrs.	Do not apply on top of Moisture Cure Polyurethane. Usually requires 5-6 coats for quality finish.
GolfWorks® Moisture Cure Dipping Polyurethane	dip or spray	12-24 hrs.	8 hrs.	Do not apply on top of Mira-Dip or Mira Filler. Can be applied over other polyurethanes or fillers.
GolfWorks® Moisture Cure Spraying Polyurethane	spray	12-24 hrs.	8 hrs.	Do not apply on top of Mira-Dip or Mira Filler. Can be applied over other polyurethanes or fillers.
GolfWorks® Moisture Cure Aerosol Polyurethane	aerosol	12-24 hrs.	8 hrs.	Do not apply on top of Mira-Dip or Mira Filler. Can be applied over other polyurethanes or fillers.

*Force dry conditions: 30% to 50% relative humidity, 90° to 100° temperature.

| | | Drying Times | | |
Product	Application	Room Temp.	Force Dry*	Compatability Comments and General Notes
TABLE 1-4 con't. **Compatibility of Various Finishing Products & Drying Times**				
CLUB-KIT SYSTEM				
Mira-Stains (alcohol base)	dip, brush, wipe or spray	3-6 hrs.	1 hr.	Can be used with anything. Dipping provides uniform coating.
Mira-Filler (polyurethane base)	dip or brush & rub	5 hrs.	2 hrs.	Use only with Mira-Dip.
Mira-Kote (polyurethane base)	spray or brush	12 hrs.	8 hrs.	Use only with Mira-Dip. Do not apply heavy coat. Several light coats superior to one heavy coat.
Mira-Kote Aerosol (polyurethane base)	aerosol	12 hrs.	8 hrs.	Same as above.
Dem-Kote Enamel	aerosol	4 hrs.	2 hrs.	Same as above.
Mira-Dip Oil Modified Polyurethane	dip or spray	8 hrs.	4 hrs.	Do not apply on top of Moisture Cure polyurethanes. Usually requires 5-6 coats for quality finish.
Mira-Spray Aerosol Oil Modified Polyurethane	aerosol	8 hrs.	4 hrs.	Do not apply on top of Moisture Cure polyurethanes.

*Force dry conditions: 30% to 50% relative humidity, 90° to 100° temperature.

How Moisture Cure Polyurethane Dries and Cures

The drying and curing information presented in the beginning of this section pertains mostly to moisture cure (mc) polyurethane. This is because a coating of moisture cure polyurethane dries from the top to the bottom. This drying action differs from a coating of oil modified polyurethane because oil modified dries from the bottom of the coat to the top. However, the information presented concerning the inter-reaction between solvents is applicable to all types of polyurethane. Also, the six tips given at the end of this section can be used to assist in trouble free refinishing, regardless of which type of polyurethane you use.

Understanding how polyurethane cures is a vital step in becoming a knowledgeable and competent golf club refinisher. With this knowledge, you will be able to troubleshoot finish problems should they occur. The following diagrams are for explanation purposes only in the way they depict the flow and movement of the polyurethane on the clubhead.

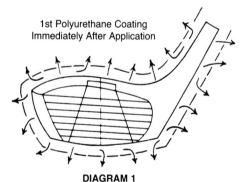

1st Polyurethane Coating Immediately After Application

DIAGRAM 1

Diagram #1 shows a wood head just after the application of the polyurethane. The dashed lines represent the solids as they flow over the head and the arrows represent the solvents that are naturally present in the polyurethane. The key to proper drying is the evaporation of all of the solvents that are in the coating. In the diagram, the solvents are beginning to evaporate or flash off the surface through the solids and out into the air. As of yet the solids have not yet begun to flow together and join to form the film coating, so there are plenty of avenues of escape for the solvents.

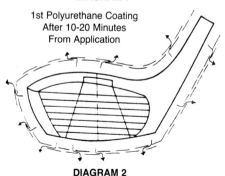

1st Polyurethane Coating After 10-20 Minutes From Application

DIAGRAM 2

In Diagram #2 the solids of the polyurethane are beginning to join together to form what is called the film coat. This is represented by the overlapping of the dashed lines seen in the diagram. This joining together begins to cut off the access to evaporation of the solvents, since at this point they have to work their way around and through the solids to get to the surface. During this time (10 to 20 minutes after application) there is a chance that many tiny bubbles may appear on the surface of the polyurethane. These bubbles are caused by a very rapid film coat set-up that "squeezes" down the solvents and naturally present gases. Not having the adequate time to come to the surface normally, these solvents and gases "collide" with the solids and burst to become bubbles on the surface. Too rapid of a film coat set-up is usually caused by humidity being too high and can be alleviated by reducing the humidity or by the addition of a retarder solvent which slows the film coat set-up.

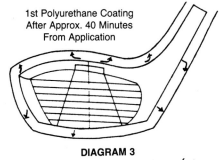

1st Polyurethane Coating
After Approx. 40 Minutes
From Application

DIAGRAM 3

Approximately 40 minutes after application of the polyurethane, the film or solid coating has joined together and shut off further evaporation of the solvents. In Diagram #3, if there are solvents remaining (arrows) they are considered to be trapped and no longer have the opportunity to evaporate into the air. This condition is called Solvent Entrapment and is the cause of over 90% of the finish application problems you have.

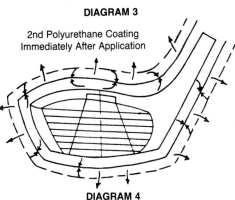

2nd Polyurethane Coating
Immediately After Application

DIAGRAM 4

Once the second coat of the polyurethane is applied, its solvents immediately begin to evaporate. At the same time its solvents are designed to penetrate or "eat" into the preceding coat. This is the real key to the adhesion properties of polyurethane. However, when the succeeding coat "eats" into the first coat and meets any unevaporated or trapped solvents, a chemical reaction occurs in the solid layer which results in a breaking down of that solid coating. This reaction may be small or quite extensive and take the form of "wrinkles" or cracking on the surface of the head. In other words, this condition can occur anywhere unevaporated solvents are trapped. In severe cases, the head will have to be started over as a result of this problem.

The preceding diagrams and explanation have covered the reasons for many of the problems seen during the application of finish coats. Now it is important to go over some of the preventative measures that may be followed to eliminate the possibility of solvent entrapment. We know the key element in the curing of the polyurethane is getting rid of the solvents present in the polyurethane. This may be accomplished by either speeding up their evaporation or by cutting down on the amount of solvents that flow over the head. The chart below covers the options available to you to control these two points.

To Speed Evaporation	To Cut Down The Volume of Solvents
• Elevation of temperature in drying area (max. 100°F)	• Keep polyurethane fresh for better flow
• Add Retarders to hold film coat open longer (in high humidity only)	• Do not use thickened or colder polyurethane
• Apply finish to warmer head (min. 70°F max. 110°F)	• Do not apply polyurethane to cold head
	• Do not add thinner to improve flow

Thinners are solvents and our goal is to rid the head of solvents.

If you study the methods of drying and understand the control you may exercise over those methods, trouble free finishing will not be difficult to achieve.

In an effort to smooth out the problems that can be caused by refinishing in a workshop environment that is colder than the suggested 70°F temperature, we recommend that you follow these tips:

1. Try to keep your clubs in a warmer area of the shop during the application of the finish coats. Primer/Sealer and Polyurethane coatings require higher temperatures to dry properly. The use of a drying box heated with small light bulbs will work well to increase the temperature around your clubs. A shallow pan of water in the box will add humidity, if necessary, for moisture cure type polyurethane. Oil modified polys do not require levels of high humidity.

2. Before applying the polyurethane, make sure the polyurethane is over 70°F. Polyurethane that is cold will not flow on the head adequately and thus a heavier coating will result. This, in turn, may cause solvent entrapment.

3. Try to keep the temperature of the heads themselves at least 70°F. Dipping or spraying a cold head can create unwanted problems in refinishing.

4. If you cannot dry the polyurethane coats at higher temperatures use this tip to aid in the cure of each finish coat. 12 to 15 hours after dipping the polyurethane, sand the entire head with 400 grit wet/dry sandpaper and set the club aside for another 12 hours to cure. This 400 sanding will break through the partially cured solid layer and help to further expose potentially trapped solvents to the air for evaporation. After the additional 12-hour dry, GENTLY 400 sand again, taking care not to break through the finish. Then steel wool and apply the next coat of polyurethane.

5. Thinning your polyurethane in colder air temperatures can create more problems than if it is done in the summer. We recommend restricting the addition of thinner in the winter unless you are able to keep the shop warm.

6. Increasing polyurethane flow may be accomplished by raising the temperature of the poly. This can be done by filling a sink with 3-4 inches of hot water. Set the can down in the sink of warm water and leave it for 20 minutes prior to using. Raising the temperature of the polyurethane will thus make the polyurethane thinner and a better flow will result.

Tips for Applying Decals

There is more to applying decals than simply sliding them in place. The position, of the decal is extremely important because if improperly positioned, the decal can make the club appear hooked or excessively open. Also, if the decal is not positioned at the middle of the insert, it gives the club an unbalanced look at address with a golf ball and may even cause problems in ball alignment and consequently solid contact at impact.

When a decal is properly positioned it should line up with the middle of the insert and tail away to an "open" position with the clubface. See Fig. 1-352.

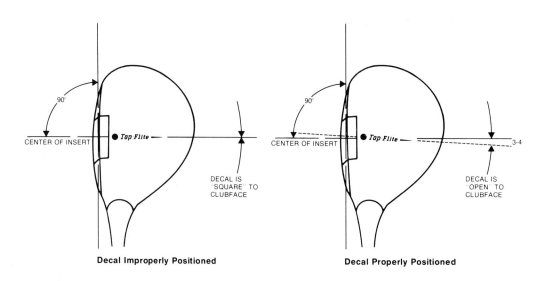

Decal Improperly Positioned   Decal Properly Positioned

Fig. 1-352
Proper decal positioning

The longer a decal happens to be, the more important it is to "tail away." Of course on the short decals such as arrows, dots, small initials or in general those less than ½" long, the importance of tilting the decal open is minimal. However, always position the decal at the center of the insert.

A problem that occurs from time to time when installing decals is the appearance of "trapped air" underneath or a blotched grayness look to the decal. This is usually caused by soaking and/or sliding the decal around too much thereby removing the water soluble glue which bonds the dedal to the head. Also, some decals have less glue than others to start with. The best remedy I have found to eliminate grayness is to put down 4 or 5 paper towels, one on top of the other, and soak them with water. See photo 1-226. Do not oversoak or to the point where water is puddling on top of the paper towels. Now, lay the decals face up on the toweling so that the water from the toweling is absorbed into the decal backing paper. This will release the decal's glue from the backing without removing the backing, so that the decal can be slid off onto the head.

NOTES

APPLYING WHIPPING TO WOODS

Applying new whipping to the neck of a golf wood is a common operation in any repair shop. Whipping will be replaced on almost every golf club that is refinished, reshafted, reheaded or needs a split neck repaired. Since the whipping is exposed on most wood and graphite hosels (and some metalwood hosels), it is susceptible to accidental breakage. Whipping is necessary on wood and graphite hosels to help prevent the hosel from splitting due to the stress on the hosel area during the golf swing. Whipping is also found on some metalwood hosels, but the whipping serves only as a cosmetic feature. The addition of whipping to a metalwood tends to make the club more appealing to some traditionalist golfers.

There are many different types and sizes of whipping available. The .022 diameter nylon whipping, available in many colors, is suggested instead of waxed or pitched linen types, mono-filament types, or the smaller .020, .019 or .016 diameter whippings. The larger .022 diameter braided nylon whipping is stronger and more durable than other whipping types, as a strand of .022 nylon whipping is composed of three smaller strands braided together and then covered with a sheathing. Also, it looks much better when installed over a hosel with minor imperfections such as small dents, dings or any unevenness that may occur with age. Also, nylon-type whippings seem to be more compatible with today's modern polyurethane wood club finishes than some of the other types, namely waxed and pitched types which tend to inhibit proper curing of modern finishing materials.

2-1 When a golf club comes in with loose or no whipping, always check to see if the shaft is loose in the hosel. Many times this is the cause for the whipping to fail. Refer to Chapter 8 for shaft tightening procedures if the shaft is loose.

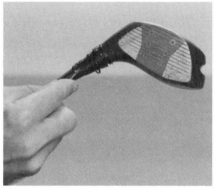

2-2 **When removing old whipping,** use a sharp knife or razor blade. When cutting through the whipping, always cut away from the clubhead. This eliminates the chance of ruining the finish should you slip.

2-3 Large irregularities or bulges on the hosel surface may be removed using a flat mill file. Follow up the filing by sanding with a fine grade of sandpaper. When shaping the hosel, the goal should be to obtain a smooth tapered look from the top of the ferrule to the bottom of the hosel where it blends into the head. **Be careful not to sand below the point where the whipping will end.**

2-4 Whipping a hosel is easier if the whipping spool is stationary. The **Insert Clamp** does double duty as a stable base from which to unravel the whipping without twisting it.

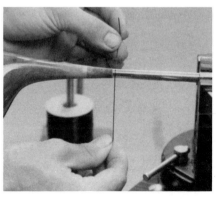

2-5 **To whip a club,** first lay the strand of whipping across the shaft approximately ⅛″ above the ferrule and . . .

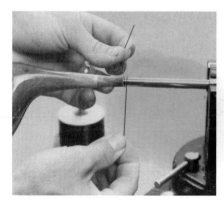

2-6 . . . completely encircle the shaft with the whipping.

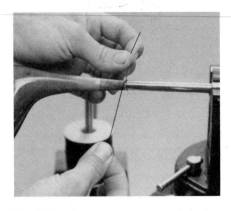

2-7 Holding the whipping as shown, take the strand held in your right hand and cross over the top of the whipping that encircles the shaft (the cut end of the whipping). This overlapping will secure the initial whipping loop to the shaft.

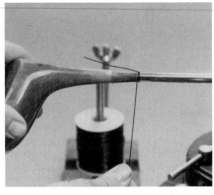

2-8 While applying light pressure with your right hand, grasp the clubhead with the left hand and turn the head, while feeding the whipping over the top of the short strand. After four turns, straighten the short strand to lay straight down the very back of the hosel and . . .

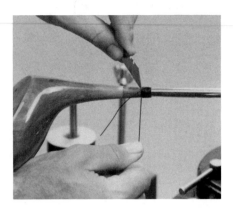

2-9 . . . continue to turn the clubhead another two revolutions. Now, cut off flush the visible portion of whipping that is laying along the back of the hosel. Doing this eliminates a possible gap in the whipping because the next turn will butt perfectly against the preceding one.

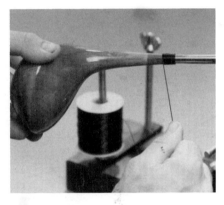

2-10 Continue to rotate the clubhead while feeding the whipping on the hosel. Note the position of the right hand in relation to the whipping already on the shaft. Feeding the whipping onto the hosel at this angle will help eliminate gaps. Use medium tension.

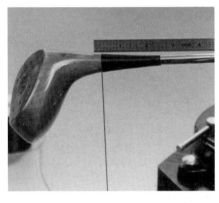

2-11 Use a ruler (6″ scale works well) to measure the finished whipping length desired. The average whipping length is 2½″, but, with various length hosels, it is better to end the whipping . . .

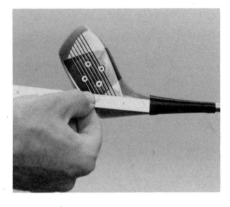

2-12 . . . at a point one inch from the top of the face measured at the heel.

2-13 When the whipping is wound to a point approx. ¼″ from the desired end, insert a **Loop Puller** (or a doubled-over piece of whipping) underneath the next turn of whipping as shown. Position the puller so that it lies alongside the centerline of the back of the hosel, not directly on it.

2-14 Wind the whipping six turns over the puller then cut the strand free from the spool while holding the whipping in place with your finger.

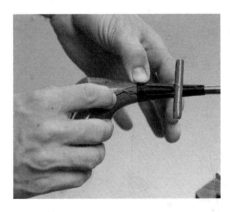

2-15 Next, feed the cut end of the whipping through the loop puller end. Continue to hold the whipping in place with your finger.

2-16 Place a thumb on the back of the hosel directly over the last strand of whipping. While holding the whipping in place, drop the end of the strand and grasp the puller with the other hand. Duplicate the hand positions as shown in the photo and . . .

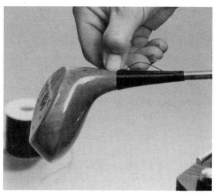

2-17 . . . quickly pull the loop through. Firmly planting the thumb on the back of the hosel will prevent the pulled-through strand from sliding to the side of the hosel.

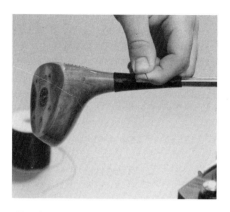

2-18 If the strand is not positioned along the back center of the hosel, pull the strand around until properly positioned.

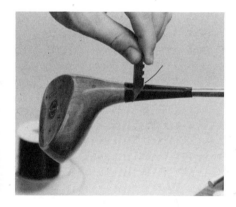

2-19 Carefully cut the excess whipping from the hosel. A sharp knife or razor blade will provide a flush cut.

2-20 If the whipping has "raised up" as a result of pulling the strand through, rub the raised part back in place with a smooth firm object such as a wooden knife handle or plastic screwdriver handle, etc.

2-21 This is how the whipping should look. Note the smoothly tapered hosel. Whipping will either enhance the look of a properly tapered hosel or magnify any irregularities.

2-22 As an alternative to the insert clamp, this **Whipping Spool Holder** will allow the whipping to be fed from the spool at a high speed. The holder can be permanently mounted so the whipping will always be ready to use.

2-23 Another way of tying off the whipping is to use the loop-over method. Once the whipping has been wound to the desired length, cut the whipping approximately 12″ longer from this point and . . .

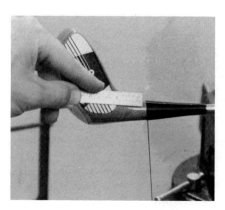

2-24 . . . unwind 9 turns of the whipping from the hosel. You should now have approximately 18″-20″ of excess whipping.

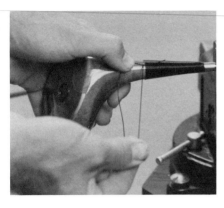

2-25 Take the very end of the whipping and lay it along the back of the neck, slightly off center and . . .

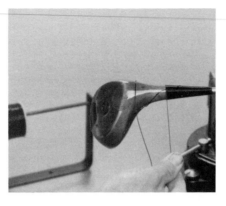

2-26 . . . wrap the whipping around the hosel over the top of the strand, thus locking the strand in place.

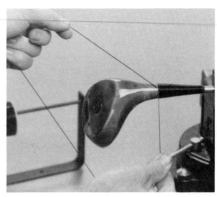

2-27 Continue to wind the whipping over the strand while, each time, passing the loop over the clubhead . . .

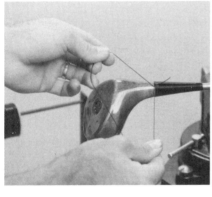

2-28 . . . until the loop of whipping will no longer pass over the head. This will leave the 9 turns of whipping over the strand. Remember, we previously unwound 9 turns of whipping.

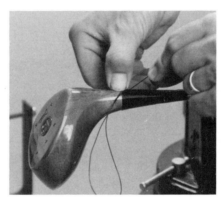

2-29 Place your thumb directly on the back of the hosel over the whipping. Grasp the end of the whipping in your hand and . . .

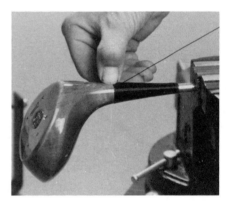

2-30 . . . pull the whipping tight underneath and through the last 9 windings. Position the strand so that it runs straight up the back of the hosel. Positioning the strand on the back of the hosel will keep this slight lump in the whipping out of sight when the golfer is addressing the ball.

2-31 Cut the strand flush with the whipping. Note: The only drawback to this method is the waste of the 12″ strand.

2-32 A quicker way of winding whipping is to fasten a spray can cap to a wall. Insert the butt of the club into the cap and support the shaft with your side as shown. Rotate the head with one hand while winding on whipping with the other. The tension created while pulling on the whipping will keep the shaft tight against your side.

2-33 If hammering a nail into your wall is not possible, attach the cap to the base of the vise or the workbench.

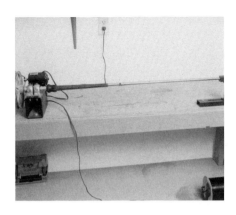

2-34 For higher volume work, the **Motorized Whipping Machine** with a variable speed drive, controlled by a foot pedal, works very well. Use of this machine will allow the operator to whip approximately 60 clubs per hour.

2-35 **The condition of this whipping cover is typical of clubs that use a plastic molded cover over a string whipping.** The plastic eventually breaks down from repeated contact with iron heads or the side of the golf bag. Replacement of a whipping cover requires removal of the shaft, so many repairman . . .

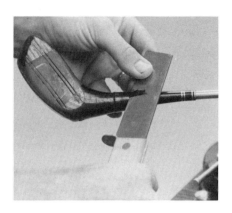

2-36 . . . choose to cut through the cover, being careful not to cut into the wood hosel or mar the finish. If only one club in a set is bad, the cover should be replaced to match the set. Of course, all this depends on the customer's desires.

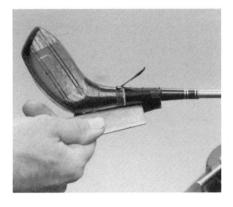

2-37 Peel the cover from the hosel, thus exposing the whipping below.

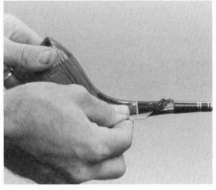

2-38 Cut through the whipping and remove it also. The whipping found below the plastic whipping cover is much thinner than the type of whipping found on most other clubs. This whipping is equivalent to 8 pound test fishing line and is usually a mono-filament type.

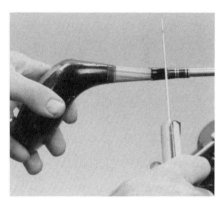

2-39 Place the knife on top of the ferrule perpendicular to the shaft. The knife should be placed ½" to ¾" from the top of the hosel. Cut through the plastic and remove the top half.

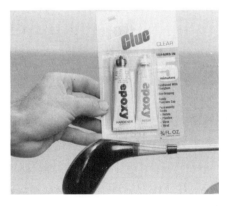

2-40 If a gap exists between the ferrule and the hosel, a quick-setting epoxy will work well to fill it.

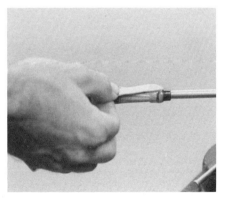

2-41 After the epoxy has been mixed, force the epoxy down into the gap and allow the epoxy to cure.

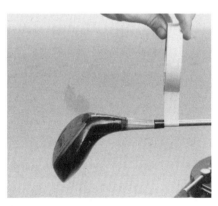

2-43 Wrap a piece of ¾" masking tape around the shaft just above the ferrule. This will protect the chrome-plated shaft during the ensuing filing steps.

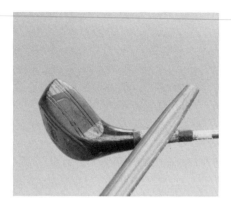

2-44 The oversized ferrule must now be filed down in diameter to provide a smooth taper from shaft to hosel for the whipping. Rough shape the ferrule with a coarse file. Do not cut into the hosel or through the tape.

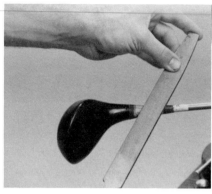

2-45 With most of the excess plastic removed, change to a fine file for final shaping. Blend the top of the ferrule into the shaft so there is no noticeable "step" between the shaft and ferrule. The bottom of the ferrule should be even or flush with the hosel.

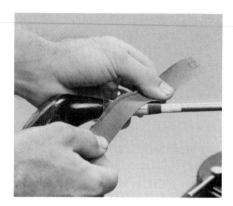

2-46 Next, use a fine grade of sandpaper to blend in the file marks and to remove any flat spots left from filing. If there is a build-up of finish at the base of the plastic cover, this too must be smoothed out. The fine file and sandpaper work well to do this.

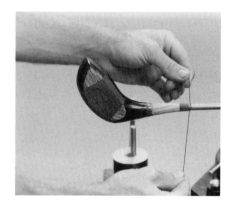

2-47 The hosel is now prepared for the application of the whipping. Now follow the same steps as performed in photos 2-5 thru 2-21.

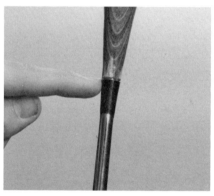

2-48 Oftentimes, whipping will loosen because the ferrule separates from the hosel. The resulting gap allows a strand of whipping to fall into it, which lessens the whipping tension, causing it to loosen and/or ultimately unravel.

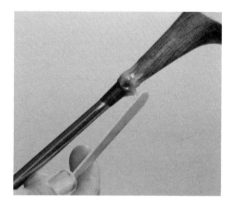

2-49 If you find a gap between the ferrule and hosel, always fill it with epoxy before whipping the hosel.

2-50 Older golf clubs require different types of whipping for proper restoration of the era. The two most common types are waxed linen and pitched linen.

2-51 Application of a modern, plastic-covered whipping to an old club would be aesthetically incorrect. To preserve the original appearance, pitched linen whipping should be used. The steps for application are the same as detailed in photos 2-5 thru 2-21.

2-52 When regripping an antique club with leather, the bottom of the leather grip should be finished off with the pitched linen whipping. Again, the same procedure is used to apply the whipping to the shaft and leather as is used for the hosel.

ADDITIONAL INFORMATION FOR
APPLYING WHIPPING TO WOOD CLUBS

Whipping is sold by the spool. The smallest amount available is 50 yards which is usually adequate to whip about 9 clubs. Table 2-1 below has been developed as an aid in purchasing the correct amount of whipping by anticipated usage. The table was calculated by using .022″ diameter whipping. It takes an average of 16 feet of whipping for each wood club.

TABLE 2-1			
Average Number Of Clubs Per Spool Of Whipping			
Spool Yardage Size	[1]Approximate Number of Clubs from Each Spool	[2]Approximate Cost Per Spool	[2]Average Cost Per Club
50 Yards	9 Clubs	$ 2.35	26¢ Per Club
200 Yards	37 Clubs	$ 6.85	18½¢ Per Club
500 Yards	93 Clubs	—	—
1000 Yards	187 Clubs	—	—
2000 Yards	375 Clubs	$49.00	13¢ Per Club
4000 Yards	750 Clubs	$79.90	10½¢ Per Club

[1]Based on .022″ diameter whipping @ 16 feet per club.

[2]Based on .022″ diameter braided or twisted nylon or orlon whipping @ 1987 prices in The GolfWorks® catalog.

NOTES

3
SOLEPLATE REMOVAL AND RESETTING LOOSE SOLEPLATES

Developing skills in removing a soleplate is important because many wood head repairs start with this operation as the first step. For instance, if a swingweight change is necessary, the soleplate is usually removed to gain access to the soleplate cavity, where weight is either added or removed. Other reasons for removing a soleplate are:

a. On a loose or open soleplate, the soleplate must be removed and then reset with epoxy to ensure good adhesion between the soleplate and the head. Also, this prevents moisture from swelling or shrinking the clubhead.

b. To repair a deep nick or gouge on a soleplate, it is best accomplished by removing the soleplate and hammering the defect from the underneath side of the soleplate.

c. An insert that is loose or needs replaced can usually only be removed by first removing the soleplate. This allows the Insert Removal Tool or chisel to be driven underneath the insert from the bottom of the insert cavity, which is normally hidden by the soleplate.

d. A rattle in the head is likely caused by a loose weight under the soleplate. Obviously, the soleplate must be removed before the loose object can be dealt with.

The time and effort required to remove a soleplate can range from fast and simple to time consuming and quite difficult. Difficulties occur because various types of high strength epoxies are now in use, and, also, golf club manufacturers have become very clever in attaching soleplates to their clubheads using various mechanical means.

To further complicate matters, some customers request that the soleplate be reset without benefit of a refinish. This means you must remove and reset the soleplate while doing as little damage as possible to the finish. If damage is done, you must then repair the damaged finish so the club is presentable to the owner. The touch-up steps without a complete refinish can be found in Chapter 15.

Soleplate removal and installation requires very little in the way of materials and equipment. You will need a size assortment of brass flathead screws, epoxy, wooden toothpicks, Phillips #1 and #2 screwdrivers, and both large and small Reed and Prince (Frearson) screwdrivers. A Reed and Prince (Frearson) screwdriver looks similar to Phillips #1 and #2 screwdrivers; however, the former has different angle points and sharper inside radiuses where the cross is formed. "Frearson" is the correct technical name used to refer to a Reed and Prince style screw or screwdriver. Most all golf clubhead manufacturers use the Reed and Prince (Frearson) type cross head screws exclusively, and most golf club repairmen use the Phillips type screwdriver to remove them. This accounts for many ruined screw heads and much frustration. Reed and Prince (Frearson) screwdrivers are usually not available in local hardware stores, and must be obtained from a golf repair supply company.

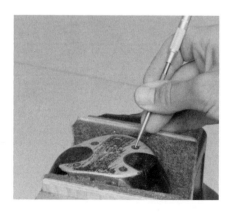

3-1 Using a sharp scriber, dental pick, awl or other pointed tool, thoroughly clean all dirt, old finish and paint from the screw head's recess. This allows the screwdriver to get a better "bite" and reduces the chance of "stripping" out the screwhead recess.

3-2 Hold the screwdriver perfectly square, press down firmly and turn the screw out (counterclockwise). It is a good idea to tap the top of the screwdriver with a hammer to be certain it seats solidly. Note: Most all soleplate screws are Reed and Prince (Frearson) and not Phillips types.

3-3 If the clubhead will not be refinished, place screws so they can be put back in their original holes. A piece of cardboard or pegboard works well for this. If the clubhead is to be refinished, discard the screws and use new ones. If the screws will not come out, refer to photos 3-25 thru 3-34. Note: Pliers protect fingers from sharp screw edges when placing screws in cardboard.

3-4 If the clubhead's finish is still covering the sole, carefully cut around the outline of the soleplate with a razor blade. This will allow the soleplate to be removed without pulling up the surrounding finish.

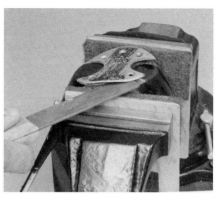

3-5 Pry up the soleplate, carefully using a strong, sharp knife. Tap the knife lightly if necessary. If the soleplate will not come off . . .

3-6 . . . tap a small wood chisel, with the bevel up, under the leading edge of the soleplate. If the soleplate still will not come off, heat will need to be applied to soften the epoxy bond.

3-7 Using a **Heat Gun**, direct heat against the soleplate keeping the nozzle elevated 1″ to 2″ from the plate. After a minute or two, the soleplate should lift off.

3-8 An alternate method is to use a **Propane Torch**, directing the tip of the flame against the middle of the soleplate. Heat will spread throughout the soleplate, softening the epoxy and allowing for easy removal. This method usually requires the club to be refinished unless great care is taken.

3-9 Still another method is to use an **Electric Screw Extractor**. Touch the electrode tips against the soleplate. If you wish to preserve the finish, place the electrode tips against the soleplate but inside the countersunk area of the screw pilot hole.

3-10 With the soleplate now removed, gently remove dirt and epoxy using a medium grade file. Be careful not to damage the sides of the soleplate cavity when filing. Do file deep enough into the cavity to remove most of the old epoxy.

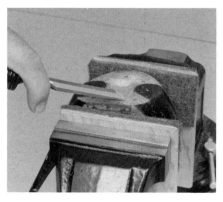

3-11 A sharp chisel also works well in removing dirt, glue or epoxy.

3-12 Remove dirt, old glue or epoxy from soleplate by using a file or chisel. Before installing the soleplate with epoxy, test fit the soleplate to the head. If the soleplate does not seat properly, further filing is needed. Refer to photo 3-40 if the soleplate is bent.

3-13 Mix epoxy and apply to both the sole-plate cavity and the back of the soleplate. In most cases, there will be a slight gap between the soleplate and the wood. A colored paste dispersion can be mixed in with the epoxy to match the color of the stained wood. This will help camouflage the epoxy line if it shows slightly.

3-14 Place the soleplate back into the sole-plate cavity. If necessary, lightly tap the soleplate with a hammer. When the soleplate screws are installed they will draw the soleplate down against the head thus eliminating small gaps.

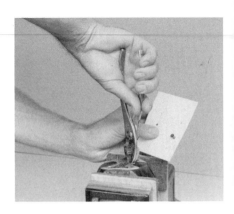

3-15 If the original screws are reused, make sure they are returned to the exact hole they came out of. Note: Pliers protect fingers from sharp screw edges when placing screws back in proper holes.

3-16 Turn the screws down until they have been turned back to their original positions. A snug fit should be achieved. If the screws are stripped, refer to photos 3-35 thru 3-39.

3-17 If the clubhead is not to be refinished, carefully wipe the excess epoxy from the head. If the club is to be refinished, the epoxy may either be wiped off or left to cure and filed from the head later.

3-18 If new screws are used, turn them into the holes until a snug fit is achieved. If the screws are stripped, refer to photos 3-35 thru 3-39.

3-19 Note the original screws have been turned down to their original positions. The heads are perfectly flush with the soleplate surface. Before returning this club to the customer, the clubhead should receive at least one coating of polyurethane. Refer to Chapter 15 for touchup steps.

3-20 If new screws have been used, file the heads flush with the soleplate using a fine mill file. Filing motion should be from heel to toe to maintain proper "graining."

3-21 Use a file cleaner to clean off any metal shaving buildup. Metal particles stuck between teeth of file will gouge the soleplate.

3-22 Pushing a piece of soft brass through the teeth of the file works amazingly well in removing stubborn metal particles or dried epoxy.

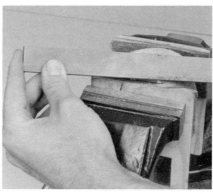

3-23 Blend in leading and trailing edges of soleplate as needed to obtain a flush fit.

3-24 Soleplate is refit and sole area is filed smooth. This club is now ready for refinishing. Refer to Chapter 1 for wood head refinishing procedures.

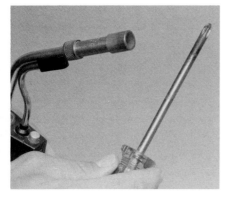

3-25 Instructions for removing difficult screws. If a soleplate screw will not turn, it is usually a result of the epoxy bond. Heat must be applied to the screw to soften the epoxy. One method is to heat the tip of an old Reed & Prince or Phillips screwdriver with a propane torch. After the tip of the screwdriver turns red . . .

3-26 . . . place the screwdriver tip inside the screw head recess. Allow the tip to rest inside the recess for 45 seconds, then try to turn the screw. Repeated application of the heated screwdriver tip may be necessary before the screw will turn.

3-27 To use a Screwheater, place the copper tube over the head of the screw. Direct the flame down the copper tube for 10-15 seconds or until the epoxy softens enough to allow the screw to be removed.

3-28 A solid copper tip, shaped to fit the screwdriver head recess, can be mounted to the tip of the propane torch. The flame from the torch heats the copper tip so the screw becomes hot without burning the finish.

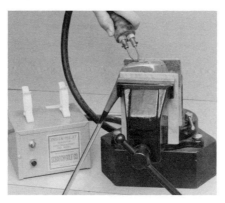

3-29 Information on use of the Screw Extractor. This is absolutely the best and fastest method to heat epoxied screws. Place both electrode tips against the head of the screw. An arc is created that instantly heats the screw. Now, simply turn out the screw.

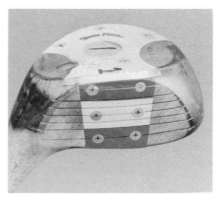

3-30 Although rare, if the soleplate screw will not turn but appears to be loose, check to see if the insert screw has been installed through the soleplate screw thus mechanically locking it in place.

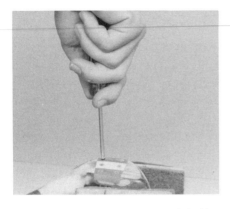

3-31 If it appears the insert screw is locking the soleplate screw, remove the suspected insert screw and then remove the soleplate screw.

3-32 To remove a screw with a ruined head, first drill a ⁵⁄₆₄″ diameter pilot hole into the center of the screwhead. Drill the hole ⅛″ to ¼″ deep. Heat the screw using one of the methods shown in photos 3-25 thru 3-29.

3-33 Next, place a #1 size screw extractor in a **"T" handle wrench.** Tap the extractor into the drilled hole to obtain a good "bite." If the extractor will not bite, drill hole deeper.

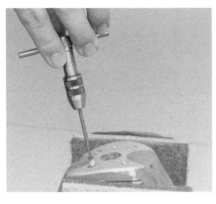

3-34 Gently and with even pressure, turn the handle counterclockwise to back the screw out. This method will also work if the head snaps off. Simply drill into the middle of the body of the screw.

3-35 If the screw threads are stripped in a wood head, push one or more toothpicks into the screw hole. Break each toothpick off flush with surface.

3-36 Dip the tip of the screw into epoxy.

3-37 Install screw in normal manner. If threads strip again, repeat procedure.

3-38 More toothpicks take up more space in the screw hole. Fine strands of steel wool can also be used. Pack the steel wool into the hole using an awl or scriber.

3-39 A Stripped Screw Repair Kit is also available. Cut one or two thin strips of perforated metal and fit them into the stripped hole. Next, insert soleplate screw in normal manner.

3-40 To rebend or to form a soleplate to make it fit properly, lay it across vise jaws and tap gently with a hammer. Repeatedly test fit the soleplate into the cavity until the proper shape is achieved.

3-41 How to remove a soleplate from a Toney Penna golf club. Photo shows the threaded steel or aluminum sleeve with brass or aluminum "Master Screw." The sleeve is epoxied into the wood head and then the Master Screw is screwed in place with epoxy.

3-42 To remove the soleplate, heat must first be applied to the Master Screw to soften the epoxy bond. Use either a Screw Heater or . . .

3-43 . . . a propane torch . . .

3-44 . . . or better yet, the **Electric Screw Extractor.**

3-45 Once the Master Screw is very hot, attempt to turn it out using a chisel that has been ground to fit the curved slot in the Master Screw or . . .

3-46 . . . use a Breaker Bar or Ratchet with a slotted socket. This creates tremendous leverage and the Master Screw will usually turn out.

3-47 If the Master Screw will not turn, insert a strong knife or chisel under the leading edge of the soleplate and slowly pry the soleplate up. Soleplate screws are removed first. If the soleplate will not come up, apply more heat until . . .

3-48 . . . the soleplate, metal sleeve and Master Screw come out as one unit. Sometimes this requires repeated heatings at higher temperatures.

ADDITIONAL INFORMATION FOR SOLEPLATE REMOVAL AND RESETTING LOOSE SOLEPLATES

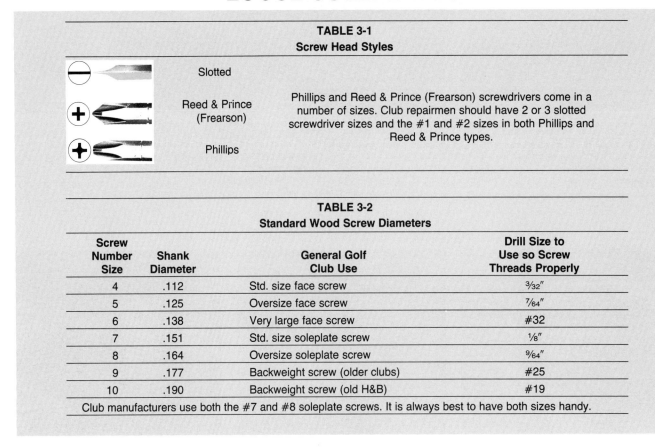

TABLE 3-1
Screw Head Styles

Slotted

Reed & Prince (Frearson)

Phillips

Phillips and Reed & Prince (Frearson) screwdrivers come in a number of sizes. Club repairmen should have 2 or 3 slotted screwdriver sizes and the #1 and #2 sizes in both Phillips and Reed & Prince types.

TABLE 3-2
Standard Wood Screw Diameters

Screw Number Size	Shank Diameter	General Golf Club Use	Drill Size to Use so Screw Threads Properly
4	.112	Std. size face screw	3/32″
5	.125	Oversize face screw	7/64″
6	.138	Very large face screw	#32
7	.151	Std. size soleplate screw	1/8″
8	.164	Oversize soleplate screw	9/64″
9	.177	Backweight screw (older clubs)	#25
10	.190	Backweight screw (old H&B)	#19

Club manufacturers use both the #7 and #8 soleplate screws. It is always best to have both sizes handy.

NOTES

INSERT REMOVAL AND RESETTING LOOSE INSERTS

Most golfers are not aware that their inserts are loose. A loose insert is usually discovered by the repairman when the club is brought in for a refinish or other clubhead work. If the club is to be refinished, a loose insert must first be repaired to eliminate insert movement. The slightest movement can cause a hairline crack to develop in the finish around the insert, usually after impact with a ball. Also, a loose insert will allow moisture to enter the head during periods of high humidity and allow moisture to leave the head during periods of low humidity. This change in moisture content causes the head to alternately swell and shrink slightly, which in turn causes cracking, delamination and general deterioration of the bonding between the head and its components.

Insert materials will usually be one of the following: original fiber, cycolac (ABS), acrylic, epoxy, phenolic laminate, graphite, aluminum, Gamma-Fire, melamine or Ferro-Ligno.

The following removal techniques will work on all of the above-mentioned insert materials, with the exception of a cast-in-place epoxy insert. Steps required for the removal of epoxy inserts are found in Chapter 5.

A number of clubs have face insert screws, although many newer models do not. If a screw is used, it is most likely a #4 or #5 brass screw. It is a good idea to keep a supply of both on hand. We stock both the #4 × ⅝″ and #5 × ¾″ sizes, and find that the larger #5 size is quite handy for replacing stripped out #4 screws.

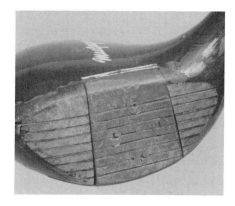

4-1 Photo shows a clubhead with a loose insert. A loose insert is identified by a gap between the insert and the insert cavity. The gap can be at the sides of the insert or along the top line of the insert or both.

4-2 First, remove the soleplate as outlined in Chapter 3.

4-3 Carefully clean out all dirt, paint and old finish from screwhead recesses with a scriber, dental pick, awl or other pointed tool.

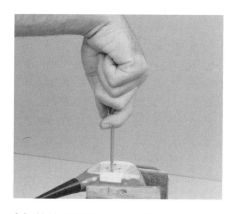

4-4 Hold screwdriver perfectly square, press down firmly and turn screw out (counterclockwise). Insert screws are usually not installed with epoxy and will therefore, turn out easily. If difficulty is experienced, refer to photos 4-5 thru 4-15 for methods of removing stubborn face insert screws.

4-5 Use of the **Electric Screw Extractor** is the fastest and easiest way to remove stubborn screws. When the two electrode tips make contact with the head of the screw, heat is immediately applied to it. After a few seconds of contact, simply turn the screw out with a screwdriver. The longer the tips make contact with the screw, the hotter the screw becomes.

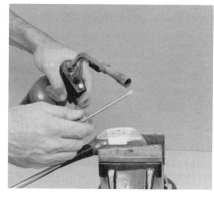

4-6 Another method is to heat the tip of an old screwdriver with a propane torch. After the tip is quite hot, place it in the screw head for 30 seconds and then try to twist the screw out. This method works surprisingly well for insert screw removal.

4-7 An **Electric Heat Gun** will also heat the screw enough to break the epoxy bond. Of course, this method heats the entire face so use care in not applying too much heat.

4-8 Method for removing a "stripped" screwhead. A stripped screwhead is generally caused by failure to properly clean the screwhead recess before attempting to turn the screw or by using the incorrect type or size of screwdriver.

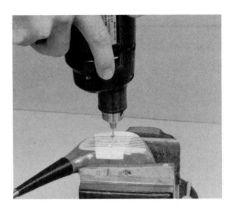

4-9 First, using a ⁵⁄₆₄″ drill bit, drill a hole at least ³⁄₁₆″ deep into the middle of the screw head. If necessary, heat the head of the screw using one of the methods already shown.

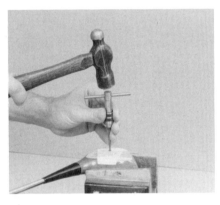

4-10 Next, place a #1 size Extractor into the drilled hole and tap lightly until it gets a good "bite." The Extractor works best when held in the **"T" handle tap wrench** as shown.

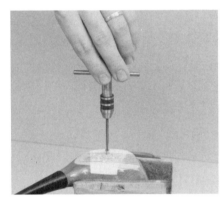

4-11 Turn the Extractor counterclockwise to remove the screw. Don't use force. If the screw will not turn, use more heat and try again.

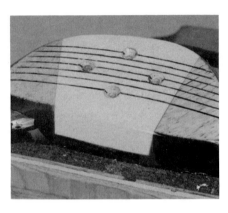

4-12 If the head of an insert screw breaks while attempting removal, the drill and extractor method will usually not work. The best method for dealing with this difficult situation is . . .

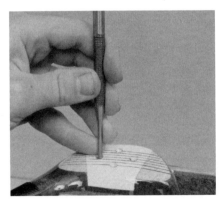

4-13 . . . place a ⅛″ or ³⁄₃₂″ **pin punch** on top of the broken screw and . . .

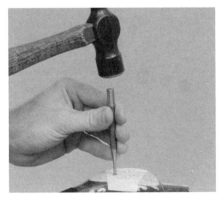

4-14 . . . drive the broken screw at least ½″ below the surface of the face.

4-15 An alternative method: Once the other insert screws are removed pry the insert over the broken screw shank. After the insert is removed, grasp the broken screw with a pair of pliers and turn it out.

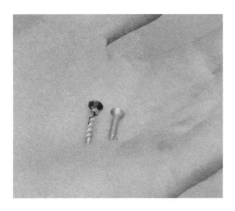

4-16 A few manufacturers use a different type of insert screw known as a drive screw. Note the difference in the threading of the two screws. The drive screw must be turned and pulled from the head simultaneously.

4-17 Unfortunately, this type of screw is not easily recognized. Experience will indicate which manufacturers use this screw. If you suspect a club has a drive screw . . .

4-18 . . . drill into the screw head as shown in photo 4-9. Next, heat the screw as shown in photos 4-5 thru 4-7. Quickly, while the screw is still hot, tap the #1 size Extractor into the hole. Once the Extractor is seated in the hole, turn the extractor counterclockwise while pulling up slightly on the screw.

4-19 After the insert screws are removed, lightly file through the polyurethane coating on the face. Concentrate the filing on the face where the insert edge meets the wood. A fine or medium grade file works best.

4-20 Polyurethane adheres very well to the face. If it is not removed from around the insert, some of the wood may be pulled from the head when the insert is removed.

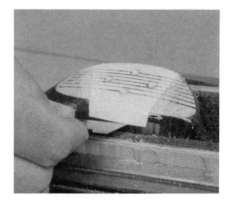

4-21 Carefully cut around the top of the insert. This step will also help prevent wood from being pulled from the head, plus, it will not allow polyurethane to be torn from the head. Only cut deep enough to penetrate the clear finish.

4-22 If you suspect there is a tight fit between the insert and the insert cavity, carefully tap a razor blade between the insert and insert cavity. This will create a very thin gap and help with insert removal. Do not tap the razor blade deeper than ⅛". Use the razor blade on both sides.

4-23 Place an **Insert Remover Tool** at the bottom of the insert cavity. Start at the side of the insert. Gently tap the top of the tool. As the insert lifts from the head, watch the sides of the face to see if any wood is coming up with the insert. If the wood begins to lift, repeat the step shown in photo 4-22.

4-24 Once approximately two-thirds of the side of the insert is free . . .

4-25 . . . remove the tool and reinsert it under the other side. Again, lightly tap until two-thirds of the insert is free.

4-26 At this point, there is a lot of pressure created at the top of the insert cavity between the insert and wood. To alleviate this pressure, tap the top of the insert lightly with a hammer. The insert should pop out. If it doesn't, repeat the previous steps. Do not attempt to pry the insert out. Serious damage to the wood around the top of the insert may result.

4-27 The method shown in the previous photos will work on every insert material with the exception of a pour-in-place epoxy insert. This type of insert is usually installed into the insert cavity in the form of a liquid which hardens and becomes solid. Most epoxy inserts can not be removed without destroying the insert. Refer to Chapter 5 for correct removal and replacement steps.

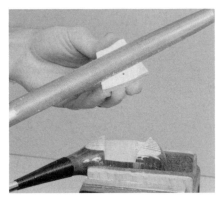

4-28 **Once the insert is removed,** file the back and sides of the insert to remove excess epoxy or any foreign material.

4-29 Excess epoxy in the insert cavity should also be removed. A file may be used to remove this excess, but be very careful when filing along the top edge of the insert cavity. Maintain a straight edge and do not file too deeply.

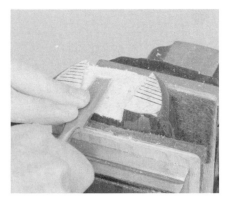

4-30 Epoxy may also be removed using a chisel. Heating the tip of the chisel before scraping will help soften the epoxy and make it much easier to remove. A propane torch is good for heating the chisel tip.

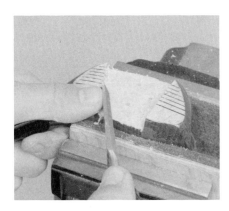

4-31 The sides of the insert cavity are also carefully cleaned. A chisel works best for this area.

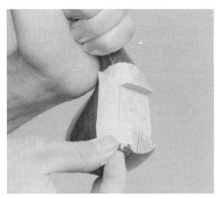

4-32 If the clubhead is not to be refinished after resetting the insert, carefully lay two layers of ¾″ masking tape around the top of the insert cavity. The tape will protect the finish from the epoxy adhesive.

4-33 **Mix an appropriate amount of epoxy.** It is a good idea to mix a colored paste dispersion with the epoxy so that the color will match the stained wood. This will camouflage an epoxy line behind the top of the insert cavity. A high shear strength epoxy is used for this step. **Conap**® or **GolfWorks**® epoxy works very well.

4-34 Apply epoxy to the back and sides of both the insert and insert cavity.

4-35 Place the insert in the bottom half of the cavity and . . .

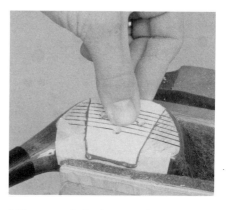

4-36 . . . push the insert up into the proper location. This will force epoxy around the sides of the insert and guarantee a good seal. Make sure the scoring lines in the insert and face are properly aligned.

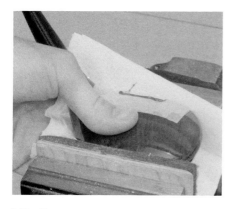

4-37 Place a paper towel across the face and position the clubhead in the vise as shown. Tighten the vise jaws until snug but not tight. Allow the epoxy to harden before removing. Note the use of a **Felt Vise Pad** to protect the back of the clubhead.

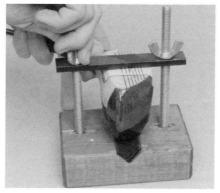

4-38 An **Insert Clamp** is the best way to tighten a newly epoxied insert into the insert cavity. Use of the Insert Clamp will keep the vise free for other activities and also allow better visibility of the clamping process. It is a good idea to have enough Insert Clamps on hand to reset an entire day's work.

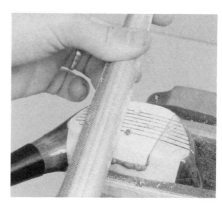

4-39 After the epoxy hardens, remove the head from the vise or Insert Clamp. Carefully file the excess epoxy from the face, using a medium cut file. Do not file into the wood yet.

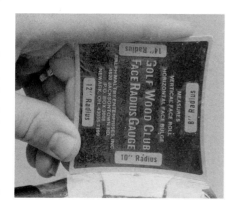

4-40 Check the bulge and roll and make any necessary corrections with the medium or fine cut file. Refer to Chapter 1, photos 1-22 thru 1-30 for correct face measuring techniques and filing steps.

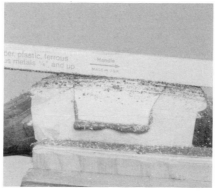

4-41 After filing, recut the scoring lines using the same technique as shown in photo 1-34 in Chapter 1.

4-42 Next, clean out the insert screw pilot holes with a ³⁄₃₂″ drill bit. The depth to drill depends upon the length of the screw to be used. See Table 4-1 for other pilot drill sizes.

4-43 After drilling, recountersink the holes if necessary. Hold the shank as shown, and twirl quickly. **DO NOT MAKE HOLES WIDER THAN THE SCREW HEADS.**

4-44 The **Automatic Countersink** is very fast and efficient for both insert and soleplate screws. It is used mainly for high volume repair or production work.

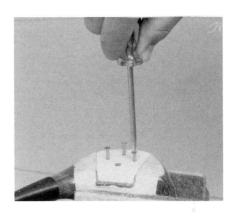

4-45   Next, install new insert screws.

4-46 A **Ratchet Screwdriver** saves time by allowing the operator to turn the screws into the head at a very fast rate.

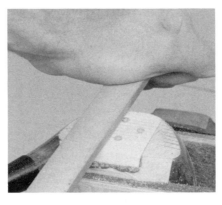

4-47   File the screw heads flush with the face. A properly countersunk hole will allow the head of the screw to be seated slightly above the face. This will give a professional look once the heads are filed down flush. Use a fine cut file when filing insert screws.

4-48   Brush the face clean with a stiff bristled brush after filing.

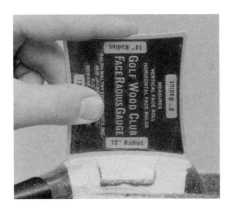

4-49   Final check the bulge and roll.

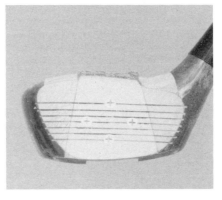

4-50 This is how the face should look after filing. Note the screw slots are positioned perpendicular and parallel to the scoring lines. If the clubhead is refinished, reinstall the soleplate as outlined in Chapter 3 and proceed with the refinishing steps as shown in Chapter 1.

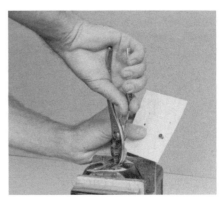

4-51 If the club must be returned to the customer without benefit of a refinish, reinstall the soleplate as outlined in Chapter 3, photos 3-10 thru 3-17. Touchup steps are shown in Chapter 15.

4-52 INFORMATION ON SPECIAL INSERTS. Some H&B Power Bilt models have three headless brass screws running through the insert and into the wood. The quickest method for removal is to first drill into the center of the screw with a 5/64" drill.

4-53 Next, heat the screw with an **Electric Screw Extractor** and then quickly tap a #1 size Extractor into the hole. Note: Alternate methods to heat the screw are to use a heat gun or a 3/16" diameter flat end heating rod and a propane torch.

4-54 Turn the Extractor and wrench counter-clockwise while pulling up. As you can see, this screw is very much like the drive screw pictured in photo 4-16.

4-55 INFORMATION ON SPECIAL INSERTS. To remove old MacGregor inserts with the screw-in aluminum firing pin, first remove the 4 screws and cut the center face line deeper with a scoring line hacksaw blade.

4-56 Heat the aluminum pin with the **Screw Heater, Electric Screw Extractor or Heat Gun.**

4-57 Place a chisel or conventional large screwdriver in the middle scoring line. Turn the aluminum pin counterclockwise and screw it out.

4-58 The aluminum pin is then removed. Note the use of a pair of pliers as the screw will be very hot. The insert can now be removed as previously shown.

4-59 INFORMATION ON SPECIAL INSERTS. To remove a two-piece insert from an old Ben Hogan head, use normal procedures and remove both the red fiber insert and the white fiber insert backing piece from the insert cavity. To reinstall, epoxy both pieces back in at the same time.

4-60 INFORMATION ON SPECIAL INSERTS. To remove all MacGregor Eye-O-Matic inserts with "V" back, proceed as follows. The insert is usually loose at its edges but the "V" is still secure to the head. Note: Some repairmen choose to simply fill any gaps around the insert with epoxy if the "V" is secure to the head. This is due to removal difficulty.

5 REPLACING OLD INSERTS WITH EPOXY CAST-IN-PLACE INSERTS AND REPAIRING DAMAGED FACES

Many times you will be faced with an unrepairable face insert which must be replaced. Epoxy, cast-in-place inserts are one alternative for replacement. This insert material was developed because it is impossible to stock the hundreds of different shapes and colors of inserts used by golf club manufacturers. The versatility of cast-in-place epoxy inserts is probably the most important characteristic of this material. Inserts can be cast in any shape or size with a myriad of color combinations available.

This high-impact strength, cast-in-place epoxy can also be used to repair damaged faces on woods. Often, due to moisture absorption and excessive toe or heel shots, a wood face will dry rot or weather. Eventually, a defect in the face develops where the rotten wood is worn from the face causing some concavity. When a ball is struck from this irregular surface, an errant shot can result. If properly repaired, the clear epoxy will reflect the wood surface beneath the epoxy, and the repair is hardly noticeable. Many valuable and cherished wood clubs have been saved using this procedure.

Epoxy inserts also allow for customizing. Photos in this chapter show how to take advantage of the versatility of this material by placing a medallion, logo, coin, photo, etc., inside the epoxy insert. Customizing inserts adds a unique touch to a club and can give the club a truly one-of-a-kind look.

5-1 Remove old insert and insert screws, if any, as outlined in Chapter 4. Also, remove the soleplate as outlined in Chapter 3.

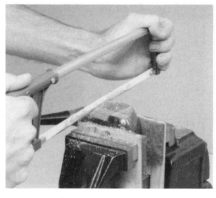

5-2 For difficult to remove inserts, make two vertical cuts approximately ⅛″ in from each side of the insert cavity. Note the use of a conventional hacksaw blade. The conventional raked teeth blade will move more freely through the insert material without binding.

5-3 Photo shows insert after cutting. **Do not cut through the top line of the insert cavity into the wood.**

5-4 Place a chisel or **Insert Remover Tool** underneath the middle of the insert. Tap the head of the tool sharply with a hammer.

5-5 The middle portion of the insert will "pop out" leaving only the sides still attached to the insert cavity.

5-6 Place a sharp knife on the line between the cavity and the insert. Tap lightly on the edge of the knife with a hammer until the sliver of insert falls into the cavity. Note: The stiff bladed "Super Knife" sold for cutting off old grips works very well for this.

4-52 INFORMATION ON SPECIAL INSERTS. Some H&B Power Bilt models have three headless brass screws running through the insert and into the wood. The quickest method for removal is to first drill into the center of the screw with a ⁵⁄₆₄″ drill.

4-53 Next, heat the screw with an **Electric Screw Extractor** and then quickly tap a #1 size Extractor into the hole. Note: Alternate methods to heat the screw are to use a heat gun or a ³⁄₁₆″ diameter flat end heating rod and a propane torch.

4-54 Turn the Extractor and wrench counter-clockwise while pulling up. As you can see, this screw is very much like the drive screw pictured in photo 4-16.

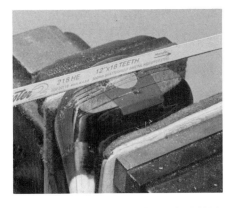

4-55 INFORMATION ON SPECIAL INSERTS. To remove old MacGregor inserts with the screw-in aluminum firing pin, first remove the 4 screws and cut the center face line deeper with a scoring line hacksaw blade.

4-56 Heat the aluminum pin with the **Screw Heater, Electric Screw Extractor or Heat Gun.**

4-57 Place a chisel or conventional large screwdriver in the middle scoring line. Turn the aluminum pin counterclockwise and screw it out.

4-58 The aluminum pin is then removed. Note the use of a pair of pliers as the screw will be very hot. The insert can now be removed as previously shown.

4-59 INFORMATION ON SPECIAL INSERTS. To remove a two-piece insert from an old Ben Hogan head, use normal procedures and remove both the red fiber insert and the white fiber insert backing piece from the insert cavity. To reinstall, epoxy both pieces back in at the same time.

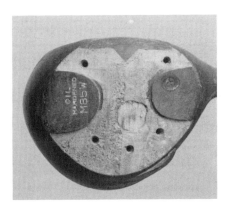

4-60 INFORMATION ON SPECIAL INSERTS. To remove all MacGregor Eye-O-Matic inserts with "V" back, proceed as follows. The insert is usually loose at its edges but the "V" is still secure to the head. Note: Some repairmen choose to simply fill any gaps around the insert with epoxy if the "V" is secure to the head. This is due to removal difficulty.

5 REPLACING OLD INSERTS WITH EPOXY CAST-IN-PLACE INSERTS AND REPAIRING DAMAGED FACES

Many times you will be faced with an unrepairable face insert which must be replaced. Epoxy, cast-in-place inserts are one alternative for replacement. This insert material was developed because it is impossible to stock the hundreds of different shapes and colors of inserts used by golf club manufacturers. The versatility of cast-in-place epoxy inserts is probably the most important characteristic of this material. Inserts can be cast in any shape or size with a myriad of color combinations available.

This high-impact strength, cast-in-place epoxy can also be used to repair damaged faces on woods. Often, due to moisture absorption and excessive toe or heel shots, a wood face will dry rot or weather. Eventually, a defect in the face develops where the rotten wood is worn from the face causing some concavity. When a ball is struck from this irregular surface, an errant shot can result. If properly repaired, the clear epoxy will reflect the wood surface beneath the epoxy, and the repair is hardly noticeable. Many valuable and cherished wood clubs have been saved using this procedure.

Epoxy inserts also allow for customizing. Photos in this chapter show how to take advantage of the versatility of this material by placing a medallion, logo, coin, photo, etc., inside the epoxy insert. Customizing inserts adds a unique touch to a club and can give the club a truly one-of-a-kind look.

5-1   Remove old insert and insert screws, if any, as outlined in Chapter 4. Also, remove the soleplate as outlined in Chapter 3.

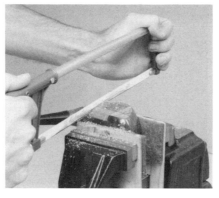

5-2   For difficult to remove inserts, make two vertical cuts approximately ⅛″ in from each side of the insert cavity. Note the use of a conventional hacksaw blade. The conventional raked teeth blade will move more freely through the insert material without binding.

5-3   Photo shows insert after cutting. **Do not cut through the top line of the insert cavity into the wood.**

5-4   Place a chisel or **Insert Remover Tool** underneath the middle of the insert. Tap the head of the tool sharply with a hammer.

5-5   The middle portion of the insert will "pop out" leaving only the sides still attached to the insert cavity.

5-6   Place a sharp knife on the line between the cavity and the insert. Tap lightly on the edge of the knife with a hammer until the sliver of insert falls into the cavity. Note: The stiff bladed "**Super Knife**" sold for cutting off old grips works very well for this.

4-52 INFORMATION ON SPECIAL INSERTS. Some H&B Power Bilt models have three headless brass screws running through the insert and into the wood. The quickest method for removal is to first drill into the center of the screw with a ⁵⁄₆₄″ drill.

4-53 Next, heat the screw with an **Electric Screw Extractor** and then quickly tap a #1 size Extractor into the hole. Note: Alternate methods to heat the screw are to use a heat gun or a ³⁄₁₆″ diameter flat end heating rod and a propane torch.

4-54 Turn the Extractor and wrench counter-clockwise while pulling up. As you can see, this screw is very much like the drive screw pictured in photo 4-16.

4-55 INFORMATION ON SPECIAL INSERTS. To remove old MacGregor inserts with the screw-in aluminum firing pin, first remove the 4 screws and cut the center face line deeper with a scoring line hacksaw blade.

4-56 Heat the aluminum pin with the **Screw Heater, Electric Screw Extractor or Heat Gun.**

4-57 Place a chisel or conventional large screwdriver in the middle scoring line. Turn the aluminum pin counterclockwise and screw it out.

4-58 The aluminum pin is then removed. Note the use of a pair of pliers as the screw will be very hot. The insert can now be removed as previously shown.

4-59 INFORMATION ON SPECIAL INSERTS. To remove a two-piece insert from an old Ben Hogan head, use normal procedures and remove both the red fiber insert and the white fiber insert backing piece from the insert cavity. To reinstall, epoxy both pieces back in at the same time.

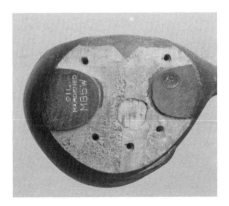

4-60 INFORMATION ON SPECIAL INSERTS. To remove all MacGregor Eye-O-Matic inserts with "V" back, proceed as follows. The insert is usually loose at its edges but the "V" is still secure to the head. Note: Some repairmen choose to simply fill any gaps around the insert with epoxy if the "V" is secure to the head. This is due to removal difficulty.

4-61 First, place an Insert Remover Tool beneath the flat back side of the insert. Tap the head of the tool several times, remove the tool and now place it under the "V" portion of the insert as shown above. Again tap the insert tool several times and continue to repeat these steps until . . .

4-62 . . . the insert comes out. Patience is the key in removing this type of insert.

4-63 INFORMATION ON SPECIAL INSERTS. This concerns old MacGregor Eye-O-Matic type inserts with three fiber dowel pins running through the insert into the wood. The best removal method is to slide the special **Insert Remover Tool** underneath the insert and cut through the dowels. Now follow the normal insert removal procedure.

4-64 The three dowels are also found in the "V" back insert type. Follow instructions as shown in photos 4-60 thru 4-62. Simply cut through the dowels while removing the insert as shown in photo 4-63.

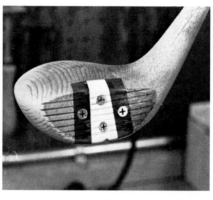

4-65 INFORMATION ON SPECIAL INSERTS. An old Spalding 3-piece insert will come out easily, but, it will come out in 3 pieces. During reassembly, epoxy the whole mess back together. Some repairmen will install each piece with an insert screw to ensure the pieces do not slide out of place.

NOTES

ADDITIONAL INFORMATION FOR
INSERT REMOVAL & RESETTING
LOOSE INSERTS

		TABLE 4-1		
		Standard Wood Screw Diameters		
Screw Number Size	Shank Diameter	General Golf Club Use	Drill Size to Use so Screw Threads Properly	
4	.112	Std. size face screw	3/32"	
5	.125	Oversize face screw	7/64"	
6	.138	Very large face screw	#32	
7	.151	Std. size soleplate screw	1/8"	
8	.164	Oversize soleplate screw	9/64"	
9	.177	Backweight screw (older clubs)	#25	
10	.190	Backweight screw (old H&B)	#19	

Golf clubs manufactured from 1940 and on use mostly #4 and #5 face insert screws. Most are brass; however, some were made of aluminum. The #6 screw was used in a few 1920's and 1930's models and is quite rare to find.

NOTES

5 REPLACING OLD INSERTS WITH EPOXY CAST-IN-PLACE INSERTS AND REPAIRING DAMAGED FACES

.   Many times you will be faced with an unrepairable face insert which must be replaced. Epoxy, cast-in-place inserts are one alternative for replacement. This insert material was developed because it is impossible to stock the hundreds of different shapes and colors of inserts used by golf club manufacturers. The versatility of cast-in-place epoxy inserts is probably the most important characteristic of this material. Inserts can be cast in any shape or size with a myriad of color combinations available.

This high-impact strength, cast-in-place epoxy can also be used to repair damaged faces on woods. Often, due to moisture absorption and excessive toe or heel shots, a wood face will dry rot or weather. Eventually, a defect in the face develops where the rotten wood is worn from the face causing some concavity. When a ball is struck from this irregular surface, an errant shot can result. If properly repaired, the clear epoxy will reflect the wood surface beneath the epoxy, and the repair is hardly noticeable. Many valuable and cherished wood clubs have been saved using this procedure.

Epoxy inserts also allow for customizing. Photos in this chapter show how to take advantage of the versatility of this material by placing a medallion, logo, coin, photo, etc., inside the epoxy insert. Customizing inserts adds a unique touch to a club and can give the club a truly one-of-a-kind look.

5-1   Remove old insert and insert screws, if any, as outlined in Chapter 4. Also, remove the soleplate as outlined in Chapter 3.

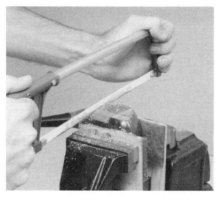

5-2   For difficult to remove inserts, make two vertical cuts approximately ⅛" in from each side of the insert cavity. Note the use of a conventional hacksaw blade. The conventional raked teeth blade will move more freely through the insert material without binding.

5-3 Photo shows insert after cutting. **Do not cut through the top line of the insert cavity into the wood.**

5-4 Place a chisel or **Insert Remover Tool** underneath the middle of the insert. Tap the head of the tool sharply with a hammer.

5-5 The middle portion of the insert will "pop out" leaving only the sides still attached to the insert cavity.

5-6 Place a sharp knife on the line between the cavity and the insert. Tap lightly on the edge of the knife with a hammer until the sliver of insert falls into the cavity. Note: The stiff bladed **"Super Knife"** sold for cutting off old grips works very well for this.

5-7 An alternative to a knife is a stiff razor blade. Employ the same technique as shown in the previous photo.

5-8 All portions of the insert are now removed. Remove any old epoxy from the cavity using a file or wood chisel.

5-9 Take note of the decorative piece inside this insert. If proper care is taken this can be saved and reused in the new insert. The existing epoxy insert can be removed using the following method.

5-10 An **Electric Heat Gun** produces anywhere from 125° to 1000° F. Directing this heat against the epoxy insert will quickly soften the epoxy. The softened epoxy can then be easily dug from the cavity using a chisel.

5-11 Continue to dig at the epoxy until . . .

5-12 . . . all the epoxy is removed. Note the medallion has been salvaged for reuse. Use care not to burn the wood with the Heat Gun.

5-13 **After the insert is removed from a club** (and if the soleplate was also removed), temporarily reinstall the soleplate without epoxy. The reinstalled soleplate will provide a perfect shaped radius for the poured insert.

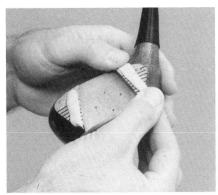

5-14 Press a tiny amount of Mortite putty in face lines on either side of the cavity. This is necessary to keep the liquid epoxy from flowing out of the cavity through the lines.

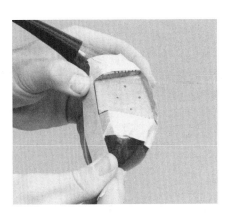

5-15 If the clubhead will not be refinished (it is strongly recommended that it be refinished), outline the entire insert cavity with ¾″ masking tape. The tape will protect the finish from the epoxy and also provide a depth gauge later on when filing the insert. Be careful not to allow the tape to lay over the cavity.

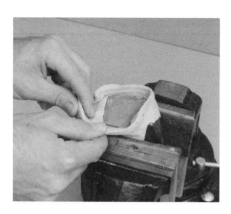

5-16 Form the Mortite putty dam. Press Mortite down tightly around the edges to prevent leaks.

5-17 The finished dam should look like this. Crude in appearance, but very effective. Be sure the putty does not occupy any space that the insert should occupy.

5-18 The club can now be placed in a vise or . . .

5-19 . . . a handy **Insert Tree.** Note the use of the **Bubble Level** to ensure the cavity will be filled evenly. Remove Bubble Level before pouring the insert.

5-20 High-impact strength epoxy is available in different colors and quantities, depending upon need. High-impact strength epoxy is used instead of high shear strength epoxy because the face must withstand the shock of the ball at impact.

5-21 Epoxy resin (base) and activator are mixed together to create the insert mixture. Resins are available in different colors. For smaller users, buy only the clear resin and mix different colored paste dispersions into it to produce the required color. When working with a precolored base, always mix the base thoroughly until . . .

5-22 . . . the coloring agent in the bottom of the can is blended in with the upper contents of the can. Note the difference in the color of the base that is on the stick compared to the previous photo. The pigment obviously settles out in the can during storage.

5-23 Pour appropriate amount of base into a container. Note the use of metric cups to ensure an accurate measurement. **Read the Additional Information on Pouring Inserts at the end of this chapter for specific amounts to use.**

5-24 Slowly stir the activator in the can. **Do not shake can since that will form bubbles.**

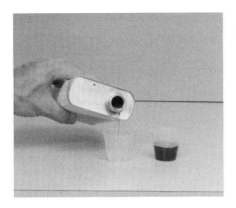

5-25 Pour the appropriate amount of activator into a separate metric cup.

5-26 Once the exact amounts have been poured, pour activator into cup holding the base.

5-27 Fold epoxy thoroughly, according to instructions. A folding motion introduces fewer air bubbles than a stirring motion. It will also do a better job of combining the base and activator.

5-28 Pour the epoxy material into the cavity approximately 1½ times the thickness of the original insert. 15 cc's of material will pour one small insert, 22½ cc's a medium insert and 30 cc's a large insert (Wilson). Some recently popular full face inserts will require an even greater amount of material.

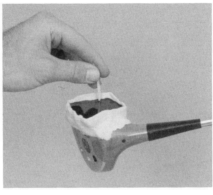

5-29 Using a toothpick or mix stick, swirl around edges of insert cavity to release any trapped air bubbles. Do not use a match or pass any open flame across insert to release bubbles. Allow insert to cure in this position, usually overnight.

5-30 After insert has cured, Mortite putty is removed and saved, as it can be used over and over again. Do not remove masking tape. **If the insert is quite soft it means the mixture quantities of base and activator were not in a proper proportion, it was not mixed well enough or the temperature was below 65°F.**

5-31 Use a medium or coarse wood rasp (I prefer 10″ length) to rough shape insert. Leave the middle of the insert "high" while filing the edges of the insert flush with the wood. Upon reaching the masking tape, when filing, provides a good indication that you should slow down and use caution so as not to file too deep and remove too much wood from the face. Always use a file handle on file to prevent possible injury to your hands.

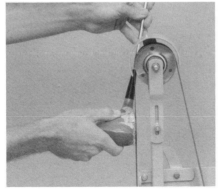

5-32 Use of a **Belt Sander** with a coarse belt is a quick alternative to filing. However, be very careful, as mistakes can occur faster, too.

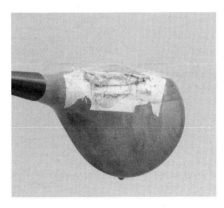

5-33 After rough shaping, the profile of the face should look like this. If there is a low spot in the middle of the insert, excessive filing of the toe and heel will be necessary to achieve the proper bulge and roll. This, in turn, will reduce the face progression and potentially ruin the look of the club.

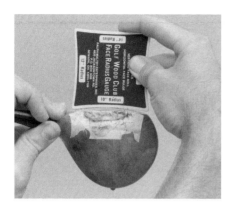

5-34 Check the horizontal face bulge with the **Face Radius Gauge.** Check at different points from top to bottom of face. Chapter 1 shows how to use this gauge properly (photos 1-22 thru 1-27).

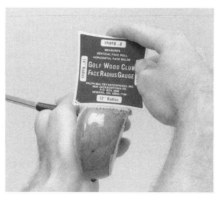

5-35 Check vertical face roll with the **Face Radius Gauge.** Check at different points from toe to heel.

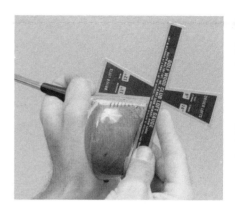

5-36 Check the loft using a protractor or a **Loft Gauge.** See Chapter 10 photos 10-1 and 10-2 for a thorough explanation of measuring loft.

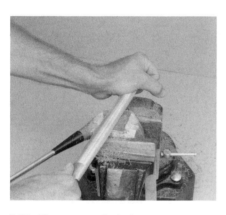

5-37 The purpose in facing the club is to bring the high spots down to the low spots without removing very much wood, if any. With that in mind, file the face with a 10″ medium cut wood file (not a rasp). Concentrate the file on the high points in the face using a radiusing motion until . . .

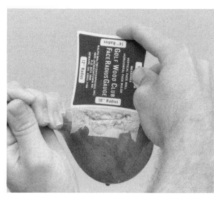

5-38 . . . the desired bulge radius is achieved and . . .

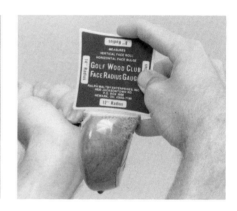

5-39 . . . the desired roll radius is achieved. Check the loft also. If the original bulge and roll are maintained, very little of the wood in the heel and toe will be filed away and as a result, the loft should be unaffected.

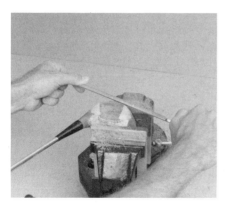

5-40 Next, radius the leading edge of the insert with the file.

5-41 Change position of club in vise pads and rough file top of insert with the medium cut wood file until the file cuts into the masking tape. The wood rasp can also be used here, but be sure to change files upon reaching or nearing the masking tape.

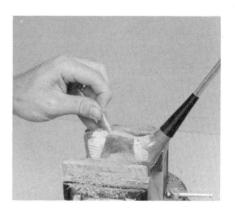

5-42 If the club will not be refinished, care must be taken not to file through the finish. Carefully peel off the tape from around the top of the insert cavity and . . .

Note: A new piece of ¾″ masking tape can be applied at this time approximately ¼″ back from the insert top edge to prevent inadvertent file nicks in the crown of the wood.

5-43 . . . lightly file the excess epoxy with a fine mill file. Continue to file the epoxy insert until . . .

5-44 . . . the top of the insert is flush with the surrounding finish. Minor surface abrasions are easily repaired. Refer to Chapter 15 for touch-up steps if the club is not to be refinished. Note: Some repairmen find it easier to shape the top of the insert with a **Detail Knife** once the level of the insert is close to the wood surface.

5-45 If the golf club is to be refinished, smooth file the top of the insert flush with the clubhead using a fine cut, flat file or mill file.

5-46 Note the shape of the top line. Care should be taken to preserve this symmetrical look.

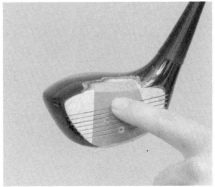

5-47 Avoid this top line shape. Too much material was removed from the middle of the insert caused by an improper filing angle.

5-48 Smooth file face with a fine cut flat or mill file. Remove all previous filing marks from the insert and face. If a medallion or other cosmetic article is to be installed, refer to photo 5-64 to begin proper steps.

5-49 Next, draw all face lines on insert using a 6″ flexible metal scale and a sharp pencil. Use care in connecting the old face lines in the toe and heel of clubface.

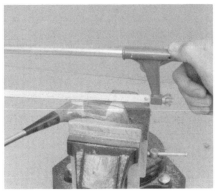

5-50 Place the hacksaw blade in the heel side scoring line. Using short cutting strokes, **cut across the face following the drawn line.** Note the use of a special made hacksaw blade with no rake or offset so proper scoring line width is maintained.

5-51 The newly cut scoring lines should look like this.

5-52 Installing insert screws. Determine the screw pattern. Most clubs use a diamond screw pattern. Place a 6″ scale on the bottom scoring line and find the midpoint between the sides of the insert. Make a mark with a pen, pencil or sharp awl. Repeat this step to the top scoring line.

5-53 Place the scale along the middle scoring line. Make a mark ¼″ in from each side of the insert.

5-54 Photo shows a properly marked insert. **Note:** The screw pattern is altered if the face has more than 7 lines. In the case of a 9 line face, the top and bottom lines are left blank. The screws are installed in the second and eighth line instead of as shown above.

5-55 Using the marks as a guide, drill into the insert with ³⁄₃₂″ bit. The depth of the hole is determined by the length of the insert screw. The #4 × ⅝″ brass cross slot screw is the industry standard for insert screws.

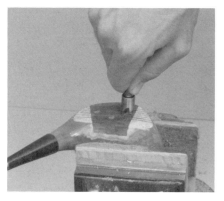

5-56 After drilling, open the holes with a countersink. Countersinking the pilot hole will allow the head of the screw to seat flush with the insert. If properly countersunk, the top of the screw head should be slightly higher than the surface of the insert before filing the screw heads.

5-57 Carefully turn in the new insert screws. Note: If desired, a small dab of epoxy can be placed on each screw tip for added security.

5-58 File the screw heads flush with the insert using a fine cut mill file. After filing, rub a finger across the face. The screw heads should not be felt.

5-59 All filing marks are removed by lightly scraping the face with the back edge of the **Detailing Knife.**

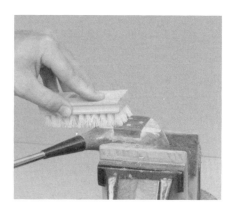

5-60 Brush dust and other particles from the scoring lines with a stiff bristled brush.

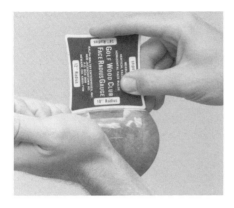

5-61 Final check for proper bulge . . .

5-62 . . . check for proper roll and . . .

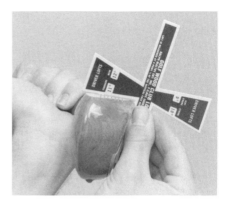

5-63 . . . check for proper loft. Club is now ready for swingweighting and soleplate installation. See Chapters 3 and 13 for these procedures. If the club is not going to be refinished, see Chapter 15 for touchup steps. See Chapter 1 if it will be refinished.

5-64 Customizing an insert. These steps are performed after the bulge, roll and loft are set but before the scoring lines are cut.

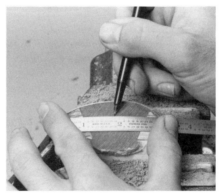

5-65 Locate the middle of the insert. Measure along a horizontal line and find the midpoint in the insert. Mark this point with a pencil or pen.

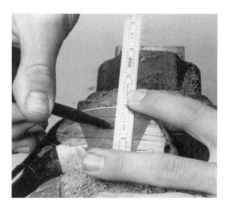

5-66 Measure on a vertical line from the top to the bottom of the insert and find the midpoint. Mark this point. If necessary, extend the points until a cross hair is formed. The cross hair determines the entry point of the drill bit.

5-67 Using the cross hair as a guide, drill into the insert using a ⅛″ bit. Drill approximately ¾″ into the insert.

5-68 Depending upon the diameter of the medallion or decorative piece, select the proper size bit. In this case a ⅝″ wood bit is used. Drill to a depth that will allow at least ⅛″ clearance between the top of the medallion and the insert surface. Do not drill through the insert into the wood unless absolutely necessary.

5-69 Place the medallion, logo, coin, emblem, photo, etc., in the recess.

5-70 Form a Mortite putty dam around the hole, mix the clear insert epoxy and pour it into the recess.

5-71 Stir a toothpick around in the epoxy to release any trapped air bubbles. Allow the epoxy to cure, usually overnight is best.

5-72 After curing, remove the Mortite putty dam.

5-73 Excess epoxy may be carefully cut from the face using a hacksaw. **DO NOT CUT INTO THE FACE.**

5-74 Using a medium to coarse cut wood rasp, file the remaining epoxy until the rasp begins to just scratch the face. Check the bulge and roll and . . .

5-75 . . . continue to file the face. Use a medium cut wood file until all of the excess is removed.

5-76 Draw and cut scoring lines as outlined in photos 5-49 thru 5-51.

5-77 The finished insert will look as good if not better than new after finishing.

5-78 MacGregor "Keysite" inserts can also be reproduced using a ⅝″ wood bit and a **Dremel** tool. Carefully draw insert outline on face before drilling and cutting.

5-79 Repairing a dry rotted face. Photo shows a fairly typical dry rotted face. The following steps illustrate the clear epoxy face repair method.

5-80 Select a sharp chisel and lightly pry and scrape the rotten wood from the face. Do not damage the insert. The unrotted or good wood will be lighter in color and hence more difficult to remove. Use this as your guide in how much and what wood should be removed.

5-81 To remove the chisel marks and create a uniform surface, file the cavity with a fine file and then lightly sand the cavity with 150 or 180 grit sandpaper.

5-82 Photo shows a properly prepared area. It is not necessary to remove the entire side of the face. Only the rotted area must be removed. Also, there is no depth limitation. Area can be very shallow or quite deep.

5-83 If the club is not to be refinished, outline the edge of the face with ¾″ masking tape to protect the finish. This step is unnecessary if the club is to be refinished.

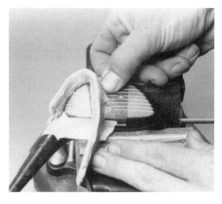

5-84 Form a Mortite putty dam around the cavity. Make sure the putty is pressed firmly around the cavity, especially into the scoring lines to prevent leaks.

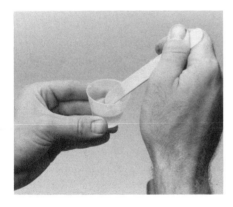

5-85 Prepare and fold the clear epoxy. Some repairmen choose to add persimmon or maple dust to the mixture. However, if the wood is properly prepared, the epoxy will reflect the wood surface underneath and the repair will hardly be noticed.

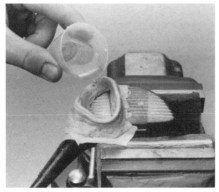

5-86 Pour the epoxy into the cavity approximately 1½ times the depth of the cavity. Allow the epoxy to cure overnight. Don't forget to stir the epoxy with a toothpick, after pouring, to free any entrapped air bubbles.

5-87 After the epoxy has cured, remove the Mortite putty. File the excess epoxy with a wood rasp.

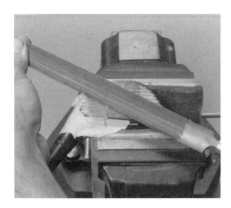

5-88 Once the rasp begins to scratch into the face, begin filing with the wood file.

5-89 Check the bulge and roll.

5-90 Continue to file, bringing down the high spots until . . .

5-91 . . . the correct face bulge and roll are achieved.

5-92 Recut the scoring lines through the epoxy face repair. Follow the steps shown in photos 5-49 thru 5-51.

5-93 This **Mini Hacksaw** is a handy tool when cutting scoring lines around the insert screws. Remember, never cut through the insert screw. This would be a sure sign of non-professional work.

5-94 File the entire face, lightly blending in all the scratches and creating a uniform surface, using a fine file.

5-95 If the face would look better by replacing the insert screws, follow these instructions.

5-96 Remove the screws as outlined in Chapter 4. If any additional filing is needed, do so now.

5-97 If necessary, recut the scoring lines.

5-98 Using a ³⁄₃₂″ drill bit, clean out each screw hole.

5-99 Re-countersink the hole. Note the use of the **Automatic Countersink.** This tool is very fast and gives precise results. You can also use a hand-held countersink as previously shown.

5-100 After installing new screws and filing the heads flush with the insert surface, remove any tape from the head and the club is now ready for finishing steps. Refer to Chapter 15 for touch-up steps if the club is not be be refinished. Chapter 1 shows complete refinishing steps.

5-101 Repairing a chip broken from the toe or heel.

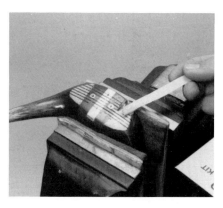

5-102 Mix and apply appropriate high shear strength epoxy to the cavity. **Conap®** or **GolfWorks®** epoxy works very well.

5-103 After applying epoxy to the chip as well, press the chip into its original location.

5-104 To ensure the piece does not move, lay a piece of masking tape across the repaired area.

5-105 After the epoxy has cured, file the excess epoxy from the face and recut any affected scoring lines. The club is now ready for complete refinishing or touch-up steps.

5-106 Photo shows a deep gouge in the face. This is often caused by hitting a rock and is commonly found in fairway woods. This may be repaired by filling with a clear, cast-in-place epoxy as shown in photos 5-79 thru 5-92. An alternative is to use . . .

5-107 . . . the **Plug Cutter** method. Using a ½″ Plug Cutter, make some laminated maple or persimmon plugs. Use old heads or turnings.

5-108 Cut through the head using a hacksaw to free the plugs.

5-109 Next, use a ½″ twist drill or speedbore flat type bit and drill out the defective area. Drill ⅜″ to ½″ deep.

5-110 Photo shows the clubface after drilling.

5-111 Apply high shear strength epoxy to the plug and hole. Use as clear an epoxy as possible to hide glue line.

5-112 Insert the wooden plug into the hole. Make sure laminations are aligned properly in the case of laminated maple heads. Allow the epoxy to cure.

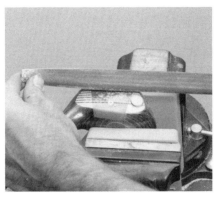

5-113 After the epoxy has cured, file plug flush with face. Use coarse rasp or medium cut wood file. Finish up with a fine file and file the entire face to blend everything in.

5-114 Face should look like this after filing.

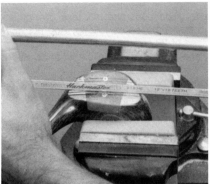

5-115 Finally, recut scoring lines as necessary.

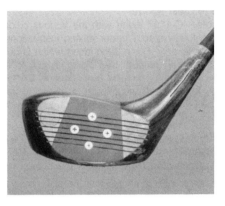

5-116 Photo shows finished club, ready for re-finishing or touchup.

NOTES

_____

_____

_____

_____

_____

_____

_____

_____

_____

ADDITIONAL INFORMATION FOR REPLACING OLD INSERTS WITH EPOXY CAST-IN-PLACE INSERTS AND REPAIRING DAMAGED FACES

Detailed Mixing Instructions for Club-Kits IC-110®

Step #1: Stir each component well (activator and base) in its original container before taking out smaller quantities to use. The coloring pigments in the base tend to settle out over a period of time making this stirring step quite important if you intend to get the same color and opacity every time you use it. Base is heavier and if not stirred properly will have a poor mix.

Step #2: Measure out desired amount of base per Table 5-1. Use a metric cup as the exact or near exact measurement is important. Next, pour in the correct amount of activator over the base.

Step #3: Immediately begin to fold the material together similar to mixing a cake batter. This procedure is very important as the lighter activator tends to float on the heavier base and normal stirring is not adequate. After one minute of folding, begin stirring. Stir for approximately 75 revolutions. Do not stir briskly or whip insert material as an excess of air bubbles will cause air entrapment during curing and the finished insert will look like a sponge. Some bubbles are normal and will float out during the cure.

Step #4: IC-110® insert material is now ready to pour.

TABLE 5-1 Volume Method Mixing Chart By Insert Size For Club-Kit IC-110®			
Insert Size	**Amount Of Base 2:1**	**Amount Of Activator 1:2**	**Total Amount**
Small (Most MacGregor and most fibre inserts)	10 cc's	5 cc's	15 cc's
Medium (Most Spalding 1962 and later and early Wilson inserts)	15 cc's	7½ cc's	22½ cc's
Large (Wilson and First Flight)	20 cc's	10 cc's	30 cc's
CC stands for cubic centimeters. Metric cups are available through golf club repair supply houses and are graduated in cc's, ounces, drams, etc.			

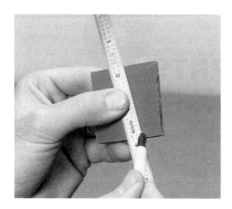

6-7 After drawing the line, a good idea is to use a straight edge to check the straightness of the line.

6-8 Sometimes the old insert is damaged or lost. In this case the **Insert Pattern Copier** simplifies insert angle copying and ensures a perfect fit into the insert cavity.

6-9 **To use this tool,** loosen the wing nut and place the arms inside the insert cavity. Spread the arms apart so each arm is flush against the side of the cavity. Tighten the wing nut.

6-10 Place the Copier against the new insert material and draw a line. Note one of the arms is flush against the side of the material eliminating one unnecessary cut.

6-11 Fasten the insert material securely in a vise so the drawn line is vertical. Using a hacksaw, cut to the outside of the line. This will ensure the new insert will be slightly larger than the cavity, allowing some modification if the insert shape is not perfect.

6-12 Test fit the insert in the cavity.

6-13 Photo shows a perfect fit along one side of the cavity but . . .

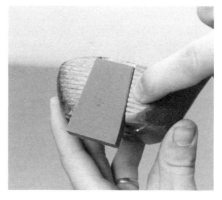

6-14 . . . a gap exists along the opposite side. Use a file to lower the high point of the insert side. This will provide a perfect fit to both sides of the insert. To do this . . .

6-15 . . . place the insert between the vise jaws with the poor fitting side up.

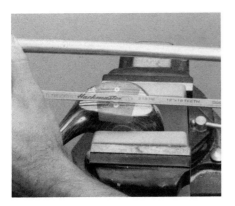

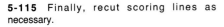

5-115 Finally, recut scoring lines as necessary.

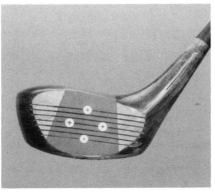

5-116 Photo shows finished club, ready for refinishing or touchup.

NOTES

_____

_____

_____

_____

_____

_____

_____

_____

ADDITIONAL INFORMATION FOR REPLACING OLD INSERTS WITH EPOXY CAST-IN-PLACE INSERTS AND REPAIRING DAMAGED FACES

Detailed Mixing Instructions for Club-Kits IC-110®

Step #1: Stir each component well (activator and base) in its original container before taking out smaller quantities to use. The coloring pigments in the base tend to settle out over a period of time making this stirring step quite important if you intend to get the same color and opacity every time you use it. Base is heavier and if not stirred properly will have a poor mix.

Step #2: Measure out desired amount of base per Table 5-1. Use a metric cup as the exact or near exact measurement is important. Next, pour in the correct amount of activator over the base.

Step #3: Immediately begin to fold the material together similar to mixing a cake batter. This procedure is very important as the lighter activator tends to float on the heavier base and normal stirring is not adequate. After one minute of folding, begin stirring. Stir for approximately 75 revolutions. Do not stir briskly or whip insert material as an excess of air bubbles will cause air entrapment during curing and the finished insert will look like a sponge. Some bubbles are normal and will float out during the cure.

Step #4: IC-110® insert material is now ready to pour.

	Amount Of Base 2:1	Amount Of Activator 1:2	Total Amount
TABLE 5-1 _Volume Method_ **Mixing Chart By Insert Size For Club-Kit IC-110®**			
Insert Size			
Small (Most MacGregor and most fibre inserts)	10 cc's	5 cc's	15 cc's
Medium (Most Spalding 1962 and later and early Wilson inserts)	15 cc's	7½ cc's	22½ cc's
Large (Wilson and First Flight)	20 cc's	10 cc's	30 cc's
CC stands for cubic centimeters. Metric cups are available through golf club repair supply houses and are graduated in cc's, ounces, drams, etc.			

Mixing Instructions for Adding Color Paste to Clear IC-110®

Many repair shops use clear non-pigmented IC-110® along with the various color paste dispersions and mix their own colors. To properly mix in the color paste dispersions, follow step 1 under mixing instructions and then proceed as follows. Add not more than 5% by weight of the desired color to the base only. For a 30cc insert which is comprised of 20 cc's base and 10 cc's activator you only need to add color paste in the approximate amount that it would take to coat one of your fingernails 1/16" thick, this is approximately 1 cc of color paste.

Mix the color paste and base thoroughly for at least one minute, scavenging the sides of the mixing container while mixing. IMPORTANT NOTE: For compatability use only Club-Kit color paste dispersions with Club-Kit IC-110® epoxy. Now proceed with steps 2 through 4 under mixing instructions.

Additional Mixing Instructions and Formulas

By Volume: Two parts of base to one part of activator. (Method of mixing shown above.)

By Weight: 68 grams of base to 27 grams of activator. (Note: This is the correct ratio by weight, hence any combination in this ratio by weight would be correct.)

Some repair shops doing large volume work prefer to weigh the base and activator on a gram scale and mix accordingly. If you prefer to use this method the following mathematics will help.

The ratio by weight stated above of 68 grams base to 27 grams activator would make an insert of 95 grams or 3.35 ounces. (95 grams divided by 28.35 grams per ounce.)

The mathematics ratio is stated as the activator being 28.4% of the base or it can be stated that the base portion is 71.6% of the activator.

By Weight:
28.4% Activator
71.6% Base

100% IC-110® mixed

So, for a 28.35 gram insert (1 ounce) which is equivalent to a Wilson size insert you would multiply 28.35 × 28.4% = 8.05 grams activator. Now subtract 8.05 grams from 28.35 grams and you get 20.3 grams of base.

By Weight:
8.05 grams activator (28.4%)
20.30 grams base (71.6%)

28.35 grams IC-110® (1 ounce) (100%)

TABLE 5-2 Weight Method Mixing Chart By Insert Size For Club Kit IC-110®			
Insert Size	**Amount Of Base (71.6%)**	**Amount Of Activator (28.4%)**	**Total Amount (100%)**
Small (Most MacGregor and most fibre inserts)	10.15 gr.	4.02 gr.	14.17 gr.
Medium (Most Spalding 1962 and later and early Wilson inserts)	15.22 gr.	6.03 gr.	21.25 gr.
Large (Wilson and First Flight)	20.3 gr.	8.05 gr.	28.35 gr.

1. To convert grams to ounces divide by 28.35.
2. To convert ounces to grams multiply by 28.35.
3. 28.35 grams = 1 ounce.

Points to Remember when Pouring Inserts

1. Never pour an insert when surrounding temperature is less than 65°F.
2. Never use a match or open flame to draw air bubbles to the surface as epoxy is flammable. Swirling with a toothpick or other object after pouring will work best to release entrapped air bubbles.
3. Never add additional activator in the hope of speeding up the cure. This will only cause the insert to remain rubbery. Follow mixing instructions exactly.
4. Never try to speed up cure by placing club in direct sunlight, under sunlamps, in an oven or on a radiator. This could cause the insert to break into flame or boil thus causing deep craters after curing.
5. If insert seems cured, but during filing it softens, DO NOT be concerned. Let insert cure for one more day then continue on. The heat build-up from filing will always soften the insert to some degree.

REPLACING OLD INSERTS WITH PREFABRICATED INSERTS

A prefabricated insert differs from an epoxy cast-in-place insert in that the prefabricated insert is solid in composition when installed into an insert cavity. Some pre-shaping of the insert is usually necessary to ensure the insert of a proper fit in the cavity. Because of this, installing a prefabricated insert requires different techniques and skills for proper installation versus the liquid epoxy cast-in-place type inserts.

Replacing an old insert with a new prefabricated insert is desirable if the old insert is not original or is worn or damaged beyond repair. For example, the older "classic" clubs were manufactured with "original" type fiber inserts. Replacing this type of insert with something other than original fiber will ordinarily lower the value of this so-called classic club.

Prefabricated inserts are available in many different materials. Cycolac, original fiber, phenolic laminate, melamine, graphite, Gamma-fire and aluminum are the most common. These insert materials are usually available in sheets, bars, squares and ready to install precut shapes.

It should be noted that even though the hardness of inserts vary, hardness makes no significant difference in the distance a ball carries. For further information on this see Ralph Maltby's books entitled *Golf Club Design, Fitting, Alteration and Repair* and *The Complete Golf Club Fitting Manual.*

6-1 Old inserts often need to be replaced because of delaminations in the insert, a large ding or a poor fit in the insert cavity caused by wood head swelling due to moisture absorption.

6-2 First, remove the soleplate as outlined in Chapter 3.

6-3 Next, remove the insert as outlined in Chapter 4.

6-4 Remove all epoxy build-up and other debris from the insert cavity. Maintain a sharp top line.

6-5 Replacement insert materials are available in various forms.

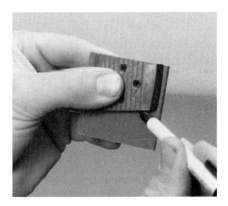

6-6 To cut out a new insert: The old insert may be used as a pattern for the new one. Place the insert against the new material. Note one side of the insert is butted up against one side of the new material. This eliminates unnecessary work in cutting two angles as only one cut will now be made. Next, draw a line down one side of the insert tracing it onto the material.

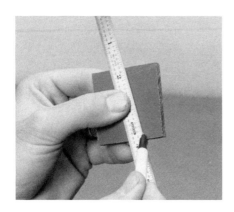

6-7 After drawing the line, a good idea is to use a straight edge to check the straightness of the line.

6-8 Sometimes the old insert is damaged or lost. In this case the **Insert Pattern Copier** simplifies insert angle copying and ensures a perfect fit into the insert cavity.

6-9 **To use this tool,** loosen the wing nut and place the arms inside the insert cavity. Spread the arms apart so each arm is flush against the side of the cavity. Tighten the wing nut.

6-10 Place the Copier against the new insert material and draw a line. Note one of the arms is flush against the side of the material eliminating one unnecessary cut.

6-11 Fasten the insert material securely in a vise so the drawn line is vertical. Using a hacksaw, cut to the outside of the line. This will ensure the new insert will be slightly larger than the cavity, allowing some modification if the insert shape is not perfect.

6-12 Test fit the insert in the cavity.

6-13 Photo shows a perfect fit along one side of the cavity but . . .

6-14 . . . a gap exists along the opposite side. Use a file to lower the high point of the insert side. This will provide a perfect fit to both sides of the insert. To do this . . .

6-15 . . . place the insert between the vise jaws with the poor fitting side up.

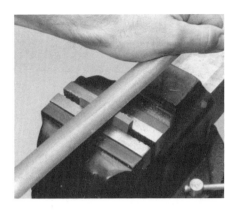

6-16 File along the side of the insert working the high spot down. Periodically test fit the insert while filing until . . .

6-17 . . . the insert fits properly. A properly fit insert will have no noticeable gaps between the insert and the insert cavity walls.

6-18 Remove the insert from the cavity and abrade the back of the insert with a wood file or sandpaper. This provides a better bonding surface for the epoxy.

6-19 Mix and apply a shear strength epoxy to the insert cavity and the back of the insert. Note that a brown paste dispersion has been added to the epoxy to camouflage any glue line.

6-20 Place the insert in the bottom half of the cavity and . . .

6-21 . . . push the insert up into the cavity until a tight fit is achieved. This method of installation ensures epoxy is forced around all sides of the insert and cavity.

6-22 Place the club in an **Insert Clamp** or vise until the epoxy cures. After the epoxy cures, follow the steps shown in photos 6-35 thru 6-53 for finishing steps.

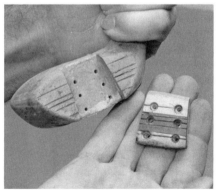

6-23 Installing 2-color horizontal bar inserts. Photo shows another classic club but, this time there is a horizontal bar running through the insert. This type of insert is a bit more difficult to duplicate.

6-24 After the soleplate and insert are removed, carefully clean the insert cavity, removing all epoxy build-up.

6-25 The horizontal bar will usually be either ½″ or ⅝″ wide. The smaller ½″ bars are commonly found in the fairway woods while the wider ⅝″ bars are found in drivers.

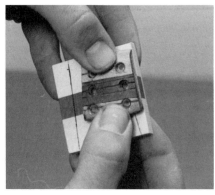

6-26 The original insert is best used as a pattern. Position the old insert on the new material so the bars are running parallel. Draw a line down both sides of the old insert onto the new material. Photo shows why one side of the old insert cannot be laid against the side of the new material. The bars would not run parallel with each other.

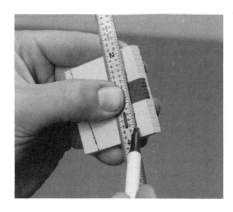

6-27 A straight edge can be used to guarantee that the lines are straight.

6-28 Place the new material between the vise jaws and tighten securely. The drawn lines should be vertical while held in the vise to make accurate cutting easier. Use a hacksaw and cut outside the drawn lines. This will ensure the insert will be larger than intended to allow for final fitting in the insert cavity itself.

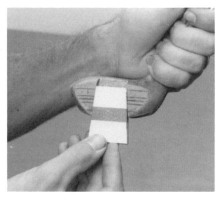

6-29 Place the insert into the cavity to check for initial fit.

6-30 File where necessary to create a tight fit without gaps between the insert and the insert cavity.

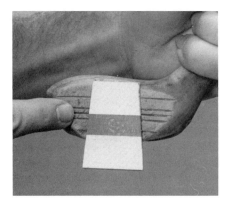

6-31 Periodically check the position of the insert within the cavity while filing. Photo shows horizontal bar running parallel with scoring lines. All that is needed now is to file an equal amount from each side of the insert so the insert will move up the cavity positioning the horizontal bar in its original location.

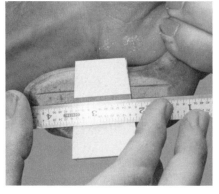

6-32 After final filing, the insert is positioned perfectly in the cavity. Note, the bar is parallel with the scoring lines. This is important for a professional look and fit.

6-33 Roughen the back of the insert with a wood file or sandpaper.

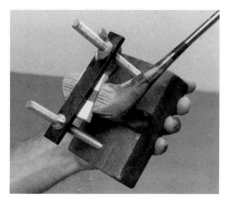

6-34 Mix and apply epoxy to both the insert and cavity. Install the insert as previously shown.

6-35 After the epoxy has cured, the excess insert material is easily removed with a hacksaw.

6-36 Use a wood file to file the remaining portion of the insert. Use a radiusing motion to follow the contour of the sole.

6-37 The bottom of the insert should look like this after filing.

6-38 Reposition the club in the vise and cut or file the top of the insert. Be careful not to mar the hosel.

6-39 Using a wood file, carefully file the remaining portion of the insert flush with the top of the head.

6-40 The top of the insert should look like this. The insert top line should blend in perfectly with the entire face topline from toe to heel.

6-41 Next, place the club in the vise as shown. Using a wood file, remove any excess insert matrial and epoxy. Concentrate filing on the sides of the insert while intentionally leaving the middle of the insert slightly higher than the rest of the face. The tendency for novices is usually to file too much from the middle of the insert.

6-42 Check horizontal face bulge and . . .

6-43 . . . vertical face roll while filing. Also check the loft with a protractor or loft gauge. Refer to tables at the end of Chapter 10 for proper bulge, roll and loft.

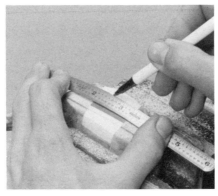

6-44 A 6″ scale is used to draw lines across the face. Make sure the drawn lines match up to the proper heel and toe scoring lines.

6-45 Carefully cut through the insert using the drawn lines as a guide. Note the use of the special hacksaw blade without sides on the teeth (no rake).

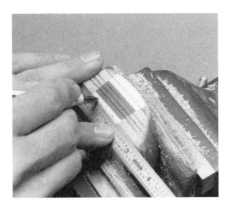

6-46 Measure and mark locations for insert screw pilot holes. A six screw configuration is used here. Marks are made ¼″ from the sides of the insert on the top, middle and bottom scoring lines. Chapter 5 shows photos for installing a four-screw diamond pattern.

6-47 Drill into the insert using a ³⁄₃₂″ **bit**. Depth of pilot hole is determined by insert screw. The #4 × ⅝″ brass screw is commonly used and is shown here.

6-48 After drilling, the pilot hole is **countersunk.** The diameter of the countersunk hole should be slightly smaller than the diameter of the insert screw head. This will allow the top of installed screw head to be seated slightly above the face, before filing.

6-49 Photo shows an **Automatic Countersink** in use. The Automatic Countersink can be set to various diameters (depths) for quick work when opening up insert or soleplate pilot holes.

6-50 To prevent a screw head from possibly snapping off, it is a good idea to drill through the insert only with a ⅛″ bit. This will alleviate excess pressure between the insert and the screw by providing clearance for the screw shank.

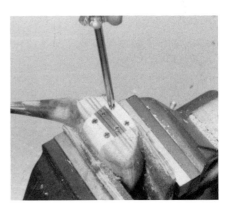

6-51 Next, install the screws. Align the slots of the screw heads parallel and perpendicular with the scoring lines. The top of the screw head should be slightly above the level of the insert.

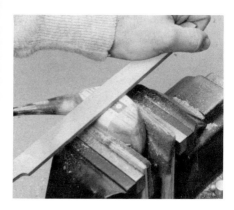

6-52 File the screw heads flush with the insert using a fine file. Rub a finger across the face. If the screw heads are filed properly, the heads will barely be felt.

6-53 Brush the face with a stiff bristled brush to remove all loose particles from the screw heads and facelines.

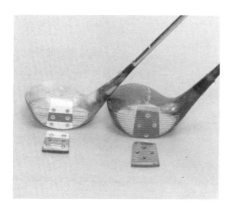

6-54 Photo shows the completed horizontal bar insert, as well as the solid color insert replaced in photos 6-5 thru 6-22. After the soleplates are reinstalled following procedures shown in Chapter 3, the clubs are ready for refinishing or touch-up. See Chapter 15 for touch-up steps or Chapter 1 for complete refinishing.

6-55 Replacing "V" back inserts. Photo shows a bar type insert with a notch in the back. This insert is commonly referred to as a three-piece "V back" insert.

6-56 First, remove the soleplate. See Chapter 3 for procedures.

6-57 Next, remove the insert following steps outlined in Chapter 4.

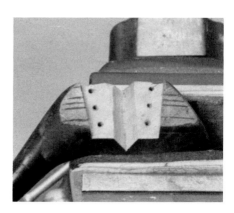

6-58 Clean the exposed insert cavity of old epoxy using a chisel and file.

6-59 Cut a ½" narrow bar of insert material. The piece should be long enough to fit entire length of "V" notch.

6-60 Mix and apply shear strength epoxy to the notch and ½" bar. Note the use of a colored paste dispersion to match insert or stain color.

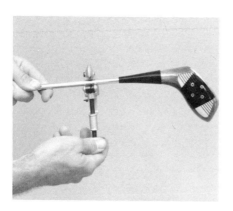

7-31 To remove the backscrew from a blind-bore club, proceed as follows. If the shaft need not be saved, cut the shaft approximately 4″ above the top of the hosel using a **tubing cutter** or a **friction cut-off wheel.** See Chapter 19, photos 19-162 thru 19-166 for information on using the friction wheel.

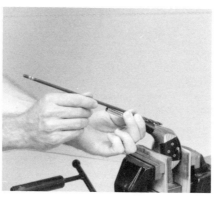

7-32 Next, place the clubhead in a vise as shown. Place the **12″ long, 7/32″ drill bit** against the outside of the hosel. The tip of the drill bit should be even with the backscrew hole.

7-33 Place a piece of masking tape around the drill bit at a point even with the top of the shaft.

7-34 Install the drill bit into the drill chuck, and then place the bit inside the shaft.

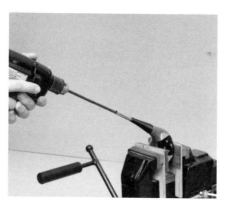

7-35 Drill inside the shaft until the wrapping of tape around the bit disappears inside the shaft. This indicates the backscrew has been drilled in half. If the tape disappears more than 1/2″ inside the shaft, the tip of the drill bit may come through the bottom of the club. If this happens, you have just turned the club into a through-bore model.

7-36 Once the backscrew has been drilled in half, place the clubhead in a vise as shown. Punch the top half of the backscrew into the shaft tip using a 1/8″ **pin punch.**

7-37 Turn the club upside down and the top half of the backscrew should tumble out of the shaft. If it does not, place the head back in the vise, redrill and repunch until the backscrew is removed.

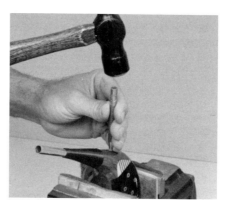

7-38 After the top half of the backscrew is removed, punch the bottom half of the backscrew into the wood head using the 1/8″ pin punch. Proceed to photo 7-44.

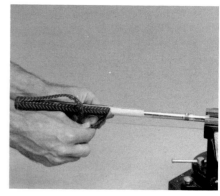

7-39 If you wish to save the shaft, as when repairing a loose head, first remove the grip. Use either a knife or, if the grip is to be saved, use a **Grip Shooter.** See Chapter 22 photos 22-31 thru 22-37 for use of the Grip Shooter.

7-40 Place the 47″ long ⁷⁄₃₂″ bit against the back of the club so that the tip of the drill is even with the backscrew.

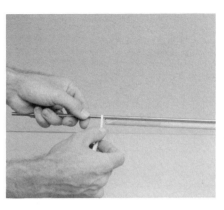

7-41 Place a wrapping of masking tape around the drill bit even with the top of the shaft.

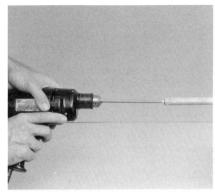

7-42 Place the long drill bit inside the shaft and drill until the wrapping of tape disappears below the top of the shaft. This indicates the backscrew has been cut in half.

7-43 Follow the punching and, if necessary, redrilling steps until the backscrew is removed as previously shown in photos 7-36 thru 7-38.

7-44 Once the backscrew is removed, the final locking mechanism must be dealt with before the shaft can be removed. On older golf clubs, white glue, fish glue or pitch tar were used allowing easy shaft removal. If epoxy was used, heat will be needed to soften the epoxy.

7-45 An Aluminum Lock Tight shaft holder is used to securely hold the shaft in the vise. Next, if necessary, use a ⁷⁄₃₂″ drill inside the shaft tip to remove any foreign material such as glue, rubber or lead, etc.

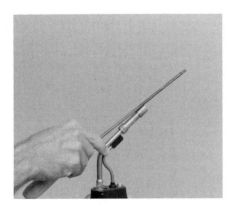

7-46 Heat the end of a **Heating Rod** using a propane torch. Note how the end of the rod is positioned in relation to the flame. This will heat a much broader portion of the rod than when the rod is placed perpendicular to the flame.

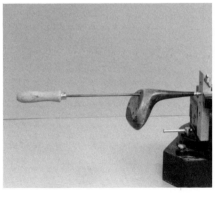

7-47 On through-bore heads, insert the rod inside the shaft from the sole. On a blind-bore head with a short shaft, insert the rod from the top of the shaft to the bottom of the hosel bore.

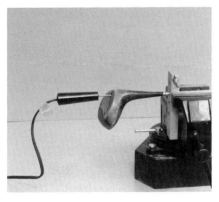

7-48 A fast alternative to the propane torch and Heating Rod method is **the Electric Heating Rod.** Plug it into an electrical outlet, wait 30 seconds and insert it into the shaft. After another few seconds, the head is ready for removal.

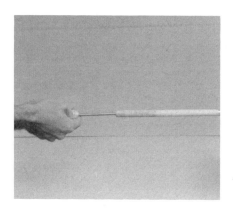

7-49 On blind-bore models with the entire shaft, heat the smooth end of a 47″ drill bit and insert into the shaft until it bottoms out. A 47″ rod can also be used.

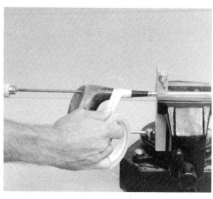

7-50 Allow heat from the heating rod to penetrate the epoxy surrounding the shaft for one to two minutes. In the meantime, apply 5 or 6 turns of masking tape to the hosel to prevent it from splitting during wood head removal.

7-51 Grasp the head with both hands and attempt to gently twist the wood head. Turn the head one complete revolution around the shaft to assure nothing is holding the head to the shaft. Now remove the head by gently, but firmly, twisting and pulling simultaneously. **Proceed to photo 7-59 if shaft comes out. Coutinue on to next photo if shaft is broken off inside hosel.**

7-52 Shaft extractors are available to fit all shaft tip diameters. Extractors represent the best way of removing shafts broken off inside wood head hosels.

7-53 To use a shaft extractor: Be certain that the backscrew is removed from the head before using the shaft extractors. The number one cause for extractor failure is a backscrew left within the walls of the shaft. Refer to photo 7-15 thru 7-30 for backscrew removal steps.

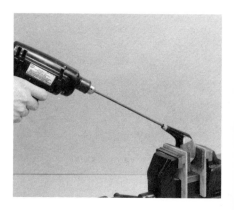

7-54 After the backscrew is removed, completely clean all epoxy or other foreign materials from inside the tip of the shaft. A 7/32″ drill bit works best. DO NOT DRILL THROUGH THE BOTTOM OF THE CLUB ON A "BLIND BORE" TYPE WOOD.

7-55 Place the smooth end of the extractor between the vise jaws and tighten securely.

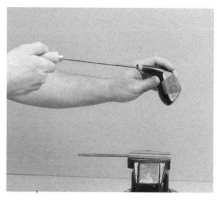

7-56 Heat the end of a **heating rod** and insert the rod inside the shaft to soften the epoxy. Make sure the tip of the rod is pushed to the bottom of the hosel. Repeated heating of the rod may be necessary to break the epoxy bond.

7-57 After heating and while the shaft is still hot, push the shaft over the extractor. Push and turn the head clockwise until you feel the shaft "lock" onto the extractor. It may require a firm push to lock the extractor into the shaft.

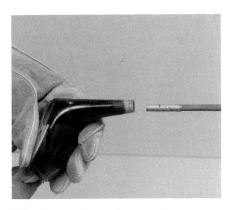

7-58 After locking in the extractor, turn the head while simultaneously pulling on the head. The head should pull free from the shaft while the shaft remains attached to the extractor as shown above. Remove the shaft from the extractor by pulling the shaft off with a pair of pliers.

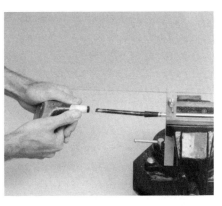

7-59 The wood head is now removed. Be sure your grasp is firm and you pull the head straight back so as not to split the hosel.

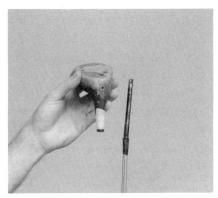

7-60 As stated before, check to see if the shaft has a bend in the tip end. This indicates a face angle change has been made either intentionally or unintentionally. Instructions for altering the face angle once the new shaft is installed are found in Chapter 12. **TIP: A bent shaft tip can be easily detected by rolling the shaft on a flat surface.**

7-61 Use the **Golf Shaft Identification Gauge, micrometer or vernier caliper** to determine the size of the removed shaft tip and replacement shaft tip.

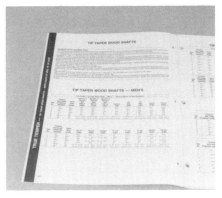

7-62 The tables in Appendix 6 give **back of heel to first step dimensions** for commercially available shafts. This measurement is vital if you want the new shaft to perform as it was designed. When this measurement is altered, the shaft will either play more flexible or more stiff.

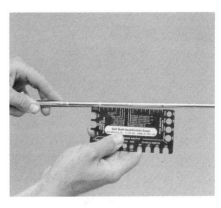

7-63 First, determine the type of shaft (Dynamic®, Pro-Fit®, TT Lite®, etc.) required. This is known either from customer input, shaft band data, use of the **Golf Shaft Identification Gauge** or measuring the shaft's step length, tip size, butt size, tip section length and tip parallel measurement, and matching these specs up with those shown in Appendices 4 and 5.

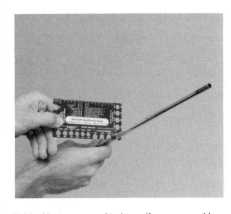

7-64 Next, you need to know if you are working with a tapered tip shaft or a parallel tip shaft. **A tapered tip shaft** is a shaft with a tip section that changes in diameter. First, take a measurement just below the first step. Measurement reads .350 dia. as shown in photo.

7-65 Another measurement is taken at the shaft's tip end. This measurement reads .294 dia. Therefore, this is a tip taper shaft.

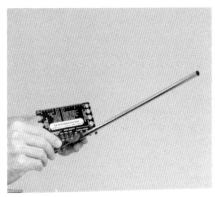

7-66 A parallel tip (unitized) shaft has a constant tip diameter from the tip to the first step. Again, a measurement is taken just below the first step. Measurement reads .335 dia. as shown in photo.

7-67 Another measurement is taken at the shaft tip. This measurement reads .335 dia. also. The tip section has a constant diameter from below the first step to its tip end, so it is a parallel tip (Unitized) shaft.

7-68 With the shaft type and tip type known, refer to the tables in Appendix 6. **The tables are divided into a tapered tip group and a parallel tip group.** Look for the grouping of tables that fits your shaft tip construction.

7-69 Then, look for the individual table that includes your type of shaft (**Dynamic®, TT Lite®, Pro Pel®, Microtaper®,** etc.).

7-70 Next, look at the first column labeled **Club Number.** Look down the column until you come across the club number with which you are working (driver, 3 wood, etc.).

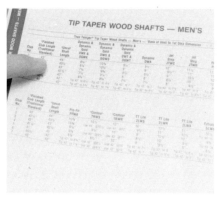

7-71 Next, look straight across the page to the next column labeled **Finished Club Length.** This reading gives you the industry standard length for your club.

7-72 The next column labeled **Uncut Shaft Length** gives the recommended raw length shaft you need to select from your stock of shafts for this length club.

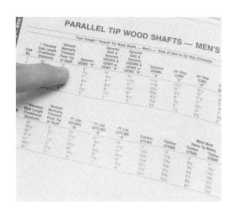

7-73 If you are working with a parallel tip shaft, you will find a column labeled **Amount Normally Trimmed From Tip Of Shaft.** Because virtually all parallel tip shafts are available in only one length, there is no reason to indicate which length shaft to choose.

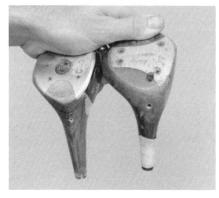

7-74 Some repairmen stop at this stage, grab the recommended shaft and install it into the head. The reason this should not be done is obvious after looking at the photo. One of the clubs is a **through-bore** and one is a **blind-bore.** If the same length shaft is installed in both clubs, without tip trimming, they will play differently.

7-75 This photo shows why. The distance from the **back of the heel to the first step** varies enough to make the club on the left play ¼ flex stiffer than the club on the right. Therefore, **the back of heel to first step dimension** must be followed closely to ensure proper shaft performance unless you specifically wish a club to perform differently.

7-76 Again, look straight across the page until you reach the column heading that describes the type and flex of shaft with which you are working. This figure is the distance you need with this shaft for **the back of the heel to the first step.**

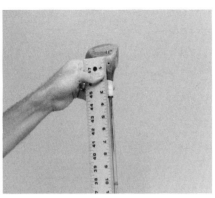

7-77 Take the recommended shaft and temporarily install it into the head and measure **the back of heel to first step distance.** (If the tip of the shaft will not penetrate to the bottom of the hosel bore, refer to photos 7-80 thru 7-88 for step drilling procedure.)

7-78 If **the back of heel to first step distance** is longer than the recommended distance, either select a shorter shaft or cut the difference from the tip of the shaft. Note: Cutting material from a tapered tip shaft may require the hosel bore to be enlarged.

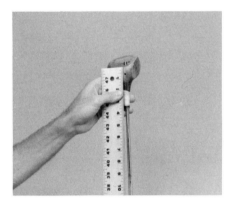

7-79 If **the back of heel to first step distance** is shorter than the recommended distance, a longer shaft is needed. This is correct because the difference in length between most shafts of the same pattern and flex is made up solely in the tip section. Hence, a longer shaft has a longer tip section.

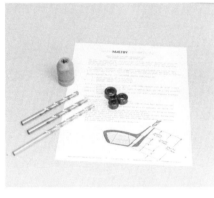

7-80 **Step drilling procedure:** Photo shows a set of 3 step drills used for cleaning out or enlarging a bore to accept **a tip taper shaft.** Drill bits are available to accommodate any tip taper or parallel tip shaft. Also shown are two types of drill stops which can be used instead of masking tape to control depth more positively.

7-81 First, place the head in the vise between a set of **felt** or **urethane vise pads.** Wrap 6 or 7 layers of ¾" masking tape tightly around the hosel to prevent possible splitting.

7-82 Using the smallest drill in set, drill to bottom of bore or completely through as necessary. Note wrapping of tape around drill bit. Premeasuring depth of hosel bore and then placing a wrapping of tape around the bit at the same length is a good idea. Stop drilling when tape is even with top of hosel.

7-83 Using the next largest size drill, drill to within a specified distance from the bottom of the first drill. Follow the instructions that came with the drill set.

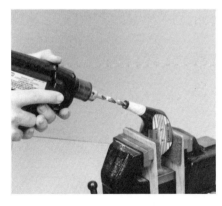

7-84 Finally, using the largest size drill, drill to within a specified distance from the depth of the 2nd drill.

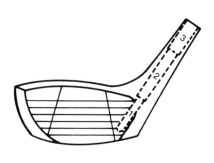

7-85 The inside of the drilled hosel will look like this, hence the term "step drilling." A blind-bore head is shown, but the step drills also work as well on through-bore types.

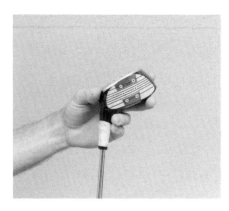

7-86 Test the shaft for proper fit. A properly fit shaft is one that is not tight or binding but snug enough so that it has no sideways movement or slop.

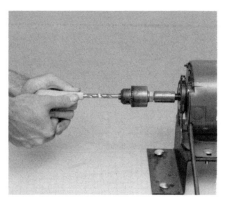

7-87 Bench motor shown with drill chuck attached by means of a "Motor Arbor." This is how we clean out bores using step drills and reamers in our repair department.

7-88 A **tapered reamer drill** is also available to enlarge existing hosel bore sizes. Reamers are very expensive and are commonly used for boring blank wood heads when making custom woods.

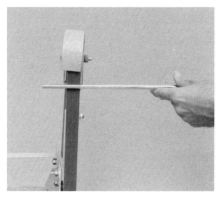

7-89 **Shaft installation:** Once the proper shaft is chosen and any needed modifications have been made, abrade the tip of the shaft with the use of a belt sander, grinding stone, emery cloth or file. Abrading the shaft tip gives the epoxy a better bonding surface.

7-90 Choose an appropriate ferrule. Ferrules are labeled according to the shaft tip size they match. Both a standard ferrule and a "shanked" ferrule are available. It is not necessary to file the top of the shanked ferrule, thus saving some time in finishing the job later on.

7-91 If the ferrule will not slide far enough up the shaft tip, refer to Chapter 19 photos 19-108 thru 19-118 for ways to do this.

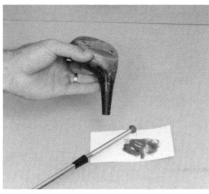

7-92 After mixing a shear strength epoxy, dip the tip of the shaft into the epoxy and then insert the shaft into the hosel. Note the use of a colored paste dispersion mixed in with the epoxy. This will help camouflage any epoxy line.

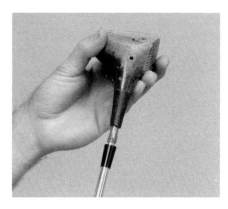

7-93 For best results, simultaneously turn and push the shaft into the hosel. This method will coat both the outside of the shaft and the inside of the hosel walls.

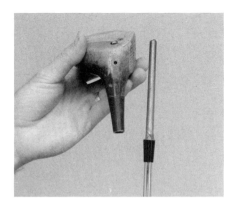

7-94 Withdraw the shaft from the hosel to ensure the tip is adequately covered with epoxy and then reinstall the shaft.

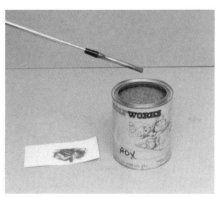

7-95 If the shaft is very loose, remove the shaft from the hosel and dip the tip of the shaft into **Aluminum Oxide Sand.**

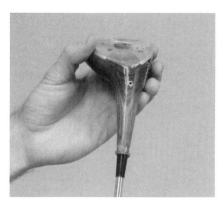

7-96 Reinstall the shaft into the hosel. The sand will take up the excess space and provide an excellent bonding surface for the epoxy.

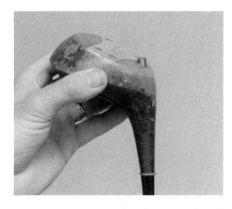

7-97 **In case of a through-bore wood,** push the shaft through the sole of the wood until the entire tip of the shaft is just protruding from the sole.

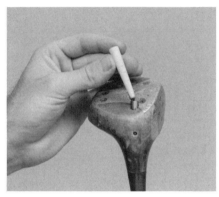

7-98 Place a tapered wood plug in the shaft opening and . . .

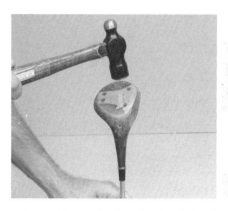

7-99 . . . drive the plug down into the shaft until the plug "mushrooms" against the sole. This indicates the plug has been driven far enough into the shaft tip.

7-100 Allow the epoxy to cure before proceeding to the next step.

7-101 To remove the excess wood plug, tap lightly until the plug breaks from the shaft tip or cut the excess with a hacksaw.

7-102 The remaining portion of the shaft tip protruding from the sole must now be removed. One way is by carefully pressing the tip against the face of a coarse or medium grit belt on a **belt sander.**

7-103 Carefully filing with a medium grade file is another way to remove the protruding shaft tip.

7-104 After the majority of the shaft tip is removed, switch to a fine cut mill file to take the shaft tip down perfectly flush with the sole.

7-105 Photo shows a properly filed shaft. Note the tapered wood plug has completely filled the inside of the shaft.

7-106 Determine the color of the head and select a color matching stain. Blot the surface of the bare wood with a towel that has been dampened with the stain.

7-107 The stained wood plug should now match the surrounding wood color.

7-108 Installing a backscrew. Using a ⅛" drill bit, (cobalt bits work best), drill into the backscrew hole cleaning out excess epoxy. Do not attempt to drill through the shaft. Instead . . .

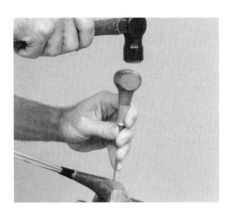

7-109 . . . insert a sharpened awl into the hole and drive the tip of the awl through the top of the shaft. Remove the awl and . . .

7-110 . . . reinstall the ⅛" bit and drill a clear passage through the top of the shaft. Do not attempt to drill through the bottom of the shaft. Instead . . .

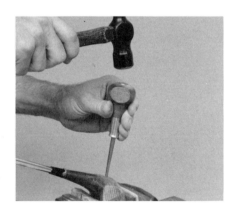

7-111 . . . insert the awl and drive it through the bottom of the shaft.

7-130 Look carefully at the [...] proper taper exists from the [...] into the base of the hosel. If th[...] ularities, file or sand as nece[...] proper blended taper.

7-112 Insert the ⅛″ bit into the hole and drill a clear passage through the shaft into the wood below the shaft. The proper depth of the hole is dependent upon the length of the backscrew (drill the hole ⅛″ deeper if you want the backscrew to be seated below the surface of the hosel after backscrew installation).

7-113 If the bit encounters an old backscrew under the shaft — have patience! The bit will seek the softer material around the backscrew and eventually will veer off to the side of the old backscrew creating a clear hole for the new backscrew.

7-114 A fast alternative to the punch and drill method is the use of a drill blank and a drill press. Install a ⅛″ **drill blank** into the chuck. Note: The drill blank tip is ground the same as a flat screwdriver tip.

7-133 To measure for [...] the club on the ground a[...] **ruler** behind the shaft and [...] pering [...] whipp[...] the m[...] sande[...]

7-115 Place the toe of the club underneath the blank. Note the use of a padded block of wood to protect the finish on the toe.

7-116 Move the drill blank into the backscrew hole and through the shaft. You'll be amazed at how fast and easy this is.

7-117 Next, select either a standard backscrew with a standard size head or, a headless backscrew. Should you ever have to remove this backscrew, the headless are much easier to remove (yes, headless) and are therefore the preferred choice.

7-15[...]
met[...]
head[...]
Shaf[...]
Note[...]
after[...]

7-136 . . . a friction [...] photos 19-162 thru 19[...] procedure.

7-118 Place the backscrew into the hole and lightly tap the head of the backscrew until it is flush with the surface of the hosel.

7-119 Some repairmen like to leave the head exposed on the back of the hosel.

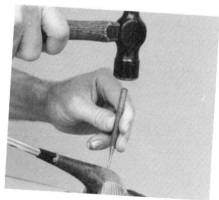

7-120 If you want the backscrew below the surface of the hosel, as is usually the case, drive it ⅛″ below the surface using a ⅛″ pin punch and hammer.

7-121 Mix a quic...
added touch, mix i...
color the epoxy to ...

7-124 . . . a sh...

7-127 Rem...
using a medi...
through the ta...

7-157 After moving the gun back and forth for two minutes, grasp the head with a gloved hand and carefully try to turn the head. Continue this action, with the gun pointed at the hosel, until the head. . .

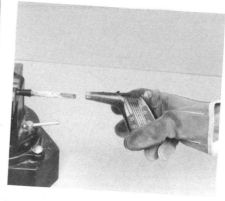

7-158 . . . turns around the shaft and can be pulled off. The real challenge with this type of reshaft is to soften the epoxy holding the shaft in place before the epoxy holding the graphite fibers together is destroyed. The success rate using this method is about 70%. No other method rates as high.

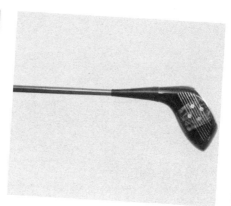

7-159 Photo shows a graphite head with a graphite shaft. Decide which of the components, head or shaft, you wish to save. There simply is no means of saving both. The heat required to soften the epoxy holding the shaft in the head will also destroy either the head or the shaft. **If the shaft is to be saved, carefully cut or saw the head from the shaft.**

7-160 If the head is to be saved, cut the shaft even with the top of the hosel and then drill the remaining portion of the shaft from the hosel. Begin with a small drill bit and then increase the size until the hosel bore is large enough to accept the new shaft. Head is then ready for shafting using normal steps.

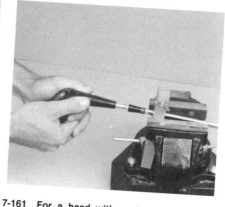

7-161 For a head with a plastic whipping cover, steps for the removal of the head are the same as demonstrated in photos 7-15 thru 7-51. The plastic whipping cover will remain on the head when the head is pulled from the shaft.

7-162 When installing the head onto the shaft, select a ferrule that is larger than the top of the whipping cover. Wipe excess epoxy from cover and ferrule. Allow the epoxy to harden.

7-163 After the epoxy hardens, file the excess plastic until the ferrule is flush with the top of the whipping cover. Use a fine file. Do not "taper" the ferrule. There should be a noticeable step from the shaft up to the top of the ferrule.

7-164 After filing, lightly sand the ferrule and whipping cover until both pieces are blended together. Remove any polyurethane from the whipping cover to ensure a uniform finish.

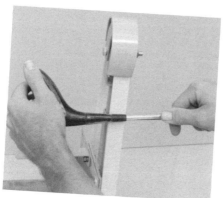

7-165 An alternative to the filing and sanding method is to use a **Cloth Linen Belt** on the belt sander. Refer to Chapter 19 photos 19-133 thru 19-136 for procedure.

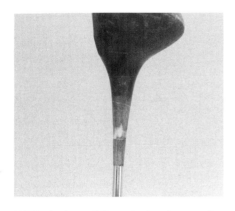

7-130 Look carefully at the hosel to see if a proper taper exists from the top of the ferrule into the base of the hosel. If there are any irregularities, file or sand as necessary to create a proper blended taper.

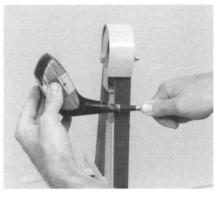

7-131 A fast alternative to the filing and sanding method is to use a belt sander. Using a medium grade belt, slowly rotate the club while pressing the hosel against the face of the sandpaper. Continue to sand until the proper taper is achieved.

7-132 Apply new whipping as shown in Chapter 2.

7-133 To measure for correct length, sole the club on the ground as shown. Slide a **48″ ruler** behind the shaft and . . .

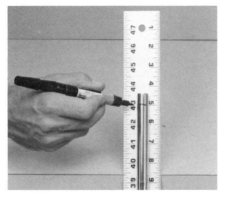

7-134 . . . make a mark on the shaft ⅛″ below the desired final length. Note: The grip cap will make up the ⅛″ difference.

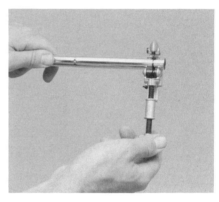

7-135 Cut the shaft using a Tubing Cutter or . . .

7-136 . . . a friction wheel. See Chapter 19 photos 19-162 thru 19-166 for correct cutting procedure.

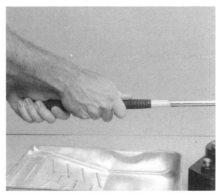

7-137 Install the proper grip following steps outlined in Chapter 22.

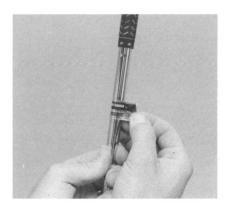

7-138 Apply the shaft band.

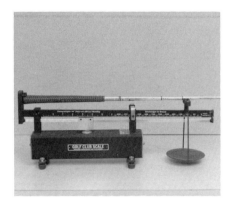

7-139 Check the swingweight. If it needs to be changed, refer to Chapter 13 for procedures.

7-140 Reshafting metalwood heads. First, determine if a rivet has been installed through the hosel and shaft. If there is a rivet, drive it through the hosel using the same procedures as shown in Chapter 19 photos 19-6 thru 19-9.

7-141 If no coating of paint and/or polyurethane is covering the hosel, heat the hosel area using a propane torch. Note the use of a wet paper towel wrapped around the ferrule. This will protect the ferrule from melting should you wish to save it. Note: A Heat Gun can also be used.

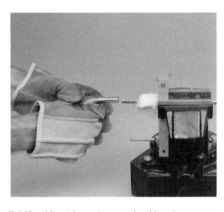

7-142 After 10 to 15 seconds of heating, grasp the head with your gloved hands and attempt to turn the head from the shaft. Apply more heat if the head will not turn.

7-143 If the hosel is covered with paint and/or polyurethane, use the **Heating Rod** and propane torch as shown in photos 7-46 thru 7-51. After heating, remove the head.

7-144 Once the head is removed, select the appropriate shaft. Refer to photos 7-61 thru 7-79 for determining proper back of heel to first step dimensions before permanently installing the shaft. Special tip-reinforced shafts are available for metalwoods. However, any parallel tip steel shaft is suitable. The tip-reinforced versions of composite shafts are absolutely necessary.

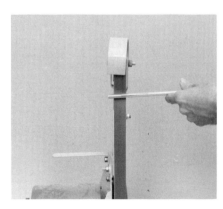

7-145 Once any corrections to the tip of the shaft have been made, abrade the tip of the shaft using a grinding stone, emery cloth, belt sander or file.

7-146 If you are working with a metalwood that had a ferrule, select the appropriate style ferrule. Slide the ferrule onto the shaft.

7-147 Mix the shear strength epoxy and dip the tip of the shaft into the epoxy.

7-148 Install the shaft into the hosel. Simultaneously turn and push the shaft inside the hosel to ensure the hosel and shaft walls are completely coated with epoxy.

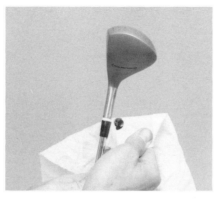

7-149 Wipe the excess epoxy from the hosel and ferrule.

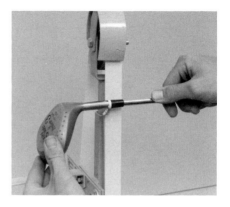

7-150 After the epoxy hardens, follow the steps shown in Chapter 19 photos 19-125 thru 19-140 for reducing the size of the ferrule. If a rivet must be installed, refer to Chapter 19 photos 19-141 thru 19-158.

7-151 If whipping is to be applied to the hosel, refer to photos 7-126 thru 7-131 for proper tapering of the ferrule prior to application of the whipping. Note: It will not be necessary to file the metal hosel, only the ferrule is filed and sanded.

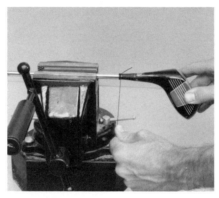

7-152 Apply the whipping as shown in Chapter 2.

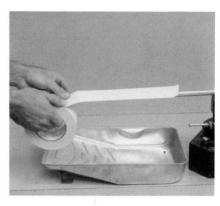

7-153 Cut the shaft butt end for proper club length following procedures shown in photos 7-133 thru 7-136. **Install the grip** as shown in Chapter 22.

7-154 Removing a graphite shaft from a metal, laminated maple or persimmon wood head. Place the graphite shaft in a **Rubber Shaft Clamp** and fasten the clamp in a vise. Note: In most cases, club will need refinished after this procedure.

7-155 Using a **Heat Gun**, apply heat to the back of the hosel working from the top to the . . .

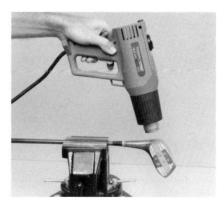

7-156 . . . bottom of the hosel (heel portion of the head). More time should be spent with the gun directed at the bottom of the hosel. The wood is much thicker in this section of the hosel and, therefore, it will take more heat to penetrate the wood to soften the epoxy.

7-157   After moving the gun back and forth for two minutes, grasp the head with a gloved hand and carefully try to turn the head. Continue this action, with the gun pointed at the hosel, until the head. . .

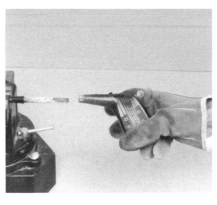

7-158   . . . turns around the shaft and can be pulled off. The real challenge with this type of reshaft is to soften the epoxy holding the shaft in place before the epoxy holding the graphite fibers together is destroyed. The success rate using this method is about 70%. No other method rates as high.

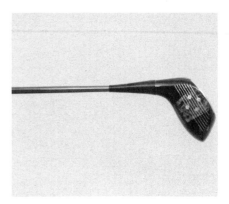

7-159   Photo shows a graphite head with a graphite shaft. Decide which of the components, head or shaft, you wish to save. There simply is no means of saving both. The heat required to soften the epoxy holding the shaft in the head will also destroy either the head or the shaft. **If the shaft is to be saved, carefully cut or saw the head from the shaft.**

7-160   If the head is to be saved, cut the shaft even with the top of the hosel and then drill the remaining portion of the shaft from the hosel. Begin with a small drill bit and then increase the size until the hosel bore is large enough to accept the new shaft. Head is then ready for shafting using normal steps.

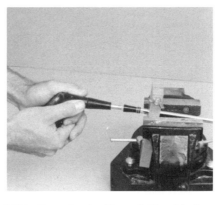

7-161   For a head with a plastic whipping cover, steps for the removal of the head are the same as demonstrated in photos 7-15 thru 7-51. The plastic whipping cover will remain on the head when the head is pulled from the shaft.

7-162   When installing the head onto the shaft, select a ferrule that is larger than the top of the whipping cover. Wipe excess epoxy from cover and ferrule. Allow the epoxy to harden.

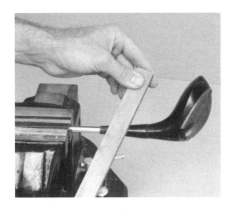

7-163   After the epoxy hardens, file the excess plastic until the ferrule is flush with the top of the whipping cover. Use a fine file. Do not "taper" the ferrule. There should be a noticeable step from the shaft up to the top of the ferrule.

7-164   After filing, lightly sand the ferrule and whipping cover until both pieces are blended together. Remove any polyurethane from the whipping cover to ensure a uniform finish.

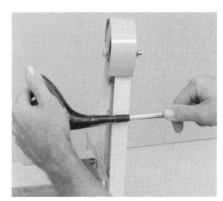

7-165   An alternative to the filing and sanding method is to use a **Cloth Linen Belt** on the belt sander. Refer to Chapter 19 photos 19-133 thru 19-136 for procedure.

7-166 Next, lightly steel wool the ferrule and cover with 000 steel wool.

7-167 Wipe the cover and ferrule with a paper towel dampened with acetone.

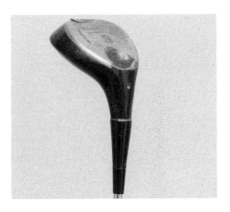

7-168 The finished ferrule and whipping cover should look like this.

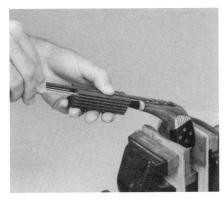

7-169 To install a backscrew in a wood head that did not have one before, use one of the following two methods. First method: Place a **Rubber Shaft Clamp** around the shaft above the ferrule and place a 12″ × 7/32″ drill bit in the Clamp so it is parallel with the shaft.

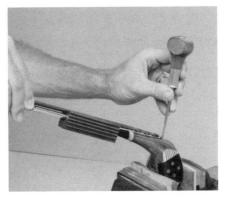

7-170 If the bit is running parallel with the shaft, it will show you exactly where the center of the shaft is in relation to the bottom of the hosel bore. Make a slight indentation into the finish with a sharpened awl or scriber ¾″ above the back of the heel.

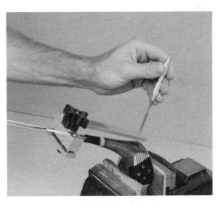

7-171 Second method: The **Backscrew Locator Tool** works under the same principle as the previous method but is easier and faster to use.

7-172 Next, after making the indentation in the finish, place a layer of cellophane tape across the mark.

7-173 Using a ⅛″ drill bit, drill through the tape into the wood. The drill bit should be angled slightly toward the sole of the club to ensure the bit doesn't drill through the top of the head. The tape will prevent the finish from tearing as the bit passes through.

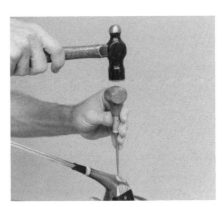

7-174 After encountering the shaft, stop drilling and use the alternating punch and drill method as shown in photos 7-108 thru 7-116 for drilling the hole for the backscrew.

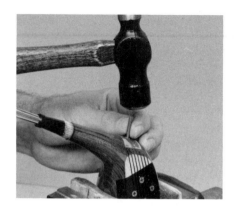

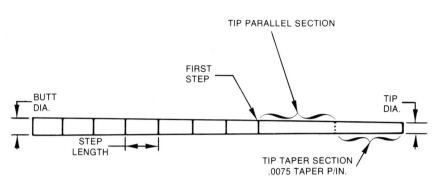

Fig. 7-176
Golf shaft terminology

7-175 Refer to photos 7-117 thru 7-125 for installation of the backscrew and camouflaging the backscrew hole.

ADDITIONAL INFORMATION FOR WOOD RESHAFTING

TABLE 7-1			
Wood Club Lengths — Men's and Ladies'			
Woods	**Men's Standard**	**Ladies' Standard**	**Ladies' Petite**
1	43″	42″	41½″
2	42½″	41½″	41″
3	42″	41″	40½″
4	41½″	40½″	40″
5	41″	40″	39½″
6	40½″	39½″	39″
7	40″	39″	38½″
8	39½″	38½″	38″
9	39″	38″	37½″

The most popular length variations for men are ½″ shorter or longer than standard and 1″ longer than standard. The most popular length variations for ladies are ½″ shorter or longer than standard.

TABLE 7-2	
Drill Selection Chart	
● Backscrew pilot drill	⅛″
● Screw extractor pilot drill	5/64″
● Drill to cut shaft backscrew	7/32″
● Pilot drill for #7 soleplate screws	⅛″
● Pilot drill for #8 soleplate screws	9/64″
● Pilot drill for #4 face screws	3/32″
● Pilot drill for #5 face screws	7/64″

TABLE 7-3		
Determining Shaft Flex by Color on Butt End of Shaft		
Designation	**Flex**	**Color**
X	Extra Stiff	Green
S	Stiff	Red
R or T	Medium	Black
A	Flexible	Yellow
L	Ladies (very flexible)	Blue

Combination flex shafts such as UDWC, UDWAL, UJWC & U2LWAL do not have a color code on the butt end.

		TABLE 7-4		
		Standard Wood Screw Diameter		
Screw Number Size	**Shank Diameter**	**General Golf Club Use**		**Drill Size to Use so Screw Threads Properly**
4	.112	Std. size face screw		3/32"
5	.125	Oversize face screw and backscrew		7/64"
6	.138	Very large face screw		#32
7	.151	Std. size soleplate screw		1/8"
8	.164	Oversize soleplate screw		9/64"
9	.177	Backweight screw (older clubs)		#25
10	.190	Backweight screw (old H&B)		#19

The majority of manufacturers use a #5 backscrew; however, some companies use a 3/32" or 1/8" headless nail.

Step Drilling Instructions and Drill Sizes by Tip Sizes

When boring hosels for new shafts or reshafting, many repair shops find it difficult or very expensive to obtain the proper size drills and reamers to match every wood shaft tip size available. Also, they run into special problems such as enlarging hosel holes to accept "tipped" shafts or hosels which need to be bored to accept another shaft size, or in most cases, hosels which just need to be cleaned out so that the replacement shaft will fit properly. Step drilling will solve this problem. See photos 7-80 thru 7-88 for procedure. Listed below are the drill sizes needed for the various shaft tip sizes.

Step Drilling Instructions and Sizes for .270" Tip Taper Shafts

Step #1: Drill to desired length or completely through with "J" (.277") diameter extra length drill.
Step #2: Drill to within 1/2" of depth as stated in *Step #1* with "L" (.290") diameter standard length drill.
Step #3: Drill to within 2½" of depth as stated in *Step #1* with "N" (.302") diameter standard length drill.

Step Drilling Instructions and Sizes for .277" Tip Taper Shafts

Step #1: Drill to desired length or completely through with 9/32" (.281") diameter extra length drill.
Step #2: Drill to within 1/2" of depth as stated in *Step #1* with "M" (.295") diameter standard length drill.
Step #3: Drill to within 2¼" of depth as stated in *Step #1* with 5/16" (.312") diameter standard length drill.

Step Drilling Instructions and Sizes for .294" Tip Taper Shafts

Step #1: Drill to desired length or completely through with 19/64" (.296") diameter extra length drill.
Step #2: Drill to within 3/8" of depth as stated in *Step #1* with 5/16" (.312") diameter standard length drill.
Step #3: Drill to within 2" of depth as stated in *Step #1* with 21/64" (.328") diameter standard length drill.

Step Drilling Instructions and Sizes for .320" Tip Taper Shafts

Step #1: Drill to desired length or completely through with "P" (.323") diameter extra length drill.
Step #2: Drill to within 1/2" of depth as stated in *Step #1* with "R" (.339") diameter standard length drill.
Step #3: Drill to within 2½" of depth as stated in *Step #1* with "T" (.358") diameter standard length drill.

Step Drilling Instructions and Size for .335" Unitized Parallel Tip Shafts

Step #1: Drill to desired length or completely through with "R" (.339") diameter extra length drill.

8

TIGHTENING LOOSE WOOD HEADS

Finding a loose wood head is fairly common, especially with persimmon woods. This is because persimmon is characterized as an open-grain wood, and therefore, is more susceptible to moisture absorption. As a wood head takes on moisture, it swells or expands. The loss of moisture in a head causes the head to shrink or contract. This movement, however slight, is sometimes enough to cause the epoxy holding the shaft in the hosel to fail. Once the epoxy bond fails, only the existence of a backscrew will keep the shaft in place. Even with the backscrew in place, some movement of the shaft is inevitable once the epoxy fails. Aside from the possibility of someone getting hurt from a flying wood head, a loose head can affect a golfer's game.

To determine if a wood head is loose, grasp the head in one hand and the grip in your other hand. Twist the grip and head in opposite directions and note if the head is loose. You may not always be able to feel or visually detect a loose head because, in many cases, the head and shaft are still firmly bonded at the bottom, but loose through the upper portion of the neck. This can usually be detected by a squeaky sound when the head and grip are twisted in opposite directions. Always check for a loose head on every club brought to you for any type of repair.

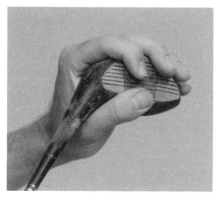

8-1 To determine if a wood head is loose, **grasp the head in one hand and the grip in your other hand** and attempt to twist each in opposite directions.

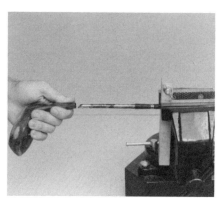

8-2 As outlined in Chapter 7 remove the head from the shaft.

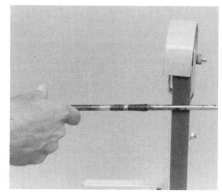

8-3 Remove old epoxy and rough up the tip of the shaft using a belt sander, grinding wheel, file or emory cloth.

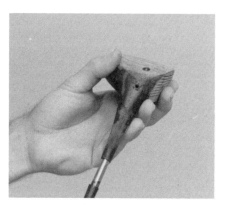

8-4 Temporarily reinstall the shaft to check the fit. If the head is very loose on the shaft, a shim must be used to take up the excess space.

8-5 The three most commonly used shimming materials are brass and paper shims, and **Aluminum Oxide Sand.**

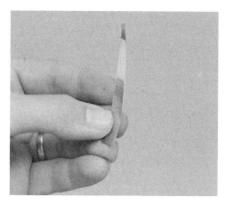

8-6 If a brass or paper shim is chosen, cut a tapered shim approximately 3″ long, as shown.

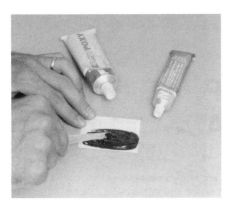

8-7 Mix a shear strength epoxy. **Conap®** or **GolfWorks® Shafting Epoxy** is extremely strong.

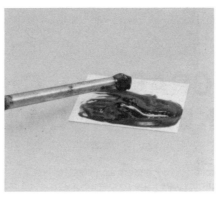

8-8 Dip the tip of the shaft into the epoxy and . . .

8-9 . . . insert the tip of the shaft into the hosel. Simultaneously push and turn the shaft to completely coat the shaft and hosel walls. **Note: It is always a good idea to wrap the hosel with masking tape to prevent splitting.**

8-10 If a tapered shim is used, apply epoxy to both sides of the shim.

8-11 Remove shaft from hosel. Press shim into hosel hole — small end first. Leave large end protruding about ¼" above end of hosel.

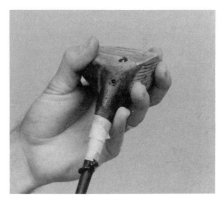

8-12 Reinstall the shaft while slowly twisting, until it bottoms out. The proturding portion of the shim should go down with the shaft.

8-13 If **Aluminum Oxide Sand** is used, coat the shaft and hosel with epoxy as detailed in photos 8-7 thru 8-9 and then dip the tip of the shaft into the sand.

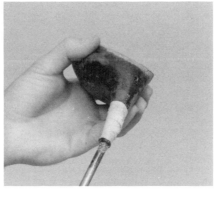

8-14 Finally, install the shaft into the hosel. The sand will effectively take up excess space while providing a good bonding surface for the epoxy.

8-15 After the epoxy has hardened, drill and install the backscrew, if the club had one before. Refer to Chapter 7 photos 7-108 thru 7-125 for procedure. **Note: Many repairmen choose to install a new backscrew regardless of whether or not a club had one before.**

9-13 Miracle-Man® epoxy manufactured by Club Kit® is an excellent bonding epoxy for broken heads. However, it does not change color very well when mixing in a colored paste dispersion.

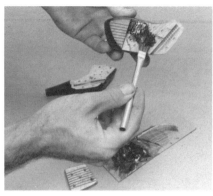

9-14 Coat one half of the broken head thoroughly with epoxy. Be sure to get epoxy in all ⅛" drilled holes.

9-15 Also coat the other half and any other pieces.

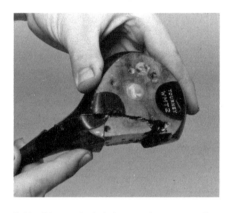

9-16 Line up both halves and press together. Do not squeeze out all of the epoxy because epoxy develops its maximum strength if it has a thin glue line.

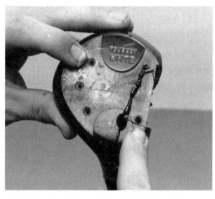

9-17 Where practical, the insert and/or soleplate can be temporarily installed to help draw the pieces in proper alignment. Photo shows the type of break that would benefit from the temporary placement of the insert and/or soleplate.

9-18 If a proper fit is achieved with the insert, it may be permanently installed with epoxy. The clubhead will require swingweighting so do not permanently install the soleplate.

9-19 Pay particular attention to the scoring lines. Installing the insert can be a great help in ensuring the lines are properly aligned.

9-20 Temporarily install the soleplate if it will help draw the pieces together.

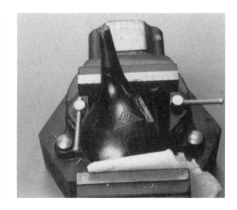

9-21 Strategically place the epoxied clubhead between the vise jaws and carefully tighten the vise until epoxy begins to ooze out. Note: A paper towel is used to protect the head from the rough surface of the vise jaws yet allowing the jaws to firmly grasp the head without slippage.

8-7 Mix a shear strength epoxy. **Conap®** or **GolfWorks® Shafting Epoxy** is extremely strong.

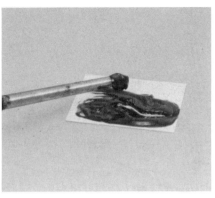

8-8 Dip the tip of the shaft into the epoxy and . . .

8-9 . . . insert the tip of the shaft into the hosel. Simultaneously push and turn the shaft to completely coat the shaft and hosel walls. **Note: It is always a good idea to wrap the hosel with masking tape to prevent splitting.**

8-10 If a tapered shim is used, apply epoxy to both sides of the shim.

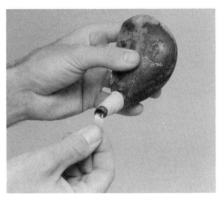

8-11 Remove shaft from hosel. Press shim into hosel hole — small end first. Leave large end protruding about ¼″ above end of hosel.

8-12 Reinstall the shaft while slowly twisting, until it bottoms out. The proturding portion of the shim should go down with the shaft.

8-13 If **Aluminum Oxide Sand** is used, coat the shaft and hosel with epoxy as detailed in photos 8-7 thru 8-9 and then dip the tip of the shaft into the sand.

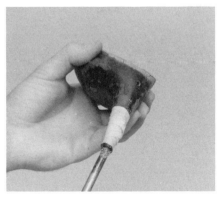

8-14 Finally, install the shaft into the hosel. The sand will effectively take up excess space while providing a good bonding surface for the epoxy.

8-15 After the epoxy has hardened, drill and install the backscrew, if the club had one before. Refer to Chapter 7 photos 7-108 thru 7-125 for procedure. **Note: Many repairmen choose to install a new backscrew regardless of whether or not a club had one before.**

REPAIRING CRACKED, CHIPPED OR BROKEN WOOD HEADS

There was a time when a cracked or broken wood head was either replaced or the entire club was discarded. This is not the case today with the availability of high strength epoxies. The proper epoxy must be a high shear strength type that cures with some flexibility. In addition, the epoxy should also accept a coloring agent such as colored paste dispersions. This will allow the repairman to alter the color of the epoxy to match the color of the stained wood. This is very effective for camouflaging an epoxy line.

Basically, there are three types of breaks which you will encounter, and all three require a different method of repair.

The first kind of break or crack, and probably the most common, is the hairline crack or cracks extending from under the whipping or ferrule down the hosel. Usually, this crack works its way down the hosel to its weakest part, namely the shaft locking screw hole. It is usually caused by a loose whipping, loose shaft-to-head bond, constant wood swelling from moisture and wood shrinking from drying out, or whoever assembled the club was not careful during the shaft installation step and cracked the hosel.

The second kind of break (usually found in persimmon heads), is one which starts on one side of the face insert, extends under the soleplate, to a backweight if one exists and then eventually around the entire head. The crack takes this route because it is always cracking in the direction of the weakest part of the head. Routing the head for the various components during manufacture weakens the wood head. This type of break will commonly break into two to five different pieces. Do not be intimidated by the prospect of refitting these back together though. If the proper epoxy is used, the club will rarely rebreak along the same cracks.

The third kind of break can really be referred to as a chip, and usually represents a piece of wood chipped out of the toe, the face or around the soleplate. Sometimes, in the case of laminated heads, it is a delamination of the wood in the sole area caused by moisture being absorbed into the wood because the finish has been chipped or worn off.

9-1 A typical crack running from behind the insert, across the head, up the side of the hosel . . .

9-2 . . . back down the hosel and under the soleplate. Cracks have a tendency to seek out the weakest parts of the head. During manufacture, the removal of wood from the head for the placement of the insert, soleplate and lead weight, will generally be where the breaks occur.

9-3 To fix a cracked wood head: First, remove the soleplate as outlined in Chapter 3.

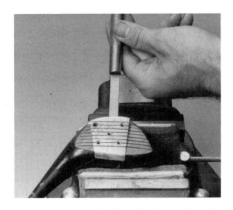

9-4 Next, remove the face insert as outlined in Chapter 4. Some cracks run parallel to the face and the removal of the insert is not necessary unless the insert is loose.

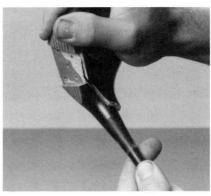

9-5 Grasp the head in both hands or in a vise and . . .

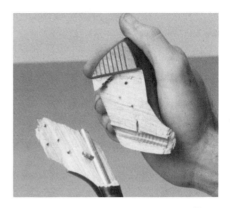

9-6 . . . break it into two or more pieces. **Note: The club must be completely broken apart at any crack to properly fix it.**

9-7 Occasionally a break must be persuaded to come apart. To do this . . .

9-8 . . . place a chisel in the crack and hammer lightly until the head comes apart. This is especially useful when a crack has not extended completely around the head. The break you create will usually follow the same line the crack would eventually develop into.

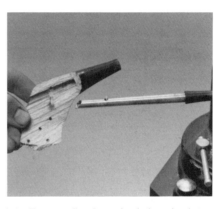

9-9 Temporarily piece the halves back together to see if the shaft interferes with a proper fit. If the shaft does interfere, remove the shaft as outlined in Chapter 7.

9-10 In one half of the broken head, drill a series of holes approximately ⅛" deep using a ⅛" diameter drill bit.

9-11 Do the same in the other half of the head. If more than two pieces exist, drill a series of holes in each piece.

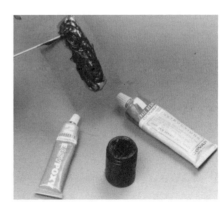

9-12 Mix up shear strength epoxy. Note the addition of a colored paste dispersion to match the stain color of the head. This will help camouflage the epoxy line when refinishing the club. If the club will be refinished in black, there is no need for concern.

9-13 Miracle-Man® epoxy manufactured by Club Kit® is an excellent bonding epoxy for broken heads. However, it does not change color very well when mixing in a colored paste dispersion.

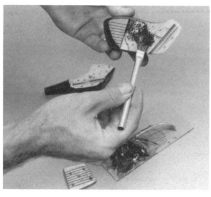

9-14 Coat one half of the broken head thoroughly with epoxy. Be sure to get epoxy in all ⅛" drilled holes.

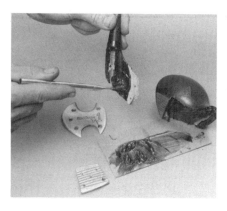

9-15 Also coat the other half and any other pieces.

9-16 Line up both halves and press together. Do not squeeze out all of the epoxy because epoxy develops its maximum strength if it has a thin glue line.

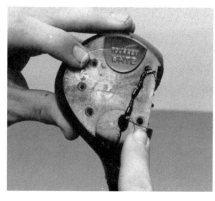

9-17 Where practical, the insert and/or soleplate can be temporarily installed to help draw the pieces in proper alignment. Photo shows the type of break that would benefit from the temporary placement of the insert and/or soleplate.

9-18 If a proper fit is achieved with the insert, it may be permanently installed with epoxy. The clubhead will require swingweighting so do not permanently install the soleplate.

9-19 Pay particular attention to the scoring lines. Installing the insert can be a great help in ensuring the lines are properly aligned.

9-20 Temporarily install the soleplate if it will help draw the pieces together.

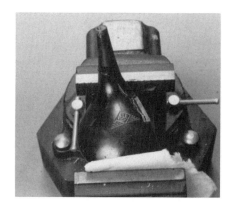

9-21 Strategically place the epoxied clubhead between the vise jaws and carefully tighten the vise until epoxy begins to ooze out. Note: A paper towel is used to protect the head from the rough surface of the vise jaws yet allowing the jaws to firmly grasp the head without slippage.

9-22 An alternative to the vise is placing a rubber band around the clubhead to hold it together and in the proper position.

9-23 A **Face Insert Clamp** works very well to hold everything together.

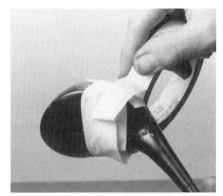

9-24 Masking tape can also be used.

9-25 After the epoxy has hardened, if the shaft was removed, clean out the hosel using the proper size drill bits and reinstall the shaft. See Chapter 7 for shaft installation procedures.

9-26 Next, remove the soleplate screws and then . . .

9-27 . . . remove the soleplate.

9-28 File excess epoxy from the face, using a medium cut or fine cut file. If the insert was not previously reset, it should now be re-epoxied.

9-29 Periodically check the bulge, roll and loft until it is correct. See Chapter 1 photos 1-22 thru 1-30 for facing procedure.

9-30 Recut the scoring lines using a proper blade with no rake on the teeth.

9-31 Redrill the screw holes using a ³/₃₂″ drill bit.

9-32 Recountersink the screw holes and install new insert screws as outlined in Chapter 4, photos 4-42 thru 4-46.

9-33 File the screw heads flush with the insert using a fine cut file. Recheck bulge, roll and loft to insure these specifications have not been changed.

9-34 Club is now ready for swingweighting and soleplate installation.

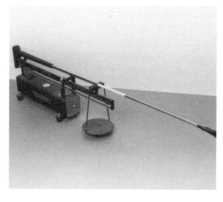

9-35 Place the soleplate in the soleplate cavity and check the swingweight. Soleplate screws can temporarily be installed or simply compensate for the lack of screws. Example: 5 #8 soleplate screws are equivalent to 3 swingweight points.

9-36 Make any necessary adjustments in swingweight following instructions from Chapter 13.

9-37 Clean soleplate cavity of excess epoxy using a medium cut file.

9-38 Temporarily reinstall the soleplate and redrill the screw holes for the soleplate screws using a ⅛″ drill bit.

9-39 Mix epoxy, apply to the cavity and the soleplate and install the soleplate. Club is now ready for refinishing. If epoxy was mixed properly, club will not break along the original crack again. However, if the wood is very brittle, clubhead may crack along a different line in the future.

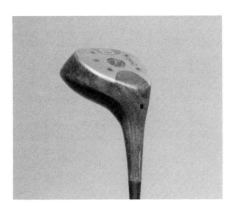

9-40 Another type of crack in a wood club is a split neck.

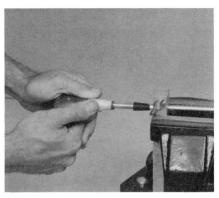

9-41 To properly repair a split neck the head must be removed as outlined in Chapter 7.

9-42 Abrade the tip of the shaft using a belt sander, grinding wheel, file or a piece of emery cloth.

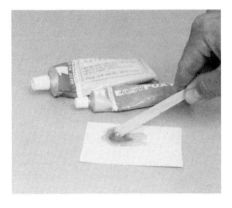

9-43 Mix appropriate shear strength epoxy such as Conap® or GolfWorks® shafting epoxy.

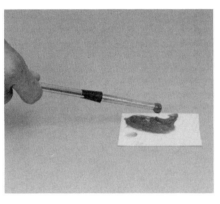

9-44 Dip the tip of the shaft into the epoxy and . . .

9-45 . . . install the shaft into the hosel. For best results, simultaneously push and turn the shaft to effectively coat the shaft tip and the hosel wall.

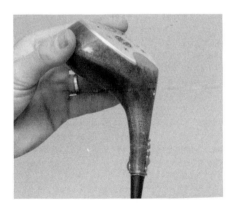

9-46 The result of turning the shaft during installation is that the epoxy is forced through and out the cracks. This effectively seals the cracks.

9-47 After the epoxy has hardened, smooth the neck, install the shaft locking screw and apply whipping.

9-48 A delamination in the sole area is quite common and usually caused by moisture absorption due to the loss of the polyurethane coating.

9-49 If the chip is removed, apply epoxy to the chip and the damaged area.

9-50 Place the chip back in place. To secure, place a piece of tape across the chip or clamp bottom of club between vise jaws.

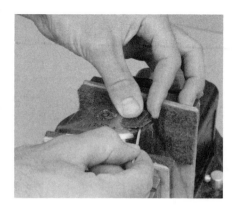

9-51 If enough epoxy can be forced underneath the delaminated piece, it is not necessary to completely remove it and then reinstall. Force epoxy under the piece with a toothpick as shown. A layer of tape should then be applied until the epoxy hardens.

9-52 If the chip from the sole is lost, make a dam around the damaged area using masking tape or . . .

9-53 . . . Mortite putty.

9-54 It is not necessary to use an impact strength epoxy for this job. Any shear strength epoxy will work. Conap® or GolfWorks® brand epoxy works well. Mix and apply enough epoxy to fill in the cavity.

9-55 After the epoxy hardens, file the excess and shape to match the contour of the head using a fine cut file.

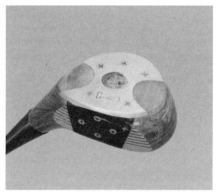

9-56 The club is now ready for touch-up or refinishing. Note that a colored paste dispersion was used to camouflage the repaired area.

NOTES

_____

_____

_____

_____

_____

_____

_____

_____

ADDITIONAL INFORMATION FOR REPAIRING CRACKED, CHIPPED OR BROKEN WOOD HEADS

EPOXY

To a golf club repairman, it is critical that any components epoxied together remain together. The thought of a customer swinging a club with a head that has just flown off the shaft is enough to make any repairman feel very uneasy. This potentially embarrassing situation need never be faced if the repairman uses the correct type of epoxy and follows a few simple rules when assembling components.

Impact strength and shear strength represent the two types of epoxies used in golf club repair. Shear strength epoxy is used whenever a component will likely experience twisting or pulling effects; i.e., shaft in or over a hosel, soleplate or insert placement, etc. . . . The twisting properties may be obvious, as in the case of the tremendous torque experienced between the shaft and hosel during impact, or not so obvious as in the case of the insert resisting movement during impact.

Impact strength epoxy is used solely when casting a new insert (see Chapter 5). The insert must be unyielding and able to withstand the impact of the ball against the insert, hence the term impact strength. Some repairmen erroneously believe they should also use an impact strength epoxy when resetting an insert. This is not true because the insert itself is impact resistant, the epoxy holding the insert in place must have shear strength properties in order to resist the oblique impact of the ball. This indirect impact produces shifting stress on the entire insert that must be avoided hence the need for shear strength epoxy.

In order to ensure the components remain epoxied together, the repairman must follow a few simple rules:
1. Make certain the quantities of base and activator are measured precisely before mixing them together.
2. Make sure the surfaces of all components are prepared properly.
3. Do not use epoxy if the contents of the epoxy container or the surrounding area are below 65°F.
4. Slowly mix the contents of each container before using whenever applicable. Depending upon the container this may not be possible in some cases.

Always follow the instructions that accompany your favorite brand of epoxy. Mixing instructions will inform you not only of the mixing ratio but also, in most cases, recommend measuring by weight or volume. Cheating on the mixing instructions (adding more activator in an attempt to speed curing) will always result in the epoxy either being too brittle or never achieving proper hardness.

When epoxying golf club components, make sure all surfaces are properly abraded following the directions found in each of the appropriate chapters of this book. Also, make sure the surfaces are free of oil, dirt, fingerprints or other surface contaminates. This is best achieved by wiping with a degreasing solvent such as Perchlorethylene (Grip Solvent), Trichlorethylene or Naphtha. Allow a few minutes drying time to allow the solvents to evaporate before applying epoxy.

The table below gives curing times for the epoxies offered by The GolfWorks® under both room temperature and heat lamp conditions. To use the heat lamp, be sure it is positioned 15″ from the repair, using a 300 or 400 watt light bulb. The strength of a heat-cured bond will not be as great as that achieved through use of moderate curing temperature.

		Conap			GolfWorks® General Purpose High Strength Epoxy	Truset APOX & BPOX	Club-Kit Miracle-Man
Type and Time to Harden and/or Cure		**K20**	**K22**	**K26**			
Rm. Temp.	Hrs. to Harden (72°F)	2	2	2	8-10	1	3
Rm. Temp.	Hrs. to Cure (72°F)	24	24	24	24	6	8
Heat Lamp	Cure (minutes)	20-30	20-30	20-30	45	60	Not Recommended

TABLE 9-1
Various Shear Strength Epoxy Curing Times

10
CHANGING LOFT, BULGE AND ROLL

Occasionally you will be required to change the loft, bulge or roll of a golf wood clubface. The amount of change which can be done to a wood face depends entirely on the particular make or model of golf club. Also, more alteration can be done on a driver face vs. a #5 wood face. This, however, should not pose a problem since most face alterations will be requested for the driver.

Before getting into the actual procedure of altering the face, it is necessary to review the exact definitions of loft, bulge and roll.

Loft: The angle of the face and a line perpendicular to the sole line measured in degrees to a point ½ the distance of the face height and located on the centerline of the face.

Horizontal Face Bulge: The radius bulge of the face is measured from the heel to toe in a horizontal plane along the face. It is usually the same at any point vertically up or down the face.

Vertical Face Roll: The radius roll of the face is measured from the top to the bottom of the face in a vertical plane. It is usually the same at any point along the face from the heel to the toe.

No matter which specification you intend to alter (loft, bulge or roll) the other two will probably be affected. Because of this it is necessary that you obtain some gauges to accurately measure loft, bulge and roll. The recommended gauges would be those specifically made to measure golf clubfaces as they save considerable time and eliminate interpolation required with other type gauges. The photos in this chapter show the proper gauges to use.

10-1 Using a machinist's protractor, hold arm of protractor tight against soleplate and adjust protractor head so it touches the face at ½ its vertical height. **Loft is always specified in degrees.**

10-2 Using a fixed loft gauge, find the loft where one arm of the gauge is resting flush against the soleplate and the other is resting against the face at ½ its vertical face height.

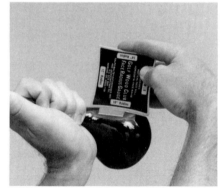

10-3 Bulge is measured with a Face Radius Gauge. See Chapter 1, photos 1-22 thru 1-27 for a thorough explanation for measuring bulge. **Bulge is always specified in inches of radius.**

10-4 Roll is also measured with the Face Radius Gauge. See Chapter 1, photos 1-22 thru 1-27 for a thorough explanation for measuring roll. **Roll is always specified in inches of radius.**

10-5 Record the loft, bulge and roll before beginning work.

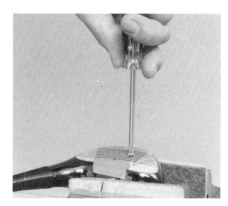

10-6 First, remove the insert screws. See Chapter 4 photos 4-3 thru 4-19 for insert screw removal procedure.

10-7 If the bulge is to be reduced (this means the amount of curvature from the heel to the toe is decreased or made flatter), concentrate your filing in the middle area of the face. A medium or coarse cut file works best depending on how much material is to be removed.

10-8 After carefully filing, the reduced horizontal face bulge is measured.

10-9 If the bulge is to be increased (this means the amount of curvature from heel to toe is increased or made more round), concentrate your filing on the heel and toe portion of the face.

10-10 After carefully filing, the increased horizontal face bulge is measured. Slide the gauge up and down the face checking it from top to bottom. On some wood head models, it is necessary for the horizontal bulge to flatten out slightly in the upper heel portion of the face. This gives a better look in the playing position and avoids filing the face into the hosel. This will not affect playability.

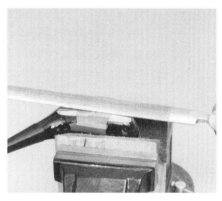

10-11 To reduce vertical face roll, concentrate your filing from the heel to the toe, along the middle of the face.

10-12 After carefully filing, the decreased vertical face roll is measured.

10-13 To increase vertical face roll, concentrate your filing from the heel to the toe, above and below the middle of the face.

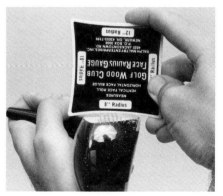

10-14 After carefully filing, the increased vertical roll is measured.

10-15 To increase loft (this adds more loft to increase ball trajectory), file as shown working along the middle of the face to the top of the face. Keep checking bulge, roll and loft as you file.

10-16 After carefully filing, the increase in loft is measured.

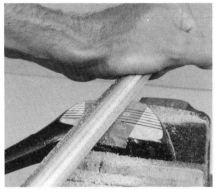

10-17 To decrease loft (this reduces loft to lower ball trajectory), concentrate your filing from the middle of the face to the bottom of the face working horizontally across the face. Keep checking bulge, roll and loft as you file.

10-18 After carefully filing, the decrease in loft is measured.

10-19 Re-cut new scoring lines if necessary.

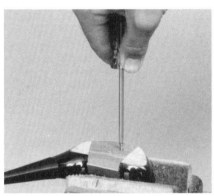

10-20 Re-install new insert screws if necessary.

10-21 Lightly sand the face with fine sandpaper and lightly scrape with a **Detailing Knife.**

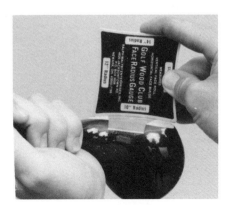

10-22 Final check the bulge, roll and loft to ensure the specifications have not changed because of the final detail steps. See Chapter 15 for finish touch-up steps.

NOTES

ADDITIONAL INFORMATION FOR CHANGING LOFT, BULGE AND ROLL

How to Read a Machinist's Protractor When Measuring Wood Head Lofts

Photo 10-1 shows how to correctly hold a protractor for measuring loft of a wood. It is important to develop a good technique that will allow you to get exact repeatability no matter how many times you recheck the same club. The method I like to use when taking a loft reading is to hold the protractor arm on the sole of the club and hold the club up directly in front of a good light source such as a window or light fixture. While in this position, I adjust the head of the protractor to touch the face at ½ its vertical height.

There are a number of different types and styles of protractors available. Some have square heads, some have round heads, and a number of them have differing graduation callout markings although every one is marked in one degree increments. Look at Fig. 10-23 which shows a head with 3 sets of callout graduations.

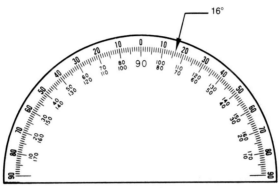

Fig. 10-23
Protractor head readings

This is not very common as most protractor heads will not have the top row with 0° in the middle and increasing to 90° in each direction. Most protractors have the bottom two rows of callout graduations thus when taking a wood loft reading with this type, you would have to do a little additional calculating.

Look again at Fig. 10-23. Most of the readings taken for loft will be on the right side of the protractor head or right of the 0° or 90° mark. When reading toward the right or left, notice you will be increasing from 90° or decreasing from 90°. If you happen to have a 0° mark you can read loft directly off this scale. However, as we earlier stated, most protractors only have the bottom two callout designations. Notice the 16° callout in Fig. 10-23. It is 16 one degree increments to the right of 90°. Hence the wood head would have 16° loft. The bottom scale callouts would have you reading 16° as either 106° or 74°. Of course, subtracting 74° from 90° would be 16° and subtracting 90° from 106° would be 16°. See Fig. 10-24. It's easiest just to count graduations in units of 10s, 5s and 1s when you are reading the protractor to obtain loft radius.

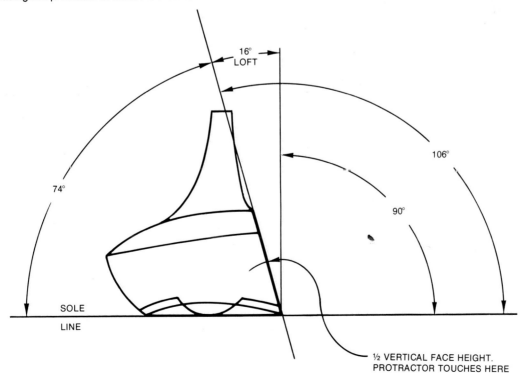

Fig. 10-24
Defining protractor readings when measuring loft

TABLE 10-1
Chart For Determining Strong, Standard and Weak Loft Specifications
Men's and Ladies' — Wood Club Lofts

Woods	Men's			Ladies'		
	Strong Lofts	Standard Lofts	Weak Lofts	Strong Lofts	Standard Lofts	Weak Lofts
1	10°	11°	12°	11°	12°	13°
2	12°	13°	14°	13°	14°	15°
3	15°	16°	17°	16°	17°	18°
4	18°	19°	20°	19°	20°	21°
5	21°	22°	23°	22°	23°	24°
6	24°	25°	26°	25°	26°	27°
7	27°	28°	29°	28°	29°	30°
8	30°	31°	32°	31°	32°	33°
9	33°	34°	35°	34°	35°	36°

TABLE 10-2
Chart For Determining Bulge and Roll Specifications
Wood Clubs

Club No.	Vertical Face Roll	Horizontal Face Bulge
1	12" Radius	10" Radius
2	14" Radius	12" Radius
3	14" Radius	12" Radius
4	14" Radius	12" Radius
5	16" Radius	14" Radius
6	16" Radius	14" Radius
7	18" Radius	16" Radius

NOTES

CHANGING LIE OF WOOD CLUBS

This chapter will show you how to alter the lie of a golf wood using a rather simple procedure of bending the shaft slightly. As golfers are learning the importance of having the clubhead in the correct lie position at impact, the demand for this service is increasing. Naturally, the most ideal solution for a golfer with an incorrect lie on his woods is to order custom woods with his own lie specifications. However, the shaft bending method described in this chapter will work very satisfactorily if you follow the detailed procedure carefully.

The amount of bend that can be made in a shaft depends upon the shaft material. Standard weight shafts made of carbon steel — i.e., True Temper's® Dynamic®, ProFit®, and Jet Step® — can be safely bent as much as four degrees. Lightweight shafts such as True Temper's® TT Lite® or Flex-Flow® should be bent a maximum of two degrees. Lightweight shafts tend to have thinner walls and larger diameters and therefore are more easily broken or kinked than a standard weight shaft. Attempting a bend of more than two degrees on a lightweight shaft should not be atttempted. Shafts that fall into the super lightweight category — i.e., True Temper's® Extralite® or Brunswick Golf's® UCV-304® — cannot be bent without breaking or kinking the shaft and as such altering these shafts should not be attempted. Shafts made of composite materials such as graphite, fiberglass or aramid-fiber, simply cannot be permanently bent and this also should not be attempted.

11-1 A bending block is the most effective way of changing a wood club's lie. This block is made from strong hardwood and has a 1″ wide × 1″ deep notch which is padded with 2 pieces of leather from an old grip. Use in vise or bolt securely to workbench as shown. Plans for making your own bending block are found at the end of this chapter.

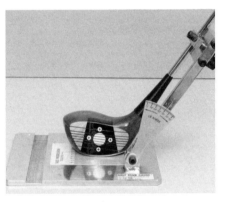

11-2 The lie can be changed by eye; however, the use of an accurate measuring gauge, such as this **Golf Club Gauge**, will eliminate guesswork.

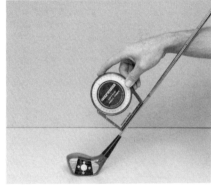

11-3 Another method for measuring lie is to rest the middle of the sole of the clubhead on a flat surface. Next, place a **Magnetic Protractor** on the tip section of the shaft. Read the lie directly off the protractor. This method is reasonably accurate.

11-4 To flatten the lie, place club in block as shown. Note location where shaft is being bent. The bend in the shaft should be made at a point where the top of the hosel meets the ferrule. Hold hands close to the block and apply short bursts of downward pressure to the shaft. **Practice on old clubs first.** Whipping should be left on the hosel to prevent the hosel from splitting.

11-5 Photo shows where the bend in the shaft is made. This point is approximately 1″ from the top of the whipping.

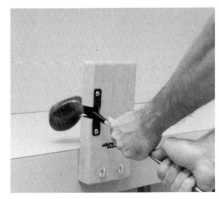

11-6 To make the lie more upright, place club in block as shown. With the toe of the club pointing downward, hold hands close to the block and apply short bursts of downward pressure to the shaft.

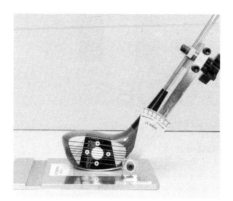

11-7 The altered club should again be measured to ensure the proper lie change has been made.

11-8 Because the shaft is being bent and not the hosel, steel shafted graphite heads may also be bent. The same steps as outlined previously apply.

11-9 Steel shafted metalwoods can also be bent. However, because of the lack of whipping to camouflage the bend, the angle created on the shaft is more obvious.

ADDITIONAL INFORMATION FOR CHANGING LIE OF WOOD CLUBS

TABLE 11-1
Wood Club Lies — Men's and Ladies'

Woods	Men's			Ladies'		
	[1]Flat Lies	[1]Standard Lies	[1]Upright Lies	[2]Flat Lies	[2]Standard Lies	[2]Upright Lies
1	53°	55°	57°	51°	53°	55°
2	53½°	55½°	57½°	51½°	53½°	55½°
3	54°	56°	58°	52°	54°	56°
4	54½°	56½°	58½°	52½°	54½°	56½°
5	55°	57°	59°	53°	55°	57°
6	55½°	57½°	59½°	53½°	55½°	57½°
7	56°	58°	60°	54°	56°	58°
8	56½°	58½°	60½°	54½°	56½°	58½°
9	57°	59°	61°	55°	57°	59°

[1] Lies shown are for standard length woods (i.e., 43" driver). For each ½" added to standard length, subtract 1° in lie (flatter) and for each ½" subtracted from standard length, add 1° in lie (upright).
[2] Same as Note 1 above but based on a standard length set with a 42" driver.

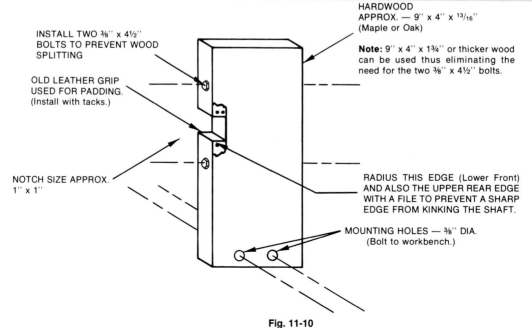

INSTALL TWO ⅜'' x 4½'' BOLTS TO PREVENT WOOD SPLITTING

OLD LEATHER GRIP USED FOR PADDING. (Install with tacks.)

NOTCH SIZE APPROX. 1'' x 1''

HARDWOOD APPROX. — 9'' x 4'' x ¹³/₁₆'' (Maple or Oak)

Note: 9'' x 4'' x 1¾'' or thicker wood can be used thus eliminating the need for the two ⅜'' x 4½'' bolts.

RADIUS THIS EDGE (Lower Front) AND ALSO THE UPPER REAR EDGE WITH A FILE TO PREVENT A SHARP EDGE FROM KINKING THE SHAFT.

MOUNTING HOLES — ⅜'' DIA. (Bolt to workbench.)

Fig. 11-10
A device you can make to alter lie of wood clubs

CHANGING THE FACE ANGLE ON WOODS (SQUARE, OPEN, CLOSED)

Adjusting the face angle on woods is accomplished by either bending the shaft or precisely removing material from certain areas of the face. This change in face angle is usually made to provide a positive change in the direction and/or shape of a golf shot. However, it should be understood that when the facing is altered, one or more other specifications may be affected significantly enough to cause an undesirable side effect in performance. For a more thorough understanding of this complex area you should read and study Chapters 11, 21, 22, 35 and 36 from Ralph Maltby's book, *Golf Club Design, Fitting, Alteration and Repair*.

The amount of bend that can be made in a shaft depends upon the shaft material. Standard weight shafts made of carbon steel — i.e., True Temper's® Dynamic®, ProFit®, and Jet Step® — can be safely bent as much as four degrees. Lightweight shafts such as True Temper's TT Lite® or Flex-Flow®, should be bent a maximum of two degrees. Lightweight shafts tend to have thinner walls and larger diameters and therefore are more easily broken or kinked than a standard weight shaft. Attempting a bend of more than two degrees on a lightweight shaft should not be attempted. Shafts that fall into the very lightweight category — i.e., True Temper's® Extralite® or Brunswick Golf's® UCV-304® — cannot be bent without breaking or kinking the shaft and as such altering these shafts should not be attempted. Shafts made of composite materials such as graphite, fiberglass or aramid-fiber, simply cannot be permanently bent and this also should not be attempted.

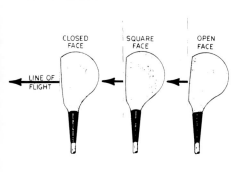

12-1 The above drawing defines a closed, square and open clubface. "Open" is sometimes referred to as "Slice" and "Closed" is referred to as "Hook." It should be noted that when the club is in the playing position, what the face angle appears to the golfer and what the face angle actually measures are two different observations.

12-2 An accurate gauge, such as the **Golf Club Gauge**, must be used to determine the actual face angle. Note the indicator shows the face to be open by 2 degrees. An actual 2° open reading will give the club the appearance of being straight-faced or "square" in the playing position.

12-3 Here is another method for determining what the face angle really is. Lean the club against a wall so the shaft is vertical but the club is in a normal lie playing position. Observe the face from the position shown in this photo (in front of the club). By looking at the clubface from this direction, you are bypassing the factors that give the club the appearance of being 2° more hooked than it really is.

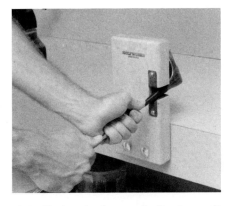

12-4 **Closing the face angle.** To close a 2° open face, the clubface is pointed downward in the shaft bending block and the shaft bent downward as shown. See Chapter 11 for bending procedure and information on the **Shaft Bending Block.**

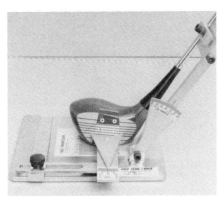

12-5 After bending the shaft, the gauge now shows the face to be 0° or square. However, when the club is placed in the playing position, it will appear to be closed to the golfer.

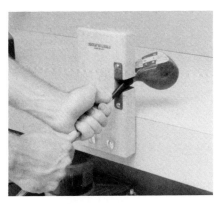

12-6 **Opening the face angle.** Point the face up and bend downward on the shaft. If the owner does not like the change, the face angle can be easily returned to its original angle.

12-7 Another way to change the face angle can be achieved by filing the face. Usually 1 or 2 degrees is the maximum and depends on each particular clubhead shape and top line progression.

12-8 **To open the face angle,** file from the middle of the insert out to the toe. Periodically check the bulge, roll and loft to ensure these face specifications remain the same. Virtually every clubface can be opened through filing. A 1° change requires approximately ⅛″ of material removed from the edge of the face. This amount decreases proportionately as you near the center of the face.

12-9 This photo shows the filed clubface. Note it is sometimes necessary to remove the insert screw(s) before filing. See Chapter 4, photos 4-3 thru 4-18 for insert screw removal. See Chapter 15 for touch-up steps after filing.

12-10 **To close the face angle,** file from the middle of the insert back toward the heel. Maintain correct bulge, roll and loft. Closing the face through filing requires some material to be removed from the top line along the hosel. Many clubfaces cannot be closed due to a lack of top line progression.

12-11 **Reboring the hosel can effect a plus or minus 1° change in face angle.** This is a difficult procedure and should only be tried by the experienced club repairman. The repairman is making use of the existing hosel bore and does not plug the bore before redrilling.

12-12 **To close the face angle,** drill into the hosel with the appropriate size drill bit. Favor the back side of the hosel with the end of the bit while drilling. **Note: Either apply whipping or masking tape around the hosel to prevent splitting during drilling.**

12-13 **To open the face angle,** drill into the hosel with the appropriate size drill bit. Favor the face side of the hosel with the end of the bit while drilling.

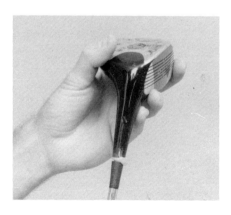

12-14 When reinstalling the shaft, make sure the shaft is shifted to the proper angle. It may be necessary to use a shim to take up the excess space in the hosel. See Chapter 8 for installing a loose shaft.

NOTES

13

CHANGING SWINGWEIGHT OF WOOD CLUBS

Changing the swingweight of woods requires the use of a swingweight scale. Other tools required are standard shop tools such as screwdrivers, a drill, drill bits and a propane torch. Weighting materials, such as various forms of lead, are needed to add weight to the head if an increase in swingweight is desired.

The most common material used by club manufacturers for weighting wood heads is lead. Lead is available at most hardware stores, plumbing supply houses, or golf repair supplies dealers.

The need to increase or decrease the swingweight will fall under two categories:

1) The owner of the club wishes to increase or decrease the total weight of the club by increasing or decreasing swingweight, or, he wishes to change the relative stiffness (flex feel) of the golf shaft by increasing or decreasing swingweight. When the swingweight is increased (weight added to the head), the shaft feels more flexible. When the swingweight is decreased (weight removed from the head), the shaft feels stiffer. Obviously, increasing or decreasing swingweight (headweight) to raise or lower the total weight will also change the relative stiffness of the shaft.

2) Virtually every repair will affect the club's swingweight. For instance, refinishing a club will usually lower the swingweight 1-2 swingweight points. Regripping can change swingweight if the new grip is not the same weight as the old grip. Reshafting a club will change the swingweight if the same shaft length and weight are not maintained. Acquiring the knowledge and skill that will allow you to change swingweight is very important.

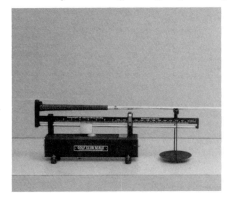

13-1 Before any change in swingweight takes place, the existing swingweight must be determined using a swingweight scale. See Chapter 17 for various types and models of swingweight scales.

13-2 It is also a good idea to check and record the golf club's total weight. Again, Chapter 17 will tell you which swingweight scales also measure total weight.

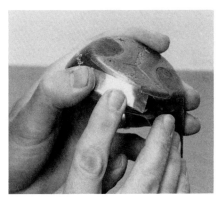

13-3 The simplest method to increase swingweight is by adding lead tape to the back of the head. This can also be used on a trial basis if the customer wishes to see what the added weight feels like before making a permanent weight increase under the soleplate. **A strip of ½″ lead tape 4½″ long will increase swingweight 1 point.**

13-4 Rub the tape to burnish it and make it conform and stick to the curved surface of the head. A wooden or plastic tool handle works well.

13-5 Swingweight can also be increased or decreased by adding or removing weight from under the soleplate. First, the soleplate must be removed, as outlined in Chapter 3.

13-6 Twist drills with ¼″ shanks or flat type wood bits work well for drilling wood heads. Sizes recommended are: ¼″, ⅜″ ⁷⁄₁₆″ and ½″ diameter twist drills or ¼″, ⅜″ ⁷⁄₁₆″, ½″, ¾″ and 1″ diameter flat bore bits.

13-25 **An alternative to the weight port** is to use a trick some manufacturers use. First, locate a number or letter stamping that is large enough to allow a ⅛″ bit to pass through. It is also helpful if the drilled hole is located in the center of the soleplate and in line with the cavity under the soleplate.

13-26 Drill through the soleplate with a ⅛″ bit.

13-27 Lead powder can be poured through the hole into the cavity.

13-28 The hole is now filled with an aluminum colored or black epoxy. Carefully cut or file excess epoxy to complete what can be a very slick method for weight increases in selected cases.

13-29 Once finished, the camouflaged hole is hardly noticed. Installing a set screw or drilling through a soleplate is an acceptable practice for some clubs and may be requested by customers wishing to make their own future changes. However, avoid the two previously described methods when working with antique or classic clubs.

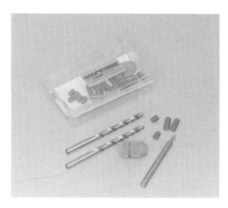

13-30 **The Changeable Swingweight Kit** allows swingweight increases without installation of a set screw.

13-31 First, remove a soleplate screw, drill a ¼″ diameter hole to accommodate either a ⁵⁄₁₆″ or ⅝″ long lead cylinder. ⁵⁄₁₆″ cylinder = 1 swingweight point. ⅝″ cylinder = 2 swingweight points.

13-32 After drilling, install the lead cylinder with a special punch which is included with the kit. It is not necessary to install the lead cylinder with epoxy since the screw will expand the lead cylinder to fit securely.

13-33 Because the lead cylinders are predrilled, simply reinstall the original screw with a dab of epoxy on the tip end of the screw. The reinstalled screw should fit flush with the soleplate.

NOTES

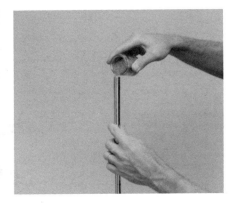

13-34 See Chapter 17 photos 17-7 thru 17-12 for steps to increase swingweight by adding lead powder or lead rod down the shaft.

ADDITIONAL INFORMATION FOR CHANGING SWINGWEIGHT OF WOOD CLUBS

TABLE 13-1
Weight Port Screw — Installation Data

[1]Weight Port Screw Size	Tap Drill Size	[2]Tap Size	Hex Key Wrench Size	Coarse or Fine Thread
#8-32 × 3⁄16″ lg.	#29	#8-32	5⁄64″	Coarse
#10-24 × 3⁄16″ lg.	#25	#10-24	3⁄32″	Coarse
#10-32 × 3⁄16″ lg.	#21	#10-32	3⁄32″	Fine
1⁄4-20 × 3⁄16″ lg.	#7	1⁄4-20	1⁄8″	Coarse
1⁄4-28 × 3⁄16″ lg.	#3	1⁄4-28	1⁄8″	Fine
5⁄16-18 × 1⁄4″ lg.	F	5⁄16-18	5⁄32″	Coarse
5⁄16-24 × 1⁄4″ lg.	I	5⁄16-24	5⁄32″	Fine

[1] Weight port screws are actually "Socket Head Set Screws."
[2] The first number is the "Outside Thread Diameter" and the second number denotes the "Threads Per Inch."

Some Helpful Hints Pertaining to Swingweight
- For every 1⁄2″ increase in a club's length, the swingweight will increase by 3 points.
- For every 1⁄2″ decrease in a club's length, the swingweight will decrease by 3 points.
- If you would like to check a club's swingweight before installing the grip and any tape, allow 9 points (10 points for leather, cord or oversize rubber). Example: Ungripped club swingweights at E-0; it will probably be D-1 after gripping with an average weight 1¾ ounce rubber grip.
- Finishing a clubhead usually increases swingweight from 1½ to 2 points (stain, filler, colorcoat, clear finish and whipping).
- Every 4 swingweights are equivalent to approximately 1⁄4 ounce (7.09 grams). A swingweight point in a wood head is approximately .065 ounce (2 grams). See Fig. 13-35.
- A swingweight point in the grip end of a wood is approximately .13 ounces (4 grams) or twice as much as is required in the head end. .13 ounce added to the grip end will decrease swingweight by 1 point. (This is called "counterbalancing") and .13 ounce taken out of the grip end will increase swingweight by 1 point. See Fig. 13-35.

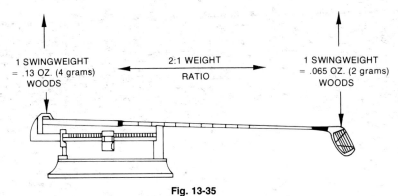

Fig. 13-35
Approximate swingweight equivalents for grip and head ends of club

• The lighter the shaft, the heavier the head weight must be to obtain the same swingweight that you would get with a heavier shaft. Even though the head weight is heavier with the lighter shaft, the total weight of the club will still be less. For a general rule of thumb, use the following: For each 1 ounce reduction in shaft weight, a wood club will lose approximately 5 swingweight points. This, of course, assumes that the grip weight and shaft length are exactly the same. Example: A set of D-2 woods with Dynamic® tip taper shafts (4⅜ ounces) are reshafted with Extralite® tip taper shafts 3⅜ ounces). Without reweighting the heads, the swingweight would now be C-7. Approximately 5/16 ounce of weight would have to be added to the heads to achieve a D-2 swingweight. The Extralite® shaft is 1 ounce lighter, leaving a net reduction in total club weight of 11/16 ounce. For a comparative look at what happened, refer to the driver example in Table 13-2. The design chapters in the *Golf Club Design, Fitting, Alteration & Repair* book will explain technically why head weights must be increased when changing to or using lighter shafts.

TABLE 13-2					
Effect of Different Weight Shafts on Driver Head Weight, Total Weight and Swingweight					
	Driver Before Change: Dynamic® Tip Taper Shaft	**Driver After Change: Extralite® Tip Taper Shaft**	**Difference From Change**	**Club Specs: Reweighted to D-2**	**Net Change In Club**
Shaft Weight (ounces)	4.37	3.37	− 1	3.37	− 1
Head Weight (ounces)	7	7	Same	7.31	+ .31
Grip Weight (ounces)	1.75	1.75	Same	1.75	None
Total Weight (ounces)	13.12	12.12	− 1	12.43	− .69
Swingweight	D-2	C-7	− 5	D-2	+ 5

Note: A 1 ounce reduction in shaft weight for an iron club would decrease swingweight by 3 points because of the shorter shaft length. Refer to Chapter 15 of *Golf Club Design, Fitting, Alteration & Repair* book.

• Installing face screws or replacing them with a larger size will affect swingweight. Table 13-3 has been developed for you to use as a guideline for face screw weights and swingweight equivalents.

TABLE 13-3								
Effect of Face Screw Weights on Swingweight								
Description:	**Brass Screw Size**	**Weight Per Screw**	**Weight of 4 Screws**	**Swingweight Equivalent[2]**	**Weight of 5 Screws**	**Swingweight Equivalent[2]**	**Weight of 6 Screws**	**Swingweight Equivalent[2]**
Standard Size Face Screw	#4 × ⅝ Lg.	.6 grams	2.4 grams	+ 1¼	3 grams	+ 1½	3.6 grams	+ 1¾
Oversize Face Screw	#5 × ¾ Lg.	.95 grams	3.8 grams	+ 1⅞	4.8 grams	+ 2⅜	5.7 grams	+ 2⅞
Standard Soleplate Screw[1]	#7 × ¾ Lg.	1.43 grams	5.7 grams	+ 2⅞	7.1 grams	+ 3½	8.6 grams	+ 4⅜

[1] In some older clubs standard soleplate screws were also used in the face.
[2] Swingweight equivalent means the number of swingweight points a club will change.

- The #5 × 1⅛″ steel shaft locking screw weighs 1.45 grams and is equivalent to ¾ of a swingweight point.
- The tapered hardwood plug on through bore shafts weighs 1.52 grams and is equivalent to ¾ of a swingweight point.
- A dollar bill weighs 1 gram and equivalent to ½ of a swingweight point. A dime weighs 2 grams and is equivalent to 1 point. A quarter weighs 6 grams and is equivalent to 3 points.
- A cycolac (ABS plastic) or fiber insert weighs approximately 14 grams in a driver or an equivalent of 7 swingweights. A Gamma Fire™ insert of the same size weighs approximately 32 grams in a driver or an equivalent of 16 swingweights. If you change a standard plastic insert to a Gamma Fire™ insert, you can plan on increasing swingweight by almost 9 points. Therefore, to maintain the original swingweight, you must remove a little over 9/16 ounce (17 grams) from the head.
- If you use ½″ wide lead tape, it takes approximately a 4½″ long piece to weigh 2 grams or be equivalent to 1 swingweight point.
- An average length whipping of .022″ braided or twisted nylon will weigh approximately 1.5 grams or an equivalent of ¾ swingweight point.
- To convert grams to ounces, divide by 28.35.
- To convert ounces to grams, multiply by 28.35. 1 ounce = 28.35 grams.

TABLE 13-4
Swingweight Conversion Chart
Official Swingweight Scale vs. Lorythmic Swingweight Scale

Official Swingweight Scale Reading	Lorythmic Scale Swingweight Woods	Irons	Official Swingweight Scale Reading	Lorythmic Scale Swingweight Woods	Irons
18.33	C0	B8	20.00	D0	C8
18.4	0.4	8.4	20.05	0.3	8.3
18.45	0.7	8.7	20.1	0.6	8.6
			20.15	0.9	8.9
18.5	C1	B9	20.17	D1	C9
18.55	1.3	9.3			
18.6	1.6	9.6	20.2	1.2	9.2
			20.25	1.5	9.5
18.65	C2	C0	20.3	1.8	9.8
18.7	2.2	0.2	20.33	D2	D0
18.75	2.5	0.5			
18.8	2.8	0.8	20.35	2.1	0.1
			20.4	2.4	0.4
18.83	C3	C1	20.45	2.7	0.7
18.85	3.1	1.1	20.5	D3	D1
18.9	3.4	1.4			
18.95	3.7	1.7	20.55	3.3	1.3
			20.6	3.6	1.6
19.00	C4	C2	20.65	D4	D2
19.05	4.3	2.3			
19.1	4.6	2.6	20.7	4.2	2.2
19.15	4.9	2.9	20.75	4.5	2.5
			20.8	4.8	2.8
19.17	C5	C3	20.83	D5	D3
19.2	5.2	3.2			
19.25	5.5	3.5	20.85	5.1	3.1
19.3	5.8	3.8	20.9	5.4	3.4
			20.95	5.7	3.7
19.33	C6	C4	21.00	D6	D4
19.35	6.1	4.1			
19.4	6.4	4.4	21.05	6.3	4.3
19.45	6.7	4.7	21.1	6.6	4.6
			21.15	6.9	4.9
19.5	C7	C5	21.17	D7	D5
19.55	7.3	5.3			
19.6	7.6	5.6	21.2	7.2	5.2
19.65	7.9	5.9	21.25	7.5	5.5
			21.3	7.8	5.8
19.66	C8	C6	21.33	D8	D6
19.7	8.2	6.2			
19.75	8.5	6.5	21.35	8.1	6.1
19.8	8.8	6.8	21.4	8.4	6.4
			21.45	8.7	6.7
19.83	C9	C7	21.5	D9	D7
19.85	9.1	7.1			
19.9	9.4	7.4	21.55	9.3	7.3
19.95	9.7	7.7	21.6	9.6	7.6
			21.65	9.9	7.9
			21.66	E0	D8

14

BRASS AND LEAD BACKWEIGHT REMOVAL, INSTALLATION & REFITTING

Many of the woods manufactured today and especially in the past have some sort of backweight. Backweights can range from a hunk of brass screwed on the back of the club to a poured lead inset routed into the back. The latter is most indicative of early and classic type MacGregor® clubs. Backweights do become loose as in the case of brass backweights and they also shift, slide and mushroom as in the case of poured lead backweights. During the course of normal repairs, you run across these situations and it is necessary to offer a concise explanation of how to repair them.

Also, with the popularizing of custom club making and component assembly, it is also necessary to cover the installation of new lead and brass backweights in both new and used clubs.

14-1   A loose brass backweight is usually identified by a rattling sound or the existence of a gap between the wood and the backweight.

14-2   To tighten a loose brass backweight, first clean out the screw head recesses using a scriber or sharpened awl.

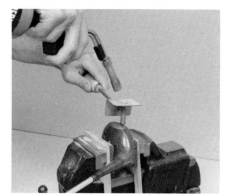

14-3   If the screws will not turn out, heat them with a propane torch and a screw heater or . . .

14-4   . . . use the **Electric Screw Extractor.**

14-5   Next, remove the screws. Screw heads may be either a straight slot, Phillips style or Frearson type.

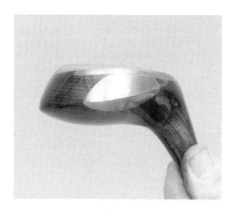

14-6   Some manufacturers are very clever in disguising the screws. The photo shows a backweight held on with a headless brass backweight screw. Virtually every backweight will have a screw of one type or another. Examine a backweight closely if it doesn't have an obvious slotted type screw.

14-7 Procedure for removing headless screws. Drill ⅛" deep into the center of the screw head with ⁵⁄₆₄" drill bit. Note: Making a slight indentation into the center of the head with an awl or a center punch will keep the bit from walking around and help start it correctly.

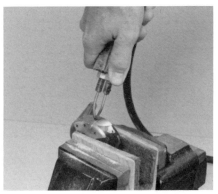

14-8 Heat the screw as previously shown.

14-9 Tap a #1 size extractor into the hole until it bites and turn the extractor counterclockwise. Note the use of the "T" handle tap Wrench.

14-10 The screw is now removed.

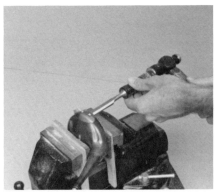

14-11 Next, insert a ½" wide or smaller wood chisel as shown and gently tap with a hammer. Heat the backweight if it will not come off easily. Avoid damaging the wood around the backweight. A heat gun works well for this.

14-12 If the backweight rests against the soleplate, remove the soleplate as outlined in Chapter 3. The only reason to remove the soleplate is to gain access to the bottom of the backweight so it can be removed with the chisel if it will not come loose otherwise.

14-13 Remove the brass backweight. Use a smooth cut file to clean off all old epoxy from flat side of the backweight.

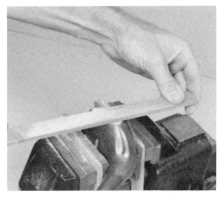

14-14 Carefully remove any glue from the flat portion of the wood. Maintain a perfectly flat surface.

14-15 Mix up some shear strength epoxy, apply it to the wood and . . .

14-16 . . . also apply epoxy to the backweight.

14-17 Place the backweight in place and install the original screws or use new screws. If the backweight turns out of place as a result of turning the screws in . . .

14-18 . . . set the backweight in the desired position and lay a couple layers of masking tape across the backweight to ensure it doesn't move. This usually only occurs when a backweight has a single screw. Most backweights utilize two screws for safety.

14-19 Wipe off all excess epoxy and reinstall soleplate (if previously removed) as outlined in Chapter 3. Club is now ready for refinishing.

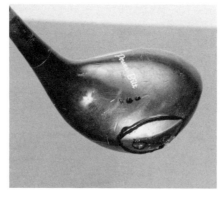

14-20 Photo shows another club with the backweight reinstalled. Note the epoxy that has been hydraulically squeezed up through the top of the club. Do not be alarmed if this happens. Persimmon is an open grain wood and the above reaction is quite common.

14-21 Installing a new brass backweight. First remove the soleplate. Also, after the soleplate is removed, check to see if any weight can be removed from the head. The addition of a brass backweight will add ½ to 1½ ounces of weight to the head. This increase needs to be offset by the removal of the same amount of weight from the head.

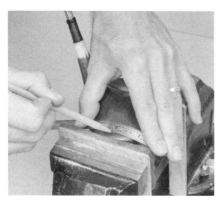

14-22 Next, mark the portion of wood to be sawed using a straight edge and pencil.

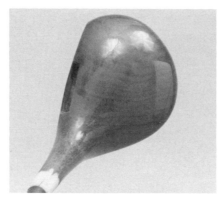

14-23 The line indicating where the cut is to be made should "appear" to be parallel to the face. In actuality, the line will be drawn slightly open to the face if it is to look parallel. If the line is drawn exactly parallel, it will appear to be closed relative to the face. See notes on this at the end of the chapter.

14-24 With a hacksaw or on a bandsaw, carefully follow the line and cut off the back portion of the wood.

14-25 Use a file or a belt sander to make sure the sawed portion of the wood is absolutely flat.

14-26 Check for absolute flatness first in one direction and . . .

14-27 . . . also in the other direction. A 6″ steel scale works well for this.

14-28 Check the backweight for proper fit and location. Minor changes can be made through filing if backweight does not appear to be in the correct location.

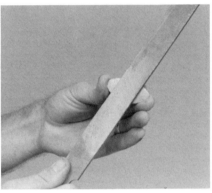

14-29 Lightly abrade the flat side of the backweight for better epoxy adhesion.

14-30 If a predrilled backweight is being used, place the backweight in place and mark the location of the screw holes using the holes in the backweight as a guide.

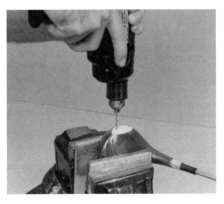

14-31 Drill the screw holes in the wood head. The drill bit size is determined by the size of the screw used. A ⅛″ bit is normally used.

14-32 After applying the epoxy to both the backweight and the wood, lay the backweight in place.

14-33 Apply a dab of epoxy to each screw and screw the backweight down tightly. A #7 brass screw is being used here.

14-52 Place several pieces of lead material in a ladle and melt it using a propane torch.

14-53 An alternative to melting lead is to use the **Electric Hot Pot with stand.** This is very handy for keeping lead molten in a repair shop.

14-54 Carefully pour molten lead into the cavity. Lead can burn the head more than is necessary if it gets too hot. Before pouring, the lead should be just above the temperature at which it solidifies.

14-55 Allow lead to cool for 5 to 10 minutes.

14-56 Remove putty from the head.

14-57 Using a ball peen hammer, mushroom lead in middle and around edges so that it becomes very tight in the cavity.

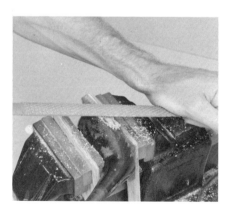

14-58 Use a "Rasp" or coarse cut file and rough shape the lead.

14-59 Next, switch to a fine file and smooth the lead so it blends perfectly with the wood.

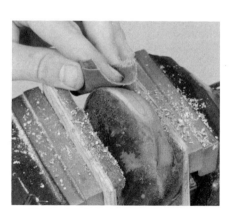

14-60 Finally, sand the lead smooth.

14-25 Use a file or a belt sander to make sure the sawed portion of the wood is absolutely flat.

14-26 Check for absolute flatness first in one direction and . . .

14-27 . . . also in the other direction. A 6″ steel scale works well for this.

14-28 Check the backweight for proper fit and location. Minor changes can be made through filing if backweight does not appear to be in the correct location.

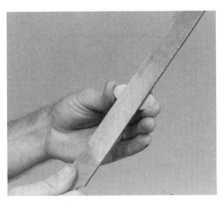

14-29 Lightly abrade the flat side of the backweight for better epoxy adhesion.

14-30 **If a predrilled backweight is being used,** place the backweight in place and mark the location of the screw holes using the holes in the backweight as a guide.

14-31 Drill the screw holes in the wood head. The drill bit size is determined by the size of the screw used. A ⅛″ bit is normally used.

14-32 After applying the epoxy to both the backweight and the wood, lay the backweight in place.

14-33 Apply a dab of epoxy to each screw and screw the backweight down tightly. A #7 brass screw is being used here.

14-34 Wipe off excess epoxy. Allow epoxy to cure. After the epoxy has cured, proceed to photo 14-42 for completion steps.

14-35 **If an undrilled backweight is used,** lay the backweight in place after applying epoxy to both the backweight and wood.

14-36 Lay a couple of layers of tape across the backweight and wood to ensure the backweight doesn't move. Allow the epoxy to cure.

14-37 After the epoxy has hardened, determine whether you wish to install one or two screws.

14-38 If one screw is installed, make a slight indentation into the center of the backweight but on the bottom half. Two screws require two indentations at points that are approximately equidistant from the center.

14-39 Drill through the backweight and into the head with a ⁹⁄₆₄" drill bit. (This is the pilot drill for a #8 screw.)

14-40 Next, countersink the pilot holes to a depth that allows most of the screw head to seat below the surface of the backweight.

14-41 Install the appropriate screw. A #8 screw is being used here. A dab of epoxy is usually applied to the screw before installation.

14-42 After the epoxy has cured, file the backweight to shape using a medium cut and then a fine cut file.

14-43 Sand the backweight smooth by hand or on a sanding machine using 150 grit to remove all scratches.

14-44 The finished backweight should look like this. Check the swingweight and make any necessary adjustments as shown in Chapter 13. Reinstall the soleplate as shown in Chapter 3 and then refer to Chapter 1 for refinishing steps.

14-45 Aluminum backweights are also used. Aluminum is lighter than brass and is sometimes more desirable for larger model drivers that will not allow the addition of a heavy brass backweight.

14-46 Procedure for repouring a lead backweight. Lead backweights sometimes fall out, become loose or mushroom and overflow like this one.

14-47 To remove this type of a backweight, drill a 7/32" hole at the point shown in the photo. Drill at angle shown. Drill another hole on the opposite side. Occasionally a center hole should be drilled if the backweight has a center plug extending into the wood head.

14-48 Using an awl or very narrow 1/4" width wood chisel, gently tap and pry all of the . . .

14-49 . . . old lead from the cavity. The three previously drilled holes should be empty of all lead and debris as they will act as a mechanical lock when the new lead backweight is repoured.

14-50 First, use "Mortite" putty to form a dam around the cavity.

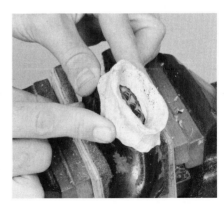

14-51 Press the putty down tight on the head and shape it like the old backweight. Do not allow any of the Mortite to rest inside the cavity.

14-52 Place several pieces of lead material in a ladle and melt it using a propane torch.

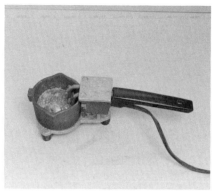

14-53 An alternative to melting lead is to use the **Electric Hot Pot with stand.** This is very handy for keeping lead molten in a repair shop.

14-54 Carefully pour molten lead into the cavity. Lead can burn the head more than is necessary if it gets too hot. Before pouring, the lead should be just above the temperature at which it solidifies.

14-55 Allow lead to cool for 5 to 10 minutes.

14-56 Remove putty from the head.

14-57 Using a ball peen hammer, mushroom lead in middle and around edges so that it becomes very tight in the cavity.

14-58 Use a "Rasp" or coarse cut file and rough shape the lead.

14-59 Next, switch to a fine file and smooth the lead so it blends perfectly with the wood.

14-60 Finally, sand the lead smooth.

14-61 Installing a new lead backweight. Use a pencil and straight edge to determine outline and location. The shape and size is left up to the individual.

14-62 Using a ⁷⁄₃₂″ drill bit, drill ⅝″ deep at angle shown.

14-63 Drill another ⁷⁄₃₂″ diameter hole in the opposite side at angle shown.

14-64 With a small round wood rasp, file back and forth to get desired shape.

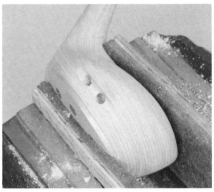

14-65 Cavity should look like this.

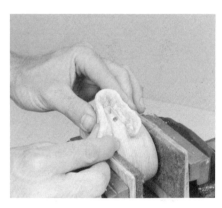

14-66 Next, form dam with "Mortite" putty. Press putty down tightly.

14-67 Be sure the dam is high enough and formed properly. Check to make sure no Mortite putty is in the cavity.

14-68 Pour in the molten lead.

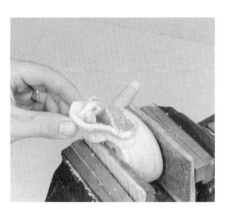

14-69 Remove putty dam.

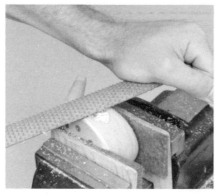

14-70 Next, peen the lead in its middle and all around the edges to lock it tightly in the cavity.

14-71 Rough shape the backweight with a "rasp" or coarse cut file. Then file the backweight with a fine cut file until smooth and flush with the wood.

14-72 The finished lead backweight should look like this after it has been hand or machine sanded smooth. Refer to Chapter 1 for refinishing steps.

ADDITIONAL INFORMATION FOR BRASS AND LEAD BACKWEIGHT REMOVAL, INSTALLATION AND REFITTING

Installing a backweight on a head which previously did not have one requires that the backweight be properly lined up with the face. The most common mistake is to install the backweight parallel with the face. This of course seems to be the logical approach, but the result will be a backweight which will appear quite hooked in relation to the face. In actual fact, a backweight should be installed 4-6° open to the face so that it appears parallel or square with the face. See Fig. 14-73.

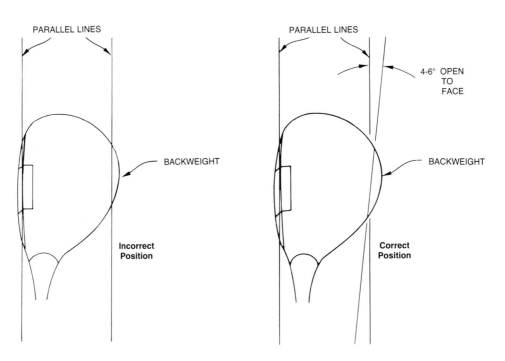

Fig. 14-73
Proper positioning for a backweight

The backweight location in the toe to heel direction should be as close to the center of the face as possible; however, this is dictated more by clubhead shape and back radius than by personal choice. The backweight will vary some from the face center position, but remember, the weight of all the head's components determines the center of gravity (center of mass) location in the heel to toe direction. Therefore, the center of gravity in the head can still be located on the face center in the heel and toe direction even though the backweight is slightly forward or back.

NOTES

15

FINISH REFURBISHING AND TOUCH-UP TECHNIQUES — WOODS

When you are working with a club that benefits from a refinish, the end result should be a club that appears as if it had just been finished at the factory. The challenge when working with a clubhead that does not benefit from a refinish is to present the repaired head in a condition that is as good if not better than when it was first given to you.

The difficulty with this challenge will range from fairly simple, i.e., touching up a reshafted club, to very difficult as when refurbishing a clubhead that has had the insert reset or replaced and the soleplate reset. As more clubhead components are removed, and consequently more of the original finish is disturbed, the more difficult the touch-up job becomes.

Touching up the finish on a repaired clubhead is absolutely necessary not only for the obvious cosmetic reasons, but also to ensure that the clubhead will not absorb moisture that results in a rotting of the wood in the exposed area. The following pages will aid you when refurbishing or touching up the finish after your clubhead repairs are complete.

15-1 Finish refurbish and whip hosel. The purpose is to take an existing club with a dull, worn or marred finish and substantially improve it, while at the same time sealing the club from moisture absorption. The procedure benefits woods that are reshafted or rewhipped or simply a wood requiring a general clean-up or winterizing service.

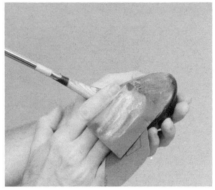

15-2 First, carefully hand sand the entire clubhead with 400 grade sandpaper. This will level an uneven surface. Be careful not to sand through the old finish.

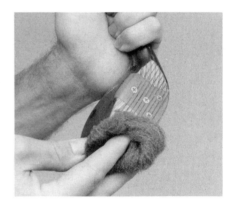

15-3 Hand or machine steel wool the head using 000 steel wool. Steel wooling will blend in the scratches left behind by the fine sandpaper. If necessary, touch up any bare spots with a matching stain color.

15-4 Next, wrap a paper towel around the shaft above the hosel. Dip the clubhead into the poly. After the poly stops flowing from the head and begins to drip . . .

15-5 . . . turn the toe upright with the face slightly open as shown. Note: Whitty Dippers, a small stretchable disc, can be used instead of paper towels to prevent the polyurethane from running down the shaft.

15-6 Allow the poly coating to cure overnight. Whipping can then be applied as shown in Chapter 2. This refurbish and new whipping can make a wood look like new.

15-7 How to touch up the face. This touch-up technique applies to a wood whose face has been filed clean of finish. Repairs that could cause this would be insert resetting or replacement, loft, bulge, roll or face angle alterations. First, remove the whipping if it is not already off the club.

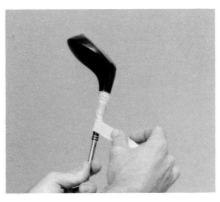

15-8 A club with a plastic whipping cover should be covered with masking tape.

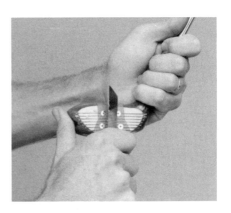

15-9 Scrape the entire face with the **Detail Knife.** This effectively removes all file or sandpaper marks and creates a smooth surface.

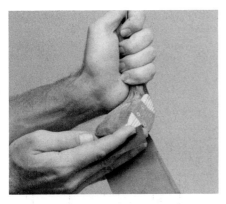

15-10 Hand sand the entire club with 400 grade sandpaper. Hand or machine steel wool the sanded surface using 000 steel wool.

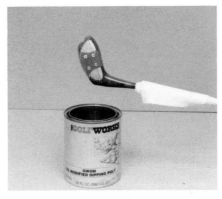

15-11 Dip a coat of polyurethane. Allow the coating to cure overnight.

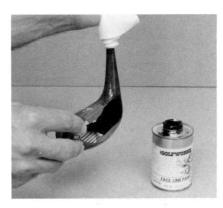

15-12 Face lines are paint filled by wiping or brushing a quick dry enamel into the grooves. Scoring line paint is available from most golf supply houses.

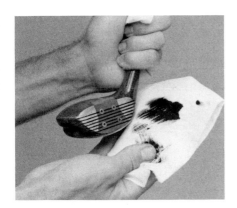

15-13 Wipe off excess scoring line paint with a paper towel which is alternately folded back and forth to expose a clean surface. Dampening the towel with Naphtha or Grip Solvent and wiping across the face will remove stubborn paint. Allow face paint to dry 12 hours.

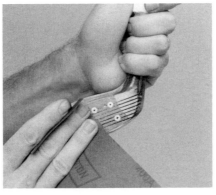

15-14 After the scoring line paint has dried, lightly hand sand the face and head with 400 grit sandpaper and then hand or machine steel wool the head with 000 steel wool.

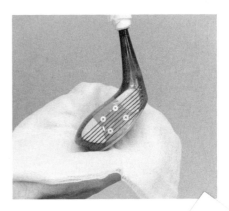

15-15 Prior to every polyurethane c lightly wipe the head with a tack rag ' all dust or steel wool particles are rer

15-16 Dip a final coat of polyurethane. This two-coat dipping process is very effective in sealing the face from moisture. Some repairmen may wish to dip an additional coat for a more even clubface surface after once again sanding and steel wooling the head.

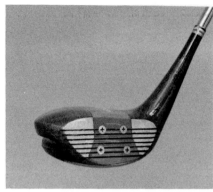

15-17 After the polyurethane has dried, the club is ready for whipping following steps shown in Chapter 2.

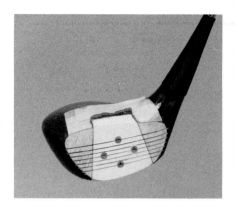

15-18 How to touch up around the top of the insert. This skill is needed when replacing or resetting an insert. Note the use of masking tape around the top of the insert. This protects the finish from epoxy.

15-19 The top of the insert must be flush with the finish. Once excess epoxy and any masking tape has been removed (see Chapter 5 photos 5-41 thru 5-44 for removal of excess epoxy and tape), lightly scrape the top of the insert with a Detail Knife to bring the top of the insert down flush to the top of the finish.

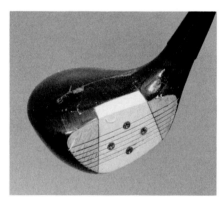

15-20 Once the level of the finish and the insert are even, minor scratches in the finish are easily removed by . . .

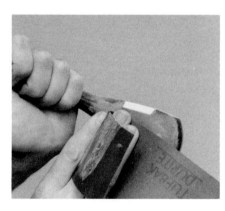

15-21 . . . hand sanding the area with 400 sandpaper. Remove whipping before sanding. If sanded properly, this will remove the scratches left from filing or scraping. DO NOT SAND THROUGH THE FINISH.

15-22 Next, lightly steel wool the sanded area with 000 steel wool.

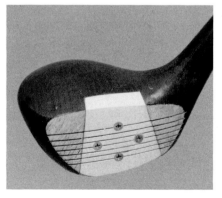

15-23 The club is now ready for touch-up steps applicable to the face as shown in photos 15-7 thru 15-17.

15-24 How to touch up a break in the finish. Photo shows an area of the club where too much filing or sanding has resulted in breaking through the finish into the bare wood. This procedure also applies when the stain or wood filler is inadvertently scraped from the head when detailing the face.

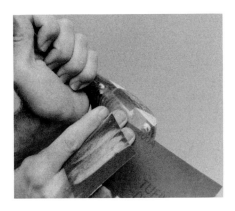

15-25 First, fine sand the damaged area with 400 grade paper to "feather in" the sharp edges of the poly. This step may enlarge the damaged area; however, it is necessary to create a smooth surface.

15-26 Next, select a stain that matches the color of the wood. Dip a paper towel or cloth into the stain and . . .

15-27 . . . blot the stained towel onto the damaged area. Open grain wood will accept stain and hopefully the newly stained area will match the rest of the club.

15-28 Often though, the newly stained area will be too light. Repeated staining will darken the color somewhat. Applying less intense black filler will help to darken the stain color slightly.

15-29 The best way to darken a light spot is as follows: Water base stains are available in dye powder form. Storing extra packets of the more popular colors in powder form will prove invaluable to you.

15-30 Dip damp paper towel or cloth into dye powder. Only a few grains are needed.

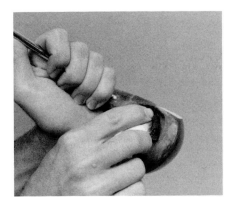

15-31 Rub the grains into the light area of the head.

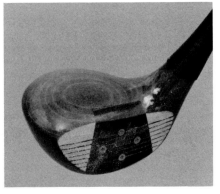

15-32 The difference in color will be dramatic. If the area is now too dark, simply rub the area with another paper towel dampened with plain water. This will dilute the intensity of the stain in the area. You will be amazed at the effectiveness of this step. This technique can be used anywhere on the clubhead.

15-33 Brush two coats of poly over any bare areas allowing an overnight dry between each coat.

15-34 Next, remove whipping if you have not already done so. Hand sand entire head with 400 grit sandpaper, steel wool with 000 steel wool and dip two coats of clear polyurethane finish.

15-35 Repaired area should match in color with the rest of the head.

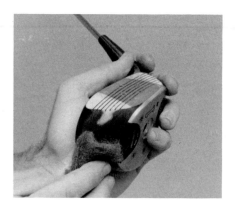

15-36 How to touch up bare spots on color-coted heads. Color-coted clubs are easier to fix than stained clubs. First, sand affected area to "feather in" finish around it. Next, 000 steel wool area and . . .

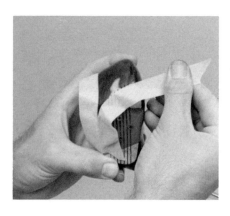

15-37 . . . apply masking tape over clubface and sole area to prevent color-cote over spray from getting on them.

15-38 Spray a couple of light coats of color-cote on bare area. Wait 15 minutes between each coat.

15-39 After 15 minutes of drying, remove the tape. Allow the color-cote to dry completely (see drying times at end of chapter for various color-cotes). Club is then ready for polyurethane coats. See photos 15-33 and 15-34 for final finishing steps.

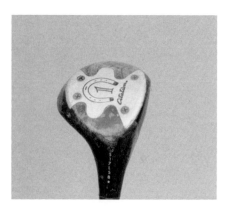

15-40 How to touch up the sole area. A skill that is required often because of the need to reset soleplates without completely refinishing the club. Also, after a through bore reshaft, the sole needs a touch-up.

15-41 One alternative is to simply hand sand the sole area and entire head with 400 sandpaper.

15-42 Next, hand or machine steel wool the entire head using 000 steel wool.

15-43 Dip a coat of polyurethane. This will properly reseal the head.

15-44 When the finish on the sole area is torn or sanded through, one must use another technique. First, using a mill or flat file, dress soleplate to blend the entire sole area smooth and flush as required.

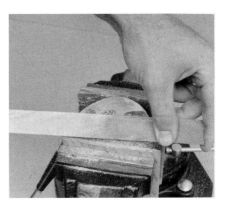

15-45 Next, blend in leading and trailing edges of soleplate as needed to obtain a flush fit.

15-46 This photo shows the sole area filed smooth and properly blended parts flush with each other.

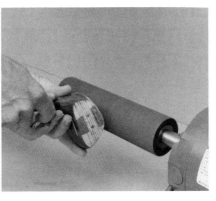

15-47 Sand the sole area by hand or machine using fine 150 grit sandpaper.

15-48 Lightly sand the edge of the polyurethane finish with 400 sandpaper. This will "feather in" the edge of the polyurethane so a smooth blending between the old and new coats will occur.

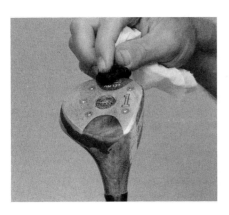

15-49 Select the color matching stain and blot the bare wood areas. Refer to photos 15-29 thru 15-32 if the stain color is too light. Allow a 4-6 hour drying time.

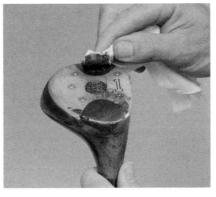

15-50 Next, apply either less intense black or natural filler to the exposed wood, depending upon whether you desire a slightly darker color or the present color. After filler has dried on the clubhead for 10 to 15 minutes, wipe excess with burlap or terry cloth. Allow to dry overnight.

15-51 After the filler has dried, refer to Chapter 1 photos 1-145 thru 1-149 for soleplate clean-up steps. Hand sand and steel wool all areas of the head except the soleplate area. Apply 2 coats of polyurethane allowing an overnight dry between each coat and 000 steel wool before the 2nd coat.

SECTION 2

GOLF IRON CLUB REPAIRS

NOTES

15-52 Photo shows finished sole area. Note how it blends in with the rest of the club after 2 coats of poly. The contents of this chapter should allow you to confidently repair the finish on any area of the club.

ADDITIONAL INFORMATION FOR FINISH REFURBISHING AND TOUCH-UP TECHNIQUES — WOODS

		Drying Times		
Product	**Application**	**Room Temp.**	**Force Dry***	**Compatibility Comments and General Notes**
GOLFWORKS® SYSTEMS				
GolfWorks® Water Base Stains	dip, brush, wipe or spray	4-6 hrs.	1 hr.	Can be used with anything. Dipping provides uniform coating.
GolfWorks® Oil Base Fillers	dip or brush & rub	12 hrs.	6 hrs.	Can be used with any polyurethane. Burnish well with burlap or coarse cloth when wiping. Do not steel wool.
GolfWorks® Rapid Dry Aerosol Colorcotes	aerosol	4-6 hrs.	2 hrs.	Must be used only with GolfWorks® Oil Modified or Moisture Cure Polyurethane. Do not apply heavy coat. Several light coats superior to one heavy coat. Do not sand or steel wool.
GolfWorks® Opaque Colorcotes	spray or brush	24 hrs.	12 hrs.	Must be used only with GolfWorks® Oil Modified or Moisture Cure Polyurethane. Do not apply heavy coat. If brushing, apply quickly to avoid streaks.
GolfWorks® Primer Sealer, Aerosol	aerosol	4 hrs.	1 hr.	Can be used with any polyurethane but specially formulated for Moisture Cure type polyurethane. Do not sand or steel wool.
GolfWorks® Primer Sealer, Spraying	spray	4 hrs.	1 hr.	Can be used with any polyurethane but specially formulated for Moisture Cure type polyurethane. Do not sand or steel wool.

TABLE 15-1
Compatibility of Various Finishing Products & Drying Times

TABLE 15-1 con't.
Compatibility of Various Finishing Products & Drying Times

Product	Application	Drying Times Room Temp.	Force Dry*	Compatibility Comments and General Notes
GolfWorks® Oil Modified Dipping Polyurethane	dip or spray	8 hrs.	4 hrs.	Do not apply on top of Moisture Cure Polyurethane. Usually requires 5-6 coats for quality finish.
GolfWorks® Moisture Cure Dipping Polyurethane	dip or spray	12-24 hrs.	8 hrs.	Do not apply on top of Mira-Dip or Mira Filler. Can be applied over other polyurethanes or fillers.
GolfWorks® Moisture Cure Spraying Polyurethane	spray	12-24 hrs.	8 hrs.	Do not apply on top of Mira-Dip or Mira Filler. Can be applied over other polyurethanes or fillers.
GolfWorks® Moisture Cure Aerosol Polyurethane	aerosol	12-24 hrs.	8 hrs.	Do not apply on top of Mira-Dip or Mira Filler. Can be applied over other polyurethanes or fillers.
CLUB-KIT SYSTEM				
Mira-Stains (alcohol base)	dip, brush, wipe or spray	3-6 hrs.	1 hr.	Can be used with anything. Dipping provides uniform coating.
Mira-Filler (polyurethane base)	dip or brush & rub	5 hrs.	2 hrs.	Use only with Mira-Dip.
Mira-Kote (polyurethane base)	spray or brush	12 hrs.	8 hrs.	Use only with Mira-Dip. Do not apply heavy coat. Several light coats superior to one heavy coat.
Mira-Kote Aerosol (polyurethane base)	aerosol	12 hrs.	8 hrs.	Same as above.
Dem-Kote Enamel	aerosol	4 hrs.	2 hrs.	Same as above.
Mira-Dip Oil Modified Polyurethane	dip or spray	8 hrs.	4 hrs.	Do not apply on top of Moisture Cure polyurethanes. Usually requires 5-6 coats for quality finish.
Mira-Spray Aerosol Oil Modified Polyurethane	aerosol	8 hrs.	4 hrs.	Do not apply on top of Moisture Cure polyurethanes.

*Force dry conditions: 30% to 50% relative humidity, 90° to 100° temperature.

NOTES

SECTION 2

GOLF IRON CLUB REPAIRS

16

REFINISHING AND RESCORING IRONS

Refinishing iron heads can be broken down into two types of procedures, namely rechroming and refurbishing.

Rechroming

It is very unlikely that any golf club repair shop will have a facility for rechroming an iron head. This is due to EPA regulations and the enormous capital investment required to start up such an operation. The two basic alternatives are:
1) Send the club to someone who specializes in rechroming irons, or
2) Send the club back to the original manufacturer for rechroming.

In many cases though, the manufacturer will send the club to a reputable shop that specializes in rechroming irons.

The rechroming process is as follows: The head is removed from the shaft; the old chrome and nickel are stripped off the head in strip tanks; the head is ground and buffed on special machinery to remove nicks and scratches; the face is outline masked and sandblasted; the head is nickel plated and the face sandblasted once more; the head is now chrome plated, the engravings in the head are paint filled and the head is reinstalled on the shaft.

Refurbishing

Refurbishing an iron head can run the gauntlet from complete repolishing of a non-chromeplated head to simple paint-filling of the head stampings in any iron head. Regardless of which steps are chosen, each can substantially improve the appearance of an iron head.

Repolishing a non-chromeplated head requires the following materials:
- Eight 8″ spiral-sewn buffing wheels; used for heavy and fine buffing work.
- Two 8″ sisal buffing wheels; used for the intermediate buffing step.
- #200 lea compound; when heavy cutting is required for the removal of nicks and scratches from the iron head.
- #173 glue compound; applied to the wheel for the sole purpose of keeping the lea compound on the wheel.
- Black sisal compound; an intermediate abrasive that evens out deep scratches left from coarser grit and/or removes minor scratches if the lea step was bypassed.
- White polishing compound; a fine abrasive with which a clubhead can be polished to a mirror finish — the last step in repolishing process.
- A double shafted ⅓ or ½ H.P. motor with a minimum R.P.M. of 3450.
- Buffing wheel rake; used to remove old compound from wheels.
- Heavy duty leather gloves; for protection because metal becomes very hot during the repolishing steps.
- Safety glasses or goggles; always wear eye protection.

Rescoring and Sandblasting Irons

The scoring lines on older clubs tend to wear, especially the lower ones on sand clubs. When an iron is being refurbished or rechromed, it is sometimes desirable to put the missing or worn lines back to like new condition. Also, it is possible to re-sandblast the face if you have the proper equipment.

This chapter shows you the methods of rescoring the traditional V-groove lines and sandblasting faces. Converting the V-groove scoring lines to the "box" groove scoring lines requires special milling equipment. The GolfWorks® offers this service.

16-1 Repolishing stainless steel heads: The following instructional steps are offered in conjunction with **The Buffing Shop,** a 20-piece buffing kit offered by The GolfWorks®. These steps are also applicable for any setup using the proper materials.

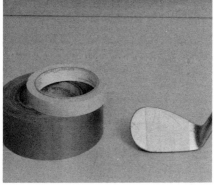

16-2 First, mask the sandblasted area of the face with duct tape or ¾″ masking tape.

16-3 Assemble four ¼″ stitched buff sections to one side of the buffer to make a 1″ wide wheel.

16-4 Apply a coating of #173 glue compound to the stitched wheels; hold the compound against the face of the wheel and turn the wheel on for 10-15 seconds while applying. Let the glue dry for one minute before proceeding. Note the use of leather gloves for this and all succeeding steps.

16-5 Next, apply the #200 lea compound, turning on the wheel for 10 seconds or until you get an even coating on the buffing sections. Wait 5 minutes before buffing. The longer the applied #200 compound is allowed to dry, the more abrasive it becomes. (This can be used to your advantage if deep nicks must be removed.)

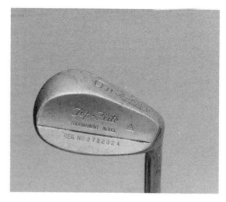

16-6 Photo shows a typical stainless steel iron head before buffing. Note the nicks in the sole.

16-7 Begin buffing the head, pressing it firmly on the wheel using a forward rolling motion. Note: Hold the head firmly in your hands; heads can sometimes be pulled from your hands.

16-8 The hosel may also need buffing. Place a screwdriver tip in the hosel. Hold the screwdriver handle while spinning the hosel against the wheel. Spin evenly to maintain proper shape of hosel.

16-9 Photo shows the same head after the buffing step. Note the nicks are removed. Take care when buffing around head stampings. The value of a classic club will drop if a head stamping is removed. Note: This finish is referred to as a satin finish and may be desired. If this is the case, proceed to photo 16-20 for final steps. If a high polish finish is desired, continue on to 16-10.

16-10 Next, assemble 2 sisal buff sections to the other side of the buffer.

16-11 Apply the black sisal compound against the face of the turning wheel. Apply a smooth coating of compound.

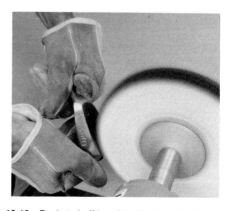

16-12 Begin to buff iron, blending in the buffing scratches from the #200 compound. Move head across face of wheel in a different direction from previous buffing step. This will effectively remove previous scratches. It is possible to begin the repolishing steps at this point if the head is free of deep scratches or nicks.

16-13 Photo shows a head after the buffing step, using the black compound and sisal wheels.

16-14 Remove wheels from either end and assemble a clean set of four stitched buff sections.

16-15 With the wheel turning, apply a smooth coating of the white polishing compound.

16-16 Buff heads to a mirror-like finish. Buffing direction should again be different from previous buffing step. This is the final step in this procedure.

16-17 Photo shows a properly polished head. Remove tape from the face of each club when the entire set is finished.

16-18 Stainless steel irons can also be refinished using an 8″ diameter stitched buffing wheel 1″ thick spinning at 1725 R.P.M. A ⅓ H.P. minimum motor is required. A set of Formax 4 bar buffing compounds work well.

16-19 Each day as you begin a new buffing job, rake the wheels clean so most of the old abrasive compound is removed from the wheels. Simply hold the rake against the face of the wheel while the wheel is turning. **Hold the rake firmly.**

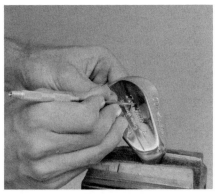

16-20 Paint-filling irons. Etch head stampings to remove old paint using a scriber or sharpened awl, if necessary. Don't slip.

16-21 First, using either lacquer sticks, lacquer paint, or fast dry enamel, brush or wipe paint into the engravings.

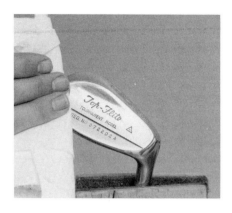

16-22 With a folded cloth or paper towel, wipe off excess paint. Let dry. If lacquer is used, apply lacquer thinner to towel before wiping off excess paint.

16-23 Lacquer sticks work best; they are not messy and come in all colors.

16-24 Rub the lacquer stick across the engraving or stamp and . . .

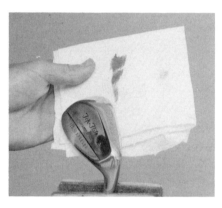

16-25 . . . immediately wipe off excess with a paper towel or clean cloth.

16-26 **Scoring lines may also be paint-filled** using the same procedure as described in photos 16-20 thru 16-25. If faces are to be sandblasted, paint-filling is performed after the sandblasting step. See photo 16-31 thru 16-34 for sandblasting steps.

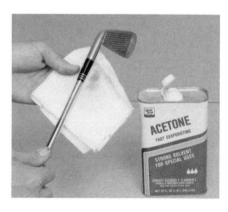

16-27 **Plastic ferrules can be made to look brand new** by wiping with an acetone dampened towel.

16-28 **Rescoring irons.** A carbide tipped rescoring tool is carefully dragged repeatedly through each groove until the proper depth is obtained. Note the use of a **Rescoring Nest** to firmly hold the head.

16-29 Iron head can also be held in aluminum or brass vise pads.

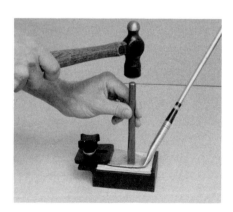

16-30 A ½″ cold chisel will also work but club must be secured in something like the Rescoring Nest. See Appendix 7 for USGA rules regarding iron face markings.

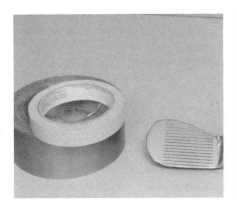

16-31 Re-sandblasting iron faces. First, use a heavy tape such as "Duct Tape" to outline the face. This will protect the toe and heel portion of the face.

16-32 A small sandblasting cabinet works best. This "Dayton" unit requires a compressor with a minimum of 6 S.C.F.M. of air to operate. Unit sells for around $700.00.

16-33 A sandblasting gun also works well and can be used with a ½ H.P. tank type compressor. This unit sells for around $50.00.

16-34 The **Power Pal air compressor** is a smaller unit that works well for sandblasting and spraying purposes. A special optional sandblast gun is available. Complete unit with sandblast gun sells for around $200.00.

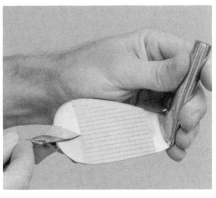

16-35 After the face has been sandblasted using a fine aluminum oxide sand, peel the protective duct or masking tape from the face.

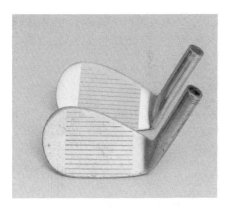

16-36 Photo shows before and after of two irons from the same set. If the head was removed from the shaft before buffing, reinstall the head following instructions in Chapter 19. In most cases, the shaft does not need to be removed.

16-37 If the clubface that was sandblasted was carbon steel and not stainless steel, then the face will have to be protected from rust. Starrett M-1 is excellent. WD-40 and C.R.C. also work well.

16-38 After buffing, winterizing, rechroming or refurbishing, it is a nice professional touch to bag the heads with a special plastic iron head bag.

16-39 This is a M.I.G. electric welder which wire feed welds in a pocket of Argon and CO_2 Gas for porosity-free welds. We use this for welding on broken hosels, fixing cracks and most general welding on damaged clubs sent to us for repair.

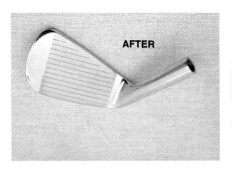

16-40 This is a T.I.G. Electric Welder (Tungsten Inert Gas). This welder uses filler rods of any material (aluminum, brass, stainless steel, carbon steel, etc.) and welds in a pocket of pure Argon Gas. It too is a specialty welder we use to give us capabilities beyond M.I.G. welding.

16-41 So, do not be intimidated by a club looking like this. A hosel that is broken — partially or completely — or has been drilled through can be repaired by us. Most all major golf club manufacturers' repair departments send this type of work to The GolfWorks®.

16-42 The same club as shown in the previous photo has been welded, ground and rechromed to play and look like new.

ADDITIONAL INFORMATION FOR REFINISHING AND RESCORING IRONS

	TABLE 16-1	
	Selecting The Proper Buffing Compound	
Grit	**Compound**	**When to Use**
Coarse	Black Emery Cake	If an extra heavy cutting action is necessary, such as removing rust, heavy nicks, deep scratches.
Medium	Tripoli Brown	For buffing items of aluminum, pewter, brass, copper, wood, bone, plastic and painted surfaces. Medium cutting action.
Fine	White Rouge	For buffing stainless steel, cast brass, aluminum, chromium, nickel and all steel articles to a bright luster. Fine cutting action.
Very Fine	Red Rouge	For buffing silverplate, gold, sterling silver and all sorts of precious metals to a bright luster. Works well on dull chrome golf shafts.

Rechroming and Refinishing:
A Way to Increase Sales and Profits

In doing golf club repair, both the golf professional and the professional club repair shop provide much needed services for the golfer. With the hustle and bustle of running the everyday operations, seldom is there time for thought on expanding and capitalizing on new areas of club repair with the sole intention of increasing sales and profits.

Rechroming irons is one such area which is virtually untapped and one which could provide a substantial increase in income. A number of people do not use the services available to them in rechroming irons because they do not understand the procedure, they are afraid of having the set ruined or they feel it just could not be profitable and worthwhile.

The profitability and economics of rechroming is probably the most important. Today, more than ever before, people are keeping and playing the older sets of irons. Many are collecting these classics and hoarding them. Also, at times it is quite difficult to sell new irons and for that matter new clubs. Let's look at the figures and see how rechroming a set of irons compares against purchasing a new set. Current 1987 prices and cost comparisons are used. Costs should increase approximately 6% per year.

First of all the wholesale cost of rechroming an iron head off the shaft is $8.75 each. If the head is sent in on the shaft, a $2.75 per club additional charge applies. The retail charge to your customer is $16.00 per club or 45% profit margin for a head off the shaft and a 28% margin for a head on the shaft. If you remove and install the head on the shaft, you can figure approximately 1 hour's labor. Some sets may take a little longer and some will take less time. However, figure a savings of $27.50 if you remove and install the heads.

Take a look at Table 16-2, read it carefully and study it. Notice in line III and IV the retail shown for rechroming, reshafting and regripping a set is an average suggested retail. The average retail throughout the United States, taken from many repair lists is $35.00 per club with the range running from $28.00 to $46.00. It is easy to see that line IV (rechroming and reshafting) compares very favorably to line V and VI (selling a new set). It also points up that you should spend the 1 to 2 hours required to do the shafting and gripping to obtain the best profit. Having a set of heads rechromed and then reshafted and regripped will give your customer a brand new set of irons for very close to the **wholesale cost** of a new set of irons. But the best part is that in many cases, you make as much and usually more profit dollars than selling the new set of irons.

Another advantage of rechroming, reshafting and regripping an old set of irons is proper custom fitting. Say an individual has a set of older irons he really likes, but through one or two changes — such as a longer or shorter length, a shaft flex or patttern change, larger or smaller grips or adjusting loft and lie — he would be even better fitted to the clubs. This can now be done quite easily and for very little or no additional cost. So, in essence, you have provided your customer with a brand new, properly fit, custom set of irons. See Ralph Maltby's *The Complete Golf Club Fitting Plan* for information on golf club fitting.

I have seen a number of golf professionals and repair shops promote rechroming successfully. This part of The GolfWorks'® business has grown dramatically to the point where we are now the largest iron refinishers and rechromers in the world. At times, during the heavy volume months, we will do more than 400 sets a week. We also do some warranty rechroming work for a few of the larger golf club manufacturers. Rechroming can take anywhere from 2 to 6 weeks depending on seasonality and the complexity of the work required.

TABLE 16-2

Rechroming Profitability and Cost Comparison Table

Line	Description	Cost Per Club	Retail Cost Per Club	Cost Per Set of 9 Clubs	Retail Cost For 9 Clubs	% Gross Margin of Profit	$ Amount of Profit (9 Clubs)
I	Rechroming a head off the shaft	$ 8.75	$16.00	$ 78.75	$144.00	45%	$ 72.50
II	Rechroming a head on the shaft	$11.50	$16.00	$103.50	$144.00	28%	$ 45.00
III	**If We Do Everything** Rechroming & Reshafting [1](Includes new grip and swingweighting)	$11.50 (rechrome) $ 9.00 (reshaft) $ 3.50 (regrip) $24.00	$16.00 $14.00 $ 5.00 $35.00	$216.00	$315.00	31.4%	$ 99.00
IV	**If We Re-chrome and You Reshaft and Regrip** Rechroming & Reshafting [1](Includes new grip and swingweighting)	$ 8.75 (rechrome) $ 3.50 (reshaft) $ 1.25 (regrip) $13.50 plus 2½ hrs. labor to reshaft, grip & swingweight	$16.00 $14.00 $ 5.00 $35.00	$121.50 plus 2½ hrs. labor	$315.00	61.4%	$193.50
V	[2]If you sell an avg. priced set of irons for avg. discounted retail	$40.00	$52.00	$360.00	$468.00	23%	$108.00
VI	[3]If you sell a so-called avg. priced set of irons for full retail	$40.00	$65.00	$360.00	$585.00	38.4%	$225.00

[1]Average retail prices nationwide for rechroming, reshafting and gripping are $35.00 per club. The range is from $28.00 to $46.00.

[2]Average discounted retail for irons in 1987 is est. @ $52.00 each. Average % gross margin based on wholesale of $40.00 to average discounted retail $52.00 is 23%.

[3]Average catalog stated retail for irons in 1987 is $65.00 each. Average wholesale for irons in 1987 is $40.00 each. This would give a 38% margin of profit.

17

CHANGING SWINGWEIGHT OF IRON CLUBS

Seldom will a golfer bring in an iron(s) specifically for a swingweight change. Usually the swingweight will need adjustment because a change in shaft weight or length, or a change in grip size or weight, has lowered or raised the swingweight.

A recent positive trend in golf club repair is the redistribution of weight within a golf club. Repairmen and golfers are discovering that lead in the tip of the shaft will adversely affect the performance of the club. Lead is often placed in the tip section by the manufacturer to increase swingweight. While this is a cosmetically acceptable practice, functionally it is not. The presence of lead in the tip of the shaft indicates the clubhead's center of gravity is no longer in the center of the head. Instead, the C of G is towards the hosel. Because of this, some clubs are virtually unplayable. A solid shot is only achieved when the ball's center of gravity is struck in line with the clubhead's center of gravity. If the club's C of G is moved too far toward the hosel, which is entirely possible, a golfer would have to almost shank the ball in order to align the C of G of both the ball and clubhead at impact. Because of this, removing lead from the hosel and re-distributing it on the back of the head in the proper position is an improvement to any golf club.

There are very few irons on the market that are designed so swingweight can be changed in the head itself, such as with a weight port. Listed below are the five methods by which the swingweight of an iron club can be changed.

Method 1: Drill a small hole(s) in the head to reduce swingweight.
Method 2: Remove shaft and drill out metal from the bottom of the hosel to reduce swingweight.
Method 3: Add lead underneath the grip to achieve a lighter swingweight reading on the swingweight scale (counterbalancing).
Method 4: Add lead tape to the back of the head to increase swingweight.
Method 5: Put weight (usually steel or lead) in the tip of the shaft to increase swingweight.

Methods 1 and 4 alter the cosmetic appearance of the iron head, but are the most effective. Because weight is either being added or subtracted directly from the head, the C of G is maintained. Methods 2 and 5 will alter the center of gravity in the head. Method 2 will move the center of gravity down and slightly toward the toe. Method 5 will move the center of gravity up and toward the hosel. Method 3 is by far the worst choice, as it does nothing but increase the overall weight of the club while only fooling the swingweight scale into thinking the clubhead has been lightened. This is called counterbalancing.

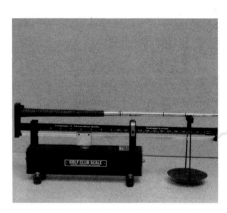

17-1 Before changing swingweight, always check the club's swingweight first. It is also a good idea to check total weight.

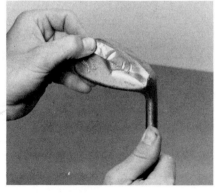

17-2 To increase swingweight, lead tape can be applied to the back of the clubhead. Be sure the tape is applied symmetrically and as low as possible behind the clubface. A 4½″ strip of ½″ wide lead tape will increase the swingweight by one point.

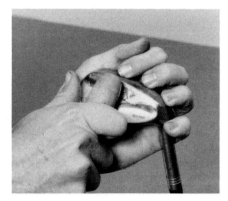

17-3 A wood or plastic tool handle is used to burnish the lead tape to the back of the iron. This helps the tape stick better and conform to any irregular surface.

17-4 Lead rod or powder can also be used to increase swingweight. Use ¼″ diameter lead rod for irons, ³⁄₁₆″ diameter lead rod for woods.

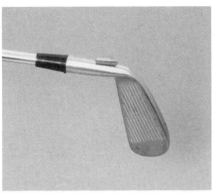

17-5 Lead rod can be first taped to the hosel while the club is on a swingweight scale to help determine proper amount to use. A ¼″ diameter rod cut to a ¼″ length will increase the swingweight by 1 point.

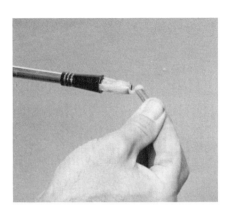

17-6 If you are making custom irons, or if the head is removed from the shaft, lead rod can be inserted directly into the tip of the shaft. Coat lead rod generously with epoxy to prevent possible future rattles.

17-7 Lead rod can also be inserted from the butt end of the shaft if the head is not removed. Apply epoxy to lead rod and drop it down shaft.

17-8 Next, drop a cork into the shaft (available from most golf repair supply dealers).

17-9 Ram the cork and lead rod as far into the tip of the shaft as possible using a **Ramrod**. The opposite end of a **47″ drill bit** will also work.

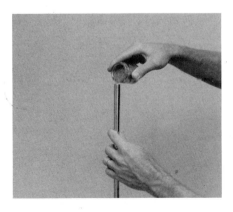

17-10 Lead shot or powder can be used instead of lead rod. First, pour the required amount through the butt end of the shaft.

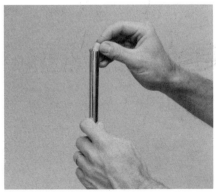

17-11 Place a cork with a glob of epoxy on its bottom end inside the shaft and . . .

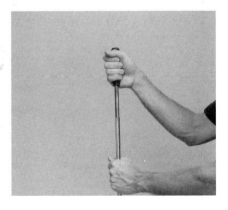

17-12 . . . ram the cork and lead powder or shot in place with the long **Ramrod** or the opposite end of a **47″ drill bit.** Note: For every four swingweights (.28 ounces or 8 grams) added to the shaft tip or hosel, the clubhead's center of gravity will move ⅛″ closer to the hosel and slightly higher up the face.

17-13 Check final swingweight. If the grip was removed from the club to add weight down the shaft, it is a good idea to check for desired swingweight before reinstalling the grip. The grip can be taped to the top of the shaft to do this.

17-14 Swingweight can be reduced in irons by drilling holes in the head. First, center punch head in desired location.

17-15 Next, drill appropriate number of holes equal distances from the face centerline. A ³⁄₁₆″ diameter hole × ¼″ deep will reduce swingweight by approximately 1 point.

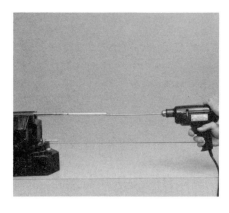

17-16 To remove weight from the hosel of an assembled club: Using a 47″ × ⁷⁄₃₂″ bit, drill into the bottom of the hosel bore. Drilling ³⁄₁₆″ deep is equivalent to a 1 swingweight point reduction. **Be careful not to drill too deep on some irons with short hosels and deep bores or you may drill through.**

17-17 If head is removed from the shaft, drill into bottom of hosel bore with a letter "T" bit. Drilling ⅛″ deep is equivalent to a 1 swingweight point reduction.

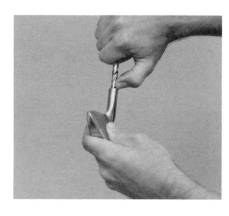

17-18 Photo shows typical iron hosel. Before drilling, always premeasure depth of hosel bore.

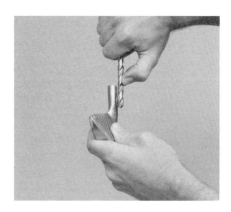

17-19 After measuring, place desired drill bit outside hosel to proper depth to determine if drilling is possible. Many repairmen have accidentally drilled through the side of the hosel. **Note: Drilling through the hosel wall can be repaired by welding.**

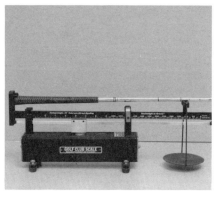

17-20 The GolfWorks® Swingweight Scale measures swingweight in Lorythmic units (D0, D1, D2, etc.) and total weight in ounces and grams. 14″ fulcrum. The scale also has a tray for weighing individual components during club assembly.

17-21 The GolfWorks® Low Cost Swingweight Scale measures swingweight in Lorythmic units (D0, D1, D2, etc.) and total weight in ounces and grams. 14″ fulcrum.

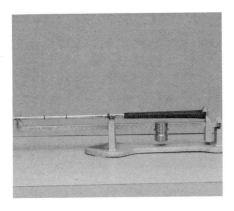

17-22 The Official Swingweight Scale measures in ounces (20.3, 20.4, 20.5, etc.) and total weight in ounces and grams. A conversion chart is used with this scale to convert readings to Lorythmic units. 12″ fulcrum. The name is a misnomer as virtually every manufacturer uses the Lorythmic reading type scales with 14″ fulcrums.

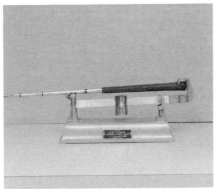

17-23 The Lorythmic Swingweight Scale measures swingweight only in Lorythmic units (D0, D1, D2, etc.). This is the original swingweight scale developed in the late 1920's. 14″ fulcrum.

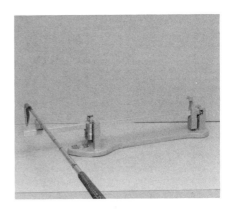

17-24 The Prorythmic Swingweight Scale measures swingweight in Lorythmic units (D0, D1, D2, etc.) and total weight in ounces and grams. 14″ fulcrum. Photo shows total weight being measured.

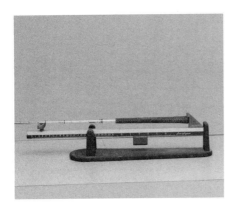

17-25 The Ben Hogan Co. Swingweight Scale measures swingweight in Lorythmic units (D0, D1, D2, etc.) and total weight in ounces and grams. 14″ fulcrum.

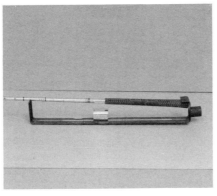

17-26 The Ping Swingweight Scale measures swingweight in Lorythmic units (D0, D1, D2, etc.) and total weight in ounces. 14″ fulcrum.

17-27 The Shadowgraph Swingweight Scale. This is an electronic scale which measures swingweight only. It is Lorythmic (D0, D1, D2, etc.) and is designed for production use because of its rapid dampening characteristic. 14″ fulcrum.

17-28 The Golfsmith Swingweight Scale measures swingweight only. Measures in Lorythmic units (D0, D1, D2, etc.). 14″ fulcrum.

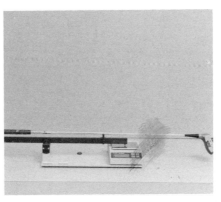

17-29 The O'Haus Electronic Swingweight Scale. This scale measures swingweight in Lorythmic units (D0, D1, D2, etc.) and total weight in ounces or grams. 14″ fulcrum.

NOTES

ADDITIONAL INFORMATION FOR CHANGING SWINGWEIGHTS OF IRON CLUBS

- For every ½″ increase in a club's length, the swingweight will increase by 3 points.
- For every ½″ decrease in a club's length, the swingweight will decrease by 3 points.
- If you would like to check a club's swingweight before installing the grip and any tape, allow 9 points (10 points for leather, cord or oversize rubber). Example: Ungripped club swingweights at E-0; it will probably be D-1 after gripping with an average-weight 1¾ ounce rubber grip.
- Every 4 swingweights are equivalent to slightly more than ¼ ounce (8 grams). A swingweight point in an iron head is approximately .07 ounce (2 grams). See Fig. 17-30.
- A swingweight point in the grip end of an iron is approximately .14 ounces (4 grams) or twice as much as is required in the head end. .14 ounces added to the grip end will decrease swingweight by 1 point (this is called "counterbalancing") and .14 ounces taken out of the grip end will increase swingweight by 1 point. See Fig. 17-30.

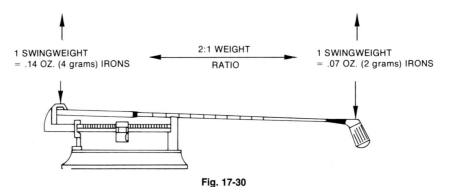

1 SWINGWEIGHT = .14 OZ. (4 grams) IRONS
2:1 WEIGHT RATIO
1 SWINGWEIGHT = .07 OZ. (2 grams) IRONS

Fig. 17-30
Approximate swingweight equivalents for grip and head ends of club

- The lighter the shaft, the heavier the head weight must be to obtain the same swingweight that you would get with a heavier shaft. Even though the head weight is heavier with the lighter shaft, the total weight of the club will still be less. For a general rule of thumb use the following: For each 1 ounce reduction in shaft weight, an iron club will lose approximately 3 swingweight points. This, of course, assumes that the grip weight and shaft length are exactly the same. Example: A set of D-2 irons with Dynamic® Tip Taper Shafts (4⅜ ounces) are reshafted with Extralite® Tip Taper Shafts (3⅜ ounces). Without reweighting the heads, the swingweight would now be C-9. Approximately ¼ ounce of weight would have to be added to the heads to achieve a D-2 swingweight. The Extralite® shaft is 1 ounce lighter than the Dynamic® Tip Taper Shaft but only ¼ ounce is added to the head leaving a net reduction in total club weight of ¾ ounce. For a comparative look at what just happened, refer to the #5 iron example in Table 17-1.

	TABLE 17-1 Effect of Different Weight Shafts on Head Weights, Total Weight and Swingweight				
	#5 Iron Before Change: Dynamic® Tip Taper Shaft	#5 Iron After Change: Extralite® Tip Taper Shaft	Difference From Change:	Club Specs: Reweighted to D-2	Net Change In Club:
Shaft Weight (ounces)	4.37	3.37	− 1	3.37	− 1
Head Weight (ounces)	9.5	9.5	Same	9.75	+ .25
Grip Weight (ounces)	1.75	1.75	Same	1.75	None
Total Weight (ounces)	15.62	14.62	− 1	14.87	− .75
Swingweight	D-2	C-9	− 3	D-2	+ 3

Note: A 1 ounce reduction in shaft weight for wood club would decrease swingweight by 5 points because of the additional shaft length. See Chapter 13, Swingweighting Woods.

- A dollar bill weighs 1 gram and is equivalent to ½ of a swingweight point. A dime weighs 2 grams and is equivalent to 1 point. A quarter weighs 6 grams and is equivalent to 3 points.
- If you use ½″ wide lead tape, it takes approximately a 4½″ long piece to weigh 2 grams or be equivalent to 1 swingweight point.
- To convert grams to ounces, divide by 28.35.
- To convert ounces to grams, multiply by 28.35.
- 1 ounce = 28.35 grams.

Official Swingweight Scale Reading	Lorythmic Scale Swingweight Woods	Irons	Official Swingweight Scale Reading	Lorythmic Scale Swingweight Woods	Irons
TABLE 17-2					
Swingweight Conversion Chart					
Official Swingweight Scale vs. Lorythmic Swingweight Scale					
18.33	C0	B8	20.00	D0	C8
18.4	0.4	8.4	20.05	0.3	8.3
18.45	0.7	8.7	20.1	0.6	8.6
			20.15	0.9	8.9
18.5	C1	B9	20.17	D1	C9
18.55	1.3	9.3			
18.6	1.6	9.6	20.2	1.2	9.2
			20.25	1.5	9.5
18.65	C2	C0	20.3	1.8	9.8
18.7	2.2	0.2	20.33	D2	D0
18.75	2.5	0.5			
18.8	2.8	0.8	20.35	2.1	0.1
			20.4	2.4	0.4
18.83	C3	C1	20.45	2.7	0.7
18.85	3.1	1.1	20.5	D3	D1
18.9	3.4	1.4			
18.95	3.7	1.7	20.55	3.3	1.3
			20.6	3.6	1.6
19.00	C4	C2	20.65	D4	D2
19.05	4.3	2.3			
19.1	4.6	2.6	20.7	4.2	2.2
19.15	4.9	2.9	20.75	4.5	2.5
			20.8	4.8	2.8
19.17	C5	C3	20.83	D5	D3
19.2	5.2	3.2			
19.25	5.5	3.5	20.85	5.1	3.1
19.3	5.8	3.8	20.9	5.4	3.4
			20.95	5.7	3.7
19.33	C6	C4	21.00	D6	D4
19.35	6.1	4.1			
19.4	6.4	4.4	21.05	6.3	4.3
19.45	6.7	4.7	21.1	6.6	4.6
			21.15	6.9	4.9
19.5	C7	C5	21.17	D7	D5
19.55	7.3	5.3			
19.6	7.6	5.6	21.2	7.2	5.2
19.65	7.9	5.9	21.25	7.5	5.5
			21.3	7.8	5.8
19.66	C8	C6	21.33	D8	D6
19.7	8.2	6.2			
19.75	8.5	6.5	21.35	8.1	6.1
19.8	8.8	6.8	21.4	8.4	6.4
			21.45	8.7	6.7
19.83	C9	C7	21.5	D9	D7
19.85	9.1	7.1			
19.9	9.4	7.4	21.55	9.3	7.3
10.95	9.7	7 7	21.6	9.6	7.6
			21.65	9.9	7.9
			21.66	E0	D8

NOTES

18 CHANGING LOFTS AND LIES OF IRON CLUBS

Altering lofts and lies of iron clubs is a relatively simple operation, but it does require special equipment. The special equipment is designed to do three things: first, to measure actual loft and lie angles; second, to provide a means of holding the head securely in position; third, to provide a tool which attaches to the hosel and exerts enough leverage to bend the hosel, thus altering loft, lie, or both.

The lie of an iron can be altered without affecting any other specifications of that iron. However, when the loft of an iron is altered, three effects on other specifications occur.

The first two of the effects, hosel offset and face progression, are relatively minor changes and are usually not given consideration when making a loft change.

The third effect is to the sole inversion. Sole inversion is defined as the angle of the sole to the ground when the shaft is perpendicular to the ground and the face is square to the target. Sole inversion, or sole angle as it is sometimes called, is defined under three possible conditions: 1) scoop or dig sole, 2) square sole, and 3) bounce (or inverted) sole. Of these three, the scoop or dig sole is to be avoided if at all possible (photos 18-1 thru 18-3 show the three conditions).

Unfortunately, most golfers who wish to have a loft adjustment will request that the loft be decreased so they can hit the ball farther. Therefore, always inspect the sole angle of the irons and determine if the decreased loft alteration will potentially ruin the clubs by creating a dig sole angle. If a loft alteration is made and you then deem it to be unfavorable, you can always bend the hosel back to its original loft position.

18-1   A scoop or dig sole. The trailing edge is lower than the leading edge. Try to avoid this as it results in fat type shots.

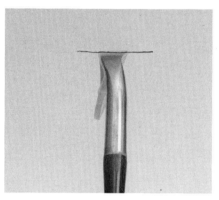

18-2   A square sole. The leading edge is even in height with the trailing edge.

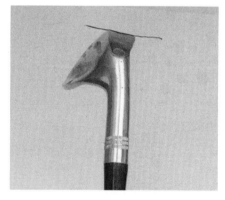

18-3   A bounce or inverted sole. The trailing edge is higher than the leading edge.

18-4 There are a number of different loft and lie machines available to fit various budgets. Shop and compare features carefully. This chapter will demonstrate the use of a loft and lie machine available from The GolfWorks®.

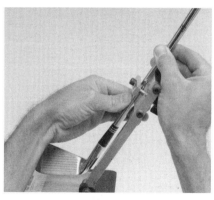

18-5   How to measure loft and lie: The clubhead must be in the correct lie position before measuring. Place the shaft in the V-Block and lower the head to the base. Pressure should be placed against the shaft while lowering the head to keep the shaft flush in the "V" groove. (The knob may be lightly tightened to accomplish this.)

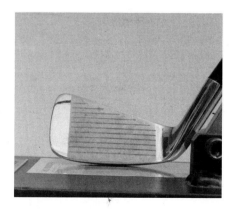

18-6 The correct lie position is achieved when the sole of the clubhead is touching the base at the center of the face. This can be determined either visually or . . .

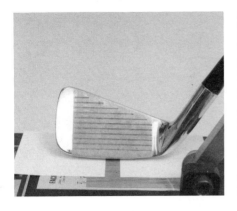

18-7 . . . by slipping two pieces of paper underneath the sole, one from the toe side and one from the heel side, until snug. The papers should either meet at the face centerline or an equal distance away from the face centerline. Photo shows the clubhead in a correct lie position. The face centerline can be determined by eye or by measuring and finding the face mid-point.

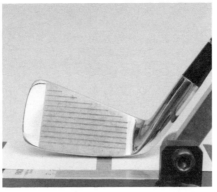

18-8 If the papers are forward or rearward of the face centerline, readjust the club until correct, using the two slips of paper as your guide.

18-9 After proper positioning of the clubhead, align the leading edge of the clubhead parallel to a line on the face progression sticker. This will ensure a correct loft reading. Now, tighten the knob holding the shaft in place.

18-10 Place the magnetic side of the Protractor against the Measuring Arm and read the actual lie angle in degrees. Record this specification on the Fitting Sheet.

18-11 Remove the Protractor from the arm. Place the Protractor's non-magnetic side on the clubface. Be sure the Protractor is flat against the face. Read and record the actual loft angle in degrees. Note: Be sure the leading edge of the face is still parallel with a line on the face progression sticker.

18-12 Continue to measure and record all loft and lie readings. Also, in the space provided on the pad, record the desired or manufacturer's specifications for comparison. Industry standard loft and lie readings are found in Tables 18-1 and 18-2 at the end of this chapter.

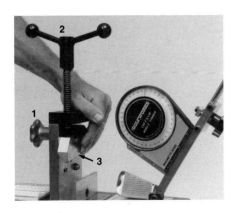

18-13 **How to bend loft and/or lie.** Loosen the steel mushroom knob (1) and unscrew the large double-handled clamping screw (2) until the Top Line Holddown (3) is raised up as far as it will go.

18-14 With the Top Line Holddown in this position, place the iron head into the Bending Unit, toe first, with the face flat against the major vertical piece (1). Be sure the toe of the club is against the Brass Acorn Head Stop Screw (2).

18-15 Lower the Top Line Holddown onto the top line of the iron head, keeping the Top Line Holddown flat against the major vertical steel piece. Be sure the Brass Plugs found on the underside of the Top Line Holddown are in contact with the top line of the head.

18-16 Secure the Top Line Holddown by tightening the steel mushroom knob until finger tight. Do not over tighten.

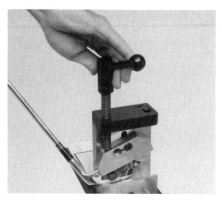

18-17 Screw the large double-handled clamping screw down to contact the Top Line Holddown and securely lock the iron head in the bending unit. Usually ½ turn of the clamping screw past snug is sufficient. The head is now secure and ready for bending.

18-18 To prevent any possibility of a small hosel nick in newer clubs, attach a brass hosel protector clip to the hosel. This is usually not necessary with older irons.

18-19 Place the bending bar around the hosel protector as low on the hosel as possible. Tighten the bending bar handle until snug around the hosel.

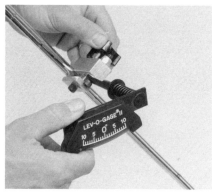

18-20 A protractor with a special clamping assembly can be placed around the shaft. This unit will allow you to see the amount of change you are making during the bending operation. This will eliminate the need to repeatedly move the club back and forth between the bending and measuring units.

18-21 Altering lie: Position the protractor so it is perpendicular to the machine as shown and rotate until the protractor reads zero degrees.

18-22 Swing the bending bar so that the bar is in line with the back of the iron's hosel. As you place each of the different lofted irons into your machine, . . .

18-23 . . . the position of the bar will always stay in line with the back of the hosel. There will be a slight change with regard to its position relative to the side of the machine. The previous photo (18-22) showed the proper positioning of the bar on a less lofted club. The photo above shows the bar's placement on a higher lofted club and in line with the hosel.

18-24 To make the lie more upright: Grasp the bar handle with both hands, as shown, and lift up towards, and in line with, the shaft of the club and the back of the hosel. Follow the lie change progress on the protractor.

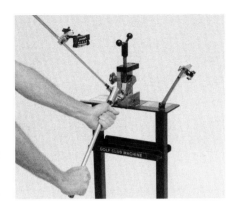

18-25 To flatten the lie: Grasp the bar handle with both hands and push directly away from the shaft and the back of the hosel. The bend is not made vertically, but is made in line with the back of the hosel.

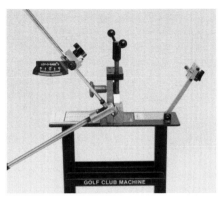

18-26 Changing the loft: Swing the measuring unit protractor around so it is parallel to the machine as shown and the protractor rotated so it reads zero degrees. Swing the bending bar around so it is even with the base of the machine or perpendicular to the face.

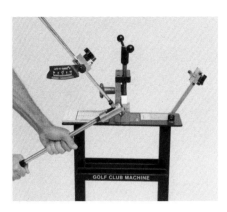

18-27 To increase the loft: Grasp the bar handle as shown and bend straight down. Follow the progress on the protractor.

18-28 To decrease the loft: Grasp the bar handle as shown and bend straight up.

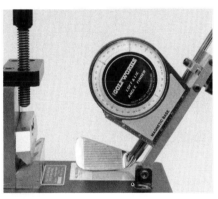

18-29 After bending, the club should be checked in the Measuring Unit for correct lie angle and . . .

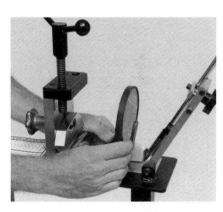

18-30 . . . checked for the correct loft angle. It takes approximately 35 minutes to check, bend and recheck an entire set of irons. Note: After you gain confidence and find that the indicator assembly attached to the shaft is always correct, you can eliminate the recheck of lofts and lies. Then it will only take 20-25 minutes per set.

18-31 This machine can also be converted to bend left-handed irons. First, the double-handled clamp is placed in the opposite hole.

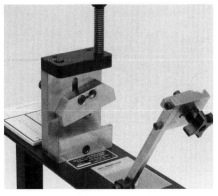

18-32 Next, the Top Line Holddown is removed, and the pivot bolt is placed in the opposite hole. Next, the Top Line Holddown is re-installed.

18-33 The brass acorn nut, which acts as a toe stop, is removed and placed in the opposite hole. This conversion takes less than 30 seconds to complete and makes this machine the most versatile on the market.

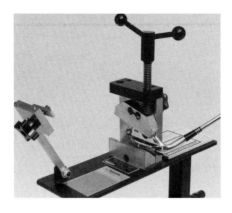

18-34 Photo shows left-handed club being clamped in Bending Unit. Left-handed clubs are measured and bent in the same manner as right-handed clubs.

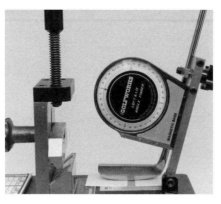

18-35 Putters can also be measured and altered in this machine. Photo shows lie angle being checked.

18-36 The loft angle is checked. Record these specifications on the Fitting Sheet.

18-37 Place the head of the putter into the Bending Unit toe first with the sole of the putter flat against the Angled Wedge Plate (1). This means the face of the putter will not be flat against the Major Vertical Piece (2), as is the case with all iron clubs.

18-38 Lower the Top Line Holddown on top of the top line of the putter and tighten the steel mushroom knob. Tighten the double-handled clamping screw.

18-39 Install the brass hosel protector on the hosel as shown in photo 18-18. Attach the special protractor to the shaft as shown above.

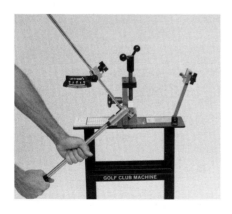

18-40 Use the bending bar as previously shown to make lie and loft alterations.

18-41 Woods can also be measured on this machine. You can easily and accurately measure both the lie angle and the loft angle of wood clubs. Use the same procedure as was shown for irons. Note: Take the loft mesurement from a wood at half the vertical face height.

18-42 Face progression is easily determined for a wood and **face angle** can be visually determined using the straight face progression lines as a visual reference.

18-43 Measuring bounce on an iron head: Place iron head properly in Measuring Unit. Measure and record the loft angle as shown above. Be sure the leading edge of the face lines up square (parallel) to the lines on the face progression sticker.

18-44 Next, rotate the iron head until the face leading edge is no longer elevated off the base but is touching the base. Another way of saying this is to simply rotate the clubhead until the sole of the club is sitting squarely (flat) on the machine base, thus eliminating all bounce.

18-45 Now, measure and record the new loft reading as shown. Subtract this reading from the previous reading to find the degree of bounce on an iron head. Example: 1st loft reading is 56°. 2nd loft reading is 48°. Then 56° − 48° = 8° bounce. Obviously we are measuring a sand club here.

NOTES

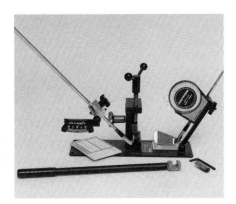

18-46 The GolfWorks® is also offering an **Economy Loft and Lie Machine.** This unit will do everything the deluxe model will do. It is offered for the less frequent user.

ADDITIONAL INFORMATION FOR CHANGING LOFT AND LIES OF IRON CLUBS

	Men's				Ladies'			
Irons	Strong Lofts	Standard Lofts	Weak Lofts	Traditional Standard	Strong Lofts	Standard Lofts	Weak Lofts	Traditional Standard
1	16°	17°	18°	17°	—	—	—	—
2	18°	20°	22°	20°	20°	21°	22°	21°
3	22°	24°	26°	23°	24°	25°	26°	24°
4	26°	28°	30°	26°	28°	29°	30°	27°
5	30°	32°	34°	30°	32°	33°	34°	31°
6	34°	36°	38°	34°	36°	37°	38°	35°
7	38°	40°	42°	38°	40°	41°	42°	39°
8	42°	44°	46°	42°	44°	45°	46°	43°
9	46°	48°	50°	46°	48°	49°	50°	47°
PW	50°	52°	54°	50°	52°	53°	54°	51°
SW	54°	56°	58°	56°	56°	57°	58°	56°

TABLE 18-1
Iron Club Lofts — Men's and Ladies'

	Men's			Ladies'		
Irons	[1]Flat Lies	[1]Standard Lies	[1]Upright Lies	[2]Flat Lies	[2]Standard Lies	[2]Upright Lies
1	53°	55°	57°	51°	53°	55°
2	54°	56°	58°	52°	54°	56°
3	55°	57°	59°	53°	55°	57°
4	56°	58°	60°	54°	56°	58°
5	57°	59°	61°	55°	57°	59°
6	58°	60°	62°	56°	58°	60°
7	59°	61°	63°	57°	59°	61°
8	60°	62°	64°	58°	60°	62°
9	61°	63°	65°	59°	61°	63°
PW	61°	63°	65°	59°	61°	63°
SW	61°	63°	65°	59°	61°	63°

TABLE 18-2
Iron Club Lies — Men's and Ladies'

[1]Lies shown are for standard men's length irons (i.e., 39″ #2 iron). For each ½″ added to standard length, subtract 1° in lie (flatter) and for each ½″ subtracted from standard length, add 1° in lie (upright).
[2]Same as Note 1 above but based on a standard length set with a 38″ #2 iron.

What Happens to an Iron When Loft and Lie Are Altered

The lie of an iron club can be altered without usually affecting any other specification of that iron. However, adjusting the lie 3 to 4 degrees flatter will increase the swingweight by 1 point and adjusting the lie 3 to 4 degrees more upright will decrease the swingweight by 1 point simply because the clubhead is extended further from or closer to the fulcrum point on the swingweight scale. However, this slight change should not be considered when altering the lie. Because if a person truly needs the lie angle changed this much, the improvement in ball striking solidness and directional control will overwhelm an insignificant 1 point swingweight change. See Fig. 18-47.

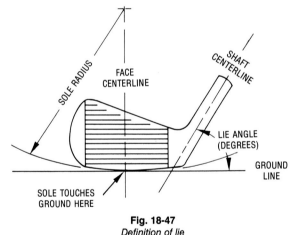

Fig. 18-47
Definition of lie

When the loft of an iron club is altered, three effects on other specifications occur with which you should be thoroughly familiar. First, the hosel offset will be progressed if the loft is decreased, and conversely, the hosel offset will be regressed if the loft is increased. As a result, the face progression has also been affected. Offset is measured differently than face progression and is illustrated in Fig. 18-48. The change in hosel offset and subsequently face progression will make the iron appear a little differently to the golfer. These two changes are rather minor though.

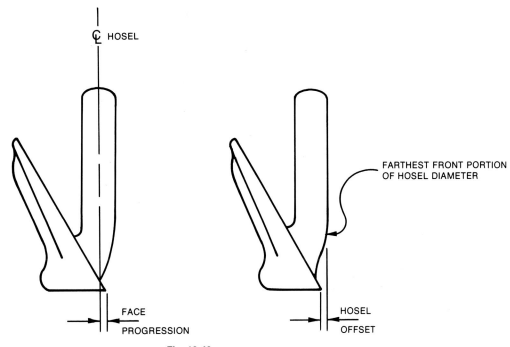

Fig. 18-48
Progression and offset comparison

The third, and more important, specification that is affected during a loft change is to the sole inversion. Sole inversion is defined as the angle of the sole to the ground when the shaft is perpendicular to the ground and the face is square to the target. See Fig. 18-49. When most iron clubs are designed, the hosel-to-face angle and the face-to-sole angle are all directly related to one another. For instance, the angle of the face to the centerline of the hosel equals the loft. Also the angle of the face to the sole minus 90 degrees would equal the loft only if 0 degree sole inversion were part of the original design. See Fig. 18-49. It should be apparent that when you bend a golf iron hosel in a bending machine, some part of this relationship of the original design specifications must be destroyed.

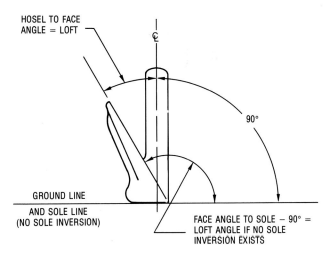

Fig. 18-49
Loft and sole inversion relationship

To more fully understand this, refer next to Fig. 18-50 which shows a before and after comparison of the same iron shown in Fig. 18-49 whose loft has been increased 3 degrees, returned to normal, and then decreased 3 degrees. Assume for discussion's sake, we have a 35 degree lofted #5 iron with no offset and a square sole angle or 0 degree sole angle. (See the top drawing in Figure 18-50.) Now look at the middle drawing in Fig. 18-50, by bending in more loft, the leading edge of the clubface has protruded slightly forward and in this example is actually ahead of the farthest front portion of the hosel, providing what is called "Regressed Offset," or in layman's golfing terms a "front porch" look. Notice also what has happened to the sole angle. We now have 3 degrees of bounce sole angle which happens to be exactly the same as the loft angle increase. Since the sole angle and loft angle are part of the same head, you cannot change either one without changing the other by the same amount.

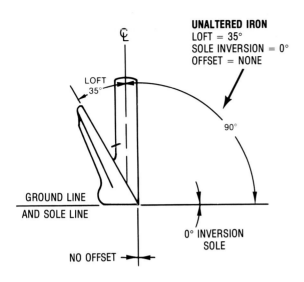

UNALTERED IRON
LOFT = 35°
SOLE INVERSION = 0°
OFFSET = NONE

LOFT 35°

90°

GROUND LINE
AND SOLE LINE

0° INVERSION
SOLE

NO OFFSET →

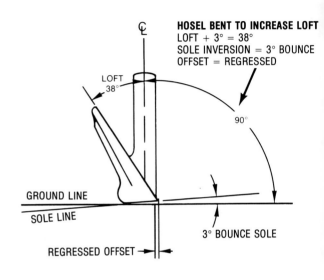

HOSEL BENT TO INCREASE LOFT
LOFT + 3° = 38°
SOLE INVERSION = 3° BOUNCE
OFFSET = REGRESSED

LOFT 38°

90°

GROUND LINE
SOLE LINE

3° BOUNCE SOLE

REGRESSED OFFSET →

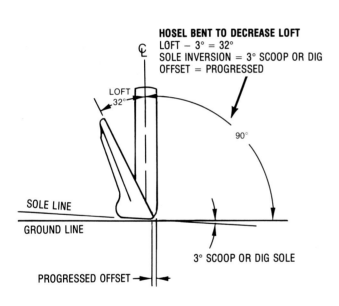

HOSEL BENT TO DECREASE LOFT
LOFT − 3° = 32°
SOLE INVERSION = 3° SCOOP OR DIG
OFFSET = PROGRESSED

LOFT 32°

90°

SOLE LINE
GROUND LINE

3° SCOOP OR DIG SOLE

PROGRESSED OFFSET →

Fig. 18-50
Effect of altering iron lofts

Now look at the bottom drawing in Fig. 18-50 where it shows the hosel bent to decrease the loft. The sole angle now has 3 degrees scoop which is not a good situation since the club will now have a greater tendency to dig into the ground. Also, the hosel offset has changed to a "Progressed Offset" where the clubhead's leading edge is behind the leading edge of the hosel. Fig. 18-50 is excellent for pointing out the importance of maintaining the proper interrelationships between specifications.

Let's go back to Fig. 18-50 and once again note that if an iron was originally designed with 0 degree sole inversion (the sole line is perpendicular to the shaft) and its loft is increased, sole inversion in the form of "bounce" is created. See photo 18-3. Conversely, if the loft is decreased, sole inversion in the form of "scoop" or "dig" is created. See photo 18-1.

Of these two sole angles, the scoop or dig condition is by far the worse and should be avoided. Unfortunately, most players ask to decrease loft so they can hit the ball farther, which can potentially create this undesirable scoop sole. Therefore, before you decide to decrease the loft on a set of irons, be sure to inspect the existing sole angle to see if the bend will unfavorably change the sole angle. To check the sole angle of any iron, hold the club in front of you as shown in Fig. 18-51 with the shaft vertical and the leading edge of the sole pointed directly away from your sight line. Note the relationship of the leading and trailing edges of the sole to the shaft. If the leading edge is even with or above the trailing edge, you will be creating a scoop sole, a condition caused by strengthening the club's loft. This is not a good situation. This can cause the player to hit heavy or fat shots.

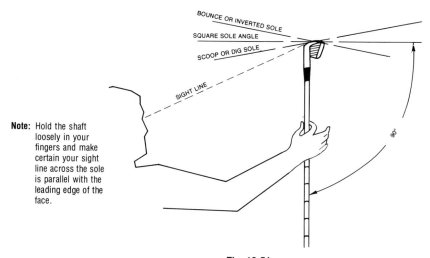

Note: Hold the shaft loosely in your fingers and make certain your sight line across the sole is parallel with the leading edge of the face.

Fig. 18-51
Visually determining sole angle

A good rule of thumb to use here is if you have various sole angles within the same set of irons (in other words a few have bounce soles, a few scoop soles and maybe a couple square soles), this would be a good indication that the lofts are out of specification. If you simply bend them back to the original loft specification, the sole angles should once again be consistent with one another throughout the set.

An advantage of altering the loft of irons is if any adverse effect on playability occurs, the iron can be restored to its original specifications quite easily. Keep in mind after reading this section that each individual manufacturer designs and builds irons in different ways. For instance, some manufacturers build an inversion or bounce sole into their iron clubs and others build their irons with a very pronounced sole camber (radius from front to back of sole and radius from heel to toe of sole). These particular sole designs would indicate slightly different results than the drawing shown here. However, the effect of each loft change can be easily calculated if you first measure an iron's original loft, offset and sole inversion, and then compare it to the altered readings. The point is, it is easy to make a club more unplayable by altering lofts without proper knowledge of the interrelationships of certain specifications. Fig. 18-52 is included here to provide additional information on the playability of various sole designs.

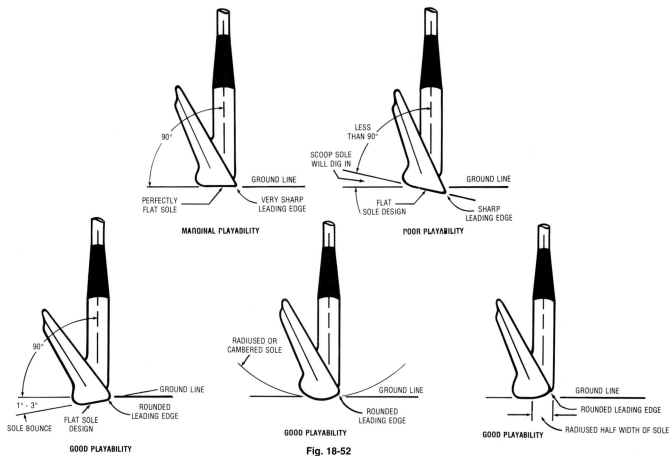

Fig. 18-52
Playability comparisons of various types of sole angles and designs

Tips and Suggestions When Altering Loft and Lie of Irons

1. Only allow authorized individuals and yourself to operate a loft and lie machine. It will generate more attention and consequently additional income if it is placed in a sales traffic area so that your customers may see and ask about it. However, it can only lead to problems if you allow just anyone to use the machine.

2. Most loft and lie machines utilize a manually operated Bending Bar while a few are motorized. With the manually operated Bending Bar, as you become more and more proficient you will obtain a feel for exactly how much pressure to exert on the Bending Bar to get the desired loft and lie.

3. 80% to 90% of all investment cast clubs can also be bent to alter loft and lie. Most cast clubs can be bent as much as 4 ° in any direction; however, it is recommended that you stay within 2° in any direction to maintain a safety margin.

   When you make the initial effort to bend the first cast club in a set that is questionable, remember that all bendable clubs will have a little springiness in the hosel as initial pressure is exerted on the Bending Bar. If this initial bend attempt produces a rigid rock hard feel with no springiness, then the set is suspect and you may break the hosel.

   Some people seem to feel that heating or warming the hosel will allow it to bend more easily. The amount of heat required to actually help would surely discolor the hosel as it would need to be almost red hot. Also, if a cast club is made of a brittle material that will not bend, it will most likely still break even though it was heated.

4. The use of a standard loft and lie chart for recording before and after readings is very helpful. The one shown in Fig. 18-53 works quite well because it has a triangular area between readings which allows the recorder to mark down differences in each successive reading. This will tell you at a glance how evenly progressed the actual readings of loft and lie are through the set and will make it much easier during bending.

CLUB NO.	LIE ACTUAL	LIE SPEC	LOFT ACTUAL	LOFT SPEC
1	55° (0)	56°	19° (0)	17°
2	55° (0)	57°	19° (+3)	20°
3	55° (+5)	58°	22° (+7)	24°
4	60° (-1)	59°	29° (+4)	28°
5	59° (+2)	60°	33° (+4)	32°
6	61° (+2)	61°	37° (+3)	36°
7	63° (-1)	62°	40° (+4)	40°
8	62° (+2)	63°	44° (+5)	44°
9	64° (+2)	64°	49° (+1)	48°
P	66° (-1)	64°	50° (+6)	52°
S	65°	64°	56°	56°

Customer's Name _John Smith_
Home Address _4820 Jacksontown Rd._
City _Newark_ State _Ohio_ Zip _43055_
Club Model _Any Brand_
Date _2/15/88_

CUSTOM FITTING CHART

LIE
☐ Flat 2°
☑ Standard
☐ Upright 2°
☐ Other _____

LOFT
☐ Strong 2°
☑ Standard
☐ Weak 2°
☐ Other _____

Fig. 18-53
Lie/Loft chart for recording specifications

5. Generally the charge for altering the loft and/or lie of each club is between $2.00 and $3.50. $2.75 per club seems to approximate a national average. Some shops charge a flat fee of $20.00 to $28.00 per set.

   When selling a new set of irons, the customer can be custom fit to a so-called stock set and of course, this service is usually on a "no charge" basis. This feature will increase your golf club sales.

6. When bending an iron club hosel, the Bending Bar exerts a tremendous pressure on it. As such, a small mark is sometimes slightly noticeable. If you are bending a brand new set, never used, you should use a Brass Hosel Protector Clip available from The GolfWorks® or you can make your own from .010" thick brass or aluminum shim stock. Using a pair of scissors cut a piece of shim stock 1½" square and roll it into a cylinder as the one pictured in photo 18-18.

The Difference in Bending Machines

Numerous bending machines are available and careful shopping is necessary before purchasing one. Bending machines fall into two categories. One type measures and bends the iron hosel in the same fixture. The other type measures the loft and lie specifications and then bends the hosel in a separate fixture. The GolfWorks® Loft and Lie machines are in this latter category. Only machines that bend and measure in separate fixtures can give the correct loft and lie for all types of irons.

Let me explain why this is a very important point. When working the type of machine that measures and bends in the same fixture, the clubhead is locked in a holding vise. The position of the shaft in relation to one, or sometimes, two fixed measuring arms determines what the loft and lie of the iron is. However, this type of machine can be inaccurate. The measuring arm gives the operator a loft or lie reading that can be off by as much as two degrees. Remember that as the hosel offset increases, the reading from this type of machine will show the loft to be weaker than what it really is. Also, as the blade length increases or decreases, or as the scoring line length increases or decreases from a standard distance built into the machine, the lie reading will be read flatter or more upright than it actually is. Look closely at photos 18-54 and 18-55 for a clear understanding of these important points.

18-54 Both #9 irons with the same degree of lie. But the lie readings are different because the length of the scoring lines vary.

18-55 Both #9 irons with the same loft. But the club on the left has a weaker loft reading because it has a greater hosel offset. (The distance from the farthest front portion of the hosel to the farthest front portion of the leading edge of the face center.)

The point is, if every iron had the same amount of hosel offset and the exact same blade length and scoring line length, then a machine that measures and bends in the same fixture would be acceptable. However, different manufactured irons vary widely with these two features and the potential for inaccurate readings is enormous. Only The GolfWorks® Golf Club Machines will provide the means to determine a truly accurate loft and lie reading, and then adjust these specifications accordingly.

The GolfWorks® Golf Club Machines allow the operator to sole the clubhead properly on the base of the machine. Remember, the definition of **lie** is *the angle of the centerline of the shaft with the ground line, tangent to the sole at the centerline of the face.* To achieve the correct lie reading, the sole of the clubhead must be resting at the point just below the center of the face. Once the club is soled properly, and only then, can the correct loft be read. The GolfWorks® Golf Club Machines enable the operator to achieve the correct soled position.

Fig. 18-56
The GolfWorks® Loft & Lie Machine

Fig. 18-57
The GolfWorks® Economy Model Loft & Lie Machine

NOTES

19

RESHAFTING IRON CLUBS AND CHANGING HOSEL BORE SIZES

Basically, reshafting irons is much easier than reshafting woods, especially if the correct equipment is used. Without correct equipment, reshafting irons can sometimes turn into a frustrating wrestling match. Fortunately, the appropriate tools and equipment are available to make even the potentially difficult reshafting job much easier.

Ninety-nine percent of all iron head assemblies fall into an assembly category referred to as a "force fit" or "slip in" assembly. This describes a shaft that is placed in the hosel and secured with epoxy, a swaged fit, and/or a rivet. The other 1% represents assemblies where the shaft screws into a threaded hosel.

It is quite important to have a good understanding of Appendices 4, 5 and 6, Golf Shaft Specifications and Reference Tables to enable you to accurately identify the shaft in a club and also the replacement shaft.

When replacing a shaft, the three most important considerations of the shaft to be determined in order to properly match it to the replaced shaft are listed below in order of importance:
1) Shaft Flex
2) Shaft Pattern or Flex Point
3) Shaft Weight

The definition of shaft flex is "a comparative measurement of a shaft's resistance to bending or deflection under a given stress and load." This measurement is commonly taken from a shaft deflection board and divided into five different flexes: L, A, R or T, S, and X, with X being the stiffest and L being the most flexible. Matching shaft flex is important so the entire set will be consistent. If one or more shafts are not matched properly in flex, the clubface may be delivered into the ball at an angle that is different from the rest of the clubs.

Shaft pattern identifies the shaft type (Dynamic®, TT-Lite®, Jet Step®, etc.) through an arrangement of step downs. Shaft type indicates the bend point (flex point) on a golf shaft. The flex point is the point on a shaft that experiences the greatest amount of bending or deflection, or, where the shaft bends the most during a swing. A golf shaft will either have a low, mid or high bend point. A high bend point means most of the bending during the swing occurs above the middle of the shaft. A mid-bend point means most of the bending occurs near the middle of the shaft and a low bend point indicates most of the bending occurs below the middle of the shaft. This is important because the bend point or flex point does much to determine both the trajectory and directional control of a golf shot.

Shaft weight simply means the total weight of the golf shaft. The weight of a golf shaft will fall into these categories: standard weight, lightweight, and very lightweight. Appendices 4 and 5 give complete information on shaft weights.

The methods, techniques and use of tools required to remove a shaft, regardless of the assembly procedure, are covered in this chapter. Also explained in the chapter is step drilling, a method utilizing 3 different drill bits to make taper tip bores in hosels or 1 drill bit for a unitized or parallel bore. Step drilling is also used to drill out broken shafts, clean out existing bores or enlarge bores to accept a different size shaft tip.

Note: Removing an iron head can be a potentially dangerous repair if certain precautions are not followed. Always wear eye protection and never stand in front of a head when applying heat to the hosel. Trapped air between the tip of the shaft and the bottom of the hosel can turn into an explosive force when heated. Occasionally a head will fly off the shaft or a rubber plug will be forced from the tip of the shaft through this rapid expansion of air.

19-1 If possible, check and record the swingweight before removing the shaft. Your goal is to return the club to the owner in as close to original condition as possible unless requested otherwise. **If the shaft is broken, check another club from the set.**

19-2 The length should also be recorded. Once again, if the shaft is broken, measure the club nearest the broken one to determine its correct set length. **(Example: #6 iron is broken. Measure length of both the #5 and #7 irons.)**

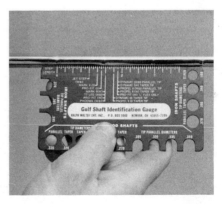

19-3 If you are to install the same type of shaft, the original shaft type must be identified. As is often the case, the shaft band may be missing. However, shafts can be easily identified using the **Golf Shaft Identification Gauge.**

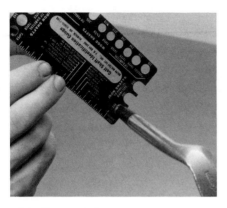

19-4 The **Golf Shaft Identification Gauge** can also be used to determine the shaft tip construction. That is, whether it is a taper tip or a parallel tip (unitized) shaft. The exact use of this gauge is explained later in this chapter.

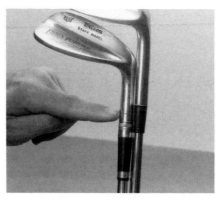

19-5 Determine if the shaft and hosel are pinned together. Sometimes a pin (rivet) will only penetrate one half of the hosel. Club on the right has no pin, while the club on the left does as indicated here.

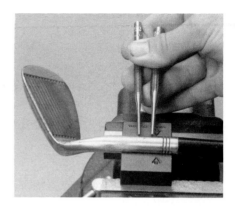

19-6 Depending upon the diameter of the pin, select either a ³/₃₂″ **or** ⅛″ **pin punch.** Note the use of a **Riveting Block.** This special tool allows the hosel to rest on a curved surface and provides a sturdy base. The pin is punched through an opening in the Block.

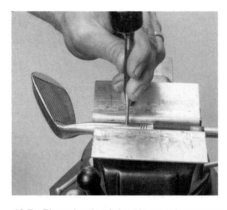

19-7 Place the tip of the **pin punch** squarely on the top of the pin. If a **Riveting Block** is not available, make sure the hosel is placed securely between a pair of **aluminum or brass vise pads** before fastening in a vise.

19-8 Drive the pin through the hosel.

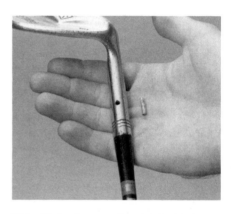

19-9 Photo shows an iron head with the pin removed. If the pin does not penetrate both sides of the hosel, then the pin must first be drilled through with a ⁷/₃₂″ drill bit from inside the shaft and the remainder of the pin punched inside the hosel.

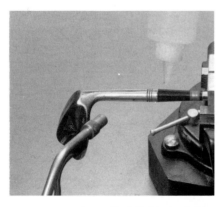

19-10 A **Lock Tight Shaft Holder** or **Rubber Shaft Clamp** should be used to hold the shaft securely. Heat the hosel at a point approximately 1″ from the top of the hosel. If you wish to save the ferrule, simultaneously squirt water onto the plastic ferrule. The squirt bottle is very handy for this purpose. A bucket can be set on the floor to catch the water.

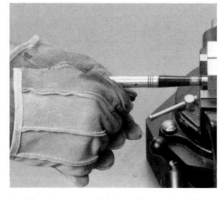

19-11 Next, grasp the head in your hands and attempt to turn and pull the head from the shaft. A pair of **leather gloves,** a pot holder glove or rags should be used to protect your hands.

19-12 If the head fails to come off the shaft, the hosel must be reheated. An alternative to the squirt bottle is to soak a paper towel with water and then wrap the towel around the ferrule.

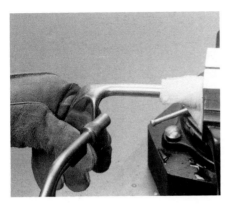

19-13 Direct more heat against the hosel. Do not worry if the hosel discolors. This is easily removed and will be shown later in this chapter.

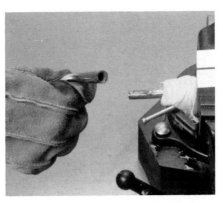

19-14 The head should now come loose from the shaft. If it does not, jump ahead to photo 19-23 and continue through the photos which apply to your particular situation.

19-15 If you wish to save the old ferrule, it will usually slip right off the shaft.

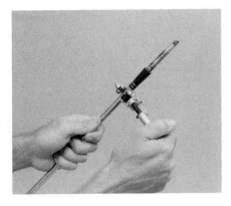

19-16 **If the ferrule will not come off, then proceed as follows:** First, cut shaft off 1″ or 2″ above the ferrule using a tubing cutter or friction wheel.

19-17 Select a hole in the **Lock Tight Shaft Holder** that will allow the shaft to slide freely through it. Gently tap the shaft through the ferrule. Note the ferrule is removed up the shaft and not from the tip end.

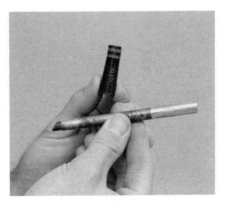

19-18 Ferrule is removed in perfect condition.

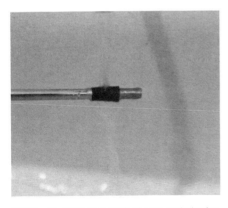

19-19 An alternative method is to soak the ferrule in hot water and attempt to remove it or wrap the ferrule with masking tape and attempt to pull it off with a pair of pliers. The hot water will soften the plastic but not burn it.

19-20 A **Heat Gun** will supply enough heat to soften the ferrule also and allow you to slide it off the shaft.

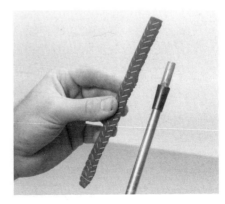

19-21 Another method for removing a ferrule is to cut a strip of rubber from an old rubber grip. The strip should be 7″ long and ¾″ wide.

19-22 Wrap the rubber strip around the ferrule and then continue to turn the strip in the same direction after tightening. This will create tremendous pressure on the ferrule and it should turn from the shaft.

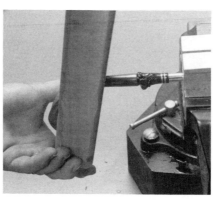

19-23 If a head fails to come off, apply more heat to the hosel. Next, place a **Hardwood Leverage Block** around the head and . . .

19-24 . . . attempt to turn the head. Once the head is turned, it will usually pull off the shaft. Note the melted condition of the plastic ferrule if not treated properly.

19-25 This **Leverage Block** allows the user to simultaneously turn and pull on the head. This is the recommended leverage block to use.

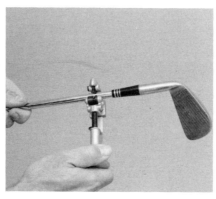

19-26 If the head would not come off as previously shown, cut the shaft off 1″ to 1½″ above the top of the hosel using a **tubing cutter.**

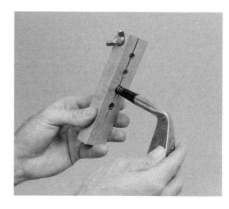

19-27 Place the protruding portion of the shaft securely in the **Lock Tight Shaft Holder.**

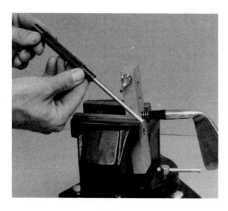

19-28 Use an **8″ Long Pin Punch** and . . .

19-29 . . . insert the punch in the shaft and drive the head off. Sometimes it is first necessary to remove any lead and other foreign matter from inside the shaft by drilling it out with a ⁷/₃₂″ or ¼″ drill bit.

19-30 The head is now driven off the shaft.

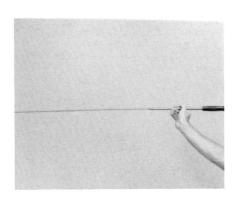

19-31 A **47″ Ramrod** is an alternative to cutting the shaft short and using the 8″ pin punch. Here's how it works.

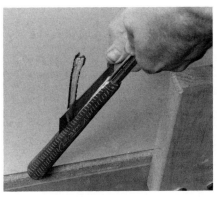

19-32 First, either cut the old grip off the shaft or . . .

19-33 . . . save the grip for future use by using the **Grip Shooter.** Chapter 22 photos 22-31 thru 22-37 shows procedure for use of the Grip Shooter.

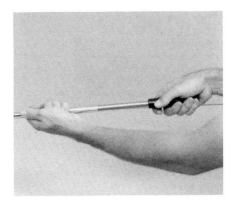

19-34 Insert the 47″ Ramrod down the shaft. Hold shaft and knock head off. Remember to first remove any foreign matter from inside the shaft tip with a **47″ drill bit.**

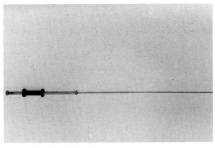

19-35 A **Sliding Weight Ramrod** works the same way as the regular ramrod except it has a heavy 6 lb. sliding weight. This produces a tremendous amount of ramming force against the bottom of the hosel.

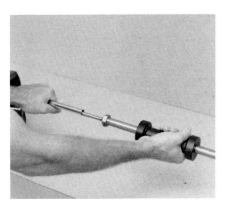

19-36 Place the **Sliding Weight Ramrod** inside the shaft, support shaft with one hand and slide weight forward against stop for hammering action.

19-37 The **Iron Head Remover Tool** will remove the most stubborn iron head from a steel shaft. Often an older shaft will rust to the hosel, making it difficult to remove.

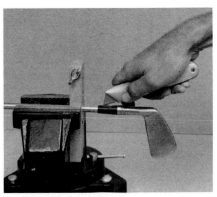

19-38 First, the ferrule must be removed from the shaft. If you wish to reuse the ferrule, split the ferrule top and bottom into two halves with a sharp knife or razor blade.

19-39 Remove the ferrule. Later, in photos 19-112 thru 19-118 you will learn how to put the split ferrule together again. If you do not wish to save the ferrule . . .

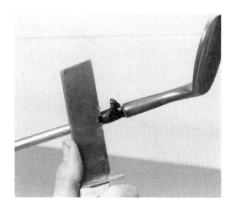

19-40 . . . simply cut it from the shaft.

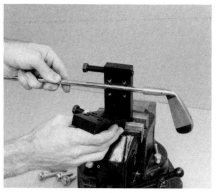

19-41 Secure the longer half of the unit in a vise. Place the shaft in the specially grooved section and place the other half of the unit around the shaft.

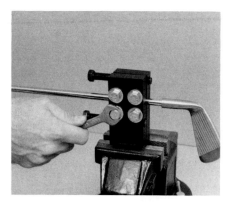

19-42 Tighten the four bolts evenly to secure the shaft. Allow at least a ¾″ gap between the top of the hosel and the unit.

19-43 Place the **forcing plate** over the shaft and tighten the drive bolts until the forcing plate is snug against the top of the hosel. Note the use of a ratchet socket wrench.

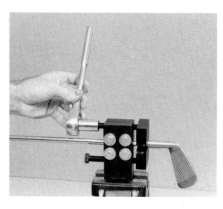

19-44 Alternately tighten the two drive bolts until the head is . . .

19-45 . . . pushed off the shaft.

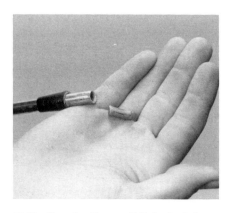

19-46 Occasionally you will find a lead slug or other weighted material inside the tip of the shaft. This indicates the manufacturer or another repairman found the swingweight too light and added weight down the shaft. If you find weight down the shaft, after reshafting, you will have to add weight to bring the swingweight back to original. See Chapter 17 for swingweighting procedures.

19-47 Some iron head models have a rubber or plastic plug extending down the hosel and through the sole. Heat the hosel as described previously. If the hosel contains a pin, refer to photos 19-6 thru 19-9.

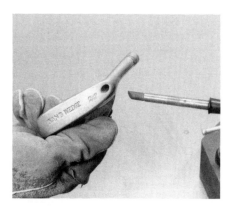

19-48 The head will pull off the shaft leaving the plug inside the shaft. If you wish to save the plug, tug at the plug with a pair of pliers. If the plug does not come out . . .

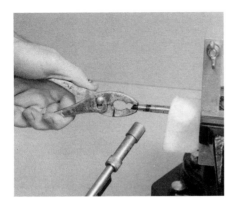

19-49 . . . apply heat to the tip of the shaft while simultaneously pulling on the plug.

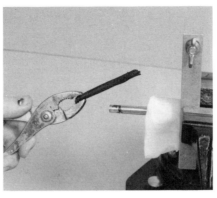

19-50 The plug is removed. As you can see, these plugs were often used in swingweighting lighter heads. Some plugs are quite short, others very long and some even had lead powder added to the rubber during molding.

19-51 Replacement plugs are available if you do not wish to save the original. See photos 19-172 thru 19-177 for installation steps. These plugs are available in both red or black colors.

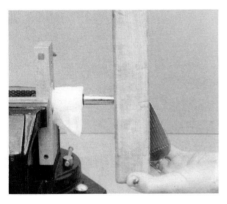

19-52 Occasionally you will encounter a model with the shaft screwed into a threaded hosel. You will note the head loosens while turning the head **clockwise** yet tightens when turned counterclockwise.

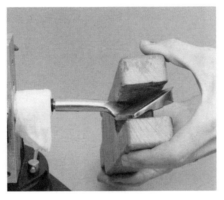

19-53 Simply continue to turn the head clockwise and . . .

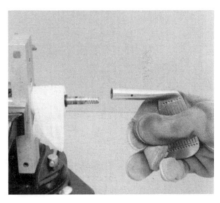

19-54 . . . the head will turn off the shaft. If you are replacing this type of shaft, be aware that the hosel must be re-bored to accept a larger tip diameter shaft. See photos 19-98 thru 19-105 for hosel bore enlarging steps using the step drills.

19-55 A shaft over hosel assembly is the easiest type to remove. You should rarely encounter a pin. Place a **Lock Tight Shaft Holder** around the shaft 3″ above the tip of the shaft. Apply heat to the shaft.

19-56 Twist head loose with a **Hardwood Leverge Block** or gloved hands. Note the post extending from the iron head. A special shaft with an enlarged over hosel tip section is needed to properly reshaft this club.

19-57 Do not be intimidated if asked to **replace a hickory shaft.** Simply punch the pin through the hosel if one is present.

19-94 This photo shows why. The distance from the **back of the heel to the first step** varies enough to make the club on the bottom play much stiffer than the club on the top. Therefore, the **back of heel to first step dimension** must be followed closely to ensure proper shaft performance unless you specifically wish a club to perform differently.

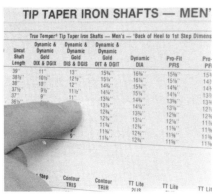

19-95 Again, look straight across the page until you reach the column heading that describes the **pattern and flex shaft** with which you are working. This measurement gives the distance you need with this shaft from **back of the heel to the first step.**

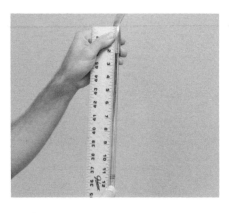

19-96 Next, take the recommended shaft, temporarily install it into the head and measure this distance. If the measurement you come up with is longer than this recommended **back of heel to first step dimension**, either select a shorter shaft or cut the difference from the tip of the shaft.

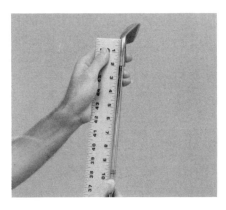

19-97 If the measurement is shorter than the recommended distance, a longer shaft is needed. This is correct because the difference in length between identical shafts is made up solely in the tip section. A longer shaft has a longer tip section.

19-98 Step drilling procedure for enlarging hosel bores: Step drilling is best performed when using a **Drill Press** in conjunction with the **Iron Head Boring and Reaming Vise.** Step drills used in this sequence are a special hard cobalt material which works best.

19-99 Place a **Brass Hosel Protector** or **Lead Tape** around the hosel to prevent possible scratches.

19-100 Fasten the hosel securely in vise's vertical "V" groove. Drill to the bottom of hosel hole using the smallest drill bit first. If working with a "through bore" model, place a wrapping of tape or a **Drill Stop** around the bit no farther than 1½" up. This will ensure that you don't drill too far.

19-101 Drill to the bottom of the bore or until the tape is even with the top of the hosel. Always use **Cutting Oil** (not machine or lubricating oil) when drilling.

19-102 Next, drill to within a specified distance of the first bit using the next largest size bit.

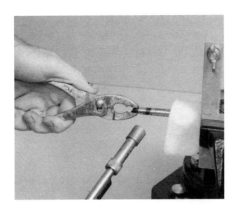

19-49 . . . apply heat to the tip of the shaft while simultaneously pulling on the plug.

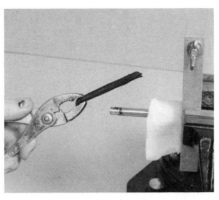

19-50 The plug is removed. As you can see, these plugs were often used in swingweighting lighter heads. Some plugs are quite short, others very long and some even had lead powder added to the rubber during molding.

19-51 Replacement plugs are available if you do not wish to save the original. See photos 19-172 thru 19-177 for installation steps. These plugs are available in both red or black colors.

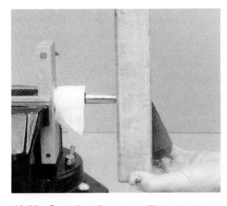

19-52 Occasionally you will encounter a model with the shaft screwed into a threaded hosel. You will note the head loosens while turning the head **clockwise** yet tightens when turned counterclockwise.

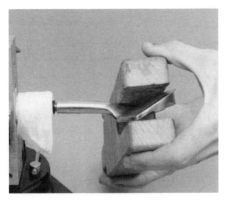

19-53 Simply continue to turn the head clockwise and . . .

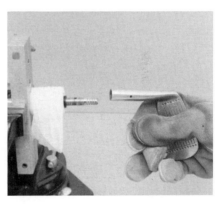

19-54 . . . the head will turn off the shaft. If you are replacing this type of shaft, be aware that the hosel must be re-bored to accept a larger tip diameter shaft. See photos 19-98 thru 19-105 for hosel bore enlarging steps using the step drills.

19-55 A shaft over hosel assembly is the easiest type to remove. You should rarely encounter a pin. Place a **Lock Tight Shaft Holder** around the shaft 3″ above the tip of the shaft. Apply heat to the shaft.

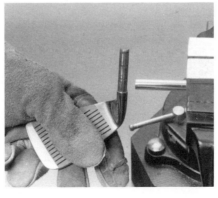

19-56 Twist head loose with a **Hardwood Leverge Block** or gloved hands. Note the post extending from the iron head. A special shaft with an enlarged over hosel tip section is needed to properly reshaft this club.

19-57 Do not be intimidated if asked to **replace a hickory shaft.** Simply punch the pin through the hosel if one is present.

19-58 Heat the hosel briefly using a propane torch and . . .

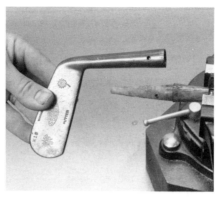

19-59 . . . turn and pull the head from the shaft.

19-60 The procedure for removing a shaft broken off inside the hosel is to first heat the hosel with a **propane torch.**

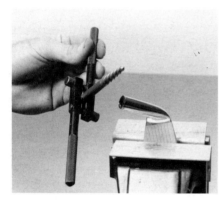

19-61 Select a screw type **extractor** of the proper size. Note the use of the special **extractor wrench.**

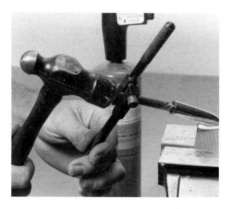

19-62 Tap the extractor inside the shaft until a snug fit is achieved.

19-63 Turn the extractor wrench counterclockwise while pulling and . . .

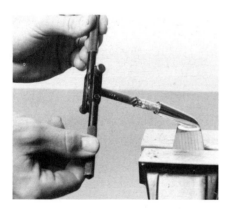

19-64 . . . the shaft should come out of the hosel. The ridges along the side of the extractor "bite" into the walls of the shaft allowing the shaft to be pulled from the head along with the extractor. If the shaft does not pull from the head, reheat the hosel and try again.

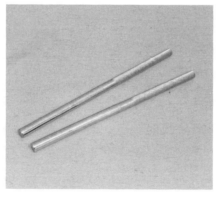

19-65 The GolfWorks® offers a set of Iron Shaft Extractors that work amazingly well. The extractors taper at the same rate as the inside of the shaft. They are available for .355 tip taper and .370 parallel tip iron shafts.

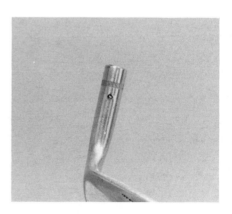

19-66 Be certain the pin (rivet) is removed from the hosel before using the **Iron Extractor.**

19-67 After the pin is removed, completely clean all epoxy or other foreign material from inside the tip of the shaft. A ¼" drill bit works best.

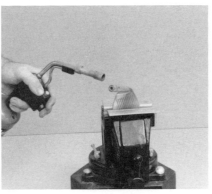

19-68 Heat the hosel using a propane torch. This will soften the epoxy and allow for easy shaft removal.

19-69 Place the smooth end of the extractor between the vise jaws and tighten securely.

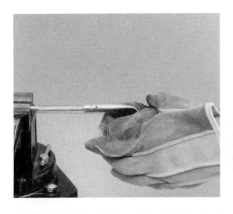

19-70 Push the shaft over the extractor. Push and turn the head clockwise until you feel the shaft "lock" onto the extractor. It may require a firm push to lock the extractor in the shaft. Note the use of leather gloves for protection from the heated hosel.

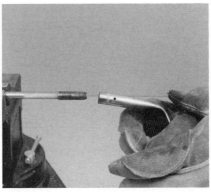

19-71 After locking in the extractor, turn the head counterclockwise while simultaneously pulling on the head. The head should pull free from the shaft while the shaft remains attached to the extractor. Remove the shaft from the extractor by pulling the shaft off with a pair of pliers.

19-72 **If the extractor methods fail, the shaft must be drilled from the head.** Use of an **Iron Head Boring and Reaming Vise** along with a **drill press** will make this job much safer, faster, easier and more accurate.

19-73 If any portion of the shaft extends out of the hosel, this must be ground flush with the top of the hosel. Do not grind into the hosel.

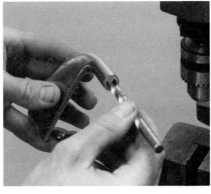

19-74 Select a drill bit that will fit snugly inside the shaft. Drill bits made from a **hard cobalt material** work best.

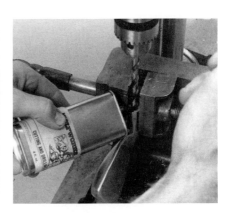

19-75 Place the hosel in the boring vise. Newer iron heads should have a brass hosel protector placed around the hosel for protection. Begin drilling and liberally apply **cutting oil** (not machine or lubricating oil) to both the drill bit and hosel hole.

19-76 Drill to bottom of hosel bore. Note: Special Wilson and Hagen models with the black or red plugs are not a true "through bore" design. The shaft is not installed completely through the hosel.

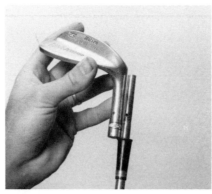

19-77 The original shaft used in this type of club is referred to as a "reduced tip" shaft. Instead of the common .355 tip diameter, this shaft is a .340. When replacing this shaft, do not re-bore the hosel to the same depth as before. Instead, bore into the hosel to a depth of 1½" maximum. Drilling farther risks the chance of the drill bit coming through the side of the hosel.

19-78 Photo shows the previously described iron head after an attempt to bore to the bottom of the hosel. Fortunately, this can be repaired by welding and rechroming. The GolfWorks® offers this service.

19-79 Next, select a drill bit that is slightly larger than the first and drill to the bottom of the hosel bore. Continue this procedure until . . .

19-80 . . . either the shaft tip comes out with the drill or the shaft is completely drilled from the hosel. Often the shaft tip will come out because of the heat created in the hosel by the spinning drill bit. Step drilling is also used to enlarge an existing bore size. See photos 19-98 thru 19-105 for procedure.

19-81 A .355 tapered reamer is great for cleaning out and resetting proper internal tapers in hosels. However, never use the reamer for removing broken shaft tips. If a drilling oil was used, clean all oil from hosel after drilling.

19-82 Iron hosels can also be super heated red hot in an attempt to remove the temper from the broken shaft tip. This is referred to as "annealing" the metal or reducing its hardness.

19-83 Apply heat to the hosel using a propane torch until the hosel turns red. Allow the hosel to return to room temp. and then drill the shaft from the hosel. This makes the shaft easier to drill. Heating the hosel does not functionally damage the hosel. Refer to photos 19-169 and 19-171 for removing the hosel discoloration.

19-84 With the head off the shaft, use a **Golf Shaft Identification Gauge**, a micrometer or vernier caliper to determine the tip size of the removed shaft and replacement shaft.

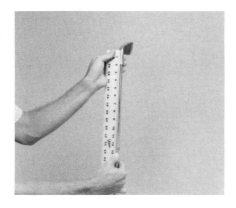

19-85 The tables in Appendix 6 give **back of heel to first step dimensions** for commercially available shafts. This measurement is important if you want the new shaft to perform as it was designed. When these measurements are altered, the shaft will either be more flexible or stiffer than original.

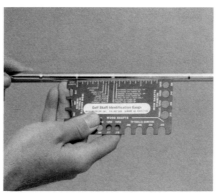

19-86 First, determine what pattern (Dynamic®, Pro-Fit®, TT Lite®, etc.) shaft you will be working with. This information will come either from customer input, your determination of the original shaft pattern, or by simply choosing a shaft to change to and try.

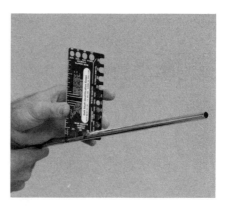

19-87 Next, you need to know if you are working with a tapered or a parallel (unitized) tip shaft. A tapered tip shaft is just that. The tip section increases in diameter from the tip to a point up from the tip. A parallel (unitized) tip shaft has a constant tip diameter from the tip to the first step. The **Shaft Identification Gauge** or a micrometer is used to determine this.

19-88 With the shaft pattern and tip construction known, refer to Appendix 6. The tables are divided into a **tapered tip group** and a **parallel tip group.** Look for the grouping of tables that fits your shaft tip construction.

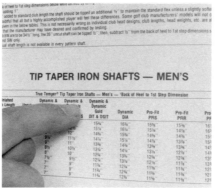

19-89 Next, look for the individual table that includes your **shaft pattern** — Dynamic®, TT Lite®, Pro Pel®, Microtaper®, etc. The tables are further subdivided into wood and iron shafts, as well as men's and ladies' shafts. Choose the table that is appropriate for your reshafting job.

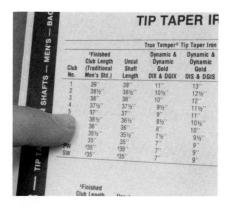

19-90 Look at the first column labeled **Club Number.** Look down the column until you come across the club number with which you are working.

19-91 Next, look straight across the page to the next column labeled **Finished Club Length.** This reading gives you the industry standard length for your club (many modern clubs have a length that is ½" longer called **Modern Standard Length.** This is easily adjusted though by following the instructions at the bottom of the tables.

19-92 The next column labeled **Uncut Shaft Length** gives the recommended raw length shaft you need to select from your stock of shafts for this length club. If you are working with a parallel tip shaft, the column will read "Amount Normally Trimmed From Tip of Shaft." Parallel tip shafts come in only 1 length for each flex, so uncut shaft length is not applicable.

19-93 Some repairmen stop at this stage, grab the recommended shaft and install it into the head. The reason this should not be done should be obvious after looking at this photograph. The two clubs have very different hosel lengths and bore depths. If the same length shafts are installed in both clubs, without tip trimming, they will play very different.

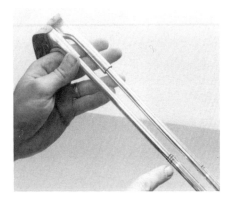

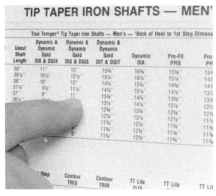

TIP TAPER IRON SHAFTS — MEN'

	True Temper® Tip Taper Iron Shafts — Men's				'Back of Heel to 1st Step Dimens	
Uncut Shaft Length	Dynamic & Dynamic Gold DIX & DGIX	Dynamic & Dynamic Gold DIS & DGIS	Dynamic & Dynamic Gold DIT & DGIT	Dynamic DIA	Pro-Fit PRS	Pro-Fit PR
39"	11"	13"	15¾"	16¾"	15¼"	15¼
38½"	10½"	12½"	15¼"	16¼"	15¼"	14¼
38"	10"	12"	14¾"	15¾"	14¾"	14¼
37½"	9½"	11½"	14¼"	15¼"	14¼"	13½
37"	9"	11"	13¾"	14¾"	13¾"	13¾
36½"			13¼"	14¼"	13¼"	12½
			12¾"	13¾"	12¾"	12¾
			12¼"	13¼"	12¼"	11½
		9"	11¾"	12¾"	11¾"	11¾
			11¾"	12¼"	11¾"	11¾
	Step	Contour TRIS	Contour TRIR	TT Lite 2LIS	TT Lite	TT Lit

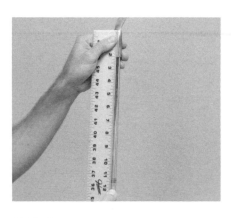

19-94 This photo shows why. The distance from the **back of the heel to the first step** varies enough to make the club on the bottom play much stiffer than the club on the top. Therefore, the **back of heel to first step dimension** must be followed closely to ensure proper shaft performance unless you specifically wish a club to perform differently.

19-95 Again, look straight across the page until you reach the column heading that describes the **pattern and flex shaft** with which you are working. This measurement gives the distance you need with this shaft from **back of the heel to the first step.**

19-96 Next, take the recommended shaft, temporarily install it into the head and measure this distance. If the measurement you come up with is longer than this recommended **back of heel to first step dimension**, either select a shorter shaft or cut the difference from the tip of the shaft.

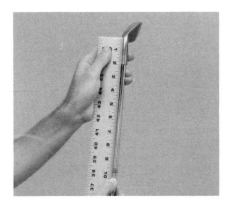

19-97 If the measurement is shorter than the recommended distance, a longer shaft is needed. This is correct because the difference in length between identical shafts is made up solely in the tip section. A longer shaft has a longer tip section.

19-98 **Step drilling procedure for enlarging hosel bores:** Step drilling is best performed when using a **Drill Press** in conjunction with the **Iron Head Boring and Reaming Vise. Step drills** used in this sequence are a special hard cobalt material which works best.

19-99 Place a **Brass Hosel Protector** or **Lead Tape** around the hosel to prevent possible scratches.

19-100 Fasten the hosel securely in vise's vertical "V" groove. Drill to the bottom of hosel hole using the smallest drill bit first. If working with a "through bore" model, place a wrapping of tape or a **Drill Stop** around the bit no farther than 1½" up. This will ensure that you don't drill too far.

19-101 Drill to the bottom of the bore or until the tape is even with the top of the hosel. Always use **Cutting Oil** (not machine or lubricating oil) when drilling.

19-102 Next, drill to within a specified distance of the first bit using the next largest size bit.

19-103 Using the largest drill bit next, measure and . . .

19-104 . . . drill to within a specified distance of the second bit. Clean hosel of any leftover cutting oil before installing the new shaft. Acetone works well for this.

19-105 The hosel has been bored to the desired depth and diameter and will now accept the larger shaft.

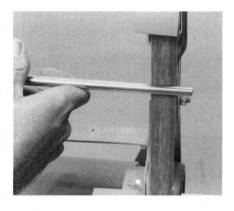

19-106 Once the proper shaft is chosen and any needed corrections have been made, abrade the tip of the shaft with the use of a belt sander, grinding stone, emery cloth or file. Abrading the shaft tip gives the epoxy an excellent bonding surface and is mandatory.

19-107 The appropriate size and style of ferrule is chosen. Ferrules have various bore sizes according to the shaft tip size they match. Slide the ferrule on the shaft.

19-108 Sometimes the new ferrule will not slide on the shaft easily. Use this method: Place the ferrule against the mouth of a can of acetone and turn the can upside down so the acetone runs into the ferrule. Keep the other end of the ferrule closed off with your finger.

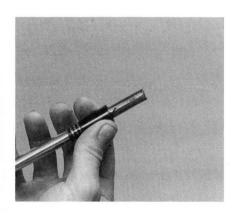

19-109 After 10 seconds, quickly remove the ferrule from the can and slide the ferrule down the shaft. If the acetone is not available in the small mouth can, drop the ferrule in an open container of acetone for a few seconds and then install it.

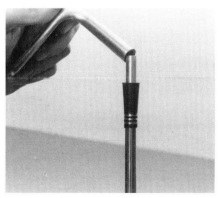

19-110 An alternative to the acetone method is to simply place the hosel over the shaft and force the ferrule down the shaft.

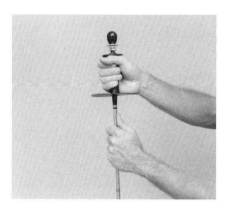

19-111 The **Ferrule Installer Tool** will accurately set an iron or wood ferrule to the proper depth. It is especially helpful when assembling more than one club and a series of ferrules must be set.

19-112 If the old ferrule was spilt with a razor knife to remove it, melt it back together with acetone. First, hold one half of the split ferrule under the shaft and . . .

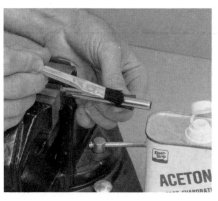

19-113 . . . apply a liberal amount of acetone to the ferrule. Note that ferrule is being assembeled up close to the shaft tip. This is important with tip taper shafts.

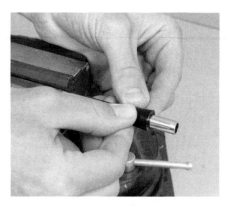

19-114 Dip the other half of the ferrule in the acetone and quickly stick the two halves together.

19-115 Rub the seams with acetone. This will further seal the 2 halves together.

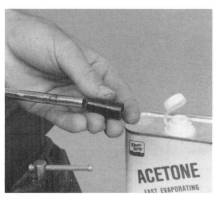

19-116 In approximately one minute, slip the ferrule off the shaft.

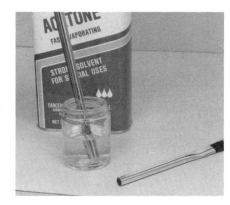

19-117 Dip the shaft tip in acetone and . . .

19-118 . . . slide ferrule up into position.

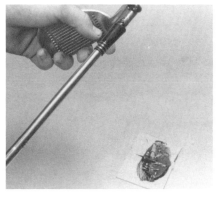

19-119 To install the shaft into the hosel: First mix your epoxy. Dip the tip of the shaft into the epoxy and then insert the shaft into the hosel. A good high shear strength shafting epoxy is best for reshafting. Conap or GolfWorks® shafting epoxy works well.

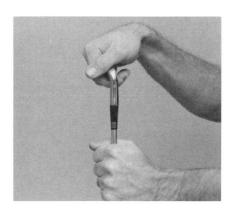

19-120 To set the shaft in place, grasp the head with one hand while supporting the shaft with the other and . . .

19-121 . . . hammer the butt of the shaft onto a steel plate or concrete floor.

19-122 A practical alternative to hammering the shaft against the floor is to tighten the head securely in a vise. Place a pair of **aluminum or brass vise pads** over the vise jaws before tightening.

19-123 Insert a **Shaft Driving Plug** in the butt end of the shaft and drive the shaft in place.

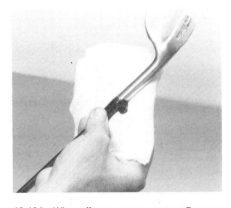

19-124 Wipe off any excess epoxy. Be sure ferrule is seated flush against hosel. If it is not, place the **Lock Tight Shaft Holder** above it and force the ferrule down into place. Allow the epoxy to cure for the recommended time.

19-125 After the epoxy has hardened, place a **Rubber Shaft Clamp** around the shaft and tighten in a vise. Wrap a piece of ¾" masking tape around the hosel just below the ferrule.

19-126 Use a flat mill or fine file and lightly file the excess plastic down flush with the tape. The tape will protect the hosel from possible scratches.

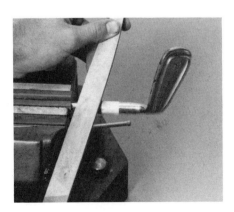

19-127 Continue to file while rotating the club. Care should be taken to ensure a proper taper in the ferrule. Do not file the top edge of the ferrule. A lip should remain.

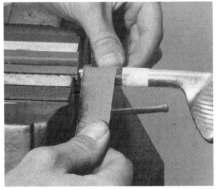

19-128 Filing will leave flat spots and ridges in the plastic. Lightly sand the ferrule with a 180 or 220 grit fine sandpaper.

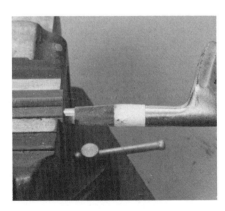

19-129 At this point the ferrule will look rough and dull in appearance. This is normal at this stage.

19-130 Rub the ferrule with 000 steel wool. This will remove some of the scratches left from the sandpaper and make the ferrule smoother.

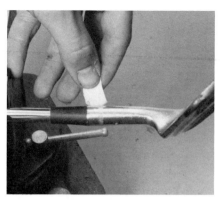

19-131 Remove the masking tape from the hosel.

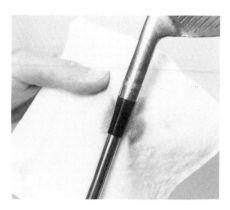

19-132 Dampen a paper towel with **Acetone** and wipe the ferrule with the paper towel. This will return the plastic ferrule to a shiny, like-new appearance.

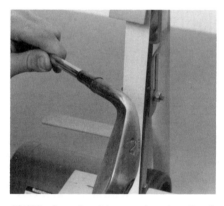

19-133 A much quicker way to reduce the diameter of the ferrule is with a **Belt Sander.** The belt used is a **Cloth Linen Belt**. This is a non-abrasive surface which removes the excess plastic through friction.

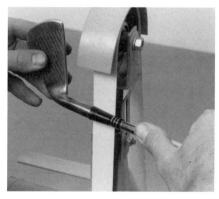

19-134 Hold the clubhead as shown and rotate the ferrule against the linen belt in . . .

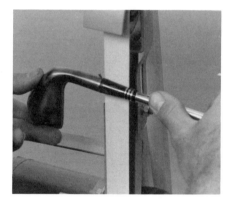

19-135 . . . the clockwise direction . . .

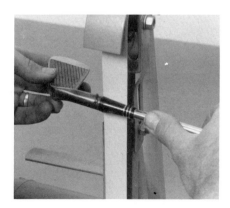

19-136 . . . as shown. This is very important. Turning the clubhead in the opposite direction will only burn and ruin the ferrule.

19-137 Photo shows a properly tapered ferrule using the **Cloth Linen Belt.**

19-138 Lightly steel wool the ferrule by hand or on the **Steel Wool Arbor.**

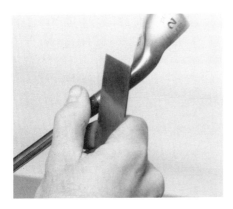

19-139 If there is any plastic or epoxy residue around the top of the hosel, carefully scrape or cut it from the hosel.

19-140 Wipe the ferrule with an **Acetone**-dampened paper towel. This makes the ferrule look like new again.

19-141 Installing a new hosel pin: Depending upon what size was previously used, select either a ⅛″ or ³⁄₃₂″ drill bit. Note the hosel is tightened securely between aluminum vise pads. Brass pads will work well also.

19-142 Drill into the existing hole to clean out the excess epoxy. Do not attempt to drill through the shaft at this point.

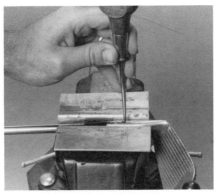

19-143 Instead, place a sharpened **Awl** or **Prick Punch** into the hole and . . .

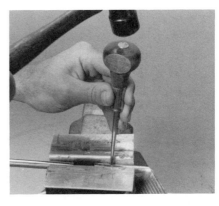

19-144 . . . drive the **Awl** through the top half of the shaft. Usually one sharp blow will do this.

19-145 After piercing the shaft, drill through the top half of the shaft. Do not attempt to drill through the bottom half. Instead . . .

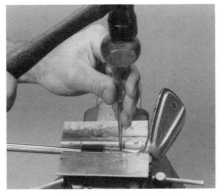

19-146 . . . turn the club around and repeat the drilling, punching and . . .

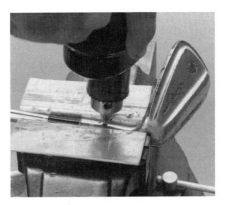

19-147 . . . drilling procedure. Once you have drilled through this half of the shaft, allow the drill bit to exit out the other side of the hosel. This will ensure there is a clear passage from one side of the hosel to the other.

19-148 Select the appropriate size hosel pin. Sharpening or beveling one end of the hosel pin will help the pin push through the hosel.

19-149 Place the pin in the hole and lightly tap the pin completely through the hosel.

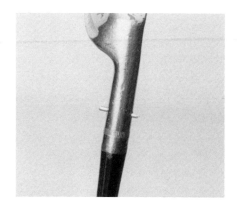

19-150 The photo shows the pin extending out both sides of the hosel.

19-151 Remove the pin excess, yet leave a small portion sticking about the surface of the hosel on both sides. Tapping a **Chisel** quickly through the pin is one way to remove this excess.

19-152 Wire snips work well also for cutting the pin.

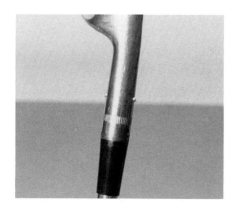

19-153 Photo shows some of the pin still extending above the surface.

19-154 Place the hosel on a hard surface such as the top of the vise jaws or vise anvil and repeatedly tap the pin lightly so it mushrooms outward against the hosel. The purpose of this step is to fill in any gap between the pin and the pin hole wall and make the pin fit tightly.

19-155 Next, gently peen the other side.

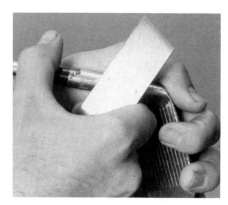

19-156 After peening, carefully cut through the flattened pin head with a sharp knife. Because the pin is made of aluminum, the pin will trim easily.

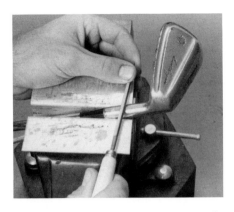

19-157 A small file works well to remove the excess pin. Do not scratch the hosel.

19-158 This photo shows a properly installed pin. The ends of the pin should camouflage well with the side of the hosel. If desired, a light buff using a white polishing compound on a set of stitched buffing wheels will hide the pin entirely.

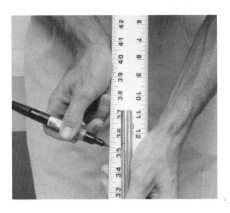

19-159 The club must now be cut to length. Lay a **48″ long ruler** behind the club with the club in a correct address position. Mark the shaft at a point ⅛″ below the desired final length (i.e., at 35⅜″ if a 35½″ length club is desired). The grip cap will account for the ⅛″ difference after the grip is installed.

19-160 Photo shows a clubhead in the correct address position for measuring with a ruler positioned directly behind the head.

19-161 Cut the shaft with either a **Tubing Cutter** or . . .

19-162 . . . a **Friction Cutoff Wheel.** Always wear safety glasses when working around machines.

19-163 Procedure for cutting a shaft with the Friction Cutoff Wheel: Make a mark on the shaft against the spinning wheel. Next, push the shaft firmly into the wheel.

19-164 Keep pushing the shaft against the cutoff wheel until the edge of the wheel is through the shaft wall and then slowly rotate the shaft counterclockwise.

19-165 Keep turning the shaft counterclockwise into the wheel until the shaft section comes off.

19-166 Lightly grind the end of the shaft to remove the rough edge. Note the shaft is positioned at a 45° angle to the grinding stone.

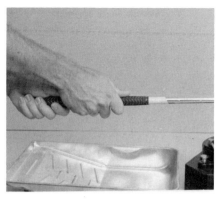

19-167 Install the grip as outlined in Chapter 22 and apply the appropriate shaft band.

19-168 Finally, check the swingweight. If swingweight correction is needed, refer to Chapter 17 for procedure.

19-169 If the hosel was blued from excess heating during shaft removal, it can be made to look like new again. **Simichrome polish** or **Blue Away** is very effective. Simply rub fluid onto hosel with a towel.

19-170 Photo shows hosel after the product **Blue Away** has been used.

19-171 Applying the hosel against the face of a **stitched** or **unstitched buffing wheel** will also remove the discoloration. The **white compound** is best used for this buffing procedure.

19-172 Procedure for installing rubber plugs: The original plug may be reinstalled or the easier step is to install an available replacement.

19-173 Dip the end of the plug into epoxy and then . . .

19-174 . . . push the plug into the hole in the sole of the club. Push until a snug fit is achieved. A **Colored Paste Dispersion** has been mixed in with the epoxy to match the color of the plug.

19-175 Wipe up the excess epoxy and allow the epoxy to cure.

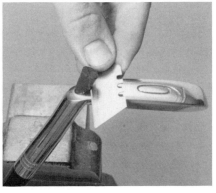

19-176 After the epoxy has hardened, slice through the protruding plug with a sharp knife or razor blade. Trim the plug as close to the sole as you can.

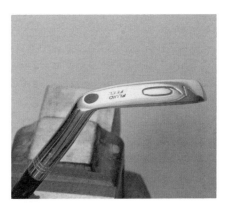

19-177 Photo shows the plug correctly trimmed.

19-178 Some Ping® model putter heads are attached to the shaft in a unique manner. In addition to epoxy, a steel ball bearing was forced into the shaft tip. This expands the tip and makes the shaft very difficult to remove. If, after heating, the shaft will not pull free . . .

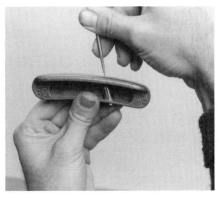

19-179 . . . determine by eye where the tip of the shaft would extend through the sole of the putter (in some models the shaft will not extend through the sole but through an offset hosel).

19-180 Make a small indentation at this point with a sharp center punch or awl. Drill through the sole of the putter with a ⅛" drill bit. Drill until the bit meets the steel ball bearing. Note the head is held in a vise using polyurethane vise pads. Aluminum or brass vise pads also work well.

19-181 Punch the ball bearing out through the shaft. The shaft will now come out easily. The hole in the sole should be filled in with a brass colored epoxy.

19-182 Photo shows the shaft tip with the hardened ball bearing. This can be a repairman's nightmare; however, it is a very clever way to ensure a shaft will not come loose.

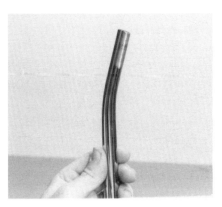

19-183 When reshafting putters, you will sometimes need to make a bend in the tip section of the new shaft to match the bend in the original.

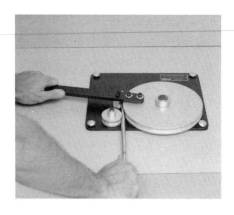

19-184   The Golf Shaft Bending Machine will make any degree bend at any point on the shaft. If you do not do enough work to justify the expense of this machine, you can have shafts custom bent for you by The GolfWorks®.

19-185   Installing a new hickory shaft in an antique iron: Photo shows a typical antique putter head with the tip of the new and old shaft.

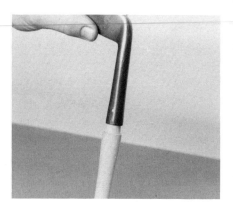

19-186   The tip of the new shaft must be shaped to fit the hosel. Test fit the shaft into the hosel and . . .

19-187   . . . file it until it fits or . . .

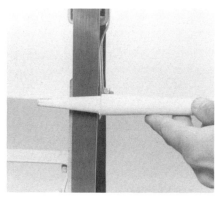

19-188   . . . sand until . . .

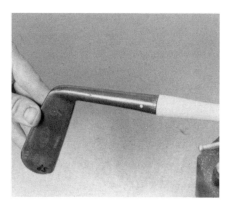

19-189   . . . the tip fits snugly inside the hosel. Have patience as this can sometimes be a time-consuming project. The results are well worth it though.

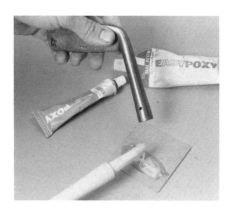

19-190   Mix up a shear strength shafting epoxy and coat the shaft tip as well as . . .

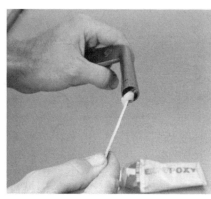

19-191   . . . the hosel.

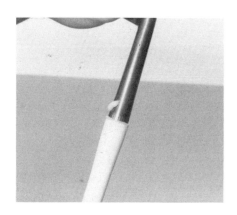

19-192   Install the shaft into the hosel and wipe off any excess epoxy. Allow the epoxy to cure.

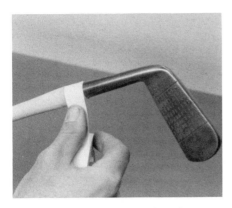

19-193 Next, wrap a layer of masking tape around the top of the hosel.

19-194 Using a **file** or preferably a **belt sander** with a **medium grade belt,** remove the excess wood so the shaft is flush with the hosel.

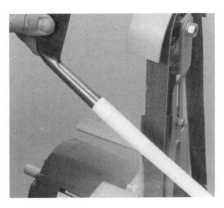

19-195 Continue to sand while maintaining a proper taper.

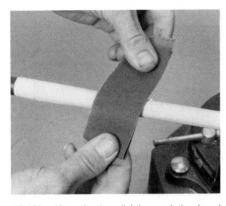

19-196 After shaping, lightly sand the hosel with a fine grade sandpaper. This will remove any irregularities in the wood surface.

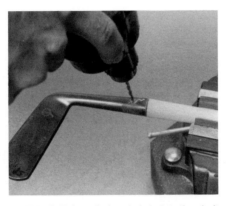

19-197 Drill through the pin hole into the shaft tip using the proper size drill bit. An ⅛″ bit is usually required. After drilling through one side of the shaft . . .

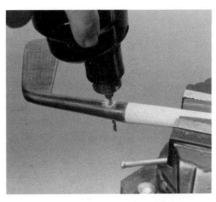

19-198 . . . turn the club in the vise and drill into the other side of the shaft tip. Allow the drill bit to pass through the opposite side to create a clear passage for the pin.

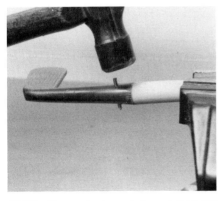

19-199 Tap an aluminum pin through the hosel and shaft.

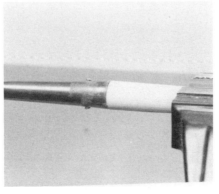

19-200 Trim the excess pin as shown in photos 19-151 thru 19-153.

19-201 Peen the end of the pin flush with the hosel so any gap around the pin is eliminated. Repeat this operation to the other side.

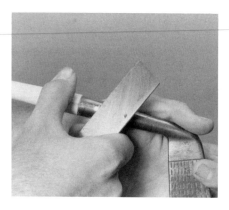

19-202 Next, cut through the excess using a sharp knife. Be careful!

19-203 Photo shows the hosel and pin area after trimming.

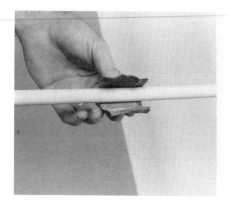

19-204 Lightly sand the entire shaft with a fine grade of sandpaper. 150 or 220 grit is preferred.

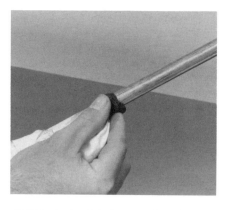

19-205 Apply a light brown stain such as walnut to the entire shaft. Allow the shaft to dry overnight.

19-206 After the shaft has dried, apply a filler to the shaft. The filler will plug up the pores of the wood and prevent moisture absorption. Leave the filler on the shaft for 7 minutes. This will allow solvents to evaporate and the filler to harden.

19-207 Vigorously wipe the excess filler from the shaft using a piece of **Burlap** or terry cloth. Allow the shaft to dry overnight. Filler used can either be a **natural** or **less intense black filler** depending upon the shade you wish to achieve. See Chapter 1 if more information on filler is needed.

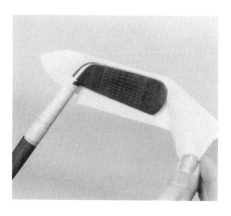

19-208 After an overnight dry, cover the head with a loose wrapping of masking tape or newspaper.

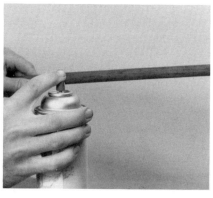

19-209 Apply a couple of light spray coats of Primer Sealer to the shaft. This will properly seal the shaft and give it a satin look. Allow the Primer Sealer to dry 30 minutes between each light coat.

19-210 Photo shows the old and new shaft. If proper care is taken, the new shaft will look similar to the old one. Note the difference in shaft thickness. This is perfectly acceptable but if you wish a more flexible feel, reduce the diameter of the shaft. Club is ready to be cut to length using a hack saw. Grip is then installed as shown in Chapter 22.

ADDITIONAL INFORMATION FOR RESHAFTING IRON CLUBS

TABLE 19-1
Iron Club Lengths — Men's and Ladies'

Irons	Men's Modern Standard	Men's Traditional Standard	Ladies' Standard	[1]Ladies' Petite
1	39½"	39"	38"	37½"
2	39"	38½"	37½"	37"
3	38½"	38"	37"	36½"
4	38"	37½"	36½"	36"
5	37½"	37"	36"	35½"
6	37"	36½"	35½"	35"
7	36½"	36"	35"	34½"
8	36"	35½"	34½"	34"
9	35½"	35"	34"	33½"
PW	35½"	35"	34"	33½"
SW	35½"	35"	34"	33½"

[1]Ladies' petite is usually ½" shorter than the traditional ladies' standard length. Some companies make ladies' petite 1" shorter than ladies' standard length.

TABLE 19-2
Drill Selection Chart

- Hosel pin drill for irons — most modern   ⅛"
- Hosel pin drill for irons — older models   ³⁄₃₂"

TABLE 19-3
Determining Shaft Flex by Color on Butt End of Shaft

Designation	Flex	Color
X	Extra Stiff	Green
S	Stiff	Red
R or T	Medium	Black
A	Flexible	Yellow
L	Ladies (very flexible)	Blue

Combination flex shafts such as UDWC, UDWAL, UJWC & U2LWAL do not have a color code on the butt end.

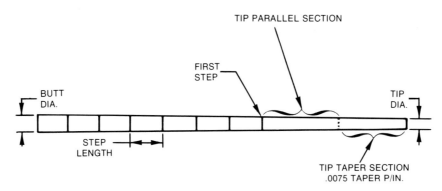

Fig. 19-211
Golf shaft terminology

Step Drilling Instructions and Drill Sizes by Tip Sizes

When boring hosels for new shafts or reshafting, many repair shops find it difficult or very expensive to obtain the proper size drills and reamers to match every iron shaft tip size available. Also, they run into special problems such as enlarging hosel holes to accept "tipped" shafts or hosels which need to be bored to accept another shaft size, or in most cases, hosels which just need to be cleaned out so that the replacement shaft will fit properly.

To solve this problem, step drilling is recommended. See Fig. 19-212. Step drilling can be described simply as a method utilizing a matched set of special drills, each a different size. The smallest drill is used first by drilling to the bottom of the hosel hole (or completely through as the case may be). The next larger size drill is then used and drilled part way down and finally the largest size is used and drilled to a lesser depth than the previous two. This system for creating the proper taper by utilizing steps has the advantge of providing areas for epoxy to collect thus eliminating the common occurrence of squeezing it all out, resulting in premature bond failure of head to shaft. Also, step drills can be easily resharpened unlike reamers and step drills are not damaged when they hit any remaining portion of the hardened shaft tip.

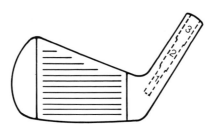

Step #1: Drill to bottom of hosel with smallest diameter cobalt drill bit.
Step #2: Drill to within a specified depth of the 1st drill using the next largest size 2nd cobalt drill bit.
Step #3: Drill to within a specified depth of the 2nd drill using the larger size 3rd cobalt drill bit.

Fig. 19-212
Step drilling procedure

Step Drilling Instructions and Sizes for .355″ Tip Taper Shafts

Step #1: Drill to bottom of hosel bore with a "T" (.358″) diameter special hard cobalt drill.
Step #2: Drill to within ⅜″ of bottom of hosel bore with a "U" (.368″) diameter special hard cobalt drill.
Step #3: Drill to within 1¼″ of bottom of hosel bore with a ⅜″ (.375″) diameter special hard cobalt drill.

Step Drilling Instructions and Sizes for .300″ Tip Taper Shafts

Step #1: Drill to bottom of hosel bore with a "N" (.302″) diameter special hard cobalt drill.
Step #2: Drill to within ⅜″ of bottom of hosel bore with a 5⁄16″ (.312″) diameter special hard cobalt drill.
Step #3: Drill to within 1¼″ of bottom of hosel bore with a "O" (.316″) diameter special hard cobalt drill.

Step Drilling Instructions and Sizes for .370″ Unitized Parallel Tip Shafts

Step #1: Drill to bottom of hosel bore with the ⅜″ (.375″) diameter special hard cobalt drill.

Equipment Required in Step Drilling Irons

A ⅜″ electric variable speed hand drill can be used to enlarge or open up hosel bores and also to clean out foreign particles before installing a new shaft. However, to drill out broken shafts it is recommended that a drill press be used in conjunction with The GolfWorks® Iron Head Boring and Reaming Vise to securely hold the hosel in a vertical position. Also, during drilling apply a liberal amount of a good quality cutting oil. DO NOT USE MOTOR OIL OR LIGHT MACHINE OIL. See Photos 19-98 thru 19-104.

Types of Drills Used in Step Drilling Irons

The best type of drills to use when step drilling irons is cobalt. The cobalt material is much tougher than high speed steel drill bits and is especially useful when drilling out broken shafts and stainless steel investment cast hosels. For irons, a standard length drill bit referred to as "jobbers length" is used. Cobalt drill bits are all but impossible to find in retail stores and with the worldwide shortage of this material, they are becoming increasingly difficult to obtain even from the drill manufacturers. The GolfWorks® sells complete sets of step drills packaged in a clear plastic box with instructions. See Fig. 19-213.

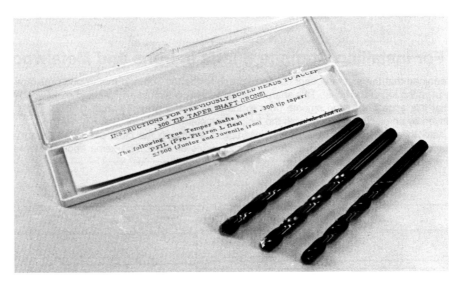

Fig. 19-213
*Sets of step drills are available from
"The GolfWorks®" for both woods and irons*

Controlling Depth When Step Drilling Irons

A piece of masking tape wrapped around the drill bit will work quite well to indicate the proper depth for drilling. Another method is to use adjustable drill stops which come in two sizes, one size to fit 1⁄16″ to ¼″ drill bits and the other size to fit ¼″ to ½″ drill bits. See Fig.19-214. Also shown here are drill stop collars which come in various sizes and are usually sold in sets. These various drill stops are available from The GolfWorks® and many hardware stores.

20

TIGHTENING LOOSE IRON HEADS

With today's modern bonding materials and assembly methods, loose iron heads on modern clubs have become more rare than in the past. This is fortunate because when a loose iron head is detected it is usually too late since the head has probably flown completely off the end of the shaft. Most of the loose iron heads you will find will be on the older clubs that have a pinned hosel. The pin, of course, will keep the head from flying completely off and it can also make it hard for you to detect if the head is loose. The best thing to do is to check the entire set by holding the clubhead in a vise equipped with aluminum or brass vise pads. With the clubhead firmly held, grasp the grip end with both hands and try to twist the shaft in both directions. If you cannot feel it move, listen carefully for a squeaking sound which indicates that the shaft is loose.

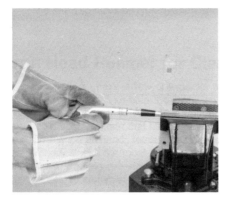

20-1 First, remove the head from the shaft. Refer to Chapter 19 for procedure.

20-2 The choices for materials to fill the excess space in a hosel are brass or aluminum shims, or **Aluminum Oxide Sand.**

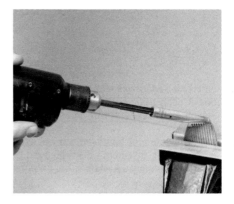

20-3 Before reinstalling the shaft, clean out all loose glue, dirt and scale from the hosel bore. A proper size hosel reamer, or step drills, work well for tapered hosel bores. A ⅜" drill bit is used for a hosel bored to fit a .370 parallel tip shaft.

20-4 If a shim is used, apply a liberal amount of epoxy to both sides of the shim and also down the hosel bore.

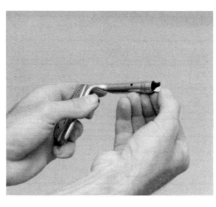

20-5 Push the shim into the hosel bore. A shim is not always necessary and sometimes epoxy alone will suffice. If the head turns freely about the shaft when the shaft is pushed to the bottom of the hosel bore, this is a good indication a shim is necessary.

20-6 Roughen the shaft tip using a belt sander, grinding stone, file or emery cloth. Removing all the old epoxy will ensure good adhesion between the epoxy and shaft.

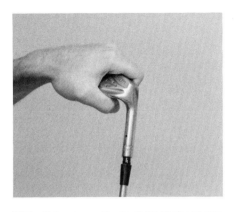

20-7 Put epoxy on the tip of the shaft and also inside the hosel. Push the shaft into the hosel hole. Make sure the shaft is turned properly so the grip is correctly aligned with the clubface. If the shaft doesn't penetrate to the bottom of the hosel bore, proceed to photo 20-8.

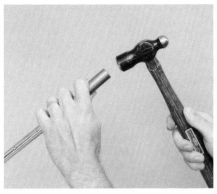

20-8 Using a **Shaft Driving Plug,** drive the shaft into the hosel as far as it will go. It is necessary to remove the grip and use the above method on "Tip Taper" shafts which are force fit. "Unitized" (parallel tip) shafts will usually bottom out in the hosel by pushing the shaft into the head or tapping the grip end against the floor.

20-9 To use Aluminum Oxide Sand, coat the inside of the hosel and the outside of the shaft with epoxy, dip only the tip of the shaft into the sand and . . .

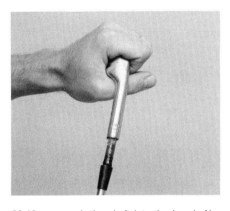

20-10 . . . push the shaft into the hosel. Aluminum Oxide Sand is an excellent material because the sand acts as a good bonding surface for the epoxy.

20-11 Another trick for ensuring the shaft is aligned properly in the hosel is to make sure the rivet hole is lined up from the outside of the hosel through the shaft. Procedure for installing a rivet is shown in Chapter 19.

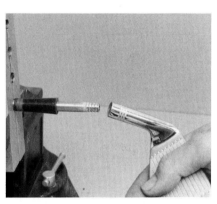

20-12 To tighten a screw-in type shaft. It is necessary to first remove it by turning the head clockwise.

20-13 Next, apply epoxy to the shaft tip and inside the hosel.

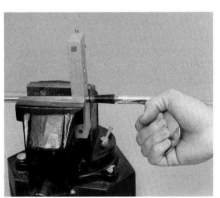

20-14 Once epoxy is applied, simply screw the head back onto the shaft. If the head is forced past its original position, it will be necessary to reposition the grip on the shaft for proper alignment.

NOTES

_____
_____
_____
_____
_____
_____
_____
_____
_____

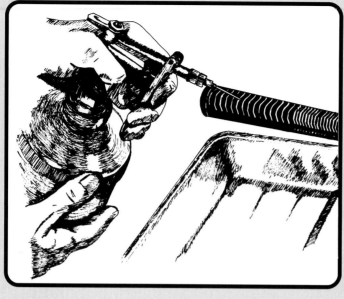

SECTION 3

COMBINED GOLF WOOD AND IRON CLUB REPAIRS

ELIMINATING RATTLES AND SQUEAKS

21

It is usually rare when a customer brings in a golf club to have an annoying noise removed from it because golfers will put up with the distraction as long as the club holds together. However, when a customer brings in a club for such a repair, you can bet that he has decided that the noise is costing him valuable strokes out on the course. In some cases it is true that the noise can be traced to something which is affecting the shot. However, nine out of ten times, the noise has no mechanical bearing on the golf club's playability.

Most common causes for rattles:

Problem #1: An adhesive particle has come loose from the shaft tip end and is sliding up and down the shaft.

Problem #2: A piece of dirt or a small stone has entered the shaft through the hole in the rubber grip's end cap.

Problem #3: Some manufacturers use plastic grip end caps with either a plastic plug or a metal screw inside. These end caps occasionally come loose or the plug falls through and slides up and down the shaft.

Problem #4: Many manufacturers add a small lead slug to the tip end of the shaft during assembly to achieve the desired swingweight. Sometimes they break loose and rattle or slide up and down inside the shaft.

Problem #5: A loose soleplate on woods can sometimes rattle.

Problem #6: A loose lead weight under the soleplate on woods is one of the most common causes of a rattle.

Problem #7: A set screw sometimes falls into the hollow cavity of a metalwood, or a piece of foam breaks loose.

Most common causes for squeaks:

Problem #8: A loose, or partially loose, shaft in a wood club or iron club will squeak.

Problem #9: A grip that is loose on the shaft. Generally this looseness will be found in the top of the grip.

21-1 To test for a rattle in the head of the club, hold the shaft loosely and tap the head gently on a hard surface.

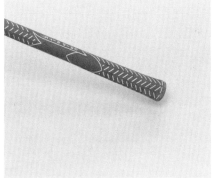

21-2 To test for a rattle in the grip end of the club, hold the head end loosely and bounce the grip on a hard surface.

21-3 Sometimes a squeak can be caused by a loose head. Grasp the head in one hand and the shaft in the other. If you detect movement between the shaft and head, the shaft will need to be removed and reinstalled properly.

21-4 To tighten a rattle under the soleplate, remove the soleplate as outlined in Chapter 3. If a lead weight is loose, it can be peened and tightened by tapping a cross point screwdriver into the lead plug.

21-5 Lead can also be peened by tapping with the round end of a ball peen hammer.

21-6 Refer to Chapter 3, photos 3-10 thru 3-24, for soleplate reinstallation procedure.

21-7 Here is an example of a club that allows access to the weight cavity without removing the soleplate.

21-8 Remove the center screw. If necessary, apply heat using methods shown in Chapter 4, photos 4-5 thru 4-7.

21-9 Lift medallion from the soleplate. Some models do not have the center screw and heat must be applied to the medallion to soften the epoxy holding it in place.

21-10 Either stuff steel wool or cotton inside the cavity to deaden the sound or . . .

21-11 . . . remove the loose lead and/or epoxy from the cavity and . . .

21-12 . . . pour lead powder or molten lead back into the cavity. Although loose, lead powder offers no sound when free inside the cavity.

21-13 Apply epoxy to the medallion and the recess that holds the medallion. If necessary, remove any old epoxy from the recess before new epoxy is applied.

21-14 Place the medallion back in the recess and install the original screw if the club had one.

21-15 Wipe off excess epoxy. If no screw holds the medallion in place, lay a piece of masking tape across the medallion until the epoxy cures.

21-16 To remove a rattle inside the shaft, either cut off the grip or remove it with the **Grip Shooter.** See Chapter 22, photos 22-31 thru 22-37. Always wear eye protection.

21-17 If particles are loose inside the shaft, pour them out.

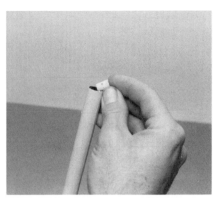

21-18 If loose particles of lead or another heavy substance is poured out of the shaft, this weight must be replaced. Ideally, the weight should be added under the soleplate and not down the shaft. Drop a cork with a glop of epoxy on it down the shaft to secure the weight.

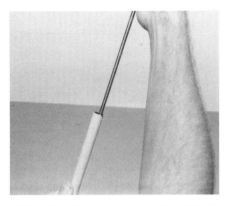

21-19 Ram the cork in place with a long drill rod or **Ramrod.** The opposite end of a **47″ Drill Bit** will also work.

21-20 To remove a rattle caused by a loose end cap, first, remove it and apply epoxy to the stem. See Chapter 22 for additional information on removing end cap assemblies.

21-21 Insert the end cap into the shaft. Be careful not to use too much epoxy as the excess may later break off and cause another rattle. It may be necessary to completely replace the end cap. See Chapter 22 for correct replacement procedure.

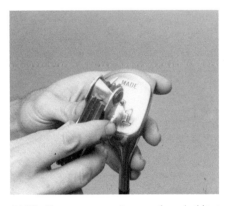

21-22 To remove a set screw from inside a metal head, it must be speared with a **Hex Key Wrench** and turned up through the threaded hole in the soleplate. This requires a degree of patience and luck.

21-23 If the set screw fails to come out, the cavity can be stuffed with cotton. This should deaden the offending sound. Steel wool can be used but be aware that swingweight will increase.

21-24 Loose foam in a metal head can be dumped out through the set screw hole if the head has one. Loss of weight can be compensated for by adding steel wool or lead powder inside the head.

22

INSTALLING GRIPS AND CHANGING GRIP SIZE

Grip replacement will probably be the most common golf club repair in your shop. Fortunately, it is also one of the most profitable and easy to perform, especially with slip-on rubber grips. And, with new materials and components recently available, even leather re-gripping has become much easier and faster than it was just a few years ago.

There will be many instances when you will be asked to re-grip a golf club with another type, style or size of grip. For instance, you may be requested to replace leather grips with rubber grips, or an 11″ rubber grip with a 10″ rubber grip, or a standard size grip with an oversize grip. When you change the grip size or change to another type or style of grip, you may unknowingly change the balance of the club by altering both the swingweight and total weight. The weight of a golf grip can vary significantly because of style, length, material, size and manufacturer. This weight variance is oftentimes significant enough to affect both swingweight and total weight.

At this point read through the tables at the end of this chapter and study the information, keeping in mind the relationships that exist between the different tables. This information is valuable as handy reference material and will also provide a better understanding of the design relationship between the grip and the entire golf club.

22-1 Before re-gripping any club, always check the swingweight. It is also a good idea to check the total weight.

22-2 If the grip size is not to be changed, the existing grip size must be accurately determined because it must be properly duplicated when installing the new grip. The **Grip Size and Shaft Butt Gauge** shown works very well and is the quickest method. Slip a gauge opening over the bottom of the grip. Slide the gauge up the grip until it becomes snug against the grip. Mark spot with your thumb and . . .

22-3 . . . slip gauge off grip and use the end of the gauge for the 2″ measurement. This gauge measures grip size at 2″ from end of grip. One of the various grip gauge openings will allow it to slide up the grip, but will stop 2″ from the top as shown in this photo. The actual size of the grip can be read at that opening.

22-4 If the gauge opening stops below the 2″ measurement, the grip is larger than the designated opening.

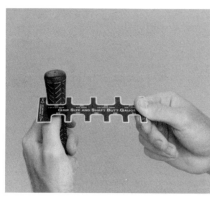

22-5 If the gauge stops above the 2″ measurement, the grip is smaller than the designated opening.

22-6 A gauge for measuring the grip size underneath the right hand is also available. The **Grip Size Under Right Hand Gauge** is used by sliding the different size openings up the grip until one becomes snug at a point 5″ from the top of the grip. The size would then be read directly from the gauge.

22-7 An alternative to a grip gauge is a micrometer. The only drawback to this method is once a reading has been taken you must refer to Table 22-2 (in the additional information section at the end of this chapter) to determine the equivalent grip size. Example: .930 = $\frac{1}{32}$″ over men's standard grip size.

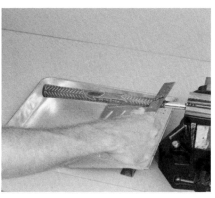

22-8 Removal of old grip. Rubber grips can be cut off using a sharp knife. Cut underneath the lip of the grip and . . .

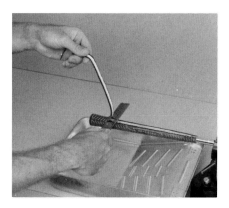

22-9 . . . pull back on the cut rubber piece while, simultaneously, slicing through the grip all the way to the grip cap. **Be very careful when using sharp knives.**

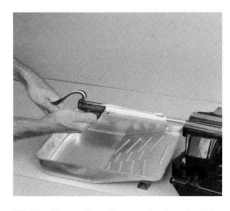

22-10 After cutting through the length of the grip, pull the remaining portion of the grip from the shaft.

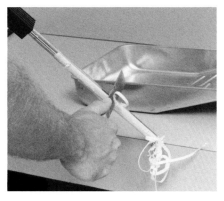

22-11 A quick way to remove any remaining tape is to place the butt of the shaft against the edge of the workbench or vise, and push the knife through the tape while rotating the shaft.

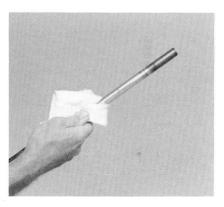

22-12 The final remaining tape residue is easily removed by wiping the butt of the shaft with a paper towel dampened in grip solvent or Naphtha.

22-13 To remove leather wrap on grips, first cut through the plastic grip collar. Note: If you are going to re-grip with leather, you can try to save the existing grip collar by grasping, twisting and pulling down simultaneously.

22-14 Next, unwrap the old leather grip and remove it.

22-15 Cut off the old underlisting and remove all old glue or tape from the shaft. Although current underlistings are made of rubber, you will find crepe paper or cardboard underlistings on many of the older clubs.

22-16 Many older clubs have plastic end caps. Sometimes, the entire end cap assembly will pull or screw out in one piece. Grasp end cap lightly in vise jaws, or with pliers, and gently twist and pull at the same time to remove it. If it will not come out all the way, warm the outside of the shaft with a propane torch on a low setting. Be careful.

22-17 Photo shows removed end cap assembly. See Fig. 22-146 in additional information section at the end of this chapter for a drawing of the anatomy of an end cap.

22-18 If the end cap will not pull out in one piece, attempt to pry out the plastic disc with a sharp knife.

22-19 In some cases, a screw will be found underneath the disc.

22-20 After turning the screw out, the end cap is easily removed. However, a tapered wooden plug extends from the shaft.

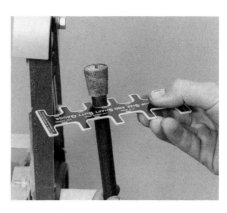

22-21 One alternative for the wooden plug is to grind it to the same diameter as the shaft butt. The **Belt Sander** shown works well. Measure the shaft with the **Grip Size and Shaft Butt Gauge** or a micrometer.

22-22 Next, grind the excess wood to the same diameter as the shaft butt.

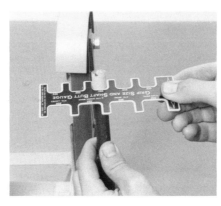

22-23 Periodically check the size until . . .

22-24 . . . the wooden plug is the same size as the shaft. The club is now ready for gripping.

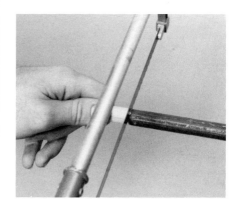

22-25 If you wish to remove the wooden plug, cut it even with the shaft using a hacksaw.

22-26 Drill through the plug with a ⅜" drill bit.

22-27 The sides of the plug are now easily collapsed inward with a scriber or awl. Dump the debris out of the shaft.

22-28 If the plug does not come out, heat the shaft butt briefly with a propane torch on a low setting.

22-29 Remains of the wood plug can then be removed with a pair of **Needle Nose Pliers.**

22-30 Sometimes, after removing the plastic disc in the end cap, you will find a plastic pin, brass pin or a hex socket set screw. Set screws will usually turn out with the proper size Hex Key wrench. Pins must be driven through the end cap assembly with a long punch as shown. The remaining end cap can then be pulled or drilled from the shaft.

22-31 If, for some reason, it is requested that the old grip be saved, it can be removed using the **Grip Shooter** as shown, or with a syringe and a large hypodermic needle. **Always wear eye protection.** Push the needle slowly into the grip at a 45 degree angle until it touches the shaft. The needle should enter the grip approx. 2" from the grip cap. **Keep your fingers away from the end of the needle.**

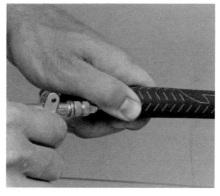

22-32 Place your thumb over the entry point in the grip and inject solvent underneath the grip. Placing your thumb over the hole will prevent the solvent from squirting out.

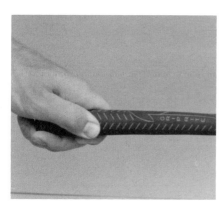

22-33 Once a portion of the grip is enlarged as a result of pumping in solvent, remove the needle. Keep your thumb over the hole.

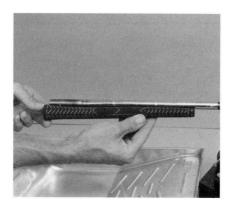

22-52 Once the build-up tape is applied, or, if no build-up tape is required, proceed as follows: Hold the new grip up to the shaft to determine the approximate length of double-coated tape needed.

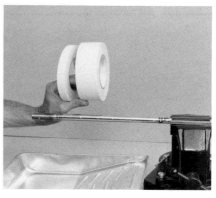

22-53 Double-coated tape is available in both ¾″ and 2″ wide tape.

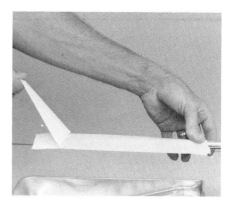

22-54 The use of 2″ wide double-coated tape is shown. This is faster and more economical than using ¾″ wide double-coated tape. Apply tape lengthwise to the shaft. The tape should be slightly shorter than the grip length, yet still have approximately 1″ extending over the butt end of the shaft.

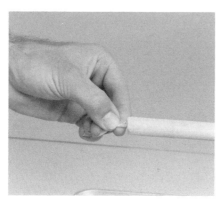

22-55 Carefully wrap tape around shaft. Twist or squeeze the end of the tape together as shown and push inside the butt end of the shaft. This prevents solvent from entering the shaft during grip installation.

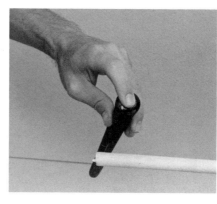

22-56 Block the vent hole in the butt end of the grip with your finger, golf tee or other pointed object.

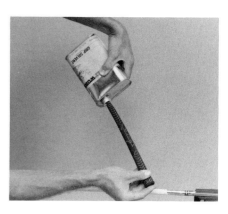

22-57 Squirt or pour a generous amount of grip solvent inside the grip. Pinch the open end of the grip with your fingers and shake to thoroughly wet the inside of the grip. **Perchlorethy-lene**, a non-flammable grip solvent, is shown. Many shops still use naphtha, gasoline or lighter fluid. These are highly flammable and danger-ous solvents and are not recommended.

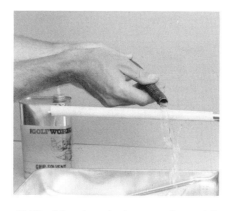

22-58 Grip solvent is then poured out of the grip over the entire length of the double-coated tape to wet it thoroughly. If necessary, squirt ad-ditional solvent onto tape.

22-59 It is vitally important that the butt end of the shaft is wet, as this will make installation easier. Working quickly, position the open end of the grip just beneath the shaft butt and . . .

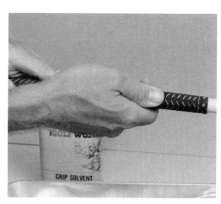

22-60 . . . start the grip up and over the shaft. Holding grip as shown, slide it on until the end of the shaft stops at the top of the grip. Work quickly.

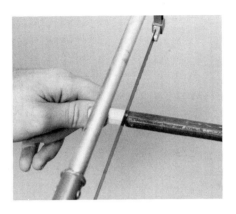

22-25 If you wish to remove the wooden plug, cut it even with the shaft using a hacksaw.

22-26 Drill through the plug with a ⅜″ drill bit.

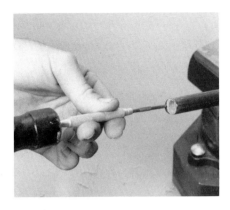

22-27 The sides of the plug are now easily collapsed inward with a scriber or awl. Dump the debris out of the shaft.

22-28 If the plug does not come out, heat the shaft butt briefly with a propane torch on a low setting.

22-29 Remains of the wood plug can then be removed with a pair of **Needle Nose Pliers.**

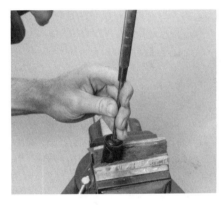

22-30 Sometimes, after removing the plastic disc in the end cap, you will find a plastic pin, brass pin or a hex socket set screw. Set screws will usually turn out with the proper size Hex Key wrench. Pins must be driven through the end cap assembly with a long punch as shown. The remaining end cap can then be pulled or drilled from the shaft.

22-31 If, for some reason, it is requested that the old grip be saved, it can be removed using the **Grip Shooter** as shown, or with a syringe and a large hypodermic needle. **Always wear eye protection.** Push the needle slowly into the grip at a 45 degree angle until it touches the shaft. The needle should enter the grip approx. 2″ from the grip cap. **Keep your fingers away from the end of the needle.**

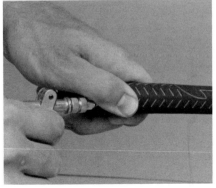

22-32 Place your thumb over the entry point in the grip and inject solvent underneath the grip. Placing your thumb over the hole will prevent the solvent from squirting out.

22-33 Once a portion of the grip is enlarged as a result of pumping in solvent, remove the needle. Keep your thumb over the hole.

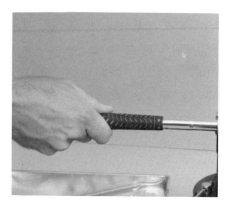

22-34 Work the solvent bubble down the length of the grip by pushing, prodding and twisting the grip at a point just below the bubble. This will allow the solvent to move down the entire length of the grip.

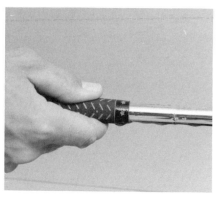

22-35 Continue to push and twist until the solvent squirts from the bottom of the grip.

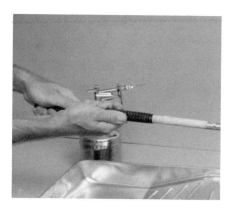

22-36 Pull the grip from the shaft.

22-37 The grip is removed in perfect condition and can be reused. **A final caution: Be very careful using hypodermic needles and always wear eye protection.**

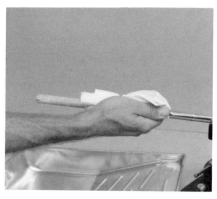

22-38 A fast way to remove slimy tape is by wrapping a paper towel around it while squeezing and pulling it towards the butt end of the shaft. You must remove all tape and residue from the shaft.

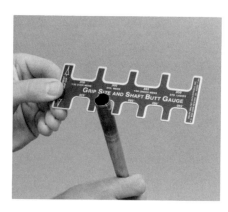

22-39 To install grips, first check the shaft butt size using the **Shaft Butt and Grip Size Gauge,** or . . .

22-40 . . use a micrometer or vernier caliper.

22-41 Next, determine grip core size by looking inside the mouth of the grip. Look for a size designation such as M58, L56, 58, 60, M62R, etc. See Tables 22-3 thru 22-6 and Fig. 22-144 in additional information section at the end of this chapter for an understanding of these codes.

22-42 The old grip and the new grip can be weighed on an accurate scale to determine if the new grip is lighter or heavier. This weight can affect the club's swingweight. Table 22-10 in additional information section at the end of this chapter gives various grip weights.

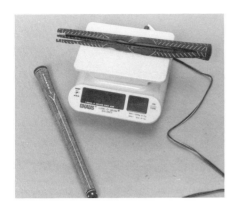

22-43 Photo shows an **O'Haus Electronic Gram-Ounce Scale** that is fast and convenient for weighing any component.

22-44 To install a slip-on rubber grip, first place shaft clamp around shaft and tighten in a vise. The face of the club should point up vertically and in a square position. Note the use of a common paint roller pan to catch excess solvent. Solvent can be reused.

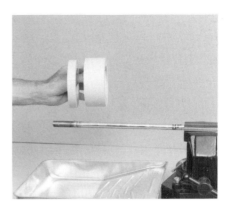

22-45 With the shaft butt size and grip core size known, additional layers of tape may be needed to achieve the desired grip size. If additional tape layers are necessary for build-up, use the regular ¾″ or 2″ wide masking tape. See tables at the end of this chapter for information on how tape thickness and multiple tape layers affect grip size.

22-46 A single layer wrap of ¾″ masking tape (not overwrapped), as shown, will increase grip size .01″ which is slightly less than ¹⁄₆₄″ (¹⁄₆₄″ = .015).

22-47 When ¾″ masking tape is overlapped half-again on itself (this is referred to as an overlap wrap), the grip size will increase by .02″, or slightly larger than ¹⁄₆₄″. Both tape wraps used together (a single layer wrap and an overlapping wrap on top of it) are exactly .03″ or ¹⁄₃₂″ oversize.

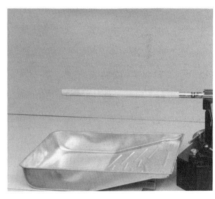

22-48 You can also use 2″ wide masking tape for build-up. One layer will increase grip size .01″ which is slightly less than ¹⁄₆₄″ (¹⁄₆₄″ = .015).

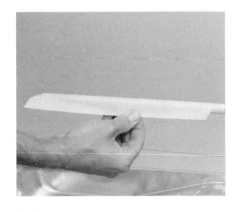

22-49 For more build-up, overlap layers of 2″ wide masking tape. Two layers will increase grip size by .02″ or slightly larger than ¹⁄₆₄″. Three layers will increase grip size by .03″ or ¹⁄₃₂″ oversize.

22-50 This photo shows a **Grip Slide Rule.** The Rule is used to calculate how to install oversize grips using build-up tape and core sizes and determine the amount of swingweight change due to the grip change. In many cases it details several ways to wrap the build-up tape and swap core sizes to achieve the desired grip size.

22-51 When placing multiple layers of tape on the shaft, stagger the length and placement of each piece of tape. This will eliminate any unsightly drop at the bottom of the grip and, also, avoid the formation of an additional rib where all pieces overlap in the same spot.

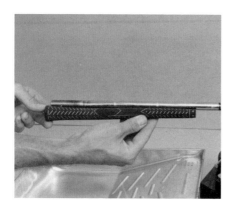

22-52 Once the build-up tape is applied, or, if no build-up tape is required, proceed as follows: Hold the new grip up to the shaft to determine the approximate length of double-coated tape needed.

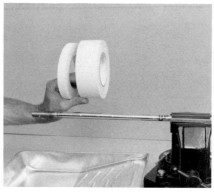

22-53 Double-coated tape is available in both ¾″ and 2″ wide tape.

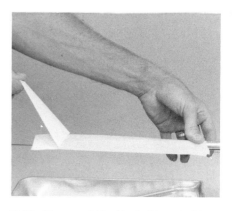

22-54 The use of 2″ wide double-coated tape is shown. This is faster and more economical than using ¾″ wide double-coated tape. Apply tape lengthwise to the shaft. The tape should be slightly shorter than the grip length, yet still have approximately 1″ extending over the butt end of the shaft.

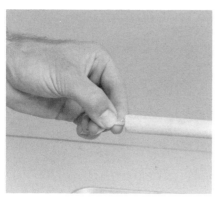

22-55 Carefully wrap tape around shaft. Twist or squeeze the end of the tape together as shown and push inside the butt end of the shaft. This prevents solvent from entering the shaft during grip installation.

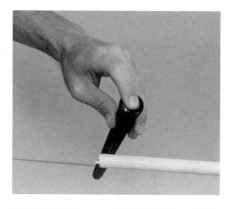

22-56 Block the vent hole in the butt end of the grip with your finger, golf tee or other pointed object.

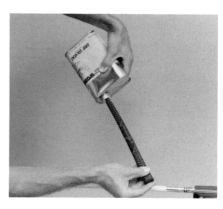

22-57 Squirt or pour a generous amount of grip solvent inside the grip. Pinch the open end of the grip with your fingers and shake to thoroughly wet the inside of the grip. **Perchlorethylene,** a non-flammable grip solvent, is shown. Many shops still use naphtha, gasoline or lighter fluid. These are highly flammable and dangerous solvents and are not recommended.

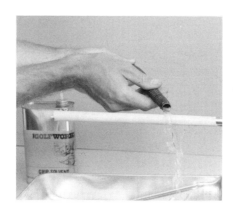

22-58 Grip solvent is then poured out of the grip over the entire length of the double-coated tape to wet it thoroughly. If necessary, squirt additional solvent onto tape.

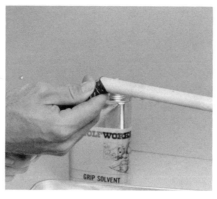

22-59 It is vitally important that the butt end of the shaft is wet, as this will make installation easier. Working quickly, position the open end of the grip just beneath the shaft butt and . . .

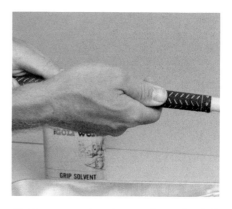

22-60 . . . start the grip up and over the shaft. Holding grip as shown, slide it on until the end of the shaft stops at the top of the grip. Work quickly.

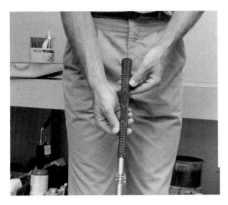

22-61 To properly align the grip, place the club in the playing position and sight down the grip and center of shaft. Grip should be aligned with the leading edge on woods and irons. Grip can be changed in alignment for 2 to 3 minutes after installation before solvent evaporates.

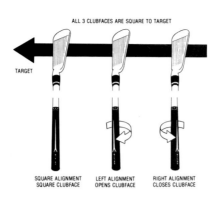

22-62 Be aware that some golfers like their grips turned slightly right or left. If possible, allow the golfer to check the first club so that he may suggest any changes in alignment. The most common installation is perfectly square.

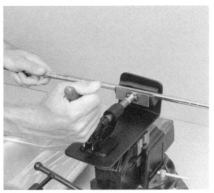

22-63 The photo shows a **Lever Action Shaft Holder.** Re-gripping can be performed much faster with this tool. The shaft is tightened and then released by simply lowering and raising the lever.

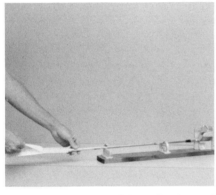

22-64 The **Automatic Gripper For Irons** will hold an iron head and most putters securely as the grip is installed. Because the face is automatically aligned properly, the grip will be in perfect alignment.

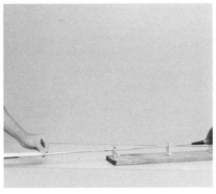

22-65 The **Automatic Gripper For Woods** works under the same principle, so grip is aligned properly.

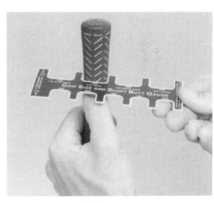

22-66 **The grip size should be final checked** before returning club to customer using the **Grip Size and Shaft Butt Gauge.**

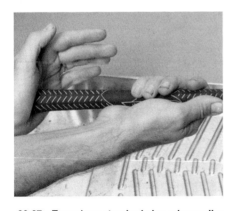

22-67 To make a standard size grip smaller, first slide grip on in normal manner. **Refer to Tables 22-4 thru 22-6 in additional information section at the end of this chapter on producing oversize and undersize grips by interchanging grip core sizes.**

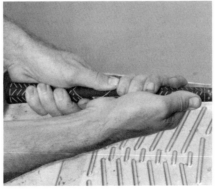

22-68 When sliding the grip on, stretch it past its normal stopping point, as shown. Use both hands to stretch the grip evenly over its entire length.

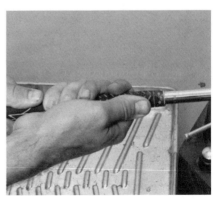

22-69 Hold it in this stretched position for approximately 1 minute or until the tape begins to set.

22-70 While still holding the grip, wrap a piece of masking tape around the bottom to hold grip in place. A grip stretched ¾" will decrease in size by ¹⁄₆₄". Leave tape on for a minimum of 2 hours. Be sure to check grip size with the gauge or micrometer before the solvent evaporates and the grip becomes firmly attached.

22-71 The **Grip Installer Tool** is very helpful when installing grips. First, slip fingers inside mouth of grip.

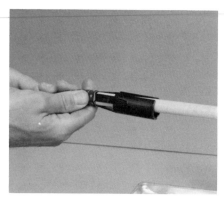

22-72 Pour solvent out of grip and onto tape. Slide Grip Installer onto the shaft butt.

22-73 Continue sliding grip on in a normal manner. The Grip Installer will slide right down with it. Also, the Grip Installer will enlarge the mouth of the grip for easier installation.

22-74 Remove club from vise and continue to slide Grip Installer down the shaft until you can remove it through the notch in the side. This tool avoids any frustration in stretching smaller grips on larger shafts.

22-75 **To install leather wrap-on grips,** first install a grip collar. Grip collars are available in two types — rigid and stretchable plastic. The rigid grip collars are available in 4 sizes to match the common butt diameters. The stretchable collar comes in one size but can be stretched over all shaft butt sizes.

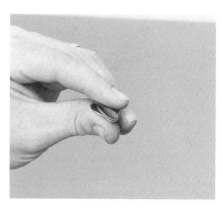

22-76 **To install a stretchable grip collar,** first roll grip collar between fingers to make it soft and pliable (or drop it in a glass of warm water for 2 minutes).

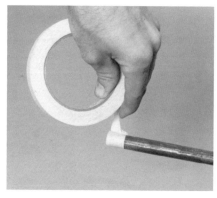

22-77 After wrapping a piece of tape around the shaft butt, push grip collar on as far as it will go.

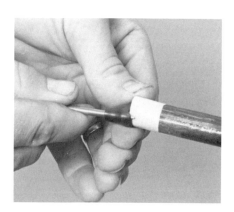

22-78 Using an awl or small screwdriver, lift and stretch remaining portion over end of shaft.

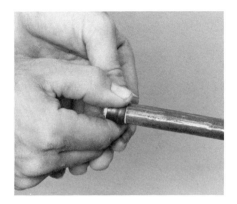

22-79 Slide grip collar down shaft.

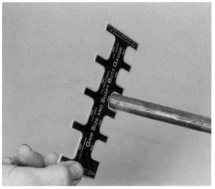

22-80 To install rigid grip collars, first, measure shaft butt and select appropriate grip collar size. Note the use of the Grip Size and Shaft Butt Gauge.

22-81 Place a **Grip Collar Starter** inside the mouth of the shaft. Slide grip collar over it and . . .

22-82 . . . onto the shaft. Fast, simple, and no cut fingers or cut grip collars. Note: The Grip Collar Starter also works well with stretchable grip collars.

22-83 As with the rubber slip-on grip, check inside the mouth of the underlisting to determine its core size. Eaton® rubber underlistings will usually be designated with a RM58, RM60 or RM62. This indicates a Men's Reminder Rib. An SM in front of the numbers indicates a round grip (with no rib). See Fig. 22-144 for more information on numeral and letter designations found inside the grip.

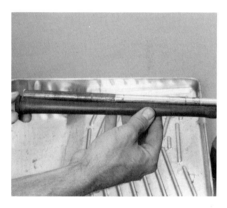

22-84 Next, hold the underlisting up to the shaft to determine the approximate tape length needed.

22-85 Use 2″ double-coated tape as shown, or, use ¾″ double-coated tape spirally wrapped around the shaft. Note: To build up size of underlisting, the same procedure applies as shown in photos 22-45 thru 22-51 for conventional rubber grips.

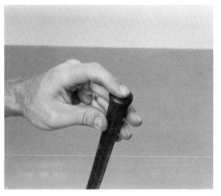

22-86 Plug vent hole in butt of underlisting with your finger, golf tee or other pointed object.

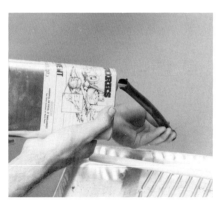

22-87 Apply grip solvent liberally inside underlisting. Pinch off the open end of the underlisting and agitate it to thoroughly wet interior of underlisting.

22-88 Pour excess solvent over double-coated tape to actuate it. Additional solvent may be necessary to completely wet the tape.

22-89 Quickly locate the rib on the underlisting and make sure it is positioned down the back of the shaft. The rib is easily identified by a series of mold markings running down the length of the back side. Note: You may wish to locate the back of the underlisting before applying solvent until you are familiar with this procedure.

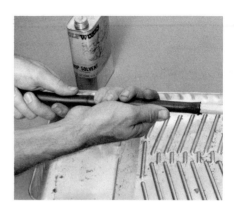

22-90 Next, slide on the underlisting. The installation procedure is the same as shown in photos 22-59 and 22-60.

22-91 After the underlisting is installed, check to make sure the rib is straight down the back of the shaft. First, adjust the grip cap so the identifying markings are vertical when the club is in the address position. Next, . . .

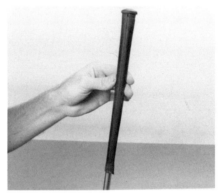

22-92 . . . twist the rest of the underlisting so the seams running down the sides of the underlisting are placed straight down the shaft. This will ensure the rib is also properly aligned. Remember, the rib should run down the back of the shaft in line with the heel of the club. The seams will be aligned down the sides of the shaft. This ensures proper rib alignment.

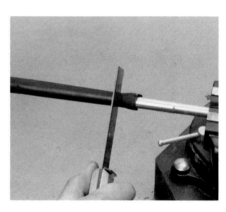

22-93 Once all of the solvent has evaporated and the grip cannot be turned, carefully cut the bell bottom off the underlisting using a sharp knife. Make a square cut.

22-94 This photo shows the bell bottom before installation. Its purpose is to aid the repairman when slipping the mouth of the grip over the shaft. Once the grip is on, it serves no other purpose and is cut off.

22-95 Now apply one strip of 2″ double-coated tape to the underlisting. Tape should extend ¼″ past bottom of the underlisting. ¾″ double-coated tape can also be used by spirally wrapping it around underlisting.

22-96 In most cases the 2″ wide double-coated tape will not wrap around the entire underlisting. Although it is not necessary, a narrow piece of double-coated tape may be applied to cover the exposed rubber.

22-97 The leather strip has a squared end and a tapered end. It is with the tapered end that the wrapping begins.

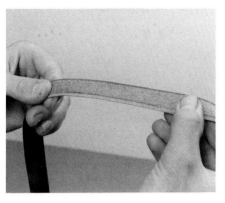

22-98 Also note the difference in the thickness of the strip. The thinner edges are referred to as the "skiving." The skiving is the part of the leather strip that is overlapped when wrapping the leather around the shaft.

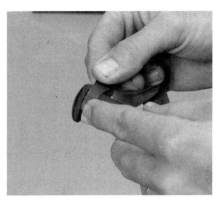

22-99 Start the tapered end of the leather strip in the rubber underlisting recess located just beneath the underlisting cap. Be sure the leather is tightly seated against the grip cap to eliminate any gaps.

22-100 The club may be held loosely in a vise for turning or it can be held in your hands. After the strip has encircled the underlisting and slightly overlapped the tapered end, start the leather in a downward direction so the top edge of the leather overlaps the bottom edge, skiving over skiving.

22-101 The correct wrapping procedure is to pull the leather strip with your right hand while turning the club with . . .

22-102 . . . your left. Wrap the grip using firm tension.

22-103 There are two different methods for wrapping a leather grip. One is called a groove or ribbed wrap, the other is called a smooth wrap. The top portion of the grip shown has been wrapped in a ribbed wrap where only a small portion of the skiving is overlapped. The bottom of the grip shown here is a smooth wrap where the entire skiving is overlapped. **Ribbed wrap is the preferred choice.**

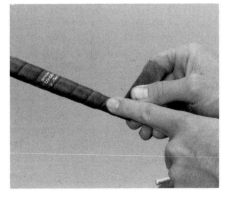

22-104 Wrap the leather 1" past the bottom of the underlisting.

22-105 Place a piece of ⅛" masking tape around the grip at a point approximately ⅜" below the bottom of the underlisting.

22-106 Using a sharp knife, cut the leather below the tape. This provides a built-in recess for positioning the grip collar.

22-107 Apply a light coating of contact cement to the bottom ⅜″ of the leather.

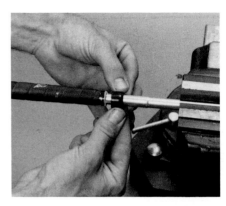

22-108 Position the grip collar below the grip.

22-109 Push the grip collar to the desired position against the bottom of the underlisting over the narrow ⅜″ leather section.

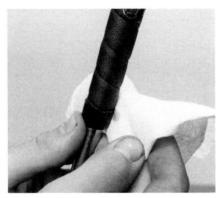

22-110 Wipe the excess cement from the collar. The rigid plastic collar gives a professional look.

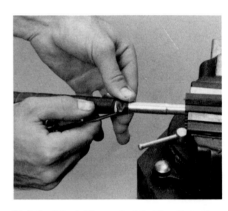

22-111 If installing a stretchable grip collar, stretch the collar over the grip, flush with the bottom of the underlisting. An awl or scriber can be used to position the collar properly.

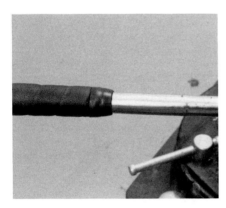

22-112 The stretch collar gives a similarly professional look.

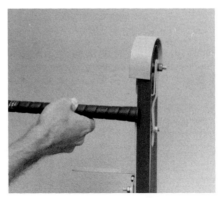

22-113 Rarely will the rubber end cap be flush with the grip diameter. It can carefully be turned down on a 1″ belt sander or filed with a medium cut wood file. If this grip is accidentally nicked with the sander or file, use appropriate color shoe polish for a touchup.

22-114 The finished grip should look like this. A groove or ribbed wrap is shown and, as was previously stated, is the preferred method of wrapping a leather grip.

22-115 Final check swingweight and make any necessary corrections as shown in Chapter 13.

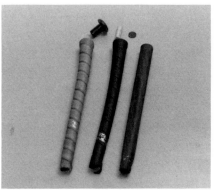

22-116 **Directions for installing leather slip-on grips.** The attraction of a leather slip-on grip is that it appears to lessen the work because the leather is already wrapped around an underlisting.

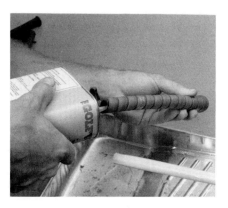

22-117 First, install grip collar and apply tape as shown in photos 22-76 thru 22-85. Plug the hole in the butt of the grip with your finger while squirting grip solvent inside grip.

22-118 Pour excess solvent over double-coated tape. Additional solvent may be necessary to completely wet the tape.

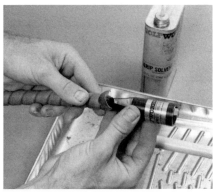

22-119 The slip-on leather grips do not have a ribbed back, so positioning is not a concern. Slip the **Grip Installer Tool** inside the mouth of the grip before installation.

22-120 Push the **Grip Installer Tool** and the mouth of the grip over the shaft. Difficulties occur when the shaft butt is larger than the grip core size. Because the leather is wrapped around the underlisting, the underlisting resists expansion. **The Grip Installer Tool is a great help with this situation and should be considered a necessity.**

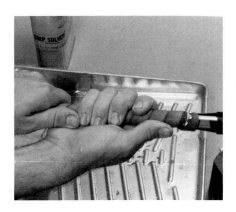

22-121 Once the grip is started on the shaft, turn the grip . . .

22-122 . . . clockwise while pushing. This helps as the wrapped underlisting will expand slightly and slide much easier down the shaft.

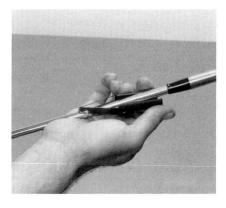

22-123 Once the top of the grip is flush with the shaft butt, slide the Installer Tool down the shaft and remove it.

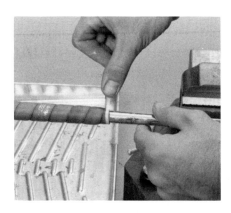

22-124 Once the solvent has evaporated and the grip can no longer turn, wrap the remaining portion of leather around the shaft. Apply a strip of ⅛″ masking tape around the bottom of the grip and finish off the bottom as shown in photos 22-105 thru 22-112.

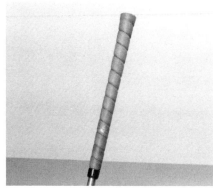

22-125 After installing the grip collar, the grip should look like this, ready for the end cap assembly.

22-126 End caps are available in four sizes: .560, .580, .600 and .620, to match the four common butt diameters. The lock pin and disc are usually included with the end cap.

22-127 Select the appropriate end cap and push the plastic plug inside the shaft until the bottom of the cap fits flush with the top of the grip.

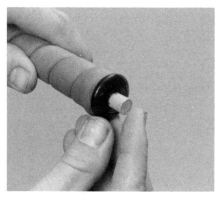

22-128 Place the lock pin inside the plug and tap in gently to the bottom of the plug. The end cap tightens as the pin is pushed farther down the plug, expanding it.

22-129 Secure the disc inside the end cap with a spot of epoxy or dampen the disc with acetone and quickly place it inside the cap. The acetone will temporarily soften the plastic and bond the plastic disc to the plastic end cap.

22-130 Rarely will the plastic end cap be flush with the outside of the grip. It can be turned down on a 1″ or 2″ **Belt Sander** as shown, or a medium cut file may be used. Use care in either procedure. If the grip is nicked with the sander or file, use appropriate color shoe polish for touchup.

22-131 Use of clear plastic poly bags give a professional touch to custom or regripped clubs. They also protect against dust, dirt, etc.

22-132 Special grip racks are available to display various grip sizes and putter grips to promote gripping services.

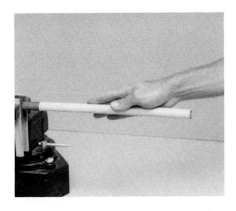

22-133 Applying leather to hickory shafts: Because of the large diameter of hickory shafts, a rubber underlisting is not necessary. Instead, apply a strip of 2″ double-coated tape to the butt. ¾″ double-coated tape can be spirally wrapped around the shaft if desired.

22-134 Place the tapered end of the leather wrap against the top of the shaft. In most cases you will be required to use a strip of leather that is longer than the standard leather strip. Extra long leather strips are available from most golf supply dealers.

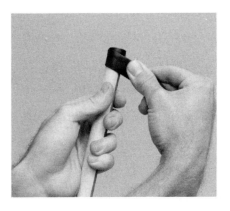

22-135 Encircle the top of the shaft with the leather. Once the beginning of the strip has been overlapped by the leather, start a downward wrapping of the leather. Follow the procedures as shown in photos 22-100 thru 22-103.

22-136 Continue to wrap the leather down the shaft to the desired stopping point.

22-137 Once the desired stopping point has been reached, wrap a piece of ⅛″ tape around the leather.

22-138 Using a sharp knife, cut through the leather and discard the excess piece.

22-139 The leather grip should now look like this. Note the sharp drop from the leather to the shaft.

22-140 Using ⅛″ masking tape, wrap tape around the shaft to create a tapered section from the shaft to the grip.

22-141 Camouflage the tape by coloring it with a black felt tip marker.

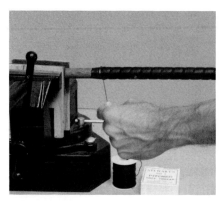
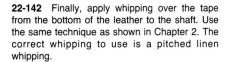

22-142 Finally, apply whipping over the tape from the bottom of the leather to the shaft. Use the same technique as shown in Chapter 2. The correct whipping to use is a pitched linen whipping.

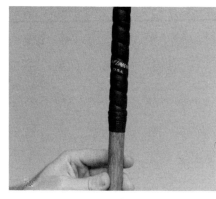

22-143 The bottom of the grip should look like this. Applying pitched whipping ensures a somewhat authentic look to the club.

NOTES

_____

_____

_____

_____

_____

_____

_____

_____

ADDITIONAL INFORMATION FOR INSTALLING GRIPS AND CHANGING GRIP SIZE

Increasing and Decreasing Grip Sizes by Interchanging Grip Core Sizes

Anyone can learn to put a grip on a golf club in a few minutes' time. However, putting the grip on to the correct size and being able to explain a possible increase or decrease in swingweight and total weight to the customer can be quite a bit more involved. Invariably, when I start off a repair class in a P.G.A. in-depth workshop with regripping, a great majority of students initially feel it is a waste of their time since they have been regripping clubs for years. However, as the lesson continues their opinions rapidly change as they find a whole new understanding in regripping. The main thrust in the repair schools concerning regripping is to be able to determine exactly what size a certain grip will install to before the club is gripped. I have seen many times someone cut off an old grip, install a new one, and if the size feels a little small they quickly slide it off and wrap on another layer of tape. This is totally unnecessary if you understand the code numbers used on grips and how they match up to various size shaft butts.

The grip core size, sometimes referred to as the mandrel size, is located just inside the mouth of the grip. See photo 22-41 and Fig. 22-144. Each grip manufacturer identifies its grips differently. Eaton® Molded Products Co. is the largest grip manufacturer and consequently, this is the most popular "after market" replacement grip used today. Eaton's® code numbers inside the mouth of their grips are easy to interpret. Usually you will find a single letter designation followed by 2 numerals. The letter designation will be either (M) men's, (L) ladies' or (J) juniors'. The 2 numerals indicate the grip core size or mandrel size such as 58, 60 or 62. The grip core size is made to match a corresponding shaft butt size such as .580, .600 or .620. The proper interpretation of all these letters and numbers is this: an M58 grip installed on a .580 diameter butt shaft will measure to a men's standard diameter when using 1 layer of double-coated tape. Men's standard diameter is defined in Table 22-1.

If an M58 grip is installed on a .600 diameter butt shaft, the grip will measure slightly over 1/64″ larger than the men's standard size. If an M58 grip is installed on a .620 diameter butt shaft, the grip will measure slightly over 1/32″ larger than men's standard size. In each case stated above, the smaller grip core size is being stretched over the larger shaft butt sizes and consequently it is being stretched to a larger than standard size according to the designation inside the mouth of the grip.

A grip can be stretched quite a bit. Hence, as long as the grip core size is smaller than the shaft butt diameter, it can be used satisfactorily assuming it is understood that it will install oversize.

A grip core size can also be selected that is actually larger than the shaft butt diameter. This will cause the grip to be installed undersize. However, the grip core size should never be more than one size larger than the shaft butt size when making a grip undersize. For example: An M60 grip installed on a .580 diameter shaft butt will measure slightly less than 1/64″ smaller than men's standard size. There are also other methods of installing grips undersize. One method is shown in photos 22-67 thru 22-70 whereby the grip is stretched farther down the shaft when installing it, causing it to decrease in size by approximately 1/64″ when stretched 3/4 to 1″ longer. The grip, however, must be stretched evenly over its entire length and not just stretched down at the bottom end.

Another method for reducing men's grip sizes is to use ladies' grips. The difference in standard men's grips and standard ladies' size grips is slightly more than 3/64″. So, as an example, if an L58 grip is installed on a .580 diameter butt shaft, the grip will measure standard ladies' size and also 3/64″ undersize men's. If an L56 grip is installed on a .580 diameter butt shaft, the grip will measure slightly over 1/64″ larger than standard ladies' size and 1/32″ undersize men's.

Now refer to Tables 22-1, 22-2, 22-3, 22-4, 22-5 and 22-6 which put this information in quick-to-use form.

TABLE 22-1
Measuring Grip Sizes

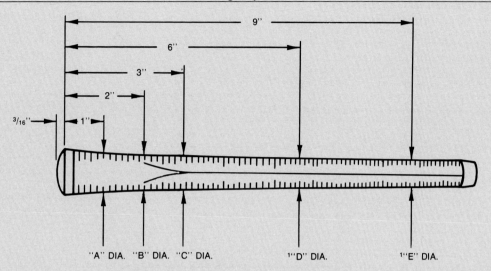

Desired Grip Size	"A" Dia.	"B" Dia.	"C" Dia.	¹"D" Dia.	¹"E" Dia.
¹⁄₆₄″ (.015) Undersize Men's	.935	.885	.845	.765	.705
STANDARD SIZE MEN'S	.950	.900	.860	.780	.720
¹⁄₆₄″ (.015) Oversize Men's	.965	.915	.875	.795	.735
¹⁄₃₂″ (.031) Oversize Men's	.980	.930	.890	.810	.750
³⁄₆₄″ (.046) Oversize Men's	.995	.945	.905	.825	.765
¹⁄₁₆″ (.062) Oversize Men's	1.010	.960	.920	.840	.780
¹⁄₆₄″ (.015) Undersize Ladies'	.885	.835	.805	.705	.630
STANDARD SIZE LADIES'	.900	.850	.820	.720	.645
¹⁄₆₄″ (.015) Oversize Ladies'	.915	.865	.835	.735	.660
¹⁄₃₂″ (.031) Oversize Ladies'	.930	.880	.850	.750	.675

¹"D" & "E" diameters can be reduced, if desired, when installing oversize grips if a slightly smaller diameter is required under the golfer's right hand. Reduce the amount of tape applied to this area to do this.

TABLE 22-2
Grip Size Table @ 2″ Down From Top of Grip

Designation	Relative Size	Measurement @ 2″ Down From Top of Grip "B" Diameter	
		Men's Diameter	Ladies' Diameter
Extra Large	¹⁄₁₆″ oversize	.960″	.910″
Very Large	³⁄₆₄″ oversize	.945″	.895″
Large	¹⁄₃₂″ oversize	.930″	.880″
Slightly Larger	¹⁄₆₄″ oversize	.915″	.865″
Average	Standard Size	.900″	.850″
Slightly Smaller	¹⁄₆₄″ undersize	.885″	.835″
Very Small	¹⁄₃₂″ undersize	.870″	.820″

TABLE 22-3
Matching Grip Size to Shaft Butt Diameter — Eaton® Grips

[2]When You Use an Eaton Grip With Identification on Mouth of Grip as Follows:	[1]Shaft Butt Diameter to Produce Standard Size Grip
"M56"	.560
"M58"	.580
"M60"	.600
"M62"	.620
"L54"	.540
"L56"	.560
"L58"	.580
"L60"	.600
#12	.375
#16 or J50	.500
#17	.560
#18	.580
#19	.600
#20	.620

[1]To determine shaft butt diameter use either a venier caliper, micrometer, or the "Grip Size and Shaft Butt Gauge" available from The GolfWorks®.
[2]M (Men's), L (Ladies'), J (Junior)

TABLE 22-4
Producing Standard and Oversize Grips By Interchanging Grip Sizes — Eaton® Grips

Men's or Ladies' Sizes	Shaft Butt Diameter	To Produce Standard Size Grip Use the Following	[1]To Produce Oversize Grip (approx. 1/64" over) Use the Following	[1]To Produce Oversize Grip (approx. 1/32" over) Use the Following
Men's	.580	M58	Use additional tape	Use additional tape
	.600	M60	M58	[3]M56
	.620	M62	M60	M58
Ladies'	.560	L56	L54	M58
	.580	L58	L56	L54 or M60
	.600	L60	L58	L56 or M62

[1]If you do not happen to have these grip sizes to produce oversize grips, refer to Table 22-7 "Tape Wrapping Information to Produce Oversize Grips."
[3]M56 grips are only available in "Men's Crown" model from Eaton®.

TABLE 22-5
Producing Standard and Undersize Grips By Interchanging Grip Sizes — Eaton® Grips

Men's or Ladies' Sizes	Shaft Butt Diameter	To Produce Standard Size Grip Use the Following	To Produce Undersize Grip (approx. 1/64" under) Use the Following	To Produce Undersize Grip (approx. 1/32" under) Use the Following
Men's	.580	M58	M60 or M58 stretched down 3/4"	L56 or M60 stretched down 3/4"
	.600	M60	M62 or M60 stretched down 3/4"	L58 or M26 stretched down 3/4"
	.620	M62	L58 or M62 stretched down 3/4"	L60 or L58 stretched down 3/4"
Ladies'	.560	L56	L58 or L56 stretched down 3/4"	L58 stretched down 3/4"
	.580	L58	L60 or L58 stretched down 3/4"	L60 stretched down 3/4"
	.600	L60	L60 stretched down 3/4"	Not Advised

For procedure on stretching grips down to reduce their size, see photos 22-67 thru 22-70.

Men's & Ladies' Sizes	Tacki-Mac® Model Number	Grip Core Size	¹Shaft Butt Diameter					GolfWorks® Catalog Code Number	Pattern on Grip	Round or Rib
			.560	.580	.600	.620	.700			
Men's Standard	Model 11	58	No	Std.	+¹⁄₆₄	+¹⁄₃₂	No	MSB 58	Knurled Wrap	Round
Men's Standard	Model 11	60	No	No	Std.	+¹⁄₆₄	No	MSB 60	Knurled Wrap	Round
Men's Standard	Model 11	62	No	No	No	Std.	No	MSB 62	Knurled Wrap	Round
Men's Oversize	Model 13	58	No	+¹⁄₃₂	+³⁄₆₄	+¹⁄₁₆	No	MOB 58	Golfer Wrap	Round
Men's Oversize	Model 13	60	No	No	+¹⁄₃₂	+³⁄₆₄	No	MOB 60	Golfer Wrap	Round
Men's Oversize	Model 13	62	No	No	No	+¹⁄₃₂	No	MOB 62	Golfer Wrap	Round
Ladies' Standard	Model 33	56	Std.	+¹⁄₆₄	+¹⁄₃₂	+¹⁄₁₆	No	LSU 56	Starburst Wrap	Round

TABLE 22-6
Producing Standard, Oversize and Undersize Grips
By Interchanging Grip Sizes — Tacki-Mac® Grips

¹Above sizes are based upon installation without the use of double-coated tape. However, sizes different from those above can be made by using build-up tape and double-coated tape. See Table 22-7.

¹**Check the letters and numbers in mouth of grip to determine size.**
Each grip has a letter and identifying number.

²**Grip Designations**

M58   Indicates that grip has a reminder rib (no "R" after number) and will install to standard men's grip size on a .580 diameter butt shaft.

M58R   Indicates that grip is round ("R" after number) and will install to standard men's grip size on a .580 diameter butt shaft.

³**Underlisting Designations**

RM58   Indicates that underlisting has a reminder rib ("R") and will install to standard men's size (after leather is installed over it) on a .580 diameter butt shaft.

SM58   Indicates that underlisting is round "S") and will install to standard men's size (after leather is installed over it) on a .580 diameter butt shaft.

Notes:

¹Not every grip model is available in every size.

²The first letter in mouth of grip indicates the general use of the grip: M-Men's, L-Ladies', J-Juniors'. Refer to these and the code markings noted above. All other numbers and letters in grips are for grip manufacturer's reference only.

³Underlistings can be built up and reduced in size using the same procedures and methods described for grips. Using build-up tape, interchanging grip core sizes and stretching down the underlisting are all acceptable methods. Remember, you should never build up a leather grip by applying multiple layers of tape on top of the underlisting.

Fig. 22-144
Information for identifying Eaton® Grips and Underlistings

Increasing Grip Sizes by Applying Additional Build-Up Tape

Build-up tape is nothing more than crepe masking tape. It is available in many widths but the most popular ones used in regripping are the ¾" and 2" widths. Each roll is 60 yards long, fairly inexpensive and easy to find in your local hardware department. A number of people use the expensive double-coated tape applied in multiple layers for building grips up. Not only is this three times more costly, but it is much more difficult to work with than ordinary masking tape.

Grip build-up procedures using masking tape are shown in photos 22-45 thru 22-51. An important point to keep in mind when building grips up using tape is that the tape has a certain amount of weight and will, depending on how much is used, counterbalance the club (reduce swingweight by increasing grip end weight) and at the same time increase total weight, again depending on the amount of tape used. Table 22-7 has been developed to provide information on how much each layer of tape increases the grip size and its equivalent reduction in swingweight and increase in total weight.

TABLE 22-7
Tape Wrapping Information to Produce Oversize Grips

Description	[1]Increase in Diameter	Weight of Tape	[2]Swingweight Equivalent
¾" masking tape (overlap wrap)	.02" slightly more than 1/64"	.1 ounce	−¾
¾" masking tape (single layer wrap)	.01" slightly less than 1/64"	.05 ounce	−⅓
¾" masking tape (overlap wrap plus single layer wrap)	.03" exactly 1/32"	.15 ounce	−1
2" masking tape (each layer lengthwise)	.01" slightly less than 1/64"	.05 ounce	−⅓
¾" or 2" width double-coated tape (single layer wrap)	.01" slightly less than 1/64"	.05 ounce	−⅓

[1]For converting decimals to fractions, use the following:
.015" = 1/64"   .031" = 1/32"   .046 = 3/64"   .062" = 1/16"

[2]Swingweight Equivalent. Example: Assume a D-2 driver with no changes other than one additional overlap wrapping of ¾" masking tape to increase the grip diameter. The resulting increased weight because of the additional tape will decrease the swingweight by approximately ¾. See Fig. 22-145. Swingweight equivalent is approximately the same for both woods and irons.

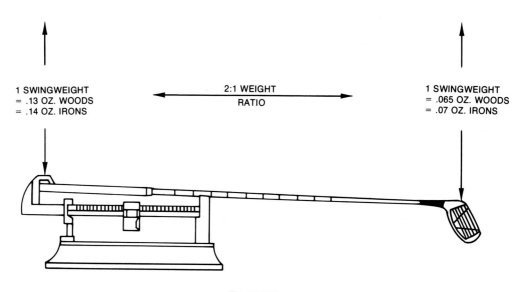

1 SWINGWEIGHT
= .13 OZ. WOODS
= .14 OZ. IRONS

2:1 WEIGHT RATIO

1 SWINGWEIGHT
= .065 OZ. WOODS
= .07 OZ. IRONS

Fig. 22-145
Equivalent head weight and grip end weight to equal 1 swingweight

Most people that regrip use the ¾" width masking tape and ¾" width double-coated tape vs. the 2" width tape. The reason for this is more tradition than anything else. Most people have learned regripping procedures using the ¾" tape and have continued to use it. There is absolutely nothing wrong with using ¾" width tapes other than they are slightly costlier in material and require substantially more labor. Study Tables 22-8 and 22-9, which provide cost comparison figures and the number of clubs you can expect to regrip from each roll of tape. One argument against using 2" tape is that some of the fine professional players feel where the tape overlaps that it increases the amount of rib under the grip. This is true; however, I made up a a number of test grip sizes using both ¾" and 2" tapes and found that it took at least a 1/32" additional build-up (3 lengths of 2" build-up plus 1 length of 2" double-coated) to be detected by feel in the reminder rib increase. For most of those detecting the increase, it was a more desirable feel. It should also be noted that during this test the individual had the opportunity to constantly switch back and forth from grip to grip thus making it easier to compare differences in feel. I seriously doubt if anyone can just pick up a regripped club and tell you that it feels as if 2" width tape was used instead of ¾". Also, you can apply the build-up tape by varying the position of the overlap so that it does not accumulatively build up in only the rib area of the grip. However, I prefer to overlap the 2" tape at the rib since, as previously stated, it gives most players a better feeling to have a little larger rib.

TABLE 22-8
¾″ and 2″ Build-Up Crepe Masking Tape: Usage and Cost Comparison

Tape Width	Tape Length	Amount of Tape Used Per Club	²Approx. Amount of Time To Apply Tape	No. of Clubs Per Roll of Tape	Cost Per Roll of Tape	Cost of Tape Per Club
¾″	60 yards	25″	30 sec.	86.4	$1.10	1.27¢
2″	60 yards	9″	10 sec.	240	$2.70	1.12¢

¹Cost based on average 1987 prices.
²Time varies with individual and technique.
Summary:
Cost wise, 2″ tape is 13% less than ¾″ when computed on a cost per club basis. If you use 2″, you save approximately 36¢ per roll on a cost vs. number of clubs comparison with ¾″.
Labor wise, 2″ tape is approximately 3 times faster to install or a 66% saving in labor vs. ¾″ tape.

TABLE 22-9
¾″ and 2″ Double-Coated Tape: Usage and Cost Comparison

Tape Width	Tape Length	Amount of Tape Used Per Club	²Approx. Amount of Time To Apply Tape	No. of Clubs Per Roll of Tape	Cost Per Roll of Tape	Cost of Tape Per Club
¾″	36 yards	25″	30 sec.	51.8	$3.40	6.56¢
2″	36 yards	9″	10 sec.	144	$6.95	4.82¢

¹Cost based on average 1987 prices.
²Time varies with individual and technique.
Summary:
Cost wise, 2″ tape is 27% less than ¾″ when computed on a cost per club basis. If you can use 2″ double-coated, you save approximately $1.55 per roll on a cost vs. number of clubs comparison with ¾″.
Labor wise, 2″ tape is approximately 3 times faster to install or a 66% saving in labor vs. ¾″ tape.

A Specific Example to Help Understand How Regripping Affects Other Club Specifications

Now that an abundant amount of information has been compiled, it is time to explain how to apply this information using a specific example.

A customer requests that you change his present "Eagle" standard size rubber grip to an "All Cord" grip $\frac{1}{32}$″ oversize on his D-3 driver. At this point, you should be able to calculate approximately what is going to happen to swingweight and total weight from this change.

1. The swingweight will decrease by approximately 3.5 swingweights.
2. The total weight or static weight will increase by approximately .45 ounces.
3. If desired, weight can be added to the head to readjust the club to its original D-3 swingweight by adding .23 ounces to head weight. Of course, the total weight will again be increased by an additional .23 ounces for a total overall weight increase of .68 ounces.

The information listed above was determined as follows:

To Determine the Swingweight Change:

First, you assume that the present "Eagle" grip weighs approximately 1.65 ounces compared to an "All Cord" grip which weighs approximately 1.95 ounces (refer to Table 22-10). Next, from Table 22-7 you determine that it will take approximately .15 ounces of additional tape to achieve a $\frac{1}{32}$″ (.031″) oversize grip. (One overlap wrap weighing .1 ounce and increasing the diameter by .02″ plus one single layer wrap weighing .05 ounce and increasing the diameter by .01″, giving a total weight increase of .15 ounce for the tape and a total size increase of $\frac{1}{32}$″ (.031″).)

Next calculate the increase in total weight:

$\frac{1}{32}$″ oversize "All Cord" total grip weight (includes tape also)	2.10 oz.
Less the original "Eagle" total grip weight	−1.65 oz.
TOTAL WEIGHT INCREASE FROM GRIP CHANGE	.45 oz.

Next, refer to Fig. 22-145 and note that a change of .13 ounce in the grip end weight or .065 ounce in head weight is equivalent to 1 swingweight (divide .45 ounces by .13 to obtain an answer of approximately a 3½ point swingweight decrease).

To Determine the Total Weight Change:

The total or static weight change has already been determined to be .45 ounce or the difference in weight between the original "Eagle" grip and the new "All Cord" grip plus the additional weight of the tape used to make it ⅟₃₂″ oversize.

Assume that it is desirable to restore the driver to its original swingweight. Again refer to Fig. 22-145 and you will see that for each swingweight decrease caused by the additional grip and weight that .065 ounce will have to be added to the head weight. So multiply the 3½ point swingweight decrease by .065 ounce to obtain an answer of .23 ounces of weight that must be added to the head to restore the original swingweight of D-3 in the example driver.

To make this more clear, a summary of the original specifications and the new specifications of the example driver are shown below to compare the net effect of the grip and size change on both swingweight and total weight.

Summary for the Example Used

Description	Swingweight	Total Weight	Total Weight Increase From Original
Original Driver w/"Eagle" grip (standard size)	D-3	13.25 oz.	0
Install ⅟₃₂″ oversize "All Cord" grip (No swingweight adjustment)	C-9½	13.70 oz.	+.45 oz.
Install ⅟₃₂″ oversize "All Cord" (Swingweight adjusted by adding head weight)	D-3	13.93 oz.	+.68 oz.

TABLE 22-10
General Information on Grips

Grip Style, Model or Pattern	Grip Material	Manufacturer	Length of Grip	[1][6]Grip Weight (Approx.)	Men's or Ladies'
Victory M58	Rubber and cork	Eaton®	10½″	1.75 oz.	Men's
Crown M58	Rubber and cork	Eaton®	10½″	1.75 oz.	Men's
Eagle M58	Rubber and cork	Eaton®	10″	1.65 oz.	Men's
Classic M58	Rubber and cork	Eaton®	11¼″	1.9 oz.	Men's
Air Cushion M58	Rubber and cork	Eaton®	10½″	1.75 oz.	Men's
[2]Arthritic M60H	Rubber and cork	Eaton®	10½″	1.9 oz.	Men's
High Tac M58	Rubber and cork	Eaton®	10½″	1.75 oz.	Men's
[3]Half Cord M58	Rubber and cord	Eaton®	10½″	1.95 oz.	Men's
[3]All Velvet Cord M58	Rubber and cord	Eaton®	10½″	1.95 oz.	Men's
[3]Crown Cord M58	Rubber and cord	Eaton®	10½″	1.95 oz.	Men's
[3]Classic Cord M58	Rubber and cord	Eaton®	10½″	1.95 oz.	Men's
[3]All Cord M58	Rubber and cord	Eaton®	10½″	1.95 oz.	Men's
Crown L56	Rubber and cork	Eaton®	10½″	1.5 oz.	Ladies'
Eagle L56	Rubber and cork	Eaton®	10½″	1.5 oz.	Ladies'
Victory L56	Rubber and cork	Eaton®	10½″	1.5 oz.	Ladies'
High Tac L56	Rubber and cork	Eaton®	10½″	1.5 oz.	Ladies'
Spiral Wrap Grip (slip-on type)	Leather	Lamkin®	10⅜″	1.75 oz.	Men's
Conquest 58	Rubber and cork	Lamkin®	10½″	1.75 oz.	Men's
Silhouette 590	Rubber and cork	Lamkin®	10½″	2.0 oz.	Men's
Silhouette 580	Rubber and cork	Lamkin®	10½″	2.0 oz.	Ladies'
Black Panel (slip-on)	Leather	Lamkin®	10½″	1.75 oz.	Men's
Ultra Tac Tour	Rubber and cork	Lamkin®	10½″	1.75 oz.	Men's
Ultra Classic	Rubber and cork	Lamkin®	10½″	1.75 oz.	Men's
Seamless	Rubber	Lamkin®	10½″	1.65 oz.	Men's
[4]Chamois CM	Rubber	Avon®	10½″	1.75 oz.	Men's
Chamois CL	Rubber	Avon®	10½″	1.5 oz.	Ladies'
Charger 58	Rubber	Avon®	10½″	1.75 oz.	Men's
Charger 56	Rubber	Avon®	10½″	1.5 oz.	Ladies'
Spiral Wrapped Grip (Hand wound type)	Cowhide or calf	Neumann®	10½″	[5]1.95 oz.	Men's
Underlisting M58	Rubber	Eaton®	10½″	1 oz.	Men's

Grip Style, Model or Pattern	Grip Material	Manufacturer	Length of Grip	[1] [6]Grip Weight (Approx.)	Men's or Ladies'
TABLE 22-10 con't.					
General Information on Grips					
Model 10 58	Krayton and rubber	Tacki-Mac®	10½"	1.75 oz.	Men's
Model 13 (Herringbone pattern) 58 (oversize)	Krayton and rubber	Tacki-Mac®	10½"	1.8 oz.	Men's
Model ST20 (Knurl pattern) 58 (standard)	Krayton and rubber	Tacki-Mac®	10½"	1.7 oz.	Men's
Model 27 58 (arthritic)	Krayton and rubber	Tacki-Mac®	10½"	2.5 oz.	Men's
Model 31 58 (standard)	Krayton and rubber	Tacki-Mac®	10½"	1.5 oz.	Ladies'

[1]Weights can vary due to the grip manufacturer's tolerances and also because of the different grip core sizes in each style that are available. As a very general rule, an M60 core size grip will weigh ⅟₂₀ ounce (1½ grams) lighter than an M58. An M62 core size grip will weigh ⅟₁₀ ounce (3 grams) lighter than an M60. Use the weights above as a comparative measure when changing from one grip type and/or size to another. (Example: The All Cord grip weighs approximately ⁵⁄₁₆ ounce more than the Eagle grip.)

[2]The "H" designation in the mouth of the grip means that the grip will install to Eaton's standard arthritic shape which utilizes 3 internal ribs, one rib on the bottom and one on each side. (Discontinued Grip)

[3]Cordline grips are only available in men's sizes.

[4]"CM" inside the mouth of a chamois grip designates "Chamois Men's Size." Likewise a "CL" indicates "Chamois Ladies' Size."

[5]1.95 ounces includes the Neumann leather strip, one layer of double-coated tape and an Eaton rubber underlisting.

[6]To convert grip weights to fractions, use the following:
    1.75 = 1¾, 1.5 = 1½, 1.65 = 1²¹⁄₃₂, 1.95 = 1⁶¹⁄₆₄, 1.45 = 1²⁹⁄₆₄, 1.6 = 1¹⁹⁄₃₂.
To convert grip weights to grams, multiply the weight shown above in ounces by 28.35.
Example: A 1.75 ounce Victory grip is 49.6 grams.

A Final Word on Regripping

The process of simply regripping a golf club takes place thousands of times every single day. It is very easy to learn how to regrip golf clubs by cutting off the old grip and slipping on a new one. However, part of the purpose of this chapter is to provide a sound working knowledge of why regripping can alter other club specifications. The information at the end of this chapter should answer the "why" aspect and give you the personal satisfaction of being able to explain to your customer what will happen to his golf club when he brings it in for regripping.

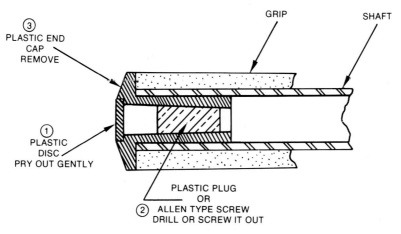

Fig. 22-146
Plastic End Cap removal

23

CHANGING LENGTHS OF GOLF CLUBS

Changing the length of a golf club is a relatively simple procedure by itself. However, when a golf club's length is changed, various other specifications of the golf club are directly affected. More specifically, total weight, swingweight, shaft flex and lie are affected enough that when a length change is made, each one of these specifications should be considered and possibly adjusted. For a basic comparison, consider the following example of an average driver changed only by increasing it ½″ in length from 43″ to 43½″.

Total weight: Increased by ³⁄₁₆ to ¼ ounce.

Swingweight: Increases 3 swingweights (shorter clubs are less affected).

Shaft Flex: Will feel slightly more flexible.

Lie: Although the actual absolute lie angle remains the same, the ½″ increase in club length will make the club appear 1° more upright and the toe will be slightly higher off the ground.

23-1   First, accurately measure the club length. Photo shows club in a normal lie position with a **48″ ruler** placed close behind it. Length is read from the top of the grip cap.

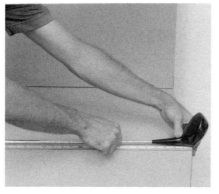

23-2   Another way to measure club length is to install a self-adhesive measuring tape to the top of a workbench. The drawback here is that this fails to pick up the distance between the bottom of the sole radius and the back of the heel. However, this method is good for comparative length checking (i.e., differences in lengths from one club to another).

23-3   Check the swingweight before changing the club length.

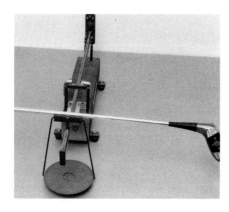

23-4   Check the total weight before changing the club length.

23-5   Check grip size if either old grip or a new one is to be installed.

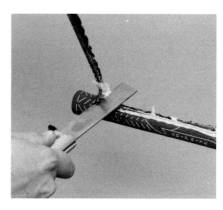

23-6   Remove grip by cutting it off, or . . .

23-7 . . . remove grip using a **Grip Shooter** which injects solvent under grip through a hypodermic needle. Wear eye protection. For procedure, see Chapter 22 photos 22-31 thru 22-37.

23-8 Determine shaft butt size. Shown is the **Grip Size and Shaft Butt Gauge.** A vernier caliper or micrometer will also work.

23-9 Check the size of a steel shaft butt extension to be sure it matches the butt size. Steel butt extensions are available to fit .560, .580, .600 and .620 shaft butts.

23-10 Light abrading of the reduced section of the shaft extension will ensure good adhesion between the epoxy and extension.

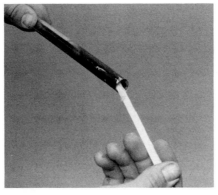

23-11 Mix and apply epoxy inside the shaft butt. Any high shear strength shafting type epoxy is sufficient.

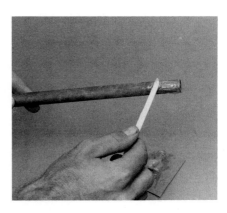

23-12 Apply epoxy to the outside of the reduced section of the shaft extension.

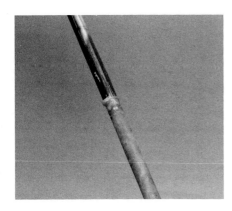

23-13 Install the reduced section of the extension inside the shaft butt. Push the extension down into the shaft until the enlarged portion of the extension rests against the shaft butt. Wipe off any excess epoxy.

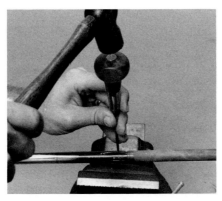

23-14 Make 2 or 3 indentations around the top of the shaft with an awl to ensure the extension will not come loose. Make marks 1″ down from the top of the shaft.

23-15 After the epoxy has cured, measure and make a mark on the extension where you wish to make your cut. Remember to make the mark ⅛″ below the desired length as the grip cap will account for an additional ⅛″.

23-16 Cut the shaft extension using a **Tubing Cutter**, the edge of a grinding wheel or a steel friction wheel.

23-17 Photo shows installed extension cut to length.

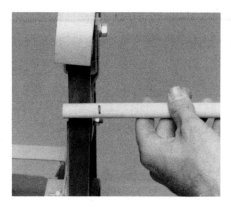

23-18 ⅝" diameter hardwood dowels can also be used as a substitute for steel shaft butt extensions. Photo shows end of dowel being turned down on a **1" × 42" Belt Sander** to fit inside shaft butt.

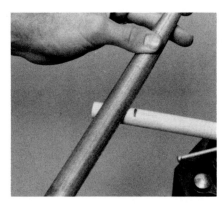

23-19 A wood rasp or coarse cut file can also be used to turn down end of wood dowel. Note the mark on the extension. Make sure the reduced section which fits inside the shaft butt is a minimum of 1½" long and preferably 2" long.

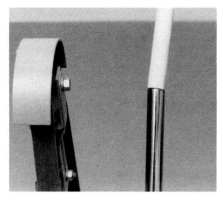

23-20 Periodically test fit the dowel in the shaft butt. When extension fits snugly inside shaft . . .

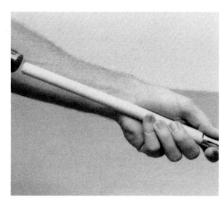

23-21 . . . mix and apply epoxy to both the inside of the shaft and to the reduced section of the dowel. Drive the reduced section of the dowel into the shaft butt.

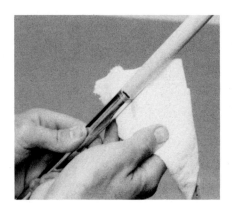

23-22 Wipe excess epoxy from the shaft and extension. Allow the epoxy to cure.

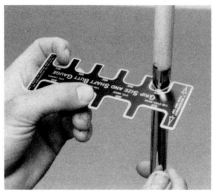

23-23 After epoxy has cured, measure the shaft butt diameter.

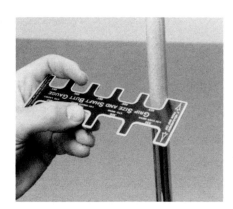

23-24 Measure the extension diameter also.

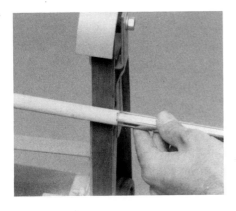

23-25 Using a file or belt sander, blend wood to conform to the outside diameter of the shaft. Make as uniform as possible.

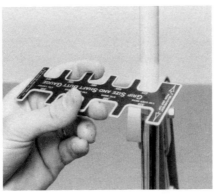

23-26 The extension has been reduced to the proper diameter.

23-27 Next, mark wood dowel at desired length and . . .

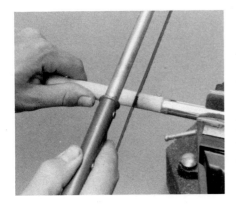

23-28 . . . cut, using a saw. Note: Lengthening clubs more than 2″ using wood dowels is not recommended.

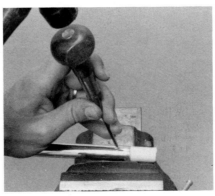

23-29 Pierce the shaft at 3 places around the shaft using a sharp **Awl** or **Prick Punch.** These punch marks are made 1″ down from the top of the steel shaft.

23-30 Composite shafts, such as graphite, can also be extended. Steel extensions are not available because of the smaller inside diameter of a graphite shaft. Instead, save old or broken graphite shafts and use these as extensions.

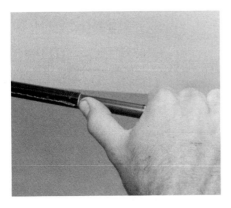

23-31 Push the old graphite shaft into the butt of the shaft to be extended until a snug fit is achieved. Mark the old shaft even with the top of the original shaft.

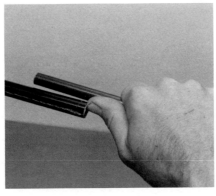

23-32 Pull the old shaft out and make another mark 3″ down from the first mark. Lightly abrade that portion of the shaft extension that will fit inside the shaft that is to be extended. Cut excess portion of shaft below 3″ mark.

23-33 Apply epoxy to the abraded section and fit inside the graphite shaft. Push the graphite extension inside the shaft until a snug fit is achieved. This should be very close to the original mark on the extension.

23-34 Remove any excess epoxy and allow the epoxy to cure.

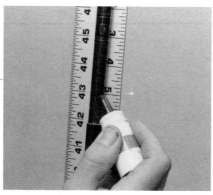

23-35 Mark the graphite extension at the point where you wish to make your cut. Remember to make the mark ⅛″ below the desired overall length as the grip cap will account for an additional ⅛″.

23-36 Cut the extension using a hacksaw.

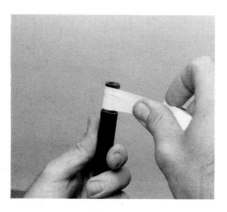

23-37 The extension can now be built up to match the outside diameter of the shaft, using several layers of masking tape.

23-38 Measure the extension diameter to ensure it is the same diameter as the shaft. No piercing is required on composite shafts as this would tend to weaken them.

23-39 **Install the grip** and check grip size as outlined in Chapter 22.

23-40 **Final check new length using a 48″ ruler.**

23-41 **Final check swingweight.** If weight is to be removed, refer to Chapter 13 for woods and Chapter 17 for irons.

23-42 **Final check total weight.**

ADDITIONAL INFORMATION FOR
CHANGING LENGTHS OF GOLF CLUBS

When it comes to golf clubs and their components, it sometimes seems that all of the different references to the use of the word "length" can be very confusing. To help you understand "length," this glossary of length terms should be studied.

Playing Length — The length of the finished golf club when measured from the ground line to the edge of the grip cap while the club is held in the playing position. This length is determined by placing a 48″ ruler in back of the club as shown in Fig. 23-43.

Fig. 23-43

Raw Shaft Length — The length of the raw, uncut golf shaft, from the tip to the butt end.

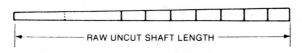

RAW UNCUT SHAFT LENGTH

Fig. 23-44

Tip Length — Also called tip section length, the distance from the raw shaft tip to the first step down.

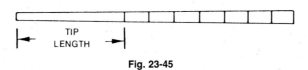

TIP LENGTH

Fig. 23-45

Traditional Length Method — The distance from the back of the heel of the golf club to the top of the grip cap. Note the difference in measuring methods as shown in Fig. 23-43 and 23-46. The playing length method compensates for sole radius and the traditional length method does not.

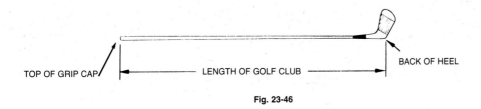

TOP OF GRIP CAP   LENGTH OF GOLF CLUB   BACK OF HEEL

Fig. 23-46

Standard Length — The golf industry's accepted playing lengths of golf clubs. See Table 23-1.

TABLE 23-1
Wood Club Lengths

Woods	Men's Standard	Ladies' Standard	Ladies' Petite
1	43″	42″	41½″
2	42½″	41½″	41″
3	42″	41″	40½″
4	41½″	40½″	40″
5	41″	40″	39½″
6	40½″	39½″	39″
7	40″	39″	38½″

Iron Club Lengths

Irons	Men's Modern Standard	Men's Traditional Standard	Ladies' Standard	¹Ladies' Petite
1	39½″	39″	38″	37½″
2	39″	38½″	37½″	37″
3	38½″	38″	37″	36½″
4	38″	37½″	36½″	36″
5	37½″	37″	36″	35½″
6	37″	36½″	35½″	35″
7	36½″	36″	35″	34½″
8	36″	35½″	34½″	34″
9	35½″	35″	34″	33½″
PW	35½″	35″	34″	33½″
SW	35½″	35″	34″	33½″

¹Ladies' petite is usually ½″ shorter than the traditional ladies' standard length. Some companies make ladies' petite 1″ shorter than ladies' standard length.

NOTES

24

STRAIGHTENING BENT SHAFTS

There are many types of bent shafts which can be straightened to like-new condition with no adverse effect in performance whatsoever. Basically, the only type of bent shafts which cannot be straightened are those with dings, dents, kinks, creases or more specifically are no longer circular in cross section. A handy device for straightening many types of bent shafts is a Shaft Straightening Block, which can be purchased from a golf repair supplies dealer or you can make your own as shown at the end of Chapter 11.

24-1 Sight down shaft to determine bend location.

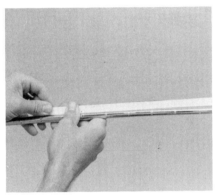

24-2 Placing a straight edge against the shaft can help you determine exactly where the bend is.

24-3 Using the **Shaft Bending Block**, apply downward pressure with hands apart as shown. Change shaft position in the Block as you slowly work along the bend.

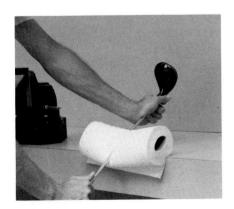

24-4 Another method may be used. Place a thick roll of paper towels against the edge of a bench. Work the bend back and forth over the towels until the bend disappears. Check for straightness constantly while alternating bending so as not to over-bend the shaft.

24-5 A crease or kink in the shaft indicates the shaft must be replaced due to structural damage.

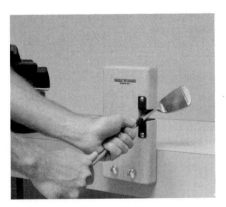

24-6 Sometimes an iron shaft will be bent at the neck. The assumption is to replace the shaft; however, the shaft can often be straightened easily as shown. Be sure the hosel just hangs over the edge of the Bending Block. Slight downward pressure will return the shaft to a straight condition.

APPENDICES

SETTING UP AND EQUIPPING THE REPAIR SHOP

Providing a good work flow is a fundamental goal when setting up a repair shop. Regardless of the shop's size or the volume of work, it should be organized to allow the work to commence at a certain point and then easily move through the shop in progressive stages until finished. With this in mind, careful positioning of the various tools and machines will contribute to a smooth operation that maximizes the use of your space and time. Examine the floor drawing for an idea of how an ideal work flow can be established.

Professionally operated repair shops typically have a desk, counter or small bench located next to the shop entrance. This serves as the nerve center for the entire shop. Here, customers are received, incoming clubs examined, records of accounts stored, outgoing clubs inspected and finally, clubs are packaged for shipment or customer pickup. Obviously, this area is a vital part of an organized shop. Once the incoming clubs have been inspected, appropriately tagged for identification and noted in a work log, they are moved to the workbench. Even if the size or location of your shop precludes a convenient customer reception space, a desk is still an important place for transacting certain business procedures in a well run shop.

Most club repair is performed at or near a vise fastened to the middle portion of the workbench. A sheet of pegboard should be attached to the back of the bench or hung on the wall behind it. Tools and gauges used most often (i.e., files, screwdrivers, face radius gauges, etc.) should be hung on pegboard hooks within easy reach of the vise. A Swingweight Scale should be conveniently located on the bench near the vise during repair operations, also. (See A.) Less frequently used tools and gauges can be hung on the outer edges of the pegboard. Larger tools can be stored along the back of the bench top. The front of the bench top should not be used for tool storage as clubhead components will be placed there during club disassembly and reassembly steps.

A small open shelving unit should be used either to the immediate right or left of the workbench. (See B.) This is used for storing screws, rivets, corks, and other sundries the repairman must have within easy reach. Adequate stock of these supplies must be continuously maintained to avoid inefficient work stoppages.

A sturdy 4' × 4' bench should be located next to the shelving unit and built sturdy enough to hold a 1" × 42" Belt Sander, Bench-type Drill Press, Club Holder, and a spare Electric Motor. (See C.) The use of this machinery

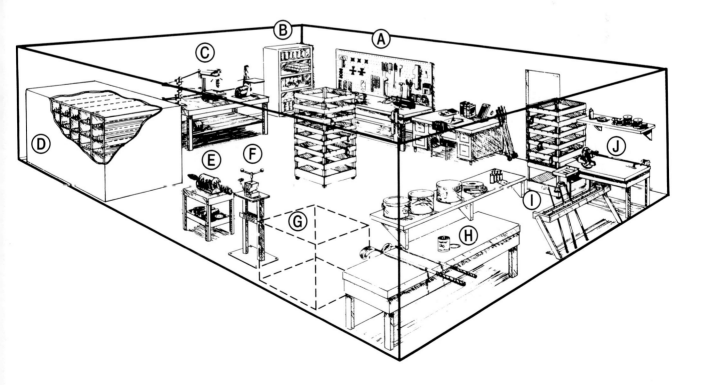

will substantially speed up many repair tasks. The Belt Sander is used to shape ferrules, sand wood hosels, abrade shaft tips, remove excess epoxy around inserts, grind indentations from soleplates and many more chores. The Drill Press is used with the Iron Head Boring and Reaming Vise for removing broken shaft tips and enlarging hosel bores in irons. Installing a drill blank into the chuck provides the repairman with a quick means of drilling back-screw holes into wood head hosels. The Club Holder will secure a club in a fixed position while the vise is used for other purposes. Specifically, clubs with freshly poured inserts must be held in the correct position until the epoxy has cured. The Electric Motor has many uses. A Drill Chuck may be attached to an arbor, which in turn, is fastened to the motor shaft. The chuck is used to hold drill bits when a wood hosel bore requires enlargement. Also, a Shaft Cut-off Wheel or Unstitched Buffing Wheel can be attached to the motor if needed.

A logical storage location for shaft and grip inventory is next to the small bench. (See D.) A large plywood rack can be built to hold both shafts and grips with enough built-in bins to sort them by type. The shaft and grip rack can be extended far enough out into the room to serve as a separating wall between the repair and finishing areas of the shop.

If space is available, a Golf Club Rack should be placed in the middle of the room to hold clubs during various drying stages in the repair/refinishing process. The rack can be set up in such a way as to allow clubs to be placed on the rack from any side of the room. For instance, clubs can be placed on the rack on the side of the room facing the workbench after the components have been reset. Clubs with a fresh coating of stain or filler may be placed on the rack until dry. It is not necessary to have clubs scattered around the shop; instead, make full use of the Golf Club Rack.

After all repairs have been performed and the wood clubs are ready for refinishing, the next step requires sanding the wood heads. The Sanding Machine is positioned next to the shaft rack. (See E.) Some repair shops place a curtain around the Sanding Machine to isolate the dust from other areas in the shop. The use of a vacuum system hooked to the sander will substantially reduce this problem. Now, it becomes obvious that the work flow is moving in a circular pattern through the shop.

The next step in the refinishing process is the application of stain, filler, and subsequent finish coats. Because clubhead sanding can create a large amount of dust, the sanding machine area should be placed as far away as possible from the finish application area. Yet, the shop must maintain an easy work flow. To accomplish this, the flow is only slightly interrupted by placing the Loft and Lie Machine next to the sanding area. (See F.) Ample space is required when using the Loft and Lie Machine, and this placement provides a good break between the sanding and finishing application stages.

To separate the two areas even more, some shops will build a drying box and place it in line next to the Loft

and Lie Machine. The drying box provides an enclosed space that is dust free for clubheads with freshly coated finishes. The box can also have heat and humidity level controls for the curing process. (See G.)

Next, in the line of flow, is a small 8' bench with a shelf mounted on top. (See H.) The bench should be placed far enough away from the wall to allow clubs to lie lengthwise across the bench top. An 8' shelf will neatly hold all the finish containers the repairman will use. A drying rack may be conveniently placed next to the finishing bench. (See I.) This rack will hold the clubs during the important room temperature flash-off period that is required before they are placed under warmer conditions.

Another 4' bench is used to hold a Whipping Machine. Also, it can be used to set up a gripping station. (See J. and note the paint pan overhanging the edge of the bench to catch excess gripping solvent for reuse.) At this point the repair/refinishing cycle is completed. After a thorough inspection, the club can be whipped and prepared for customer delivery or pickup. The rack conveniently located next to the door serves as a holding area until delivery.

While we have used an advanced repair shop as our model, those repairmen wishing to get started on a smaller scale should utilize as many of these ideas as is practical to achieve a smooth work flow.

HOW MUCH SPACE IS NEEDED?

Now we will discuss things in what I like to refer to as "Specific Generalities." This means that it is virtually impossible to cover each and every situation in exact quantitative terms on how to get properly set up repairing golf clubs.

In many instances the question, "How much space is needed?" should have been asked, "How much space is available?"

In a very general way, the following minimum square footages for each situation should be used as a guideline only.

(A) Regripping, rewhipping, fixing loose inserts and sole plates, minor touch-up and dipping 1 coat of finish to seal clubhead.
Minimum: 60 sq. ft.
Examples of adequate room sizes would be:
10' × 6', 8½' × 7', etc.
Comments: Room would contain bench, vise, wall pegboard, tools & supplies to do above operations.

(B) Everything listed in (A) plus re-shafting.
Minimum: 84 sq. ft.
Examples of adequate room sizes would be:
10' × 8½', 12' × 7', etc.
Additional space is needed for shaft storage and additional tools and supplies needed for re-shafting.

(C) Everything listed in both (A) and (B) plus refinishing.
Minimum: 144 sq. ft.
Examples of adequate room sizes would be:
12' × 12', 10' × 14½', 8' × 18', etc.

Comments: Addition of refinishing supplies, shelves, and sanding equipment. Drying between coats must be in another location. If drying is included in the same room, 200 sq. ft. would be minimum.

(D) A full service repair shop doing virtually all repairs including re-shafting, refinishing, adjusting lofts and lies of irons.

1. Small volume full service shop with mostly hand tools, some motorized equipment, and minimum supplies.
   Minimum: 324 sq. ft.
   Examples of adequate room sizes would be:
   18′ × 18′, 12′ × 27′, etc.

2. Medium volume full service shop with additional motorized equipment, and good stock of supplies.
   Minimum: 400 sq. ft.
   Examples of adequate room sizes would be:
   20′ × 20′, 13′ × 30′, 16′ × 25′, etc.

3. Large volume full service shop complete with most specialized equipment available. Excellent stock of supplies.
   Minimum: 600 sq. ft.
   Examples of adequate room sizes would be:
   20′ × 30′, 25′ × 24′, 18′ × 34′, etc.

WHAT MACHINES, TOOLS, COMPONENTS AND SUPPLIES ARE NEEDED?

This listing consists of three groups — machines and tools, supplies, and components. Each group is then sub-divided into three categories — beginning, intermediate and advanced. This will help the repairman determine his needs when equipping a repair shop. Each category is specifically geared toward the needs of a beginning, intermediate or advanced repair shop.

Do not feel you must confine yourself to only one category throughout the groups. For instance, if you wish to concentrate on the most profitable repairs — reshafting and regripping — you may want to outfit yourself with those machines, tools, supplies and components from the advanced categories for reshafting and regripping. Selections for other repairs can be made from the beginning or intermediate categories. Realistically consider the services you will be offering and make your choices from the appropriate category.

Beginning Category: regripping, reshafting, changing club lengths and club assembly. Bulge, roll, loft and face angle alterations also.

Intermediate Category: regripping, reshafting, refinishing woods, club assembly and all club alterations. Machines are introduced to speed club repair services and a larger inventory of components and supplies are listed to provide greater variety for a larger clientele.

Advanced Category: regripping, reshafting, refinishing woods, stainless steel irons and metalwoods, club assembly and all club alterations. Wide array of machinery

to provide very efficient operation. Large variety of components and supplies to cover virtually any request.

MACHINES AND TOOLS
Beginning

1 Clubmaker's Vise	1 Screwdriver	1 "U" Cobalt Standard Length Drill
1 Propane Torch Kit	1 Mini Hacksaw w/Blade	1 ⅜" Cobalt Standard Length Drill
1 Locktight Shaft Holder	1 Mill Knife	
1 Screw Heater	1 ⅛" Pin Punch	1 1/16" Drill
1 Whipping Loop Puller	1 3/32" Pin Punch	1 ⅛" Drill
1 Swingweight Scale	1 Scratch Awl	1 3/32" Drill
1 Speed Drill	1 8" Long Punch	1 7/32" Drill
1 pr. Wooden Vise Pads	1 pr. Leather Buffing Gloves	1 12" × 7/32" Extension Drill
1 pr. Aluminum Vise Pads	1 Driving Plug	1 47" × 7/32" Drill
1 Shaft Vise Clamp	1 19/64" Taper Length Drill	1 #1 Extractor & Wrench Set
1 Shaft Bending Block	1 5/16" Standard Length Drill	1 Heating Rod
1 Grip Size and Shaft Butt Gauge	1 21/64" Standard Length Drill	1 Golf Shaft Cutter
1 Leverage Block	1 "R" Taper Length Drill	1 Ball Peen Hammer
1 Face Radius Gauge		1 Grip Collar Starter
1 Shaft I.D. Gauge	1 "T" Standard Length Drill	1 Hacksaw Blade
1 Grip Slide Rule		1 Drill Stand
1 Aluminum Ruler	1 "T" Cobalt Standard Length Drill	1 Protractor
1 Wood File		1 Shaft Tipping Gauge
1 Flat File		1 Grip Size Under Right Hand Gauge
1 File Cleaner		

Intermediate

1 Clubmaker's Vise	1 Golf Club Gauge	1 21/64" Standard Length Drill
1 Propane Torch Kit	1 Face Radius Gauge	
1 Locktight Shaft Holder	1 Loft Gauge	1 "T" Cobalt Standard Length Drill
1 Screw Heater	1 Shaft I.D. Gauge	
1 Propane Torch Tip	1 Grip Slide Rule	1 "U" Cobalt Standard Length Drill
1 Whipping Loop Puller	1 48" Aluminum Ruler	
	1 Insert Pattern Copier	1 ⅜" Cobalt Standard Length Drill
1 Economy Loft & Lie Machine	1 Insert Remover Tool	1 "T" Standard Length Drill
1 Swingweight Scale	1 Wood File	
1 Economy Sanding Machine	1 Flat File	1 "R" Taper Length Drill
1 1" × 42" Belt Sander	1 File Cleaner	1 12" × 7/32" Extension Drill
2 Ferrule Turning Belt	1 #1 Phillips Screwdriver	1 47" × 7/32" Drill
2 1" × 42" Fine Sanding Belts	1 #2 Phillips Screwdriver	1 Ram Rod
2 1" × 42" Coarse Sanding Belts	1 Hacksaw w/Blade	1 Tap Wrench
1 Buffing Wheel Rake	1 Hacksaw Blade	1 Screw Ext. Set
2 Unstitched Buffing Wheels	1 Mini Hacksaw w/Blade	1 Countersink
1 Speed Drill	1 Mill Knife	1 Drill Stand
1 pr. Wooden Vise Pads	2 ⅛" Pin Punch	1 ½" Wood Chisel
1 pr. Aluminum Vise Pads	2 3/32" Pin Punch	1 Heating Rod
1 Rubber Shaft Vise Clamp	1 Scratch Awl	1 6" Scale With Clip
1 Shaft Bending Block	1 8" Long Punch	1 Weight Checker Rod
1 Grip Size Shaft Butt Gauge	1 Backscrew Hook & Scriber	1 Ball Peen Hammer
1 Leverage Block	1 pr. Leather Buffing Gloves	1 Grip Collar Starter
1 Squarehead Protractor	1 Driving Plug	1 Rasp
	1 19/64" Taper Length Drill	1 Round File
	1 5/16" Standard Length Drill	1 Fractional Drill Set
		1 Shaft Tipping Gauge
		1 Grip Size Under Right Hand Gauge

Advanced

1 Clubmaker's Vise
1 Sure Fire Propane Torch
1 Super Tight-Lock Shaft Holder
1 Electric Extractor
1 Whipping Loop Puller
1 Motorized Whipping Machine
1 Golf Club Machine
1 Golf Club Scale
1 Accurate Shop Scale
1 Sanding Machine
1 Sanding Sleeve for XL550 Sanding Machine
1 Sanding Machine Stand
4 Face Insert Clamps
1 1″ × 42″ Belt Sanding Machine
5 1″ × 42″ Linen Ferrule Turning Belts
5 1″ × 42″ Sanding Belts - Fine
5 1″ × 42″ Sanding Belts - Coarse
1 ⅓ H.P. Motor
1 Buffing Wheel Rake
2 Unstitched Loose Buffing Wheels
1 Scotchbrite Wheel
1 Speed Drill
1 Motor Switch
1 8′ Motor Cord
1 4-Outlet Plug Box
1 Club Holder
1 pr. Bent Nose Pliers
1 Eaton Metal Shaft Clamp
1 Lever Action Shaft Holder
1 Shaft Bending Block

1 Grip Size and Butt Gauge
1 Leverage Block
1 Protractor
1 Golf Club Gauge
1 Face Radius Gauge
1 Driver Loft Gauge
1 Fairway Loft Gauge
1 Shaft I.D. Gauge
1 Grip Slide Rule
1 48″ Aluminum Ruler
1 Golf Club Drying Rack
1 Electric Heat Gun
1 Bench Grinder
1 Drill Press
1 Insert Pattern Copier
1 Insert Remover Tool
1 Ferrule Installer Tool
1 Wood Rasp
1 Round Wood File
1 Flat File
4 File Handles
1 File Cleaner
1 Wood File
1 Spiral Ratchet Screwdriver
1 #1 Phillips Screwdriver
1 #2 Phillips Screwdriver
1 Small Reed and Prince Screwdriver
1 Large Reed and Prince Screwdriver
1 Hacksaw w/Blade
1 Hacksaw Blade
1 Mini Hacksaw w/ Blade
1 Mill Knife
2 ⅛″ Pin Punch
2 ³⁄₃₂″ Pin Punch

1 Scratch Awl
1 8″ Long Punch
1 Backscrew Hook & Scriber
1 Binocular Magnifier
1 Pressurized Grip Remover
1 Driving Plug
1 .294 Set Step Drills
1 .320 Set Step Drills
1 .335 Set Step Drills
1 .355 Set Step Drills
1 Iron Head Reamer
1 ⅛″ Drill Blank
1 12″ × ⁷⁄₃₂″ Extension Drill
1 47″ × ⁷⁄₃₂″ Drill
1 47″ Ram Rod
1 Cutting & Drilling Oil
1 Extractor Wrench
1 Screw & Shaft Extractor Set
1 Countersink
1 Drill Stand
1 Drill Chuck & Key
1 Motor Shaft Arbor
1 ½″ Wood Chisel
1 Heating Rod
1 6″ Steel Scale
1 Iron Head Boring and Reaming Vise
1 Dremel Moto Tool
1 Ball Peen Hammer
1 Grip Collar Knife
1 Fractional Drill Set
1 Electric Heating Rod
1 Shaft Extractor Set
1 Power Pal Compressor & Accessories
1 Buffing Shop
1 Weight Checker Rod

Note: All of the above items are available through The GolfWorks® Full Line Catalog.

SUPPLIES
Beginning

Wood and Iron Ferrules to fit: .277, .294, .335, .355 and .370 shaft tip diameters (1 doz. of each)
1 qt. - Acetone
End Cap Assemblies to fit: .560, .580, .600 and .620 shaft butt diameters (1 doz. of each)
Plastic Bell Grip Collars to fit: .560, .580, .600 and .620 shaft butt diameters (1 doz. of each)

50 yards - Whipping
4 - Molded Whipping Covers
50 - #8 × ⅝″ Brass Screws
50 - #4 × ⅝″ Brass Screws
50 - #5 × 1¼″ Steel Backscrews
25 - Wood Corks
25 - Iron Corks
1 roll - Lead Tape
1 lb. - Powdered Lead
12 - Tapered Wood Plugs
25 - ⅛″ Hosel Rivets
1 can - Oil Modified or Moisture Cure Polyurethane

1 - Black Faceline Scoring Paint
10 sheets - 400 grit Sandpaper
000 Steel Wool
5 - Epoxy Application Brushes
1 - Tack Rag
1 - Shear Strength Epoxy
1 roll - Single Coated 2″ Wide Tape
1 roll - Double Coated 2″ Wide Tape
1 qt. - Grip Solvent
1 qt. - Aluminum Oxide Sand
100 - Repair Tags

Intermediate

12 - Cycolac Inserts
4 squares - Fiber Inserts
Wood and Iron Ferrules to fit: .277, .294, .335, .355 and .370 shaft tip diameters (3 doz. of each)
End Cap Assemblies to fit: .560, .580, .600 and .620 shaft butt diameters (1 doz. of each)
Plastic Bell Grip Collars to fit: .560, .580, .600 and .620 shaft butt diameters (1 doz. .560, 2 doz. .580, .600, and .620)
Trim Rings (assortment of colors to match all shaft sizes)
200 yards - Whipping
4 - Whipping Covers
50 - #7 × ¾″ Steel Screws
50 - #5 × ¾″ Aluminum Screws
50 - #7 × ¾″ Brass Screws
100 - #8 × ⅝″ Brass Screws
50 - #5 × ¾″ Brass Screws
100 - #4 × ⅝″ Brass Screws
100 - #5 × 1¼″ Steel Backscrews
25 - Wood Corks
25 - Iron Corks
1 roll - Lead Tape

Lead Rod - 1lb. ¼″ diameter
1 lb. - Powdered Lead
100 - Tapered Wood Plugs
100 - ⅛″ Hosel Rivets
100 - ³⁄₃₂″ Hosel Rivets
12 - Black Rubber Hosel Plugs
12 - Red Rubber Hosel Plugs
4 - Brass Backweights
3 - 1″ × 42″ Linen Ferrule Turning Belts
1 can - Contact Adhesive
10 sheets - 100 grit Sandpaper
10 sheets - 150 grit Sandpaper
10 sheets - 240 grit Sandpaper
20 sheets - 400 grit Sandpaper
1 lb. roll - 000 Steel Wool
1 pr. - Leather Gloves
Stains: cherry, black, walnut, armour mahogany and burgundy
Fillers: natural and less intense black
Color Cotes: black and blue - aerosol
1 can - Polyurethane
1 can - Polyurethane Preservative
Faceline Scoring Paint — black and white
1 qt. - Acetone
1 qt. - Paste Stripper
1 tube - Chrome Polish

1 bar - Glanz Wach
3 - 1″ × 42″ Coarse Sanding Belts
100 - Epoxy Mix Sticks
7 - Dipping Containers (for stains and fillers)
20 pairs - Plastic Gloves
25 - Metric Cups
5 - Stiff Bristled Brushes
3 - Face Masking Brushes
10 - Epoxy Application Brushes
3 - Tack Rags
30 yards - Burlap Cheesecloth
Pour-in-place Epoxy — red, black, clear
Mortite Putty
Shear Strength Epoxy
1 gal. - Grip Solvent
1 roll - Single Coated 2″ Wide Tape
1 roll - Single Coated ¾″ Wide Tape
2 rolls - Double Coated 2″ Wide Tape
Color Paste Dispersions — black, brown
Lacquer Rub-in Sticks — white, red, black and gold
1 qt. - Aluminum Oxide Sand
100 - Poly Grip Protector Bags
50 - Poly Wood Head Bags
50 - Repair Brochures
100 - Repair Tags

Advanced

12 - Cycolac Inserts
4 squares - Fiber Inserts
4 squares - Phenolic Inserts
4 squares - Fiber Two-color Inserts
1 - Graphite Insert
1 - Aluminum Insert
Wood and Iron Ferrules to fit: .277, .294, .335, .355 and .370 shaft tip diameters (100 of each)
End Cap Assemblies to fit: .560, .580, .600 and .620 shaft butt diameters (1 doz. of each)
Plastic Bell Grip Collars to fit: .560, .580, .600

100 - Tapered Wood Plugs
100 - ⅛″ Hosel Rivets
100 - ³⁄₃₂″ Hosel Rivets
12 - Black Rubber Hosel Plugs
12 - Red Rubber Hosel Plugs
4 - Brass Backweights
5 - 1″ × 42″ Linen Ferrule Turning Belts
1 can - Contact Adhesive
10 sheets - 100 grit Sandpaper
10 sheets - 150 grit Sandpaper
10 sheets - 240 grit Sandpaper
40 sheets - 400 grit Sandpaper
1 lb. roll - 000 Steel Wool

20 pairs - Plastic Gloves
25 - Metric Cups
5 - Stiff Bristled Brushes
3 - Face Masking Brushes
10 - Epoxy Application Brushes
5 - Tack Rags
30 yards - Burlap Cheesecloth
Pour-in-place Epoxy — red, black, clear
Mortite Putty
1 gal. - Grip Solvent
1 roll - Single Coated 2″ Wide Tape
1 roll - Single Coated ¾″ Wide Tape
2 rolls - Double Coated 2″ Wide Tape
Color Paste

and .620 shaft butt diameters (1 doz. .560, 2 doz. .580, .600 and .620)

Trim Rings — assortment of colors to match all shaft sizes

200 yards - Whipping

4 - Whipping Covers

50 - #7 × ¾" Steel Screws

50 - #5 × ¾" Aluminum Screws

50 - #7 × ¾" Brass Screws

100 - #8 × ⅝" Brass Screws

50 - #5 × ¾" Brass Screws

100 - #4 × ⅝" Brass Screws

100 - #5 × 1¼" Steel Backscrews

25 - Wood Corks

25 - Iron Corks

1 roll - Lead Tape

Lead Rod - 1 lb. ¼" diameter

1 lb. - Powdered Lead

1 pr. - Leather Gloves

Stains: cherry, black, walnut, armour mahogany, burgundy, buckskin, dark blue and rosewood

Fillers: natural and less intense black

Color Cotes: black and blue - aerosol

1 can - Polyurethane

1 can - Polyurethane Preservative

Faceline Scoring Paint — black, red and white

1 qt. - Acetone

1 qt. - Paste Stripper

1 tube - Chrome Polish

1 bar - Glanz Wach

10 - 1" × 42" Coarse Sanding Belts (for belt sander)

100 - Epoxy Mix Sticks

10 - Dipping Containers (for stains and fillers)

Dispersions — black, brown

Lacquer Rub-in Sticks — white, red, black and gold

1 qt. - Aluminum Oxide Sand

100 - Poly Grip Protector Bags

50 - Poly Wood Head Bags

50 - Repair Brochures

200 - Repair Tags

1 - Dust Respirator

1 pr. - Soft Flex Goggles

8 - 8" Spiral-sewn Buffing Wheels

2 - 8" Sisal Buffing Wheels

1 bar - White Polishing Compound

1 bar - Sisal Compound

1 bar - Lea Compound

1 bar - Glue Compound

COMPONENTS
(Shafts & Grips)
Beginning Grips

24 - VG60	14 - MSN60	4 - GRI58
14 - VVC60	14 - CHMS	4 - HTP59
14 - CRM60	14 - SIH	12 - LVGG58
4 - JBV	4 - POP58	12 - LVGW58
14 - MSB60		

Intermediate Grips

48 - VG60	5 - POP58	14 - HTM59
12 - VG62	5 - GRI58	14 - BHTM59
24 - VGR60	5 - PAB58	14 - MSB60
24 - CRM60	12 - LVGG58	12 - MSN60
12 - CLSC60	12 - LVGW58	4 - FMAC
24 - VVC60	1 - RTG	14 - CPCU
4 - VG70	12 - NBL	14 - CHMS
14 - VHC60	12 - RU60	14 - SIH
12 - XPC	12 - SM60	5 - OMPG
4 - JBV		

Advanced Grips

48 - VG58	9 - JRV50	10 - BHTP59
1 case - VG60	14 - MSN60	5 - BHTP59
48 - VG62	14 - MSB60	5 - HTP59
24 - VGR60	14 - FMAC	24 - LVGG58
24 - CRM60	14 - CPCU	12 - LVGW58
14 - CLSC60	24 - CHMS	14 - NBL
48 - VVC60	24 - SIH	14 - NPL
14 - CRC60	14 - UTT60	14 - NML
14 - EAG60	10 - OMPG	14 - KNC
14 - VGB60	5 - CHPS	2 - L60
14 - XPC	10 - POP58	24 - SM60
14 - JBV	10 - GRI58	48 - RU60
24 - HTM59	5 - PGB58	14 - TSO60
24 - BHTM59	5 - PAN58	14 - BSO60

Beginning Shafts

Taper Tip Woods	Parallel Tip Woods
2 - 44" DWS	2 - UDWC
2 - 44" DWT	4 - UTTLWC
1 - 44" 2LWS	1 - U2LWAL
1 - 44" 2LWR	1 - UPMWC
1 - 43" 2LWL	
Irons	**Irons**
2-35", 1-35½", 1-36", 1-36½", 1-37", 1-37½", 1-38", 1-38½", 1-39" - DIS	1 - UDIC
	2 - UTTLIC
1-35", 1-37", 1-39" - DIT	1 - UDICO
1-35" - 2LIS	1 - U2LIAL
1-35" - 2LIR	1 - UPMIC
1 - YSTG	1 - YSTGF

Total Shafts = 38

Intermediate Shafts

Taper Tip Woods	Parallel Tip Woods
1-44" - DGWS300	UDGWS300
1 - DWX	3 - UDWC
2-44", 1-43", 1-42" - DWS	1 - U2LWAL
2-44", 1-42" - DWT	3 - UTTLWC
1-44" - NDWS	1 - UPMWC
1-44" - 2LWS	
1-44" - 2LWR	
1-43" - 2LWL	
1-44" - PFWR	
1-44" - SDLWS	
Irons	**Irons**
1 - 35" - DIX	2 - UDIC
1-35", 1-36", 1-37", 1-38", 1-39" - DIS	1 - U2LIAL
	1 - UDICO
1-35", 1-36", 1-37", 1-38", 1-39" - DIT	5 - UTTLIC
1-35" - PFIS	1 - UPMIC
1-35" - PFIR	2 - YSTGF
1-35", 1-37", 1-39" - 2LIS	
1-35", 1-37", 1-39" - 2LIR	
2 - YSTG	

Total Shafts = 57

Advanced Shafts

Taper Tip Woods	Parallel Tip Woods
1-44" - DGWS100	3 - UDGWS300
1-44" - DGWS300	2 - UDWX
1-44" - DGWS500	4 - UDWC
2-44" - DWX	3 - UDWAL
3-44", 1-43", 1-42½", 1-42" - DWS	4 - UTTLWC
2-44", 1-43", 1-42" - DWT	3 - U2LWAL
3-44" - 2LWS	1 - UJWC
3-44" - 2LWR	3 - UPMWC
1-43" - 2LWL	1 - ALD-LTWS
1-44" - SDLWS	
1-44" - 3DLWR	
1-44" - UCV-304WS	
1-44" - PFWS	
1-44" - PFWR	
Irons	**Irons**
1-35", 1-37", 1-39" - DGIS100	1 - UDGIS100
1-35", 1-37", 1-39" - DGIS300	1 - UDGIS300
1-35", 1-37", 1-39" - DGIS500	1 - UDGIS500
1-35", 1-37", 1-39" - DIX	1 - UDIX
1-35" thru 39" increments (9) - DIS	10 - UDIC
2-35", 1-36", 1-37", 1-38", 1-39" - DIT	1 - UDIAL
	2 - UDICO
1-35", 1-37", 1-39" - PFIS	1 - UDIALO
1-35", 1-37", 1-39" - PFIR	10 - UTTLIC
2-35", 2-37", 2-39" - 2LIS	2 - UPMIC
2-35", 2-37", 2-39" - 2LIR	2 - YSTGF
1-35", 1-36", 1-37", 1-38" - 2LIL	2 - UYSTG
2 - YSTG	

Total Shafts = 136

HOW TO EXPAND AND GET ADDITIONAL BUSINESS

Once you have entered the hobby/business of club repair, quality work will inevitably attract more and more business. However, there are proven ways of accelerating this process. Some methods involve branching off into related areas such as custom club making and fitting. The following ideas and tips are offered to help with the expansion effort.

Regripping Specials

1. Offer a discount when regripping a full set of clubs.
2. Regrip the putter for free if the entire set is regripped.
3. Offer a special regripping service on one type of grip. Most grips can be purchased at a reduced cost when ordering in case quantities. These savings can be passed on to the customer in the form of a "special," when clubs are regripped with this particular grip.
4. Fit the customer to the proper grip size for free, before regripping a set of clubs. This service can improve the golf game not only through the use of new grips, but also by using grips that are the correct size.

Grip Promotion

1. Display racks are available that promote different grip types on shaft butts. This allows the golfer to choose from not only different styles but also materials (see Chapter 22 photo 22-132).
2. Another display rack can be filled with all conceivable grip sizes. Golfers are naturally curious about different grip sizes and are attracted to this display. Golfers are fitted for correct grip size using the grips from this display.

Reshafting Specials

1. Offer a discount when reshafting a full set.
2. Offer a reshafting service for one shaft type. As with grips, shafts may be purchased in larger quantities at a reduced cost. Pass these savings to the customer in the form of a "special."

Shaft Promotion

1. Build 4 or 5 drivers with identical shaft patterns but each with a different flex. Strike a deal with the local pro-shop to display these clubs. Allow golfers to take the clubs to the range or course for a trial. This is a great way to increase reshafting services. A profitable arrangement can be worked out so both you and the golf professional can benefit.
2. Same concept as above but build 4 or 5 drivers with different shaft patterns and materials. Best way to increase reshafting services is to not use all conventional shafts. Try the new fibrous or very lightweight shafts.

Loft & Lie Specials

1. Offer to check loft and lie for free. Most sets will require adjusting. When customer sees the recorded specifications, he will usually want to take advantage of your bending service.
2. Offer a free lie fitting service in return for loft and lie adjustment.

Loft & Lie Promotion

1. Demonstrate the importance of correctly fitted lofts and lies with a professional presentation at the golf course range or organizational meetings. The most effective demonstration is using an iron with a hole drilled through the face and a shaft pushed into the hole. See GolfWorks® literature for more information.
2. Build a very upright and very flat 5 iron. Allow golfer to hit shots with both to see the effect on ball flight.

General Promotions and Specials

1. Place a small advertisement in the Monday edition of your newspaper's sports section. Monday sports pages carry all of the final results of the weekend's events including the final round coverage of professional golf tournaments. The ad will be seen by a great number of golfers.
2. Use promotional items. Buttons and/or shirts can be worn describing your service. Caps can be worn or passed out with the same information. Signs can be placed on the side of your car or truck to promote inquiries from golfers. Ball markers can be printed on and then passed out (some repairmen will intentionally leave a ball marker on every green so the groups playing behind him will receive this promotion). Business cards can be made up and left at local golf courses, restaurants or businesses. Promotional posters are commercially available promoting golf repair and fitting services.
3. Contact golf courses or clubs with bag storage facilities and arrange to offer winterizing to all of the bags in storage over the winter. For example, the club can bill the members a small additional charge on top of their bag storage fee. You can split an agreed percentage with the club or professional.
4. If a winterizing service cannot be worked out, arrange a time when you may look through each bag and inspect all the clubs. If all clubs are in need of repair leave a tag behind detailing the necessary work. Many times the owner will be appreciative of the attention given to their equipment and will contact you for the work.

5. Assemble examples of your refinishing, reshafting and regripping work. Go out and talk with golf professionals, sporting goods or department stores and show them the examples of your work. Emphasize service and quality with a turnaround on repairs of 5 working days on normal repairs and 10 working days on wood head refinishes.

6. Keep at least one set of partially finished custom clubs in your shop. For example, the heads would be finished and assembled on shafts but no other work performed. The customer who is attracted to the set can be fit for length, grip type and size, swingweight, face angle on woods (through slight bending of the shaft) and lie of both the woods and irons (again through bending).

7. Accepting trade-ins or shopping around for used sets is a great way to increase sales and profit. It is relatively easy to put your repair skills to work to turn a used set of clubs into like-new condition. Don't forget rechroming or repolishing services for used irons. The results can be fantastic.

8. Offer a gift certificate for repair or fitting services. This can be a great gift for the golfer who has everything.

9. Contact major golf club manufacturers to discuss the need for an authorized repair center in your area. The company may send a representative around to your shop to evaluate the quality of your work and whether you can handle the work load. This can be the source of tremendous prestige if successful.

NOTES

THE GOLFWORKS®
GOLF CLUB REPAIR WORKSHOPS

April of 1982 saw The GolfWorks® embark upon what has become the most successful series of golf club repair workshops held anywhere. Initially, we looked upon the club repair workshops as a short-term run to handle what was felt to be a limited number of requests by club repair enthusiasts. However, as word spread of the educational and enjoyable time had by all at The GolfWorks'® unique setting, it was soon realized that this "short term" affair would have no end. The workshop schedule has grown from eight per year in 1982, 12 in '86, 25 in '88 and to 40 tentatively scheduled for 1989.

The students have come not only from within the borders of the U.S. but also from without. A list of countries represented at our workshops would include Canada, West Germany, Great Britain, South Africa, Argentina, Saudi Arabia, Italy and India. These foreign students have given the workshops an international flavor not only with their presence but also with their stories of working conditions in their own countries. So, it is not unusual for a "local" student to come to a GolfWorks® Repair Workshop and find himself working alongside someone who has traveled 2500 miles just to learn the skills of club repair.

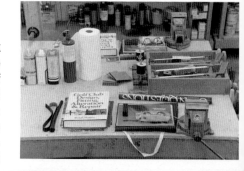

When students arrive at The GolfWorks®, they settle into their own work environment that includes individual work stations and tools. Surrounding the work stations are all the machinery necessary to perform any steps in the golf club repair process. This would include four different sanding machines and three different bending machines — all to give the student a wide variety when choosing what is best for his individual club repair needs. In addition to the normal array of machines, the student is also exposed to the machinery necessary for performing the unconventional repairs — refinishing stainless steel irons and metalwoods. Finishing off the room are tables and pegboards that hold virtually every club repair item shown in The GolfWorks® catalog. These tools, gauges and supplies are used throughout the week. Whatever the needs of the student, the workshop is set up and equipped to handle those needs.

Adjacent to the workshop is an audio/visual room. Timely breaks in the work schedule enable the students to seat themselves in a comfortable setting to view movies, slides and listen to lectures that pertain to club repair, alteration and design. The students are also introduced to golf club fitting and how changes in equipment can bring about positive and negative effects in ball flight. Regardless of the student's prior experience in club repair, at the end of the week he leaves with a well-rounded education in the art of repairing golf clubs.

GOLF SHAFT MANUFACTURERS' PUBLISHED SPECIFICATIONS

The following specifications provide valuable information for identifying, specifying and selecting the proper golf shaft. The golf shaft manufacturers publish this data in their price lists, normally on an annual basis. The information provided here is the latest available at the time of publication.

Every clubfitter should be able to identify any stock type and pattern golf shaft. A micrometer or vernier caliper along with a 48″ ruler will work well to do this. The best way, however, is with the "Shaft Identification Gauge," which used in conjunction with a 48″ ruler and the "Shaft Butt Gauge" available from The GolfWorks®, will identify most shafts by type and pattern.

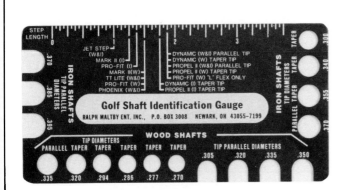

Golf Shaft Identification Gauge.

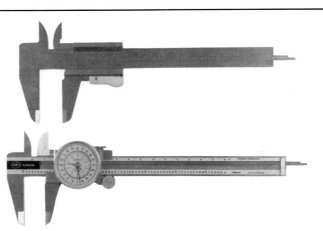

Two types of Vernier Calipers, dial type and non-dial type.

Golf Shaft Tipping Gauge.

Shaft Butt Diameter Gauge.

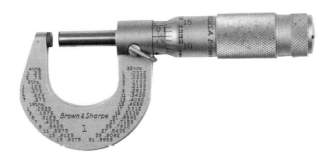

Micrometer 0″ to 1″ capacity.

48″ aluminum or wood ruler.

TRUE TEMPER STANDARD WEIGHT SHAFTS TAPERED TIP

PRO WOODS
FIT

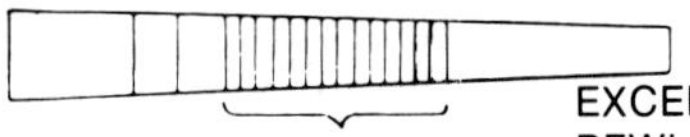

1½" STEPS
EXCEPT
PFWL @
1⅞" STEPS

PRO IRONS
FIT

1⅜" STEPS

DYNAMIC® WOODS

1⅞" STEPS

DYNAMIC® IRONS

1¾" STEPS

JET STEP® WOODS

1" STEPS

JET STEP® IRONS

1" STEPS

DYNAMIC GOLD™ WOODS

1⅞" STEPS

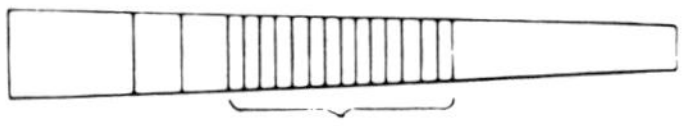

DYNAMIC GOLD™ IRONS

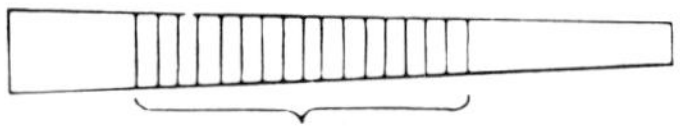

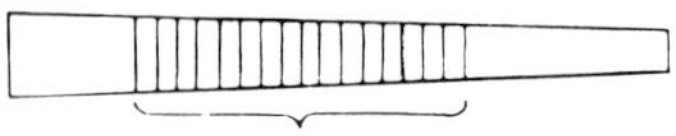

1¾" STEPS

Pattern	Flex	Butt Dia.	Tip Dia.	Tip Parallel	Length (Specify)	Nominal Weight (Ounces)	Weight Tolerance (Ounces)
PFWS	S	.620	.286	.340	42" — 45"	4.37	±⅛
PFWR	R	.600	.277	.335	42" — 45"	4.37	±⅛
PFWA	A	.580	.277	.320	42" — 45"	4.25	±⅛
PFWL	L	.580	.270	.305	42" — 44"	4.10	±⅛
PFIS	S	.600	.355	.395	35" — 39"	4.37	±⅛
PFIR	R	.580	.355	.385	35" — 39"	4.25	±⅛
PFIA	A	.560	.355	.380	35" — 39"	4.25	±⅛
PFIL	L	.580	.300	.335	34" — 38"	4.10	±⅛
DWX	X	.620	.294	.350	42" — 45"	4.50	±⅛
DWS	S	.620	.294	.350	42" — 45"	4.37	±⅛
DWT	T	.600	.277	.335	42" — 45"	4.37	±⅛
DWA	A	.580	.277	.320	42" — 45"	4.25	±⅛
DIX	X	.600	.355	.395	35" — 39"	4.50	±⅛
DIS	S	.600	.355	.395	35" — 39"	4.37	±⅛
DIT	T	.580	.355	.395	35" — 39"	4.25	±⅛
DIA	A	.560	.355	.380	35" — 39"	4.25	±⅛
JTWS	S	.620	.277	.320	42" — 45"	4.37	±⅛
JTWR	R	.600	.277	.320	42" — 45"	4.37	±⅛
JTIS	S	.580	.355	.392	35" — 39"	4.25	±⅛
JTIR	R	.580	.355	.380	35" — 39"	4.25	±⅛
DGWX	X100	.620	.294	.350	42" — 45"	4.38	±.03 oz.
DGWX	X200	.620	.294	.350	42" — 45"	4.44	±.03 oz.
DGWX	X300	.620	.294	.350	42" — 45"	4.50	±.03 oz.
DGWX	X400	.620	.294	.350	42" — 45"	4.56	±.03 oz.
DGWX	X500	.620	.294	.350	42" — 45"	4.63	±.03 oz.
DGWS	S100	.620	.294	.350	42" — 45"	4.25	±.03 oz.
DGWS	S200	.620	.294	.350	42" — 45"	4.31	±.03 oz.
DGWS	S300	.620	.294	.350	42" — 45"	4.37	±.03 oz.
DGWS	S400	.620	.294	.350	42" — 45"	4.43	±.03 oz.
DGWS	S500	.620	.294	.350	42" — 45"	4.50	±.03 oz.
DGWT	T100	.600	.277	.335	42" — 45"	4.25	±.03 oz.
DGWT	T200	.600	.277	.335	42" — 45"	4.31	±.03 oz.
DGWT	T300	.600	.277	.335	42" — 45"	4.37	±.03 oz.
DGWT	T400	.600	.277	.335	42" — 45"	4.43	±.03 oz.
DGWT	T500	.600	.277	.335	42" — 45"	4.50	±.03 oz.
DGIX	X100	.600	.355	.395	35" — 39"	4.38	±.03 oz.
DGIX	X200	.600	.355	.395	35" — 39"	4.44	±.03 oz.
DGIX	X300	.600	.355	.395	35" — 39"	4.50	±.03 oz.
DGIX	X400	.600	.355	.395	35" — 39"	4.56	±.03 oz.
DGIX	X500	.600	.355	.395	35" — 39"	4.63	±.03 oz.
DGIS	S100	.600	.355	.395	35" — 39"	4.25	±.03 oz.
DGIS	S200	.600	.355	.395	35" — 39"	4.31	±.03 oz.
DGIS	S300	.600	.355	.395	35" — 39"	4.37	±.03 oz.
DGIS	S400	.600	.355	.395	35" — 39"	4.43	±.03 oz.
DGIS	S500	.600	.355	.395	35" — 39"	4.50	±.03 oz.
DGIT	T100	.580	.355	.395	35" — 39"	4.13	±.03 oz.
DGIT	T200	.580	.355	.395	35" — 39"	4.19	±.03 oz.
DGIT	T300	.580	.355	.395	35" — 39"	4.25	±.03 oz.
DGIT	T400	.580	.355	.395	35" — 39"	4.31	±.03 oz.
DGIT	T500	.580	.355	.395	35" — 39"	4.37	±.03 oz.

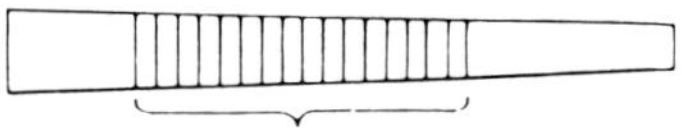

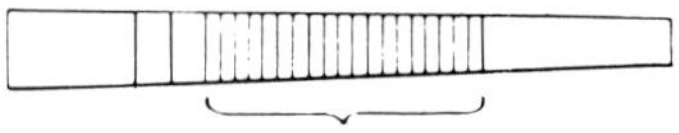

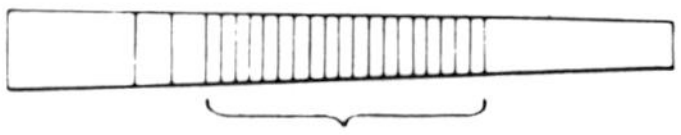

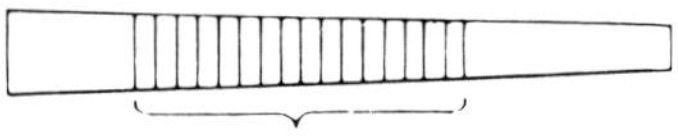

[1]Available in ½" increments

TRUE TEMPER LIGHT WEIGHT SHAFTS
TAPERED TIP AND PARALLEL TIP

	Pattern	Flex	Butt Dia.	Tip Dia.	Length (Specify)	Nominal Weight (Ounces)	Weight Tolerance (Ounces)
ExtraLite WOODS & IRONS	SDLWS	S	.600	.320	44", 43", 42"	3.40	±⅛
	SDLWR	R	.600	.320	44", 43", 42"	3.30	±⅛
	SDLWL	L	.580	.300	43", 42"	3.30	±⅛
	SDLIS	S	.600	.355	35" — 39"	3.50	±⅛
	SDLIR	R	.600	.355	35" — 39"	3.40	±⅛
	SDLIL	L	.580	.355	34" — 38"	3.37	±⅛
LITE™ WOODS							
PARALLEL TIP	U2LWS	S	.620	.335	45"	4.125	±⅛
	U2LWR	R	.620	.335	45"	4.000	±⅛
	U2LWAL	A & L	.580	.335	46"	4.000	±⅛
REINFORCED TIP	U2LWRH	R	.620	.335	43"	4.000	±⅛
	U2LWSH	S	.620	.335	43"	4.125	±⅛
TAPERED TIP	2LWS	S	.620	.294	42" — 45"	4.125 @ 45"	±⅛
	2LWR	R	.620	.294	42" — 45"	4.000 @ 45"	±⅛
	2LWA	A	.580	.294	42" — 45"	3.92 @ 45"	±⅛
	2LWL	L	.580	.294	42" — 45"	3.83 @ 45"	±⅛
LITE™ IRONS							
PARALLEL TIP	U2LIS	S	.620	.370	39"	4.000	±⅛
	U2LIR	R	.620	.370	39"	3.875	±⅛
	U2LIAL	A & L	.580	.370	40"	3.875	±⅛
TAPERED TIP	2LIS	S	.620	.355	35" — 39"	4.125 @ 39"	±⅛
	2LIR	R	.620	.355	35" — 39"	3.875 @ 39"	±⅛
	2LIL	L	.580	.355	34" — 38"	3.675 @ 38"	±⅛

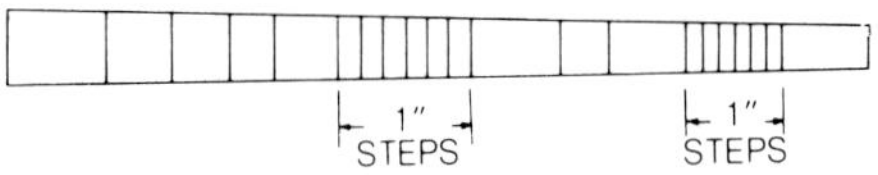

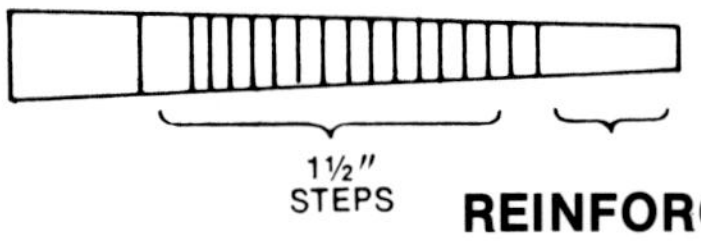

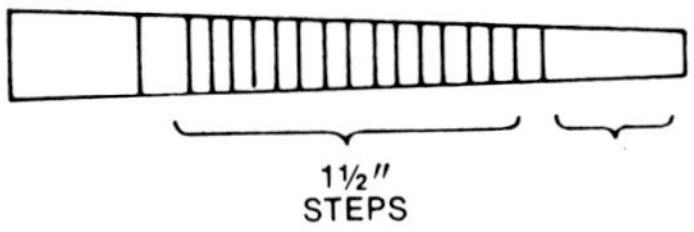

NOTE — Lite Woods & Iron shafts be they parallel or tapered tip are unitized shafts — in trimming for overall club length shafts will lose approx. 2.8 grams per inch.

LITE™ COMBINATION FLEX — R & S (FEATURING: .600 BUTT DIAMETER)

	Pattern	Flex	Butt Dia.	Tip Dia.	Length	Nominal Weight	Weight Tolerance
PARALLEL WOOD	UTTLWC	R&S	.600	.335	47"	4.31 @ 47"	±⅛
REINFORCED TIP	UTTLWCH	R & S	.600	.335	45"	4.25 @ 45"	±⅛
PARALLEL IRON	UTTLIC	R & S	.600	.370	41"	4.19 @ 41"	±⅛

GOLF SHAFT LENGTHS
1st Quality TAPERED TIP

Woods — All Flexes 45", 44½", 44", 43", 42½", 42"

Irons — X-S-R-A Flexes 39", 38½", 38", 37½", 37", 36½", 36", 35½", 35"

Irons — L Flex 38", 37½", 37", 36½", 36", 35½", 35", 34½", 34"

TRUE TEMPER FLEX FLOW
TAPERED TIP AND PARALLEL TIP
PROGRESSIVE FLEX POINTS

	Pattern	Flex	Butt Dia.	Tip Dia.	Length*	Nominal Weight (Grams)	Weight Tolerance (Grams)
Flex Flow™ WOODS **TAPERED TIP**	TFFWS	S	.600	.294	41½'' — 44''	110	±3
	TFFWR	R	.600	.294	41½'' — 44''	106	±3
	TFFWA	A	.580	.294	41½'' — 44''	106	±3
	TFFWL	L	.580	.294	41½'' — 44''	106	±3
PARALLEL TIP	UTFFWS	S	.600	.335	41½'' — 44''	110	±3
	UTFFWR	R	.600	.335	41½'' — 44''	106	±3
	UTFFWA	A	.580	.335	41½'' — 44''	106	±3
	UTFFWL	L	.580	.335	41½'' — 44''	106	±3
PARALLEL REINFORCED TIP	UTFFWSH	S	.600	.335	40½'' — 43''	110	±3
	UTFFWRH	R	.600	.335	40½'' — 43''	106	±3
	UTFFWAH	A	.580	.335	40½'' — 43''	106	±3
	UTFFWLH	L	.580	.335	40½'' — 43''	106	±3
Flex Flow™ IRONS **TAPERED TIP**	TFFIS	S	.600	.355	35'' — 39''	110	±3
	TFFIR	R	.600	.355	35'' — 39''	106	±3
	TFFIA	A	.580	.355	35'' — 39''	106	±3
	TFFIL	L	.580	.355	34½'' — 38½''	106	±3
PARALLEL TIP	UTFFIS	S	.600	.370	35'' — 39''	110	±3
	UTFFIR	R	.600	.370	35'' — 39''	106	±3
	UTFFIA	A	.580	.370	35'' — 39''	106	±3
	UTFFIL	L	.580	.370	34½'' — 38½''	106	±3

Available in ½'' increments only, in both tapered and parallel tip.

Special Note: Discrete Shafts are Recommended for each Club in a Set to Achieve Best Results.

True Temper's Recommendation:	WOODS					IRONS									
Club:	#1	#3	#4	#5	#7	#2	#3	#4	#5	#6	#7	#8	#9	PW	SW
Purchased Shaft Length in Both Parallel & Tapered Tip:	44''	43''	42½''	42''	41½''	39''	38½''	38''	37½''	37''	36½''	36''	35½''	35''	35''

Product Information on Flex Flow Shafts: The Flex Flow™ Shaft is designed to give each club in a set a different flex point. The Flex Flow™ Shaft provides a low flex point in the longer irons, a mid flex point in the middle irons and a higher flex point in the short irons. With woods, the driver will have the lower flex point and the fairway woods will be progressively higher in flex point location.

TRUE TEMPER PARALLEL TIP SHAFTS

DYNAMIC® WOODS

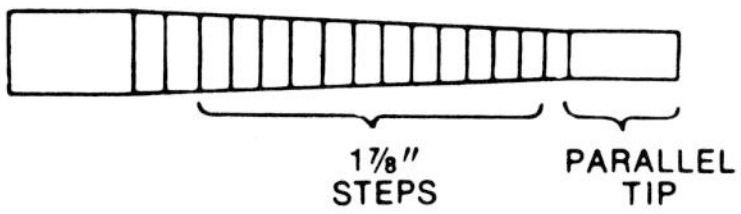

1⅞" STEPS / PARALLEL TIP

Pattern	Flex	Butt Dia.	Parallel Tip	Length	Nominal Weight (Ounces)	Weight Tolerance (Ounces)
UDWX	X	.600	.335	45"	4.375	±⅛
UDWC	R & S	.600	.335	47"	4.625	±⅛
UDWR	R	.600	.335	45"	4.312	±⅛
UDWS	S	.600	.335	45"	4.375	±⅛
UDWAL	A & L	.560	.335	46"	4.375	±⅛
UDWRH (Tip Reinforced)	R	.600	.335	43"	4.19	±⅛
UDWSH (Tip Reinforced)	S	.600	.335	43"	4.25	±⅛

DYNAMIC® IRONS

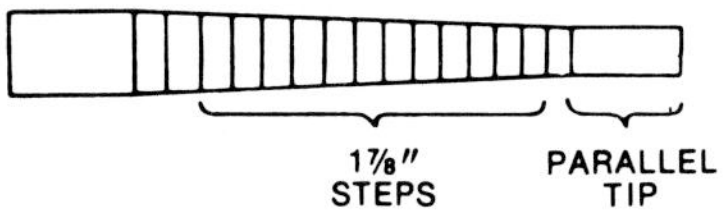

1⅞" STEPS / PARALLEL TIP

Pattern	Flex	Butt Dia.	Parallel Tip	Length	Nominal Weight (Ounces)	Weight Tolerance (Ounces)
UDIX	X	.600	.370	39"	4.500	±⅛
UDIC	R & S	.600	.370	41"	4.562	±⅛
UDIR	R	.600	.370	39"	4.250	±⅛
UDIS	S	.600	.370	39"	4.375	±⅛
UDIAL	A & L	.560	.370	40"	4.312	±⅛
UDICO	R & S	.600	.395	41"	4.562	±⅛
UDIALO	A & L	.560	.395	40"	4.375	±⅛

DYNAMIC GOLD™ WOODS

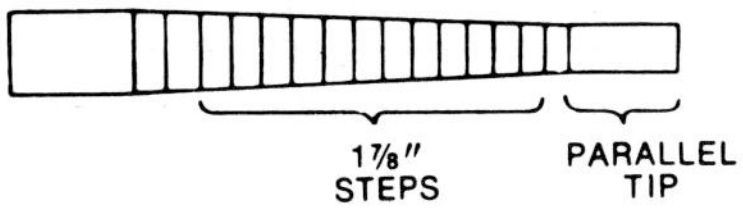

1⅞" STEPS / PARALLEL TIP

DYNAMIC GOLD™ IRONS

1⅞" STEPS / PARALLEL TIP

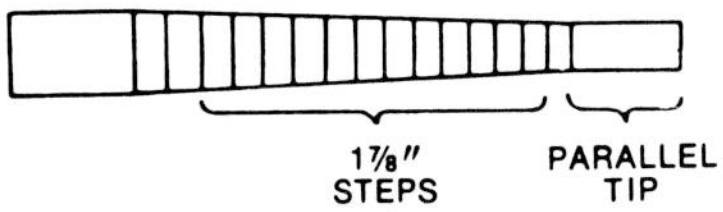

Pattern	Flex Category	Flex	Butt Diameter	Tip Diameter	Length	Nominal Weight (Ounces)	Weight Tolerance (Ounces)
UDGWS	S	S200	.600	.335	45"	4.31	±.03 oz.
		S300	.600	.335	45"	4.37	±.03 oz.
		S400	.600	.335	45"	4.43	±.03 oz.
UDGWR	R	R200	.600	.335	45"	4.25	±.03 oz.
		R300	.600	.335	45"	4.31	±.03 oz.
		R400	.600	.335	45"	4.37	±.03 oz.
UDGIS	S	S200	.600	.370	39"	4.31	±.03 oz.
		S300	.600	.370	39"	4.37	±.03 oz.
		S400	.600	.370	39"	4.43	±.03 oz.
UDGIR	R	R200	.600	.370	39"	4.19	±.03 oz.
		R300	.600	.370	39"	4.25	±.03 oz.
		R400	.600	.370	39"	4.31	±.03 oz.

JET STEP® WOODS

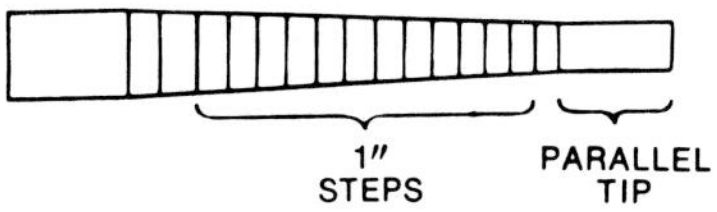

1" STEPS / PARALLEL TIP

Pattern	Flex	Butt Dia.	Tip Dia.	Length	Nominal Weight (Ounces)	Weight Tolerance (Ounces)
UJWC	R & S	.600	.335	47"	4.580	±⅛

JET STEP® IRONS

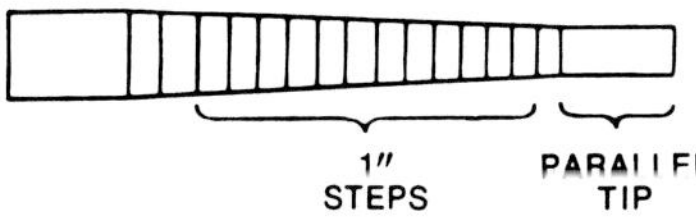

1" STEPS / PARALLEL TIP

Pattern	Flex	Butt Dia.	Tip Dia.	Length	Nominal Weight (Ounces)	Weight Tolerance (Ounces)
UJIC	R & S	.600	.370	41"	4.562	±⅛
UJICO	R & S	.600	.395	41"	4.562	±⅛

PUTTER SHAFTS

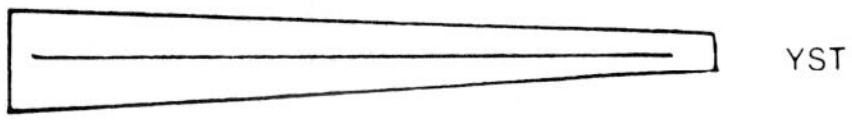

YST

Code	Description	Butt Dia.	Tip Dia.
YSTLSP	Str. Taper (Discontinued)	.500	.281
YST	Str. Taper	.580	.355
YSTG	Str. Taper Fluted	.580	.355
UYST	Unitized (Parallel Tip)	.580	.395
UYSTG	Unitized, Fluted (Parallel Tip)	.580	.395
YLCP	Step Down, No Heat Treat	.580	.355

PUTTER SHAFTS (cont.)

Code	Description	Butt Dia.	Tip Dia.
YSTGD	YSTG in Satin Chrome	.580	.355
UYSTGD	UYSTG in Satin Chrome	.580	.395
YESTGFD	Flared Tip, Fluted, Satin Chrome	.580	—
YESTF	Flared Tip, Bright Chrome	.580	—

NOTE: Putters are available in 35" only. Customer may trim from butt for shorter lengths.

BUTT EXTENSIONS

Used to increase length of shafts for longer length clubs.
Steel — Butt Size   .620 - .600 - .580 - .560

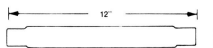

12"

Double length, cut in half

TRUE TEMPER PROMOTIONAL AND COMMERCIAL GRADE GOLF SHAFTS

		Pattern	Flex	Butt Dia.	Tip Dia.	Length (Specify)	Nominal Weight (Ounces)	Weight Tolerance (Ounces)
COMET₀ WOODS	PARALLEL TIP	URWR	R	.600	.335	45"	4.375	±¼
		URWL	L	.560	.320	44"	4.250	±¼
	TAPER TIP	URWRX	R	.600	.294	44"	4.375	±¼
		URWLX	L	.560	.270	44"	4.250	±¼
COMET₀ IRONS		URIR	R	.600	.370	39"	4.375	±¼
	PARALLEL TIP	URIL	L	.560	.320	38"	4.250	±¼
		URILM	L	.560	.370	39"	4.250	±¼
	TAPER TIP	URIRX	R	.600	.355	39"	4.375	±¼
		URILX	L	.560	.300	38"	4.250	±¼
CENTURY™ WOODS	PARALLEL TIP	U3W	R	.600	.335	44"	4.375	±¼
		U3WL	L	.560	.320	44"	4.250	±¼
	TAPER TIP	U3WX	R	.600	.277	44"	4.375	±¼
		U3WLX	L	.560	.277	44"	4.250	±¼
CENTURY™ IRONS		U3I	R	.600	.370	39"	4.375	±¼
	PARALLEL TIP	U3IL	L	.560	.320	38"	4.250	±¼
		U3ILM	L	.560	.370	38"	4.250	±¼
	TAPER TIP	U3IX	R	.600	.355	39", 37", 35"	4.375	±¼
		U3ILX	L	.560	.300	38" & 36"	4.250	±¼

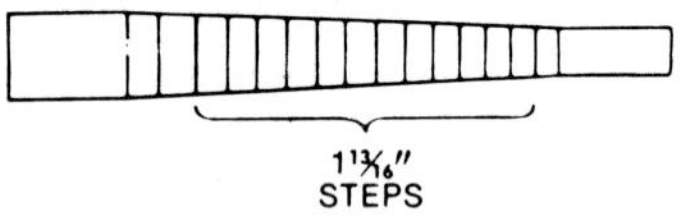

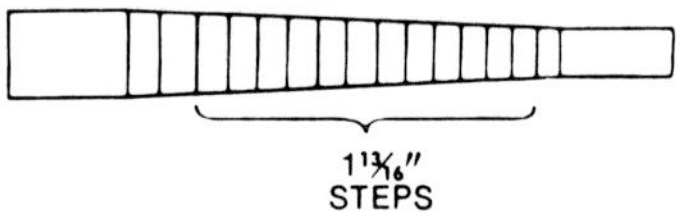

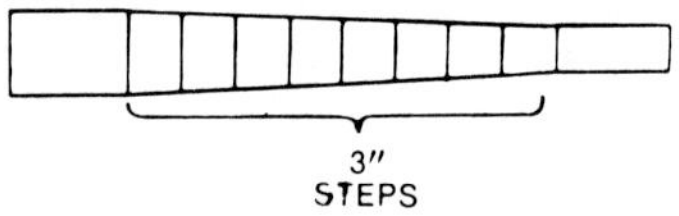

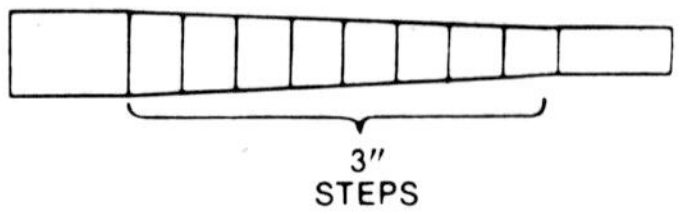

Step markings: COMET WOODS 1¹³⁄₁₆" STEPS; COMET IRONS 1¹³⁄₁₆" STEPS; CENTURY WOODS 3" STEPS; CENTURY IRONS 3" STEPS

JUNIOR & JUVENILE PARALLEL BUTT & TAPERED TIP

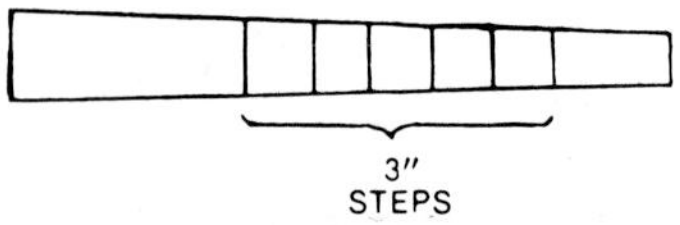

Pattern	Butt Parallel	Tip Taper	Length
Wood SJ500 — 39	.500	.300	39"
Iron SJ500 — 35	.500	.300	35"

3" STEPS

DRIVING RANGE WOOD

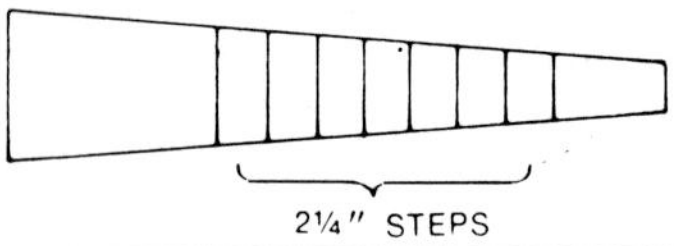

Pattern	Butt Dia.	Tip Dia.	Length	Nominal Weight (Ounces)	Weight Tolerance (Ounces)
MWH	.600	.320	44"	5.00	±¼

2¼" STEPS

TRUE TEMPER DISCONTINUED GOLF SHAFTS

Kinetic™ WOODS (DISCONTINUED IN 1981)

	Pattern	Flex	Butt Dia. Taper 10"	Tip Dia.	Length (Specify)	Nominal Weight (Ounces)	Weight Tolerance (Ounces)
PARALLEL TIP	U704WC	R & S	.704-.600	.335	47"	4.375	±3/16
TAPERED TIP	704WS	S	.704-.616	.294	42" — 45"	4.000	±3/16
	704WR	R	.704-.600	.294	42" — 45"	3.875	±3/16

1⅞" STEPS

Kinetic™ IRONS (DISCONTINUED IN 1981)

	Pattern	Flex	Butt Dia. Taper 10"	Tip Dia.	Length (Specify)	Nominal Weight (Ounces)	Weight Tolerance (Ounces)
PARALLEL TIP	U704IC	R & S	.704-.600	.370	41"	4.375	±3/16
TAPERED TIP	704IS	S	.704-.600	.355	35" — 39"	4.000	±3/16
	704IR	R	.704-.560	.355	35" — 39"	3.875	±3/16

1¾" STEPS

SUPER LITE™ WOODS (DISCONTINUED IN 1980)

TAPERED TIP

Pattern	Flex	Butt Dia. Taper 10"	Tip Dia.	Length (Specify)	Nominal Weight (Ounces)	Weight Tolerance (Ounces)
TTSWX	X	.620	.320	44" & 42"	3.75	±1/8
TTSWS	S	.620	.320	44" & 42"	3.65	±1/8
TTSWR	R	.620	.320	44" & 42"	3.55	±1/8
TTSWA	A	.580	.320	43" & 41"	3.45	±1/8
TTSWL	L	.580	.320	43" & 41"	3.45	±1/8

44" & 43" for Driver; 42" & 41" for Fairway Woods

BUTT 1½" STEPS

CONTOUR™ WOODS
3" RECESSED SECTION IN TIP SECTION

Pattern	Flex	Butt Dia. Taper 10"	Tip Dia.	Length (Specify)	Nominal Weight (Ounces)	Weight Tolerance (Ounces)
TRWS	S	.600	.294	—	42" — 45"	4.250	±3/16
TRWR	R	.600	.294	—	42" — 45"	4.125	±3/16
TRWL	L	.560	.277	—	42" — 44"	4.000	±3/16

1½" & 1" STEPS

CONTOUR™ IRONS
3" RECESSED SECTION IN TIP SECTION

Pattern	Flex	Butt Dia. Taper 10"	Tip Dia.	Length (Specify)	Nominal Weight (Ounces)	Weight Tolerance (Ounces)
TRIS	S	.600	.355	—	35" — 39"	4.125	±3/16
TRIR	R	.600	.355	—	35" — 39"	4.000	±3/16
TRIL	L	.560	.355	—	35" — 38"	3.875	±3/16

1½" & 1" STEPS

CONTOUR™ WOODS
3" RECESSED SECTION IN TIP SECTION

Pattern	Flex	Butt Dia. Taper 10"	Tip Dia.	Length (Specify)	Nominal Weight (Ounces)	Weight Tolerance (Ounces)
UTRWS	S	.600	.335	45"	4.250	±3/16
UTRWR	R	.600	.335	45"	4.125	±3/16
UTRWL	L	.560	.335	44"	4.000	±3/16

1½" & 1" STEPS — PARALLEL TIP

CONTOUR™ IRONS
3" RECESSED SECTION IN TIP SECTION

Pattern	Flex	Butt Dia. Taper 10"	Tip Dia.	Length (Specify)	Nominal Weight (Ounces)	Weight Tolerance (Ounces)
UTRIS	S	.600	.370	39"	4.125	±3/16
UTRIR	R	.600	.370	39"	4.000	±3/16
UTRIL	L	.560	.370	38"	3.875	±3/16

1½" & 1" STEPS — PARALLEL TIP

BRUNSWICK GOLF SHAFTS
TAPERED TIP AND PARALLEL TIP

	Model No.	Flex	Butt Dia., In.	[1]Tip Dia., In.	[2]Nominal Wt., Oz.
Bruns Lite™ Wood (Chrome Vanadium Alloy) Variable Steps / Tapered Tip	8568WV (UBLWV) Lengths 44'', 43'', 42½'', 42''.	V	.600	.294	2.90
Bruns Lite Iron Variable Steps / Tapered Tip	8568IV (UBLIV) Lengths 38½'', 38'', 37½'', 36½'', 36'', 35½'', 35''.	V	.600	.355	2.90
UCV-304® Wood (Chrome Vanadium Alloy) Variable Steps / Tapered Tip	6588WX (UCVWX)	X	.620	.294	3.80
	6578WS (UCVWS)	S	.600	.294	3.60
	6568WR (UCVWR)	R	.600	.294	3.40
	6528WL (UCVWL)	L	.560	.286	3.40
	Lengths X, S, R Flex 45'', 44'', 43'', 42''. L Flex 44'', 43'', 42'', 41''.				
UCV-304 Iron Variable Steps / Tapered Tip	6588IX (UCVIX)	X	.600	.355	3.80
	6578IS (UCVIS)	S	.600	.355	3.60
	6568IR (UCVIR)	R	.580	.355	3.40
	6528IL (UCVIL)	L	.540	.355	3.60
	Lengths X Flex 39'', 38'', 37'', 36'', 35''. S, R Flex 39'', 38½'', 38'', 37½'', 37'', 36½'', 36'', 35½'', 35''. L Flex 38'', 37'', 36'', 35''.				
Vanadium Sonic™ Wood (Chrome Vanadium Alloy) (Discontinued) Variable Steps / Parallel Tip	8488WX (UVSWX)	X	.590	.335	4.50
	8478WS (UVSWS)	S	.590	.335	4.40
	8468WR (UVSWR)	R	.590	.335	4.30
	8428WL (UVSWL)	L	.560	.335	4.10
	Lengths X, S, R Flex 45''. L Flex 44''.				
Vanadium Sonic Iron (Discontinued) Variable Steps / Parallel Tip	8488IX (UVSIX)	X	.590	.370	4.50
	8478IS (UVSIS)	S	.590	.370	4.40
	8468IR (UVSIR)	R	.590	.370	4.30
	8428IL (UVSIL)	L	.560	.370	4.10
	Lengths X, S, R Flex 39''. L Flex 38''.				
Phoenix™ Woods Parallel Tip	7578WS (UPHWS)	S	.620	.335	4.12
	7568WR (UPHWR)	R	.620	.335	4.00
	7556WAL (UPHWAL)	A/L	.580	.335	4.00
	Lengths S & R Flex 45''. A/L Flex 46''.				
1½'' Steps / Tapered Tip	7278WS (PHWS)	S	.620	.294	4.02
	7268WR (PHWR)	R	.620	.294	3.90
	7228WL (PHWL)	L	.580	.294	3.73
	Lengths S & R Flex 44'', 43'', 42½'', 42''. L Flex 44'', 43''. Nominal Weight Applies to 44'' Length.				
Phoenix Irons Parallel Tip	7578IS (UPHIS)	S	.620	.370	4.00
	7568IR (UPHIR)	R	.620	.370	3.87
	7556IAL (UPHIAL)	A/L	.580	.370	3.90
	Lengths S & R Flex 39''. A/L Flex 40''.				
1½'' Steps / Tapered Tip	7278IS (PHIS)	S	.620	.355	4.00
	7268IR (PHIR)	R	.620	.355	3.87
	7228IL (PHIL)	L	.580	.355	3.70
	Lengths S & R Flex 39'', 38½'', 38'', 37½'', 37'', 36½'', 36'', 35½'', 35''. L Flex 38'', 37'', 36'', 35''. Nominal Weight Applies to Longest Length in Each Flex.				

[1]Tip diameters have a tolerance of ±.002''
[2]Weight tolerance on all shafts above is ±1/10 ounce.
Standard length tolerance is ±1/16''.

BRUNSWICK GOLF SHAFTS
TAPERED TIP AND PARALLEL TIP

	Model No.	Flex	Butt Dia., In.	Tip Dia., In.	¹Nominal Wt., Oz.
Propel®II Woods	8088WX	X	.600	.335	4.50
	8076WRS (UPWC)	R/S	.600	.335	4.60
	8056WAL (UPWAL)	A/L	.560	.335	4.40
Parallel Tip	Lengths R/S Flex 47''. A/L Flex 46''.				
1⅞" Steps Tapered Tip	5088WX (PWX)	X	.620	.294	4.50
	5078WS (PWS)	S	.600	.294	4.40
	5068WR (PWR)	R	.600	.294	4.30
	5058WA (PWA)	A	.600	.294	4.12
	Lengths X Flex 44'', 43'', 42''. S, R & A Flex 44'', 43'', 42½'', 42''.				
Propel II Irons	7876IRS (UPIC)	R/S	.600	.370	4.58
	7856IAL (UPIAL)	A/L	.560	.370	4.30
1⅞" Steps Parallel Tip	Lengths R/S Flex 41''. A/L Flex 40''.				
	5088IX (PIX)	X	.600	.355	4.50
	5078IS (PIS)	S	.600	.355	4.40
	5068IR (PIR)	R	.600	.355	4.30
1¾" Steps Tapered Tip	5058IA (PIA)	a	.560	.355	4.12
	Lengths X Flex 39'', 38'', 37'', 36'', 35''.				¹Weight tol.
	S, R & A Flex 39'', 38½'', 38'', 37½'', 37'', 36½'', 36'', 35½'', 35''.				±¹⁄₁₀ ounce.

	Model No.	Flex	Butt Dia., In.	Tip Dia., In.	Length In.	Nominal Wt., Oz.
Mark II™ Woods	2763WR (UM2WR)	R	.600	.335	44	4.30
Parallel Tip	2423WL (UM2WL)	L	.560	.335	44	4.30
1½" Steps Tapered Tip	3263WR (M2WR)	R	.600	.294	44	4.25
	3223WL (M2WL)	L	.560	.286	44	4.20
Mark II Irons Parallel Tip	2463IR (UM2IR)	R	.600	.370	39	4.30
	3723IL (UM2IL)	L	.560	.370	39	4.30
1¼" Steps Tapered Tip	2763IR (M2IR)	R	.600	.355	38 & 36	4.30
Super Champion™ Woods Parallel Tip	2863WR (USCWR)	R	.600	.335	44	4.30
	2823WL (USCWL)	L	.560	.320	43	4.20
1¹³⁄₁₆" Steps Tapered Tip	2663WR (SCWR)	R	.600	.270	44	4.30
	2623WL (SCWL)	L	.560	.270	44	4.30
Super Champion Irons Parallel Tip	2663IR (USCIR)	R	.600	.370	39	4.25
	3523IL (USCIL)	L	.560	.370	38	4.25
1¹³⁄₁₆" Steps Tapered Tip	3863IR (SCIR)	R	.600	.355	38 & 36	4.30
	3823IL (SCIL)	L	.560	.300	38 & 36	4.10
Champion™ Woods Parallel Tip	2263WR (UCWR)	R	.600	.335	44	4.30
	2223WL (UCWL)	L	.560	.320	44	4.30
3" Step Tapered Tip	2563WR (CWR)	R	.600	.277	44	4.40
	2523WL (CWL)	L	.560	.277	44	4.30
Champion Irons Parallel Tip	2263IR (UCIR)	R	.600	.370	39	4.30
	2223IL (UCIL)	L	.560	.320	38	4.10
3" Step Tapered Tip	2563IR (CIR)	R	.600	.355	38 & 36	4.30
	2523IL (CIL)	L	.560	.300	38 & 36	4.10

BRUNSWICK GOLF SHAFTS
TAPERED TIP AND PARALLEL TIP

PUTTER SHAFTS

Model No.	Butt Dia., In.	Tip Dia. In.	Length In.	Description
9493P (QSTF)	.580	.382 I.D.	35	Straight Taper/Flared Tip
9093P (QST)	.580	.355	35	Straight Taper
9993P (QSTG)	.580	.355	35	Straight Taper/Flute
9893P (UQSD)	.580	.395	35	Variable Steps
2363P (QM2) (Discontinued)	.600	.355	36	1¼'' Steps
3863P (QSC)	.600	.355	36	1¹³/₁₆'' Steps
2563P (QC)	.600	.355	36	3'' Steps
1063P (QNHT) (Discontinued)	.580	.355	35	4'' (No Heat Treat)
2763P	.600	.355	36	1¼'' Steps

Model 3863, 2563, available in .370 parallel tip.

[3]Propel Micro Taper Woods

Parallel Tip
¾'' Steps
¼'' Taper Sections
Tapered Tip

Model No.	Flex	Butt Dia., In.	[1]Tip Dia., In.	[2]Nominal Wt., Oz.
8676WRS (UPMWC)	R/S	.600	.335	4.20
8656WAL (UPMWAL)	A/L	.580	.335	4.10

Lengths — R/S Flex 47''; A/L Flex 46''.

7678WS (PMWS)	S	.600	.294	4.10
7668WR (PMWR)	R	.600	.294	4.00
7658WA (PMWA)	A	.580	.286	4.00
7628WL (PMWL)	L	.580	.286	3.88

Lengths — S, R, and A Flex 44'', 43'', 42½'' and 42''; L Flex 43'', 42'' and 41''.

[3]Propel Micro Taper Irons

Parallel Tip
¾'' Steps
¼'' Taper Sections
Tapered Tip

8676IRS (UPMIC)	R/S	.600	.370	4.20
8656IAL (UPMIAL)	A/L	.560	.370	4.10

Lengths — R/S Flex 41''; A/L Flex 40''.

7678IS (PMIS)	S	.600	.355	4.05
7668IR (PMIR)	R	.600	.355	3.95
7658IA (PMIA)	A	.560	.355	4.00
7628IL (PMIL)	L	.560	.355	3.88

Lengths — S, R, and A Flex 39'', 38½'', 38'', 37½'', 37'', 36½'', 36'', 35½'' and 35''; L Flex 38'', 37'', 36'' and 35''.

[1]Tip diameters have a tolerance of ± .002''.
[2]Weight tolerance is ±¹/₁₀ ounce. Standard length tolerance is ±¹/₁₆''.
[3]The Propel Micro Taper is a new stock pattern shaft, introduced by Brunswick in its 1982 line.

METALWOOD HEAD SHAFTS .335'' PARALLEL, REINFORCED TIP

Model No.	Flex	Butt Dia., In.	Tip Dia., In.	Length In.	Nominal Wt., Oz.
Propel Microtaper Woods ¾'' Steps / ¼'' Taper Sections					
8976WRS	R/S	.600	.335	45	4.30
8956WAL	A/L	.580	.335	44	4.20
Propel®II Woods 1⅞'' Steps					
8088WX	X	.600	.335	45	4.50
8076WRS	R/S	.600	.335	47	4.60
8056WAL	A/L	.560	.335	46	4.40
Mark II™ Woods 1½'' Steps					
2763WR	R	.600	.335	44	4.30
2423WL	L	.560	.335	44	4.30
Super Champion™ Woods 1¹³/₁₆'' Steps					
2863WR	R	.600	.335	44	4.30
Champion™ Woods 3'' Step					
2263 WR	R	.600	.335	44	4.30

TI APOLLO TAPER TIP

MODEL	Flex	Step	Diameters Butt (inches)	Diameters Tip (inches)	45	44½	44	43½	43	42½	42	39	38½	38	37½	37	36½	36	35½	35	34½	Nominal Weight (ounces)
PHANTOM																						
Wood	S	GPS	·620	·294	●		●	●	●													4⅛
	R	GPS	·620	·294	●		●		●	●	●											4
Iron	S	GPS	·620	·355								●		●	●	●	●	●	●	●		4
	R	GPS	·620	·355								●		●	●	●	●	●	●	●		3⅞
SPECTRE																						
Wood	S	1½″	·620	·294	●	●	●	●	●													4⅛
	R	1½″	·620	·294		●	●	●	●													4
	L	1½″	·580	·294				●	●	●												4
Iron	S	1½″	·620	·355								●	●	●	●	●	●	●	●	●	●	4
	R	1½″	·620	·355									●	●	●	●	●	●	●	●	●	3⅞
	L	1½″	·580	·355										●	●	●	●	●	●	●	●	3⅞
AP 25																						
Wood	S	1″	·620	·277		●		●														4⅜
	R	1″	·600	·277			●		●													4⅜
Iron	S	1″	·580	·355								●	●	●	●	●	●	●	●	●		4¼
	R	1″	·580	·355								●	●	●	●	●	●	●	●	●	●	4¼
AP 35																						
Wood	S	1½″	·620	·286		●	●	●														4½
	R	1½″	·600	·277		●	●	●	●	●												4⅜
Iron	S	1⅜″	·600	·355								●	●	●	●	●	●	●	●	●		4⅜
	R	1⅜″	·580	·355									●	●	●	●	●	●	●	●	●	4¼
AP 44																						
Wood	X	1⅞″	·620	·294		●		●														4⅝
	S	1⅞″	·620	·294		●	●	●														4½
	R	1⅞″	·600	·277		●	●	●	●	●												4⅜
	L	1⅞″	·580	·277			●	●	●	●												4⅛
Iron	X	1¾″	·600	·355									●		●		●		●			4½
	S	1¾″	·600	·355								●	●	●	●	●	●	●	●	●		4⅜
	R	1¾″	·580	·355									●	●	●	●	●	●	●	●	●	4¼
	L	1¾″	·560	·355										●		●		●		●		4⅛
AP 46																						
Wood	R	1 13/16″	.600	.277			●															4⅜
	L	1 13/16″	.560	.270			●															4¼
Iron	R	1 13/16″	.600	.355										●				●				4¼
	L	1 13/16″	.560	.300										●				●				4¼
AP 83																						
Wood	R	3″	·600	·277			●															4⅜
	L	3″	·560	·277			●															4¼
Iron	R	3″	·600	·355								●				●				●		4⅜
	L	3″	·560	·300										●				●				4¼
					45	44½	44	43½	43	42½	42	39	38½	38	37½	37	36½	36	35½	35	34½	

PATTERN [1]TORSION MATCHED	Flex	Diameters Butt (inches)	Diameters Tip (inches)	45	44	43	42	39	38	37	36	35	34	Nominal Weight (ounces)
TAPER TIP														
Wood	S	·600	·294	●	●	●	●							4 5/16
	R	·600	·294	●	●	●	●							4 3/16
	L	·580	·277		●	●	●							4
Iron	S	·600	·365					●	●	●	●	●		4¼
	R	·600	·355					●	●	●	●	●		4⅛
	L	·580	·355						●	●	●	●	●	3¾

[1]Torsion matched shafts have alternating 1½″ and ½″ step lengths.

TI APOLLO GOLF SHAFTS
TAPERED TIP AND PARALLEL TIP

MASTERFLEX
Parallel Woods and Irons (All dimensions in inches)

	Code	Flex	Category	Length	Butt Diam.	Tip Diam.	Nominal Wt. oz.	gm.	Kickpoint
Woods	II	R	Regular	45	.600	.335	4.00	113	High
Irons	II	R	Regular	39	.600	.370	4.00	113	High
Woods	III	RS	Firm	45	.600	.335	4.19	119	High
Irons	III	RS	Firm	39	.600	.370	4.19	119	High
Woods	IV	S	Stiff	45	.600	.335	4.38	124	High
Irons	IV	S	Stiff	39	.600	.370	4.38	124	High
Woods	V	TS	Tourstiff	45	.620	.335	To special		High
Irons	V	TS	Tourstiff	39	.620	.370	customer order		High
Woods	VI	X	Xtrastiff	45	.620	.335	To special		High
Irons	VI	X	Xtrastiff	39	.620	.370	customer order		High

Taper Woods and Irons (All dimensions in inches)

	Code	Flex	Category	Length	Butt Diam.	Tip Diam.	Nominal Wt. oz.	gm.	Kickpoint
Woods	II	R	Regular	45-42	.600	.294	3.98	113	High
Irons	II	R	Regular	39-35	.600	.355	3.99	113	High
Woods	III	RS	Firm	45-42	.600	.294	4.16	118	High
Irons	III	RS	Firm	39-35	.600	.355	4.18	119	High
Woods	IV	S	Stiff	45-42	.600	.294	4.35	123	High
Irons	IV	S	Stiff	39-35	.600	.355	4.36	124	High
Woods	V	TS	Tourstiff	45-42	.620	.294	To special		High
Irons	V	TS	Tourstiff	39-35	.620	.355	customer order		High
Woods	VI	X	Xtrastiff	45-42	.620	.294	To special		High
Irons	VI	X	Xtrastiff	39-35	.620	.355	customer order		High

Stated weight is nominal for 39″ taper tip iron shaft. To achieve nominal weight for other shaft lengths, subtract 0.06 oz. (1.7 gms) for each ½″ increment.

Stated weight is nominal for 45″ taper tip wood shaft. To obtain nominal weight for other shaft lengths, subtract 0.10 oz. (2.83 gms) for each 1″ increment.

Taper Tip shaft lengths: Woods 1″ Increments
                         Irons ½″ Increments

Matchflex Woods and Irons (All dimensions in inches)

	Code	Flex	Category	Length	Butt Diam.	Tip Diam.	Nominal Wt. oz.	gm.	Kickpoint
Woods	1	AR	Flexible	45	.600	.335	3.88	110	Low
Irons	1	AR	Flexible	39	.600	.370	3.90	111	Low
Woods	2	R	Regular	45	.600	.335	4.20	119	Lo-mid
Irons	2	R	Regular	39	.600	.370	3.95	112	Lo-mid
Woods	3	RS	Firm	45	.600	.335	4.20	119	Hi-mid
Irons	3	RS	Firm	39	.600	.370	4.30	122	Hi-mid
Woods	4	S	Stiff	45	.600	.335	4.60	130	High
Irons	4	S	Stiff	39	.600	.370	4.45	126	High

TI APOLLO PARALLEL TIP

MODEL		[1]Flex	Step Length	Diameter Butt	Diameter Tip	Length	Nominal Weight
Phantom	Woods	S/R	Groups	.620	.335	47	4½
		A/L	Groups	.580	.335	46	3⅞
	Irons	S/R	Groups	.620	.370	41	4⅛
		A/L	Groups	.580	.370	40	3⅞
Spectre	Woods	S	1½	.620	.335	45	4⅛
		R	1½	.620	.335	45	4
		A/L	1½	.580	.335	46	4
	Irons	S	1½	.620	.370	39	4
		R	1½	.620	.370	39	3⅞
		A/L	1½	.580	.370	40	3⅞
AP25	Woods	S/R	1	.600	.335	47	4⅝
	Irons	S/R	1	.600	.370	41	4⁹/₁₆
AP35	Woods	S/R	1½	.600	.335	47	4⅝
	Irons	S/R	1½	.600	.370	41	4⁹/₁₆
[2]AP44	Woods	S/R	1⅞	.600	.335	47	4⅝
		A/L	1⅞	.560	.335	46	4⅜
	Irons	S/R	1⅞	.600	.370	41	4⁹/₁₆
		A/L	1⅞	.560	.370	40	4⁵/₁₆
AP46	Woods	R	1¹³/₁₆	.600	.335	44	4⅜
		L	1¹³/₁₆	.560	.320	44	4¼
	Irons	R	1¹³/₁₆	.600	.370	39	4¼
		L	1¹³/₁₆	.560	.320	38	4¼
AP83	Woods	R	3	.600	.335	44	4⅜
		L	3	.560	.320	44	4¼
	Irons	R	3	.600	.370	39	4⅜
		L	3	.560	.320	38	4¼

[1]S/R or A/L indicates a combination flex shaft.
[2]AP44 irons are also available in a combination S/R flex .395 over-hosel tip diameter.

PATTERN [1]TORSION MATCHED	Flex	Diameters Butt (inches)	Diameters Tip (inches)	STANDARD LENGTHS (inches) 45	44	43	42	39	38	37	36	35	34	Nominal Weight (ounces)
[2]PARALLEL TIP Wood	S	·600	·335	●	●	●	●							4⁵/₁₆
	R	·600	·335	●	●	●	●							4³/₁₆
	L	·580	·335		●	●	●							4
Iron	S	·600	·370					●	●	●	●	●		4¼
	R	·600	·370					●	●	●	●	●		4⅛
	L	·580	·370						●	●	●	●	●	3¾

[1]Torsion matched shafts have alternating 1½'' and ½'' step lengths.
[2]To preserve the torsion matching, it is essential to trim parallel tip shafts in this model only, from the butt end. Therefore, it is required that various lengths of shafts be available.

PATTERN SHADOW	Flex	Diameters Butt (inches)	Diameters Tip (inches)	STANDARD LENGTHS (inches) 47	46	45	41	40	39	38	37	36	35	Nominal Weight (ounces)
PARALLEL TIP Wood	S/R	.600	.335	●										4⅜
	A/L	.580	.335		●									4⅛
	Lite	.600	.335			●								3⅞
Iron	S/R	.600	.370				●							4⅛
	A/L	.580	.370					●						4¹/₁₆
	Lite	.600	.370						●					3⅞

SANDVIK SPECIAL METALS

PARALLEL WOODS

	Flex	Butt Dia.	Tip Dia.	Length		Nominal Weight	Weight Tolerance
Ti SHAFT — WOODS	X	.620	.335	45''	(at 45'' length)	3.81 oz.	±2 grams
TITANIUM	S	.600	.335	45''		3.70 oz.	±2 grams
	R	.600	.335	45''		3.63 oz.	±2 grams
	A	.600	.335	45''		3.25 oz.	±2 grams
	L	.580	.335	45''		3.14 oz.	±2 grams

PARALLEL & TIP TAPER IRONS

	Flex	Butt Dia.	Tip Dia.	Length		Nominal Weight	Weight Tolerance
Ti SHAFT — IRONS*	X	.620	.355	39'' — 35''	(at 39'' length)	3.75 oz.	±2 grams
TITANIUM	S	.600	.355	39'' — 35''		3.45 oz.	±2 grams
	R	.600	.355	39'' — 35''		3.45 oz.	±2 grams
	A	.600	.355	39'' — 35''		3.45 oz.	±2 grams
	L	.600	.355	39'' — 35''		3.44 oz.	±2 grams

*Also available in .370 tip for irons.

GRAPHITE GOLF SHAFT
SPECIFICATIONS BY MANUFACTURER

There have been quite a number of graphite shaft manufacturers since graphite was first introduced in 1973. Some lasted only a few months and others a number of years. By 1985, the graphite shaft industry in the United States had basically been reduced to two manufacturers, Aldila and Grafalloy. However, due to the increased demand for graphite shafts, the manufacturers' ranks have again swollen. Kunnan and Carbon Fiber Products are the latest companies to offer quality graphite shafts. The Pow-

erflex Corporation also makes a graphite shaft but they are better known for three golf shafts made from Aramid fibers that have unique flexing characteristics.

Reproduced here are tables that will provide useful reference information for removing, installing and identifying Aldila, Grafalloy and Powerflex Corporation shafts. The older graphite shafts are still quite common and on occasion new, unused ones can be found.

974 GRAPHITE SHAFT SPECIFICATIONS BY MANUFACTURER

Manufacturer	Woods					Irons				
	Length (In.)	Weight (Oz.)	Tip Dia.	Butt Dia.	Flex Desig.	Length (In.)	Weight (Oz.)	Tip Dia.	Butt Dia.	Flex Desig.
Aldila (Original)	45	2.3	.275	.590	1-6	—	—	—	—	—
	45	2.5	.287	.600	7-9					
	45	3.0	.305	.625	10-14					
	45	3.6	.325	.635	15					
Aldila (Alda 8)	45	2.2	.277	.580	8(L)	37	2.2	.350	.580	13(SD)
	45	2.4	.277	.580	12(SD)	38	2.3	.350	.600	14(SD)
	45	2.9	.300	.600	15(XXX)	38	2.7	.350	.600	16(XXX)
						39	2.8	.350	.600	16(XXX)
						39	2.2	.350	.580	8(L)
Carbonite	45	2.8-3.2	.315	.600	L,A,R,S,X,XX	39	2.75	.370	.600	Trim from tip end
Durafiber	45		.280	.585	L	39		.355		
	45		.287	.595	A	38		.355		
	45	3.2	.290	.605	R	37	—	.355	—	—
	45		.300	.615	S	36		.355		
	45		.307	.620	X, XX	35		.355		
Graftek (Exxon Entpr. Inc.)	45	3.1	.300	.608	L,A,R,S,X,XX	41½	2.9	.350	.608	L,A,R,S,X,XX
Fansteel	45	2.5	.270	.570	L	39	2.6	.355	.600	R,S
	45	2.8	.300	.600	A,R,S,X					
Grafalloy (Composite Development Corp.)	44	2.6	.295	.595	L	40	2.6	.355	.595	S
	44	2.6	.295	.595	R					
	44	2.7	.295	.595	S					
	44	2.8	.295	.595	X					
	45	3.2	.295	.595	Pro X					
Sigma - Sigma 580 (Shakespeare)	45	3.1	.360	.620	X	38	2.7	.360	.580	X
	45	3.1	.360	.580	X					
Skyline	45	2.7	.300	.621	L,A,R,S,X,XX	—	—	—	—	—
Graphite 100 (U.S. Fiberwood Corp.)	45	3.0	.290	.590	A,R,S,X	40	2.9	.355	.590	No Flex Specified

1982 GRAFALLOY GRAPHITE SHAFT SPECIFICATIONS

Model	Description	[2]Flex	Tip Dia.	[1]Taper Tip or Parallel	Butt Dia.	Length	Weight (Grams)
M-54 RLT (Woods)	Low torque Graphite with high flex point. For stronger players, lower handicaps.	X	.320''	[1]Both	.580''	45''	88 gr.
		S	.320''	[1]Both	.580''	45''	86 gr.
		R	.320''	[1]Both	.580''	45''	84 gr.
		A	.320''	[1]Both	.580''	45''	82 gr.
		L	.320''	[1]Both	.580''	45''	80 gr.
M-6 (Woods)	2° more torque than M-54, Graphite with mid flex point for average players.	X	.320''	[1]Both	.580''	45''	82 gr.
		S	.320''	[1]Both	.580''	45''	80 gr.
		R	.320''	[1]Both	.580''	45''	78 gr.
		A	.320''	[1]Both	.580''	45''	76 gr.
		L	.320''	[1]Both	.580''	45''	74 gr.
M-3 (Woods)	3° more torque than M-54, Graphite with low flex point for women, seniors, and easy or smooth swingers.	X	.300''	[1]Both	.580''	45''	82 gr.
		S	.300''	[1]Both	.580''	45''	80 gr.
		R	.300''	[1]Both	.580''	45''	78 gr.
		A	.300''	[1]Both	.580''	45''	76 gr.
		L	.300''	[1]Both	.580''	45''	74 gr.
M-80 HC (Woods)	1° more torque than M54, Graphite. Thinnest profile shaft available from Grafalloy.	X	.300''	[1]Both	.580''	45''	82 gr.
		S	.300''	[1]Both	.580''	45''	80 gr.
		R	.300''	[1]Both	.580''	45''	78 gr.
		A	.300''	[1]Both	.580''	45''	76 gr.
		L	.300''	[1]Both	.580''	45''	74 gr.
M-24 HC (Woods)	1½° more torque than M-54, Graphite with a slightly thicker profile than M-80.	X	.320''	[1]Both	.580''	45''	84 gr.
		S	.320''	[1]Both	.580''	45''	82 gr.
		R	.320''	[1]Both	.580''	45''	80 gr.
		A	.320''	[1]Both	.580''	45''	78 gr.
		L	.320''	[1]Both	.580''	45''	76 gr.
M-29 (Woods)	5° more torque than M-54. Least expensive 100% Graphite shaft in Grafalloy's line	X	.320''	[1]Both	.580''	45''	78 gr.
		S	.320''	[1]Both	.580''	45''	76 gr.
		R	.320''	[1]Both	.580''	45''	74 gr.
		A	.320''	[1]Both	.580''	45''	72 gr.
		L	.320''	[1]Both	.580''	45''	70 gr.
I-54 (Irons)	Low torque Graphite with high flex point. For stronger players, lower handicaps.	X	.370''	[1]Both	.580''	40''	88 gr.
		S	.370''	[1]Both	.580''	40''	86 gr.
		R	.370''	[1]Both	.580''	40''	84 gr.
		A	.370''	[1]Both	.580''	40''	82 gr.
		L	.370''	[1]Both	.580''	40''	80 gr.
370-14-HC	1½° more torque than I-54 Graphite.	X	.370''	[1]Both	.580''	40''	82 gr.
		S	.370''	[1]Both	.580''	40''	80 gr.
		R	.370''	[1]Both	.580''	40''	78 gr.
		A	.370''	[1]Both	.580''	40''	76 gr.
		L	.370''	[1]Both	.580''	40''	74 gr.
350-D14 (Irons)	1½° more torque than I-54 Graphite. Only difference from 370-14-HC is tip diameter.	X	.355''	[1]Both	.580''	40''	82 gr.
		S	.355''	[1]Both	.580''	40''	80 gr.
		R	.355''	[1]Both	.580''	40''	78 gr.
		A	.355''	[1]Both	.580''	40''	76 gr.
		L	.355''	[1]Both	.580''	40''	74 gr.
Putter	100% Graphite.	—	.355''	[1]Both	.580''	35'' - 36½''	74-85 gr.

[1]Grafalloy manufactures a .005 inches per inch taper tip. This is done so the shaft will fit both tip taper and the parallel tip bores.
[2]XX Flex is also available in any model on special order.

1982 ALDILA GRAPHITE SHAFT SPECIFICATIONS

Model	Description	Model Code Number	Flex	Tip Dia.	Taper Tip or Parallel	Butt Dia.	Length	WEIGHT Grams	WEIGHT Ounces
VELOCITOR (Wood)	Boron/Graphite and Sicon; Flex point underneath grip	JSVWLL	Light	.310''	Taper	.595''	44''	72±4	2.53±.14
		JSVWRR	Reg.	.310''	Taper	.595''	44''	74±4	2.60±.14
		JSVWFF	Firm	.310''	Taper	.595''	44''	76±4	2.68±.14
VELOCITOR (Iron)	Boron/Graphite and Sicon; Flex point underneath grip	JSVILL	Light	.370''	Parallel 4''	.595''	39''	70±4	2.46±.14
		JSVIRR	Reg.	.370''	Parallel 4''	.595''	39''	74±4	2.60±.14
		JSVIFF	Firm	.370''	Parallel 4''	.595''	39''	76±4	2.68±.14
ALDA VIII (Wood)	Boron/Graphite Versatile shaft lowest flex point	JSW8LL	Light	.300''	Taper	.600''	44''	68±4	2.40±.14
		JSW8RR	Reg.	.300''	Taper	.600''	44''	72±4	2.54±.14
		JSW8FF	Firm	.300''	Taper	.600''	44''	76±4	2.68±.14
		JSW8XX	Strong	.300''	Taper	.600''	44''	80±4	2.82±.14
ALDA VIII (Iron) (.355 Tip)	Boron/Graphite Versatile shaft lowest flex point	JSI8LL	Light	.355''	Parallel 4''	.600''	39''	68±4	2.40±.14
		JSI8RR	Reg.	.355''	Parallel 4''	.600''	39''	72±4	2.54±.14
		JSI8FF	Firm	.355''	Parallel 4''	.600''	39''	76±4	2.68±.14
		JSI8XX	Strong	.355''	Parallel 4''	.600''	39''	80±4	2.82±.14
ALDA VIII (Iron) (.370 Tip)	Boron/Graphite Versatile shaft lowest flex point	DSI7LL	Light	.370''	Parallel 4''	.600''	39''	68±4	2.40±.14
		DSI7RR	Reg.	.370''	Parallel 4''	.600''	39''	72±4	2.54±.14
		DSI7FF	Firm	.370''	Parallel 4''	.600''	39''	76±4	2.68±.14
		DSI7XX	Strong	.370''	Parallel 4''	.600''	39''	80±4	2.82±.14
LOW TORQUE (Wood)	Boron/Graphite stiffer shaft for stronger player	JSWLLL	Light	.320''	Taper	.620''	44''	73±4	2.57±.14
		JSWLRR	Reg.	.320''	Taper	.620''	44''	76±4	2.68±.14
		JSWLFF	Firm	.320''	Taper	.620''	44''	81±4	2.85±.14
		JSWLXX	Strong	.320''	Taper	620''	44''	84±4	2.96±.14
LOW TORQUE (Iron)	Boron/Graphite stiffer shaft for stronger player	JSILLL	Light	.370''	Parallel 2''	.620''	39''	72±4	2.54±.14
		JSILRR	Reg.	.370''	Parallel 2''	.620''	39''	75±4	2.64±.14
		JSILFF	Firm	.370''	Parallel 2''	.620''	39''	79±4	2.78±.14
		JSILXX	Strong	.370''	Parallel 2''	.620''	39''	81±4	2.85±.14
ALDALITE (Wood)	Boron/Graphite Aldila's lightest shaft	JSWALL	Light	.320''	Taper	.620''	44''	64±4	2.25±.14
		JSWARR	Reg.	.320''	Taper	.620''	44''	66±4	2.32±.14
		JSWAFF	Firm	.320''	Taper	.620''	44''	69±4	2.43±.14
		JSWAXX	Strong	.320''	Taper	.620''	44''	73±4	2.57±.14
HMG3 (Wood)	Boron/Graphite, High Modulus Graphite 3° Torque	JHW3LL	Light	.320''	Taper	.610''	44''	79±4	2.78±.14
		JHW3RR	Reg.	.320''	Taper	.610''	44''	82±4	2.89±.14
		JHW3FF	Firm	.320''	Taper	.610''	44''	86±4	3.03±.14
G-4 (Wood)	Total Graphite Aldila's most inexpensive shaft	JGW4LL	Light	.320''	Taper	.620''	44''	83±6	2.93±.21
		JGW4RR	Reg.	.320''	Taper	.620''	44''	85±6	3.00±.21
		JGW4FF	Firm	.320''	Taper	.620''	44''	87±6	3.07±.21

To install irons with parallel 4'' tips: Install #2 iron shaft with no tipping, tip #3 iron ½'', #4 iron 1'', #5 iron 1½'' and so on down to #9 iron. Do not trim more than 3½'' from tip. Cut to desired club length from the butt after installation.

1982 POWERFLEX AND SWINGRITE ARAMID FIBER SHAFT SPECIFICATIONS

Model	Description	Flex	Tip Dia.	Tip Taper or Parallel	Butt Dia.	Length	Weight (Grams)
Powerflex (Woods)	This shaft is extremely flexible and whippy. Made from Aramid & other compatible fibers.	Uniflex	.295''	Parallel	.580''	45''	75 gr.
Powerflex (Irons)		Uniflex	¹.355''	Parallel	.580''	40''	75 gr.
Swingrite (Woods)	This shaft is stiffer than the Powerflex. It is moderately flexible. Made from Aramid & other compatible fibers.	Uniflex	.310''	Parallel	.580''	45''	95 gr.
Swingrite (Irons)		Uniflex	¹.355''	Parallel	.580''	40''	95 gr.

¹.370'' tip also available.

1986 GRAFALLOY GRAPHITE SHAFT SPECIFICATIONS — WOOD

Model	Description	[2]Flex	Tip Dia.	[1]Taper Tip or Parallel	Butt Dia.	Length	Weight (Grams)	Flex Point
M-54RLT (Woods)	Low torque Graphite with high flex point. For stronger players, lower handicaps.	X	.320"	[1]Both	.590"	44" - 45"	88 gr.	High
		S	.320"	[1]Both	.590"	44" - 45"	86 gr.	High
		R	.320"	[1]Both	.590"	44" - 45"	84 gr.	High
		A	.320"	[1]Both	.590"	44" - 45"	82 gr.	High
		L	.320"	[1]Both	.590"	44" - 45"	80 gr.	High
M-54 BLT* (Woods)	Low torque Graphite Same as M-54 RLT, but with Boron reinforced tip.	X	.335"	[1]Both	.590"	44" - 45"	88 gr.	High
		S	.335"	[1]Both	.590"	44" - 45"	86 gr.	High
		R	.335"	[1]Both	.590"	44" - 45"	84 gr.	High
		A	.335"	[1]Both	.590"	44" - 45"	82 gr.	High
		L	.335"	[1]Both	.590"	44" - 45"	80 gr.	High
M-6 (Woods)	2° more torque than M-54, Graphite with mid flex point for average players.	X	.320"	[1]Both	.590"	44" - 45"	82 gr.	Mid
		S	.320"	[1]Both	.590"	44" - 45"	80 gr.	Mid
		R	.320"	[1]Both	.590"	44" - 45"	78 gr.	Mid
		A	.320"	[1]Both	.590"	44" - 45"	76 gr.	Mid
		L	.320"	[1]Both	.590"	44" - 45"	74 gr.	Mid
M-3 (Woods)	3° more torque than M-54, Graphite with low flex point for women, seniors, and easy or smooth swingers.	X	.300"	[1]Both	.590"	44" - 45"	82 gr.	Low
		S	.300"	[1]Both	.590"	44" - 45"	80 gr.	Low
		R	.300"	[1]Both	.590"	44" - 45"	78 gr.	Low
		A	.300"	[1]Both	.590"	44" - 45"	76 gr.	Low
		L	.300"	[1]Both	.590"	44" - 45"	74 gr.	Low
M-24 HC (Woods)	1½° more torque than M-54, Graphite with a slightly thicker profile than M-80.	X	.320"	[1]Both	.590"	44" - 45"	84 gr.	High
		S	.320"	[1]Both	.590"	44" - 45"	82 gr.	High
		R	.320"	[1]Both	.590"	44" - 45"	80 gr.	High
		A	.320"	[1]Both	.590"	44" - 45"	78 gr.	High
		L	.320"	[1]Both	.590"	44" - 45"	76 gr.	High
M-29 (Woods)	5° more torque than M-54. Least expensive 100% Graphite shaft in Grafalloy's line.	X	.320"	[1]Both	.590"	44" - 45"	82 gr.	Mid
		S	.320"	[1]Both	.590"	44" - 45"	80 gr.	Mid
		R	.320"	[1]Both	.590"	44" - 45"	78 gr.	Mid
		A	.320"	[1]Both	.590"	44" - 45"	76 gr.	Mid
		L	.320"	[1]Both	.590"	44" - 45"	74 gr.	Mid
M-29 P5 (Woods)	Same as M-29 with 5° more torque than M-54, but tip is parallel for first 5".	X	.320"	[1]Both	.590"	44" - 45"	82 gr.	Mid
		S	.320"	[1]Both	.590"	44" - 45"	80 gr.	Mid
		R	.320"	[1]Both	.590"	44" - 45"	78 gr.	Mid
		A	.320"	[1]Both	.590"	44" - 45"	76 gr.	Mid
		L	.320"	[1]Both	.590"	44" - 45"	74 gr.	Mid
M-29 BP* (Woods)	Same as M-29 P5, but tip is Boron.	X	.335"	[1]Both	.590"	44" - 45"	90 gr.	Mid
		S	.335"	[1]Both	.590"	44" - 45"	88 gr.	Mid
		R	.335"	[1]Both	.590"	44" - 45"	86 gr.	Mid
		A	.335"	[1]Both	.590"	44" - 45"	84 gr.	Mid
		L	.335"	[1]Both	.590"	44" - 45"	82 gr.	Mid
M-29 BLT* (Woods)	5° more torque than M-54 BLT, but has Boron tip.	X	.335"	[1]Both	.590"	44" - 45"	86 gr.	Mid
		S	.335"	[1]Both	.590"	44" - 45"	82 gr.	Mid
		R	.335"	[1]Both	.590"	44" - 45"	78 gr.	Mid
		A	.335"	[1]Both	.590"	44" - 45"	74 gr.	Mid
		L	.335"	[1]Both	.590"	44" - 45"	70 gr.	Mid
M-45 MR* (Woods)	This shaft has more carbon than any of the others with 6.5° torque.	X	.335"	[1]Both	.590"	44" - 45"	92 gr.	High
		S	.335"	[1]Both	.590"	44" - 45"	88 gr.	High
		R	.335"	[1]Both	.590"	44" - 45"	86 gr.	High
		A	.335"	[1]Both	.590"	44" - 45"	84 gr.	High
		L	.335"	[1]Both	.590"	44" - 45"	80 gr.	High
M-79 BC (Woods)	This is the lowest torque shaft at 4.5° Made of Boron.	X	.320"	[1]Both	.580"	44" - 45"	93 gr.	Mid-High
		S	.320"	[1]Both	.580"	44" - 45"	91 gr.	Mid-High
		R	.320"	[1]Both	.580"	44" - 45"	89 gr.	Mid-High
		A	.320"	[1]Both	.580"	44" - 45"	87 gr.	Mid-High
		L	.320"	[1]Both	.580"	44" - 45"	85 gr.	Mid-High

*The tips of these shafts are reinforced with Boron, and are designed for metalwoods.
[1]Grafalloy manufactures a .005 inches per inch taper tip. This is done so the shaft will fit both tip taper and the parallel tip bores.
[2]XX Flex is also available in any model on special order.

1986 GRAFALLOY GRAPHITE SHAFT SPECIFICATIONS — IRONS

Model	Description	²Flex	Tip Dia.	¹Taper Tip or Parallel	Butt Dia.	Length	Weight (Grams)	Flex Point
I-54 (Irons)	Low torque Graphite with high flex point. For stronger players, lower handicaps.	X	.370''	¹Both	.590''	39'' - 40''	88 gr.	Low
		S	.370''	¹Both	.590''	39'' - 40''	86 gr.	Low
		R	.370''	¹Both	.590''	39'' - 40''	84 gr.	Low
		A	.370''	¹Both	.590''	39'' - 40''	82 gr.	Low
		L	.370''	¹Both	.590''	39'' - 40''	80 gr.	Low
I-54 BLT (Irons)	Low torque Graphite. Same as I-54, but with Boron reinforced tip.	X	.350''	¹Both	.590''	39'' - 40''	88 gr.	High
		S	.350''	¹Both	.590''	39'' - 40''	86 gr.	High
		R	.350''	¹Both	.590''	39'' - 40''	84 gr.	High
		L	.350''	¹Both	.590''	39'' - 40''	82 gr.	High
		A	.350''	¹Both	.590''	39'' - 40''	80 gr.	High
I-4 (Irons)	1½° more torque than I-54 Graphite.	X	.370''	¹Both	.590''	39'' - 40''	82 gr.	Mid
		S	.370''	¹Both	.590''	39'' - 40''	80 gr.	Mid
		R	.370''	¹Both	.590''	39'' - 40''	78 gr.	Mid
		A	.370''	¹Both	.590''	39'' - 40''	76 gr.	Mid
		L	.370''	¹Both	.590''	39'' - 40''	74 gr.	Mid
I-4 BLT (Irons)	Same as I-4, but with reinforced tip.	X	.350''	¹Both	.590''	39'' - 40''	82 gr.	Mid
		S	.350''	¹Both	.590''	39'' - 40''	80 gr.	Mid
		R	.350''	¹Both	.590''	39'' - 40''	78 gr.	Mid
		A	.350''	¹Both	.590''	39'' - 40''	76 gr.	Mid
		L	.350''	¹Both	.590''	39'' - 40''	74 gr.	Mid
I-10 BLT (Irons)	Low torque Graphite reinforced with Boron.	X	.350''	¹Both	.590''	39'' - 40''	98 gr.	High
		S	.350''	¹Both	.590''	39'' - 40''	94 gr.	High
		R	.350''	¹Both	.590''	39'' - 40''	90 gr.	High
		A	.350''	¹Both	.590''	39'' - 40''	86 gr.	High
		L	.350''	¹Both	.590''	39'' - 40''	80 gr.	High
Putter	100% Graphite	—	.350''	¹Both	.580''	35'' - 36½''	74-85 gr.	—
		—	.370''	¹Both	.580''	35'' - 36½''	74-85 gr.	—

¹Grafalloy manufactures a .005 inches per inch taper tip. This is done so the shaft will fit both the tip taper and the parallel tip bores.
²XX Flex is also available in any model on special order.

1986 ALDILA GRAPHITE SHAFT SPECIFICATIONS — IRONS

Model	Description	Flex	Tip Dia.	Taper Tip or Parallel	Butt Dia.	Length	WEIGHT Grams	Ounces
VELOCITOR (.370 Tip)	Boron/Graphite and Sicon; Flex point underneath grip	Ladies'	.370"	Parallel 5"	.595"	39"	68 ± 4	2.40 ± .14
		Light	.370"	Parallel 5"	.595"	39"	70 ± 4	2.46 ± .14
		Reg.	.370"	Parallel 5"	.595"	39"	74 ± 4	2.60 ± .14
		Firm	.370"	Parallel 5"	.595"	39"	76 ± 4	2.68 ± .14
		Strong	.370"	Parallel 5"	.595"	39"	78 ± 4	2.75 ± .14
ALDA VIII (.355 Tip)	Boron/Graphite Versatile shaft lowest flex point	Light	.355"	Parallel 4"	.600"	39"	68 ± 4	2.40 ± .14
		Reg.	.355"	Parallel 4"	.600"	39"	72 ± 4	2.54 ± .14
		Firm	.355"	Parallel 4"	.600"	39"	76 ± 4	2.68 ± .14
		Strong	.355"	Parallel 4"	.600"	39"	80 ± 4	2.82 ± .14
ALDA VIII (.370 Tip)	Boron/Graphite Versatile shaft lowest flex point	Light	.370"	Parallel 4"	.600"	39"	68 ± 4	2.40 ± .14
		Reg.	.370"	Parallel 4"	.600"	39"	72 ± 4	2.54 ± .14
		Firm	.370"	Parallel 4"	.600"	39"	76 ± 4	2.68 ± .14
		Strong	.370"	Parallel 4"	.600"	39"	80 ± 4	2.82 ± .14
LOW TORQUE II (.355 Tip)	Boron/Graphite stiffer shaft for stronger players	Light	.355"	Parallel 5"	.020"	39"	72 ± 4	2.54 ± .14
		Reg.	.355"	Parallel 5"	.620"	39"	75 ± 4	2.64 ± .14
		Firm	.355"	Parallel 5"	.620"	39"	79 ± 4	2.78 ± .14
		Strong	.355"	Parallel 5"	.620"	39"	81 ± 4	2.85 ± .14
LOW TORQUE II (Iron) (.370 Tip)	Boron/Graphite stiffer shaft for stronger players	Light	.370"	Parallel 5"	.620"	39"	72 ± 4	2.54 ± .14
		Reg.	.370"	Parallel 5"	.620"	39"	75 ± 4	2.64 ± .14
		Firm	.370"	Parallel 5"	.620"	39"	79 ± 4	2.78 ± .14
		Strong	.370"	Parallel 5"	.620"	39"	81 ± 4	2.85 ± .14
TRUE TOUCH (Putter)	Graphite and High Modulus Graphite Excellent feel	Light	.355"	Parallel 1"	.590"	35"	95 ± 4	3.35 ± .14
		Reg.	.355"	Parallel 1"	.590"	35"	96 ± 4	3.38 ± .14
		Firm	.355"	Parallel 1"	.590"	35"	97 ± 4	3.42 ± .14
PUTTER M	100% Graphite Recommended for all golfers	—	.355"	Parallel 1"	.590"	35"	96 ± 4	3.36 ± .14
HM-40 (.370 Tip)	High Modulus Graphite and Boron	Reg.	.370"	Parallel 2"	.620"	39"	94 ± 4	3.31 ± .14
		Firm	.370"	Parallel 2"	.620"	39"	98 ± 4	3.46 ± .14
		Strong	.370	Parallel 2"	.620"	39"	101 ± 4	3.56 ± .14

1986 ALDILA GRAPHITE SHAFT SPECIFICATIONS — WOODS

Model	Description	Flex	Tip Dia.	Taper Tip or Parallel	Butt Dia.	Length	WEIGHT	
							Grams	Ounces
VELOCITOR	Boron/Graphite and	Ladies'	.310″	Taper	.595″	44″	70 ± 4	2.46 ± .14
(.310 Tip)	Sicon; Flex point	Light	.310″	Taper	.595″	44″	72 ± 4	2.53 ± .14
	underneath grip	Reg.	.310″	Taper	.595″	44″	74 ± 4	2.60 ± .14
		Firm	.310″	Taper	.595″	44″	76 ± 4	2.68 ± .14
		Strong	.310″	Taper	.595″	44″	78 ± 4	2.75 ± .14
VELOCITOR	Boron/Graphite and	Ladies'	.335″	Parallel 4″	.595″	44″	70 ± 4	2.46 ± .14
(.335 Tip)	Sicon; Flex point	Light	.335″	Parallel 4″	.595″	44″	72 ± 4	2.53 ± .14
	underneath grip	Reg.	.335″	Parallel 4″	.595″	44″	74 ± 4	2.60 ± .14
		Firm	.335″	Parallel 4″	.595″	44″	76 ± 4	2.68 ± .14
		Strong	.335″	Parallel 4″	.595″	44″	78 ± 4	2.75 ± .14
ALDA VIII	Boron/Graphite	Light	.300″	Taper	.600″	44″	68 ± 4	2.40 ± .14
(.300 Tip)	Versatile shaft	Reg.	.300″	Taper	.600″	44″	72 ± 4	2.54 ± .14
	lowest flex point	Firm	.300″	Taper	.600″	44″	76 ± 4	2.68 ± .14
		Strong	.300″	Taper	.600″	44″	80 ± 4	2.82 ± .14
ALDA VIII	Boron/Graphite	Light	.335″	Parallel 2″	.600″	44″	68 ± 4	2.40 ± .14
(.335 Tip)	Versatile shaft	Reg.	.335″	Parallel 2″	.600″	44″	72 ± 4	2.54 ± .14
	lowest flex point	Firm	.335″	Parallel 2″	.600″	44″	76 ± 4	2.68 ± .14
		Strong	.335″	Parallel 2″	.600″	44″	80 ± 4	2.82 ± .14
LOW TORQUE II	Boron/Graphite	Light	.320″	Taper	.620″	44″	73 ± 4	2.57 ± .14
(.320 Tip)	stiffer shaft for	Reg.	.320″	Taper	.620″	44″	76 ± 4	2.68 ± .14
	stronger players	Firm	.320″	Taper	.620″	44″	81 ± 4	2.85 ± .14
		Strong	.320″	Taper	.620″	44″	84 ± 4	2.96 ± .14
LOW TORQUE II	Boron/Graphite	Light	.335″	Parallel 5″	.620″	44″	73 ± 4	2.57 ± .14
(.335 Tip)	stiffer shaft for	Reg.	.335″	Parallel 5″	.620″	44″	76 ± 4	2.68 ± .14
	stronger players	Firm	.335″	Parallel 5″	.620″	44″	81 ± 4	2.85 ± .14
		Strong	.335″	Parallel 5″	.620″	44″	84 ± 4	2.96 ± .14
HMG	Graphite/High	Light	.320″	Taper	.620″	44″	81 ± 4	2.85 ± .14
(.320 Tip)	Modulus Graphite	Reg.	.320″	Taper	.620″	44″	84 ± 4	2.96 ± .14
	2° torque	Firm	.320″	Taper	.620″	44″	87 ± 4	3.07 ± .14
		Strong	.320″	Taper	.620″	44″	90 ± 4	3.17 ± .14
HMG	Graphite/High	Light	.335″	Parallel 2″	.620″	44″	81 ± 4	2.85 ± .14
(.335 Tip)	Modulus Graphite	Reg.	.335″	Parallel 2″	.620″	44″	84 ± 4	2.96 ± .14
	2° torque	Firm	.335″	Parallel 2″	.620″	44″	87 ± 4	3.07 ± .14
		Strong	.335″	Parallel 2″	.620″	44″	90 ± 4	3.17 ± .14
HM-40	Graphite/High	Reg.	.335″	Parallel 2″	.620″	44″	94 ± 4	3.31 ± .14
(.335 Tip)	Modulus Boron	Firm	.335″	Parallel 2″	.620″	44″	98 ± 4	3.46 ± .14
	Graphite 1.9° torque	Strong	.335″	Parallel 2″	.620″	44″	101 ± 4	3.56 ± .14

1986 KERBAND GRAPHITE SHAFT SPECIFICATIONS

Model	Description	Flex	Tip Dia.	Taper Tip or Parallel	Butt Dia.	Length	Weight (Grams)
SUPRA (Wood)	Lightweight Graphite over steel, mid shaft flex point, low torque	X	.335"	Parallel	.590"	[1]45½"	100 gr.
		S	.335"	Parallel	.590"	[1]45½"	96 gr.
		R	.335"	Parallel	.590"	[1]45½"	92 gr.
		L	.335"	Parallel	.590"	[1]45½"	88 gr.
SUPRA (Iron)	Lightweight Graphite over steel, mid shaft flex point, low torque	S	.370"	Parallel	.590"	39½"	88 gr.
		R	.370"	Parallel	.590"	39½"	88 gr.

[1]When used on metalwoods tip 2½" for desired flex.

1986 POWERFLEX ARAMID FIBER SHAFT SPECIFICATIONS

Model	Description	Flex	Tip Dia.	Tip Taper or Parallel	Butt Dia.	Length	Weight (Grams)
[1]Powerflex (Woods)	This shaft is extremely flexible and whippy. Made from Aramid & other compatible fibers.	Uniflex	.295"	Parallel	.580"	45"	75 gr.
Powerflex (Irons)		Uniflex	.370"	Parallel	.580"	40"	75 gr.
[1]Swingrite (Woods)	This shaft is stiffer than the Powerflex. It is moderately flexible. Made from Aramid & other compatible fibers	Uniflex	.310"	Parallel	.580"	45"	95 gr.
Swingrite (Irons)		Uniflex	.370"	Parallel	.580"	40"	95 gr.
[1]Proflex (Woods)	The shaft flex is similar in feel to a soft steel shaft.	Uniflex	.310"	Parallel	.580"	45"	87 gr.
Proflex (Irons)		Uniflex	.310"	Parallel	.580"	40"	87 gr.

[1]For metalwoods designation is Powerflex MTL, Swingrite MTL, and Proflex MTL. All then have .335 tip.

1986 POWERFLEX GRAPHITE SHAFT SPECIFICATIONS

Model	Flex	Tip Dia.	Tip Taper or Parallel	Butt Dia.	Length	Weight (Grams)
100% Graphite (Woods)	X	.310"	Parallel	.580"	45"	85 gr.
100% Graphite (Woods)	S	.310"	Parallel	.580"	45"	85 gr.
100% Graphite (Woods)	R	.310"	Parallel	.580"	45"	85 gr.
100% Graphite (Woods)	L	.310"	Parallel	.580"	45"	85 gr.
100% Graphite (Irons)	X	[1].355"	Taper & Parallel Tip	.580"	40"	85 gr.
100% Graphite (Irons)	S	[1].355"	Taper & Parallel Tip	.580"	40"	85 gr.
100% Graphite (Irons)	R	[1].355"	Taper & Parallel Tip	.580"	40"	85 gr.
100% Graphite (Irons)	L	[1].355"	Taper & Parallel Tip	.580"	40"	85 gr.

[1].370 available on request.

GOLF SHAFT COMPARISON AND IDENTIFICATION CHARTS

STANDARD AVAILABLE SHAFT PATTERNS

Manufacturer	Model	Flex Point	Weight	Irons	Woods	Shaft Grade
True Temper	Extralite	Low	Very Lightweight	1″, Random	1″, Random	1st
True Temper	TT Lite	Mid	Lightweight	1½″	1½″	1st
True Temper	Pro Fit	Mid	Standard	1⅜″	1½″	1st
True Temper	Dynamic (Taper Tip)	High	Standard	1¾″	1⅞″	1st
True Temper	Dynamic (Parallel Tip)	High	Standard	1⅞″	1⅞″	1st
True Temper	Dynamic Gold (Taper Tip)	High	Standard	1¾″	1⅞″	1st
True Temper	Dynamic Gold (Parallel Tip)	High	Standard	1⅞″	1⅞″	1st
True Temper	Jet Step	Low	Standard	1″	1″	1st
True Temper	Driving Range	Mid	Standard	—	2¼″	1st
True Temper	Flex Flow	Progressive	Lightweight	1¼″	1¼″	1st
True Temper	TT Lite (Combination)	Mid	Lightweight	1½″	1½″	1st
True Temper	Comet	Mid	Standard	1¹³⁄₁₆″	1¹³⁄₁₆″	2nd
True Temper	Century	Mid	Standard	3″	3″	2nd
True Temper	Junior	Mid	Standard	3″	3″	2nd
True Temper (Discontinued)	Contour	Low	Lightweight	1½″, 1″	1½″, 1″	1st
True Temper (Discontinued)	Kinetic	Mid	Lightweight	1¾″	1⅞″	1st
True Temper (Discontinued)	Super Lite	Low	Lightweight	—	1½″	1st
True Temper (Discontinued)	Dynalite	Mid	Lightweight	1¼″	1½″	1st
True Temper (Discontinued)	Rocket	Mid	Standard	1⅜″	1½″	1st
True Temper (Discontinued)	Meteor	Mid	Standard	1¼″	1¼″	2nd
True Temper (Discontinued)	325 Series	Mid	Standard	3¼″	3¼″	2nd
True Temper (Discontinued)	Classic	Mid	Standard	4″	4″	2nd
Brunswick Golf	FM	High	Lightweight	Variable	Variable	1st
Brunswick Golf	FM (Featherlite)	High	Lightweight	Variable	Variable	1st
Brunswick Golf	UCV-304	Mid	Lightweight	Variable	Variable	1st
Brunswick Golf	Phoenix	Mid	Lightweight	1½″	1½″	1st
Brunswick Golf	Propel Microtaper	Low	Lightweight	—	¾″	1st
Brunswick Golf	Propel II (Taper Tip)	High	Standard	1¾″	1⅞″	1st
Brunswick Golf	Propel II (Parallel Tip)	High	Standard	1⅞″	1⅞″	1st
Brunswick Golf	Mark II	Mid	Standard	1¼″	1½″	2nd
Brunswick Golf	Super Champion	Mid	Standard	1¹³⁄₁₆″	1¹³⁄₁₆″	2nd
Brunswick Golf	Champion	Mid	Standard	3″	3″	2nd
Brunswick Golf (Discontinued)	Vanadium Sonic	Mid	Lightweight	Variable	Variable	1st
Brunswick Golf (Discontinued)	Brunslite	Mid	Lightweight	Variable	Variable	1st
Apollo	Masterflex	High	Standard	Variable	Variable	1st
Apollo	Matchflex (1)	Low	Lightweight	Variable	Variable	1st
Apollo	Matchflex (2)	Lo-Mid	Lightweight	Variable	Variable	1st
Apollo	Matchflex (3)	Mid-Hi	Lightweight	Variable	Variable	1st
Apollo	Matchflex (4)	High	Standard	Variable	Variable	1st
Apollo	Torsion Matched	High	Standard	1½″, ½″	1½″, ½″	1st
Apollo	Shadow	Low	Lightweight	1⅞″, ½″	1⅞″, ½″	1st
Apollo	AP44	High	Standard	1¾″	1⅞″	1st
Apollo	AP46	Mid	Standard	1¹³⁄₁₆″	1¹³⁄₁₆″	1st
Apollo	Spectre	Mid	Lightweight	1½″	1½″	1st
Apollo	AP83	Mid	Standard	3″	3″	2nd
Apollo (Discontinued)	Phantom	Low	Lightweight	Groups	Groups	1st
Apollo (Discontinued)	AP25	Low	Standard	1″	1″	1st
Apollo (Discontinued)	AP32	Mid	Standard	1¼″	1½″	1st
Apollo (Discontinued)	AP35	Mid	Standard	1⅜″	1½″	1st
Apollo (Discontinued)	AP57	Mid	Standard	2¼″	2¼″	2nd

1st grade shafts are usually characterized by having the most shaft steps, closer weight tolerances, a number of choices in shaft flex, a top quality scratch free chrome plating and a higher cost per shaft to the manufacturer. 2nd grade shafts usually have less shaft steps, wider weight tolerances, limited choice of shaft flex as most are available in medium flex only, chrome plating is sometimes a lesser quality and may show slight dullness and a few scratches and will cost the manufacturer less than 1st grade shafts.

PROPRIETARY SHAFT PATTERN IDENTIFICATION

Company	Shaft Name	Flex Point	Weight
Acushnet	Power-Step	Low	Standard
	Power Flo	High	Standard
	Title-Lite II	Mid	Lightweight
Browning	System 350	High	Lightweight
Confidence	Plus Lite	Mid	Lightweight
Daiwa	TRX-T	High	Very Lightweight
	TRX	Mid	Very Lightweight
	TR	Low	Very Lightweight
Dunlop	Alta	High	Lightweight
	Maxpower	Low	Standard
	Max Lite	Mid	Lightweight
Walter Hagen	Control Flex	High	Standard
H & B	Dynasty Plus	Variable	Lightweight
	Dynasty	Mid	Very Lightweight
	Propower	Mid	Standard
	Duopower	Mid	Standard
Ben Hogan	Apex	Low	Lightweight
	Apex Pro	Low	Standard
	Apex D	Low	Standard
	Apex Extra	Mid	Lightweight
	Vector	High	Lightweight
	Legend	Low	Lightweight
	Saber	High	Standard
Karsten	ZZ Lite	High	Lightweight
	ZZZ Lite	High	Lightweight
	K	Mid	Lightweight
	Olympic	High	Very Lightweight
	TTT	High	Standard
Lynx	Lynx Lite	High	Lightweight
MacGregor	Response	Mid	Very Lightweight
	Velocitized Dual Action	Low	Lightweight
	Tourney Action	High	Standard
	Microstep	Low	Standard
	Propel (1958-68)	Low	Standard
Mizuno	Dynaflex 1100	Low	Lightweight
	Dynaflex 2200	Mid	Lightweight
	Dynaflex 3300	High	Lightweight
Northwestern	Power Kick	Low	Lightweight
	Proaction Plus	Low	Standard
	Micro Lite 400	Mid	Lightweight
PGA	Concept	Mid	Lightweight
Pinseeker	Pin Lite	Mid	Lightweight
Pro Group	Hex Flex	High	Lightweight
	Pro-Lite	Mid	Lightweight
	Axiom-Lite	Low	Lightweight
Ram	Reactive Rhythm	Mid	Lightweight
	Ramlite	Mid	Lightweight
Toney Penna	Flex Plus	Low	Standard
Sigma	Pinpoint	High	Lightweight
Soundor	Sounder Flex	Mid	Lightweight
Wilson	V2	Low	Lightweight
	Aggressor	Low	Lightweight
	Dynapower	Low	Lightweight
	Counter Torque	Low	Lightweight
	Dynamic	High	Standard

GOLF SHAFT INSTALLATION PRINCIPLES, PROCEDURES AND REFERENCE TABLES

This will be one of the most used sections in club repair because it contains most all of the reference data needed to check for proper shaft installation and to properly install a golf shaft. It should be read carefully and studied thoroughly. A mastery of this information will provide the key to understanding proper shaft installation.

One of the biggest problems in checking for proper shaft installation has been the non-availability of information concerning the distance from the tip end of the shaft to the first step. In addition to this, the information has never been converted to show the proper distance from the back of the heel on both woods and irons to the first shaft step. This is the most important measurement because with everything else being equal, it is the main factor in determining just how a shaft will flex and feel.

This reference section provides shaft installation information based on what is referred to as "traditional standards." For example, the traditional standard for irons is a shaft in head assembly where the tip of the shaft bottoms out 1″ from the back of the heel. See Figure 1. This standard was determined after measuring hundreds of different iron head shaft penetrations and hosel lengths in irons produced from 1940 to present. Therefore, this traditional standard is an average or mean, to show the predominant distance usually found from the tip of the shaft (or bottom of the hosel hole) to the back of the heel. Remember, this traditional standard is being established as a benchmark and caution should be used not to draw any conclusions regarding other clubmakers' or club manufacturers' shaft installation procedures. In many cases there may be sound reason for a different installation than those described in the tables in this section. Certain head designs, club lengths, head weights and test data may have dictated this. Also, many clubfitters, clubmakers and club repairmen are unaware of the fact that some club manufacturers purchase standard shaft types and patterns but will change one of the specifications so the shaft is designed exactly as they want it. It may be a tip diameter change, weight change, a wall thickness change or moving the step pattern down or up. Visually the shaft may look like a standard available pattern but it may not be. A good example to use here is the fact that some manufacturers are ordering their medium flex tip taper wood shafts in a .294 tip size so they do not have to change their head boring setup during manufacture; they now stock only 1 ferrule size, etc. Normally, most medium flex tip taper wood shafts have a .277 tip size.

It was far easier to determine the "traditional standard" for woods. This would be a "through bore" with the shaft tip extending ½″ beyond the back portion of the heel. See Figure 2.

Keep in mind that with the tables in this appendix, it does not matter whether a wood is "through bore" or "blind bore" or what the hosel length and bore depth is on an iron. The tables give the installed back of heel to 1st step dimensions based on the "traditional standards" already discussed for woods and irons in Figures 1 and 2. As stated earlier, this information provides a benchmark or starting point for installing a given shaft type and step pattern to the defined traditional standard.

SHAFT OVER HOSEL ASSEMBLY

TIP END OF SHAFT TO 1ST STEP

BACK OF HEEL TO 1ST STEP

BACK OF HEEL TO TIP OF SHAFT

1″

SHAFT IN HOSEL ASSEMBLY

TIP END OF SHAFT TO 1ST STEP

BACK OF HEEL TO 1ST STEP

BACK OF HEEL TO TIP END OF SHAFT

1″

Fig. 1
Iron shaft installation terminology.

① This dimension will vary depending on hosel length and bore depth and should be calculated as shown in Fig. 3. The 1″ dimension is considered the traditional standard.

Sole Radius and Back of Heel Location

If two golf clubs of the same length were measured in the traditional manner from the back of the heel to the

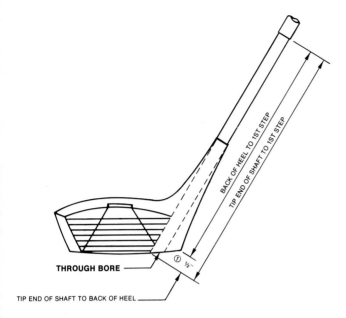

Fig. 2
Wood shaft installation terminology.

① This dimension on through bores will vary slightly and should be calculated as shown in Fig. 4. The ½" dimension is considered the traditional standard.

woods, should be thoroughly understood. The information given thus far coupled with the tables in this section will give the reader proper procedures to check shaft installations, install new shafts or correct improper shaft installations.

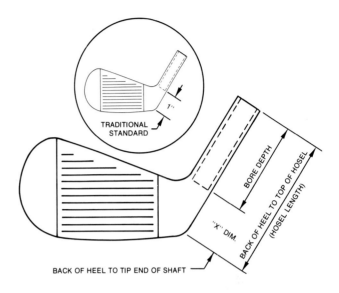

To find back of heel to tip end of shaft dimension ("X" Dim.):
A. Measure hosel length and bore depth.
B. Hosel length minus bore depth = "X" Dim.
C. Example: 2¼" Hosel length minus 1¼" bore depth = 1" dimension from back of heel to tip end of shaft.

NOTE: All tables in this section are based on a 1" dimension from back of heel to tip end of shaft. This dimension is an average of most irons ever built and it is considered the traditional shaft installation standard to obtain normal flex characteristics. However, be cautioned that varying head weights, club lengths, individual head designs, etc., can affect the feel of a given shaft flex.

Fig. 3
Calculating back of heel to tip end of shaft dimension.

top of the grip cap, the club with less sole radius would be shorter than the club with more sole radius.

A similar problem exists in this section concerning the back of heel to 1st shaft step distance. As was the case with club length, the less the sole radius, the stiffer the shaft; and the greater the sole radius, the weaker the shaft. This assumes, of course, that the 1st step location from the back of the heel would be the same in both clubs with either more or less sole radius. The reader should be aware of this but in most cases the sole radiuses are quite similar from model to model and only make very slight differences. The standards in this section are based on a 6" sole radius for woods (5" & 7" radiuses make very little difference) and a 10" sole radius for irons (8" to 12" radiuses make very little difference).

Back of Heel to 1st Step
Installation Procedure

When checking installed golf shafts according to the tables in this section, it may have been necessary to cut the tip end of the shaft shorter. I hesitate to refer to this as "tipping" because its only purpose is to adjust the tip length of the shaft so it can be installed in hosels of varying penetration and still have the desired back of heel to 1st step location. Depending on hosel design and bore depth, two identical golf shafts can be installed to have the same flex feel even though one of the shafts may have had ½" cut from its tip. An example of this could be a comparison between a blind bore wood vs. a through bore wood. The blind bore wood may need ½" cut from its tip to install with the proper back of heel to 1st shaft step dimension listed in the tables of this section.

There are a number of ways to predetermine, before a shaft is assembled, the back of heel to 1st step location. One method, shown in Figure 3 for irons and Figure 4 for

Understanding Tip Taper Shaft Installations in Woods

Trimming tip taper shafts is easy to understand since they are normally only trimmed from the butt end. Therefore, unlike parallel tip shafts, tip taper shafts can usually be installed in the wood head and then cut to length. Tip taper wood shafts are either .270", .277", .286", .294" or .320" tip size with a .0075 inches per inch of taper. This means that the shaft diameter gradually increases by 7½ thousandths of an inch for each inch up from the tip end. The length of the taper in the tip varies from shaft to shaft depending on the tip parallel diameter which is the parallel portion of every tip taper shaft just before the 1st step. See Figure 5.

For example, take a 44" Dynamic® Wood Stiff (DWS 44") shaft. It has a .294" tip taper, a .350" tip parallel and an 11¼" tip length (length from tip to 1st step). The change in diameter from the tip (.294") to the tip parallel (.350") is .056". Divide .056" by .0075" and the answer is that this shaft has 7½" of taper and 3¾" of tip parallel (11¼" − 7½" = 3¾"). The reason for explaining this is to obtain a better understanding of changes in tip diameter if a shaft is tipped. "Tipping" refers to precutting a certain amount from the tip end of the shaft to increase its stiffness. As you can

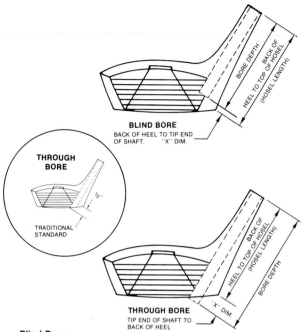

Blind Bore

To find back of heel to tip end of shaft dimension ("X" Dim.):

A. Measure hosel length and bore depth

B. Hosel length minus bore depth = "X" Dim. (Note that sometimes the bored depth is equal to or greater than the hosel length. If this is the case then bore depth minus hosel length = "X" Dim.)

Through Bore

To find tip end of shaft to back of heel dimension ("X" Dim.):

A. Measure hosel length and bore depth

B. Bore depth minus hosel length = "X" Dim.

NOTE: All tables in this section are based on a ½" dimension from the tip end of the shaft to the back of the heel. This dimension is the most common found on through bore heads and is considered the traditional shaft installation standard to obtain normal flex characteristics. However, be cautioned that varying head weights, club lengths, individual head designs, etc., can affect the feel of a given shaft flex.

Fig. 4
Calculating back of heel to tip end of shaft dimension.

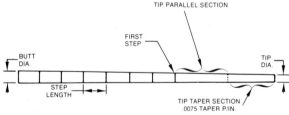

Fig. 5
Golf shaft terminology.

see, if a wood hosel is bored to accept a .294" tip taper shaft and you tip it, the shaft will not fit properly and the hosel must be bored out to a slightly larger size. Table 1 was developed to provide the tip diameters of tipped shafts and also the amount of stiffness increase.

An important consideration in "tipping" or for that matter when installing any wood shaft is whether or not the head is "blind" bored (shaft does not go completely through head) or "through" bored (shaft is bored completely through head). For example: if you are building two

TABLE 1			
"Tipped" Shafts, Their Stiffness Increase and New Tip Diameters			
Original Shaft Tip Size	Amount of "Tipping"	Approximate Amount of Flex Change	"Tipped" Tip Diameter
.277"	½"	+ ¼ Stiffer	.281"
.277"	1"	+ ½ Stiffer	.285"
.277"	1½"	+ ¾ Stiffer	.288"
.277"	2"	+ 1 Stiffer	.292"
.294"	½"	+ ¼ Stiffer	.298"
.294"	1"	+ ½ Stiffer	.302"
.294"	1½"	+ ¾ Stiffer	.305"
.294"	2"	+ 1 Stiffer	.309"
.320"	½"	+ ¼ Stiffer	.324"
.320"	1"	+ ½ Stiffer	.328"
.320"	1½"	+ ¾ Stiffer	.331"
.320"	2"	+ 1 Stiffer	.335"

Example Tipping a DWS shaft (Dynamic Wood Stiff) 2" will produce a relative stiffness approximating an "X" flex in that same pattern. However, the tipped "S" shaft will be ²⁄₁₀ ounce lighter than the standard "X" flex weight. Experimentation in actual hitting on an individual basis is the best way to confirm which may feel best or give desired performance.

identical drivers and one is bored and shafted to within ½ of the bottom of the club and the other is bored and shafted completely through, the one that is bored through will feel one quarter flex stiffer than the blind bored head. The reason for this is that the distance from the back of the heel to the 1st step is longer on the blind bored club than the through bored club. This is sort of an "untipped" effect. See Figure 6. Of course, both clubs would probably feel the same, (all other specifications being the same) if the blind bored shaft was "tipped" ½" before installation.

Keep in mind that "through" bored clubs play no better than "blind" bored clubs and vice-versa as long as the blind bored club has its shaft properly installed. The main understanding to be obtained from this is to evaluate the different wood club bore types and then use the information here to make a relative playability comparison, if one exists. This is particularly useful in reshafting work.

Understanding Tip Taper Shaft Installations in Irons

As with woods, trimming tip taper shafts is easy to understand because they are also normally only trimmed from the butt end. Therefore, unlike parallel tip shafts, tip taper shafts can be installed in the iron head and then cut to length. Most all tip taper shafts have a .355" tip diameter with a .0075 inches per inch of taper. This means that the shaft diameter gradually increases by 7½ thousandths of an inch for each inch away from the tip. The length of the taper in the tip varies from shaft to shaft depending on the tip parallel diameter which is the parallel portion of every tip taper shaft just before the 1st step. Refer back to Figure 5. For example, take a 39" Dynamic® Iron Stiff (DIS 39") shaft. It has a .355" diameter tip taper, a .395" diameter tip parallel, and a 12" tip length (length from tip to 1st step). The change in diameter from the tip (.355") to the tip parallel (.395") is .040". Divide .040" by .0075" and the answer is that this shaft has 5⅓" of taper and 6⅔" of tip parallel

The follo
to provide a
incremental l
bles provided
mensions als
as to the incre
The reason f
manufactured
to 1st step di
½″ from the
step as if it w
ences now b
(approx. four
and the shaft
per ½″ cut fro
shaft or those

Understan
Installatior

When th
duced by Tru
trimming cha
brochure. Th
shaft a firmer
flex and was

During t
present, True
ming method
align the pro
flex standard
method softe
shaft and mo
tip taper shaf
two shafts ca
significantly c
fering club to

The met
parallel tip sh
ming method
revised trimm
exception. T
the adjustme
other words,
apply to para
step dimensi
amount to ge
1st step tabl
club length.
remember e
the "tradition
tablished at
through bore
set of woods
ard" shaft pe
recommende
be exactly th
"Maltby Clut
12. So you s
adjusts for n

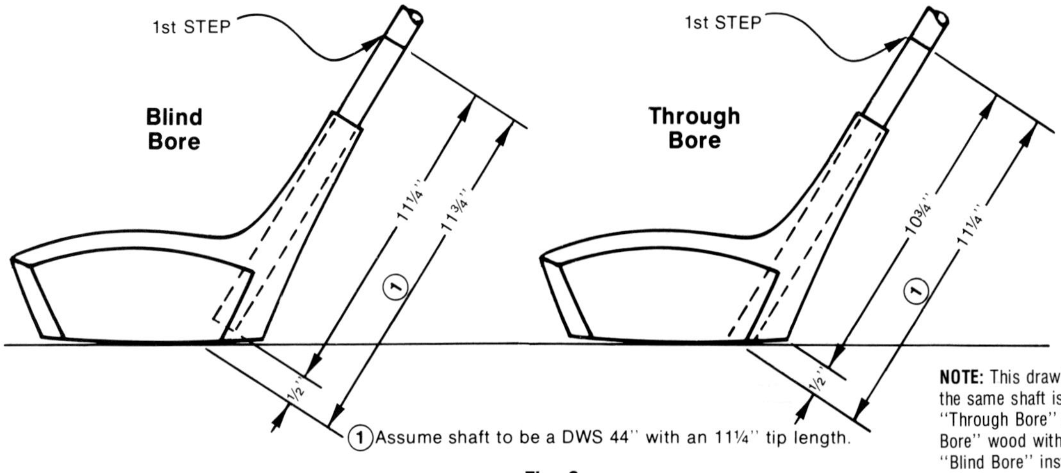
1st STEP
Blind
Bore
11¼''
11¾''
½''
1st STEP
Through
Bore
10¾''
11¼''
½''
①Assume shaft to be a DWS 44'' with an 11¼'' tip length.

NOTE: This drawing shows that if the same shaft is installed in a "Through Bore" and "Blind Bore" wood without tipping, the "Blind Bore" installation will be ¼ flex weaker than the "Through Bore" installation.

Fig. 6
"Through" bore and "Blind" bore effect on shaft stiffness.

TABLE 2
"Tipped" Shafts, Their Stiffness Increase, New Tip Diameters and Step Drill Sizes to Properly Install Them (For .355" Tip Taper Shafts Only)

Amount of "Tipping"	[2]Approximate Amount of Flex Change	"Tipped" Tip Diameter	[1]1st Drill to Bottom	[1]2nd Drill to Within ⅜" of Bottom	[1]3rd Drill Within 1" of Bottom
½''	+ ¼ Stiffer	.359''	23/64''	"U"	⅜''
1''	+ ½ Stiffer	.363''	"U"	⅜''	"V"
1½''	+ ¾ Stiffer	.366''	"U"	⅜''	"V"
2''	+ 1 Stiffer	.370''	⅜''	Not Req.	"W"

[1]Cobalt drill bits work best but high speed steel is okay. Use cutting and drilling oil during drilling. Dull drills tend to drill larger holes so some variance may occur.
[2]Example: Tipping a DIS staff (Dynamic Iron Stiff) 2" will produce a relative stiffness approximating an "X" flex in that same pattern. However, the tipped "S" shaft will be ²/₁₀ ounce lighter than the standard "X" flex weight. Experimentation in actual hitting on an individual basis is the best way to confirm which may feel best or give desired performance.

(12″ − 5⅓″ = 6⅔″). Again, the reason for explaining this is to obtain a better understanding of changes in tip diameter if a shaft is tipped. "Tipping" refers to precutting a certain amount from the tip end of the shaft to increase its stiffness. As you can see, if an iron hosel is bored to accept a .355″ tip taper shaft and you tip it, the shaft will not fit properly and the hosel must be bored out to a slightly larger size. Table 2 was developed to give you the tip diameters of tipped shafts and the proper drill bit size to use so the shaft will fit in the hosel.

Table 2 also shows the approximate amount a shaft stiffens when it is tipped. An important consideration in tipping, or for that matter when installing any iron shaft, is hosel length and shaft penetration. Manufacturers bore irons in varying depths, design some irons with long hosels and some irons with short hosels. See Figure 7. In the Figure 7 example, the long hosel with a 1½″ back of heel to shaft tip end penetration will feel more flexible than the

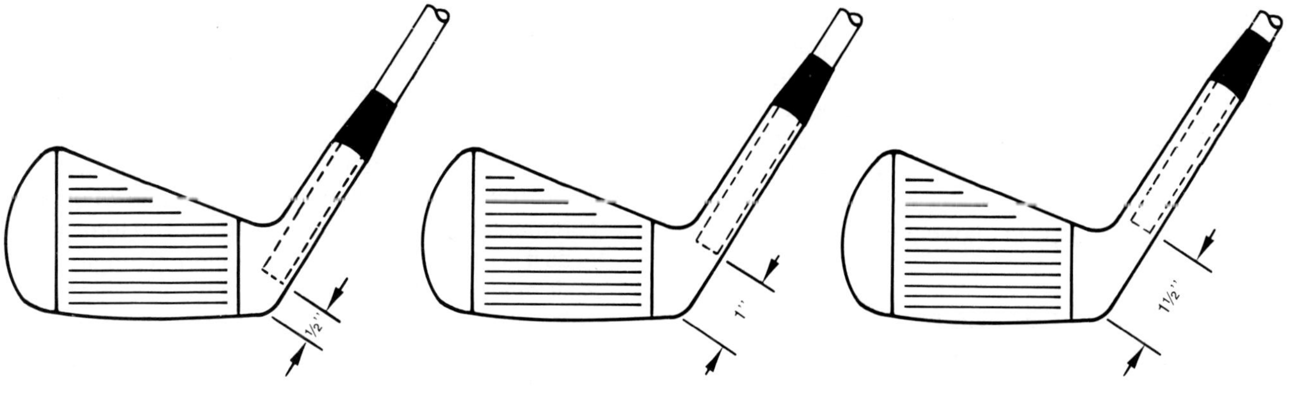
½''
1''
1½''

Slightly Stronger Than Standard Flex | **Standard Flex (Traditional Standard)** | **Slightly Weaker Than Standard Flex**

The dimension shown above is from the back of the heel to the tip of the shaft. 1'' is considered the traditional standard.

Fig. 7
The effect of different bore depths on shaft flex.

Understanding Parallel Tip Shaft Installations in Irons

As was stated for woods, all of the golf shaft manufacturers also have parallel tip iron shafts available. Brunswick Golf® and True Temper® are the only ones that use a fairly logical coding system whereby it is much easier to immediately identify a certain type of shaft. For instance with True Temper's® system, a UDIS shaft is a "Unitized Dynamic® Iron Stiff" flex and a UDIC is a "Unitized Dynamic® Iron Combination R or S" flex. UDICO is a "Unitized Dynamic® Iron Combination R or S Flex Over-The Hosel." Unitized simply means "parallel tip."

Some confusion has always existed concerning where to trim unitized parallel tip shafts. Many parallel tip shafts are available in specific flexes such as X, S, R, A and L. The specific flex parallel tip shaft is identified by a spot of color on the butt end and also by having a .370" parallel tip for shaft-in hosel assemblies and a .395" parallel tip for shaft-over hosel assemblies. Trimming on the specific flex parallel tip shafts is quite easy and is shown in its simplest form in Table 10. This table represents True Temper's® recommended trimming method which is also shown in Figure 9. Once again, the drawback to this trimming method is its disregard for variations in shaft installation depth. Each individual iron design may have differing dimensions from the back of the heel to the tip of the shaft thus causing a difference in flex feel, i.e., weaker flex, standard flex or stronger flex. Refer back to Figure 7.

Trimming the "combination flex" unitized parallel tip shafts is similar to trimming the "specific flex" types but an adjustment in tip trimming is required to obtain this stiffer flex. First of all, you have to understand that a combination flex shaft such as the UDIC, which is a combination "R" or "S" flex in the Dynamic® pattern, is manufactured in the weaker flex or "R" flex. In the case

TABLE 8
Trimming Chart for Specific Flex (Non-combination Flex) Unitized Parallel Tip Wood Shafts

Club No.	[1]Amount to Pretrim from Tip	Amount to Trim from Butt
1	0"	
2	½"	Trim butt to obtain
3	1"	desired club lengths
4	1½"	after shaft is tipped
5	2"	and installed in head.
6	2½"	
7	3"	

[1]To obtain a weaker or stiffer flex feel, this dimension can be changed. For example, cutting an additional ½" from the tip makes the shaft ¼ flex stiffer. Conversely, leaving an additional ½" on the tip will make this shaft ¼ flex weaker or softer.

If a shaft is tipped an additional 2" it will produce the equivalent of one full flex stiffer. However, the feel of the tipped shaft to one made in the stiffer flex will usually not be the same due to different shaft weights and flex points.

TABLE 9
[1]Trimming Chart for "Combination Flex" Unitized Parallel Tip Wood Shafts

Club No.	[2]Tip Trimming for Weaker Flex	[2]Tip Trimming for Stiffer Flex	Amount to Trim from Butt
1	0"	2"	
2	½"	2½"	Trim butt to obtain
3	1"	3"	desired club lengths
4	1½"	3½"	after shaft is tipped
5	2"	4"	and installed in head.
6	2½"	4½"	
7	3"	5"	

[1]Combination flex shafts are usually identified by a "C" or "AL" in the code number. For example: UDWC is a combination "R" or "S" flex shaft and a UDWAL is a combination "A" or "L" flex.
[2]In-between flexes, stiffer flexes and weaker flexes can be obtained by tipping less or tipping more. For example: Trimming the tip 1" on a driver with a UDWC shaft will give you a flex between R and S.

TABLE 10
Trimming Chart for Specific Flex (Non-combination Flex) Unitized Parallel Tip Iron Shafts

Club No.	[2]Amount to Pre-Trim from Tip	Amount to Trim from Butt
1	0"	
2	½"	
3	1"	
4	1½"	Trim butt to obtain
5	2"	desired club length
6	2½"	after shaft is tipped
7	3"	and installed in head.
8	3½"	
9	4"	
PW	[1]4"	
SW	[1]4"	

[1]If the PW & SW are made the same length as the #9 iron then the 4" dimension applies. If however, they are made ½" shorter, then 4½" of tipping would apply.
[2]To obtain a weaker or stiffer flex feel, this dimension can be changed. For example, cutting an additional ½" from the tip makes the shaft ¼ flex stiffer. Conversely, leaving an additional ½" on the tip will make this shaft ¼ flex weaker or softer.

If a shaft is tipped an additional 2" it will produce the equivalent of one full flex stiffer; however, the feel of the tipped shaft to one made in the stiffer flex will usually not be the same due to different shaft weights and flex points.

TABLE 11
[1]Trimming Chart For "Combination Flex Unitized Parallel Tip Iron Shafts

Club No.	[2]Tip Trimming For Weaker Flex	[2][3]Tip Trimming For Stiffer Flex	Amount to Trim from Butt
1	0"	2"	
2	½"	2½"	
3	1"	3"	
4	1½"	3½"	Trim butt to obtain
5	2"	4"	desired club length
6	2½"	4½"	after shaft is tipped
7	3"	5"	and installed in head.
8	3½"	5½"	
9	4"	6"	
PW	[3]4"	[3]6"	
SW	[3]4"	[3]6"	

[1]Combination flex shafts are usually identified by a "C" or "AL" in the code number. For example: UDIC is a combination "R" or "S" flex shaft and a UDIAL is a combination "A" or "L" flex.
[2]In-between flexes, stiffer flexes and weaker flexes can be obtained by tipping less or tipping more. For example: trimming the tip 1" from a UDIC shaft will give you a flex between R and S.
[3]If the PW and SW are made the same length as the #9 iron then the 4" and 6" dimensions above apply. If, however, they are made ½" shorter then 4½" and 6½" of tipping respectively would apply.

The following tables should be used for reference and to provide a better understanding on how to install non-incremental lengths. Keep in mind, however, that the tables provided which give the back of heel to 1st step dimensions also apply to non-incremental lengths as well as to the incremental lengths shown in the following tables. The reason for this is simple: most all tip taper shafts are manufactured in the different lengths by changing the tip to 1st step distance in ½" increments. Therefore, cutting ½" from the tip of a shaft will give it the same tip to 1st step as if it were made in that length. The only two differences now being that the tip diameter is slightly larger (approx. four-thousandths of an inch per ½" cut from it) and the shaft weight is lighter (approximately 1.4 grams per ½" cut from the tip) than the proper incremental length shaft or those shafts purchased in ½" increments.

Understanding Parallel Tip Shaft Installations — Introduction

When the unitized parallel tip shaft was first introduced by True Temper® in the early 70s, a unitized shaft trimming chart and drawing was included in their sales brochure. This method of installation gave the parallel tip shaft a firmer feel than its tip taper counterpart in the same flex and was not satisfactory.

During the latter part of the mid 70s and up to the present, True Temper® changed their recommended trimming method on unitized parallel tip shafts to more closely align the proper flex feel according to their overall shaft flex standards. See Figures 9 and 10. This "revised" method softened or weakened the flex feel of the installed shaft and more closely aligned the flex feel to that of the tip taper shaft. It should be stated here, however, that the two shafts can really never feel the same because of their significantly differing design characteristics resulting in differing club total weights and swingweights.

The method now recommended for trimming unitized parallel tip shafts is called the "Maltby Club Design" trimming method. In actuality it is the same as True Temper's® revised trimming method of the mid 70s with one important exception. The "Maltby Club Design" method allows for the adjustment of differing shaft in hosel penetrations. In other words, the tables that follow in this section which apply to parallel tip shafts provide back of heel to 1st shaft step dimensions. You simply trim the shaft tip the required amount to get the dimension shown in the back of heel to 1st step tables, and then trim the butt end to the desired club length. One last point on this to aid the reader: remember earlier in this section when it was stated that the "traditional standards" for shaft penetration were established at 1" from back of heel to tip of shaft in irons and through bores on woods? Well, if you were reshafting a set of woods and irons that had these "traditional standard" shaft penetrations, then the trimming dimensions as recommended by True Temper® in Figures 9 and 10 would be exactly the same as a set of shafts installed using the "Maltby Club Design" method shown in Figures 11 and 12. So you see, the "Maltby Club Design" method simply adjusts for non-traditional back of heel to shaft tip dimen-

TABLE 4
Men's Tip Taper Iron Shafts
[1]Tipping Table for Proper Installation of Incremental and Non-Incremental Uncut Shaft Lengths

Club No.	[2]Finished Club Length (Traditional Standard)	Column 1 Uncut Shaft Length	Amount of Tipping	Column 2 Uncut Shaft Length	Amount of Tipping	Column 3 Uncut Shaft Length	Amount of Tipping	Column 4 Uncut Shaft Length	Amount of Tipping
1	39"	39"	0"	39"	0"	39"	0"	—	
2	38½"	38½"	0"	39"	½"	39"	½"	38"	0"
3	38"	38"	0"	38"	0"	39"	1"	38"	½"
4	37½"	37½"	0"	38"	½"	39"	1½"	37"	0"
5	37"	37"	0"	37"	0"	37"	0"	37"	½"
6	36½"	36½"	0"	37"	½"	37"	½"	36"	0"
7	36"	36"	0"	36"	0"	37"	1"	36"	½"
8	35½"	35½"	0"	36"	½"	37"	1½"	35"	0"
9	35"	35"	0"	35"	0"	35"	0"	35"	½"
PW	35"	35"	0"	35"	0"	35"	0"	35"	½"
SW	35"	35"	0"	35"	0"	35"	0"	35"	½"

[1]This table gives standard iron shaft flexes based on a 1" dimension from back of heel to tip end of shaft when installed in a head. See Figure 1. Column 1 uses 9 lengths, column 2 uses 5 lengths, column 3 uses 3 lengths and column 4 uses 4 lengths. The one exception to the so-called standard flex is column 4. Many companies have used 4 lengths of shafts starting with a 38" #2 iron shaft. This can also be considered a standard but keep in mind that on a comparative basis, a set of clubs shafted as shown in column 4 will feel about ¼ flex stiffer than those in column 1, 2 or 3.
Another point to keep in mind is this: Although column 2 and 3 show the closest way to match flex and feel to the ideal installation of column 1, it would be impossible to be perfectly exact. However, in most cases gained through practical application, I have found very few tour players or other accomplished players who could feel any difference. The final proof is always in actually hitting the clubs.
[2]For each ½" added to standard club length the shaft should be tipped an additional ½" to maintain the standard flex unless a slightly softer feel is desired. In most cases it is doubtful that all but a highly accomplished player will feel these differences.

TABLE 5
Men's Tip Taper Wood Shafts
[1]Tipping Table for Proper Installation of Incremental and Non-Incremental Uncut Shaft Lengths

Club No.	[2]Finished Club Length (Traditional Standard)	Column 1 Uncut Shaft Length	Amount of Tipping	Column 2 Uncut Shaft Length	Amount of Tipping	Column 3 Uncut Shaft Length	Amount of Tipping
1	43"	44"	0"	44"	0"	44"	0"
2	42½"	43½"	0"	44"	½"	44"	½"
3	42"	43"	0"	43"	0"	44"	1"
4	41½"	42½"	0"	43"	½"	44"	1½"
5	41"	42"	0"	42"	0"	44"	2"
6	40½"	42"	½"	42"	½"	44"	2½"
7	40"	42"	1"	42"	1"	44"	3"

[1]This table gives standard wood shaft flexes based on a through head shaft bore which is considered the traditional standard. See Figure 2.
[2]For each ½" added to standard club length the shaft should be tipped an additional ½" to maintain the standard flex unless a slightly softer feel is desired. In most cases it is doubtful that all but a highly accomplished player will feel the differences.

sions to make all parallel shaft installations have a predictable flex feel.

These four figures, Figures 9 through 12, provide for a graphic or visual interpretation of trimming parallel tip shafts in both woods and irons. The following also provides the reader with more in-depth reference information on installing parallel tip shafts in irons and woods.

TABLE 6
Ladies' Tip Taper Iron Shafts
[1]Tipping Table for Proper Installation of
Incremental and Non-Incremental Uncut Shaft Lengths

Club No.	[2]Finished Club Length (Traditional Standard)	Column 1 Uncut Shaft Length	Amount of Tipping	Column 2 Uncut Shaft Length	Amount of Tipping	Column 3 Uncut Shaft Length	Amount of Tipping
2	37½''	38''	0''	38''	0''	38''	0''
3	37''	37½''	0''	38''	½''	38''	½''
4	36½''	37''	0''	37''	0''	38''	1''
5	36''	36½''	0''	37''	½''	38''	1½''
6	35½''	36''	0''	36''	0''	36''	0''
7	35''	35½''	0''	36''	½''	36''	½''
8	34½''	35''	0''	35''	0''	36''	1''
9	34''	34½''	0''	35''	½''	34''	0''
PW	34''	34½''	0''	35''	½''	34''	0''
SW	34''	34½''	0''	35''	½''	34''	0''

[1]This table gives standard iron shaft flexes based on a 1'' dimension from back of heel to tip end of shaft when installed in a head. See Figure 1.
[2]For each ½'' added to standard club length the shaft should be tipped an additional ½'' to maintain the standard flex unless a slightly softer feel is desired. In most cases it is doubtful that all but a highly accomplished player will feel these differences.

TABLE 7
Ladies' Tip Taper Wood Shafts
[1]Tipping Table for Proper Installation of
Incremental and Non-Incremental Uncut Shaft Lengths

Club No.	[2]Finished Club Length (Tradtional Standard)	Column 1 Uncut Shaft Length	Amount Tipping	Column 2 Uncut Shaft Length	Amount Tipping	[3]Column 3 Uncut Shaft Length	Amount Tipping
1	42''	43''	0''	43''	0''	44''	0''
2	41½''	42½''	0''	43''	½''	44''	½''
3	41''	42''	0''	43''	1''	44''	1''
4	40½''	42''	½''	43''	1½''	44''	1½''
5	40''	42''	1''	43''	2''	44''	2''
6	39½''	42''	1½''	43''	2½''	44''	2½''
7	39''	42''	2''	43''	3''	44''	3''

[1]This table gives standard wood shaft flexes based on a through head shaft bore which is considered the traditional standard. See Figure 2.
[2]For each ½'' added to standard club length the shaft should be tipped an additional ½'' to maintain the standard flex unless a slightly softer feel is desired. In most cases it is doubtful that all but a highly accomplished player will feel the differences.
[3]A 44'' ''L'' flex shaft will produce a weaker ladies' flex than the so-called traditional standard. It should be noted here that this more flexible set-up will many times improve the shotmaking ability of beginning, less accomplished, non-athletic, weaker in strength, women golfers.

Understanding Parallel Tip Shaft Installations in Woods

All of the golf shaft manufacturers have parallel tip shafts available. However, Brunswick Golf® and True Temper® are the only ones to use a fairly logical coding system whereby it is much easier to immediately identify the type of shaft. For instance, with True Temper's® system, a UDWS shaft is a "Unitized Dynamic® Wood Stiff" flex and a UDWAL is a "Unitized Dynamic® Wood Combination A or L" flex. A UJWR is a "Unitized Jet Step Wood R" flex. Unitized simply means "parallel tip." This now gives you a pretty good idea of interpreting the code and understanding its meaning.

Some confusion has also existed concerning where to trim parallel tip shafts. Many parallel tip shafts are available in specific flexes such as X, S, R, A, and L. The specific flex parallel tip shaft is identified by a spot of color on the butt end, usually under the grip, and also by having a .335 parallel tip. Trimming on these specific flex parallel tip shafts is quite easy and is shown in its simplest form in Table 8. This table represents True Temper's® recommended trimming method also shown in Figure 10. The only drawback to this trimming method, as has already been stated, is its disregard for shaft installation depth in the hosel such as blind bore or through bore type assemblies.

Trimming the "Combination Flex" unitized parallel tip shafts is similar to trimming "Specific Flex" types but an adjustment in tip trimming is required to obtain the stiffer flex. First of all, you have to understand that a combination flex shaft such as the UDWC, which is a combination "R" or "S" flex in the Dynamic® pattern, is manufactured in the weaker flex or "R" flex. In the case of the UDWC, the tip length (tip to 1st step) is 12½" or exactly the same as the UDWR. However, the UDWR is made 45" long, while the UDWC is 47" long. Hence, the butt section on the UDWC is lengthened by 2". So, to properly trim a UDWC shaft to make it an "R" flex, you simply pretrim the tip end by the amount shown in Table 9 and then trim the rest from the butt end to get the desired length for that particular wood. If you want an "S" flex from a UDWC shaft, you cut an additional 2" from the tip end and trim the butt to the desired club length. For a detailed trimming explanation on combination flex shafts, see Table 9 which is also shown in Figure 10 in a more graphic presentation.

Remember, parallel tip shafts in combination flexes do not have color coding mark on the butt end. The reason for this is quite obvious since the shaft can be made into either of the two flexes.

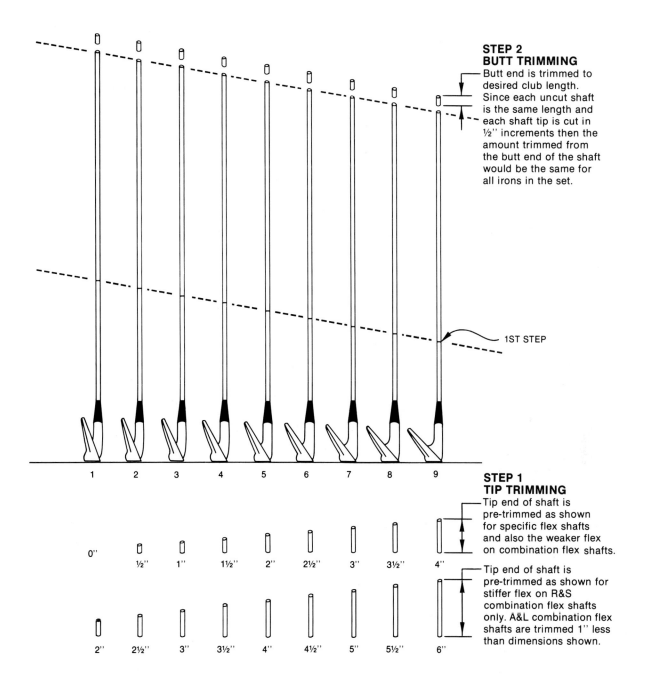

STEP 2
BUTT TRIMMING
Butt end is trimmed to desired club length. Since each uncut shaft is the same length and each shaft tip is cut in ½'' increments then the amount trimmed from the butt end of the shaft would be the same for all irons in the set.

1ST STEP

STEP 1
TIP TRIMMING
Tip end of shaft is pre-trimmed as shown for specific flex shafts and also the weaker flex on combination flex shafts.

Tip end of shaft is pre-trimmed as shown for stiffer flex on R&S combination flex shafts only. A&L combination flex shafts are trimmed 1'' less than dimensions shown.

Fig. 9
Revised True Temper® Parallel Tip Shaft Trimming Method.

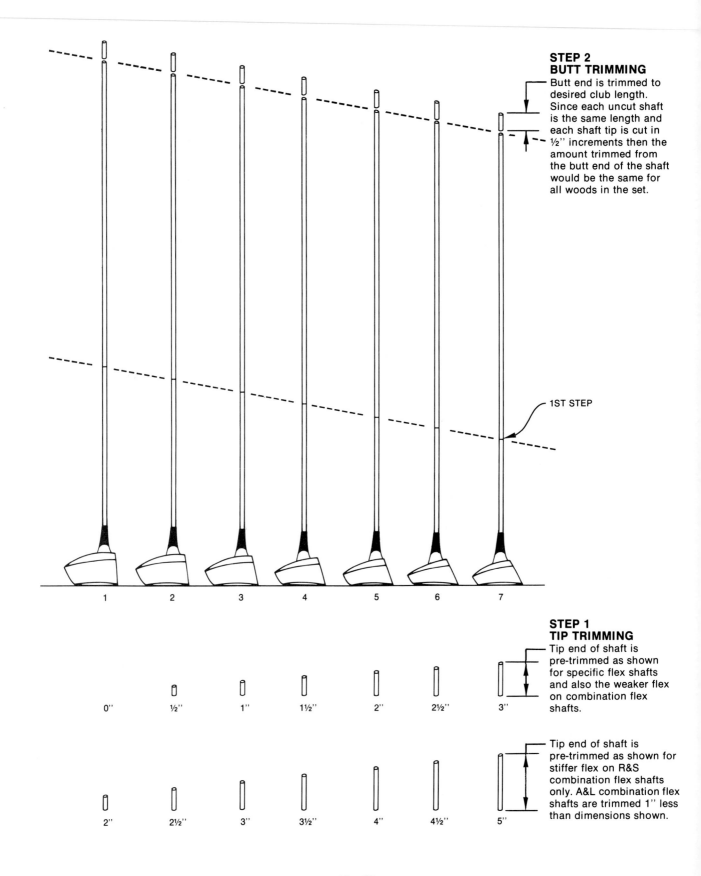

**STEP 2
BUTT TRIMMING**
Butt end is trimmed to desired club length. Since each uncut shaft is the same length and each shaft tip is cut in ½'' increments then the amount trimmed from the butt end of the shaft would be the same for all woods in the set.

1ST STEP

**STEP 1
TIP TRIMMING**
Tip end of shaft is pre-trimmed as shown for specific flex shafts and also the weaker flex on combination flex shafts.

0''   ½''   1''   1½''   2''   2½''   3''

Tip end of shaft is pre-trimmed as shown for stiffer flex on R&S combination flex shafts only. A&L combination flex shafts are trimmed 1'' less than dimensions shown.

2''   2½''   3''   3½''   4''   4½''   5''

Fig. 10
Revised True Temper® Parallel Tip Shaft Trimming Method.

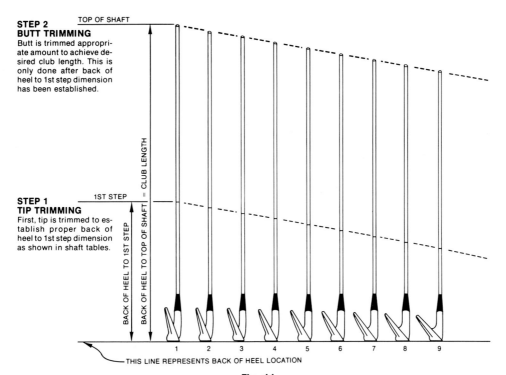

STEP 2
BUTT TRIMMING
Butt is trimmed appropriate amount to achieve desired club length. This is only done after back of heel to 1st step dimension has been established.

STEP 1
TIP TRIMMING
First, tip is trimmed to establish proper back of heel to 1st step dimension as shown in shaft tables.

Fig. 11
Maltby "Club Design" Parallel Tip Shaft Trimming Method.

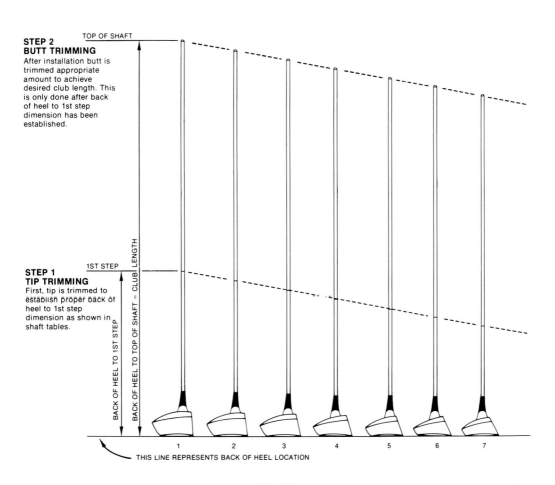

STEP 2
BUTT TRIMMING
After installation butt is trimmed appropriate amount to achieve desired club length. This is only done after back of heel to 1st step dimension has been established.

STEP 1
TIP TRIMMING
First, tip is trimmed to establish proper back of heel to 1st step dimension as shown in shaft tables.

Fig. 12
Maltby "Club Design" Parallel Tip Shaft Trimming Method.

Understanding Parallel Tip Shaft Installations in Irons

As was stated for woods, all of the golf shaft manufacturers also have parallel tip iron shafts available. Brunswick Golf® and True Temper® are the only ones that use a fairly logical coding system whereby it is much easier to immediately identify a certain type of shaft. For instance with True Temper's® system, a UDIS shaft is a "Unitized Dynamic® Iron Stiff" flex and a UDIC is a "Unitized Dynamic® Iron Combination R or S" flex. UDICO is a "Unitized Dynamic® Iron Combination R or S Flex Over-The Hosel." Unitized simply means "parallel tip."

Some confusion has always existed concerning where to trim unitized parallel tip shafts. Many parallel tip shafts are available in specific flexes such as X, S, R, A and L. The specific flex parallel tip shaft is identified by a spot of color on the butt end and also by having a .370″ parallel tip for shaft-in hosel assemblies and a .395″ parallel tip for shaft-over hosel assemblies. Trimming on the specific flex parallel tip shafts is quite easy and is shown in its simplest form in Table 10. This table represents True Temper's® recommended trimming method which is also shown in Figure 9. Once again, the drawback to this trimming method is its disregard for variations in shaft installation depth. Each individual iron design may have differing dimensions from the back of the heel to the tip of the shaft thus causing a difference in flex feel, i.e., weaker flex, standard flex or stronger flex. Refer back to Figure 7.

Trimming the "combination flex" unitized parallel tip shafts is similar to trimming the "specific flex" types but an adjustment in tip trimming is required to obtain this stiffer flex. First of all, you have to understand that a combination flex shaft such as the UDIC, which is a combination "R" or "S" flex in the Dynamic® pattern, is manufactured in the weaker flex or "R" flex. In the case

TABLE 8
Trimming Chart for Specific Flex (Non-combination Flex)
Unitized Parallel Tip Wood Shafts

Club No.	[1]Amount to Pretrim from Tip	Amount to Trim from Butt
1	0"	
2	½"	Trim butt to obtain
3	1"	desired club lengths
4	1½"	after shaft is tipped
5	2"	and installed in head.
6	2½"	
7	3"	

[1]To obtain a weaker or stiffer flex feel, this dimension can be changed. For example, cutting an additional ½" from the tip makes the shaft ¼ flex stiffer. Conversely, leaving an additional ½" on the tip will make this shaft ¼ flex weaker or softer.

If a shaft is tipped an additional 2" it will produce the equivalent of one full flex stiffer. However, the feel of the tipped shaft to one made in the stiffer flex will usually not be the same due to different shaft weights and flex points.

TABLE 9
[1]Trimming Chart for "Combination Flex"
Unitized Parallel Tip Wood Shafts

Club No.	[2]Tip Trimming for Weaker Flex	[2]Tip Trimming for Stiffer Flex	Amount to Trim from Butt
1	0"	2"	
2	½"	2½"	Trim butt to obtain
3	1"	3"	desired club length
4	1½"	3½"	after shaft is tipped
5	2"	4"	and installed in head.
6	2½"	4½"	
7	3"	5"	

[1]Combination flex shafts are usually identified by a "C" or "AL" in the code number. For example: UDWC is a combination "R" or "S" flex shaft and a UDWAL is a combination "A" or "L" flex.
[2]In-between flexes, stiffer flexes and weaker flexes can be obtained by tipping less or tipping more. For example: Trimming the tip 1" on a driver with a UDWC shaft will give you a flex between R and S.

TABLE 10
Trimming Chart for Specific Flex (Non-combination Flex)
Unitized Parallel Tip Iron Shafts

Club No.	[2]Amount to Pre-Trim from Tip	Amount to Trim from Butt
1	0"	
2	½"	
3	1"	
4	1½"	Trim butt to obtain
5	2"	desired club length
6	2½"	after shaft is tipped
7	3"	and installed in head.
8	3½"	
9	4"	
PW	[1]4"	
SW	[1]4"	

[1]If the PW & SW are made the same length as the #9 iron then the 4" dimension applies. If however, they are made ½" shorter, then 4½" of tipping would apply.
[2]To obtain a weaker or stiffer flex feel, this dimension can be changed. For example, cutting an additional ½" from the tip makes the shaft ¼ flex stiffer. Conversely, leaving an additional ½" on the tip will make this shaft ¼ flex weaker or softer.

If a shaft is tipped an additional 2" it will produce the equivalent of one full flex stiffer; however, the feel of the tipped shaft to one made in the stiffer flex will usually not be the same due to different shaft weights and flex points.

TABLE 11
[1]Trimming Chart For "Combination Flex
Unitized Parallel Tip Iron Shafts

Club No.	[2]Tip Trimming For Weaker Flex	[2 3]Tip Trimming For Stiffer Flex	Amount to Trim from Butt
1	0"	2"	
2	½"	2½"	
3	1"	3"	
4	1½"	3½"	Trim butt to obtain
5	2"	4"	desired club length
6	2½"	4½"	after shaft is tipped
7	3"	5"	and installed in head.
8	3½"	5½"	
9	4"	6"	
PW	[3]4"	[3]6"	
SW	[3]4"	[3]6"	

[1]Combination flex shafts are usually identified by a "C" or "AL" in the code number. For example: UDIC is a combination "R" or "S" flex shaft and a UDIAL is a combination "A" or "L" flex.
[2]In-between flexes, stiffer flexes and weaker flexes can be obtained by tipping less or tipping more. For example: trimming the tip 1" from a UDIC shaft will give you a flex between R and S.
[3]If the PW and SW are made the same length as the #9 iron then the 4" and 6" dimensions above apply. If, however, they are made ½" shorter then 4½" and 6½" of tipping respectively would apply.

of the UDIC, the tip length (tip to 1st step) is 12⅛″ or exactly the same as the UDIR. However, the UDIR is made 39″ long while the UDIC is 41″ long. Hence, the butt section of the UDIC is lengthened by 2″. So, to properly trim a UDIC shaft to make it an "R" flex, you simply pretrim the tip end by the amount shown in Table 11 and then trim the rest from the butt end to get the desired length for that particular iron. If you want an "S" flex from the UDIC, you cut an additional 2″ from the tip end and trim the butt for the desired club length.

For a detailed trimming explanation on combination flex shafts, see Table 11. Also shown in Figure 9 is a more graphic presentation of the same data. Remember, parallel tip shafts in combination flexes do not have a color coding mark on the butt end. The reason for this is quite obvious since the shaft can be made into either of the two flexes.

Tables — Back of Heel to 1st Step for Wood and Iron Shafts

The back of heel to 1st shaft step dimensions given in the following tables were calculated by taking the tip to 1st step distance from the shaft manufacturer's blueprints and adjusting the dimension according to the "traditional standards" shown in Figure 1 for irons and Figure 2 for woods. Each table has a corresponding footnotes explanation on how the dimensions were derived and other applicable information. These tables include virtually all stock shafts available today.

One last point to reiterate, if you are checking a raw shaft for shaft tip to 1st step distance to determine what type shaft you have, simply subtract ½″ from the actual shaft tip to 1st step distance and look the shaft up in the tables in this section. See Figure 2. (For irons add 1″ to the shaft tip to 1st step distance. See Figure 1.)

Here is an example of this: Suppose you are trying to identify a golf shaft which is 44″ long, has a .620 butt diameter, .294 tip diameter and a .350 tip parallel section. You also determine that the distance between steps is 1⅞″. Most of you will realize already that this is a Taper Tip Dynamic® shaft. However, it could be a "Stiff" or "X-Stiff" flex because both these shafts have the same dimensions we just listed. However, there is a dimension that will immediately tell us this shaft's flex. Simply measure the shaft's tip length or that dimension from the shaft tip to the 1st step. Let's say this shaft measures 9¼″ from its tip to the 1st step. Next, subtract ½″ from 9¼″ which gives us 8¾″. Turn to page 308 and look up the back of heel to 1st step dimension for both Dynamic® "X" and Dynamic® "S" tip taper 44″ wood shafts. The table shows 8¾″ for an "X" flex and 10¾″ for an "S" flex. So, our shaft is an "X" flex DWX 44″ shaft (Dynamic® wood X-stiff, 44″ long). Go ahead and practice with a few wood and iron shafts and you will see that it is quite easy to do.

NOTES

_____
_____
_____
_____
_____
_____
_____
_____
_____
_____
_____
_____
_____
_____
_____
_____
_____
_____
_____
_____

TIP TAPER IRON SHAFTS

FOOTNOTES FOR THE FOLLOWING TABLES

[1]The following tables give standard iron shaft flexes based on a 1″ dimension from back of heel to tip end of shaft when installed in a head. This is considered to most closely approximate the traditional standard assembly. See Figure 1. Shafts installed in iron heads with a greater dimension than 1″ may sometimes have to be tipped slightly (usually ⅛″ to ⅜″) to make the back of heel to 1st step dimension conform.

The back of heel to 1st step dimensions below were derived by taking the actual shaft manufacturer's blueprint dimensions of uncut shafts from the tip end to the 1st step and adding 1″.

[2]For each ½″ added to standard club length, the shaft should be tipped an additional ½″ to maintain the standard flex unless a slightly softer feel is desired. In most cases it is doubtful that all but a highly accomplished player will feel these differences. Some golf club manufacturers' models will not conform exactly to those dimensions given in the below tables. This is not necessarily wrong as individual club head designs, club lengths, head weights, etc. are all part of the overall club performance that the manufacturer may have desired and confirmed by testing.

[3]If the PW and SW are to be 34½″ long, the 35″ uncut shaft can be tipped ½″; then, subtract ½″ from the back of heel to 1st step dimensions shown in the tables below for the PW and SW only.

[4]Each individual shaft length is not available in every pattern shaft.

[5]"X" - Extra Stiff   "TS" - Tour Stiff   "S" - Stiff   "RS" - Mid Stiff   "R" - Regular

TIP TAPER IRON SHAFTS — MEN'S

True Temper® Tip Taper Iron Shafts — Men's — [1]Back of Heel to 1st Step Dimension

Club No.	[2]Finished Club Length (Traditional Men's Std.)	Uncut Shaft Length	Dynamic & Dynamic Gold DIX & DGIX	Dynamic & Dynamic Gold DIS & DGIS	Dynamic & Dynamic Gold DIT & DGIT	Dynamic DIA	Pro-Fit PFIS	Pro-Fit PFIR	Pro-Fit PFIA	Jet Step JTIS
1	39″	39″	11″	13″	15¾″	16¾″	15⅝″	15⅜″	16⅞″	15½″
2	38½″	38½″	10½″	12½″	15¼″	16¼″	15⅛″	14⅞″	16⅜″	15″
3	38″	38″	10″	12″	14¾″	15¾″	14⅝″	14⅜″	15⅞″	14½″
4	37½″	37½″	9½″	11½″	14¼″	15¼″	14⅛″	13⅞″	15⅜″	14″
5	37″	37″	9″	11″	13¾″	14¾″	13⅝″	13⅜″	14⅞″	13½″
6	36½″	36½″	8½″	10½″	13¼″	14¼″	13⅛″	12⅞″	14⅜″	13″
7	36″	36″	8″	10″	12¾″	13¾″	12⅝″	12⅜″	13⅞″	12½″
8	35½″	35½″	7½″	9½″	12¼″	13¼″	12⅛″	11⅞″	13⅜″	12″
9	35″	35″	7″	9″	11¾″	12¾″	11⅝″	11⅜″	12⅞″	11½″
PW	[3]35″	[3]35″	7″	9″	11¾″	12¾″	11⅝″	11⅜″	12⅞″	11½″
SW	[3]35″	[3]35″	7″	9″	11¾″	12¾″	11⅝″	11⅜″	12⅞″	11½″

Club No.	[2]Finished Club Length (Traditional Men's Std.)	Uncut Shaft Length	Jet Step JTIR	Contour TRIS	Contour TRIR	TT Lite 2LIS	TT Lite 2LIR	TT Lite 2LIA	Extralite SLIS	Extralite SLIR
1	39″	39″	16½″	13″	14½″	10″	12″	10″	11½″	13½″
2	38½″	38½″	16″	12½″	14″	9½″	11½″	9½″	11″	13″
3	38″	38″	15½″	12″	13½″	9″	11″	9″	10½″	12½″
4	37½″	37½″	15″	11½″	13″	8½″	10½″	8½″	10″	12″
5	37″	37″	14½″	11″	12½″	8″	10″	8″	9½″	11½″
6	36½″	36½″	14″	10½″	12″	7½″	9½″	7½″	9″	11″
7	36″	36″	13½″	10″	11½″	7″	9″	7″	8½″	10½″
8	35½″	35½″	13″	9½″	11″	6½″	8½″	6½″	8″	10″
9	35″	35″	12½″	9″	10½″	6″	8″	6″	7½″	9½″
PW	[3]35″	[3]35″	12½″	9″	10½″	6″	8″	6″	7½″	9½″
SW	[3]35″	[3]35″	12½″	9″	10½″	6″	8″	6″	7½″	9½″

TI Apollo Masterflex Tip Taper Iron Shafts — Men's — [1]Back of Heel to 1st Step Dimension

Club No.	[2]Finished Club Length (Traditional Men's Std.)	Uncut Shaft Length	VI [5]"X"	V [5]"TS"	IV [5]"S"	III [5]"RS"	II [5]"R"
1	39″	39″	12¼″	12¾″	13⁴⁄₁₀″	13½″	13⁷⁄₁₀″
2	38½″	38½″	11¾″	12¼″	12⁹⁄₁₀″	13″	13²⁄₁₀″
3	38″	38″	11¼″	11¾″	12⁴⁄₁₀″	12½″	12⁷⁄₁₀″
4	37½″	37½″	10¾″	11¼″	11⁹⁄₁₀″	12″	12²⁄₁₀″
5	37″	37″	10¼″	10¾″	11⁴⁄₁₀″	11½″	11⁷⁄₁₀″
6	36½″	36½″	9¾″	10¼″	10⁹⁄₁₀″	11″	11²⁄₁₀″
7	36″	36″	9¼″	9¾″	10⁴⁄₁₀″	10½″	10⁷⁄₁₀″
8	35½″	35½″	8¾″	9¼″	9⁹⁄₁₀″	10″	10²⁄₁₀″
9	35″	35″	8¼″	8¾″	9⁴⁄₁₀″	9½″	9⁷⁄₁₀″
PW	35″	35″	8¼″	8¾″	9⁴⁄₁₀″	9½″	9⁷⁄₁₀″
SW	35″	35″	8¼″	8¾″	9⁴⁄₁₀″	9½″	9⁷⁄₁₀″

TIP TAPER IRON SHAFTS — MEN'S

Brunswick Golf® Tip Taper Iron Shafts — Men's — ¹Back of Heel to 1st Step Dimension

Club No.	²Finished Club Length (Traditional Men's Std.)	Uncut Shaft Length	Bruns Lite IV "V"	UCV-304 IX "X"	UCV-304 IS "S"	UCV-304 IR "R"	Phoenix IS "S"	Phoenix IR "R"
1	39"	39"	N/A	12"	14"	15"	10"	12"
2	38½"	38½"	12¾"	Tip 39" to 11½"	13½"	14½"	9½"	11½"
3	38"	38"	12¼"	11"	13"	14"	9"	11"
4	37½"	37½"	11¾"	Tip 38" to 10½"	12½"	13½"	8½"	10½"
5	37"	37"	11¼"	10"	12"	13"	8"	10"
6	36½"	36½"	10¾"	Tip 37" to 9½"	11½"	12½"	7½"	9½"
7	36"	36"	10¼"	9"	11"	12"	7"	9"
8	35½"	35½"	9¾"	Tip 36" to 8½"	10½"	11½"	6½"	8½"
9	35"	35"	9¼"	8"	10"	11"	6"	8"
PW	³35"	³35"	9¼"	8"	10"	11"	6"	8"
SW	³35"	³35"	9¼"	8"	10"	11"	6"	8"

Club No.	²Finished Club Length (Traditional Men's Std.)	⁴Uncut Shaft Length	Propel II IX "X"	Propel II IS "S"	Propel II IR "R"	Propel II IA "A"	Mark II IR "R"	Super Champion IR "R"
1	39"	39"	11"	13"	14½"	16¾"	—	—
2	38½"	38½"	Tip 39" to 10½"	12½"	14"	16¼"	—	—
3	38"	38"	10"	12"	13½"	15¾"	12"	12¹⁵/₁₆"
4	37½"	37½"	Tip 38" to 9½"	11½"	13"	15¼"	—	—
5	37"	37"	9"	11"	12½"	14¾"	—	—
6	36½"	36½"	Tip 37" to 8½"	10½"	12"	14¼"	—	—
7	36"	36"	8"	10"	11½"	13¾"	10"	10¹⁵/₁₆"
8	35½"	35½"	Tip 36" to 7½"	9½"	11"	13¼"	—	—
9	35"	35"	7"	9"	10½"	12¾"	—	—
PW	³35"	³35"	7"	9"	10½"	12¾"	—	—
SW	³35"	³35"	7"	9"	10½"	12¾"	—	—

TIP TAPER IRON SHAFTS — LADIES'

Brunswick Golf® Tip Taper Iron Shafts — Ladies' — ¹Back of Heel to 1st Step Dimension

Club No.	²Finished Club Length (Traditional Ladies' Std.)	⁴Uncut Shaft Length	UCV-304 IL "L"	Phoenix IL "L"	Super Champion IL "L"	Champion IL "L"
2	37½"	38"	13½"	11"	13"	11"
3	37"	38"	Tip 38" to 13"	Tip 38" to 10½"	—	—
4	36½"	37"	12½"	10"	—	—
5	36"	37"	Tip 37" to 12"	Tip 37" to 9½"	—	—
6	35½"	36"	11½"	9"	11"	9"
7	35"	36"	Tip 36" to 11"	Tip 36" to 8½"	—	—
8	34½"	35"	10½"	8"	—	—
9	34"	35"	Tip 35" to 10"	Tip 35" to 7½"	—	—
PW	34"	35"	Tip 35" to 10"	Tip 35" to 7½"	—	—
SW	34"	35"	Tip 35" to 10"	Tip 35" to 7½"	—	—

True Temper® Tip Taper Iron Shafts — Ladies' — ¹Back of Heel to 1st Step Dimension

Club No.	²Finished Club Length (Traditional Ladies' Std.)	Uncut Shaft Length	Pro-Fit PFIL	Contour TRIL	TT Lite 2LIL	Extralite SLIL
2	37½"	38"	12½"	14"	11"	14½"
3	37"	37½"	12"	13½"	10½"	14"
4	36½"	37"	11½"	13"	10"	13½"
5	36"	36½"	11"	12½"	9½"	13"
6	35½"	36"	10½"	12"	9"	12½"
7	35"	35½"	10"	11½"	8½"	12"
8	34½"	35"	9½"	11"	8"	11½"
9	34"	34½"	9"	10½"	7½"	11"
PW	34"	34½"	9"	10½"	7½"	11"
SW	34"	34½"	9"	10½"	7½"	11"

TRUE TEMPER & BRUNSWICK GOLF — TIP TAPER IRON SHAFTS — MEN'S & LADIES' BACK OF HEEL TO 1ST STEP

TIP TAPER WOOD SHAFTS

FOOTNOTES FOR THE FOLLOWING TABLES

[1]The following tables give standard wood shaft flexes based on a through head shaft bore which is considered the traditional standard assembly. Shafts installed in blind bore wood heads may sometimes have to be tipped slightly (usually ¼" to ½") to make the back of heel to 1st step dimension conform.

The back of heel to 1st step dimensions below were derived by taking the actual shaft manufacturer's dimensions of uncut shafts from the tip end to the 1st step and subtracting ½". The ½" is that distance from the back of the heel to the shaft tip. See Figure 2.

[2]For each ½" added to standard club length, the shaft should be tipped an additional ½" to maintain the standard flex unless a slightly softer feel is desired. In most cases it is doubtful that all but a highly accomplished player will feel these differences. It should also be noted that most manufacturers of blind bore woods simply install the shaft to the bottom of the hole and do not tip it. This is not necessarily wrong as individual club head designs, club lengths, head weights, etc. are all part of the overall club performance that the manufacturer may have desired and confirmed by testing.

[3]The Countour shaft has a recessed section in its tip which is a constant distance from the tip for all available lengths. Therefore, if the shaft is tipped, this recessed section would vary up and down in relation to the back of the heel.

[4]Each individual shaft length is not available in every pattern shaft.

[5]The Bruns Lite™ shaft is made with a constant tip length. The various raw uncut shaft lengths are made by shortening the butt length by the appropriate amount. If a #2 wood is desired, use a 44" shaft and install in the normal manner, maintaining the 8½" distance from the back of heel to 1st step. Trim to overall club length from the butt.

[6]The UCV-304® shaft is made similar in design to the Bruns Lite™. Read Note 5. The UCV-304® shaft is also available in a 45" length.

[7]Mark II and Super Champion can be tipped ½" for each successively shorter club.

[8]The UCV-304® "L" flex is made with a constant tip length. The various raw uncut shaft lengths are made by shortening the butt length by the appropriate amount. Use the uncut shaft lengths shown below and install in the normal manner, maintaining the 7½" distance from the bck of heel to 1st step. Trim to overall club length from the butt.

[9]"X" - Extra Stiff   "TS" - Tour Stiff   "S" - Stiff   "RS" - Mid Stiff   "R" -Regular

TIP TAPER WOOD SHAFTS — MEN'S

True Temper® Tip Taper Wood Shafts — Men's — [1]Back of Heel to 1st Step Dimension

Club No.	[2]Finished Club Length (Traditional Standard)	[4]Uncut Shaft Length	Dynamic & Dynamic Gold DWX & DGWX	Dynamic & Dynamic Gold DWS & DGWS	Dynamic & Dynamic Gold DWT & DGWT	Dynamic DWA	Jet Step JTWS	Jet Step JTWR	Pro-Fit PFWS	Pro-Fit PFWR
1	43"	44"	8¾"	10¾"	9½"	9½"	10"	11½"	11½"	11¼"
2	42½"	43½"	8¼"	10¼"	9"	9"	9½"	11"	11"	10¾"
3	42"	43"	7¾"	9¾"	8½"	8½"	9"	10½"	10½"	10¼"
4	41½"	42½"	7¼"	9¼"	8"	8"	8½"	10"	10"	9¾"
5	41"	42"	6¾"	8¾"	7½"	7½"	8"	9½"	9½"	9¼"
6	40½"	42"	Tip 42" to 6¼"	Tip 42" to 8¼"	Tip 42" to 7"	Tip 42" to 7"	Tip 42" to 7½"	Tip 42" to 9"	Tip 42" to 9"	Tip 42" to 8¾"
7	40"	42"	Tip 42" to 5¾"	Tip 42" to 7¾"	Tip 42" to 6½"	Tip 42" to 6½"	Tip 42" to 7"	Tip 42" to 8½"	Tip 42" to 8½"	Tip 42" to 8¼"

Club No.	[2]Finished Club Length (Traditional Standard)	[4]Uncut Shaft Length	Pro-Fit PFWA	[3]Contour TRWS	[3]Contour TRWR	TT Lite 2LWS	TT Lite 2LWR	TT Lite 2LWA	Extralite SLWS	Extralite SLWR
1	43"	44"	10⅞"	10½"	12"	10"	11½"	11"	10½"	12½"
2	42½"	43½"	10⅜"	Use 44" @10½"	Use 44" @12"	9½"	11"	10½"	Tip 44" to 10"	Tip 44" to 12"
3	42"	43"	9⅞"	9½"	11"	9"	10½"	10"	9½"	11½"
4	41½"	42½"	9⅜"	Use 43" @9½"	Use 43" @11"	8½"	10"	9½"	Tip 43" to 9"	Tip 43" to 11"
5	41"	42"	8⅞"	8½"	10"	8"	9½"	9"	8½"	10½"
6	40½"	42"	Tip 42" to 8⅜"	Use 42" @8½"	Use 42" @10"	Tip 42" to 7½"	Tip 42" to 9"	Tip 42" to 8½"	Tip 42" to 8"	Tip 42" to 10"
7	40"	42"	Tip 42" to 7⅞"	Use 42" @8½"	Use 42" @10"	Tip 42" to 7"	Tip 42" to 8½"	Tip 42" to 8"	Tip 42" to 7½"	Tip 42" to 9½"

TI Apollo Masterflex Tip Taper Wood Shafts — Men's — [1]Back of Heel to 1st Step Dimension

Club No.	[2]Finished Club Length (Traditional Men's Std.)	[4]Uncut Shaft Length	VI [9]"X"	V [9]"TS"	IV [9]"S"	III [9]"RS"	II [9]"R"
1	43"	44"	13¹⁄₁₀"	13⁹⁄₁₆"	12½"	12½"	12³⁄₁₀"
2	42½"	43½"	12⁶⁄₁₀"	13¹⁄₁₆"	12"	12"	11⁸⁄₁₀"
3	42"	43"	12¹⁄₁₀"	12⁹⁄₁₆"	11½"	11½"	11³⁄₁₀"
4	41½"	42½"	11⁶⁄₁₀"	12¹⁄₁₆"	11"	11"	10⁸⁄₁₀"
5	41"	42"	11¹⁄₁₀"	11⁹⁄₁₆"	10½"	10½"	10³⁄₁₀"
6	40½"	41½"	10⁶⁄₁₀"	11¹⁄₁₆"	10"	10"	9⁸⁄₁₀"
7	40"	41"	10¹⁄₁₀"	10⁹⁄₁₆"	9½"	9½"	9³⁄₁₀"

TIP TAPER WOOD SHAFTS — MEN'S

Brunswick Golf® Tip Taper Wood Shafts — Men's — ¹Back of Heel to 1st Step Dimension

Club No.	²Finished Club Length (Traditional Standard)	⁴Uncut Shaft Length	⁵Bruns Lite IV "V"	⁶UCV-304 WE "X"	⁶UCV-304 WS "S"	⁶UCV-304 WR "R"	Phoenix WS "S"	Phoenix WR "R"
1	43''	44''	8½''	8¼''	9½''	10½''	10''	11½''
2	42½''	43½''	Use 44'' Maintain 8½''	Use 44'' Maintain 8¼''	Use 44'' Maintain 9½''	Use 44'' Maintain 10½''	Tip 44'' to 9½''	Tip 44'' to 11''
3	42''	43''	8½''	8¼''	9½''	10½''	9''	10½''
4	41½''	42½''	8½''	Use 43'' Maintain 8¼''	Use 43'' Maintain 9½''	Use 43'' Maintain 10½''	8½''	10''
5	41''	42''	8½''	8¼''	9½''	10½''	8''	9½''
6	40½''	42''	8½''	Use 42'' Maintain 8¼''	Use 42'' Maintain 9½''	Use 42'' Maintain 10½''	Tip 42'' to 7½''	Tip 42'' to 9''
7	40''	42''	8½''	Use 42'' Maintain 8¼''	Use 42'' Maintain 9½''	Use 42'' Maintain 10½''	Tip 42'' to 7''	Tip 42'' to 8½''

Club No.	²Finished Club Length (Traditional Standard)	⁴Uncut Shaft Length	Propel II WX "X"	Propel II WS "S"	Propel II WR "R"	Propel II WA "A"	⁷Mark II WR "R"	⁷Super Champion WR "R"
1	43''	44''	8¾''	9¾''	8½''	10⅞''	12''	9¹⁵/₁₆''
2	42½''	43½''	Tip 44'' to 8¼''	Tip 44'' to 9¼''	Tip 44'' to 8''	Tip 44'' to 10⅜''	—	—
3	42''	43''	7¾''	8¾''	7½''	9⅞''	—	—
4	41½''	42½''	Tip 43'' to 7¼''	8¼''	7''	9⅜''	—	—
5	41''	42''	6¾''	7¾''	6½''	8⅞''	—	—
6	40½''	42''	Tip 42'' to 6¼''	Tip 42'' to 7¼''	Tip 42'' to 6''	Tip 42'' to 8⅜''	—	—
7	40''	42''	Tip 42'' to 5¾''	Tip 42'' to 6¾''	Tip 42'' to 5½''	Tip 42'' to 7⅞''	—	—

TIP TAPER WOOD SHAFTS — LADIES'

True Temper® Tip Taper Wood Shafts — Ladies' — ¹Back of Heel to 1st Step Dimension

Club No.	²Finished Club Length (Traditional Ladies' Std.)	⁴Uncut Shaft Length	Pro-Fit PFWL or DWL	³Contour TRWL	TT Lite 2LWL	Extralite SLWL
1	42''	43''	8½''	12½''	12''	14''
2	41½''	42½''	8''	Use 43'' @12½''	11½''	Use 43'' Tip to 13½''
3	41''	42''	7½''	11½''	11''	13''
4	40½''	42''	Use 43'' Tip to 7''	Use 42'' @11½''	Use 42'' Tip to 10½''	Use 42'' Tip to 12½''
5	40''	42''	Use 42'' Tip to 6½''	Use 42'' @11½''	Use 42'' Tip to 10''	Use 42'' Tip to 12''
6	39½''	42''	Use 42'' Tip to 6''	Use 42'' @11½''	Use 42'' Tip to 9½''	Use 42'' Tip to 11½''
7	39''	42''	Use 42'' Tip to 5½''	Use 42'' @11½''	Use 42'' Tip to 9''	Use 42'' Tip to 11''

Brunswick Golf® Tip Taper Wood Shafts — Ladies' — ¹Back of Heel to 1st Step Dimension

Club No.	²Finished Club Length (Traditional Ladies' Std.)	⁴Uncut Shaft Length	⁶UCV-304 WL "L"	Phoenix WL "L"	Super Champion WL "L"	Champion WL "L"
1	42''	44''	7½''	13''	Use 43'' Maintain 14¹⁵/₁₆''	15½''
2	41½''	44''	Use 44'' Maintain 7½''	Tip 44'' to 12½''	Tip 43'' to 14⁷/₁₆''	Tip 44'' to 15''
3	41''	43''	7½''	12''	Tip 43'' to 13¹⁵/₁₆''	Tip 44'' to 14½''
4	40½''	43''	Use 43'' Maintain 7½''	Tip 43'' to 11½''	Tip 43'' to 13⁷/₁₆''	Tip 44'' to 14''
5	40''	42''	7½''	11''	Tip 43'' to 12¹⁵/₁₆''	Tip 44'' to 13½''
6	39½''	42''	Use 42'' Maintain 7½''	Tip 43'' to 10½''	—	—
7	39''	41''	7½''	Tip 43'' to 10''	—	—

TRUE TEMPER & BRUNSWICK GOLF — TIP TAPER WOOD SHAFTS MEN'S & LADIES' — BACK OF HEEL TO 1ST STEP

TIP TAPER IRON & WOOD SHAFTS — MEN'S

True Temper® Special NDIS Iron Shaft — Tip Taper — Back of Heel to 1st Step Dimension

Club No.	[2]Finished Club Length (Traditional Standard)	Uncut Shaft Length	[1]Dynamic NDIS (Modified) GolfWorks®	If Uncut Shaft Length Is this; Then . . .	Tip This Amount	If Uncut Shaft Length Is This; Then . . .	Tip This Amount
1	39"	39"	16¾"	39"	0"	39"	0"
2	38½"	38½"	16¼"	39"	½"	39"	½"
3	38"	38"	15¾"	38"	0"	39"	1"
4	37½"	37½"	15¼"	38"	½"	39"	1½"
5	37"	37"	14¾"	37"	0"	37"	0"
6	36½"	36½"	14¼"	37"	½"	37"	½"
7	36"	36"	13¾"	36"	0"	37"	1"
8	35½"	35½"	13¼"	36"	½"	37"	1½"
9	35"	35"	12¾"	35"	0"	35"	0"
PW	35"	35"	12¾"	35"	0"	35"	0"
SW	35"	35"	12¾"	35"	0"	35"	0"

[1]NDIS is the True Temper code designation for "New Dynamic Iron Stiff." This shaft was developed many years ago by True Temper. The shaft, however, was thought to be too flexible by touring professionals and better players so the above modified version was developed in the early 1960's to have a firmer feel. It is a special order shaft and is usually only available in 3 or 5 lengths and not in ½" increments. The above table shows proper tipping for these lengths. Regardless of the lengths used, the distance shown above from back of heel to the 1st step would apply for a standard flex. Tour players and harder hitting, lower handicap players usually prefer this shaft tipped ½" to 1½".
[2]For each ½" added to standard club length the shaft should be tipped ½" to maintain the standard flex, unless a slightly softer flex is desired.

True Temper® Special NDWS Wood Shaft — Tip Taper — Back of Heel to 1st Step Dimension

Club No.	[2]Finished Club Length (Traditional Standard)	Uncut Shaft Length	[1]Dynamic NDWS
1	43"	44"	11⅜"
2	42½"	44"	10⅞"
3	42"	44"	10⅜"
4	41½"	44"	9⅞"
5	41"	44"	9⅜"
6	40½"	44"	8⅞"
7	40"	44"	8⅜"

[1]NDWS is the True Temper code designation for "New Dynamic Wood Stiff." This shaft was actually developed in 1946. It is a special order shaft and is usually only available from suppliers in the 44" length. For tour players and exceptionally hard hitting low handicap players the driver shaft is usually tipped from ½" to 1½ ".
[2]For each ½" added to standard club length the shaft should be tipped ½" to maintain the standard flex, unless a slightly softer flex is desired.

FLEX FLOW TIP TAPER WOOD & IRON SHAFTS — MEN'S & LADIES'

True Temper® Tip Taper Wood and Iron Shafts — Men's & Ladies' — Back of Heel to First Step Dimension

Club No.	Finished Club Length (Traditional Standard) Men's	Ladies'	Uncut Shaft Length Men's	Ladies'	Flex Flow TFFWS "S"	Flex Flow TFFWR "R"	Flex Flow TFFWA "A"	Flex Flow TFFWL "L"
1	43"	42"	44"	44"	9"	10½"	11½"	13½"
2	42½"	41½"	43½"	43½"	8½"	10"	11"	13"
3	42"	41"	43"	43"	8"	9½"	10½"	12½"
4	41½"	40½"	42½"	42½"	7½"	9"	10"	12"
5	41"	40"	42"	42"	7"	8½"	9½"	11½"
6	40½"	39½"	41½"	41½"	6½"	8"	9"	11"
7	40"	39"	41½"	41½"	6½"	8"	9"	11"

Club No.	Finished Club Length (Modern Standard) Men's	Ladies'	Uncut Shaft Length Men's	Ladies'	Flex Flow TFFIS "S"	Flex Flow TFFIR "R"	Flex Flow TFFIA "A"	Flex Flow TFFIL "L"
2	39"	38"	39"	38"	11¾"	13"	14"	15"
3	38½"	37½"	38½"	37½"	11¼"	12½"	13½"	14½"
4	38"	37"	38"	37"	10¾"	12"	13"	14"
5	37½"	36½"	37½"	36½"	10¼"	11½"	12½"	13½"
6	37"	36"	37"	36"	9¾"	11"	12"	13"
7	36½"	35½"	36½"	35½"	9¼"	10½"	11½"	12½"
8	36"	35"	36"	35"	8¾"	10"	11"	12"
9	35½"	34½"	35½"	34½"	8¼"	9½"	10½"	11½"
PW	35½"	34½"	35"	34"	7¾"	9"	10"	11"
SW	35½"	34½"	35"	34"	7¾"	9"	10"	11"

TORSION MATCHED TIP TAPER OR PARALLEL TIP
IRON & WOOD SHAFTS — MEN'S

TI Apollo Torsion Matched Wood Shafts — Tip Taper and Parallel Tip — [1]Back of Heel to 1st Step Dimension

Club No.	Finished Club Length (Traditional Standard)	Uncut Shaft Length	[2]Torsion Matched "S"	[2]Torsion Matched "R"
1	43"	44"	11"	13"
2	42½"	44"	Use 44" Maintain 11"	Use 44" Maintain 13"
3	42"	43"	11"	13"
4	41½"	43"	Use 43" Maintain 11"	Use 44" Maintain 13"
5	41"	42"	11"	13"
6	40½"	42"	11"	13"
7	40"	42"	11"	13"

[1]This table gives standard wood shaft flexes based on a through head shaft bore which is considered the traditional standard assembly. Shafts installed in blind bore wood heads may sometimes have to be tipped slightly (usually ¼" to ½") to make the back of heel to 1st step dimension conform to the above.

The back of heel to 1st step dimensions above were derived by taking the actual shaft manufacturer's dimensions of uncut shafts from the tip end to the 1st step and subtracting ½". The ½" is that distance from the back of the heel to the shaft tip. See Figure 2.

[2]All trimming to length must be from the butt end only to maintain the torsion matching properties. This applies to both parallel tip and tip taper models. For this reason, both parallel tip and tip taper shafts must be purchased in the standard 1" incremental lengths offered.

TI Apollo Torsion Matched Iron Shafts — Tip Taper and Parallel Tip — [1]Back of Heel to 1st Step Dimension

Club No.	Finished Club Length (Traditional Men's Std.)	Uncut Shaft Length	[2]Torsion Matched "S"	[2]Torsion Matched "R"
1	39"	39"	11½"	14"
2	38½"	39"	Use 39" Maintain 11½"	Use 39" Maintain 14"
3	38"	38"	11½"	14"
4	37½"	38"	Use 38" Maintain 11½"	Use 38" Maintain 14"
5	37"	37"	11½"	14"
6	36½"	37"	Use 37" Maintain 11½"	Use 37" Maintain 14"
7	36"	36"	11½"	14"
8	35½"	36"	Use 36" Maintain 11½"	Use 36" Maintain 14"
9	35"	35"	11½"	14"
PW	[3]35"	[3]35"	11½"	14"
SW	[3]35"	[3]35"	11½"	14"

[1]This table gives standard iron shaft flexes based on a 1" dimension from back of heel to tip end of shaft when installed in a head. This is considered to most closely approximate the traditional standard assembly. See Figure 1. Shafts installed in iron heads with a greater dimension than 1" may sometimes have to be tipped slightly (usually ⅛" to ⅜") to make the back of heel to 1st step dimension conform to the above.

The back of heel to 1st step dimensions above were derived by taking the actual shaft manufacturer's blueprint dimensions of uncut shafts from the tip end to the 1st step and adding 1".

[2]All trimming to length must be from the butt end only to maintain the torsion matching properties. This applies to both parallel tip and tip taper models. For this reason, both parallel tip and tip taper shafts must be purchased in the standard 1" incremental lengths offered.

MATCHFLEX PARALLEL TIP
IRON & WOOD SHAFTS — MEN'S

TI Apollo Matchflex Wood Shafts — Parallel Tip — [1]Back of Heel to 1st Step Dimension

Club No.	Finished Club Length (Traditional Standard)	Amount Normally Trimmed From Tip of Shaft	4 [2](S)	3 [2](RS)	2 [2](R)	1 [2](AR)
1	43"	0"	12¾"	9¾"	13⁸⁄₁₀"	13¼"
2	42½"	½"	12¼"	9¼"	13³⁄₁₀"	12¾"
3	42"	1"	11¾"	8¾"	12⁸⁄₁₀"	12¼"
4	41½"	1½"	11¼"	8¼"	12³⁄₁₀"	11¾"
5	41"	2"	10¾"	7¾"	11⁸⁄₁₀"	11¼"
6	40½"	2½"	10¼"	7¼"	11³⁄₁₀"	10¾"
7	40"	3"	9¾"	6¾"	10⁸⁄₁₀"	10¼"

[1]This table gives standard wood shaft flexes based on a through head shaft bore which is considered the traditional standard assembly. Shafts installed in blind bore wood heads may sometimes have to be tipped slightly (usually ¼" to ½") to make the back of heel to 1st step dimension conform to the above.

The back of heel to 1st step dimensions above were derived by taking the actual shaft manufacturer's dimensions of uncut shafts from the tip end to the 1st step and subtracting ½". The ½" is that distance from the back of the heel to the shaft tip. See Figure 2.

[2]"S" — Stiff   "RS" — Mid Stiff   "R" — Regular   "AR" — Flexible.

TI Apollo Matchflex Iron Shafts — Parallel Tip — [1]Back of Heel to 1st Step Dimension						
Club No.	Finished Club Length (Traditional Standard)	Amount Normally Trimmed From Tip of Shaft	4 [2](S)	3 [2](RS)	2 [2](R)	1 [2](AR)
1	39″	0″	12½″	12½″	12¹/₁₆″	13¾″
2	38½″	½″	12″	12″	11⁹/₁₆″	13¼″
3	38″	1″	11½″	11½″	11¹/₁₆″	12¾″
4	37½″	1½″	11″	11″	10⁹/₁₆″	12¼″
5	37″	2″	10½″	10½″	10¹/₁₆″	11¾″
6	36½″	2½″	10″	10″	9⁹/₁₆″	11¼″
7	36″	3″	9½″	9½″	9¹/₁₆″	10¾″
8	35½″	3½″	9″	9″	8⁹/₁₆″	10¼″
9	35″	4″	8½″	8½″	8¹/₁₆″	9¾″
PW	35″	4″	8½″	8½″	8¹/₁₆″	9¾″
SW	35″	4″	8½″	8½″	8¹/₁₆″	9¾″

[1]This table gives standard iron shaft flexes based on a 1″ dimension from back of heel to tip end of shaft when installed in a head. This is considered to most closely approximate the traditional standard assembly. See Figure 1. Shafts installed in iron heds with a greater dimension than 1″ may sometimes have to be tipped slightly (usually ⅛″ to ⅜″) to make the back of heel to 1st step dimension conform to the above.

The back of heel to 1st step dimensions above were derived by taking the actual shaft manufacturer's blueprint dimensions of uncut shafts from the tip end to the 1st step and adding 1″.

[2]"S" — Stiff   "RS" — Mid Stiff   "R" — Regular   "AR" — Flexible.

MASTERFLEX PARALLEL TIP
IRON & WOOD SHAFTS — MEN'S

TI Apollo Masterflex Wood Shafts — Parallel Tip — [1]Back of Heel to 1st Step Dimension						
Club No.	Finished Club Length (Traditional Standard)	Amount Normally Trimmed From Tip of Shaft	VI [2](X)	V [2](TS)	IV [2](S)	III [2](RS)	II [2](R)
1	43″	0″	13¹/₁₀″	13⁹/₁₆″	12½″	12½″	12³/₁₀″
2	42½″	½″	12⁶/₁₀″	13¹/₁₆″	12″	12″	11⁸/₁₀″
3	42″	1″	12¹/₁₀″	12⁹/₁₆″	11½″	11½″	11³/₁₀″
4	41½″	1½″	11⁶/₁₀″	12¹/₁₆″	11″	11″	10⁸/₁₀″
5	41″	2″	11¹/₁₀″	11⁹/₁₆″	10½″	10½″	10³/₁₀″
6	40½″	2½″	10⁶/₁₀″	11¹/₁₆″	10″	10″	9⁸/₁₀″
7	40″	3″	10¹/₁₀″	10⁹/₁₆″	9½″	9½″	9³/₁₀″

[1]This table gives standard wood shaft flexes based on a through head shaft bore which is considered the traditional standard assembly. Shafts installed in blind bore wood heads may sometimes have to be tipped slightly (usually ¼″ to ½″) to make the back of heel to 1st step dimension conform to the above.

The back of heel to 1st step dimensions above were derived by taking the actual shaft manufacturer's dimensions of uncut shafts from the tip end to the 1st step and subtracting ½″. The ½″ is that distance from the back of the heel to the shaft tip. See Figure 2.

[2]"X" — Extra Stiff   "TS" — Tour Stiff   "S" — Stiff   "RS" — Mid Stiff   "R" — Regular.

TI Apollo Masterflex Iron Shafts — Parallel Tip — Amount to Trim From Tip			
Club No.	[1]Finished Club Length (Traditional Standard)	Uncut Shaft Length	[2]Amount to Trim From Tip [3]For X, TX, S, RS and R Flexes
1	39″	39″	0″
2	38½″	39″	⅛″
3	38″	39″	¼″
4	37½″	39″	⅜″
5	37″	39″	½″
6	36½″	39″	⅝″
7	36″	39″	¾″
8	35½″	39″	⅞″
9	35″	39″	1″
PW	35″	39″	1″
SW	35″	39″	1″

[1]After tip trimming and installation of shaft in head, trim butt of shaft to overall club length.

[2]For each ½″ added to standard club length, the shaft should be tipped an additional ⅛″ to maintain the standard flex unless a slightly softer feel is desired.

[3]"X" — Extra Stiff   "TS" — Tour Stiff   "S" — Stiff   "RS" — Mid Stiff   "R" — Regular.

PARALLEL TIP IRON SHAFTS

FOOTNOTES FOR THE FOLLOWING TABLES

[1]The following tables give standard iron shaft flexes based on a 1'' dimension from back of heel to tip end of shaft when installed in a head. This is considered to most closely approximate the traditional standard assembly. See Figure 1. Parallel tip shafts installed in iron heads with a greater dimension than 1'' may sometimes need a slight amount of additional tipping (usually ⅛'' to ⅜'') to make the back of heel to 1st step dimension conform to the below.

The back of heel to 1st step dimensions below were derived by taking the actual shaft manufacturer's blueprint dimension of uncut shafts from the tip end to the 1st step and adding 1''. Since these shafts are parallel tip and only come in one length, the blueprint tip length only applies to the #1 iron. Therefore the below 1st step dimensions for the #2 thru #9 iron through SW were derived by subtracting an additional ½'' for each successively shorter club.

[2]For each ½'' added to standard club length the shaft should be tipped an additional ½'' to maintain the standard flex unless a slightly softer feel is desired. In most cases it is doubtful that all but a highly accomplished player will feel these differences. It should also be noted that most manufacturers, regardless of shaft tip to back of heel dimension, trim in ½'' increments and install the shaft to the bottom of the hole. This is not necessarily wrong as individual club head designs, club lengths, head weights, etc. are all part of the overall club performance that the manufacturer may have desired and confirmed by testing.

[3]After the shaft is installed in a head with the back of heel to 1st step dimensions as shown below (normal installation) the finished club length is obtained by trimming from the shaft butt.

[4]For men, if the PW and SW are to be 34½'' long, then an additional ½'' should be cut from the shaft tip (4½'' vs. 4'').

[5]To maintain the proper flexing characteristics in the tip area, the parallel tip Contour shaft should only be tip trimmed in ⅛'' increments for each ½'' reduction in club length.

[6]For ladies', if the PW and SW are to be 33½'' long, then an additional ½'' should be cut from the shaft tip (4'' vs. 3½'').

PARALLEL TIP IRON SHAFTS — MEN'S

True Temper® Parallel Tip Iron Shafts — Men's — [1]Back of Heel to 1st Step Dimension

Club No.	[2] [3]Finished Club Length (Traditional Standard)	[1]Amount Normally Trimmed From Tip of Shaft	Dynamic UDIX "X"	Dynamic Gold & Dynamic UDGDS & UDIS or UDIC "S"	Dynamic Gold & Dynamic UDGIR & UDIR or UDIC "R"	Dynamic UDIAL "A"	Dynamic UDIXO "X"	Dynamic UDICO "S"	Dynamic UDICO "R"	Dynamic UDIALO "A"	TT Lite UTTLIC "S"	TT Lite UTTLIC "R"
1	39''	0''	11⅛''	11⅛''	13⅛''	14⅞''	11''	13''	15''	16¾''	10''	12''
2	38½''	½''	10⅝''	10⅝''	12⅝''	14⅜''	10½''	12½''	14½''	16¼''	9½''	11½''
3	38''	1''	10⅛''	10⅛''	12⅛''	13⅞''	10''	12''	14''	15¾''	9''	11''
4	37½''	1½''	9⅝''	9⅝''	11⅝''	13⅜''	9½''	11½''	13½''	15¼''	8½''	10½''
5	37''	2''	9⅛''	9⅛''	11⅛''	12⅞''	9''	11''	13''	14¾''	8''	10''
6	36½''	2½''	8⅝''	8⅝''	10⅝''	12⅜''	8½''	10½''	12½''	14¼''	7½''	9½''
7	36''	3''	8⅛''	8⅛''	10⅛''	11⅞''	8''	10''	12''	13¾''	7''	9''
8	35½''	3½''	7⅝''	7⅝''	9⅝''	11⅜''	7½''	9½''	11½''	13¼''	6½''	8½''
9	35''	4''	7⅛''	7⅛''	9⅛''	10⅞''	7''	9''	11''	12¾''	6''	8''
PW	35''	[4]4''	7⅛''	7⅛''	9⅛''	10⅞''	7''	9''	11''	12¾''	6''	8''
SW	35''	[4]4''	7⅛''	7⅛''	9⅛''	10⅞''	7''	9''	11''	12¾''	6''	8''

Club No.	[2] [3]Finished Club Length (Traditional Standard)	[1]Amount Normally Trimmed From Tip of Shaft	TT Lite U2LIS "S"	TT Lite U2LIR "R"	TT Lite U2LIAL "A"	Jet Step UJIC "S"	Jet Step UJIC "R"	Jet Step UJICO "S"	Jet Step UJICO "R"	[5]Contour UTRIS "S"	[5]Contour UTRIR "R"
1	39''	0''	10''	12''	10''	12''	14''	13''	15''	13''	14½''
2	38½''	½''	9½''	11½''	9½''	11½''	13½''	12½''	14½''	12⅞''	14⅜''
3	38''	1''	9''	11''	9''	11''	13''	12''	14''	12¾''	14¼''
4	37½''	1½''	8½''	10½''	8½''	10½''	12½''	11½''	13½''	12⅝''	14⅛''
5	37''	2''	8''	10''	8''	10''	12''	11''	13''	12½''	14''
6	36½''	2½''	7½''	9½''	7½''	9½''	11½''	10½''	12½''	12⅜''	13⅞''
7	36''	3''	7''	9''	7''	9''	11''	10''	12''	12¼''	13¾''
8	35½''	3½''	6½''	8½''	6½''	8½''	10½''	9½''	11½''	12⅛''	13⅝''
9	35''	4''	6''	8''	6''	8''	10''	9''	11''	12''	13½''
PW	35''	[4]4''	6''	8''	6''	8''	10''	9''	11''	12''	13½''
SW	35''	[4]4''	6''	8''	6''	8''	10''	9''	11''	12''	13½''

POWER KICK PARALLEL TIP IRON & WOOD SHAFTS
MEN'S & LADIES'

Northwestern "Power Kick®" Parallel Tip Iron Shaft — [4]Amount to Trim from Tip

Club No.	[2] [3]Finished Club Length (Traditional Std. Men's)	[3]Finished Club Length (Traditional Std. Ladies')	Uncut Shaft Length	[1]Power Kick® NWKI [4](Amount to Trim from Tip)
1	39''	—	39''	0''
2	38½''	37½''	39''	⅛''
3	38''	37''	39''	¼''
4	37½''	36½''	39''	⅜''
5	37''	36''	39''	½''
6	36½''	35½''	39''	⅝''
7	36''	35''	39''	¾''
8	35½''	34½''	39''	⅞''
9	35''	34''	39''	1''
PW	35''	34''	39''	1''
SW	35''	34''	39''	1''

[1]Northwestern's trimming instructions are the same for all flexes (X, S, R, A & L).
[2]If the PW & SW are cut to 34½'', then trim 1⅛'' from the shaft tip vs. 1'' as shown. (Men's)
[3]After tip trimming and installation of shaft in head; trim butt of shaft to overall club length.
[4]For each ½'' added to standard club length the shaft should be tipped an additional ⅛'' to maintain the standard flex unless a slightly softer feel is desired.

Northwestern "Power Kick®" Parallel Tip Wood Shaft — [3]Amount to Trim from Tip

Club No.	[2]Finished Club Length (Traditional Std. Men's)	[2]Finished Club Length (Traditional Std. Ladies')	Uncut Shaft Length	[1]Power Kick® NWKW [3](Amount to Trim from Tip)
1	43''	42''	44''	0''
2	42½''	41½''	44''	⅛''
3	42''	41''	44''	¼''
4	41½''	40½''	44''	⅜''
5	41''	40''	44''	½''
6	40½''	39½''	44''	⅝''
7	40''	39''	44''	¾''

[1]Northwestern's trimming instructions are the same for all flexes (X, S, R, A & L).
[2]After tip trimming and installation of shaft in head; trim butt or shaft to overall club length.
[3]For each ½'' added to standard club length the shaft should be tipped an additional ⅛'' to maintain the standard flex unless a slightly softer feel is desired.

PARALLEL TIP WOOD SHAFTS — MEN'S

FOOTNOTES FOR THE FOLLOWING TABLES

[1]The following tables give standard wood shaft flexes based on a through head shaft bore which is considered the traditional standard assembly. Shafts installed in blind bore wood heads may sometimes need additional tipping (usually ¼'' to ½'') to make the back of heel to 1st step dimension conform to the below.

The back of heel to 1st step dimensions below were derived by taking the actual shaft manufacturer's blueprint dimension of uncut shafts from the tip end to the 1st step and subtracting ½''. The ½'' is that distance from the back of the heel to the shaft tip. See Figure 2. Since these are parallel tip shafts which only come in one length, the blueprint tip length only applies to the driver. Therefore the above 1st step dimensions for the #2 through #7 woods were derived by subtracting an additional ½'' for each successively shorter club.

[2]For each ½'' added to standard club length the shaft should be tipped an additional ½'' to maintain the standard flex unless a slightly softer feel is desired. In most cases it is doubtful that all but a highly accomplished player will feel these differences. It should also be noted that most manufacturers of blind bore woods simply pretrim the tip end in ½'' increments and install the shaft to the bottom of the hole. This is not necessarily wrong as individual club head designs, club lengths, head weights, etc. are all part of the overall club performance that the manufacturer may have desired and confirmed by testing.

[3]After the shaft is installed in a head with the back of heel to 1st step dimensions as shown below (normal installation) the finished club length is obtained by trimming from the shaft butt.

[4]To maintain the proper flexing characteristics in the tip area, the parallel tip Contour shaft should only be tip trimmed to ⅛'' increments for each ½'' reduction in club length.

True Temper® Parallel Tip Wood Shafts — Men's — [1]Back of Heel to 1st Step Dimension

Club No.	[2] [3]Finished Club Length (Traditional Standard)	[1]Amount Normally Trimmed From Tip of Shaft	Dynamic UDWX "X"	Dynamic Gold & Dynamic UDGWS & UDWS or UDWC "S"	Dynamic Gold & Dynamic UDGWR & UDWR or UDWC "R"	Dynamic UDWAL "A"	Jet Step UJWC "S"	Jet Step UJWC "R"	TT Lite U2LWS	TT Lite U2LWR
1	43''	0''	8''	10''	12''	11⅞''	10½''	12½''	11''	12½''
2	42½''	½''	7½''	9½''	11½''	11⅜''	10''	12''	10½''	12''
3	42''	1''	7''	9''	11''	10⅞''	9½''	11½''	10''	11½''
4	41½''	1½''	6½''	8½''	10½''	10⅜''	9''	11''	9½''	11''
5	41''	2''	6''	8''	10''	9⅞''	8½''	10½''	9''	10½''
6	40½''	2½''	5½''	7½''	9½''	9⅜''	8''	10''	8½''	10''
7	40''	3''	5''	7''	9''	8⅞''	7½''	9½''	8''	9½''

PARALLEL TIP WOOD SHAFTS

Club No.	[2][3]Finished Club Length (Traditional Standard)	[1]Amount Normally Trimmed From Tip of Shaft	TT Lite U2LWAL "A"	TT Lite UTTLWC "S"	TT Lite UTTLWC "R"	[4]Contour UTRWS	[4]Contour UTRWR	Metal Wood Heavy Tip Models [4]Contour UTRWS	Metal Wood Heavy Tip Models [4]Contour UTRWR
1	43"	0"	12"	10"	12"	11"	13"	9"	11"
2	42½"	½"	11½"	9½"	11½"	10⅞"	12⅞"	8⅞"	10⅞"
3	42"	1"	11"	9"	11"	10¾"	12¾"	8¾"	10¾"
4	41½"	1½"	10½"	8½"	10½"	10⅝"	12⅝"	8⅝"	10⅝"
5	41"	2"	10"	8"	10"	10½"	12½"	8½"	10½"
6	40½"	2½"	9½"	7½"	9½"	10⅜"	12⅜"	8⅜"	10⅜"
7	40"	3"	9"	7"	9"	10¼"	12¼"	8¼"	10¼"

PARALLEL TIP IRON SHAFTS — MEN'S

Brunswick Golf® Parallel Tip Iron Shafts — Men's — [1]Back of Heel to 1st Step Dimension

Club No.	[2][3]Finished Club Length (Traditional Standard)	[1]Amount Normally Trimmed From Tip of Shaft	Vanadium Sonic IX "X"	Vanadium Sonic IS "S"	Vanadium Sonic IR "R"	Phoenix IS "S"	Phoenix IR "R"	Phoenix IAL "A"	Microtaper UPMIC "S"	Microtaper UPMIC "R"
1	39"	0"	9⅞"	11⅜"	12⅞"	10"	12"	9"	13¼"	15¼"
2	38½"	½"	9⅜"	10⅞"	12⅜"	9½"	11½"	8½"	12¾"	14¾"
3	38"	1"	8⅞"	10⅜"	11⅞"	9"	11"	8"	12¼"	14¼"
4	37½"	1½"	8⅜"	9⅞"	11⅜"	8½"	10½"	7½"	11¾"	13¾"
5	37"	2"	7⅞"	9⅜"	10⅞"	8"	10"	7"	11¼"	13¼"
6	36½"	2½"	7⅜"	8⅞"	10⅜"	7½"	9½"	6½"	10¾"	12¾"
7	36"	3"	6⅞"	8⅜"	9⅞"	7"	9"	6"	10¼"	12¼"
8	35½"	3½"	6⅜"	7⅞"	9⅜"	6½"	8½"	5½"	9¾"	11¾"
9	35"	4"	5⅞"	7⅜"	8⅞"	6"	8"	6"	9¼"	11¼"
PW	35"	[4]4"	5⅞"	7⅜"	8⅞"	6"	8"	6"	9¼"	11¼"
SW	35"	[4]4"	5⅞"	7⅜"	8⅞"	6"	8"	6"	9¼"	11¼"

Club No.	[2][3]Finished Club Length (Traditional Standard)	[1]Amount Normally Trimmed From Tip of Shaft	Microtaper UPMIAL "A"	Propel II IRS "S"	Propel II IRS "R"	Propel II IAL "A"	Mark II IR "R"	Super Champion IR "R"	Champion IR "R"
1	39"	0"	N/A	11⅛"	13⅛"	13⅞"	13"	13¹⁵⁄₁₆"	12"
2	38½"	½"	14¾"	10⅝"	12⅝"	13⅜"	12½"	13⁷⁄₁₆"	11½"
3	38"	1"	14¼"	10⅛"	12⅛"	12⅞"	12"	12¹⁵⁄₁₆"	11"
4	37½"	1½"	13¾"	9⅝"	11⅝"	12⅜"	11½"	12⁷⁄₁₆"	10½"
5	37"	2"	13¼"	9⅛"	11⅛"	11⅞"	11"	11¹⁵⁄₁₆"	10"
6	36½"	2½"	12¾"	8⅝"	10⅝"	11⅜"	10½"	11⁷⁄₁₆"	9½"
7	36"	3"	12¼"	8⅛"	10⅛"	10⅞"	10"	10¹⁵⁄₁₆"	9"
8	35½"	3½"	11¾"	7⅝"	9⅝"	10⅜"	9½"	10⁷⁄₁₆"	8½"
9	35"	4"	11¼"	7⅛"	9⅛"	9⅞"	9"	9¹⁵⁄₁₆"	8"
PW	35"	[4]4"	11¼"	7⅛"	9⅛"	9⅞"	9"	9¹⁵⁄₁₆"	8"
SW	35"	[4]4"	11¼"	7⅛"	9⅛"	9⅞"	9"	9¹⁵⁄₁₆"	8"

PARALLEL TIP IRON SHAFTS — LADIES'

True Temper® Parallel Tip Iron Shafts — Ladies' — [1]Back of Heel to 1st Step Dimension

Club No.	[2][3]Finished Club Length (Traditional Std.)	[1]Amount Normally Trimmed From Tip of Shaft	Dynamic UDIAL "L"	Dynamic UDIALO "L"	TT Lite U2LIAL "L"	[5]Contour UTRIL "L"
2	37½"	0"	15⅞"	17¾"	11"	14½"
3	37"	½"	15⅜"	17¼"	10½"	14⅜"
4	36½"	1"	14⅞"	16¾"	10"	14¼"
5	36"	1½"	14⅜"	16¼"	9½"	14⅛"
6	35½"	2"	13⅞"	15¾"	9"	14"
7	35"	2½"	13⅜"	15¼"	8½"	13⅞"
8	34½"	3"	12⅞"	14¾"	8"	13¾"
9	34"	3½"	12⅜"	14¼"	7½"	13⅝"
PW	34"	[6]3½"	12⅜"	14¼"	7½"	13⅝"
SW	34"	[6]3½"	12⅜"	14¼"	7½"	13⅝"

(left margin, vertical) **TRUE TEMPER & BRUNSWICK GOLF — PARALLEL TIP WOOD & IRON SHAFTS — MEN'S AND LADIES' — BACK OF HEEL TO 1ST STEP**

Brunswick Golf® Parallel Tip Iron Shafts — Ladies' — ¹Back of Heel to 1st Step Dimension

Club No.	² ³Finished Club Length (Traditional Standard)	¹Amount Normally Trimmed From Tip of Shaft	Vanadium Sonic IL "L"	Phoenix IAL "L"	Propel II IAL "L"	Mark II IL "L"	Super Champion IL "L"	Champion IL "L"	Microtaper UPMIAL "L"
2	37½"	0"	13"	11"	15⅞"	13½"	16⅞"	11"	16¾"
3	37"	½"	12½"	10½"	15⅜"	13"	16⅜"	10½"	16¼"
4	36½"	1"	12"	10"	14⅞"	12½"	15⅞"	10"	15¾"
5	36"	1½"	11½"	9½"	14⅜"	12"	15⅜"	9½"	15¼"
6	35½"	2"	11"	9"	13⅞"	11½"	14⅞"	9"	14¾"
7	35"	2½"	10½"	8½"	13⅜"	11"	14⅜"	8½"	14¼"
8	34½"	3"	10"	8"	12⅞"	10½"	13⅞"	8"	13¾"
9	34"	3½"	9½"	7½"	12⅜"	10"	13⅜"	7½"	13¼"
PW	34"	⁶3½"	9½"	7½"	12⅜"	10"	13⅜"	7½"	13¼"
SW	34"	⁶3½"	9½"	7½"	12⅜"	10"	13⅜"	7½"	13¼"

PARALLEL TIP WOOD SHAFTS — MEN'S

Brunswick Golf® Parallel Tip Wood Shafts — Men's — ¹Back of Heel to 1st Step Dimension

Club No.	² ³Finished Club Length (Traditional Standard)	¹Amount Normally Trimmed From Tip of Shaft	Vanadium Sonic WX "X"	Vanadium Sonic WS "S"	Vanadium Sonic WR "R"	Phoenix WS "S"	Phoenix WR "R"	Phoenix WAL "A"	Microtaper UPMWC "S"	Microtaper UPMWC "R"
1	43"	0"	8½"	10¼"	12"	11"	12½"	11"	11¾"	13¾"
2	42½"	½"	8"	9¾"	11½"	10½"	12"	10½"	11¼"	13¼"
3	42"	1"	7½"	9¼"	11"	10"	11½"	10"	10¾"	12¾"
4	41½"	1½"	7"	8¾"	10½"	9½"	11"	9½"	10¼"	12¼"
5	41"	2"	6½"	8¼"	10"	9"	10½"	9"	9¾"	11¾"
6	40½"	2½"	6"	7¾"	9½"	8½"	10"	8½"	9¼"	11¼"
7	40"	3"	5½"	7¼"	9"	8"	9½"	8"	8¾"	10¾"

Club No.	² ³Finished Club Length (Traditional Standard)	¹Amount Normally Trimmed From Tip of Shaft	Microtaper UPMWAL "A"	Propel II WRS "S"	Propel II WRS "R"	Propel II WAL "A"	Mark II WR "R"	Super Champion WR "R"	Champion WR "R"
1	43"	0"	14"	10"	12"	10⅞"	10½"	9 15/16"	9½"
2	42½"	½"	13½"	9½"	11½"	10⅜"	10"	9 7/16"	9"
3	42"	1"	13"	9"	11"	9⅞"	9½"	8 15/16"	8½"
4	41½"	1½"	12½"	8½"	10½"	9⅜"	9"	8 7/16"	8"
5	41"	2"	12"	8"	10"	8⅞"	8½"	7 15/16"	7½"
6	40½"	2½"	11½"	7½"	9½"	8⅜"	8"	7 7/16"	7"
7	40"	3"	11"	7"	9"	7⅞"	7½"	6 15/16"	6½"

PARALLEL TIP WOOD SHAFTS — LADIES'

True Temper® Parallel Tip Wood Shafts — Ladies' — ¹Back of Heel to 1st Step Dimension

Club No.	² ³Finished Club Length (Traditional Std.)	¹Amount Normally Trimmed From Tip of Shaft	Dynamic UDWAL "L"	TT Lite U2LWAL "L"	⁴Contour UTRWL "L"	Metal Wood Heavy Tip Model ⁴Contour UTRWL "L"
1	42"	0"	12⅞"	13"	13½"	11½"
2	41½"	½"	12⅜"	12½"	13⅜"	11⅜"
3	41"	1"	11⅞"	12"	13¼"	11¼"
4	40½"	1½"	11⅜"	11½"	13⅛"	11⅛"
5	40"	2"	10⅞"	11"	13"	11"
6	39½"	2½"	10⅜"	10½"	12⅞"	10⅞"
7	39"	3"	9⅞"	10"	12¾"	10¾"

Brunswick Golf® Parallel Tip Wood Shafts — Ladies' — ¹Back of Heel to 1st Step Dimension

Club No.	² ³Finished Club Length (Traditional Standard)	¹Amount Normally Trimmed From Tip of Shaft	Vanadium Sonic WL "L"	Phoenix WAL "L"	Propel II WAL "L"	Mark II WL "L"	Super Champion WL "L"	Champion WL "L"	Microtaper UPMWAL "L"
1	42"	0"	12¼"	13"	12⅞"	12"	16¾"	15½"	15"
2	41½"	½"	11¾"	12½"	12⅜"	11½"	16¼"	15"	14½"
3	41"	1"	11¼"	12"	11⅞"	11"	15¾"	14½"	14"
4	40½"	1½"	10¾"	11½"	11⅜"	10½"	15¼"	14"	13½"
5	40"	2"	10¼"	11"	10⅞"	10"	14¾"	13½"	13"
6	39½"	2½"	9¾"	10½"	10⅜"	9½"	14¼"	13"	12½"
7	39"	3"	9¼"	10"	9⅞"	9"	13¾"	12½"	12"

METAL WOOD REINFORCED PARALLEL TIP SHAFTS — MEN'S & LADIES'

Club No.	Finished Club Length (Traditional Std.)	Uncut Shaft Length	Dynamic UDWRH "R"	Dynamic UDWSH "S"	TT Lite UTTLWCH "R"	TT Lite UTTLWCH "S"	TT Lite U2LWRH "R"	TT Lite U2LWSH "S"
1	43"	43"	9"	7"	9½"	7½"	11½"	9½"
2	42½"	43"	8½"	6½"	9"	7"	11"	9"
3	42"	43"	8"	6"	8½"	6½"	10½"	8½"
4	41½"	43"	7½"	5½"	8"	6"	10"	8"
5	41"	43"	7"	5"	7½"	5½"	9½"	7½"
6	40½"	43"	6½"	4½"	7"	5"	9"	7"
7	40"	43"	6"	4"	6½"	4½"	8½"	6½"

True Temper® Metal Wood Reinforced Parallel Tip Shafts — Men's and Ladies' — Back of Heel to 1st Step Dimension

Club No.	Finished Club Length (Traditional Std.)	Uncut Shaft Length for Flex Flow	Flex Flow UTFFWRH "R"	Flex Flow UTFFWSH "S"	Flex Flow UTFFWLH (Use Ladies' Std. Club Lengths)
1	43"	43"	10¼"	8¾"	11½"
2	42½"	43"	9¾"	8¼"	11"
3	42"	42"	9¼"	7¾"	10½"
4	41½"	41½"	8¾"	7¼"	10"
5	41"	41"	8¼"	6¾"	9½"
6	40½"	40½"	7¾"	6¼"	9"
7	40"	40½"	7¼"	5¾"	8½"

FLEX FLOW PARALLEL TIP WOOD & IRON SHAFTS — MEN'S & LADIES'

True Temper® Parallel Tip Wood and Iron Shafts — Men's and Ladies' — Back of Heel to 1st Step Dimension

Club No.	Finished Club Length (Traditional Standard) Men's	Ladies'	Uncut Shaft Length Men's	Ladies'	Flex Flow UTFFWS "S"	Flex Flow UTFFWR "R"	Flex Flow UTFFWA "A"	Flex Flow UTFFWL "L"
1	43"	42"	44"	44"	7¾"	9¼"	11½"	11½"
2	42½"	41½"	44"	44"	7¼"	8¾"	11"	11"
3	42"	41"	43"	43"	6¾"	8¼"	10½"	10½"
4	41½"	40½"	42½"	42½"	6¼"	7¾"	10"	10"
5	41"	40"	42"	42"	5¾"	7¼"	9½"	9½"
6	40½"	39½"	41½"	41½"	5¼"	6¾"	9"	9"
7	40"	39"	41½"	41½"	4¾"	6¼"	8½"	8½"

Club No.	Finished Club Length (Modern Standard) Men's	Ladies'	Uncut Shaft Length Men's	Ladies'	Flex Flow UTFFIS "S"	Flex Flow UTFFIR "R"	Flex Flow UTFFIA "A"	Flex Flow UTFFIL "L"
2	39"	38"	39"	38"	10½"	11¾"	12¾"	15"
3	38½"	37½"	38½"	37½"	10"	11¼"	12¼"	14½"
4	38"	37"	38"	37"	9½"	10¾"	11¾"	14"
5	37½"	36½"	37½"	36½"	9"	10¼"	11¼"	13½"
6	37"	36"	37"	36"	8½"	9¾"	10¾"	13"
7	36½"	35½"	36½"	35½"	8"	9¼"	10¼"	12½"
8	36"	35"	36"	35"	7½"	8¾"	9¾"	12"
9	35½"	34½"	35½"	34½"	7"	8¼"	9¼"	11½"
PW	35½"	34½"	35"	34"	6½"	7¾"	8¾"	11"
SW	35½"	34½"	35"	34"	6½"	7¾"	8¾"	11"

7 UNITED STATES GOLF ASSOCIATION RULES GOVERNING GOLF CLUB AND BALL DESIGN

The following Rules of Golf which apply to golf equipment have been reprinted through the courtesy of The United States Golf Association.

Rule 4. Clubs

If there may be any reasonable basis for doubt as to whether a club which is to be manufactured conforms with Rule 4 and Appendix II, the manufacturer should submit a sample to the United States Golf Association for a ruling, such sample to become its property for reference purposes. If a manufacturer fails to do so, he assumes the risk of a ruling that the club does not conform with the Rules of Golf.

A player in doubt as to the conformity of a club should consult the United States Golf Association.

4-1. Form and Make of Clubs

A club is an implement designed to be used for striking the ball.

A putter is a club designed primarily for use on the putting green.

The player's clubs shall conform with the provisions of this Rule and with the specifications and interpretations set forth in Appendix II.

a. GENERAL

The club shall be composed of a shaft and a head. All parts of the club shall be fixed so that the club is one unit. The club shall not be designed to be adjustable except for weight. The club shall not be substantially different from the traditional and customary form and make.

b. SHAFT

The shaft shall be generally straight, with the same bending and twisting properties in any direction, and shall be attached to the clubhead at the heel either directly or through a single plain neck or socket. A putter shaft may be atttached to any point in the head.

c. GRIP

The grip consists of that part of the shaft designed to be held by the player and any material added to it for the purpose of obtaining a firm hold. The grip shall be substantially straight and plain in form and shall not be molded for any part of the hands.

d. CLUBHEAD

The distance from the heel to toe of the clubhead shall be greater than the distance from the face to the back. The clubhead shall be generally plain in shape.

The clubhead shall have only one face designed for striking the ball, except that a putter may have two such faces if their characteristics are the same, they are opposite each other and the loft of each is the same and does not exceed 10 degrees.

e. CLUBFACE

The face shall not have any degree of concavity and, in relation to the ball, shall be hard and rigid. It shall be generally smooth except for such markings as are permitted by Appendix II. If the basic structural material of the head and face of a club, other than a putter, is metal, no inset or attachment is permitted.

f. WEAR

A club which conforms to Rule 4-1 when new is deemed to conform after wear through normal use. Any part of a club which has been purposely altered is regarded as new

and must conform, in the altered state, to the Rules.

g. DAMAGE

If a player's club ceases to conform with Rule 4-1 because of damage sustained in the normal course of play, the player may:

(i) use the club in its damaged state, but only for the remainder of the <u>stipulated round</u> during which such damage was sustained; or

(ii) without unduly delaying play, repair it.

A club which ceases to conform because of damage sustained other than in the normal course of play shall not subsequently be used during the round.

(Damage changing playing characteristics of club — see Rule 4-2.)

CLUBS

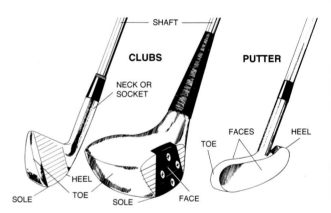

4-2. Playing Characteristics Changed

During a <u>stipulated round</u>, the playing characteristics of a club shall not be purposely changed.

If the playing characteristics of a player's club are changed during a round because of damage sustained in the normal course of play, the player may:

(i) use the club in its altered state; or

(ii) without unduly delaying play, repair it.

If the playing characteristics of a player's club are changed because of damage sustained other than in the normal course of play, the club shall not subsequently be used during the round.

Damage to a club which occurred prior to a round may be repaired during the round, provided the playing characteristics are not changed and play is not unduly delayed.

4-3. Foreign Material

No foreign material shall be applied to the clubface for the purpose of influencing the movement of the ball.

PENALTY FOR BREACH OF RULE 4-1, -2 or -3:
Disqualification.

Appendices II and III

Any design in a club or ball which is not covered by Rules 4 and 5 and Appendices II and III, or which might significantly change the nature of the game, will be ruled on by the United States Golf Association and the Royal and Ancient Golf Club of St. Andrews.

Note: Equipment approved for use or marketed prior to January 1, 1984 which conformed to the Rules in effect in 1983 but does not conform to the 1984 Rules may be used until December 31, 1989; thereafter all equipment must conform to the current Rules.

Appendix II
DESIGN OF CLUBS

Rule 4-1 prescribes general regulations for the design of clubs. The following paragraphs, which provide some detailed specifications and clarify how Rule 4-1 is interpreted, should be read in conjunction with this Rule.

4-1b. Shaft

GENERALLY STRAIGHT

The shaft shall be at least 18 inches (457mm) in length. It shall be straight from the top of the grip to a point not more than 5 inches (127mm) above the sole, measured along the axis of the shaft and the neck or socket.

BENDING AND TWISTING PROPERTIES

The shaft must be so designed and manufactured that at any point along its length:

(i) it bends in such a way that the deflection is the same regardless of how the shaft is rotated about its longitudinal axis; and

(ii) it twists the same amount in both directions.

ATTACHMENT TO CLUBHEAD

The neck or socket must not be more than 5 inches (127mm) in length, measured from the top of the neck or socket to the sole along its axis. The shaft and the neck or socket must remain in line with the heel, or with a point to the right or left of the heel, when the club is viewed in the address position. The distance between the axis of the shaft or the neck or socket and the back of the heel must not exceed 0.625 inches (16mm).

Exception for Putters: The shaft or neck or socket of a putter may be fixed at any point in the head and need not remain in line with the heel. The axis of the shaft from the top to a point not more than 5 inches (127mm) above the sole must diverge from the vertical in the toe-heel plane by at least 10 degrees when the club is in its normal address position.

4-1c. Grip

(i) For clubs other than putters, the grip must be generally circular in cross-section, except that a continuous, straight, slightly raised rib may be incorporated along the full length of the grip.

(ii) A putter grip may have a non-circular cross-section, provided the cross-section has no concavity and remains generally similar throughout the length of the grip.

(iii) The grip may be tapered but must not have any bulge or waist.

(iv) For clubs other than putters the axis of the grip must coincide with the axis of the shaft.

GRIPS

CLUB GRIP CIRCULAR

PUTTER GRIP FLAT SIDE (Permitted on putters only)

4-1d. Clubhead

DIMENSIONS

The dimensions of a clubhead (see diagram) are measured, with the clubhead in its normal address position, on horizontal lines between vertical projections of the outermost points of (i) the heel and the toe and (ii) the face and the back. If the outermost point of the heel is not clearly defined, it is deemed to be 0.625 inches (16mm) above the horizontal plane on which the club is resting in its normal address position.

PLAIN IN SHAPE

The clubhead shall be generally plain in shape. All parts shall be rigid, structural in nature and functional.

Features such as holes through the head, windows or transparencies, or appendages to the main body of the head such as plates, rods or fins for the purpose of meeting dimensional specifications, for aiming or for any other purpose are not permitted. Exceptions may be made for putters.

Any furrows in or runners on the sole shall not extend into the face.

4-1e. Clubface

HARDNESS AND RIGIDITY

The clubface must not be designed and manufactured to have the effect at impact of a spring which would unduly influence the movement of the ball.

MARKINGS

Except for specified markings, the surface roughness must not exceed that of decorative sandblasting. Markings must not have sharp edges or raised lips, as determined by a finger test. Markings within the area where impact is intended (the "impact area") are governed by the following:

(i) *Grooves.* A series of straight grooves with diverging sides and a symmetrical cross-section may be used. (See diagram.) The width and cross-section must be generally consistent across the face of the club and along the length of the grooves. Any rounding of groove edges shall be in the form of a radius which does not exceed 0.020 inches (0.5mm). The width of the grooves shall not exceed 0.035 inches (0.9mm), using the 30 degree method of measurement on file with the United States Golf Association. The distance between edges of adjacent grooves must not be less than three times the width of a groove, and not less than 0.075 inches (1.9mm). The depth of a groove must not exceed 0.020 inches (0.5mm).

GROOVES

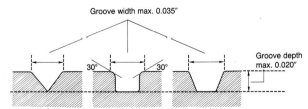

Groove width max. 0.035″

Groove depth max. 0.020″

EXAMPLES OF PERMISSIBLE GROOVE CROSS-SECTIONS

(ii) *Punch Marks.* Punch marks may be used. The area of any such mark must not exceed 0.0044 square inches (2.8 sq. mm). A mark must not be closer to an adjacent mark than 0.168 inches (4.3mm), measured from center to center. The depth of a punch mark must not exceed 0.040 inches (1.0mm). If punch marks are used in combination with grooves, a punch mark may not be closer to a groove than 0.168 inches (4.3mm), measured from center to center.

DECORATIVE MARKINGS

The center of the impact area may be indicated by a design

within the boundary of a square whose sides are 0.375 inches (9.5mm) in length. Such a design must not unduly influence the movement of the ball. Markings outside the impact area must not be greater than 0.040 inches (1.0mm) in depth and width.

NON-METALLIC CLUBFACE MARKINGS

The above specifications for markings do not apply to non-metallic clubs with loft angles less than 24 degrees, but markings which could unduly influence the movement of the ball are prohibited. Non-metallic clubs with a loft or face angle exceeding 24 degrees may have grooves of maximum width 0.040 inches (1.0mm) and maximum depth 1½ times the groove width, but must otherwise conform to the markings specifications above.

Appendix III
THE BALL

a. WEIGHT
The weight of the ball shall not be greater than 1.620 ounces avoirdupois (45.93gm).

b. SIZE
The diameter of the ball shall be not less than 1.680 inches (42.67mm). This specification will be satisfied if, under its own weight, a ball falls through a 1.680 inches diameter ring gauge in fewer than 25 out of 100 randomly selected positions, the test being carried out at a temperature of 23±1°C.

c. SPHERICAL SYMMETRY
The ball shall be designed and manufactured to perform in general as if it were spherically symmetrical.

As outlined in procedures on file at the United States Golf Association, differences in peak angle of trajectory, carry and time of flight will be measured when 40 balls of the same type are launched, spinning 20 about one axis and 20 about another axis.

These tests will be performed using apparatus approved by the United States Golf Association. If in two successive tests differences in the same two or more measurements are statistically significant at the 5% level of significance and exceed the limits set forth below, the ball type will not conform to the symmetry specification.

MEASUREMENT	MAXIMUM ABSOLUTE DIFFERENCE OF THE MEANS
Peak angle of trajectory	0.9 grid units (approx. 0.4 degrees)
Carry distance	2.5 yards
Flight time	0.16 seconds

Note: Methods of determining whether a ball performs as if it were generally spherically symmetrical may be subject to change as instrumentation becomes available to measure other properties accurately, such as the aerodynamic coefficient of lift, coefficient of drag and moment of inertia.

d. INITIAL VELOCITY
The velocity of the ball shall not be greater than 250 feet (76.2m) per second when measured on apparatus approved by the United States Golf Association. A maximum tolerance of 2% will be allowed. The temperature of the ball when tested shall be 23±1°C.

e. OVERALL DISTANCE STANDARD
A brand of golf ball, when tested on apparatus approved by the USGA on the outdoor range at the USGA Headquarters under the conditions set forth in the Overall Distance Standard for golf balls on file with the USGA, shall not cover an average distance in carry and roll exceeding 280 yards plus a tolerance of 6%. *Note:* The 6% tolerance will be reduced to a minimum of 4% as test techniques are improved.

Exception: In international team competitions, the size of the ball shall not be less than 1.620 inches (41.15mm) in diameter and the Overall Distance Standard shall not apply if the diameter of the ball is less than 1.680 inches (42.67mm).

Note: The Rules of the Royal and Ancient Golf Club of St. Andrews provide for the same specifications as those set forth above except that the size of the ball must not be less than 1.620 inches (41.15mm) in diameter and there is no Overall Distance Standard.

NOTES

GOLF CLUB MANUFACTURERS' STANDARD LENGTH, LOFT AND LIE SPECIFICATIONS

This reference material includes most manufacturers' standard specifications and will save time in comparing, checking or resetting lofts, lies and lengths of both men's and ladies' woods and irons.

The information here includes the original published loft, lie and length specifications from the 1974 and 1982 editions of *Golf Club Design, Fitting, Alteration & Repair* and it also includes the latest available specifications from the golf club manufacturers. In this manner, as additional editions of this book are published in the future, the historical information will expand using these easy-to-use reference tables.

The specifications were derived from the latest manufacturers' published data or obtained from phone calls to the companies. In some cases manufacturers do not make this information available or they have recently stopped publishing part or all of this information. If this was the case, the latest published specifications were used.

Listed in the manufacturers' name column is the model year for which the data applies. Remember that manufacturers' specifications are not often changed, thus making the data valid for a number of years. Since most manufacturers' standard specifications of loft, lie and length apply to 90 to 100% of the models they offer, the information here is mostly listed by manufacturer; however, many individual models are also listed.

It is very interesting to study and compare the specifications from manufacturer to manufacturer listed here.

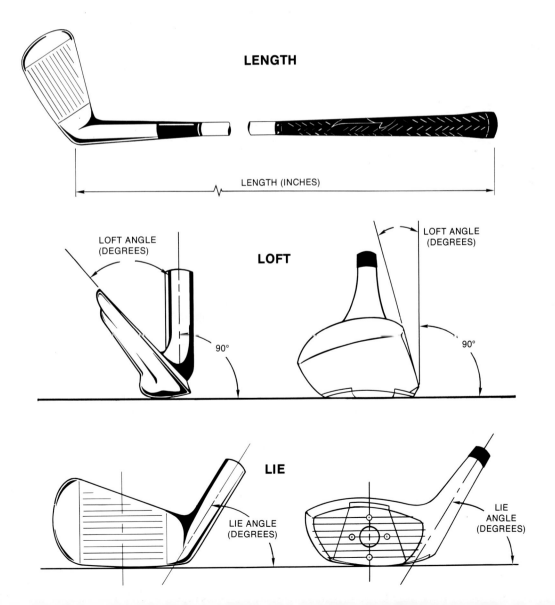

LENGTH — MEN'S

GOLF CLUB MANUFACTURERS' STANDARD SPECIFICATIONS — DATA FROM 1974 DESIGN BOOK

Mfgr. & Year Specs. Published		#1 Wood	#2 Wood	#3 Wood	#4 Wood	#5 Wood	#2 Iron	#3 Iron	#4 Iron	#5 Iron	#6 Iron	#7 Iron	#8 Iron	#9 Iron	Pitch Wedge	Sand Wedge
Acushnet	(1973)	43	43	42½	42	41¾	38¾	38¼	37¾	37¼	36½	36¾	36¼	35¾	35¼	35¼
Dunlop	(1973)	48⅜	42⅞	42⅜	41⅞	41⅝	38½	38	37½	37	36½	36	35¾	35½	35	35
Faultless	(1974)	43	42½	42	41½	41	38½	38	37½	37	36½	36	35½	35	35	35
H & B	(1973)	43	42½	42	41½	41½	38½	38	37½	37	36½	36	35½	35	35	35
MacGregor	(1972)	43	42¾	42½	42	42	38½	38	37½	37	36½	36	35¾	35½	35	35
Northwestern	(1973)	43	42½	42	41½	41	38½	38	37½	37	36½	36	35½	35	35	35
P.G.A.	(1972)	43	42½	42	41½	41¼	38½	38	37½	37	36½	36	35¾	35½	35	35
First Flight	(1974)	43	42½	42	41½	41	38½	38	37½	37	36½	36	35½	35	35	35
Pro-Dyn	(1974)	43	—	42	41½	41¼	38½	38	37½	37	36½	36	35½	35	35	35
Ram	(1973)	43	—	42	41½	41	38½	38	37½	37	36½	36	35½	35	35	35
Royal	(1974)	43	42½	42	41½	41¼	38½	38	37½	37	36½	36	35½	35	35	35
Spalding	(1974)	43	42⁹/₁₆	42⅛	41¹¹/₁₆	41¼	38⅝	38³/₁₆	37¾	37⁵/₁₆	36⅞	36⁷/₁₆	36	35⁹/₁₆	35⅛	34⅝
Hagen	(1974)	43	42½	42	41½	41¼	38½	38	37½	37	36½	36¼	35¾	35¼	35	35
Wilson	(1974)	43	42½	42	41½	41¼	38½	38	37½	37	36½	36¼	35¾	35¼	35¼	35¼

LOFT — MEN'S

GOLF CLUB MANUFACTURERS' STANDARD SPECIFICATIONS — DATA FROM 1974 DESIGN BOOK

Mfgr. & Year Specs. Published		#1 Wood	#2 Wood	#3 Wood	#4 Wood	#5 Wood	#2 Iron	#3 Iron	#4 Iron	#5 Iron	#6 Iron	#7 Iron	#8 Iron	#9 Iron	Pitch Wedge	Sand Wedge
Acushnet	(1973)	11	14	17	20	22	22	25	28	31	35	39	43	47	51	55
Dunlop	(1973)	11	14	17	19	22	21	24	28	32	36	40	44	48	52	56
Faultless	(1974)	12	—	15	18	21	20	24	28	32	36	40	44	48	52	56
H & B	(1973)	11	13	16	19	21	20	24	28	32	36	40	44	48	52	58
MacGregor	(1972)	11	13	15½	18½	22	22	25	28	32	36	38½	43	45	49	56
Northwestern	(1973)	11	14	16	19	22	21	24	27	31	35	39	43	47	51	55
P.G.A.	(1972)	11	14	17	20	22	21	23	26	29	33	37	41	45	50	54
First Flight	(1974)	12½	14	17	20	23	21	24	27	31	35	39	43	47	51	55
Pro-Dyn	(1974)	12	—	16½	19½	22½	21	24	27	30	34	38	42	46	51	57
Ram	(1973)	11	—	16.5	19.2	22	21	24.3	27.8	31.5	35.3	39.2	43.3	47.5	51.6	56.7
Royal	(1974)	11	14	17	19	21	21	24	27	31	35	39	43	47	51	57
Spalding	(1974)	11	13	16	19	22	20	23	27	31	35	39	43	47	52	58
Hagen	(1974)	11	16	17	19	21	21	24	27	31	35	39	43	47	51	55
Wilson	(1974)	11	14	16	19	21	21	24	27	31	35	39	43	47	51	55

LIE — MEN'S

GOLF CLUB MANUFACTURERS' STANDARD SPECIFICATIONS — DATA FROM 1974 DESIGN BOOK

Mfgr. & Year Specs. Published		#1 Wood	#2 Wood	#3 Wood	#4 Wood	#5 Wood	#2 Iron	#3 Iron	#4 Iron	#5 Iron	#6 Iron	#7 Iron	#8 Iron	#9 Iron	Pitch Wedge	Sand Wedge
Acushnet	(1973)	54	54	55	56	56	57	58	59	60	61	62	63	63	64	64
Dunlop	(1973)	55	55	56	56	57	58	59	60	61	62	63	64	65	65	64
Faultless	(1974)	54	54½	55	55½	56	57	58	59	60	61	62	63	64	64	64
H & B	(1973)	55	55	56	57	57	57	58	59	60	61	62	63	64	64	64
MacGregor	(1972)	53	53	54	54½	54½	58	59	60	60½	61	62	62	62	62	63
Northwestern	(1973)	53	53½	54	54½	55	58	59	60	61	62	63	64	65	65	65
P.G.A.	(1972)	54	54	55	55	55	58	59	60	61	61½	62	62½	63	63	63
First Flight	(1974)	54	54	55	56	56	57	58	59	60	61	62	63	63	63	63
Pro-Dyn	(1974)	54	—	55	55	55	57	58	59	60	61	62	63	63	64	64
Ram	(1973)	54	—	55.6	56	56.3	56.7	57.5	58.2	59	60	60.9	61.7	62.6	62.6	62.6
Royal	(1974)	56	56	57	57	57	56	57	58	59	60	61	62	62	63	63
Spalding	(1974)	56	—	56¾	57	57¼	58½	58¾	59¼	59¾	60¼	60½	61¼	62	63	63
Hagen	(1974)	56	56	57	57	57	57	58	59	60	61	62	63	63	64	64
Wilson	(1974)	55	55	55½	56	56	57	58	59	60	61	62	63	63	64	64

LENGTH — LADIES'

GOLF CLUB MANUFACTURERS' STANDARD SPECIFICATIONS — DATA FROM 1974 DESIGN BOOK

Mfgr. & Year Specs. Published	#1 Wood	#2 Wood	#3 Wood	#4 Wood	#5 Wood	#2 Iron	#3 Iron	#4 Iron	#5 Iron	#6 Iron	#7 Iron	#8 Iron	#9 Iron	Pitch Wedge	Sand Wedge
Length:															
Acushnet (1973)	41½	41½	41	40½	40¼	37½	37	36½	36	35½	35¼	35	34½	34½	34½
Dunlop (1973)	42	41½	41	40½	40¼	37½	37	36½	36	35½	35	34¾	34½	34	34
Faultless (1974)	42	—	41	40½	40	—	37½	37	36½	36	35½	35	34½	34½	34½
MacGregor (1972)	42	41¾	41½	41	41	38	37½	37	36½	36	35½	35¼	35	34½	34½
P.G.A. (1972)	42	41½	41	40½	40	—	37½	37	36½	36	35½	35¼	35	34½	34½
Ram (1973)	41½	41	40½	40	39	37½	37	36½	36	35½	35	34½	34	34	34
Royal (1974)	42	—	41½	41	40½	—	—	—	—	—	—	—	—	—	—
Spalding (1974)	42	41⁹⁄₁₆	41⅛	40¹¹⁄₁₆	40¼	37⅝	37³⁄₁₆	36¾	36⁵⁄₁₆	35⅞	35⁷⁄₁₆	35	34⁹⁄₁₆	34⅛	33⅝

LOFT — LADIES'

GOLF CLUB MANUFACTURERS' STANDARD SPECIFICATIONS — DATA FROM 1974 DESIGN BOOK

Mfgr. & Year Specs. Published	#1 Wood	#2 Wood	#3 Wood	#4 Wood	#5 Wood	#2 Iron	#3 Iron	#4 Iron	#5 Iron	#6 Iron	#7 Iron	#8 Iron	#9 Iron	Pitch Wedge	Sand Wedge
Loft															
Acushnet (1973)	12	15	18	21	23	21	24	27	31	35	39	43	47	51	55
Dunlop (1973)	12	15	17	19	22	20	22½	26½	30½	34½	38½	42½	46½	50½	56
Faultless (1974)	12	—	17	20	23	—	24	28	32	36	40	44	48	52	56
MacGregor (1972)	12	15	18	20	23	22	25	28	32	36	38½	43	45	50	55
P.G.A. (1972)	13	15	18	20	22	—	23	26	29	33	37	41	45	50	54
Ram (1973)	12.5	14	16.5	19.2	22	21	24.3	27.8	31.5	35.3	39.2	43.3	47.5	56.6	56.7
Royal (1974)	12	—	17	20	22	—	24	27	31	35	39	43	47	51	57
Spalding (1974)	13	—	19	—	22	20	23	27	31	35	39	43	47	52	58

LIE — LADIES'

GOLF CLUB MANUFACTURERS' STANDARD SPECIFICATIONS — DATA FROM 1974 DESIGN BOOK

Mfgr. & Year Specs. Published	#1 Wood	#2 Wood	#3 Wood	#4 Wood	#5 Wood	#2 Iron	#3 Iron	#4 Iron	#5 Iron	#6 Iron	#7 Iron	#8 Iron	#9 Iron	Pitch Wedge	Sand Wedge
Lie:															
Acushnet (1973)	54	54	55	56	56	57	58	59	60	61	62	63	63	64	64
Dunlop (1973)	55	55	56	56	57	58	59	60	61	62	63	64	65	65	64
Faultless (1974)	54	—	55	55½	56	—	57	58	59	60	61	62	63	63	63
MacGregor (1972)	53	53	53½	54½	54	58	59	60	60½	61	62	62	62	64	65
P.G.A. (1972)	54	54	55	55	55	—	59	60	61	61½	62	62½	63	63	63
Ram (1973)	55.5	55.8	56	56.5	57	57.6	58.4	59.1	60	61	61.9	62.6	63.5	63.5	63.5
Royal (1974)	56	—	57	57	57	—	58	59	60	61	62	63	63	64	64
Spalding (1974)	55	—	56	—	56½	58½	58¾	59¼	59¾	60¼	60½	61¼	62	63	63

NOTE: Some manufacturers who publish men's specifications do not publish ladies' specifications.

LADIES' — LENGTH, LOFT & LIE — EARLY & MID 1970'S

LENGTH — MEN'S

GOLF CLUB MANUFACTURERS STANDARD SPECIFICATIONS

Mfgr. & Year Specs. Published		#1 Wood	#2 Wood	#3 Wood	#4 Wood	#5 Wood	#6 Wood	#7 Wood	#1 Iron	#2 Iron	#3 Iron	#4 Iron	#5 Iron	#6 Iron	#7 Iron	#8 Iron	#9 Iron	Pitch Wedge	Sand Wedge
Ajay Double Eagle	(1977)	43	—	42	41½	41	—	—	—	38½	38	37½	37	36½	36	35½	35	35	35
Browning	(1980)	43	—	42	41½	41	—	—	39½	39	38½	38	37½	37	36½	36	35½	35½	—
Cobra Low Profile	(1982)	—	—	—	—	—	—	—	39½	39	38½	38	37½	37	36½	36	35½	35¼	35
Cobra Premier Iron	(1982)	—	—	—	—	—	—	—	39½	39	38½	38	37½	37	36½	36	35½	35¼	35
Cobra Tour Model	(1982)	—	—	—	—	—	—	—	39½	39	38½	38	37½	37	36½	36	35½	35½	35¼
Confidence	(1977)	43	—	42	41½	41	—	—	39	38½	38	37½	37	36½	36	35½	35	35	35
Dunlop Australian Blade	(1978)	—	—	—	—	—	—	—	39½	39	38½	38	37½	37	36½	36	35½	35	35
Dunlop Maxfli Woods	(1978)	43⅜	42⅞	42⅜	41⅜	41⅛	—	41⅛	39½	39	38½	38	37½	37	36½	36	35½	35	35
Walter Hagen The Haig	(1982)	43	42½	42	41½	41¼	—	41	—	39	38½	38	37½	37	36¾	36¼	35¾	35½	35½
Hogan Apex	(1978)	43¼	—	42¼	41¾	41¼	—	—	39¾	39¼	38¾	38½	37¾	37¼	36¾	36¼	35¾	35½	—
Hogan Director	(1978)	43¼	—	42¼	41¾	41¼	—	—	—	39¼	38¾	38¼	37¾	37¼	36¾	36¼	35¾	35½	—
Hogan Medallion	(1978)	43¼	—	42¼	41¾	41¼	—	—	—	39¼	38¾	38¼	37¾	37¼	36¾	36¼	35¾	35½	—
Hogan Producer	(1978)	43¼	42¾	42¼	41¾	41¼	—	40¼	—	39¼	38¾	38¼	37¾	37¼	36¾	36¼	35¾	35½	—
MacGregor M693 Woods	(1982)	43¼	—	42¾	42¾	42¼	—	—	—	—	—	—	—	—	—	—	—	—	—
MacGregor M85 Woods	(1982)	43¼	—	42¾	42¼	41¼	—	—	—	—	—	—	—	—	—	—	—	—	—
MacGregor MT Woods/Irons	(1982)	43¼	—	42¾	42¼	42¼	—	—	39¾	39¼	38¾	38¼	37¾	37¼	36¾	36½	36¼	35¾	35¾
MacGregor MCX Woods/Irons	(1982)	43¼	—	42¾	42¼	42¼	—	42¼	—	39¼	38¾	38¼	37¾	37¼	36¾	36½	36¼	36	35¾
MacGregor Limited Edition	(1982)	43¼	—	42¾	42¼	42¼	—	—	39¾	39¼	38¾	38¼	37¾	37¼	36¾	36½	36¼	35¾	35¾
Northwestern	(1982)	43	42½	42	41½	41	—	40	39	38½	38	37½	37	36½	36	35½	35	35	35
P.G.A. Emblem	(1982)	43¼	—	42¼	41¾	41¼	—	40¾	—	38½	38	37½	37	36½	36	35½	35	35	35
P.G.A. Tommy Armour	(1982)	43½	—	42½	42	41¾	—	—	39½	39	38½	38	37½	37	36½	36	35½	35	35
P.G.A. Performer	(1982)	43¼	—	42¼	41¾	41¼	—	40¾	—	39	38½	38	37½	37	36½	36	35½	35½	35½
P.G.A. Concept LCG	(1982)	43	—	42	41½	41¼	—	40¾	—	38½	$38\frac{1}{16}$	37⅝	$37\frac{3}{16}$	36¾	$36\frac{5}{16}$	35⅞	$35\frac{7}{16}$	35	35
P.G.A. Ryder Cup II	(1982)	43	—	42	41½	41¼	—	40¾	—	39	38½	38	37½	37	36½	36	35½	35	35
Pedersen	(1978)	43	42¾	42¼	42	41½	—	41	39	38½	38	37½	37	36½	36	35½	35	35	35
Toney Penna	(1980)	43	—	42½	42	41½	—	—	39½	39	38½	38	37½	37	36½	36	35½	35	35
Penna Driver Model JS	(1980)	43	—	—	—	—	—	—	—	—	—	—	—	—	—	—	—	—	—
Penna Driver Model I	(1980)	43	—	—	—	—	—	—	—	—	—	—	—	—	—	—	—	—	—

GOLF CLUB MANUFACTURERS STANDARD SPECIFICATIONS

Mfgr. & Year Specs. Published		#1 Wood	#2 Wood	#3 Wood	#4 Wood	#5 Wood	#6 Wood	#7 Wood	#1 Iron	#2 Iron	#3 Iron	#4 Iron	#5 Iron	#6 Iron	#7 Iron	#8 Iron	#9 Iron	Pitch Wedge	Sand Wedge
Penna Driver Model 2 + 65	(1980)	43	—	—	—	—	—	—	—	—	—	—	—	—	—	—	—	—	—
Penna Driver Model 12	(1980)	43	—	—	—	—	—	—	—	—	—	—	—	—	—	—	—	—	—
Pinseeker (Length only)	(1978)	43	42½	42	41½	41¼	—	—	39½	39	38½	38	37½	37	36½	36	35½	35½	35¼
PowerBilt/All	(1982)	43	42½	42	41½	41½	—	—	39½	39	38½	38	37½	37	36½	36	35½	35½	35½
Pro-Dyn	(1977)	43	—	42	41½	41	—	40½	39	38½	38	37½	37	36½	36	35½	35	35	35
Pro Group	(1982)	43	42½	42	41½	41	—	—	39½	39	38½	38	37½	37	36½	36	35½	35½	—
Ram Accubar	(1982)	43½	—	42½	42	41½	—	—	—	39	38½	38	37½	37	36½	36	35½	35½	35½
Ram Golden Ram, Tour Grind	(1982)	43½	—	43	42½	42	—	—	39½	39	38½	38	37½	37	36½	36	35½	35½	35½
Rawlings RXP	(1980)	43	—	42	41½	41	—	—	—	39	38½	38	37½	37	36½	36	35½	35½	35½
Royal Edge	(1978)	43½	—	42½	42	41¾	—	—	—	39	38½	38	37½	37	36½	36	35½	35	35
Royal Impact	(1978)	43½	—	42½	42	41¾	—	41	—	39	38½	38	37½	37	36½	36	35½	35	35
Sigma Tiger Shark	(1982)	41½	—	41	—	40½	—	40	—	—	37¼	37	36¾	36½	36¼	36	35¾	35½	35⅛
Slotline	(1982)	43	—	42	41½	41	—	—	39½	39	38½	38	37½	37	36½	36	35½	35¼	35⅛
Spalding Elite	(1982)	43¼	—	42¼	41¾	41¼	—	—	39½	39	38½	38	37½	37	36½	36	35½	35	35
Spalding XL4	(1982)	43¼	—	42¼	41¾	41¼	—	—	39½	39	38½	38	37½	37	36½	36	35½	35	35
Spalding Top Flite	(1982)	43¼	—	42¼	41¾	41¼	—	—	39½	39	38½	38	37½	37	36½	36	35½	35	35
Spalding Executive	(1982)	43	—	42⅛	$41\frac{11}{16}$	41¼	—	—	$39\frac{1}{16}$	38⅝	$38\frac{3}{16}$	37¾	$37\frac{5}{16}$	36⅞	$36\frac{7}{16}$	36	$35\frac{9}{16}$	35⅛	$34\frac{11}{16}$
Square Z	(1978)	43	—	42	41½	41	—	—	39	38½	38	37½	37	36½	36	35½	35	35½	35½
Taylor Made Golf	(1982)	43	—	42	41½	41	—	41	39½	39	38½	38	37½	37	36½	36	35½	35½	35½
Titleist Pro 100	(1976)	43	43	42½	42	41¾	—	—	39½	39	38½	38	37½	37	36½	36	35½	35½	—
Titleist AC-108	(1976)	43	43	42½	42	41¾	—	—	—	38¾	38¼	37¾	37¼	36⅞	36½	36	35½	35¼	35¼
Unique	(1982)	43	—	42	41½	41	—	—	39½	39	38½	38	37½	37	36½	36	35½	35½	35½
Wilson Staff	(1982)	43	42½	42	41½	41¼	—	41	39	38½	38	37½	37	36½	36¼	35¾	35¼	35	35
Wilson Aggressor	(1982)	43	42½	42	41½	41¼	—	41	39	38½	38	37½	37	36½	36¼	35¾	35¼	35	35
Wilson X-31	(1982)	43	42½	42	41½	41¼	—	41	—	39	38½	38	37½	37	36½	36	35½	35	35
Wilson 1200 GE	(1982)	43	42½	42	41½	41¼	—	41	—	39	38½	38	37½	37	36½	36	35½	35	35½
Wilson Reflex	(1982)	43	42½	42	41½	41¼	—	41	—	39	38½	38	37½	37	36¾	36¼	35¾	35	35½
Stan Thompson	(1982)	43	43	42½	42	41½	—	41	—	39	38½	38	37½	37	36½	36	35½	35½	35½

LOFT — MEN'S

GOLF CLUB MANUFACTURERS STANDARD SPECIFICATIONS

Mfgr. & Year Specs. Published		#1 Wood	#2 Wood	#3 Wood	#4 Wood	#5 Wood	#6 Wood	#7 Wood	#1 Iron	#2 Iron	#3 Iron	#4 Iron	#5 Iron	#6 Iron	#7 Iron	#8 Iron	#9 Iron	Pitch Wedge	Sand Wedge
Ajay Double Eagle	(1977)	11	—	16	19	21	—	—	—	21	24	27	31	35	39	43	47	51	55
Browning	(1980)	11	—	16	19	22	—	—	17	20	23	26	29	32	36	40	44	49	—
Cobra Low Profile	(1982)	—	—	—	—	—	—	—	17	20	23	26	29	32	36	40	44	48	55
Cobra Premier Iron	(1982)	—	—	—	—	—	—	—	17	19	22	25	29	33	37	41	45	49	56
Cobra Tour Model	(1982)	11	14	16	19	22	—	—	17	19	22	25	29	33	37	41	45	49	56
Confidence	(1977)	11	—	17	19	21	—	—	17	20	23	26	29	33	37	41	45	49	54
Dunlop Australian Blade	(1978)	—	—	—	—	—	—	—	17	20	23	27	31	35	39	42	47	51	57
Dunlop Maxfli	(1978)	11	14	16	19	22	—	28	17	20	23	27	31	35	39	42	47	51	57
Walter Hagen The Haig	(1982)	11	14	16	19	21	—	25	17	20	23	26	30	34	38	42	46	50	55
Hogan Apex	(1978)	10½	—	15½	18½	21½	—	—	—	19½	23	26½	30	33½	37	41	45	50	—
Hogan Director	(1978)	11	—	17	19	21½	—	—	—	19½	23	26½	30	33½	37	41	45	50	—
Hogan Medallion	(1978)	11½	—	17	19	21½	—	—	—	19½	23	26½	30	33½	37	41	45	50	—
Hogan Producer	(1978)	12	15	17	19	21½	—	25½	—	19½	23	26½	30	33½	37	41	45	50	—
MacGregor M693 Woods	(1982)	10	—	15	18	21	—	—	—	—	—	—	—	—	—	—	—	—	—
MacGregor M85 Woods	(1982)	10	—	15½	18½	22	—	—	—	—	—	—	—	—	—	—	—	—	—
MacGregor MT Woods/Irons	(1982)	10	—	15	18	21	—	—	17	20	23	26	29	33	37	41	46	51	56
MacGregor MCX Woods/Irons	(1982)	12	—	15½	18½	22	—	24½	—	18	21	24	27	31	36	40	44	48	55
MacGregor Limited Edition	(1982)	10	—	15	18	21	—	—	17	20	23	26	29½	33	37	41	45	51	55
Northwestern	(1982)	11	13	16	19	21	—	24	17	20	23	27	31	35	39	43	47	51	56
P.G.A. Emblem	(1982)	12	—	17	20	22	—	25	—	19	22	25	28½	32	36	40	44	48	55
P.G.A. Tommy Armour	(1982)	11	—	16	19	21	—	—	18	20	23	26	29	32	36	40	44	49	56
P.G.A. Performer	(1982)	12	—	17	20	22	—	25	—	19	22	25	28½	32	36	40	44	48	55
P.G.A. Concept LCG	(1982)	12	—	17	20	22	—	25	—	20	23	26	30	34	38	42	46	51	56
P.G.A. Ryder Cup II	(1982)	12	—	17	20	22	—	25	—	21	23	26	29	33	36	39	42	47	54
Pedersen	(1978)	11½	15	18	21	24	—	29	18	20	23	26	30	34	38	42	46	50	55
Toney Penna	(1980)	11	—	15	18	21	—	—	13	15	18	21	25	28	31	34	37	42	47
Penna Driver Model JS	(1980)	11	—	—	—	—	—	—	—	—	—	—	—	—	—	—	—	—	—
Penna Driver Model I	(1980)	9½	—	—	—	—	—	—	—	—	—	—	—	—	—	—	—	—	—

GOLF CLUB MANUFACTURERS STANDARD SPECIFICATIONS

Mfgr. & Year Specs. Published		#1 Wood	#2 Wood	#3 Wood	#4 Wood	#5 Wood	#6 Wood	#7 Wood	#1 Iron	#2 Iron	#3 Iron	#4 Iron	#5 Iron	#6 Iron	#7 Iron	#8 Iron	#9 Iron	Pitch Wedge	Sand Wedge
Penna Driver Model 2 + 65	(1980)	11	—	—	—	—	—	—	—	—	—	—	—	—	—	—	—	—	—
Penna Driver Model 12	(1980)	12	—	—	—	—	—	—	—	—	—	—	—	—	—	—	—	—	—
PowerBilt/All	(1982)	11	14	17	20	22	—	—	18	20	24	28	32	35	38	41	44	50	56
Pro-Dyn	(1977)	12	—	16½	19½	22½	—	28	18	21	24	27	30	34	38	42	46	51	57
Pro Group	(1982)	11½	14	17	20	23	—	—	18	21	24	27	30	34	38	41	45	49	—
Ram Accubar	(1982)	11	—	16¼	19¼	22	—	—	—	19½	23.2	27	30.5	34.2	37	42	45.8	49.5	55.5
Ram Golden Ram, Tour Grind	(1982)	11	—	16	19	22	—	—	16	19.5	23	26.5	30	33.5	37	41	45	49	55
Rawlings RXP	(1980)	11	—	17	20	23	—	—	—	19	23	27	30	35	39	43	47	51	56
Royal Edge	(1978)	12	—	17	20	22	—	—	—	21	23	26	29	33	37	41	45	50	54
Royal Impact	(1978)	12	—	17	20	22	—	26	—	19	22	25	29	33	37	41	45	49	55
Slotline	(1982)	11	—	16	19	22	—	—	17	20	23	26	29	32	36	40	44	49	56
Spalding Elite	(1982)	12	—	16	18	20	—	—	17	19	22	25	29	33	37	41	45	49	54
Spalding XL4	(1982)	12	—	16	18	20	—	—	17	19	22	25	28	32	36	40	44	48	54
Spalding Top Flite	(1982)	11	—	16	18	20	—	—	17	19	22	26	30	34	38	41	46	49	56
Spalding Executive	(1982)	12	—	17	20	23	—	—	17½	19½	22½	26	30	34	38	41½	46½	52	58
Square 2	(1978)	11	—	16	19	22	—	—	—	20	23	26	29	32	35³/₁₀	38⁹/₁₀	43	49	55
Taylor Made Golf	(1982)	9½	—	19	21	23	—	27	18	21	24	27	30	33	37	41	45	49	57
Titleist Pro 100	(1976)	11	14	17	20	22	—	—	19	21	24	27	30	33	36	40	44	48	—
Titleist AC-108	(1976)	11	14	17	20	22	—	—	—	22	25	28	30	33½	36	40	43	47	55
Unique	(1982)	11	—	16	19	22	—	—	17	20	23	26	29	33	37	41	45	50	57
Wilson Staff	(1982)	11	14	16	19	21	—	25	17	20	23	26	30	34	38	42	46	50	55
Wilson Aggressor	(1982)	12	—	16	19	21	—	25	—	20	23	26	30	34	38	42	46	50	55
Wilson X-31	(1982)	12	14	16	19	21	—	26	—	20	23	26	30	34	38	42	46	50	55
Wilson 1200 GE	(1982)	11	14	16	19	21	—	25	—	20	23	26	30	34	38	42	46	50	55
Wilson Reflex	(1982)	11	14	16	19	21	—	25	—	20	23	26	30	34	38	42	46	50	55
Stan Thompson	(1982)	11	14	17	20	23	—	29	—	21	24	27	30	34	38	42	46	51	56

LIE — MEN'S

GOLF CLUB MANUFACTURERS STANDARD SPECIFICATIONS

Mfgr. & Year Specs. Published		#1 Wood	#2 Wood	#3 Wood	#4 Wood	#5 Wood	#6 Wood	#7 Wood	#1 Iron	#2 Iron	#3 Iron	#4 Iron	#5 Iron	#6 Iron	#7 Iron	#8 Iron	#9 Iron	Pitch Wedge	Sand Wedge
Ajay Double Eagle	(1977)	55	—	55½	55¾	56	—	—	—	57	58	59	60	61	62	63	63	64	64
Browning	(1980)	55	—	56	57	57	—	—	56½	57	58	59	60	61	62	63	64	64	—
Cobra Low Profile	(1982)	—	—	—	—	—	—	—	56½	57	58	59	60	61	62	63	63	64	64
Cobra Premier Iron	(1982)	—	—	—	—	—	—	—	56	57	58	59	60	61	62	63	64	64	64
Cobra Tour Model	(1982)	54	54	54½	55	55	—	—	56	57	58	59	60	61	62	63	64	64	64
Confidence	(1977)	54	—	55	55	55	—	—	56	56	57	58	59	60	61	62	62	63	63
Dunlop Australian Blade	(1978)	—	—	—	—	—	—	—	56	57	58	59	60	61	62	63	64	65	65
Dunlop Maxfli Woods	(1978)	55	55	56	56	57	—	57	56	57	58	59	60	61	62	63	64	65	65
Walter Hagen The Haig	(1982)	55	55	56	57	57	—	57	—	57	58	59	60	61	62	63	63	64	65
Hogan Apex	(1978)	55½	—	57	57	58	—	—	—	57	58	59	60	61	62	62½	63	64½	—
Hogan Director	(1978)	55½	—	57	57	58	—	—	—	57	58	59	60	61	62	62½	63	64½	—
Hogan Medallion	(1978)	55½	—	57	57	58	—	—	—	57	58	59	60	61	62	62½	63	64½	—
Hogan Producer	(1978)	55½	56	57	57	58	—	59	—	56½	57½	58½	59½	60½	61½	62	62½	64	—
MacGregor M693 Woods	(1982)	54	—	55	56	56	—	—	—	—	—	—	—	—	—	—	—	—	—
MacGregor M85 Woods	(1982)	54	—	55	56	56	—	—	—	—	—	—	—	—	—	—	—	—	—
MacGregor MT Woods/Irons	(1982)	54	—	55	56	56	—	—	58	59	60	61	62	63	63	64	64	64	65
MacGregor MCX Woods/Irons	(1982)	54	—	55	56	56	—	57	—	58	59	60	61	61½	62	62½	63	63½	65
MacGregor Limited Edition	(1982)	55	—	55½	56½	56½	—	—	59	59½	60	60½	61	61½	62½	62½	63½	65	66
Northwestern	(1982)	55	55¼	55½	55¾	56	—	56½	55	56	57	58	59	60	61	62	63	63	63
P.G.A. Emblem	(1982)	54	—	55	55	56	—	—	—	57	58	59	60	60½	61	62	63	64	64
P.G.A. Tommy Armour	(1982)	54	—	55	55	55	—	—	57	57	58	59	60	60½	61	62	63	64	64
P.G.A. Performer	(1982)	54	—	55	55	56	—	—	—	56½	57½	58½	59½	60	61	62	63	64	64
P.G.A. Concept LCG	(1982)	54	—	55	55	56	—	56	—	58	59	60	60½	61	62	63	63	64	64
P.G.A. Ryder Cup II	(1982)	54	—	55	55	55	—	56	—	58	59	60	61	61½	62	62½	63	63	63
Pedersen	(1978)	56	56½	57	57½	58	—	58	56	57	58	59	60	61	62	63	64	64	64
Toney Penna/All	(1980)	54	—	56	57	58	—	—	56	56½	56½	57	58	59	59½	60	60½	61	61
Penna Driver Model JS	(1980)	54	—	—	—	—	—	—	—	—	—	—	—	—	—	—	—	—	—
Penna Driver Model I	(1980)	54	—	—	—	—	—	—	—	—	—	—	—	—	—	—	—	—	—

GOLF CLUB MANUFACTURERS STANDARD SPECIFICATIONS

Mfgr. & Year Specs. Published		#1 Wood	#2 Wood	#3 Wood	#4 Wood	#5 Wood	#6 Wood	#7 Wood	#1 Iron	#2 Iron	#3 Iron	#4 Iron	#5 Iron	#6 Iron	#7 Iron	#8 Iron	#9 Iron	Pitch Wedge	Sand Wedge
Penna Driver Model 2 + 65	(1980)	54	—	—	—	—	—	—	—	—	—	—	—	—	—	—	—	—	—
Penna Driver Model 12	(1980)	54	—	—	—	—	—	—	—	—	—	—	—	—	—	—	—	—	—
PowerBilt/All	(1982)	55	55	56	57	57	—	—	56	57	58	59	60	61	62	63	64	64	64
Pro-Dyn	(1977)	54	—	55	55	55	—	55	56	57	58	59	60	61	62	63	63	64	64
Pro Group	(1982)	54	54	55	56	—	—	—	57	57	58	59	60	61	61	62	62	63	—
Ram Accubar	(1982)	55	—	56	56½	57	—	—	—	57½	58	58½	59	60	61	62	63	63	63
Ram Golden Ram, Tour Grind	(1982)	55	—	56	56½	57	—	—	56½	57½	58½	59½	60½	61½	62½	63½	64½	65½	65½
Rawlings RXP	(1980)	56	—	57	58	58	—	—	—	57	58	59	60	61	62	63	64	64	64
Royal Edge	(1978)	54	—	55	55	55	—	—	—	57	58	59	60	60½	61	61½	62	62	62
Royal Impact	(1978)	54	—	55	55	55	—	56	—	58	59	60	61	62	63	64	64	64	64
Slotline	(1982)	55	—	56	57	57	—	—	56½	57	58	59	60	61	62	63	64	64	64
Spalding Elite	(1982)	54½	—	54¾	55¼	55¾	—	—	57¾	58¼	58¾	59¼	59¾	60¼	60¾	61¼	62	63	63
Spalding Executive	(1982)	55	—	55¼	55½	56	—	—	58¼	58¼	58¾	59¼	59¾	60¼	61	61¾	62¼	63	63
Spalding Top Flite	(1982)	54	—	54½	55	55½	—	—	58	58	59¼	59¾	60	60¾	61	61¾	62½	63½	63½
Spalding XL4	(1982)	55	—	55½	56	56½	—	—	57¾	58¼	58¾	59¼	59¾	60¼	60¾	61¼	62	63	63
Square 2	(1978)	55	—	56	56½	57	—	—	—	58	59	60	61	62	62½	63	63½	63½	63½
Taylor Made Golf	(1982)	54	—	55	55	55	—	55	56	57	58	59	60	61	62	63	64	64	64
Titleist Pro 100	(1976)	54	54	55	56	56	—	—	56	57	58	59	60	61	62	63	63	64	—
Titleist AC-108	(1976)	54	54	55	56	56	—	—	—	57	58	59	60	61	62	63	63	64	64
Unique	(1982)	55	—	55½	56	56½	—	—	58	58	59	60	61	62	63	64	65	65	65
Wilson Staff	(1982)	—	—	—	—	—	—	—	56	57	58	59	60	60	61	62	62	63	64
Wilson Aggressor	(1982)	55	55	56	57	57	—	57	—	56	57	58	59	60	61	62	62	63	64
Wilson X-31	(1982)	54	54	55	56	56	—	56	—	57	58	59	60	60	61	62	62	63	64
Wilson 1200 GE	(1982)	54	54	55	56	56	—	56	—	57	58	59	60	61	62	62	62	63	64
Wilson Reflex	(1982)	54	54	55	56	56	—	56	—	57	58	59	60	61	62	63	63	64	65
Stan Thompson	(1982)	54	54	55	56	57	—	58	—	57	58	59	60	61	62	63	64	64	64

LENGTH — LADIES'

GOLF CLUB MANUFACTURERS STANDARD SPECIFICATIONS

Mfgr. & Year Specs. Published		#1 Wood	#2 Wood	#3 Wood	#4 Wood	#5 Wood	#6 Wood	#7 Wood	#1 Iron	#2 Iron	#3 Iron	#4 Iron	#5 Iron	#6 Iron	#7 Iron	#8 Iron	#9 Iron	Pitch Wedge	Sand Wedge
Ajay Double Eagle	(1977)	42	—	41	40½	40	—	—	—	—	37	36½	36	36½	35	34½	34	34	34
Browning	(1980)	42	41	40½	40	—	—	—	38½	38	37½	37	36½	36	35½	35	34½	34½	—
Cobra Ladies' Low Profile	(1982)	—	—	—	—	—	—	—	38½	38	37½	37	36½	36	35½	35	34½	34½	34
Confidence	(1977)	42	—	41	40½	40	—	—	—	38	37½	37	36½	36	35½	35	34½	34½	34½
Dunlop	(1978)	42	—	41	40½	40¼	—	—	—	38	37½	37	36½	36	35½	35	34½	34	34
Walter Hagen AM-Lady	(1979)	41	—	40½	40	39¾	—	39½	—	37	36½	36	35½	35	34¾	34½	33¾	33½	33½
Walter Hagen Onyx	(1979)	42	—	41½	41	40¾	—	40½	—	38	37½	37	36½	36	35¾	35¼	34¾	34½	34½
Walter Hagen Lady Ultra	(1979)	42	—	41½	41	40¾	—	40½	—	38	37½	37	36½	36	35¾	35¼	34¾	34½	34½
Hogan Champion Woods	(1978)	42	—	41½	41	40½	—	39½	—	—	—	—	—	—	—	—	—	—	—
Hogan Medallion Irons	(1978)	—	—	—	—	—	—	—	—	38	37½	37	36½	36	35½	35	34½	34¼	—
Hogan Director Irons	(1978)	—	—	—	—	—	—	—	—	38	37½	37	36½	36	35½	35	34½	34¼	—
MacGregor Finesse	(1982)	42¼	—	41¾	41½	41½	—	41¼	—	—	37¾	37¼	36¾	36¼	35¾	35½	35¼	34¾	34¾
P.G.A. Butterfly	(1982)	41½	—	40½	40	39½	—	39	—	—	37 1/16	36 5/8	36 3/16	35¾	35 5/16	34⅞	34 7/16	34	34
P.G.A. Lady Ryder Cup II	(1982)	42	—	41	40½	40	—	39	—	—	37½	37	36½	36	35½	35	34½	34	34
Pedersen	(1978)	41½	—	40¾	40½	40	—	39½	38	37½	37	36½	36	35½	35	34½	34	34	34
Pinseeker (Length only)	(1978)	42	—	41½	41	40½	—	40	—	38	37½	37	36½	36	35½	35	34½	34½	34½
Pro-Dyn	(1977)	42	—	41	40½	40	—	39½	38	37½	37	36½	36	35½	35	34½	34	34	34
Pro Group	(1982)	42	—	41	40½	40	—	39	—	—	37½	37	36½	36	35½	35	34½	34½	34½
Royal	(1978)	42	—	41	40½	40	—	39	—	—	37½	37	36½	36	35½	35	34½	34½	34½
Spalding Ladies' Executive	(1982)	42	—	41⅛	—	40¼	—	39⅜	—	—	37 3/16	36¾	36 5/16	35⅞	35 7/16	35	34 9/16	34⅛	33 11/16
Taylor Made Golf	(1982)	41½	—	40½	40	39½	—	39½	38½	38	37½	37	36½	36	35½	35	34½	34½	34½
Unique	(1982)	42	—	41	40½	40	—	39	38½	38	37½	37	36½	36	35½	35	34½	34½	34½
Wilson Berg Staff	(1982)	42	—	41½	41	40¾	—	40½	—	38	37½	37	36½	36	35¾	35¼	34¾	34½	34½
Wilson Tiara	(1982)	41½	—	40½	—	39½	—	38½	—	—	37	36½	36	35½	35¼	34¾	34¼	34*	
Stan Thompson	(1982)	42	42	41½	41	40½	—	40	—	37½	37	36½	36	35½	35	34½	34	34	34

*Dual Wedge Only

LOFT — LADIES'

GOLF CLUB MANUFACTURERS STANDARD SPECIFICATIONS

Mfgr. & Year Specs. Published		#1 Wood	#2 Wood	#3 Wood	#4 Wood	#5 Wood	#6 Wood	#7 Wood	#1 Iron	#2 Iron	#3 Iron	#4 Iron	#5 Iron	#6 Iron	#7 Iron	#8 Iron	#9 Iron	Pitch Wedge	Sand Wedge
Ajay Double Eagle	(1977)	11	—	16	19	21	—	—	—	—	24	27	31	35	39	43	47	51	55
Browning	(1980)	14	18	21	24	—	—	—	17	20	23	26	29	32	36	40	44	49	—
Cobra Low Profile	(1982)	--	—	—	—	—	—	—	17	20	23	26	29	32	36	40	44	48	55
Confidence	(1977)	13	—	18	20	22	—	—	—	20	23	26	29	33	37	41	45	49	54
Dunlop	(1978)	13	—	16	19	22	—	—	—	20	23	27	31	35	39	43	47	51	57
Hagen AM-Lady	(1979)	13	—	19	22	25	—	31	—	—	24	27	31	35	39	43	47	51	55
Hagen Onyx	(1979)	14	—	17	20	22	—	20			25	28	31	35	39	43	47	51	55
Hagen Lady Ultra	(1979)	14	—	17	20	22	—	26	—	—	24	27	31	35	39	43	47	51	55
Hogan Champion	(1978)	13	—	17	19	21½	—	25½	—	—	—	—	—	—	—	—	—	—	—
Hogan Medallion	(1978)	—	—	—	—	—	—	—	—	19½	23	26½	30	33½	37	41	45	50	—
Hogan Director	(1978)	—	—	—	—	—	—	—	—	19½	23	26½	30	33½	37	41	45	50	—
MacGregor Finesse	(1982)	12½	—	15½	18½	22	—	30	—	—	23	25	29	33	37	41	44	51	57
P.G.A. Butterfly	(1982)	13	—	17	20	22	—	25	—	—	23	26	29	33	37	41	45	52	57
P.G.A. Lady Ryder Cup II	(1982)	13	—	18	20	22	—	26	—	—	23	26	29	33	36	39	42	47	54
Pedersen	(1978)	13	—	18	21	24	—	29	18	20	23	26	30	34	38	42	46	50	55
Pro-Dyn	(1977)	13	—	18	20	22½	—	28	18	21	24	27	30	34	38	42	46	51	57
Pro Group	(1982)	14	—	18	21	24	—	27	—	—	24	27	31	35	39	43	47	51	—
Royal	(1978)	13	—	18	20	22	—	26	—	—	23	26	29	33	37	41	45	49	56
Spalding Ladies' Executive	(1982)	13	—	18	—	24	—	29	—	—	22½	26	30	34	38	41½	46½	52	58
Taylor Made Golf	(1982)	12	—	19	21	23	—	27	18	21	24	27	30	33	37	41	45	49	57
Unique	(1982)	13	—	16	19	22	—	28	17	20	23	26	29	33	37	41	45	50	57
Wilson Berg Staff	(1982)	13	—	17	20	22	—	26	—	20	23	26	30	34	38	42	46	50	55
Wilson Tiara	(1982)	14	—	18	—	23	—	27	—	20	23	26	30	34	38	42	46	50	55
Stan Thompson	(1982)	12	15	18	21	24	—	30	—	21	24	27	30	34	38	42	46	51	56

LADIES' — LIE — LATE 1970's & EARLY 1980's

LIE — LADIES'

GOLF CLUB MANUFACTURERS STANDARD SPECIFICATIONS

Mfgr. & Year Specs. Published		#1 Wood	#2 Wood	#3 Wood	#4 Wood	#5 Wood	#6 Wood	#7 Wood	#1 Iron	#2 Iron	#3 Iron	#4 Iron	#5 Iron	#6 Iron	#7 Iron	#8 Iron	#9 Iron	Pitch Wedge	Sand Wedge
Ajay Double Eagle	(1977)	55	—	55½	55¾	56	—	—	—	—	58	59	60	61	62	63	63	64	64
Browning	(1982)	55	56	57	57	—	—	—	56½	57	58	59	60	61	62	63	64	64	—
Cobra Low Profile	(1982)	—	—	—	—	—	—	—	56½	57	58	59	60	61	62	63	64	64	64
Confidence	(1977)	54	—	55	55	55	—	—	—	57	58	59	60	61	62	63	63	64	64
Dunlop	(1978)	55	—	56	56	57	—	—	—	57	58	59	60	61	62	63	64	64	65
Hagen AM-Lady	(1979)	55	—	56	57	57	—	57	—	—	58	59	60	61	62	63	64	64	64
Hagen Onyx	(1979)	55	—	56	57	57	—	57	—	—	58	59	60	61	62	63	64	64	64
Hagen Lady Ultra	(1979)	55	—	56	57	57	—	57	—	—	58	59	60	61	62	63	64	64	64
Hogan Champion	(1978)	55½	—	57	57	58	—	58	—	—	—	—	—	—	—	—	—	—	—
Hogan Medallion Irons	(1978)	—	—	—	—	—	—	—	—	57	58	59	60	61	62	62½	63	64½	—
Hogan Director Irons	(1978)	—	—	—	—	—	—	—	—	57	58	59	60	61	62	62½	63	64½	—
MacGregor Finesse	(1982)	54	—	55	56	56	—	58	—	—	59	59½	60	61	62	62½	63	63	65
P.G.A. Butterfly	(1982)	53	—	54	54	55	—	55	—	—	58	59	60	60½	61	61½	62	62½	63
P.G.A. Lady Ryder Cup II	(1982)	54	—	55	55	56	—	56	—	—	59	60	61	61½	62	62½	63	63	63
Pedersen	(1978)	56	—	57	57½	58	—	58	56	57	58	59	60	61	62	63	64	64	64
Pro-Dyn	(1977)	54	—	55	55	55	—	55	56	57	58	59	60	61	62	63	63	64	64
Pro Group	(1982)	54	—	55	56	56	—	56	—	—	58	59	60	61	62	63	64	64	—
Royal	(1978)	54	—	55	55	55	—	56	—	—	58	59	60	61	62	63	64	64	64
Spalding Ladies' Executive	(1982)	55	—	55½	—	56	—	56½	—	—	58¾	59¼	59¾	60¼	61	61¾	62¼	63	63
Taylor Made Golf	(1982)	54	—		55	55	—	55	56	57	58	59	60	61	62	63	64	64	64
Unique	(1982)	55	—	55½	56	56½	—	57½	58	58	59	60	61	62	63	64	65	65	65
Wilson Berg Staff	(1982)	54	—	55	56	56	—	56	—	57	58	59	60	60	61	62	62	63	64
Wilson Tiara	(1982)	54	—	55	—	56	—	56	—	—	57	58	59	60	61	62	62	64	Dual Wedge
Stan Thompson	(1982)	54	54	55	56	57	—	58	—	57	58	59	60	61	62	63	64	64	64

LENGTH, LOFT & LIE — CUSTOM MFGR.'S — LADIES'

GOLF CLUB MANUFACTURERS STANDARD SPECIFICATIONS

Mfgr. & Year Specs. Published		#1 Wood	#2 Wood	#3 Wood	#4 Wood	#5 Wood	#6 Wood	#7 Wood	#1 Iron	#2 Iron	#3 Iron	#4 Iron	#5 Iron	#6 Iron	#7 Iron	#8 Iron	#9 Iron	Pitch Wedge	Sand Wedge
Length:																			
Mario Cesario	(1982)	42	41½	41	40½	40	—	39	—	37½	37	36½	36	35½	35	34½	34	34	34
Bert Dargie	(1982)	42	41½	41	40½	40	—	—	38	37½	37	36½	36	35½	35	34½	34	34	34
George Izett	(1982)	42	42	41	40½	40	—	39	—	38	37½	37	36½	36	35½	35	34½	34½	34½
Irving King	(1982)	42	41½	41	40½	40	—	39	—	37½	37	36½	36	35½	35	34½	34	34	34
Louisville Golf	(1982)	41½	41	40½	40	39½	—	39	—	37½	37	36½	36	35½	35	34½	34	34	34
Ralph Maltby	(1982)	42	—	41	40½	40	39½	39	38½	38	37½	37	36½	36	35½	35	34½	34½	34½
John Ofer	(1982)	42	—	41½	41	41	40	40	—	—	37½	37	36½	35¾	35⅝	35¼	34¾	34½	34½
Orlimar	(1982)	42	41¾	41	40½	40	—	39	38¾	38¼	37¾	37¼	36¾	36¼	35¾	35¼	34¾	34½	34½
Kenneth Smith	(1979)	41½	41	40½	40	39½	—	38	38	37½	37	36½	36	35½	35	34½	34	33½	33½
Bob Toski	(1982)	42	41½	41	40½	40	—	39	38½	38	37½	37	36½	36	35½	35	34½	34½	34½
Loft:																			
Mario Cesario	(1982)	12½	14	17	20	23	—	29	—	20	24	28	32	36	40	44	48	52	56
Bert Dargie	(1982)	11	13	16	19	22	—	—	18	21	24	27	31	35	39	43	47	51	55
George Izett	(1982)	12	14	16	19	22	—	—	—	20	22½	25	27½	30	32½	35	37½	40	42½
Louisville Golf	(1982)	12	14	16	19	22	—	28	—	20	23	26	30	34	38	42	46	50	55
Ralph Maltby	(1982)	13	—	17	20	23	26	29	17	20	23	26	30	34	38	42	46	50	56
John Ofer	(1982)	13	—	17	20	22	25	27	—	—	24	27	31	35	39	43	47	51	56
Orlimar	(1982)	13	14½	18½	21½	24½	—	31	16	19	22	25½	29	33	37	41	45	50	58
Kenneth Smith	(1979)	12	15	18	21	24	—	30	18	21	24	28	32	36	40	44	48	52	57
Bob Toski	(1982)	13	15	18	20	22	—	27	22	24	26½	29	31½	35	38½	41½	45	48½	51½
Lie:																			
Mario Cesario	(1982)	53	54	56	56	56	—	56	—	56	57	58	59	60	61	62	63	64	64
Bert Dargie	(1982)	54	54	55	56	56	—	—	57	58	59	60	61	62	63	64	64	65	65
George Izett	(1982)	53	53	54	55	56	—	57	—	56	57	58	59	60	61	62	63	63	63
Irving King	(1982)	55	55½	56	56½	57	—	58	—	57	58	59	60	61	62	63	64	64	64
Louisville Golf	(1982)	54	54	55	56	56	—	57	—	54	55	56	57	58	59	60	60	61	61
Ralph Maltby	(1982)	53	—	54	54½	55	55½	56	55	56	57	58	59	60	61	62	63	63	63
John Ofer	(1982)	54	—	55	56	56	56	56	—	—	57	58	59	60	61	61	62	63	
Kenneth Smith	(1979)	53	54	55	56	57	—	59	56	57	58	59	60	61	62	63	64	64	64
Bob Toski	(1982)	53	53	54	55	56	—	56	56½	57	57½	58	58½	60	61	61½	62	63	63

LENGTH, LOFT & LIE — CUSTOM MFGR.'S — MEN'S

GOLF CLUB MANUFACTURERS STANDARD SPECIFICATIONS

Mfgr. & Year Specs. Published		#1 Wood	#2 Wood	#3 Wood	#4 Wood	#5 Wood	#6 Wood	#7 Wood	#1 Iron	#2 Iron	#3 Iron	#4 Iron	#5 Iron	#6 Iron	#7 Iron	#8 Iron	#9 Iron	Pitch Wedge	Sand Wedge
Length:																			
Mario Cesario	(1982)	43	42½	42	41½	41	—	40	39	38½	38	37½	37	36½	36	35½	35	35	35
Bert Dargie	(1982)	43	42½	42	41½	41	—	40	39	38½	38	37½	37	36½	36	35½	35	35	35
George Izett	(1982)	43	43	42	41½	41	—	40	39½	39	38½	38	37½	37	36½	36	35½	35½	35½
Irving King	(1982)	43	42½	42	41½	41	—	—	—	38½	38	37½	37	36½	36	35½	35	35	35
Louisville Golf	(1982)	43	42½	42	41½	41	—	40	—	38½	38	37½	37	36½	36	35½	35	35	35
Ralph Maltby	(1982)	43	42½	42	41½	41	40½	40	39½	39	38½	38	37½	37	36½	36	35½	35½	35½
John Ofer	(1982)	43	42½	42	41½	41	41	41	—	39	38½	38	37½	37	36⅝	36¼	35¾	35½	35½
Orlimar	(1982)	43	42¾	42	41½	41	—	—	39¾	39¼	38¾	38¼	37¾	37¼	36¾	36¼	35¾	35½	35½
Kenneth Smith	(1979)	43	42½	42	41½	41	—	39½	39	38½	38	37½	37	36½	36	35½	35	34½	34½
Bob Toski	(1982)	43	42½	42	41½	41	—	40	39½	39	38½	38	37½	37	36½	36	35½	35½	35½
Loft:																			
Mario Cesario	(1982)	11	13	16	19	22	—	28	17	20	24	28	32	36	40	44	48	52	58
Bert Dargie	(1982)	11	13	16	19	22	—	28	18	21	24	27	31	35	39	43	47	51	55
George Izett	(1982)	10	13	16	19	22	—	28	17	20	22½	25	27½	30	32½	35	37½	40	42½
Irving King	(1982)	11	13	16	19	21	—	—	—	20	24	28	32	36	40	44	48	52	56
Louisville Golf	(1982)	10½	13	16	19	22	—	28	—	20	23	26	30	34	38	42	46	50	55
Ralph Maltby	(1982)	11	13	16	19	22	25	28	17	20	23	26	30	34	38	42	46	50	56
John Ofer	(1982)	10½	13	16	19	22	25	27	—	20	23	26	30	34	38	42	46	50	55
Orlimar	(1982)	11	14	17	20	23	—	—	16	19	22	25½	29	33	37	41	45	50	58
Kenneth Smith	(1979)	11	14	17	20	23	—	29	17	20	23	27	31	35	39	43	47	51	56
Bob Toski	(1982)	12	15	18	20	22	—	27	22	24	26½	29	31½	35	38½	41½	45	48½	51½
Lie:																			
Mario Cesario	(1982)	54	55	56	57	57	—	57	56	57	58	59	60	61	62	63	64	65	65
Bert Dargie	(1982)	54	54	55	56	56	—	57	57	58	59	60	61	62	63	64	64	65	65
George Izett	(1982)	55	55	56	57	58	—	59	56	57	58	59	60	61	62	63	64	64	64
Irving King	(1982)	55	55½	56	56½	57	—	—	—	57	58	59	60	61	62	63	64	64	64
Louisville Golf	(1982)	55	55	56	57	57	—	58	—	55	56	57	58	59	60	61	61	62	62
Ralph Maltby	(1982)	55	55½	56	56½	57	57½	58	55	56	57	58	59	60	60	61	62	63	63
John Ofer	(1982)	55	55	56	57	57	57	57	—	57	58	59	60	60	61	62	62	63	65
Orlimar, Pers. (Lam. 1° Flatter)	(1982)	56	56¼	56¾	57	57¼	—	—	58¼	58¼	58¾	59¼	59¾	60¼	60½	61¼	62	62¼	62½
Kenneth Smith	(1979)	54	55	56	57	58	—	60	56	57	58	59	60	61	62	63	64	64	64
Bob Toski, Cast (Forged 1° Upright)	(1982)	54	54	55	56	57	—	57	56½	57	57½	58	58½	60	61	61½	62	63	63

CUSTOM MFGR.'S — MEN'S & LADIES' LENGTH, LOFT & LIE LATE 1970's & EARLY 1980's

LENGTH — MEN'S

MEN'S — LENGTH — MID 1980's

GOLF CLUB MANUFACTURERS STANDARD SPECIFICATIONS

Mfgr. & Year Specs. Published		#1 Wood	#2 Wood	#3 Wood	#4 Wood	#5 Wood	#6 Wood	#7 Wood	#1 Iron	#2 Iron	#3 Iron	#4 Iron	#5 Iron	#6 Iron	#7 Iron	#8 Iron	#9 Iron	Pitch Wedge	Sand Wedge
Armour Golf T-Line BC	(1986)	43¼	—	42¼	41¾	41¼	—	40¾	39½	39	38½	38	37½	37	36½	36	35½	35½	35½
Browning 440	(1986)	43	—	42	41½	41	—	41	—	39	38½	38	37½	37	36½	36	35½	35½	35½
Browning Automatic	(1986)	43	—	42	41½	41	—	41	—	39	38½	38	37½	37	36½	36	35½	35½	35½
Daiwa Exceler	(1986)	43¼	—	42¼	41¾	41¼	—	40¾	—	39	38½	38	37½	37	36½	36	35½	35½	35½
Dunlop 357	(1986)	43⅜	—	42⅜	—	41⅝	—	41⅛	39½	39	38½	38	37½	37	36½	36	35½	35½	35½
The GolfWorks® Bio-Mech	(1986)	43	42½	42	41½	41	40½	40	39½	39	38½	38	37½	37	36½	36	35½	35½	35½
The GolfWorks® RMH	(1986)	43	42½	42	41½	41	40½	40	39½	39	38½	38	37½	37	36½	36	35½	35½	35½
H & B All	(1986)	43	—	42	41½	41½	—	—	—	39	38½	38	37½	37	36½	36	35½	35½	35½
Hogan Apex	(1986)	43¼	—	42¼	41¾	41¼	—	—	—	39¼	38¾	38¼	37¾	37¼	36¾	36¼	35¾	35½	35
Hogan Radial	(1986)	43¼	—	42¼	41¾	41¼	—	—	—	39	38½	38	37½	37	36½	36	35½	35¼	35¼
Lynx - Parallax	(1986)	43	—	42	41½	41	—	40	39½	39	38½	38	37½	37	36½	36	35½	35½	35¼
Lynx - Liberty	(1986)	43	—	42	41½	41	—	40	—	39	38½	38	37½	37	36½	36	35½	35½	35¼
MacGregor Muirfield	(1986)	43½	—	42¾	42¼	41¾	—	—	39¾	39¼	38¾	38¼	37¾	37¼	36¾	36½	36¼	35¾	35¾
MacGregor CG1800	(1986)	43½	—	42¾	42¼	41¾	—	—	39¾	39¼	38¾	38¼	37¾	37¼	36¾	36½	36¼	35¾	35¾
Mizuno MS-5	(1986)	43¼	—	42¾	42½	42	—	—	39¾	39¼	38¾	38¼	37¾	37¼	36¾	36½	36¼	36	35¾
Mizuno MS-4	(1986)	43¼	—	42¾	42½	42	—	—	39¾	39	38¾	38¼	37¾	37¼	36¾	36½	36¼	36	35¾
Northwestern 241 Tour	(1986)	43	—	42	41½	41	—	—	39	38½	38	37½	37	36½	36	35½	35	35	35
Northwestern 865GR	(1986)	43	—	42	41½	41	—	—	39	38½	38	37½	37	36½	36	35½	35	35	35
Northwestern 965	(1986)	43	—	42	42½	41	—	—	39	38½	38	37½	37	36½	36	35½	35	35	35
Penna Golf Original	(1986)	43	—	42½	42	41	—	—	—	39	38½	38	37½	37	36½	36	35½	35	35
Penna Golf Innovater	(1986)	43	—	42½	42	41	—	—	—	39	38½	38	37½	37	36½	36	35½	35	35
Pinseeker Fireball	(1986)	43	—	42	41½	41¼	41	—	39½	39	38½	38	37½	37	36½	36	35½	35½	35½
Pinseeker Olympian	(1986)	43	—	42	41½	41¼	41	—	39½	39	38½	38	37½	37	36½	36	35½	35½	35½
Pro Group Axiom	(1986)	43	—	42	41¾	41½	—	41¼	39½	39	38½	38	37½	37	36½	36	35½	35½	35½
Pro Group Peerless	(1986)	43	—	42	41¾	41½	—	41¼	39½	39	38½	38	37½	37	36½	36	35½	35½	35½
Ram Tour Grind	(1986)	43¼	—	42¼	41¾	41¼	—	—	39½	39	38½	38	37½	37	36½	36	35½	35½	35
Ram Accubar	(1986)	43¼	—	42¼	41¾	41¼	—	—	—	39	38½	38	37½	37	36½	36	35½	35½	35
Spalding Cannon	(1986)	43	—	42	41½	41	—	40	—	39	38½	38	37½	37	36½	36	35½	35½	35½
Spalding Executive	(1986)	43	—	42	41½	41	—	40	—	38⅝	38⅛	37⅝	37⅛	36⅝	36⅛	35⅝	35⅛	35⅛	35⅛
Taylor Metalwoods	(1986)	43	—	42	41½	41	41	41	—	—	—	—	—	—	—	—	—	—	—
Taylor Technician	(1986)	42½	—	41¾	41½	41	—	—	38½	38⅛	37¾	37⅜	37	36⅝	36⅛	35¾	35¼	35	35
Taylor Iron Cleek	(1986)	—	—	—	—	—	—	—	39½	39	38½	38	37½	37	36½	36	35½	35½	35½
Taylor Tour Preferred	(1986)	—	—	—	—	—	—	—	39½	39	38½	38	37½	37	36½	36	35½	35½	35½
Titleist Tour Model	(1985)	43	—	42½	42	41¾	—	—	39½	39	38½	38	37½	37	36⅝	36¼	35⅞	35½	35½
Titleist Pinnacle	(1985)	43	—	42½	—	41¾	—	—	—	38¾	38¼	37¾	37¼	36¾	36⅜	36	35⅝	35¼	35
Wilson Aggressor	(1984)	43	—	42	41½	41¼	—	41	—	38½	38	37½	37	36½	36¼	35¾	35¼	35	35
Wilson Staff	(1986)	43	—	42	41½	41¼	41	41	—	39	38½	38	37½	37	36½	36	35½	35	35
Wilson 1200LT	(1986)	43	—	42	41½	41¼	41	41	—	39	38½	38	37½	37	36½	36	35½	35	35
Wilson 1200GE	(1986)	43	—	42	41½	41¼	41	41	—	39	38½	38	37½	37	36½	36	35½	35	35
Yahama Spada	(1986)	43½	—	42½	42	41½	—	—	—	—	—	—	—	—	—	—	—	—	—
Yamaha Y-45	(1986)	43½	—	42½	42	41½	—	—	—	—	—	—	—	—	—	—	—	—	—
Yamaha ST-30	(1986)	—	—	—	—	—	—	—	39½	39	38½	38	37½	37	36½	36	35½	35	35
Yamaha EX-22	(1986)	—	—	—	—	—	—	—	39½	39	38½	38	37½	37	36½	36	35½	35	35

LOFT — MEN'S

GOLF CLUB MANUFACTURERS STANDARD SPECIFICATIONS

Mfgr. & Year Specs. Published		#1 Wood	#2 Wood	#3 Wood	#4 Wood	#5 Wood	#6 Wood	#7 Wood	#1 Iron	#2 Iron	#3 Iron	#4 Iron	#5 Iron	#6 Iron	#7 Iron	#8 Iron	#9 Iron	Pitch Wedge	Sand Wedge
Armour Golf T-Line BC	(1986)	10	—	12½	18½	21½	—	24½	16	18½	21½	25	28½	32½	36½	40½	44½	49	52
Browning 440	(1986)	10	—	16	19	22	—	25	—	21	24	27	30	34	38	42	46	50	56
Browning Automatic	(1986)	10	—	16	19	22	—	25	—	21	24	27	30	34	38	42	46	50	56
Daiwa Exceler	(1986)	11½	—	16½	19	21	—	25	—	17	19	22	25	29	33	37	41	45	50
Dunlop 357	(1986)	12	—	15	—	20	—	23	15	18	21	24	28	32	36	40	44	50	55
The GolfWorks® Bio-Mech	(1986)	11	13	16	19	22	25	28	17	19	22	25	29	33	37	41	45	49	55
The GolfWorks® RMH	(1986)	11	13	16	19	22	25	28	17	20	23	26	30	34	38	42	46	50	56
H & B All	(1986)	11	—	17	20	22	—	—	—	20	24	28	32	35	38	41	44	50	56
Hogan Apex	(1986)	10½	—	15	17½	21	—	—	—	19½	23	26½	30	33½	37	41	45	49	—
Hogan Radial	(1986)	10½	—	15	17½	21	—	—	—	19½	23	26½	30	33½	37	41	45	49	—
Lynx - Parallax	(1986)	10	—	17	20	23	—	26	16	19	22	25	29	33	37	41	45	49	57
Lynx - Liberty	(1986)	11	—	16	19	22	—	26	—	19	22	25	29	33	37	41	45	49	57
MacGregor Muirfield	(1986)	10	—	14	17	21	—	—	18	20	23	26	29	33	37	41	45	50	56
MacGregor CG1800	(1986)	13	—	16	19	21½	—	—	16	18	21	24	27½	32	37	41	45	50½	57
Mizuno MS-5	(1986)	10½	—	16	19	22	—	—	16	18	21	25	29	33	37	41	45	50	56
Mizuno MS-4	(1986)	11	—	16	19	22	—	—	16	18	21	25	29	33	37	41	45	50	56
Northwestern 241 Tour	(1986)	10	—	15	18	20	—	—	16	19	22	26	30	34	38	42	46	50	52
Northwestern 865GR	(1986)	10	—	15	18	20	—	—	16	19	22	26	30	34	38	42	46	50	52
Northwestern 965	(1986)	10	—	15	18	20	—	—	16	19	22	26	30	34	38	42	46	50	52
Penna Golf Original	(1986)	11	—	15	18	21	—	—	—	20	23	27	31	35	39	43	47	51	56
Penna Golf Innovator	(1986)	9½	—	15	18	21	—	—	—	20½	23	26	28½	31½	36	39	43	48	56
Pinseeker Fireball	(1986)	9	—	15	20	—	—	25	—	17	20	24	27	31	35	39	44	49	56
Pinseeker Olympian	(1986)	9	—	15	—	21	—	—	16	18	21	24	27	31	35	39	44	49	56
Pro Group Axiom	(1986)	12½	—	16	19	21	—	25	19	22	24	27	29	32	36	40	44	48	54
Pro Group Peerless	(1986)	10½	—	16	19	21	—	25	17	20	23	27	31	35	38	42	46	51	56
Ram Tour Grind	(1986)	11	—	16	19	22	—	—	16	19½	23	26½	30	33½	37	41	45	49	55
Ram Accubar	(1986)	12	—	17	—	22	—	26	—	17½	23½	27	30½	34½	37	42	46	50	55
Spalding Cannon	(1986)	11	—	16	—	21	—	26	17	19	22	25	28	32	36	40	45	50	—
Spalding Executive	(1986)	12	—	16	—	21	—	—	17½	19½	22	26	30	34	38	41½	46½	52	—
Taylor Metalwoods	(1986)	10	—	17	20	23	25	27½	—	—	—	—	—	—	—	—	—	—	—
Taylor Technician	(1986)	10	—	17	20	23	25	27½	16	19	22	25	28	32	36	40	44	48	54
Taylor Iron Cleek	(1986)	—	—	—	—	—	—	—	16	18	21	25	29	33	37	41	45	50	—
Taylor Tour Preferred	(1986)	—	—	—	—	—	—	—	16	19	22	25	29	33	37	41	45	49	55
Titleist Tour Model	(1985)	10½	—	16	19	22	—	—	18	20	23	26	30	33	37	41	45	49	54
Titleist Pinnacle	(1985)	12	—	17	—	23	—	—	—	19	22	26	30	33	36	40	44	48	55
Wilson Aggressor	(1984)	12	—	16	19	21	—	25	—	20	23	26	30	34	38	42	46	50	55
Wilson Staff	(1986)	12	—	16	19	21	—	—	—	20	23	26	30	34	38	42	46	50	55
Wilson 1200LT	(1986)	12	—	16	19	21	—	—	—	20	23	26	30	34	38	42	46	50	55
Wilson 1200GE	(1986)	12	—	16	19	21	—	—	—	19	22	25	29	33	37	41	45	49	54
Yahama Spada	(1986)	10½	—	16½	19	21½	—	—	—	—	—	—	—	—	—	—	—	—	—
Yamaha Y-45	(1986)	11	—	15	18	21	—	—	—	—	—	—	—	—	—	—	—	—	—
Yamaha ST-30	(1986)	—	—	—	—	—	—	—	19	21	24	27	31	35	39	43	47	51	56
Yamaha EX-22	(1986)	—	—	—	—	—	—	—	—	—	23	26	29	32	36	40	45	50	58

LIE — MEN'S

GOLF CLUB MANUFACTURERS STANDARD SPECIFICATIONS

Mfgr. & Year Specs. Published		#1 Wood	#2 Wood	#3 Wood	#4 Wood	#5 Wood	#6 Wood	#7 Wood	#1 Iron	#2 Iron	#3 Iron	#4 Iron	#5 Iron	#6 Iron	#7 Iron	#8 Iron	#9 Iron	Pitch Wedge	Sand Wedge
Armour Golf T-Line BC	(1986)	55	—	55	55½	56	—	56½	56	56¾	57¾	58¾	59¾	60¾	61¾	62¾	63¾	63¾	63¾
Browning 440	(1986)	55	—	56	57	57	—	57	—	57	58	59	60	61	62	63	64	64	64
Browning Automatic	(1986)	55	—	56	57	57	—	57	—	57	58	59	60	61	62	63	64	64	64
Daiwa Exceler	(1986)	54	—	55	56	56	—	56	—	57	58	59	60	61	62	63	64	64	64
Dunlop 357	(1986)	55	—	55½	—	56½	—	57	57	58	59	60	61	62	63	64	65	65	65
The GolfWorks® Bio-Mech	(1986)	55	55½	56	56½	57	57½	58	58	58½	59	59½	60	60½	61	61½	62	63	63
The GolfWorks® RMH	(1986)	55	55½	56	56½	57	57½	58	55	56	57	58	59	60	61	62	63	63	63
H & B All	(1986)	55	—	56	57	57	—	—	—	57	58	59	60	61	62	63	64	64	64
Hogan Apex	(1986)	55	—	56	56	57	—	—	—	57	58	59	60	61	62	62½	63	63½	—
Hogan Radial	(1986)	55	—	56	56	57	—	—	—	57	58	59	60	61	62	63	63½	64	—
Lynx - Parallax	(1986)	54	—	55	56	57	—	58	57	57	58	59	60	61	62	63	64	64	64
Lynx - Liberty	(1986)	55	—	56	56	57	—	58	—	57	58	59	60	61	62	63	64	64	64
MacGregor Muirfield	(1986)	55	—	56	56½	56½	—	—	57	57½	58	59	60	60½	61	61½	62	63	63
MacGregor CG1800	(1986)	55	—	56	56	56	—	—	57	57½	58	59	60	60½	61	61½	62	63	63
Mizuno MS-5	(1986)	55	—	56	56½	57	—	—	56	57	58	59	60	60½	61	62	63	63	63
Mizuno MS-4	(1986)	55	—	56	56½	57	—	—	56	57	58	59	60	60½	61	62	63	63	63
Northwestern 241 Tour	(1986)	55	—	55½	55¾	56	—	—	55	56	57	58	59	60	61	62	63	63	63
Northwestern 865GR	(1986)	55	—	55½	55¾	56	—	—	55	56	57	58	59	60	61	62	63	63	63
Northwestern 965	(1986)	55	—	55½	55¾	56	—	—	55	56	57	58	59	60	61	62	63	63	63
Penna Golf Original	(1986)	55	—	56	56	57	—	—	—	58	58½	59	59½	60	60½	61	61½	61½	61½
Penna Golf Innovator	(1986)	55	—	56	56	57	—	—	—	58	59	59½	60	61	61½	62½	63	63½	61
Pinseeker Fireball	(1986)	54	—	55	55½	55½	—	—	55	56	57	58	59	60	61	62	63	63	63
Pinseeker Olympian	(1986)	54	—	55	55½	55½	—	—	55	56	57	58	59	60	61	62	63	63	63
Pro Group Axiom	(1986)	55½	—	56	57	57	—	58	56	56	57	58	59	60	61	62	63	63	64
Pro Group Peerless	(1986)	54½	—	55	56	56	—	—	56	56	57	58	59	60	61	62	63	63	64
Ram Tour Grind	(1986)	55	—	56	56½	57	—	—	55½	57½	58	59½	60½	61½	62½	63½	64½	65½	65½
Ram Accubar	(1986)	55	—	56	—	57	—	58	—	57½	58	58½	59	60	61	62	63	63	64
Spalding Cannon	(1986)	55	—	55½	—	56	—	56½	58	58½	59	59½	60	60½	61	61½	62	63	—
Spalding Executive	(1986)	55	—	55½	—	56	—	—	58¼	58¼	58¾	59¼	59¾	60¼	61	61¾	62¼	63	—
Taylor Metalwoods	(1986)	54	—	55	55	55	55	55	—	—	—	—	—	—	—	—	—	—	—
Taylor Technician	(1986)	54	—	55	55	55	55	55	57½	58¼	59	59¾	60½	61¼	62	63	63	64	64
Taylor Iron Cleek	(1986)	—	—	—	—	—	—	—	56½	57	58	59	60	61	62	63	64	64	—
Taylor Tour Preferred	(1986)	—	—	—	—	—	—	—	56½	57	58	59	60	61	62	63	64	64	—
Titleist Tour Model	(1985)	54	—	55	56	56	—	—	56	57	58	59	60	61	62	63	63	64	64
Titleist Pinnacle	(1985)	54	—	56	—	57	—	—	—	57	58	59	59	60	61	61	62	62	64
Wilson Aggressor	(1984)	55	—	56	57	57	57	—	—	56	57	58	59	60	61	62	62	63	64
Wilson Staff	(1986)	54	—	55	56	56	56	—	—	57	58	59	60	60	61	62	62	63	64
Wilson 1200LT	(1986)	55	—	56	57	57	—	—		57	58	59	60	60	61	62	62	63	64
Wilson 1200GE	(1986)	54	—	55	56	56	56	—	—	57	58	59	60	60	61	62	62	63	64
Yahama Spada	(1986)	55	—	56	56½	57	—	—	—	—	—	—	—	—	—	—	—	—	—
Yamaha Y-45	(1986)	55	—	56	56½	57	—	—	—	—	—	—	—	—	—	—	—	—	—
Yamaha ST-30	(1986)	—	—	—	—	—	—	—	57	57	58	59	60	61	62	63	63½	64	64
Yamaha EX-22	(1986)	—	—	—	—	—	—	—	—	—	58	58½	59	60	61	62	63	63½	64

LADIES' — LENGTH, LOFT & LIE — MID 1980's

LENGTH LADIES'

GOLF CLUB MANUFACTURERS STANDARD SPECIFICATIONS

Mfgr. & Year Specs. Published		#1 Wood	#2 Wood	#3 Wood	#4 Wood	#5 Wood	#6 Wood	#7 Wood	#1 Iron	#2 Iron	#3 Iron	#4 Iron	#5 Iron	#6 Iron	#7 Iron	#8 Iron	#9 Iron	Pitch Wedge	Sand Wedge
Armour Golf BC	(1986)	42	—	41	40½	40	—	39½	—	—	37¾	37¼	36¾	36¼	35¾	35¼	34¾	34¾	34¾
Browning 440	(1986)	42	—	41	—	40	—	39½	—	38	37½	37	36½	36	35½	35	34½	34½	34½
Daiwa Exceler	(1986)	42	—	41	40½	40	—	39½	—	—	37½	37	36½	36	35½	35	34½	34½	34½
H & B All	(1986)	41½	—	40½	40	40	—	39½	—	—	37	36½	36	35½	35	34½	34	34	34
Lynx - Tigress SP	(1986)	42	—	41	—	40	—	39	—	—	37½	37	36½	36	35½	35	34½	34½	34½
MacGregor L. Finesse	(1986)	42½	—	41¾	41¼	40¾	—	—	—	—	37¾	37¼	36¾	36¼	35¾	35½	35¼	34¾	34¾
Mizuno Quad	(1986)	42	—	41½	—	40¾	—	—	—	—	37½	37	36½	36	35½	35¼	35	34¾	34½
Northwestern Micro-Lite	(1986)	42	—	41	40½	40	—	—	—	—	37	36½	36	35½	35	34½	34	34	34
Penna Golf Original	(1986)	42	—	41½	41	40	—	—	—	—	37½	37	36½	36	35½	35	34½	34	34
Pinseeker Fireball	(1986)	42	—	41	40½	40½	40	—	—	38	37½	37	36½	36	35½	35	34½	34½	34½
Pro Group Axiom	(1986)	42	—	41	40¾	40½	—	40¼	—	—	37½	37	36½	36	35½	35	34½	34½	34¼
Ram Patty Sheehan	(1986)	42	—	41	—	40	—	40	—	—	38	37½	37	36½	36	35½	35	34½	34½
Spalding Cannon	(1986)	42	—	41¼	—	40½	—	39¾	—	—	37½	37	36½	36	35½	35	34½	34	—
Taylor Metal	(1986)	42	—	41	40½	40	—	—	—	—	—	—	—	—	—	—	—	—	—
Taylor Technician	(1986)	41½	—	40¾	—	40	—	—	37½	37½	36¾	36⅜	36	35⅝	35¼	34¾	34¼	34	34
Taylor Iron Cleek	(1986)	—	—	—	—	—	—	—	38½	38	37½	37	36½	36	35½	35	34½	34½	—
Titleist Titlette	(1985)	42	—	41½	—	40¾	—	—	—	—	—	37	36½	36	35⅝	35¼	34⅞	34½	—
Wilson Patty Berg	(1986)	42	—	41½	41	40¾	—	40½	—	—	37½	37	36½	36	35½	35	34½	34	34
Wilson Tiara	(1986)	41½	—	40½	40	39½	—	38½	—	—	37½	37	36½	36	35½	35	34½	34	34
Yamaha C-100	(1986)	42¼	—	41	40½	40	—	—	—	—	—	—	—	—	—	—	—	—	—
Yamaha Image	(1986)	—	—	—	—	—	—	—	—	—	37½	37	36½	36	35½	35	34½	34	34

LOFT LADIES'

GOLF CLUB MANUFACTURERS STANDARD SPECIFICATIONS

Mfgr. & Year Specs. Published		#1 Wood	#2 Wood	#3 Wood	#4 Wood	#5 Wood	#6 Wood	#7 Wood	#1 Iron	#2 Iron	#3 Iron	#4 Iron	#5 Iron	#6 Iron	#7 Iron	#8 Iron	#9 Iron	Pitch Wedge	Sand Wedge
Armour Golf BC	(1986)	12½	—	15½	18½	21½	—	25	—	—	21½	25	28½	32½	36½	40½	44½	49	52
Browning 440	(1986)	13	—	19	—	22	—	25	—	21	24	27	30	34	38	42	45	50	56
Daiwa Exceler	(1986)	14	—	16½	19	21	—	25	—	17	19	22	25	29	33	37	41	45	50
H & B All	(1986)	14	—	20	22	24	—	27	—	—	24	28	32	35	38	41	44	50	56
Lynx - Tigress SP	(1986)	12	—	16	—	22	—	26	—	—	22	25	29	33	37	41	45	44	56
MacGregor L. Finesse	(1986)	15½	—	18	22	25½	—	—	—	—	23	26	29	33	37	41	45	50	56
Mizuno Quad	(1986)	11½	—	17	—	23	—	—	—	—	21	24	27	30	34	38	42	47	54
Northwestern Micro-Lite	(1986)	11	—	15	18	20	—	—	—	—	22	26	30	34	38	42	46	50	52
Penna Golf Original	(1986)	11	—	15	18	21	—	—	—	—	23	27	31	35	39	43	47	51	56
Pinseeker Fireball	(1986)	11	—	15	20	—	—	25	—	—	20	24	27	31	35	39	44	49	56
Pro Group Axiom	(1986)	12½	—	16	19	21	—	25	—	22	24	27	29	32	36	40	44	48	54
Ram Patty Sheehan	(1986)	13	—	17	—	22	—	26	—	—	23½	27	30½	34½	37	42	46	50	55
Spalding Cannon	(1986)	13	—	16	21	26	—	—	—	—	22	25	28	32	36	40	44	48	—
Taylor Metal	(1986)	12	—	17	20	23	25	27½	—	—	—	—	—	—	—	—	—	—	—

LADIES' — LENGTH, LOFT & LIE — MID 1980's

LOFT LADIES' *(cont.)*

GOLF CLUB MANUFACTURERS STANDARD SPECIFICATIONS

Mfgr. & Year Specs. Published		#1 Wood	#2 Wood	#3 Wood	#4 Wood	#5 Wood	#6 Wood	#7 Wood	#1 Iron	#2 Iron	#3 Iron	#4 Iron	#5 Iron	#6 Iron	#7 Iron	#8 Iron	#9 Iron	Pitch Wedge	Sand Wedge
Taylor Technician	(1986)	12	—	17	20	23	25	27½	16	19	22	25	28	32	36	40	44	48	54
Taylor Iron Cleek	(1986)	—	—	—	—	—	—	—	16	18	21	25	29	33	37	41	45	50	—
Titleist Titlette	(1985)	12	—	16	—	21	—	—	—	—	—	26	30	34	38	42	46	53	—
Wilson Patty Berg	(1986)	13	—	17	20	22	—	26	—	—	23	26	30	34	38	42	46	50	55
Wilson Tiara	(1986)	14	—	18	—	23	—	27	—	—	23	26	30	34	38	42	46	50	55
Yamaha C-100	(1986)	14	—	19	22	25	—	—	—	—	—	—	—	—	—	—	—	—	—
Yamaha Image	(1986)	—	—	—	—	—	—	—	—	—	—	26	30	34	38	42	46	50	56

LIE LADIES'

GOLF CLUB MANUFACTURERS STANDARD SPECIFICATIONS

Mfgr. & Year Specs. Published		#1 Wood	#2 Wood	#3 Wood	#4 Wood	#5 Wood	#6 Wood	#7 Wood	#1 Iron	#2 Iron	#3 Iron	#4 Iron	#5 Iron	#6 Iron	#7 Iron	#8 Iron	#9 Iron	Pitch Wedge	Sand Wedge
Armour Golf BC	(1986)	54	—	55	55½	56	—	56½	—	—	57¾	58¾	59¾	60¾	61¾	62¾	63¾	63¾	63¾
Browning 440	(1986)	55	—	57	—	57	—	57	—	57	58	59	60	61	62	63	64	64	64
Daiwa Exceler	(1986)	54	—	55	56	56	—	56	—	—	58	59	60	60	61	62	62	63	64
H & B All	(1986)	55	—	57	57	57	—	—	—	—	58	59	60	61	62	63	64	64	64
Lynx - Tigress SP	(1986)	55	—	56	—	56½	—	57	—	—	58	59	60	61	62	63	64	64	64
MacGregor L. Finesse	(1986)	56	—	57	57	57	—	—	—	—	58	59	60	60½	61	61½	62	63	63
Mizuno Quad	(1986)	55	—	56	—	57	—	—	—	—	58	59	60	61	61½	62	63	64	64
Northwestern Micro-Lite	(1986)	55	—	55½	55¾	56	—	—	—	—	57	58	59	60	61	62	63	63	63
Penna Golf Original	(1986)	55	—	56	56	57	—	—	—	—	58½	59	59½	60	60½	61	61½	61½	61½
Pinseeker Fireball	(1986)	54	—	55	55½	55½	—	—	—	—	57	58	59	60	61	62	63	63	63
Pro Group Axiom	(1986)	55½	—	56	57	57	—	—	—	—	57	58	59	60	61	62	63	63	64
Ram Patty Sheehan	(1986)	55½	—	56½	—	57½	—	58½	—	—	58	58½	59	60	61	62	63	63	64
Spalding Cannon	(1986)	55	—	55½	—	56	—	56½	—	—	58¾	59¼	59¾	60¼	60¾	61¼	62	63	—
Taylor Metal	(1986)	54	—	55	55	55	55	55	—	—	—	—	—	—	—	—	—	—	—
Taylor Technician	(1986)	54	—	55	55	55	55	55	57½	58¼	59	59¾	60½	61¼	62	63	63	64	64
Taylor Iron Cleek	(1986)	—	—	—	—	—	—	—	56½	57	58	59	60	61	62	63	64	64	—
Titleist Titlette	(1985)	54	—	55	—	57	—	—	—	—	—	59	60	60	61	62	62	63	—
Wilson Patty Berg	(1986)	54	—	55	56	56	56	—	—	—	58	59	60	60	61	62	62	63	64
Wilson Tiara	(1986)	54	—	55	56	56	56	—	—	—	57	58	59	60	61	62	62	—	—
Yamaha C-100	(1986)	52	—	53	53½	54	—	—	—	—	—	—	—	—	—	—	—	—	—
Yamaha Image	(1986)	—	—	—	—	—	—	—	—	—	—	58	59	60	61	62	63	64	64

LENGTH — MEN'S

GOLF CLUB MANUFACTURERS STANDARD SPECIFICATIONS

Mfgr. & Year Specs. Published	#1 Wood	#2 Wood	#3 Wood	#4 Wood	#5 Wood	#6 Wood	#7 Wood	#1 Iron	#2 Iron	#3 Iron	#4 Iron	#5 Iron	#6 Iron	#7 Iron	#8 Iron	#9 Iron	Pitch Wedge	Sand Wedge
Length:																		
Mario Cesario (1986)	43	42½	42	41½	41	—	40	39	38½	38	37½	37	36½	36	35½	35	35	35
Cobra (1986)	43	42¾	42½	42	41½	41¼	41	39½	39	38½	38	37½	37	36½	36	35½	35½	35¼
Bert Dargie (1982)	43	42½	42	41½	41	—	40	39	38½	38	37½	37	36½	36	35½	35	35	35
The GolfWorks® (1986)	43	42½	42	41½	41	40½	40	39½	39	38½	38	37½	37	36½	36	35½	35½	35½
George Izett (1986)	43	43	42	41½	41	—	40	39½	39	38½	38	37½	37	36½	36	35½	35½	35½
Irving King (1982)	43	42½	42	41½	41	—	—	—	38½	38	37½	37	36½	36	35½	35	35	35
Louisville Golf (1986)	43	42½	42	41½	41	—	40	39½	39	38½	38	37½	37	36½	36	35½	35½	35½
John Ofer (1986)	43	42½	42	41½	41	41	41	—	39	38½	38	37½	37	36⅝	36¼	35¾	35½	35½
Orlimar (1982)	43	42¾	42	41½	41	—	—	39¾	39¼	38¾	38¼	37¾	37¼	36¾	36¼	35¾	35½	35½
Pederson (1986)	43	42¾	42¼	42	41½	41	40½	39	38½	38	37½	37	36½	36	35½	35	35	35
Kenneth Smith (1986)	43	42½	42	41½	41	—	39½	39	38½	38	37½	37	36½	36	35½	35	34½	34½
Bob Toski (1986)	43	42½	42	41½	41	—	40	39½	39	38½	38	37½	37	36½	36	35½	35½	35½

LOFT — MEN'S

GOLF CLUB MANUFACTURERS STANDARD SPECIFICATIONS

Mfgr. & Year Specs. Published	#1 Wood	#2 Wood	#3 Wood	#4 Wood	#5 Wood	#6 Wood	#7 Wood	#1 Iron	#2 Iron	#3 Iron	#4 Iron	#5 Iron	#6 Iron	#7 Iron	#8 Iron	#9 Iron	Pitch Wedge	Sand Wedge
Loft:																		
Mario Cesario (1986)	11	13	16	19	22	—	28	17	20	24	28	32	36	40	44	48	52	58
Cobra (1986)	10	14	16	19	22	25	27	17	20	23	27	31	36	40	44	48	52	56
Bert Dargie (1982)	11	13	16	19	22	—	28	18	21	24	27	31	35	39	43	47	51	55
The GolfWorks® (1986)	11	13	16	19	22	25	28	17	20	23	26	30	34	38	42	46	50	56
George Izett (1986)	10	13	16	19	22	—	28	17	20	22½	25	27½	30	32½	35	37½	40	42½
Irving King (1982)	11	13	16	19	21	—	—	—	20	24	28	32	36	40	44	48	52	56
Louisville Golf (1986)	11	13½	16	18½	21½	24	26½	—	20	23	26	29	33	37	41	45	50	55
John Ofer (1986)	10½	13	16	19	22	25	27	—	20	23	26	30	34	38	42	46	50	55
Orlimar (1982)	11	14	17	20	23	—	—	16	19	22	25½	29	33	37	41	45	50	58
Pederson (1986)	11	13	16	19	22	24	26	18	22	23	26	30	34	38	42	46	50	55
Kenneth Smith (1986)	11	14	17	20	23	—	29	17	20	23	27	31	35	39	43	47	51	56
Bob Toski (1986)	12	15	18	20	22	—	27	22	24	26½	29	31½	35	38½	41½	45	48½	51½

LIE — MEN'S

GOLF CLUB MANUFACTURERS STANDARD SPECIFICATIONS

Mfgr. & Year Specs. Published	#1 Wood	#2 Wood	#3 Wood	#4 Wood	#5 Wood	#6 Wood	#7 Wood	#1 Iron	#2 Iron	#3 Iron	#4 Iron	#5 Iron	#6 Iron	#7 Iron	#8 Iron	#9 Iron	Pitch Wedge	Sand Wedge
Lie:																		
Mario Cesario (1986)	54	55	56	57	57	—	57	56	57	58	59	60	61	62	63	64	65	65
Cobra (1986)	54	54	55	55½	56	55	55½	57	57½	58	59	59½	60	61	62	63	63	64
Bert Dargie (1982)	54	54	55	56	56	—	57	57	58	59	60	61	62	63	64	64	65	65
The GolfWorks® (1986)	55	55½	56	56½	57	57½	58	55	56	57	58	59	60	61	62	63	63	63
George Izett (1986)	55	55	56	57	58	—	59	56	57	58	59	60	61	62	63	64	64	64
Irving King (1982)	55	55½	56	56½	57	—	—	—	57	58	59	60	61	62	63	64	64	64
Louisville Golf (1986)	55	55½	56	56½	57	57½	58	56	57	58	59	60	61	62	63	64	64	64
John Ofer (1986)	55	55	57	57	57	57	57	—	57	58	59	60	60	61	62	62	63	63
Orlimar (1982)	56	56¼	56¾	57	57¼	—	—	58¼	58¼	58¾	59¼	59¾	60¼	60½	61¼	62	62¼	62½
Pederson (1986)	54	54½	55	56	56½	57	57½	56	57	58	59	60	61	62	63	64	64	64
Kenneth Smith (1986)	54	55	56	57	58	—	60	56	57	58	59	60	61	62	63	64	64	64
Bob Toski (1986)	54	54	55	56	57	57	57	56½	57	57½	58	58½	60	61	61½	62	63	63

CUSTOM MFGR.'S — LADIES' — LENGTH, LOFT & LIE — MID 1980's

LENGTH — LADIES'

GOLF CLUB MANUFACTURERS STANDARD SPECIFICATIONS

Mfgr. & Year Specs. Published		#1 Wood	#2 Wood	#3 Wood	#4 Wood	#5 Wood	#6 Wood	#7 Wood	#1 Iron	#2 Iron	#3 Iron	#4 Iron	#5 Iron	#6 Iron	#7 Iron	#8 Iron	#9 Iron	Pitch Wedge	Sand Wedge
Length:																			
Mario Cesario	(1986)	42	41½	41	40½	40	—	39	—	37½	37	36½	36	35½	35	34½	34	34	34
Cobra	(1986)	42	41¾	41½	41	40½	40¼	40	38½	38	37½	37	36½	36	35½	35	34½	34½	34½
Bert Dargie	(1982)	42	41½	41	40½	40	—	—	38	37½	37	36½	36	35½	35	34½	34	34	34
The GolfWorks®	(1986)	42	—	41	40½	40	39½	39	38½	38	37½	37	36½	36	35½	35	34½	34½	34½
George Izett	(1986)	42	42	41	40½	40	—	39	—	38	37½	37	36½	36	35½	35	34½	34½	34½
Irving King	(1982)	42	41½	41	40½	40	—	39	—	37½	37	36½	36	35½	35	34½	34	34	34
Louisville Golf	(1986)	42	41½	41	40½	40	39½	39	38½	38	37½	37	36½	36	35½	35	34½	34½	34½
John Ofer	(1986)	42	—	41½	41	41	40	40	—	—	37½	37	36½	35¾	35⅝	35¼	34¾	34½	34½
Orlimar	(1982)	42	41¾	41	40½	40	—	39	38¾	38¼	37¾	37¼	36¾	36¼	35¾	35¼	34¾	34½	34½
Pederson	(1986)	41½	41¼	40¾	40½	40	39½	39	38	37½	37	36½	36	35½	35	34½	34	34	34
Kenneth Smith	(1986)	41½	41	40½	40	39½	—	38	38	37½	37	36½	36	35½	35	34½	34	33½	33½
Bob Toski	(1986)	42	41½	41	40½	40	—	39	38½	38	37½	37	36½	36	35½	35	34½	34½	34½

LOFT — LADIES'

GOLF CLUB MANUFACTURERS STANDARD SPECIFICATIONS

Mfgr. & Year Specs. Published		#1 Wood	#2 Wood	#3 Wood	#4 Wood	#5 Wood	#6 Wood	#7 Wood	#1 Iron	#2 Iron	#3 Iron	#4 Iron	#5 Iron	#6 Iron	#7 Iron	#8 Iron	#9 Iron	Pitch Wedge	Sand Wedge
Loft:																			
Mario Cesario	(1986)	12½	14	17	20	23	—	29	—	20	24	28	32	36	40	44	48	52	56
Cobra	(1986)	11	14	16	19	22	25	27	17	20	23	27	31	36	40	44	48	52	56
Bert Dargie	(1982)	11	13	16	19	22	—	—	18	21	24	27	31	35	39	43	47	51	55
The GolfWorks®	(1986)	13	—	17	20	23	26	29	17	20	23	26	30	34	38	42	46	50	56
George Izett	(1986)	12	14	16	19	22	—	—	—	20	22½	25	27½	30	32½	35	37½	40	42½
Louisville Golf	(1986)	12	14½	17	19½	22½	25	27½	18	21	24	27	30	34	38	42	46	51	56
John Ofer	(1986)	13	—	17	20	22	25	27	—	—	24	27	31	35	39	43	47	51	56
Orlimar	(1982)	13	14½	18½	21½	24½	—	31	16	19	22	25½	29	33	37	41	45	50	58
Pederson	(1986)	12	13	16	19	22	24	26	18	20	23	26	30	34	38	42	46	50	55
Kenneth Smith	(1986)	12	15	18	21	24	—	30	18	21	24	28	32	36	40	44	48	52	57
Bob Toski	(1986)	13	15	18	20	22	—	27	22	24	26½	29	31½	35	38½	41½	45	48½	51½

LIE — LADIES'

GOLF CLUB MANUFACTURERS STANDARD SPECIFICATIONS

Mfgr. & Year Specs. Published		#1 Wood	#2 Wood	#3 Wood	#4 Wood	#5 Wood	#6 Wood	#7 Wood	#1 Iron	#2 Iron	#3 Iron	#4 Iron	#5 Iron	#6 Iron	#7 Iron	#8 Iron	#9 Iron	Pitch Wedge	Sand Wedge
Lie:																			
Mario Cesario	(1986)	53	54	56	56	56	—	56	—	56	57	58	59	60	61	62	63	64	64
Cobra	(1986)	54	54	55	55½	56	55	55½	57	57½	58	59	59½	60	61	62	63	63	64
Bert Dargie	(1982)	54	54	55	56	56	—	—	57	58	59	60	61	62	63	64	64	65	65
The GolfWorks®	(1986)	53	—	54	54½	55	55½	56	55	56	57	58	59	60	61	62	63	63	63
George Izett	(1986)	53	53	54	55	56	—	57	—	56	57	58	59	60	61	62	63	63	63
Irving King	(1986)	55	55½	56	56½	57	—	58	—	57	58	59	60	61	62	63	64	64	64
Louisville Golf	(1986)	54	54½	55	55½	56	56½	57	55	56	57	58	59	60	61	62	63	63	63
John Ofer	(1986)	54	—	55	56	56	56	56	—	—	57	58	59	59	60	61	61	62	63
Pederson	(1986)	53	53½	54	55	55½	56	56½	55	56	57	58	59	60	61	62	63	63	63
Kenneth Smith	(1986)	53	54	55	56	57	—	59	56	57	58	59	60	61	62	63	64	64	64
Bob Toski	(1986)	53	53	54	55	56	—	56	56½	57	57½	58	58½	60	61	61½	62	63	63

MEN'S — LENGTH, LOFT & LIE — FILL IN YOUR OWN TO KEEP UPDATED

GOLF CLUB MANUFACTURERS STANDARD OR CUSTOM SPECIFICATIONS

Manufacturer & Model	Year Specs. Published	#1 Wood	#2 Wood	#3 Wood	#4 Wood	#5 Wood	#6 Wood	#7 Wood	#1 Iron	#2 Iron	#3 Iron	#4 Iron	#5 Iron	#6 Iron	#7 Iron	#8 Iron	#9 Iron	Pitch Wedge	Sand Wedge	Third Wedge

Length:

Loft:

Lie:

LADIES' — LENGTH, LOFT & LIE — FILL IN YOUR OWN TO KEEP UPDATED

GOLF CLUB MANUFACTURERS STANDARD OR CUSTOM SPECIFICATIONS

Manufacturer & Model	Year Specs. Published	#1 Wood	#2 Wood	#3 Wood	#4 Wood	#5 Wood	#6 Wood	#7 Wood	#1 Iron	#2 Iron	#3 Iron	#4 Iron	#5 Iron	#6 Iron	#7 Iron	#8 Iron	#9 Iron	Pitch Wedge	Sand Wedge	Third Wedge
Length:																				
Loft:																				
Lie:																				

NOTES

NOTES